ARCHITECTURE

DESIGN · ENGINEERING · DRAWING

McKNIGHT & McKNIGHT PUBLISHING COMPANY

This publication was prepared by the McKnight &
McKnight Editorial Staff under the direction of:

Ronald E. Dale
Managing Editor

Elizabeth Purcell
Art Editor

Donna Faull
Production Editor

John Lee
Cover Design

Bettye King
Copy Editor

Gorman Typesetting
Bradford, Illinois
Compositor

ARCHITECTURE

DESIGN • ENGINEERING • DRAWING

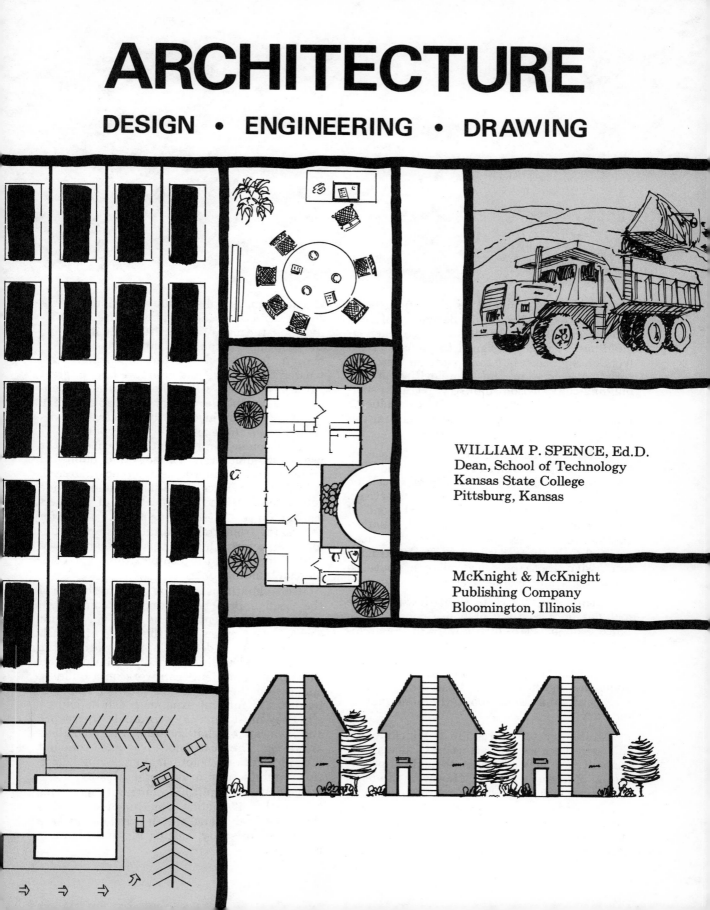

WILLIAM P. SPENCE, Ed.D.
Dean, School of Technology
Kansas State College
Pittsburg, Kansas

McKnight & McKnight
Publishing Company
Bloomington, Illinois

INTRODUCTION

This text is designed as a comprehensive study of the planning and designing of residences and small, single-story, commercial buildings. It is not designed to prepare architects or engineers, but to provide an introductory experience in the complexities of the building-construction industry. It has sufficient scope and depth to be of great value to junior college and college design and drafting classes.

The text is designed to enable members of the class to go as far as they have time. The experiences to be offered in the class can be varied and selected to meet course objectives. The use of the class activities at the end of each chapter reinforces the student's understanding of the text material. No class need complete all these activities. The instructor can assign those he feels will contribute to meeting his course objectives.

Frequently, an architectural drawing course includes only a study of house construction. Since a major share of the work of the architect and contractor is in commercial work, this area should comprise a large segment of an architectural drawing course. If this is not done, the youth in these classes are given an erroneous impression about the construction industry.

Multistory structures are not included in this text because the structural calculations generally are beyond the mathematical preparation of most students. However, students should realize that multistory commercial buildings are the mainstay of the construction industry. An exposure to the design and construction of small commercial buildings prepares the way for this understanding.

The commercial building section utilizes simple structural calculations and relies heavily upon the use of stock items. It is beyond the scope of this course to furnish design information for items such as open-web steel trusses. These are manufactured in a great variety of sizes with the span and load-carrying capabilities available in tables. Small commercial buildings can be successfully designed using these and other stock parts.

This course can be greatly enriched by the use of manufacturers' catalogs and published architectural standards as reference material. Additional resource materials should include complete plans and specifications of commercial buildings. These are usually available for the asking from architectural firms and building contractors. Only in this way can a class fully understand the complexities of a commercial building.

Consideration should be given to the use of the team approach to designing commercial buildings. Frequently, time will not permit each student to research the needs of a business, develop a defensible plan, design the structure and utilities and draw the plans. If three or four students can work on a building and divide the design and drawing responsibilities, a significant experience can be had by all. They must carefully coordinate their work and be aware of what the other team members are doing. They can pool ideas and work out several solutions before making a final decision. Architectural firms work this way.

One of the significant contributions of this text is that it enables the student to realize that the final plans are drawn only after a great deal of study, calculation and planning are done.

ACKNOWLEDGMENTS

The preparation of a text of this scope requires the cooperation of individuals, companies and organizations. Following is a listing of those making some contribution.

Companies

Alley, Williams, Carmen and King, Inc., Engineers and Achitects
Alliance Ware, Inc.
Alsynite Division of Reichhold Chemicals, Inc.
American Builder Magazine
American of Martinsville
American Terra Cotta Corporation
AMF Pinspotters, Inc.
Anaconda American Brass Company
Andersen Corporation
Architectural Forum Magazine
Architectural Record Magazine
Arkla Air Conditioning Company
Armstrong Cork Co.
Azrock Floor Products
Bastian-Blessing Company
William Bayley Company
Bell and Gossett Company
Bestwall Certain-Teed Sales Corporation
Bethlehem Steel Company
Bilco Company
G. S. Blakeslee Company
Bostitch
Boston Plaza Cleaners
Bowman Steel Corporation
Brunswick Corporation
Bryant Manufacturing Company
Builders Structural Steel Company
Butler Manufacturing Company
Callaghan and Seiler, Architectural Models
Caloric Architectural Porcelain
Campbell and Wong Associates
Caradco, Inc.
Carrier Corporation
CECO Corp.
Ceramic Tile Panels, Inc.
Champion Dish Washing Machine Company

Chapman's Shoes
Cole Steel Equipment Co.
Columbia Lighting Co.
Cold Spring Granite Co.
Concrete Plank Company, Inc.
Coppes Napanee
Crane Company
Del Webb's Ocean House
Diebold, Inc.
Eugene Dietzgen Company
Diffusa-Lite Company
Ditzen, Rowland, Mueller and Associates, Architects
F. W. Dodge Corporation
Donley Brothers Company
Dow Chemical Company
Burton W. Duehke Building Company
E. I. duPont de Nemours and Company
Durham, Anderson, Freed, Architects
Eckerd Drug Stores
Edwards Engineering Company
Electromode
Marshall Erdman and Associates, Inc.
Feathercock, Inc.
Flintkote Company
Friedes, Inc.
Garlinghouse Co., Inc.
Geifer's Barber Shop
General Electric Co.
General Plywood Corporation
Geneva Modern Kitchens
Gerber Plumbing and Fixture Corporation
Granco Steel Products Company
Harnischfeger Homes, Inc.
Haven-Busch Company
Hobart Manufacturing Company

Holiday Inns, Inc.
Homasote Company
Home Planners, Inc.
Jack Horner Studios
House and Home Magazine
Icard, Merrill, Cullis and Timm, Attorneys
Infinity, Inc., Photographers
International Business Machines Corporation
Intrusion-Prepakt, Inc.
Iron Fireman Manufacturing Company
Jordan Commercial Refrigerator Company
Kansas Gas and Electric Company
Kawneer Company
Kitchen Kompact, Inc.
Stanley Knight Corporation
Lally Column Company, Inc.
Libby-Owens-Ford Glass Company
R. C. Mahon Company
Majestic Company, Inc.
McGraw-Hill Book Company
Herman Miller, Inc.
Mirawal, Birdsboro Corporation
Montgomery Elevator Company
Morgan Company
Mosaic Tile Company
Motel/Motor Inn Journal
Natcor Store Fronts
National Gypsum Company
National Homes Corporation
Northrop Architectural Systems
Nutone, Inc.
Olson Manufacturing Company
Ordan Publishing Company, Inc.
Owens-Corning Fiberglass Corporation
Panel Structures, Inc.
Phillips Petroleum Company
Pittsburgh Corning Corporation
Plywood Fabricators Service, Inc.
Prescolite Manufacturing Company
Progressive Metal Equipment, Inc.

George Rackle and Sons, Company
Rambusch, Designers, Craftsmen and Lighting Engineers
Raymond Concrete Pile Company, Ltd.
Reflector Hardware Corporation
Reinhold Publishing Corporation
Republic Steel Corporation
Revco, Inc.
Reynolds Metals Company
H. H. Robertson Company
Rowe Manufacturing Company
Sahara Motor Hotel
Scholtz Homes
Sears, Roebuck and Company
Sellars Department Store
Shlargo Steel Products Company
Shokokusha Publishing Company, Japan
Simpson Engineering
Simpson Timber
Smart Shop
Southern Cast Stone Company, Inc.
Southern Homes, Inc.
Tappan Range Co.
Tectum Corporation
Temco, Inc.
Timber Engineering Company
Tyler Refrigeration Corporation
Union Carbide Corporation
United States Air Conditioning Corporation
United States Rubber Company
United States Steel Homes
Vega Industries, Inc.
Wesix Electric Heater Company
Whirlpool Corporation
John Wiley and Sons, Inc.
Wiremold Company
Wood Conversion Company
Woodall Industries, Inc.
Lee Woodward and Sons, Inc.
Young Radiator Company

Organizations

American Baptist Home Mission Societies
American Institute of Architects, Kansas City
American Institute of Steel Construction, Inc.
American Institute of Timber Construction
American Motel, Hotel, Resort Magazine
American Motor Hotel Association
American Society of Civil Engineers
Better Kitchens Institute
Board of Church Extension, Presbyterian Church in the United States
Board of Missions of the Methodist Church
Brazilian Government Trade Bureau
British Columbia Lumber Manufacturers Association
British Information Services
California Redwood Association
Canadian Consul
Canadian Wood Development Council
Chapel of the Holy Cross
Colonial Williamsburg
Commission on Synagogue Administration
Concrete Reinforcing Steel Institute
Copper and Brass Research Association
Cornell University, Food Facilities Engineering
Danish Information Service
Douglas Fir Plywood Association
Embassy of Nigeria
Embassy of Spain
Embassy of the Union of Soviet Socialist Republics
Essex Institute
Flexicore Manufacturers Association
Greene County Historical Society, Inc.
Harvard University Press
Housing and Home Finance Agency
I B C Homes
Industry Committee on Interior Wiring Design
Information Service of India
Insulation Board Institute
Italian Embassy
Lead Industries Association
Lumber Dealers Research Council
Mexican Embassy
Mo Sai Institute, Inc.
Mount Vernon Ladies Association
National Association of Retail Grocers of the United States
National Council of the Church of Christ in the U.S.A.
National Forest Products Association
Netherlands Information Service
New York State Department of Commerce
Old Sturbridge Village
Pan American Union
Porcelain Enamel Institute
Portland Cement Association
Precast Concrete Institute
Prestressed Concrete Institute
Royal Swedish Embassy
St. Luke's Episcopal Church
The Society for the Preservation of New England Antiquities
Southern Pine Association
Steel Joist Institute
Structural Clay Products Institute
The Sunday School Board of the Southern Baptist Church
Sycamore Homes
Union of American Hebrew Congregations
United States Department of the Interior
West Coast Lumbermen's Association
Western Wood Products Association
Wood Office Furniture Institute

Individuals

Allgeier, Martin and Associates
A. O. Brown, Electronics Instructor
Robert E. Buchner, AIA
Norman F. Carver, Designer
J. R. Flanigan, AIA
Robert H. Ford, Photographer
Ulrich Franzen, AIA
Jules Gregory, AIA
Dow Gumerson, AIA
William Hankhammer, Designer
Don Heuchan, Photographer
Louis C. Kingscott, Sr.
Louis C. Kingscott, Jr.
W. Milt Santee, Food Service Consultant
Joseph M. Seiler, Architect
James Seitz, Building Design Instructor
Frank Folson Smith and Associates, Architects
Penrose K. Spohn, AIA
J. Earl Trudeau, AIA
Lawrence S. Williams, Photographer
Beverly Willis, Industrial Designer

CONTENTS

CHAPTER ONE   Getting Started on the Plan 1

General Considerations 1
Developing the Floor Plan 1
Traffic Patterns 4
Zoning the House 6
Planning Stairs and Halls 7
Basic House Types 11
Common House Shapes 12
The Building Codes 13
The Building Site 14
Topography 15
Prevailing Winds 17
The View and Privacy 17
Orientation 18
Vocabulary, Activities, References 23

CHAPTER TWO   Planning the Individual Rooms 25

Designing the Individual Rooms 25
Planning the Living Room 31
Planning the Dining Area 33
Planning the Kitchen 34
Planning the Bedrooms 38
Planning Closets and Storage Walls 39
Planning a Bath 41
Planning Laundry Facilities 45
Planning Utility Rooms 46
Planning Core Units 47
Planning Garages and Carports 47
Planning the Basement 49
Activities, References 58

Evaluating Designs 59
Basic Principles of Building Design 60
Factors Influencing Styling 62
Common Roof Types 63
The Development of Architectural Styles Influencing Residential Design   64
Old World Residential Architecture 64
Early American Residential Architecture 69
Residential Architecture in the United States Since 1900 81
Houses Around the World 93
Architecture in Transition 97
Activities, References 100

Preparing for Work 102
Drawing to Scale 102
Reading the Architect's Scale 103
Architectural Symbols 103
Dimensioning a Working Drawing 103
Lettering 111
Drawing the Floor Plan 112
Drawing the Foundation or Basement Plan 113
Drawing the Elevations 113
Drawing the Sections 114
Drawing the Details 114
Drawing the Roof and Plot Plan 116
Specifications 116
Vocabulary, Questions, References 121

How a Conventional House is Built 131
Frame House Construction Details 132
Sheathing the Walls 134
Siding 135
Stucco 138
Solid Masonry Construction 140
Masonry Veneer over Frame Construction 142
Framing the Roof 143
Post, Plank, and Beam Construction 143
Steel House Framing 148
The Factory-Manufactured·House 150
Buildings from Modular Components 150
Building from Modular Units 157
Mobile Homes 174
New Developments in House Construction 180
Vocabulary, Activities, References 185

CHAPTER SIX   Footing, Foundation and Basement Construction   187

Footings 187
How to Ascertain Foundation Footing Sizes 188
Foundations 195
Piers, Columns and Curtain Walls 198
Pilasters 200
Grade Beam on Piling Foundation 201
Slab Foundation and Floor 202
Soil Investigation 205
Vocabulary, Activities, References 206

CHAPTER SEVEN   Structural Members Commonly Used   207

Loads and Strengths of Materials 207
Selecting Joists 207
Selecting Rafters 209
Collar Beams 211
Roof Trusses 211
Sheathing Spans 211
Heavy Decking for Plank-and-Beam Roofs 213
Columns 215
Stressed-Skin Panels 216
Girders 216
Lintels 228
Vocabulary, Activities, References 234

CHAPTER EIGHT   Electrical Features   236

Wiring Characteristics and Service Requirements 236
Planning the Electrical System 241
Kinds of Light Fixtures 247
Signal and Communication Systems 249
Surface-Mounted Wiring 250
Low-Voltage, Remote-Control Wiring 251
Vocabulary, Activities, References 253

CHAPTER NINE   Plumbing   255

Waste Disposal System 255
The Water System 265
Vocabulary, Activities, References 267

CHAPTER TEN   Heating, Cooling and Insulating   269

Placement of Heating and Cooling Units 269
Forced-Air Heating Systems 270
Forced-Air Cooling Units 273
Electric Cooling Units 273
Electric Heat 278
The Heat Pump 281
Gas All-Year Air Conditioning 282
Hot-Water Heat 286

Cold-Water Air-Cooling Systems 292
Steam Heat 293
Heat Loss Calculations 295
Fireplaces 298
Insulation 309
Condensation Control 313
Sound Control 315
Vocabulary, Activities, References 318

CHAPTER ELEVEN   Getting the House Built 320

Plans and Specifications 320
Getting Bids and Selecting a Contractor 321
Owner-Architect Relationships 321
Owner-Contractor Relationships 322
Estimating the Cost of a House 322
Fitting the House into Your Budget 323
Insurance 324
Financing a House 324
Trade-In House Sales 326
Vocabulary, Activities, References 327

CHAPTER TWELVE   Architectural Rendering and Model Construction 328

Architectural Perspective 328
Presentation Drawings 334
Architectural Models 336
Rendering Architectural Drawings 338
Black and White Illustrations 343
Principles of Light and Shade 344
Color Media 345
The Use of Values 345
The Use of Hue and Intensity 346
Complementary Color Schemes 347
Vocabulary, Activities, References 347

PLANNING COMMERCIAL BUILDINGS 349

CHAPTER THIRTEEN   Planning Merchandising Facilities 351

An Efficient and Atttractive Sales Area 351
Service Areas 356
Materials and Color 358
Exterior Design 358
Shoe Stores 362
Jewelry Stores 365
Furniture Stores 366
Appliance Stores 368
Men's Clothing Stores 370
Women's Clothing Stores 371
Hardware and Building Supply Stores 373

Retail Cleaning Shops 376
Florist and Nursery Shops 377
Barber Shops 378
Service Stations 379
Drugstores 383
Vocabulary, Activities, References 386

CHAPTER FOURTEEN   Planning Offices, Banks and Medical Offices and Clinics   388

Office Planning 388
Data Processing Centers 396
Planning Banks 397
Medical and Dental Offices and Clinics 404
Vocabulary, Activities, References 410

CHAPTER FIFTEEN   Planning Food Stores, Restaurants and Cafeterias   412

Food Stores 412
Restaurants 423
Cafeterias 429
Luncheonette and Short-Order Facilities 431
Drive-In Restaurants 433
Activities, References 435

CHAPTER SIXTEEN   Planning Motels and Parking Facilities   436

Motel Planning 436
Parking Facility Design 446
Activities, References 451

CHAPTER SEVENTEEN   Planning Shopping Centers   452

Shopping Centers 452
Activities, References 458

CHAPTER EIGHTEEN   Planning Churches   460

General Planning Considerations 460
The Narthex 466
The Nave 467
The Chancel 469
The Sacristy 470
The Chapel 471
Choir and Organ Placement 472
Furnishings 473
Color 474
Lighting 475
Art in Church Buildings 476
The Church School 477
Designing the Exterior 479
Vocabulary, Activities, References 480

CHAPTER NINETEEN   Structural Systems   482

Footings 482
Pile Foundations 482
Precast Concrete Structural Systems for Large Spans and Heavy Loads 485
Precast Bents 499
Monolithic Reinforced Concrete Construction 502
A Precast Concrete Floor and Roof System 509
Poured Gypsum Roof Systems 512
Tilt-Up Concrete Construction 515
Structural Steel Members 517
Structural Steel Drawings 534
Steel Roof Decking and Wall Panels 547
Cellular-Steel Floor Systems 551
Glued, Laminated Wood Structural Members 552
Wood-Fiber Roof Planks 561
Factory-Manufactured Commercial Buildings 563
Vocabulary, Problems, References 565

CHAPTER TWENTY   Curtain-Wall Systems   567

Porcelain-Enamel Curtain-Wall Systems 567
Stainless-Steel Curtain Walls 571
Copper and Copper-Alloy Curtain-Wall System 572
Steel Wall Panels 573
Aluminum Wall Panels 573
Translucent Plastic Curtain-Wall Panels 573
Cement-Asbestos Curtain-Wall Panels 573
Ceramic-Tile-Faced Curtain-Wall Panels 574
Glass Curtain-Wall Panels 575
Glass-Block Curtain Walls 576
Precast Concrete Facing and Curtain-Wall Panels 578
Vocabulary, Activities 581

CHAPTER TWENTY-ONE   Working Drawings for Small Commercial Buildings   582

Placement of Drawings on the Sheets 582
A Set of Working Drawings 584

Reference List   618

Books 618
Government Publications 620
Magazines 620
Association and Industrial Publications 620

Index   623

TABLES

Table	1	Commonly Used Tread and Riser Sizes	9
Table	2	Overhang Width for Sun Protection	20
Table	2A	Typical Frame Siding Materials	136
Table	3	Standard Footing Sizes for Residential Construction	189
Table	4	Common Design Loads for Live Loads	189
Table	5	Average Weights of Conventional Construction Materials	190
Table	6	Example of Load Calculations for a Residence	191
Table	7	Average Safe Loads of Soils	191
Table	8	Example of Load Calculation on Pier Footing	193
Table	10	Standard Thicknesses of Residence Foundation Walls	195
Table	11	Standard Pier Design Data for Single-Story Residences on Average Soil	199
Table	12	Design Data for Structural Slab on the Ground	203
Table	13	Perimeter Insulation Design Data for Heating Requirements	204
Table	14	Permissible Spans for Southern Pine Floor and Ceiling Joists	208
Table	15	Permissible Spans for Southern Pine Roof Joists and Rafters	210
Table	16	Joist Spacing Standards for Plywood Sheathing	211
Table	17	Joist Spacing Standards for Plywood Subfloor	213
Table	18	Maximum Spans for Decking Used in Plank and Beam Roofs	214
Table	19	Allowable Spans for Fiberboard Decking	215
Table	20	Maximum Loads for Steel Columns	216
Table	21	Steel Column Base Dimensions	216
Table	22	Maximum Loads for Wood Columns	216
Table	23	Compressive Strengths of Various Types of Wood Used for Columns	218
Table	24	Permissible Spans of Solid Wood Girders (1600 psi)	220
Table	25	Permissible Spans of Solid Wood Girders (1400 psi)	221

Table 26   Permissible Spans of Solid Wood Girders (1200 psi) 222
Table 27   Permissible Spans of Solid Wood Girders (900 psi) 223
Table 28   Allowable Unit Stresses for Structural Lumber and Timber 224
Table 29   Typical Glued Laminated Beam and Purlin Sizes 225
Table 30   Typical Sizes of Glued Laminated Beams and Purlins 226

Table 31   Safe Loads for Open-Web Steel Joists 229
Table 32   Precast Reinforced Concrete Lintels in Masonry Walls 231
Table 33   Carrying Capacity of Reinforced Concrete Lintels 232
Table 34   Loads for Regular Series Angle Beams 233
Table 35   Allowable Current Carrying Capacities (in Amperes)
            of Insulated Copper Conductors 240

Table 36   Unit Values of Plumbing Fixtures 260
Table 37   Trap Sizes and Estimated Fixture Unit Values 260
Table 38   Capacities of Building Drains and Sewers 260
Table 39   Capacities of Horizontal Fixture Branches and Stacks 261
Table 40   Commonly Used Trap Sizes 262

Table 41   Sizes and Lengths of Vents 263
Table 42   Usual Residential Vent Sizes 264
Table 43   Recommended Distances from Fixture Traps to Vents 264
Table 44   Minimum Capacities for Septic Tanks 264
Table 45   Minimum Sizes of Water Supply Pipes 265

Table 46   Selected Coefficients of Heat Transmission for
            Typical Wall, Ceiling and Floor Sections 299
Table 47   Dimensions for Conventionally Built,
            Single-Opening Fireplace 301
Table 48   Dimensions for Conventionally Built,
            Projecting Corner Fireplace 302
Table 49   Dimensions for Conventionally Built,
            Three-Way Fireplace 303
Table 50   Dimensions for Conventionally Built,
            Double-Opening Fireplace 303

Table 51   Common Sizes of Prefabricated Steel
            Heat-Circulating Fireplaces 304
Table 55   Typical Medical and Dental Space Requirements 407
Table 56   Suggested Aisle Widths for Parking 446
Table 57   Ramp Length for Straight Ramps 447
Table 60   Design Data for Precast Concrete Columns 486

Table 61   Safe Superimposed Loads for Prestressed Beams 487
Table 62   Safe Loads for Rectangular Concrete Beams 487
Table 63   Safe Superimposed Loads for Precast Concrete Tee Joists 488
Table 64   Safe Superimposed Loads for
            Six-Inch Concrete Roof Channels 489
Table 65   Safe Superimposed Loads for
            Longspan Concrete Roof Channels 489

Table 66	Safe Superimposed Loads for Double Tee Concrete Roof Decking	490
Table 67	Design Data and Construction Details for Precast Concrete Planks	491
Table 68	Design Data and Loads for Joists and Slab Designed as T-Beams (No Shoring)	492
Table 69	Design Data and Loads for Joists and Slab Designed as T-Beams (Shoring at Midspan)	494
Table 70	Design Data and Loads for Joists Designed as Independent Beams (No Shoring)	496
Table 71	Maximum Safe Superimposed Working Loads for 6″ x 16″ Precast Concrete Decking	509
Table 72	Weights of Bulb Tees Per Foot	513
Table 73	Design Data and Safe Loads for Bulb Tee Subpurlins	513
Table 74	Data on Component Parts of Typical Poured Gypsum Deck	514
Table 75	Allowable Unit Stresses for Structural Steel with 36,000 psi Specified Yield Point (A-36 Steel)	519
Table 76	Allowable Loads for American Standard Beams	523
Table 77	Allowable Loads for Wide Flange Beams	525
Table 78	Allowable Loads for Miscellaneous and Junior Beams	526
Table 79	Allowable Loads for Columns	527
Table 80	Design Properties and Dimensions for Detailing Wide Flange Shapes	528
Table 81	Design Properties and Dimensions for Detailing Miscellaneous Shapes and Light Beams	529
Table 82	Design Properties and Dimensions for Detailing Miscellaneous Columns and Channels	530
Table 83	K Factors	531
Table 84	Allowable Loads for Wide Flange Columns	532
Table 85	Allowable Loads for Concrete-Filled Steel Columns	533
Table 86	Design Data for Corrugated Panels	533
Table 87	Allowable Loads for Steel Roof Decking	547
Table 88	Design Data for Steel Roof Decking and Insulating Concrete Slab	550
Table 89	Design Data for Floor Construction with Steel Decking and Concrete Slab	550
Table 90	Design Data for Laminated Structural Members — Rigid Frame Units	553
Table 91	Design Data for Two-Hinged Arches	555
Table 92	Design Data for Selected Three-Hinged Arches	556
Table 93	Design Data for Typical Bowstring Trusses with Dimensions of Bearings	557
Table 94	Design Data for Box Section Subpurlins	561
Table 95	Maximum Spans for Three Span Bulb Tees	562

Table 96   Data for Stock, Rigid Frame Steel Buildings 564

Table 97   Safe Limits for Aluminum Mullions —
Rectangular Loading 571

Table 98   Design Data for Cement-Asbestos Curtain-Wall Panels 573

Table 99   Design Data for Ceramic-Tiled Curtain-Wall Panels
Over Insulated Concrete Units 574

Table 100   Design Data for Ceramic-Tiled Curtain-Wall Panels
Over Insulated Metal Panels 575

Table 101   Heat Transmission "U" Values of Glass Blocks 576

CHAPTER ONE

GETTING STARTED ON THE PLAN

The planning of a new home is usually the most important and exciting event in the life of the average family. Everyone has a "dream house" in mind and hopes to plan and build it some day. Families are willing to spend hours reading magazines and books and visiting homes to find ideas for their new house. However, the planning of a house is not this simple. Many factors must be considered before working drawings can be started.

General Considerations

A good way to start planning a house is to list all the features wanted. Specific items must be studied, such as the kinds of rooms, size of family, hobbies of family, personal likes and dislikes, and the style of the house. The lot upon which the house is to be built should be selected before planning progresses too far. The slope of the lot and the houses in the neighborhood influence the planning. The climate and the section of the country in which the house is to be built should be considered; a house designed for southern California would not be suitable for northern Wisconsin. Building codes, trends in style, advanced methods of construction and new building materials all deserve consideration as a house is planned.

Perhaps more than any other single factor influencing house planning is the amount of money available. Information concerning financing can be found in Chapter 11.

Developing the Floor Plan

As previously mentioned, a good way to get started on planning is to list all the things desired in the house. This will give a word picture of the house. The following is a sample list developed by one family.

> Three bedrooms
> Eat in kitchen
> Living room at least 12 x 20 feet
> No dining room
> Full walk-out basement (lot slopes to rear)
> Recreation room in basement
> Fireplace in living room and recreation room
> One and one-half baths
> Two-car garage
> Prefer ranch-type home
> Price cannot be over $18,000 with the lot
> Brick exterior
> Gable roof, wide overhang
> Washer and dryer in basement
> Oil hot air heat
> Plastered walls
> Room for a workshop

With the preliminary information concerning the house gathered, it is time to develop a floor plan. Several approaches are in use. Probably the most common method for people not trained in home planning and design is to use plan books, to examine magazines, or to look at plans already prepared. Certainly this is a sound approach. However, it is folly to copy a ready-made plan if it does not meet your needs. Try to "live" in a plan in your imagination. Always keep in mind the question, "Will it meet all of the needs of the family?" Usually it will not, and a process of revision must begin. This involves the application of the principles of room planning, traffic patterns, orientation of the house on the lot, as well as many personal considerations.

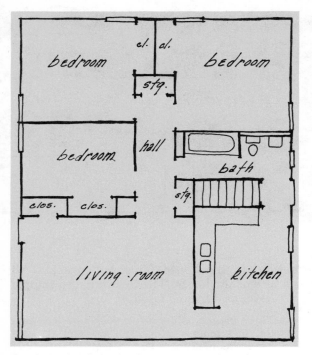

Fig. 1. Freehand sketch of a preliminary floor plan.

The revision can be facilitated by sketching the floor plan on ¼-inch squared graph paper. Allow each square to represent one square foot, and represent walls with a single line. See Fig. 1. Add wall thickness later, after the plan has "firmed up" and is in the final form. Remember that interior walls will consume 5 inches of floor space, and exterior walls 6 to 8 inches.

Check the pattern of traffic through the house. The supreme test of a house is the ease with which people can move about in it.

Before finalizing the plan, carefully examine the lot and determine how sun, wind, view, and privacy will necessitate changes in the plan. This costs nothing, but is worth much in comfort and liveability.

As the floor plan is developed, a new factor enters in — the exterior styling of the house. Many changes in locations of interior wall partitions, closets, and halls can be made without changing the exterior, but as soon as a window or fireplace is moved, the exterior appearance is affected. If the house is made larger or an ell added, the exterior styling is greatly changed. It is not a matter of whether the exterior or interior should be planned first — they must be planned together. Therefore,

as each change in a floor plan is made, consider its effect on the exterior styling.

A decision as to the type of house desired should be made early in the planning stage. This frequently dictates the layout of the floor plan. For example, the floor plan of a two-story colonial house is as fixed as its exterior styling. A rambling ranch-type house permits greater planning freedom, but generally eliminates attic rooms. Such problems should be recognized and resolved early in the planning.

Once the floor plan has been developed to what seems to be a final form, it is well to check each room to see if it meets the principles of room planning. (See Chapter 2.) This can be done by making scale templates of the furniture expected to be in the room. Arrange these in their locations on the scale floor plan. Now check the aisles of traffic in each room. See if windows need to be moved or rooms made larger. Determine if there is sufficient room between furniture to walk freely. Such a check frequently makes additional changes in the floor plan necessary.

As the width and length of the house and its rooms are being decided, use the principles of modular planning. A *module* is a standard unit of measure. This concept is explained in detail in Chapter 5. Modular planning saves materials and reduces labor costs because most construction materials are made on a 4-inch standard modular unit. Buildings are designed using 16 inches and 24 inches as minor modules and 48 inches as the major module. For example, sheets of sheathing material are 4'-0" x 8'-0". The 4'-0" width is three 16-inch or two 24-inch modules.

By designing room sizes to fit the 16-inch module, the interior partitions can be constructed utilizing the regular studs. This results in a saving of one extra stud at each partition. See Fig. 2. Note that the regular studs are spaced 16 inches on center. If a window or door opening occurs, extra studs are inserted, since the 16-inch spacing is not broken by an opening. See Fig. 3.

Another factor to consider before finalizing the plan is to see if the width of the house affords the most economical use of lumber for floor and ceiling joists. Lumber is sold in lengths by two-foot increments, such as 10'-0", 12'-0", 14'-0". If a joist 12'-3" is needed, a 14'-0" joist must be purchased, and 1'-9" of it must be cut off and thrown away. Careful

planning permits the use of as much of a joist as possible and enables the most house to be built for the money.

Consider the example in Fig. 4. The width of the house is 26'-4". This requires one 12'-0" joist and one 14'-0" joist. No waste is involved. If the width of this house were increased to 26'-6", the 12'-0" joist would not reach, and a 14'-0" joist would be necessary. This would cause a waste of 22 inches on each joist. Multiply this by the number of joists needed, and the amount of waste becomes considerable.

If the house is to be constructed from factory assembled modular wall components, design the length and width to use the modular measure. Details on a modular component system are in Chapter 5.

Some houses are constructed from factory assembled modular units. A modular unit is a room size or larger part of a building that is completely finished in a factory. It is moved to the building site much like a mobile home. Details for this system are also in Chapter 5. When making a floor plan for such a house, the rooms have to be planned so the modular units will fit together.

Once the width of the house has been decided, it is time to put in wall thicknesses on the sketch. Exterior frame walls are usually 6 inches, solid masonry walls 8 inches, masonry veneer walls 10 inches, and interior partitions 5 inches. This will reduce floor area and will especially affect closet space and stair openings. Since closets should be at least 2'-0" clear inside, the sketch must provide 2'-5" between centers of studs for closet depth; the extra 5 inches is allowance for the thickness of the partition. With a little practice, this addition for wall thickness will become habitual.

Before drawing the final, detailed, floor plan on vellum, it is wise to make several freehand sketches of the exterior of the house and to work out the details of the roof. Occasionally, an unbalanced or unpleasant exterior has

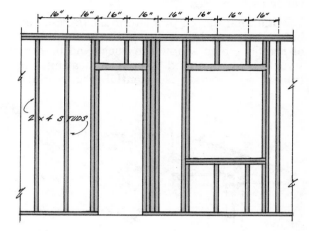

Fig. 3. Framing detail indicating stud locations at door and window openings.

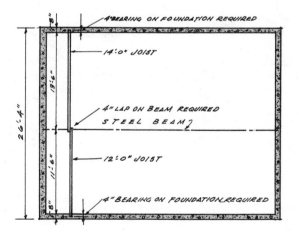

Fig. 4. Foundation plan illustrating maximum use of joist length.

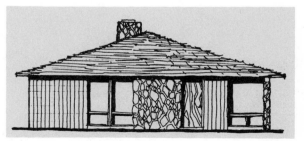

Fig. 5. Freehand preliminary sketch of a possible house elevation.

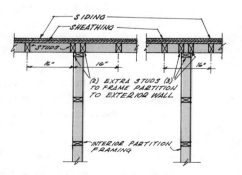

Fig. 2. Horizontal wall section showing details of framing an interior partition to studs 16" o.c.

been created by quirks of interior planning. Also, some very difficult and expensive roof-framing problems can occur and must be corrected before proceeding. This will change the floor plan and, sometimes, the basic shape of the house. See Fig. 5.

One final design problem must be resolved before it is safe to proceed with the final draft of the floor plan — how the house will be constructed. A freehand sketch indicating the typical wall section is essential, Fig. 6. Such

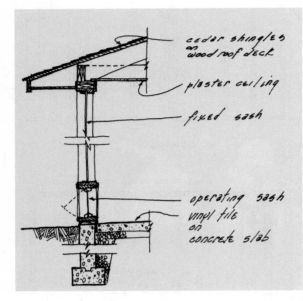

Fig. 6. Freehand trial sketch of a wall section.

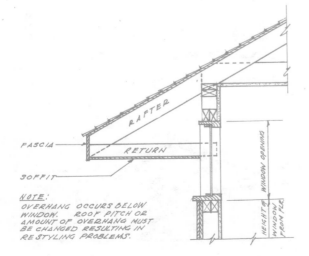

Fig. 7. Section illustrating a cornice error that must be corrected before planning can continue.

preliminary planning will frequently correct errors that will influence the elevations. A recurring error is to have a large overhang at the eaves, with the return ending below the head of the window. See Fig. 7.

After the floor plan is finalized, the elevations planned, and the wall section decided upon, it is safe to proceed with the drafting of the final floor plan.

Summary of Planning Steps

1. List all the things wanted in the house.
2. Examine existing plans for one near to what you want.
3. Try to "live in" the plan.
4. Revise the plan to better meet your needs.
5. Study traffic problems.
6. Apply principles of planning to each room as explained in Chapter 2.
7. Consider the proper orientation of the house.
8. Check to see if stock parts such as joists can be used with little waste.
9. Sketch wall thickness on revised plan.
10. Sketch exterior elevations. (See Chapter 3.)
11. Examine roof for problems. (See Chapter 3.)
12. Ascertain wall construction. (See Chapter 5.)
13. If all checks, then begin drafting final floor plan.

Traffic Patterns

As the house is being planned, constant attention must be given to the flow of traffic through the house. Considerable inconvenience can be caused by poor room relationship. People must be able to move from room to room and from one part of the house to another with a minimum of congestion and unnecessary steps. Rooms can be rendered useless by having a main traffic aisle directed through them.

Following is a list of factors to observe as the flow of traffic between rooms is considered.

1. In most homes, the heaviest flow of traffic will occur between the kitchen and dining areas, the bedrooms and bath, and the living and dining areas.
2. The dining area should be next to the kitchen and easily accessible. This eases the task of serving a meal and cleaning up. No hall should separate these areas.

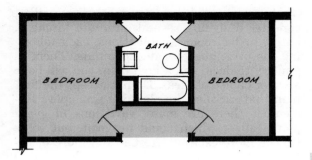

Fig. 8. A bathroom situation lacking privacy.

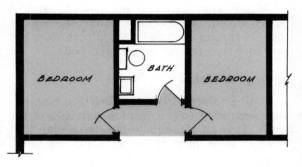

Fig. 9. A satisfactory solution permitting privacy in the bath.

3. It should be possible to enter the kitchen
    without crossing the dining area. An aisle
    of traffic through a dining room could be
    completely blocked, if the family were
    seated at the table.
4. The kitchen should have an outside door.
    This is necessary for removing trash and
    taking laundry to the line. It also gives
    the children an entrance to use, so they
    do not soil the carpets.
5. The garage or carport should be near the
    kitchen and have an entrance permitting
    easy access into it. This facilitates bring-
    ing in supplies and entering the house in
    bad weather.
6. Each bedroom should have easy and quick
    access to a bath — no other room should
    come between these. The location of a
    bath between two bedrooms with en-
    trances from each room is very unsatis-
    factory. See Fig. 8 for an example. This
    robs everyone of privacy. If the door to
    one bedroom is locked, then those in that
    bedroom cannot use the bath without
    going through the other bedroom. All
    things considered, it is not a good solu-
    tion. Fig. 9 illustrates a more satisfactory
    solution.

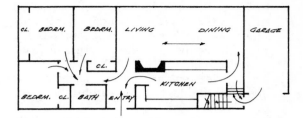

Fig. 10. A plan with a good traffic pattern.

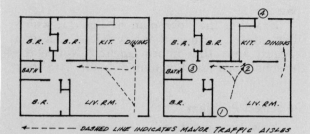

Fig. 11. A plan and a revision to improve the flow of traffic. Such revisions do not increase the cost of the house.

	Revision	*Reason*
1.	Moved front entrance	Eliminates traffic through center of living room.
2.	Put in kitchen door	Can get to bath and bedrooms without going through dining room and living room.
3.	Moved bath door over	Adds to privacy of bath. People cannot sit in living room and see in bath.
4.	Added rear door	Essential to be able to get to rear of house from inside. Without this, trash must be carried out front door.

7. Each bedroom should have access to a
    hall. It is very poor to have to go through
    one bedroom to reach another.
8. It is desirable to be able to go to the
    front entrance without crossing through
    the dining area or living area. This prin-
    ciple of traffic flow is occasionally violated
    under the guise of economy. If the front
    entrance opens directly into the living
    area, the expense of an entrance hall or
    foyer is eliminated, but the effective
    space in the living area is also cut.
9. It is ideal to be able to enter a house
    and go to the bedroom area or bath
    without crossing through the living area.
    This is desirable for the sake of privacy.
10. An inside means of reaching the basement
    is vital. This is best if it can be built off
    the kitchen area. It is also very helpful

to have this inside basement access so situated that a person can go directly outside from the basement, without passing through the living or dining areas or front entrance hall.

11. An outside entrance to a basement is highly desirable, but not absolutely essential.

Fig. 10 illustrates a well planned house. The arrows indicate the heaviest traffic patterns. Can you find any way to improve the traffic pattern?

Examine the floor plan in Fig. 11, which illustrates a plan and its revision. Can you suggest any other improvements? Notice the reasons given for the changes made. Are they valid?

Required Problem

Now try your hand at improving the following floor plans (Fig. 12). It probably will take several tries before you are satisfied with a plan. Remember it usually is necessary to revise a plan several times. Submit the revised plan to others for their opinions. Sometimes, another person can see things you have overlooked. Constantly apply the principles of planning for traffic movement as presented in this chapter.

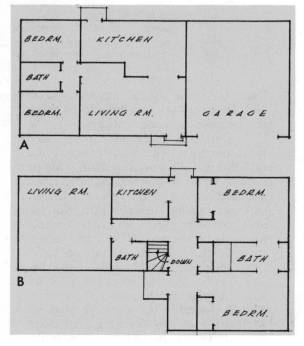

Fig. 12.

As you work on your plan revisions, consider designing several alternate kitchens, baths, or bedroom combinations, each following the principles of sound planning. Then, as you try to decide on a final plan, you will have a wider choice of ideas. Do not accept the first plan that satisfies the planning principles. Remember there are many variations of every plan — all of which could be good, but some will be more exciting, fresher and more pleasing to you. This is your goal — a plan that is not just sound, but one that pleases you and is stimulating, fresh and exciting.

Sketch your revisions on ¼-inch squared paper, letting each square equal one square foot. Be careful that the revised plan does not introduce new factors considered poor.

Zoning the House

Zoning refers to the dividing of a house in areas according to the various activities of the family. It is an attempt to develop a plan that provides some privacy for each person. Obviously, some activities in a home conflict. Noise from children playing is not conducive to sleep. However, a house can usually be divided into the quiet area, including the sleeping and study areas, and the noisy area, such as the living room, recreation and food areas. When the zoning of activities is considered, the bedrooms are usually placed in one end of the house or in a wing away from the living area. Placing a sound barrier between the sleeping area and the living area, reduces transmission of noises. A stair, hall, or a closet provides an effective sound barrier to help isolate the sleeping area.

Usually, formal and quiet entertaining take place in the living room. This means that some provision should be made for the more active recreation activities. A basement recreation room is an excellent location for noisy activities, although a ground-level recreation room, located off or near the kitchen, is good.

If a family desires quiet and privacy for reading, a den or study should be provided. Again, this must be away from the living area. In most houses, it is closely related to the sleeping area.

The kitchen and dining areas are best separated from the other areas. This reduces the annoyance of cooking odors and the disturbances from running water and the clatter of dishes.

The formal dining area usually is very near the kitchen, but separated from its view and traffic. This insures a relaxed and pleasant environment for dining. However, in many homes, these areas are combined.

Fig. 13 illustrates a plan that takes advantage of zoning considerations.

Planning Stairs and Halls

Stairs and halls are the means utilized for assisting the flow of traffic through a house and between levels of a house. They are not classified as living space. Other than facilitating movement about a house, they are wasted space and, therefore, should be kept to a minimum.

Halls

The average hall should be at least 3'-0" wide from finished wall to finished wall. A wider hall is nice, but becomes expensive because it serves as little more than a passageway. Sometimes, building in a storage wall or

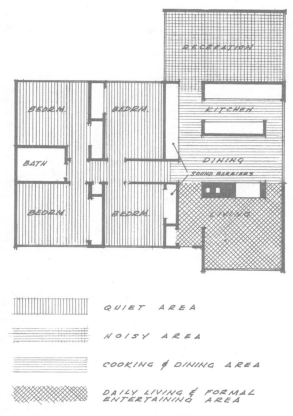

Fig. 13. A plan with activities carefully zoned to improve livability.

Fig. 14. A simple stair in a contemporary Hawaiian house.

closets along one side of a hall makes it more useful.

Usually, a long hall becomes a rather dark tunnel-like area. In flat-top contemporary homes, skylights are used to combat this, but most homes must rely on electric lighting. The best solution is to try to eliminate the long hall during the planning stage.

As mentioned earlier, an entrance hall or foyer improves a plan and the traffic flow. However, it does consume space and, therefore, costs money.

Probably, the most frequent use for a hall is to provide access to bedrooms and baths.

Stairs

Almost every house, except a one-story house with no basement, has a stairway of some kind. Most stairs in recently built houses are very simple in design. See Fig. 14. The

stairs found in some of the traditional homes are massive and very ornate. Such stairs are ready masterpieces of design, but they are expensive and rarely used today.

Fig. 15 illustrates the parts involved in a simple stair and the proper name for each. Fig. 16 indicates how stair treads and risers are secured with wedges.

The tread is the portion of the stair that is stepped upon, while the riser is the vertical member running between treads. These are fastened into grooves, cut in long side boards called stringers.

Interior stairways between floors should have a minimum continuous head clearance of 6'-8'', while basement stairways should have a minimum of 6'-4''. This distance is measured vertically from the edge of each tread, as indicated in Fig. 17.

The main stairs should have a minimum width of 2'-8'' clear of the handrail, while basement stairs should be at least 2'-6'' clear of the handrail. There must be enough width to allow the passage of large pieces of furniture such as beds and dressers, when these are moved. If a stair has a sharp turn, such as a 90° turn, this, together with a minimum width, could prevent the passage of furniture from floor to

floor. As stairs are planned, ascertain if such passage is possible.

If a stair is in a location where it must frequently accommodate the passage of two people, it should be at least 3'-6'' wide.

Any stair having a door that opens toward the run of the stair must have a landing provided. This is necessary for the safety of persons using the stair. To open a door and, immediately, have to step down one tread is extremely dangerous. Notice the landing in Fig. 17.

All stairs should have a handrail on at least one side. This prevents falls and assists older people in ascending and descending.

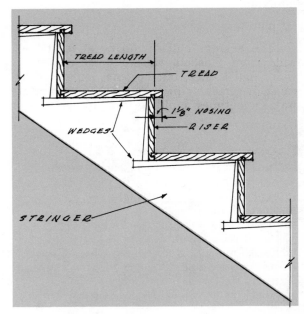

Fig. 16. Stair construction.

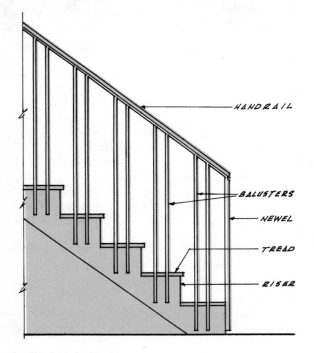

Fig. 15. Stair terminology.

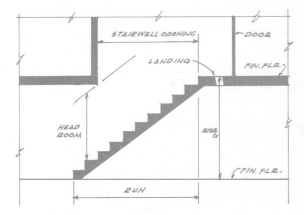

Fig. 17. How headroom, rise and run are measured.

The pitch of the stair relates to the slope of the stringer. The steeper the pitch, the steeper the stair, and the shorter the run. The lower the pitch, the longer the run. See Fig. 17 for an indication of total run and total rise. For use in a home, stairs should be no steeper than 9:8 pitch or less than 5:16 pitch. A 5:16 pitch means 5 inches of rise for every 16 inches of run.

The stairway in Fig. 17 has ten treads, each 9 inches long, and eleven risers, each 8 inches high. The total run, then, is 10 times 9 inches or 90 inches, or 7'-8''. The total rise is 11 times 8 inches, or 88 inches, or 7'-4''. Note that there is always one more riser than tread.

The nosing overhangs the riser and is not included as part of the tread width; therefore, a 9-inch tread is really 10-1/8 inches wide, as most nosings are 1-1/8 inches. A 9-inch tread is minimum for use in main and basement stairs.

As the height of the riser increases, the standard tread size decreases. Table 1 lists commonly used tread and riser sizes. To read this table, determine what the tread or riser size will be; then pick the proper size for the unknown part. For example, a stair with a 10-inch tread should have a 7½-inch riser. If the total rise does not exactly fit this table so the number of risers works out even, the size of the riser can be varied. For example, if a stair has a 10-inch tread, but needs a riser of 7-3/4 inches to make the steps all equal in size, this is quite acceptable. However it would be poor planning to use a 9-inch riser with a 10-inch tread.

Table 1
Commonly Used Tread and Riser Sizes

Tread	Riser
8''	9''
9''	8''
10''	7½''
11''	7''

A riser 8-1/4 inches is considered maximum for use in a home. Risers above this height are too uncomfortable to use in places frequently traveled. The most commonly used risers are from 6-5/8'' to 7-5/8''.

Types of Stairs

The most commonly used types of stairs in homes are the straight, the *L* and *U*.

The straight flight is the least expensive to install and the easiest to move large articles up and down. If room is available on the floor plan, a long flight of straight stairs can be improved by placing a landing halfway in the flight. This gives the person ascending a spot to pause and rest.

If floor space is not available for a straight stair, an *L* or *U* stair can be used. The location of the landings can be varied to suit the conditions of the house and permit the necessary headroom.

Winders are triangular-shaped treads used to turn a corner in a stair without using a landing. They utilize less floor space than that required by a stair with a landing. Such stairs are not advised, however, because they are very dangerous. The tread at the turn is so narrow only a small portion of the foot can

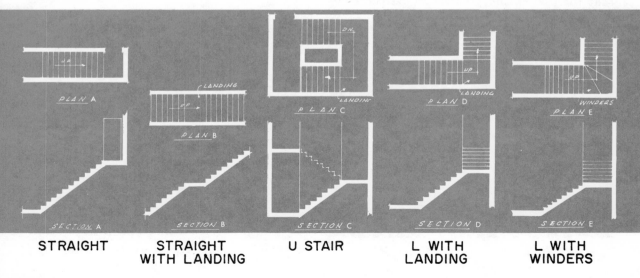

| STRAIGHT | STRAIGHT WITH LANDING | U STAIR | L WITH LANDING | L WITH WINDERS |

Fig. 18. Common types of stairs.

be rested upon it; this may result in slipping and bad falls. It is also very difficult to move furniture on such a stair, because of the tight turn.

These and other common types of stairs are illustrated in Fig. 18.

How to Figure a Stairway

Assume a straight stair is going to run from the first floor to the basement. Two things must be ascertained before riser and tread sizes can be decided. First, the *total rise* must be found, and, second, the amount of space available for the *total run* must be determined. Then a drawing such as Fig. 19 should be made. This sets forth the total rise.

The total rise is the basement ceiling height of 7'-3" plus 7-1/2" for the actual joist size plus 1-1/2" for the subfloor and finish floor. This equals a total rise of 8'-0".

An examination of a table of stair sizes[1] indicates that twelve 8-inch risers will equal the 8'-0" distance. This can also be ascertained by dividing the total rise, 8'-0", by the selected riser height, 8 inches. Further examination of the stair table (or Table 1) indicates that an 8-inch riser requires a 9-inch tread. Since there is always one or more riser than tread, this stairway will have eleven treads of 9 inches each, which gives a total run for the stair of 99 inches or 8'-3".

In summary, a stair with twelve 8-inch risers and eleven 9-inch treads would solve this stair problem.

An examination of a stair table indicates that there are other possible riser-tread combinations that also will be satisfactory. For example, if the above stair is considered too

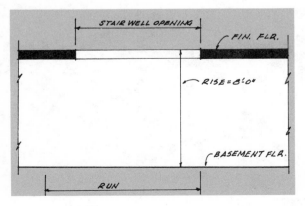

Fig. 19. Stair problem.

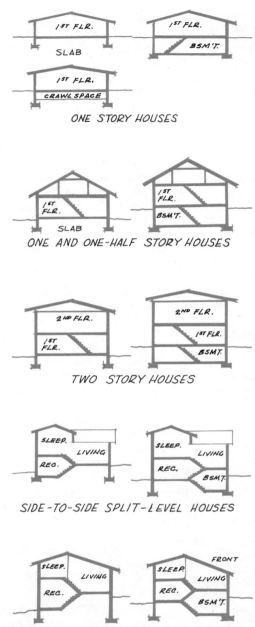

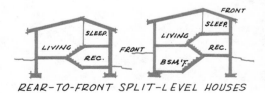

Fig. 20. Typical house types.

steep, fifteen risers of 6.4 inches with fourteen treads of 12.5 inches would be satisfactory. Use of a stair table such as that presented in the *Time Saver Standards*[1] saves calculation and aids in designing a comfortable stairway.

Basic House Types

As choices are being made during the planning stages, an early, essential decision is the type of house to build. See Fig. 20. The thinking of the planner must be centered about a specific, basic type. Ideas for a good split-level type may not be at all suitable for a ranch-house type.

One Story

A one-story house has all the habitable rooms on one level. A ranch house is an example. Most long, low, contemporary homes are of this type. An advantage is that any room can be reached without ascending or descending stairs. Some one-story houses have a basement with a flight of stairs, while others are built on a concrete slab or over a crawl space. The attic space is small and not usable for expansion of living area, but is useful for limited storage. A house of this type usually has a low-pitched or flat roof. See Fig. 21.

Fig. 21. A one-story house.

One-and-One-Half-Story

The one-and-one-half-story house is similar to a one-story, except it has a high-pitched roof, making the attic space useful for living area. Generally, it has two bedrooms and a bath on the first floor and additional bedrooms and a bath on the second floor. About half of the total square footage of the attic floor is useful living area; space with less than 5-foot

[1]*Time Saver Standards, Architectural Record* (Editorial Staff).

headroom is not considered useful. The walls and ceiling slant, and knee walls are necessary. Dormers on the front and a shed dormer off the rear are common.

This is an economical house to build, because it offers a considerable number of square feet of living area, with only the extra cost of the higher roof, dormers, and stair. This type of home is desirable as an expansion house. The Cape Cod is a popular one-and-one-half-story house, Fig. 22.

Two Story

The two-story house has been a favorite for years. It consists of a first floor and full second floor of the same square footage as the first floor. It affords certain economies, the most important being a large number of square feet of living area with a minimum of foundation and roof being required. Any heat loss through the first-floor ceiling benefits the rooms on the

Fig. 22. A one-and-one-half-story house.

Fig. 23. A two-story house.

second floor. Also, this type house can be built on a smaller lot than the long, rambling homes. See Fig. 23.

While most two-story houses are of a traditional style, architects have designed excellent contemporary two-story houses.

Cost of two-story houses can be slightly reduced and styling influenced by dropping the eaves below the ceiling line of the second-floor rooms. This usually makes the addition of dormers necessary, which, while changing styling, could negate the savings of lowering the eaves. Nevertheless, it does make an interesting house exterior. Note Fig. 24.

The long flight of stairs to the second floor is somewhat of a disadvantage, especially since all bedrooms are on the second floor in most two-story houses. A half-bath located on the first floor is an essential item.

The two-story house can be built with or without a basement.

Split-Level

A split-level is really a one-story house with a basement, which has had one portion of it pushed up so the basement is about halfway out of the ground. The living area, generally, is on the ground level, with a deep basement below. The bedrooms are on the highest level, with a garage, utility area, recreation room, or additional bedrooms in the raised portion of the basement below. Such a plan converts what, generally, is a large, wasted, basement space into light, well-ventilated, living space. See Fig. 25.

The split-level house is admirably suited for sloping lots. Some people build this type on flat lots and fill in around them. This usually results in a high, off-balance exterior and should be avoided for the sake of esthetics.

There are a number of frequently used variations of the split-level. Most commonly used is the side-to-side split. This is well suited for lots sloping to the right or left. Such a house can have three or four levels.

The front-to-rear split is well suited for lots sloping away from the street. From the street, the house appears as a one-story, while from the rear, it appears as a two-story.

A similar split is from rear to front, giving the street elevation the appearance of a two-story house. This is well suited for lots sloping toward the street.

Common House Shapes

The shape of a house influences the layout of the floor plan, exterior styling, and cost.

The most common shapes are the square, rectangle, *L*, *U*, and *T*. Projections from a house, at right angles to the length of the main portion of the house, are called *ells*.

Ells or breaks in a long elevation do much to improve the appearance, but they do increase the cost, for each break causes extra corners. The more the house deviates from the square shape, the more *lineal feet* of wall and footings are required. See Fig. 26. Notice that the square house has 1600 feet of floor space, 4 corners, and 160 lineal feet of wall and footing. Both rectangular houses have the same square footage of floor space, but one has 174 lineal feet of wall and footing, and the other has 200 lineal feet. The less square the house, the more expensive it will become. The *L* plan also has 1600 square feet of floor space, but has 6 corners and 200 lineal feet of wall and footing. Thus can be seen the reason for considering cost as house shape changes.

The rectangular shape is used more frequently than the square shape, because it makes it easier to develop a satisfactory floor plan. A good, square floor plan is very difficult to devise.

Fig. 24. Two-story house with eave below second-story ceiling height.

Fig. 25. Split-level house.

The *L* shape costs a little more, mainly because of the extra corners and more expensive roof framing; but the extra cost is well spent when the exterior styling is considered. This same reasoning can apply to houses built in other shapes; the cost is increased, but there is more freedom for interior planning and exterior styling.

Building Codes

Most localities, especially in and around cities, have building codes which must be ob-

served by the designer and contractor. *Building codes* are statements (established by community officials), indicating the minimum acceptable standard of quality in construction. They are enforced by inspectors who come to the building site and check the house during the various phases of construction.

In addition to local building codes, certain other organizations, such as mortgage and loan companies and the Federal Housing Administration, set minimum acceptable requirements for home construction. These codes must be

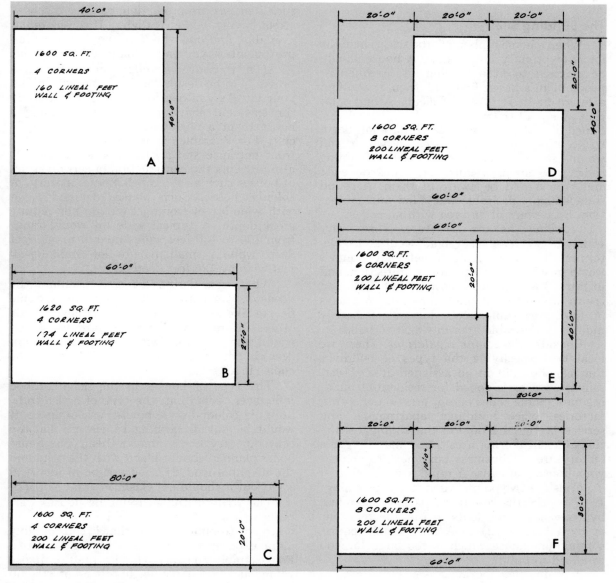

Fig. 26. Typical house shapes.

met by the builder before an organization will loan money to construct the house.

Another possible place to look for building requirements is in the deed to the land upon which a house is to be built. A *deed* is a written contract which conveys the title of ownership of a piece of real estate to the purchaser. A deed frequently contains building restrictions. For example, it may require the house to be one story, or brick, or to have a basement; or it may require all houses built on the land involved to be two stories high. The deed deserves careful examination.

The Building Site

When a home is planned, the selection of the lot is of primary importance. A house should be planned to fit a specific lot. Frequently, people plan a house first and, then, try to find a lot to fit it. It is very difficult to find a lot that meets all the requirements of a predetermined plan. In making a search for a lot, begin by locating the general area in which you would like to live. Investigate the building codes, for harsh or outdated codes do exist and you should be aware of them. A sound code is highly desirable and is for your protection. So beware of an area with no codes.

Examine the tax structure. Taxes vary widely between areas, even adjacent areas. Determine if you are going to get your money's worth in schools, streets, police protection, and utilities. Visit the local government office and try to find out what the future holds for taxes in that area. Low taxes do not necessarily indicate a desirable area in which to build.

Consider the *zoning regulations*. These are local laws specifying the types of buildings that can be built in an assigned area. Ascertain if an area is zoned for residential building only. Some zones permit erection of stores, factories, office buildings, apartments, and service stations. Examine the zoning restrictions of neighboring areas. You may border a factory area; a business built next to or near your house can cause a rapid loss of value.

Consider two points when studying zoning: (1) How are the zoning regulations amended; by vote of the residents in the affected zone or by a board? (2) Does the zoning require a minimum house which is too large for you to afford to build?

Examine neighboring areas. Drive around the streets bordering the area of interest to you. Look for objectionable factors such as noisy, busy thoroughfares, dumps, swamps, railroads, or substandard sections of houses. Is the neighborhood on the downgrade? All these factors will lower the future value of your house and the pride you will have living there.

Look for the conveniences you desire. These could include easy access to shopping centers, schools, bus service, and churches. The availability of utilities (gas, water, sewers, and electricity), as well as telephone service, should be considered. It is wise to check into such items as fire protection, garbage disposal, street paving, and streetlights. If these are not available, find out who is to pay for these improvements — you individually or the public.

If a thorough examination of the area proves it to be desirable, you are ready to find your lot. As you consider various sites, study the size and shape of the lots. Planning a house to fit a narrow, deep lot is quite difficult. For example, it is hard to locate the front entrance and a garage on such a lot. It also prevents the construction of certain styles of houses such as the ranch, contemporary, or colonial house. Such houses demand a lot with wide street frontage, but do not require great depth. A typical wide lot would range from 100 to 130 feet wide and 130 to 150 feet deep, while a small, narrow lot could be 40 feet wide by 125 feet deep.

When considering lot size, examine the needs of your family and their interests. Some people like gardens and spacious lawns while others desire a minimum of yard work and would not be happy with a large yard. Children in the family may also influence the choice in lot size.

The type of houses in the neighborhood influences, somewhat, the type of house to be built. If colonial-style houses predominate, it would be out of keeping to place a flat-top contemporary house among them. The house being planned should blend with the others in the neighborhood. It need not be of identical style, but it should not clash.

The value of the surrounding houses warrants consideration. It would be a risky investment to build a house that is considerably more expensive than any other in the area. For example, if a contractor built a house valued at $25,000 in a neighborhood of $15,000 houses, it would be very difficult to sell, be-

cause the family able to afford the more expensive house would also prefer to live with other families in a similar income bracket. Many families in the lower income bracket would like to purchase the expensive house, but probably would have great difficulty in raising the down payment and making the monthly payments. Most loaning organizations would refuse to issue them a loan, because of their lower income.

Sloping land can present advantages as well as difficulties. A flat lot is easiest to build upon, but most difficult to landscape interestingly. A lot with some slope aids in drainage of the yard and could make the basement partially or fully exposed even to the point of having a walk-out basement. Steeply sloped lots frequently make retaining walls and expensive fills necessary. Low-lying lots usually should be avoided, because dampness problems frequently are encountered.

An examination of the portion of this chapter illustrating the basic house types shows why some types of homes are better adapted to lots with a particular slope. It would be a mistake to plan and draw a long, low, ranch-style house and, then, purchase a lot with a steep slope. This would not be in keeping with the character of the house.

The condition of the soil should be examined. A layer of topsoil at least a foot thick is excellent. Sand or clay below the topsoil is fine. Watch for indications of rock close beneath the surface. The occurrence of rock may eliminate the possibility of having a basement, and it may make footings expensive and septic tanks almost impossible. Recently filled lots should be avoided, because they will not support a house, and the walls will crack due to settling.

Examine the deed of the lot for building restrictions and possible easements. An *easement* is the right granted by the owner of land to utility companies to cross portions of this land with gas and water mains and electric lines, and it, also, grants them the right to come on the land to service or repair them. If there are easements, see if any will cause inconvenience, expense, or difficulty after the house is built.

Upon being satisfied that the lot is the one you want, make a minimum down payment and sign a sales agreement. Do not pay for the lot in full until you have a lawyer search the title and have the property surveyed. When you are certain the title is clear, with no prior liens, it is safe to pay the balance.

Accept only a warranty deed. A good safety device is to get a title guarantee from a guarantee insurance firm. Such a firm will guarantee the title to be clear and will pay any liens against it, should they occur.

Topography

Plot Plans

Before buying or building on a piece of ground, the owner should have it surveyed. For a fee, a surveyor will come to the property and carefully ascertain the information desired. From this information, he will draw a plot plan. A *plot plan* is a top view of the lot, which usually shows the lot and block number, if the lot is in a development; the dimensions of the lot; the north point; the dimensions of the front, rear and side yard; the location and dimensions of the garage, carport or other accessory buildings; the location of walks, driveways and approaches, steps, terraces, porches, fences and retaining walls; and the location and size of easements and required setbacks from the street, or lot boundries. A typical plan is shown in Fig. 27.

The plot plan also should indicate the elevation above the local datum level of the first floor of the house, the garage or carport floor and other buildings, the elevation of the finished curb and crown of the street, and the finish grade level at each principal corner of the house. The *datum level* is an assumed basic level, used as a reference for reckoning heights. In various areas, especially cities, this datum level is established as a part of the building code, and it controls all building standards for that area or city.

If special grading, drainage provisions or foundations are necessary, their elevations must be specified on the plot plan. Each corner of the lot should have the existing grade and the finish grade after the special grading is done. If grading involves the immediate area around a house (such as a house on a steeply sloping lot requiring a back fill), the existing grade at each corner of the house should be indicated.

The finish grade on both sides of retaining walls should be given.

Some indication as to how the lot drains should be given. If a private well is on the property or a private sewage disposal system is to be used, this should be indicated on the plot plan.

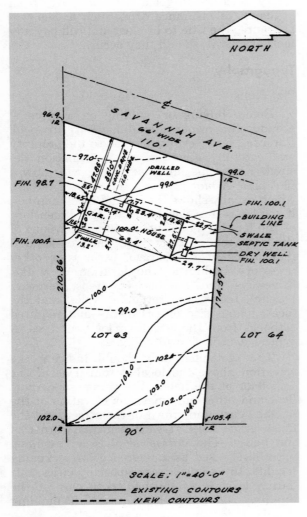

Fig. 27. Surveyor's plot plan.

This drawing was accompanied by signed statements that "the undersigned, a Registered Civil Engineer under the laws of the State of Michigan, certifies that he has made a survey of Lot 63, Plat of 'Broan Addition', Section 6, T.2 S., R. 10 W., Township of Comstock, County of Kalamazoo, State of Michigan, as recorded in the Office of the Register of Deeds for Kalamazoo County. Measurements were made and corners perpetuated in accordance with the true and established lines of the property as described, and the dimensions and lines of the property are indicated on the following Plat. The above Survey, Plat and Certificate are hereby certified correct as described. Surveyed December 29, 1958; Survey No. 2929 - 97."

Contour Plans

More complete information about the existing and finished slope of a lot can be obtained by having a surveyor establish contour lines. On a plan of a piece of land, *contour lines* connect points having the same elevation above or below an established level, such as the datum level or sea level. Refer again to Fig. 27.

Contour lines are very useful in orienting a house on a lot, for they indicate amount of slope. For example, widely spaced contour lines indicate a gradual slope; closely spaced lines define a steep slope.

Landscape Plans

A *landscape plan* indicates the location of the house, garage, and drives and walks. It also shows the location and, frequently, the species of the plantings that are to be made on the lot.

Such a plan is made by a landscape architect. His services are most often engaged by owners of expensive houses, because he charges

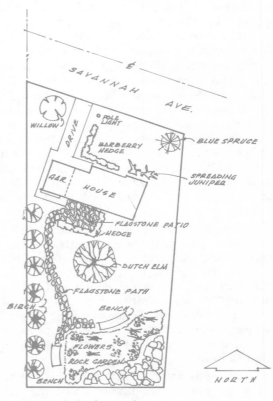

Fig. 28. A simple landscape plan.

An eating area can be designed as part of the kitchen. (Coppes Napanee)

A counter provides an eating area that occupies only a small floor area. (Azrock Floor Products)

An island counter gives extra working and storage space. (Tappan)

This kitchen has the fixtures in an L-shaped plan with storage on a third wall. Notice the direct access to the dining area. (Kitchen Kompact, Inc.)

This tight U counter puts storage, preparation, and serving areas close together. Notice the planning desk. (Tappan)

A minimum L-shaped kitchen. Notice that counter space is provided on each side of the cooking unit and sink. (Tappan)

The water closet is located in a private alcove. (Kohler)

A comfortable seat and counter is provided for personal grooming. Notice the water closet in a separate compartment. (Kohler)

This bath has a spacious plan. Notice the bathtub is open on both sides. (Kohler)

This bath occupies a minimum of space. (Kohler)

16C

Book shelves and a wall storage cabinet can add to the atmosphere of a room. (Coppes Napanee)

A fireplace can serve as the center of attention in a living area. (Vega Industries, Inc.)

The laundry area requires a sink and counter space. It can have a bright, cheery atmosphere. (General Electric Co.)

a fee. Many nurseries offer free landscaping services and advice to their customers. This enables most persons to have some assistance in planning the plantings that will surround their house.

Since the plan as drawn by the landscape architect indicates the species of the plantings, it can be used to obtain competitive bids on the plantings and their installation. Fig. 28 illustrates a simple landscape plan.

Prevailing Winds

A little time spent in a study to determine the direction from which the prevailing winds blow will pay big dividends.

In the summer, the air should blow through the living area and sleeping area. If something blocks these breezes, one must resort to fans or air conditioning. Examine your site to see if a hill or growth of trees will block the summer breeze. A house in a hollow may miss all breeze and be stifling.

Undesirable winter winds present an entirely different problem. Every attempt should be made to block them. See Fig. 29. Place the garage and utility room so they will receive the brunt of winter storms. This greatly increases the comfort and ease of heating a home. A planting of trees or tall shrubs helps break the force of the wind and settle the snow. A northwest winter wind driving against a garage door will pile it high with snow and increase the difficulty of moving the automobile.

Winds can bring smoke and odors from nearby factories and make living objectionable

in what would be, otherwise, an acceptable area. In areas where high winds are common, construction must be strengthened to resist damage.

Prevailing Winds in the United States

Fig. 30 indicates the major normal surface wind directions in January and July. It presents an interesting study of the influence of mountains or bodies of water on the direction of prevailing winds. As a house is being planned for a particular location, check with the local weather bureau for specific information concerning the directions and peculiarities of the local winds.

The View and Privacy

If a lot presents a pleasant view, the living area should be placed to take advantage of it. The master bedroom, frequently, can be located to share the view or look upon another that is pleasing. Some families consider the view from the dining area of great importance. Occasionally, the best view will conflict with

Normal surface wind directions in January.

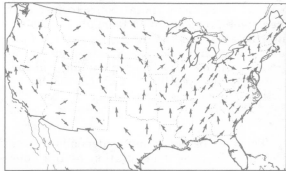

Normal surface wind directions in July.

Fig. 30. Normal surface winds (from *Climatic Atlas of the United States*, Visher, Harvard University Press, Cambridge, Mass.)

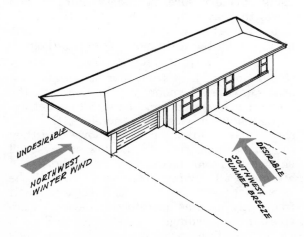

Fig. 29. A house oriented to the prevailing winds.

the orientation of the house in relation to the sun or the prevailing winds. A compromise must then be reached.

Many contemporary homes have few or no windows on the street side. A row of houses across the street usually is not the best view. A large glass area toward a street only exposes the activities in the house to the public. It is an intrusion upon the privacy of the occupants.

For the sake of privacy, fences can be built around glass window walls, or clusters of shrubbery can be planted.

Privacy in a bedroom can be attained by using long, narrow windows, placed approximately 5'-0" above the floor. This permits some light and ventilation, but guarantees privacy. However, other plans include full-length glass walls for the bedrooms. Such a plan requires special consideration in lot selection and landscaping to insure privacy.

Orientation

The orientation of a house on a lot is of great importance. This is something that must be considered as the house is being planned, because orientation influences the location of the rooms on the plan as well as the positioning of the house on the lot.

Orientation involves a consideration not only of the prevailing winds, views and privacy as already discussed, but also of the sun. Each of these affects the livability of the house. Generally it is not possible to incorporate all the best factors involved, but each should be considered and some provision made to help ease a bad situation. For example, if the hot western summer sun will bear on the bedroom wing in the evening, and if it is not possible to reorient these rooms to face east, then some provision must be made for sheltering this area. A large overhang, trees, a fence or some such device should be planned to break the sun's rays. Such planning will help overcome disagreeable factors caused by unfortunate orientation.

The Sun

The comfort of a home depends a great deal upon a careful orientation of the house to the sun. In the summer, the sun can make a poorly oriented house unbearably hot. In the winter, a poorly oriented house could lose the benefit of free solar heat.

The *south wall* of a house receives a sustained and intense exposure to the summer sun. This means that this side of the house will be bright and well illuminated all day, receiving considerable heat from the direct rays of the sun.

Proper orientation requires that the living area face south. It is desirable for the master bedroom to face south also. It is necessary, however, to provide a deep overhang or some other means of breaking the sun's rays during the heat of the day.

This southern wall could use large areas of glass to advantage. In the winter, it will benefit from the low rays of the sun by using this light to make the living area cheery and by using the heat to warm the room. Such an orientation can reduce winter fuel bills.

The *north wall* of a house receives only a small amount of direct sunlight. It needs little overhang or shading devices. The northern light is uniform and free from the glare. For this reason, artists value northern light. Generally, the garage, kitchen or utility room is placed to the north. Such rooms do not require a great deal of solar light or are affected considerably by solar heat. If a view is to the north, however, large areas of glass can be used to advantage to secure the even light, but there are few other advantages to this exposure.

The *east wall* of the house receives the early morning sunshine, which is usually moderate and pleasant. Bedrooms, kitchens and dining areas can be placed to advantage, using this exposure. A cheery morning sun starts the day right and brightens the breakfast table. It is wise to keep these windows high, so only the early morning rays will enter.

The *west wall* of the house receives intensive periods of heat from rays striking at low angles in the afternoon. As the sun sets, the angles get lower, causing the rays to penetrate any windows in this wall; therefore, this wall should have a minimum of windows, and they should be high, so only the lowest rays will enter. Any rooms facing west will be hot every afternoon all summer. Devices to control the rays of the sun are needed. A large porch is frequently used as a protective device, as are trees, fences, awnings and trellises. See Fig. 31. Deciduous trees are excellent, because they shade the house in the summer and shed their

leaves in the winter to permit the desirable winter sunlight to enter.

Fig. 32 illustrates why the south wall receives sunlight all day, the east wall in the morning, the west in the afternoon and why the north wall receives little or no sunlight at any time.

In the deep South and hot Southwest, the problem of orienting the house in relation to the sun is, somewhat, reversed. Usually, the living area faces north, and a wall with few or no windows faces south. A large roof overhang and trees are much desired on the hot, southern side.

There are two factors that directly influence the relationship between the sun and a house. One of these is the angle of the sun, called the *altitude*, and the other is the direction from which the sun rises and sets during the various seasons. This is called the *azimuth*.

The Altitude

The altitude is the angle formed by the rays of the sun and the earth's surface. Fig. 33 illustrates the maximum and minimum angles of the sun for the 40° parallel of latitude (sighting on Milwaukee). Angle *A* is 73°-30', and this occurs at noon June 22. From this date the angle gets lower each day until it reaches its minimum on December 22, when it is in position *B*. This angle would be 26°-30' for the 40° parallel of latitude.

Maximum and minimum altitudes for selected parallels of latitude can be found in architectural standards books.

It can be seen that the altitude of the sun is considerably lower in the winter than in the summer. This fact enables a designer to utilize the sun to warm the house in winter, yet to use such devices as a large roof overhang to shield the interior of the house from the hot, summer sun. See Fig. 34.

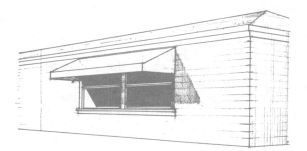

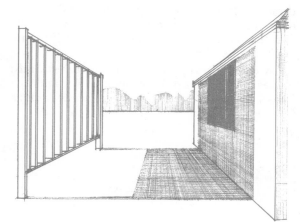

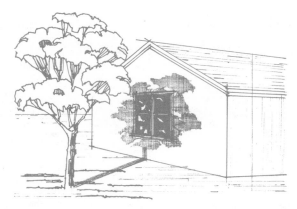

Fig. 31. Sun protective devices.

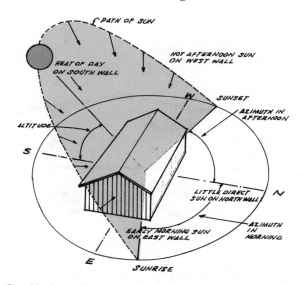

Fig. 32. Sun strikes east side of house in the morning, the south side through the middle of the day, and the west side in the late afternoon.

Since the altitude varies with the parallel of latitude, the amount of overhang needed also varies. Table 2 indicates the size overhang necessary to protect windows from the summer sun, but still permit the winter sun to enter. It can be seen that as the house is turned southeast or southwest, the amount of overhang must be increased to afford protection from the low-angle, early morning, east rays and the low-angle, late afternoon rays of the sun.

Table 2
Overhang Width for Sun Protection

Latitude	South Windows	Windows 30° E or 30° W of South
45°	3'-6"	6'-0"
40°	3'-0"	5'-4"
35°	2'-5"	4'-8"
30°	1'-10"	4'-1"
25°	1'-3"	3'-8"

The Azimuth

The sun rises from an easterly direction and sets in a westerly direction. It does not rise due east and set due west everyday. As the earth turns on its axis and revolves about the sun, the angle of inclination of the axis to the sun varies a little each day. This causes the direction from which the sun rises and sets to vary a few degrees each day.

This angle is measured from the north-south axis and is called the azimuth. In the morning, the azimuth is measured from the north-south axis in an easterly direction, and in the afternoon, it is measured in a westerly direction from the same axis. In Fig. 35, selected azimuth readings are recorded for the 40° parallel of latitude at sunrise, 11:00 a.m., 1:00 p.m., and sunset on June 22.

A complete report of altitude and azimuth angles can be found in architectural standards books and the *American Nautical Almanac*.

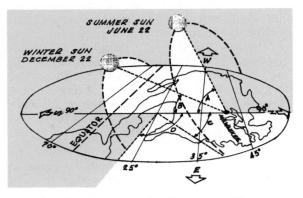

Fig. 33. Angle A is the altitude of the sun at Milwaukee at noon on June 22.

Angle B is the altitude on December 22.

Angle C is the azimuth at sunrise in Milwaukee on June 22.

Angle D is the azimuth on December 22.

(*House and Home* magazine)

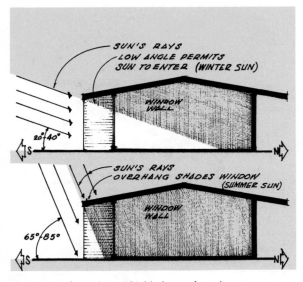

Fig. 34. Roof overhang shields house from hot summer sun, yet permits desirable winter sun rays to enter.

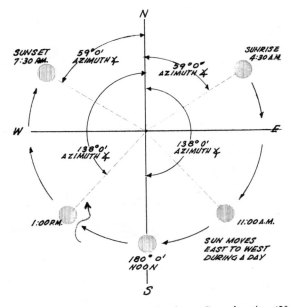

Fig. 35. Plan view showing azimuth readings for the 40° parallel of latitude on June 22.

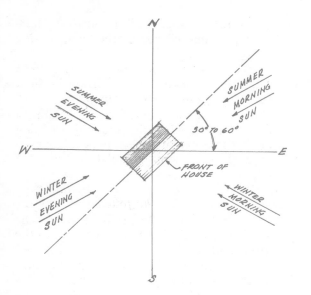

Fig. 36. Desirable orientation in relation to the sun in northern climates.

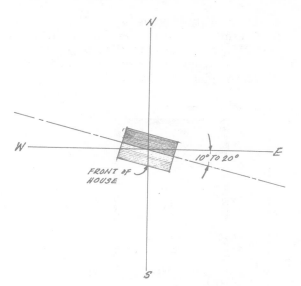

Fig. 37. Alternate position useful when orienting house in northern climates.

Positioning the House

In the northern states, the long axis of a house should be along a northeast to southwest angle. Usually, this angle is from 30° to 60°. This will cause the sunlight to strike the northern side of the house and help melt snow and ice. See Fig. 36.

Fig. 37 illustrates an alternate direction to orient a house in a northern climate. Such a location permits use of the southern exposure and takes advantage of some of the western heat in the winter. Any angle over 20° northwest to southeast would allow too much hot summer sun to hit the front of the house in the afternoon.

In the extreme South, the house can approach a true east-west direction with its major axis. This keeps the hot afternoon summer sun away from the living area. See Fig. 38.

How to Find the Shadow Cast by Overhang Using the Altitude and Azimuth

It is possible, to locate the shadow cast by the overhang on a house graphically, by using the altitude and azimuth of the house location.

For example, assume a cottage was built along the 45° parallel of latitude. To find where the shadow will fall on a particular day, refer to a table of altitudes and azimuth angles for that day. Let us assume the day to be

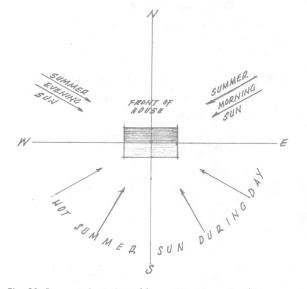

Fig. 38. Proper orientation of house in extreme South.

June 22, the longest day of the year, and the time 10 a.m. The tables indicate that the altitude is 57°-30', and the azimuth is 121°-30'. Now, follow these steps, shown in Fig. 39.

1. Lay out the plan of the building.
2. Locate the north-south axis.
3. Draw a line 121°-30' east of the north-south axis. It is east because it is in the morning. It would be west in the afternoon.

4. Draw altitude angle of 57°-30′.
5. On the plan, draw a ray line parallel to the 121°-30′ azimuth line. This passes through the extreme corner of the roof overhang on the plan (labeled *A*).

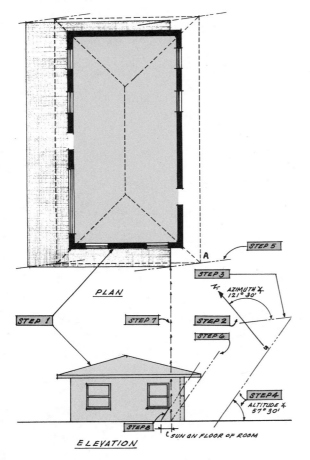

PLAN

ELEVATION

Fig. 39. How to find the shadow cast by a house.
1. Draw plan view and side view.
2. Locate north-south axis.
3. Draw azimuth (in this problem 121° 30′ E of N).
4. Draw altitude angle (in this problem 57° 30′).
5. Draw ray line parallel to azimuth through the corner of roof in plan view.
6. Draw ray line parallel to altitude through the same corner of roof in side view.
7. Project the point of intersection between the altitude ray and the ground line to plan view intersecting the azimuth ray.
Note: The shadow cast by any point may be found similarly. All horizontal planes (or lines) cast a shadow parallel to themselves and all vertical lines or planes cast a shadow parallel to the azimuth; therefore, the shadow is constructed by the intersection of azimuth rays and parallel lines.
8. To locate where the sun will fall inside a room, draw only a simple wall section instead of a side view.

6. Draw ray line parallel to altitude line, through same corner of the roof, in side view.
7. Project the altitude line from the point where it crosses the azimuth line until it cuts the azimuth line on the plan.
8. This intersection between the azimuth line and the altitude line on the plan locates the shadow line. The shadow runs through this point parallel to the roof edges.

If shadows for all sides of a building are desired, continue with the following steps:

9. Draw the front elevation. Project the shadow line into the front elevation to the ground line.
10. Connect the shadow line with the edge of the overhang. This gives the shadow angle.
11. Transfer this shadow angle to any other part of this elevation, where it is desired to find another shadow location.
12. Project this new shadow line from where it hits the ground line to the plan view. Where it cuts the azimuth line is another point of the shadow. This gives the location of the shadow on the plan.

Such a procedure even permits the location of the sun's rays inside a house. The length of the sun's rays inside the house is terminated by the head of the window casting a shadow on the floor.

If shadows are to be found for latitudes not given in the tables, refer to more elaborate tables, or use the *process of interpolation.* Following is an example:

Assume shadows were to be found for 43°-0′ latitude at 10 a.m., June 22. The tables indicate that for 45° latitude (the same time and date), the altitude is 57°-30′, and the azimuth is 121°-30′; for 40° latitude, the altitude is 60°-0′, and the azimuth is 114°-0′.

To find the altitude by interpolation, set up the problem as follows:

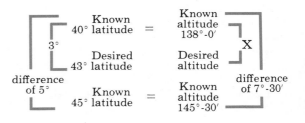

The altitude for 43° of latitude is desired. The 43° of latitude is ⅗ of the difference between 40° and 45° latitude. Therefore, the altitude angle is ⅗ of the difference between their known altitudes, 138°-0′ and 145°-30′. Let the unknown altitude be represented by the letter X.

Since the difference in latitudes is in the same proportion as the difference in altitudes, it can be said that 3 is to 5 as X is to 7°-30′. The solution follows:

$$\frac{3}{5} = \frac{X}{7°\text{-}30′}$$

$$5X = 22°\text{-}30′ \quad (60′ = 1°)$$

$$X = \frac{22°\text{-}30′}{5}$$

$$X = 4°\text{-}30′$$

Since 40° of latitude has an altitude of 138°-0′, 43° latitude would have an altitude of 138°-0′ plus the amount X, 4°-30′, or be equal to 142°-30′.

The same process can be used to find azimuth angles not given in tables.

Build Your Vocabulary

Following are words that you should understand and use as a part of your working vocabulary. Write a brief explanation of what each means.

    Traffic pattern
    Zoning
    Stair pitch and run
    Stair riser, tread, nosing
    Building code
    Contour lines
    Orientation
    Altitude
    Azimuth

Class Activities

1. List all the factors that need to be considered as you plan your house.
2. Examine local building codes and the Federal Housing Administration requirements to see how they will influence the plan.
3. Try to visit homes representative of the basic types mentioned in this chapter. After discussing the home with the occupant, write

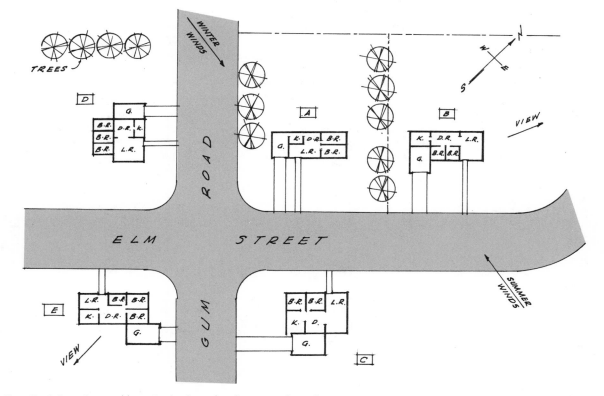

Fig. 40. Orientation problem. Study these five houses and list the principles of orientation that each violates. Revise the floor plan or reorient the existing plan on each lot to improve the overall position.

a brief report, indicating the favorable and unfavorable aspects mentioned for each type.

4. Study the deed to your house. Look for building restrictions, and report these to the class.

5. Visit the local office of the Recorder of Deeds, and ask to read the restrictions placed on lots in subdivisions in your area.

6. Visit a subdivision under development. Have the realtor explain the merits and drawbacks of the various lots for sale. From his discussion, choose the lot upon which you would like to build your desired house. As you design your house, be certain it will fit the size and slope of this lot.

7. Design a house floor plan that will meet the needs set forth in activity one above. Consider orientation and exterior styling, as you proceed.

8. Sketch the floor plan of your house on $1/4$-inch graph paper. Criticize the arrangement of rooms as it influences the patterns of traffic flow. Improve the plan, if possible.

9. Examine the neighborhood in which you live. List the advantages and disadvantages that exist due to the location of the lot upon which your home was built.

Additional Reading

Architectural Record (Editorial Staff), *Time Saver Standards.*

Aronin, Jeffrey E., *Climate and Architecture.*

International Conference of Building Officials, "Uniform Building Codes."

Koeppe, Clarence E., and DeLong, G. C., *Weather and Climate.*

National Board of Fire Underwriters, "The National Building Code."

National Lumber Manufacturers Association, "Fabrication of Components," Manual No. 2.

————, "The Unicom Method of House Construction," Manual No. 1.

Pollman, R. B., *123 Unicom Modular Component Designs.*

Ramsey, Charles G., and Sleeper, H. R., *Architectural Graphic Standards.*

Simon, Maron J. (ed.), and Libbey-Owens-Ford Glass Co., *Your Solar House.*

U.S. Federal Housing Administration, "Minimum Property Standards for One and Two Living Units."

Visher, Stephen S., *Climatic Atlas of the United States.*

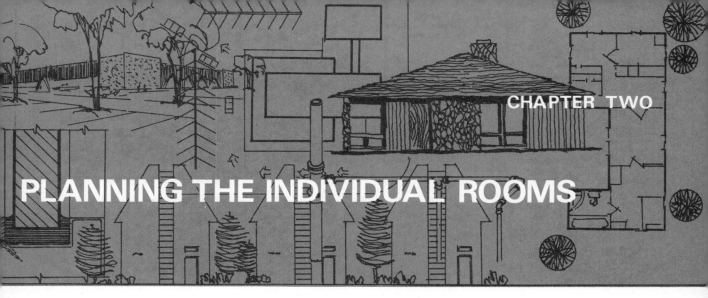

CHAPTER TWO

PLANNING THE INDIVIDUAL ROOMS

The planning of a house to best serve the needs of a family involves many factors. Some of the preliminary considerations were discussed in Chapter 1.

In this chapter, attention will be given to the requirements of planning each room. While it will not be possible to incorporate all the suggestions in a house plan, certainly each deserves careful consideration.

Designing the Individual Rooms

To begin planning the individual rooms, first, decide upon the desired size of each room. Then, decide upon the furniture to be in each room, and ascertain the dimensions of each piece. Make a scale freehand sketch of each room on ¼-inch graph paper. Allow each square to represent one square foot. Make templates of each piece of furniture, using the scale ¼″=1'-0″, and arrange them in their places on the scale, room drawing. Move and adjust the templates until you have a furniture arrangement that seems satisfactory. Then, try to imagine the room being used for various activities. Decide if the furniture arrangement is convenient for day to day living, entertaining, or other activities for which the room may be used. Is the room large enough to comfortably accommodate the furniture? Consider other possible door and window locations.

Once such an arrangement is deemed satisfactory, paste the templates to the plan, or sketch around them, so their locations will not be forgotten.

Once such an arrangement is deemed satisfactory, paste the templates to the plan, or sketch around them so their locations will not be forgotten. Typical furniture sizes are shown in Fig. 60A.

Fig. 60. Furniture arranged in front of window wall. Notice the pleasant view and open feeling in the room. (Andersen Corp.)

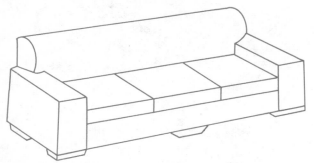

SOFA		
Width	Depth	Height
78 to 86	30 to 36	26 to 38

END TABLES		
Width	Depth	Height
28	21	20
20	20	15

RECLINING CHAIR		
Width	Depth	Height
33	36	42

TELEVISION			
	Width	Depth	Height
20" Portable	26	20	20
23" Cabinet	36	18	30

OCCASIONAL CHAIR		
Width	Depth	Height
24 to 33	29 to 35	29 to 37

COCKTAIL TABLE		
Width	Depth	Height
48 to 60	20	15

Fig. 60A. Typical furniture sizes.

DINING TABLES		
Width	**Depth**	**Height**
48″ Round extends to 72″ long		29
48	42	29
60	42	29
72	40	29

ORGAN AND PIANO			
	Width	**Depth**	**Height**
Organ	39	35	21
Spinet Piano	58	24	34

COMMODES		
Width	**Depth**	**Height**
26 Diameter		20
28	22	20

DINING CHAIRS		
Width	**Depth**	**Height**
19	21	30

BUFFET		
Width	**Depth**	**Height**
48	16	31

HUTCH		
Width	**Depth**	**Height**
30	14	39

Fig. 60A. (cont.) Typical furniture sizes.

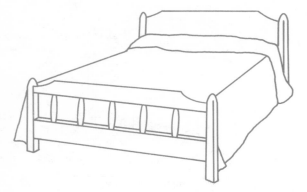

BEDS (MATTRESS SIZE)		
	Width	Depth
Twin	75	39
Full	75	54
Queen	60	80
King	76	80

DOUBLE DRESSER		
Width	Depth	Height
40 - 48	16 - 18	30 - 36

BEDSIDE TABLE		
Width	Depth	Height
20	15	25

SINGLE DRESSER		
Width	Depth	Height
30 - 36	16 - 18	24 - 30

DESK CHAIR		
Width	Depth	
24	18	

DESK		
Width	Depth	Height
45	22	30
54	26	24

Fig. 60A. (cont.) Typical furniture sizes.

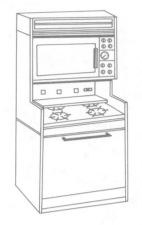

DISHWASHER			
	Width	Depth	Height
Built-In	24	24	34
Portable	24	26	36

COOKING CENTER		
Width	Depth	Height
30	28	59

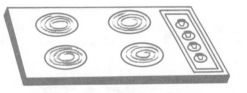

SURFACE COOKING UNIT	
26, 28, 33, 35	30

DINETTE SETS — TABLE		
Width	Depth	Height
66	42	29
54	42	29
42″ round extends to 60″ oval		29

BUILT-IN OVEN		
Width	Depth	Height
24	24	39

Fig. 60A. (cont.) Typical furniture sizes.

FREEZERS, UPRIGHT			
Cubic Ft.	Width	Depth	Height
15.8	32	31	65
17.0	32	31	71
30.0	35	32	72

REFRIGERATORS			
Cubic Ft.	Width	Depth	Height
7.7	23	21	50
8.6	24	21	57
10.0	31	24	57
12.3	32	28	59
14.0	32	25	65
16.3	33	26	65

HOOD		
Width	Depth	Height
30 , 36 , 42	20	6

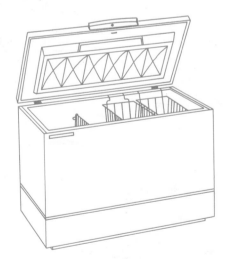

DROP-IN RANGE		
Width	Depth	Height
30	24	24

FREEZERS, HORIZONTAL			
Cubic Ft.	Width	Depth	Height
17.0	48	29	37
22	60	28	38

Fig. 60A. (cont.) Typical furniture sizes.

POOL TABLE		
Width	Depth	Height
100	56	31

TABLE TENNIS		
Width	Depth	Height
96	60	30

SEWING MACHINE		
Width	Depth	Height
CLOSED 22	16	30
OPEN 44	16	30

IRONING BOARD	
Width	Depth
54	15

CLOTHES WASHER (DRYER SAME SIZE)		
Width	Depth	Height
29	26	44

Planning the Living Room

The living room is the most versatile room in the house. It serves as a sitting room, dining room, television room, extra bedroom (if you have a sofa bed), music room, den (if your desk is there) and library. Usually, it is the largest room in the house and is the best furnished. When people come to visit, their first impression of your house is made when they enter the living room.

As the living room is being planned, consider the following:

1. When locating windows, remember that large picture windows reduce the amount of wall space for furniture. In homes with window walls, much of the furniture is arranged out in the room, rather than backed up to the window wall. See Fig. 60.

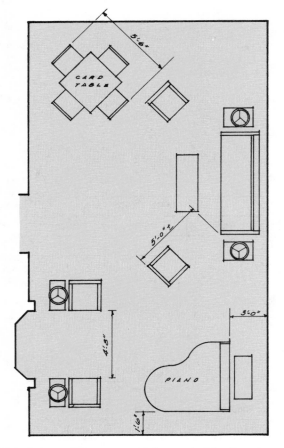

Fig. 61. Large living room with four typical furniture groupings.

2. Center the room about some focal point such as a fireplace or a picture window. Chairs and sofas normally are grouped about the focal point. A living room may have a second, less important grouping, such as several chairs in one end or one corner. A very large room may have three or four groupings, such as a piano and chair grouping or a card table and chair grouping. See Fig. 61.

3. Locate living rooms with picture windows toward a view; if there is no view, then there is no need for a picture window.

4. Have the front entrance open into a foyer. As an economy measure, it could open into the living room. The long entrance hall of yesterday's houses has been eliminated, because of the expense.

5. Design wide openings between living rooms and dining rooms and halls. Usually, these openings have no doors. A frequent combination in contemporary homes is the living room, dining room, and kitchen, with little or no division separating them. A fireplace, wall of cabinets, or a bar can be used as a divider. A folding door can form a convenient divider, as shown in Fig. 62.

6. Locate dining area (when a part of the living room) next to the kitchen.

7. Consider the need for built-in units such as bookcases, television and record cabinets, log boxes by the fireplace, and planters. These influence furniture arrangement and traffic patterns.

Fig. 62. Folding doors make excellent dividers between rooms with large connecting openings. (Wood Conversion Co.)

Fig. 63. Living room with open-beam ceiling and wood paneling. (Timber Structures, Inc.)

Fig. 64. A sunken living room provides an exciting change. (Wood Conversion Co.)

Fig. 65. A kitchen-dining area combination. Notice the nearness of the cooking area of the kitchen. (Caradco, Inc.)

8. Constantly be aware of patterns of traffic in the living room. This can influence room size and shape, as well as furniture arrangement.

9. Decide upon the finish of the interior walls. A living room that is panelled and has an open-beam ceiling needs an entirely different treatment than the usual flat ceiling and plaster walls. See Fig. 63.

10. Consider comfortable spacing of furniture to facilitate movement about the room. Refer to a book of standards. A comfortable major aisle should be approximately 3'-6", while a minor aisle should be approximately 2'-0". The allowance for an aisle from the front entrance to the main seating area, usually the focal point, should be from 3'-6" to 4'-6".

11. Consider comfortable spacing of furniture for conversation. Pieces of furniture facing each other in a conversation grouping should be from 4'-6" to 6'-0" apart. Anything over 6'-0" makes conversation a bit difficult because of the distance.

12. For standard furniture sizes, see an architectural standards book.

Planning the Dining Area

Currently, the separate dining room can be found in expensive homes, but it frequently is omitted, as an economy measure, in smaller homes. Popular substitutes include a dining area set up at the end of the living room and kitchens with dining space. See Fig. 65.

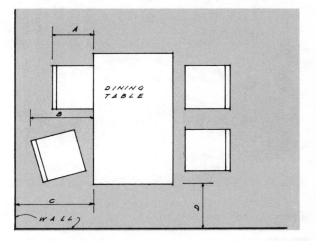

Fig. 66. Dining room space requirements.

A. Seated person occupies 1'-6" to 1'-10".

B. Average person requires 2'-6" to 3'-1" to rise from table.

C. If an aisle for passage behind chair is required, 3'-4" to 3'-6" space is needed.

If an aisle for tray service is required, 4'-10" to 5'-4" space is needed.

D. If only an aisle is needed, 2'-0" is sufficient. If a chair is to be at this end of the table, apply parts A, B and C above.

As the dining area is being planned, consider the following:

1. Locate it next to the kitchen to facilitate serving.

2. Make it large enough to handle the required furniture and to enable persons to be comfortably seated. See Figs. 66 and 67.

3. Provide sufficient window area to make it a bright, cheery area.

4. Provide access to the kitchen without requiring persons to go through dining area.

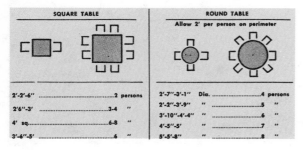

Fig. 67. Standard table sizes and seating requirements.

Fig. 68. Wood folding doors dividing the kitchen and dining areas. (Wood Conversion Co.)

Fig. 69. Dining space built into kitchen. (Andersen Corp.)

5. Locate linens and dishes near dining area.

6. Use folding doors or similar devices to screen kitchen from dining area, when they are together on an open plan. See Fig. 68.

7. Provide dining space for light meals. See the snack bars in Fig. 69.

Planning the Kitchen

The kitchen has received considerable attention from home planners the past few years. It has become quite mechanized and is planned with close attention to efficiency and a minimum of walking for the housewife. Kitchens are planned for food preparation, laundry activities, sewing and mending, and, frequently, are combined with the family room, making a modern version of the former large, family kitchen with sofa, television,

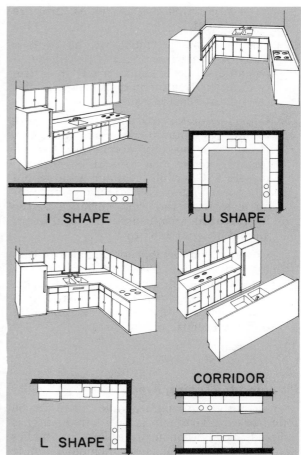

Fig. 70. Basic kitchen shapes.

Fig. 71. An open kitchen with a bar serving as a room divider. Notice the wood paneling, the storage for small items below wall cabinets, and the surface unit. (Geneva Modern Kitchens)

Fig. 72. The three basic centers around which a kitchen is planned. (Geneva Modern Kitchens)

Fig. 73. A high window used in a kitchen. This same window frequently is used in bedrooms for the sake of privacy and to increase wall space. (Andersen Corp.)

hobby space, and other provisions for family activity. The kitchen serves as a snack bar, food storage space, utensil storage, freezer room, and informal location for buffet parties. Sometimes it becomes a greenhouse.

As a kitchen is being planned, consider the following:

1. Kitchens are frequently arranged in *I, L, U,* and corridor shapes. See Fig. 70. The corridor-type requires at least 4 feet of floor space between appliances on opposite walls.
2. Kitchens (a) may be completely contained in a room by themselves, (b) may open into the dining area, or (c) may open into the living area. The open kitchen is an especially valuable plan in a small house, because even though it may be small, it does not seem crowded. See Fig. 71.
3. A kitchen should be arranged around three appliances — the refrigerator, stove, and sink. These are sometimes referred to, respectively, as the food-storage center, the cooking center and the clean-up center. See Fig. 72. Cabinets are built between these appliances for storage of supplies and utensils and to provide table-top area.
4. In most kitchens, the refrigerator-freezer and other food storage is located near the outside door, for convenience in unloading and putting away groceries.

5. The sink, generally, is placed next to the food storage. It is used in connection with food preparation and cleaning up after a meal. A central location, therefore, is recommended.
6. Some kitchens place the sink on an outside wall, under a window, as in Fig. 73. Other variations place it in a peninsula, or in an island installation with the dish washer. Sinks can be placed anywhere. In a large kitchen, a small, single-bowl sink (in addition to the usual double-bowl sink) is very useful, if placed near the food-preparation or cooking area.
7. The stove is best placed near the dining area to facilitate serving.
8. Separate ovens and surface cooking units are available so that the two need not be kept side by side. Since the oven is not used as much as the surface cooking unit, it can be placed in a location providing less valuable wall space. Note Fig. 74.
9. Most families desire a dining space in the

kitchen. Fig. 75 illustrates a spacious, well planned kitchen with a nice dining area.

10. Helpful in a kitchen is a section of counter with leg room beneath so a person can sit on a stool and work.

11. Dish washers are best located next to the sink. For right-handed persons, locate it to the left of the sink; for left-handed people, to the right. See Fig. 76.

12. A garbage disposal unit is a very convenient appliance.

13. When a family has young children, the kitchen should be located so it affords a view of the outside play area.

14. It is essential to have one kitchen access near the garage or carport, to facilitate the unloading of groceries.

15. If much outdoor living is planned, facilities for simplifying the movement from kitchen to patio should be furnished.

16. Fumes and kitchen odors can be easily removed by exhaust fans or hoods. Refer again to Fig. 74.

17. If you desire an all-gas or all-electric kitchen, manufacturers of these items can provide considerable assistance for kitchen planning.

18. The kitchen should be bright and well lighted.

19. Electrical outlets should be plentiful, especially along the counter for use with minor appliances.

20. If it is difficult to work a satisfactory kitchen arrangement in the space allotted on the plan, the floor plan should be rearranged.

21. No thru traffic should be permitted through kitchen work areas.

22. The number of doors opening off the kitchen should be limited. Exterior doors opening into the kitchen can block cabinet doors and make them difficult to use.

23. Easy access to the front entrance from kitchen should be provided, preferably, not routing traffic through the dining room or the living room.

Fig. 74. An I-shaped kitchen. Notice the dishwasher to the right of the stainless steel sink and the liberal counter space allowed on either side of the sink. The surface unit with hood and the double ovens are separated. (Geneva Modern Kitchens)

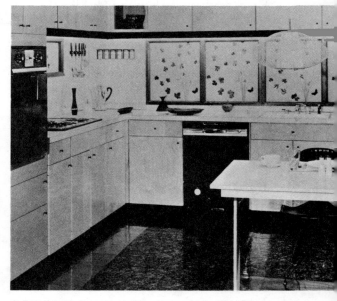

Fig. 76. A kitchen can be made unusual and exciting with a little imagination in the use of decorating materials. Notice the placement of the dishwasher to the left of the sink. (Caradco, Inc.)

Fig. 75. An L-shaped kitchen. Notice the counter space on both sides of the surface unit, the corner sink and the dishwasher to the right of the sink. Allowance has also been made for an attractive eating area. (Caradco, Inc.)

24. Enough cabinet space must be provided to store articles in use in each of the work areas of the kitchen. The area in which food is cooked and served should have space to store cooking utensils, silver, china and spices.

25. Windows are important in a kitchen, but they reduce the amount of wall-cabinet, storage space. Window area should be approximately 15 percent of floor area.

26. The average kitchen should have not less than 15'-0" lineal of free, clear, wall space, available for use of cabinets and appliances. This does not include corners.

27. Allow sufficient room between appliances to permit location of counter space. Ap-

pliances that are too close together reduce storage below the minimum needed; appliances too far apart result in wasted space and too much walking. See Fig. 77.

28. Allow a minimum of 1'-0" of counter space beside the refrigerator, to hold articles being taken from it.

29. Allow 2'-0" to 3'-0" counter space on each side of the sink, on which to stack dishes.

30. Allow approximately 2'-0" counter space beside the range, for pans and dishes.

31. Allow 3'-0" to 4'-0" clear, counter space, for food preparation.

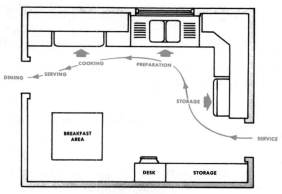

Fig. 77. The basis of kitchen planning is a pattern of work flow for storing, processing, cooking and serving foods and cleaning up after the meal. Notice how the major appliances have been located for ease of work, with storage facilities for utensils and equipment near the point of use. (Geneva Modern Kitchens)

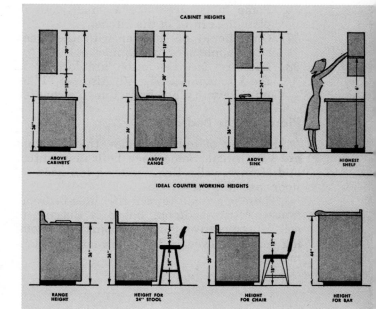

Fig. 78. Kitchen cabinet planning standards.

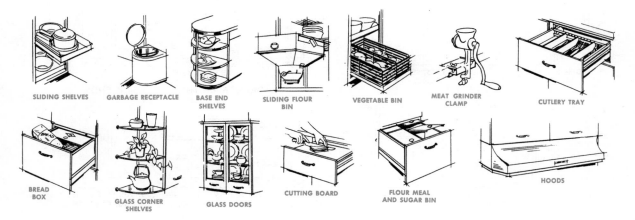

Fig. 79. Carefully selected accessories can add much to the efficiency of a kitchen. (Geneva Modern Kitchens)

32. Allow 2'-0" clear, counter space to one side of oven, if it is a separate unit.

33. The straight-line distance from stove to refrigerator to sink should not be over 22 feet. Distances between sink and refrigerator should be 4 to 7 feet; between sink and range, 4 to 6 feet; between range and refrigerator, 4 to 9 feet.

34. Base cabinets are usually 3'-0" high and 2'-0" deep. Wall cabinets are usually 2'-6" high and 1'-0" deep. See Figs. 78 and 78A for cabinet-planning standards.

35. The use of accessories often will increase the efficiency of the kitchen. See Fig. 79.

36. Some housewives like a small desk or planning center in the kitchen.

37. One should be familiar with the many stock appliances on the market.

38. Laundry facilities often are located in the kitchen. See Fig. 80. Also see "Planning Laundry Facilities," in this chapter.

Planning the Bedrooms

In many of today's homes, the bedrooms are very small. Some have built-in furniture and storage walls, thus reducing the need for floor space for these items.

There is a trend toward the three-bedroom house. A two-bedroom house is difficult to sell. In some areas, four bedrooms are becoming common, even in large, low-cost developments.

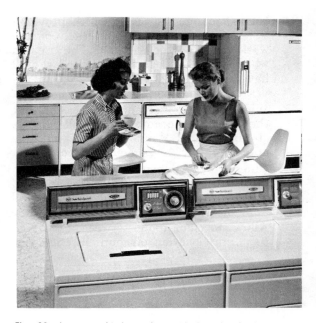

Fig. 80. An open kitchen plan with laundry facilities conveniently built-in. (Whirlpool Corp.)

As the bedrooms are being planned, consider the following:

1. Be certain furniture will fit into the room and will leave sufficient aisle and dressing space. Aisles of at least 24" are necessary. See Figs. 81 and 82.

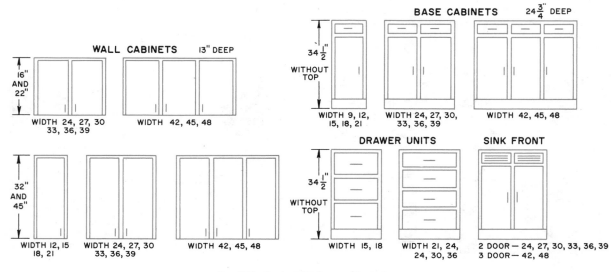

Fig. 78A. Typical kitchen cabinet sizes.

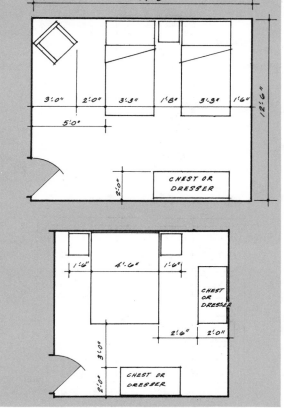

Fig. 81. Minimum spacing for twin beds and double bed.

2. Allow for two windows in every bedroom. Try to get cross ventilation; corner rooms are ideal.

3. Try to prevent drafts from blowing across bed.

4. Locate bedrooms so that they can be entered from a hall. Never locate a bedroom so that one must go through another room to get into it.

5. Consider high windows, with sill approximately 5'-0" from the floor. Although this increases privacy and permits arrangement of furniture on all walls, it does prevent easy escape in case of fire.

6. Consider glass sliding doors to private patio. This opens up the room to the outdoors and makes small rooms seem larger.

7. Provide sufficient closet space.

8. Consider full or half-bath off master bedroom.

9. Locate mirrors and dressing table to take advantage of natural light.

Planning Closets and Storage Walls

Perhaps one of the most important hidden values in a well planned house is the amount and location of closet space. A closet by the front entrance, for the coats and rubber footware of the family and guests, is essential. Every bedroom needs at least one large closet. Master bedrooms are enhanced by having two closets — his and hers. Shallow linen closets in halls or baths are vital. They take little space and are well worth their cost. A closet near the rear entrance is helpful. This is the perfect place for storing so many things, including a gardening jacket and favorite old hat.

Many contemporary homes line one wall of a long hall with closets. This provides excellent, readily available, dry, warm, storage space. Basement and attic storage, while valuable, is not suitable for many things and is not convenient. Fig. 83 illustrates various types of closets.

As closet space is being planned, consider the following:

1. The bedroom closets and the entrance closet should be, at least, 2'-0" deep inside x 4'-0" wide, or larger. Walk-in closets off the master bedroom are nice. They should average 5'-0" x 5'-0" to 5'-0" x 7'-0".

2. Linen closets should be, at least, 1'-0" to 1'-6" deep by 2'-0" to 4'-0" wide.

Fig. 82. A spacious bedroom with comfortable chairs and pleasant view. (Andersen Corp.)

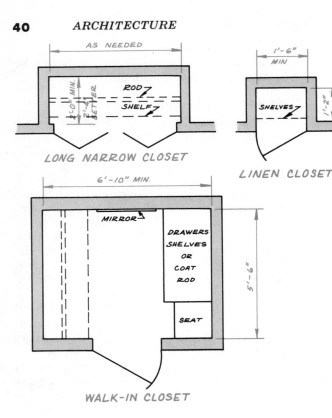

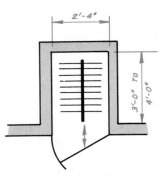

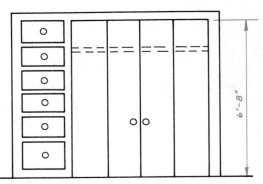

LONG, DEEP, CLOSET WITH
SLIDING COAT ROD

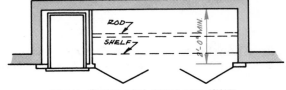

Fig. 83. Types of closets.

The long, narrow closet with a completely open front is most frequently used. It can have folding, sliding, or accordion doors.

A walk-in closet is placed off the master bedroom. It can serve as a dressing room.

Linen closets are located near the bedrooms and baths.

Deep, narrow closets require a sliding coat rod to give access to clothing. Avoid this type of closet whenever possible.

Built-in bedroom storage units make economical use of storage space. Shown here is only one design. There are many other design possibilities.

3. The usual, hinged door is falling into disfavor for large closets. Sliding doors have become extremely popular, and folding doors of wood and metal are gaining popularity. See Figs. 84 through 86. Accordion doors are also used. The hinged door requires much floor space and becomes a liability to the planner. The other types permit better use of the floor space around a closet.

4. Occasionally, closet storage space is built under a stairway. This is satisfactory for general storage.

5. The coat rod should be at least 5'-7" above the floor.

6. A shelf should be provided above the coat rod.

7. A light in each closet is highly desirable. It can be a pull-chain or switch-operated.

8. In contemporary homes, storage walls, which contain built-in drawer space, are frequently used. These make better use of the area set aside for storage and reduce the need for large pieces of furniture.

Fig. 84. Sliding door extending from floor to ceiling saves expense of furring down to regular door height. (Woodall Industries, Inc.)

Fig. 85. Louvered folding closet doors. Doors are floor to ceiling high, speeding installation and eliminating air trapped at ceiling. (Simpson Timber Co.)

Fig. 86. Wood folding closet doors. (General Plywood Corp.)

Planning a Bath

A full-bath in a home today is expected. A distinct trend is to provide a bath and a half or two full baths. Many houses have a bath off the master bedroom and a second bath for the remaining bedrooms. A four-bedroom house should have two full baths in the sleeping area. A house built on several levels should have a half-bath on the living level and at least one full bath on the sleeping level. It is desirable to have a half-bath convenient to the entertainment area; this could be the living room, family room, or basement recreation room.

As the baths are being planned, consider the following:

1. For the sake of economy, both kitchen and laundry plumbing should be located

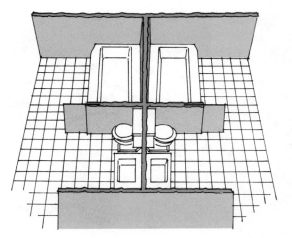

Fig. 87. Two full baths utilizing a common wall.

on the same wall, in a back-to-back arrangement; or two baths should be planned back-to-back. Figs. 87 through 90 are examples of good planning.

2. Second-story baths should be located over first-story baths, to cut plumbing costs.

3. A "mud room" with sink and water closet near the rear entrance is convenient for children to clean up in before they enter the house.

4. If only one bath can be afforded, consider two lavatories. See Fig. 91.

5. Consider locating the water closet in a private compartment from the remainder of the bath, if only one can be afforded. This greatly expands the use of the facilities. See Fig. 92.

6. A small lavatory installed in master bedroom will relieve strain on main bath facilities.

7. A bath that can be entered from two bedrooms is inconvenient. It is difficult to tell if someone is in the bath or if the last user forgot to unlock the door.

8. Many new materials are available for bath walls. In addition to the usual plaster or a variety of tiles, other materials such as plastic-covered wallpaper, corrugated plastic sheets, wood paneling, marble, terrazzo, glass, and mirror panels are used. Small mosaic tiles are very decorative and durable. Since the bath is small, the use of such impressive materials is not expensive.

9. A window in a bath is highly desirable,

but not essential. A good exhaust fan will satisfactorily change the air in a bath without windows.

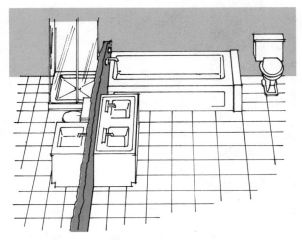

Fig. 89. Economical arrangement of full bath and private bath off a master bedroom.

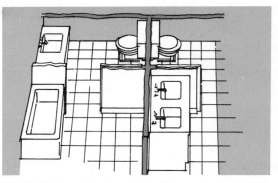

Fig. 90. Economical plan for a bath and a one-half bath which utilize a common wall.

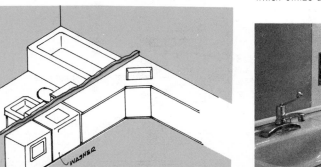

Fig. 88. Kitchen, laundry and bath plumbing located in a common wall.

Fig. 91. A double lavatory expands the use of a bathroom. Notice the auxiliary electric heater. (Alliance Ware, Inc.)

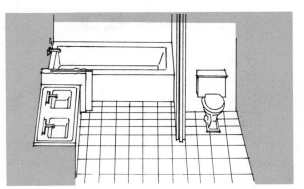

Fig. 92. Two lavatories and dividers make one bath more useful. Actually, three persons could use this bath in privacy.

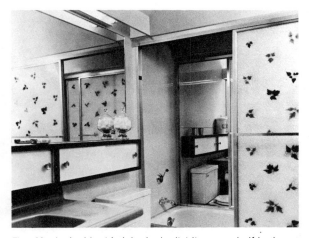

Fig. 93. A double-sided bathtub dividing two half-baths — used in NAHB Research House. (Alliance Ware, Inc.)

10. Locating a bath tub beneath a window should be avoided. It tends to be a chilly place to bathe in the winter.

11. The water closet should be located so it is not seen when the bathroom door is open.

12. A shower in the second bath requires less floor space than a tub. Refer to Fig. 89.

13. The tub should be located so the faucets can be accessible from the rear. Most frequently, an access door is made available in a closet. This enables the faucets to be repaired or replaced.

14. Industry is offering new developments constantly. Study magazines and manufacturers' catalogs for these innovations. Figs. 93 and 94 illustrate some new thinking in bathroom planning.

15. The space allowed for fixtures must provide for some clearance to make them visible. Figs. 95 and 96 illustrate satisfactory, but tight, placement of fixtures. Fig. 97 indicated minimum spacing requirements for bathroom fixtures. Fig. 97A gives the standard bathroom fixture sizes.

16. The rooms requiring plumbing should be located near the point of entrance of water and sewer services to the house. Fig. 98 illustrates the extra materials and resulting labor due to differences in location of baths and kitchens. See Chapter 9 for piping details.

Fig. 94. A bathtub with a center drain, making cleaning easier. (Alliance Ware, Inc.)

Fig. 95. Fixtures located in a minimum of space. Notice the sliding glass shower doors. (Alliance Ware, Inc.)

Fig. 96. Satisfactory, compact bath unit in a 5'-6" by 6'-6" space. (Alliance Ware, Inc.)

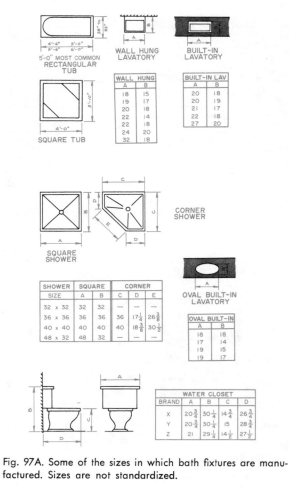

Fig. 97A. Some of the sizes in which bath fixtures are manufactured. Sizes are not standardized.

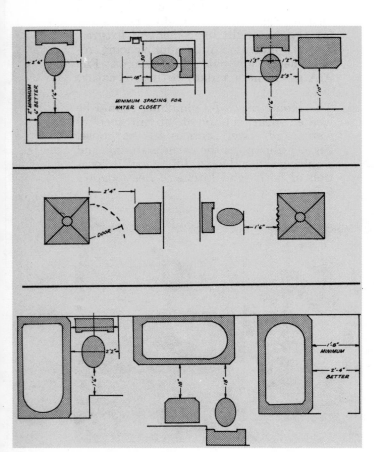

Fig. 97. Minimum space requirements for bathroom fixtures.

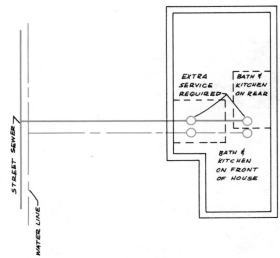

Fig. 98. Location of bath and kitchen on floor plan influences plumbing costs.

Planning Laundry Facilities

The automatic washer and dryer are common appliances in today's homes. Space should be provided for these, as well as for sorting and ironing clothing.

A primary consideration is convenience. The most common location for laundry facilities is in a utility room or basement. Some homes have the washer and dryer in the kitchen or bathroom. These appliances even could be located in a recessed space in a hall. See Fig. 99. Folding doors can close them from view, when not in use. In milder climates, the garage or carport serves as a laundry area.

As the laundry facilities are planned, consider the following:

Fig. 99. Washer and dryer off a hall near bedroom area. Notice folding doors. (Whirlpool Corp.)

Fig. 100. A washer and dryer can fit neatly into a kitchen or utility room. Notice these back up to the wall separating the utility room from the kitchen, thus utilizing a common wall for plumbing. Convenient storage cabinets are located above these appliances. (Caradco, Inc.)

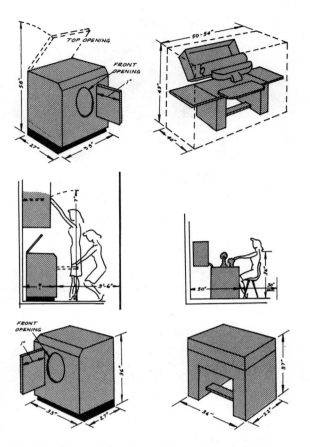

Fig. 101. Standard laundry appliance sizes and space requirements.

1. The washer and dryer should be located side-by-side; this requires a 5'-6" wall space and a 3'-6" aisle. See Fig. 100. A washer and dryer located opposite each other require a 4'-0" passage. Fig. 101 gives standard appliance sizes and spacing requirements. Some washers and dryers can be stacked one above the other, and a combination washer-dryer in one cabinet is available. See Fig. 102.
2. A sink is necessary in a laundry area.
3. A countertop is very helpful, when sorting and arranging clothes. Wall cabinets are necessary for storage purposes.
4. The laundry facilities should be arranged in a sequence, so the clothes move toward the place they are to be dried. The usual sequence is to have a sorting counter, then a sink for removal of difficult stains, then the washer, followed by the dryer, and, finally, the ironing area. If the wash-

Fig. 102. A combination washer-dryer neatly located in a kitchen. Cabinets on each side hold soiled clothing. (Whirlpool Corp.)

Fig. 104. A spacious, well planned utility room in a house without a basement. It provides laundry facilities as well as workshop space. (Caradco, Inc.)

er door opens to the left, it is convenient to have the dryer door open to the right. See Fig. 103.

5. Dryers are often placed on outside walls, to aid in their venting.
6. If the laundry area is in the basement, a laundry chute is a real convenience.
7. Easy access to an outdoor clothes line is desirable.
8. About 6 inches space should be allowed between the wall and the laundry appliances, for pipes and wiring.

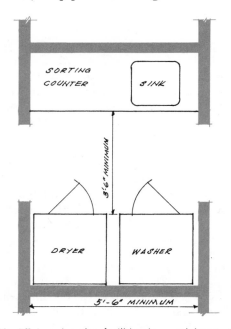

Fig. 103. Efficient laundry facilities in a minimum space. Ironing must be done elsewhere.

Planning Utility Rooms

In homes without basements, a ground-level space for the furnace, laundry, and water heater is necessary. Such a room is called a utility room. It frequently has a lavatory and a water closet.

It is becoming popular for homes with basements to have a ground-level utility room for laundry and toilet facilities, with the furnace and water heater in the basement. This makes housework easier, since the housewife does not have to run down to the basement to tend the washer and dryer. It also enables homes with septic tanks to deposit wash water directly in the sewer. Otherwise, a sump pump would be necessary to raise the water up from the basement to the septic tank.

As a utility room is being planned, consider the following:

1. The utility room should be located next to the kitchen, for convenience and economy.
2. It is desirable to have an outside door from the utility room.
3. If a furnace is included, the proximity of a chimney should be considered.
4. Some means of ventilation should be provided, either by a window or an exhaust fan.
5. The room must be placed so a dryer can be vented, if necessary.
6. Equipment should be located so it may be serviced, and room should be allowed around the furnace, for cleaning and adjusting. Since laundry equipment is heavily used, it should be most accessible.

7. If laundry facilities are to be in the utility room, refer to previous section, "Planning Laundry Facilities."

8. A home workshop can be located in a utility room. See Fig. 104.

Planning Core Units

As the kitchen, bath, and utility rooms are planned, it is well to consider them as the core of the house around which the remainder of the house is planned. Such a core enables the builder to keep plumbing costs at a minimum. It also facilitates the use of a factory-produced plumbing unit which can lower costs further. Obviously, it necessitates a new look at planning the floor plan and will influence the exterior styling as well. Fig. 105 illustrates a typical core unit.

Planning Garages and Carports

Climate influences the type of storage facility needed for automobiles. In warm, dry climates, a carport provides adequate shelter and permits space for the storage of yard tools and lawn furniture. (A carport is a covered roof with one or more open sides or ends and no doors.) In areas having some cold weather, rain, or snow, an enclosed garage is desirable.

Consideration should be given to a two-car garage. This is becoming a standard part of homes in northern areas. Many families now

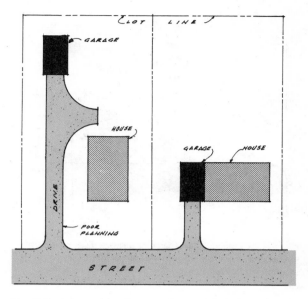

Fig. 106. A long drive is expensive and is inconvenient in inclement weather. Notice the advantage of a short drive and attached garage.

have two cars, or a boat or trailer. The extra money invested in the second garage space is quite wise. It, also, is an attraction to help sell a house. Just as three bedrooms are becoming standard, the two-car garage is expected by many home buyers.

As the garage is being planned, consider the following:

1. The garage is a good location for laundry equipment, a clothesline, the family workshop, a play space, and an outdoor porch for family living.

2. The garage should be located on the side of the house receiving winter winds, to provide a buffer against these winds and snows.

3. A carport can be used, if climate is mild and only shelter from sun is desired.

4. A carport is cheaper to build than a garage.

5. Building a one-car garage with a single carport beside it provides car shelter and also serves as a covered, outdoor, living area.

6. The garage should be located so one can reach the kitchen door and front entrance without going out into the weather.

7. Prevailing summer breezes should not be blocked by a garage.

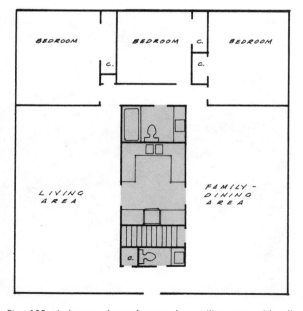

Fig. 105. A house planned around a utility core with all plumbing concentrated in the shaded area.

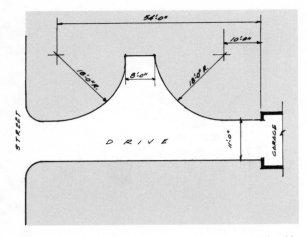

Fig. 107. A typical Y turn. Such a turn requires considerable space and must be considered when planning a garage location on the lot plan.

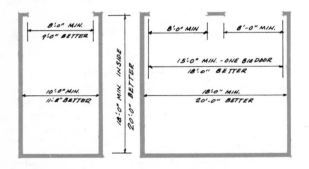

Fig. 108. Minimum and recommended garage sizes.

8. If garage is detached from the house, it should be connected to the house with a covered walk or breezeway.

9. Garage should be located so a long drive is not necessary. Turning room should be allowed for, if needed. See Figs. 106 and 107.

10. A parking area for cars of guests should be provided.

11. Minimum inside dimensions for a one-car garage should be 10'-0" x 18'-0", and for a two-car garage, 18'-0" x 18'-0". These dimensions do not allow much space for storage. See Fig. 108.

12. The garage door should be in keeping with the style of the house. Doors should be simple, so they do not stand out or over-balance the design. Bright, contrasting colors are undesirable. See Fig. 109.

13. For best appearance, the garage should be constructed from the same material as

the house; it should not be a sharp contrast.

14. Most contemporary house styles are enhanced by the garage roof being a continuation of the house. Lining up the ridge or the eaves gives the house a long, low, impressive appearance. A break in the roof line or eave line can make the house more interesting, provided it is not too severe. Projecting the garage forward can be enhancing.

15. Standard sizes for garage doors are found in manufacturers' catalogs.

16. The *type* of door should be considered. The use of one large door for a two-car garage is popular. Some prefer to use two single doors. This allows a car to be removed, without exposing all the miscellaneous items stored in a garage. See Fig. 110.

17. An 8-foot, single garage door is minimum. Wider sizes are quite desirable. A 15-foot width is minimum for two-car garages. Refer again to Fig. 108.

18. Overhead types of doors are very desirable. Swinging or folding doors are difficult to operate, take wall space, and frequently are blocked by snow.

19. A single, 3'-0" x 7'-0" door is desirable to permit persons to enter without having to open the large car door.

Fig. 109. A simple, two-car garage door that blends well with the style of the house. (Rowe Manufacturing Co.)

An A-frame provides a spacious living area. (Western Wood Products Association)

An open living-dining area. Notice the attention given to the use of color in the furniture. (American of Martinsville)

Wood ceiling, wall paneling, and exposed structural members provide a warm, comfortable atmosphere. (Western Wood Products Association)

An exciting, comfortable living area. The glass gable end permits a wide view of the outside. The large overhang affords protection from the sun. The fireplace has a wide raised hearth which serves as a bench. The artificial lighting provides a dramatic touch. (Armstrong Cork Co.)

A cheerful, pleasant dining room. The vinyl floor requires little maintenance. (Armstrong Cork Company)

A bright, cheerful dining room. The room is large enough to permit the table to be expanded to seat additional guests. (Western Wood Products Association)

A formal dining room. The furniture sets the character of the room. This is enhanced by the wall color and decoration. (American of Martinsville)

A dining area and game room gives flexibility in space utilization. (Azrock Floor Products)

48B

A child's bedroom requires a durable floor covering. Bright colors add to the cheerful atmosphere.
(Azrock Floor Products)

A contemporary style of bedroom. (American of Martinsville)

48C

Light colors give a cool, clean feeling. (Azrock Floor Products)

This corner of a living area has a mixture of oriental design and contemporary furnishings. (Azrock Floor Products)

This open floor plan uses dividers to give areas of privacy. (Azrock Floor Products)

Rooms can be planned around carefully selected furniture units and art pieces. (Azrock Floor Products)

Fig. 110. Two single doors on a two-car garage. (Rowe Manufacturing Co.)

20. High windows to provide natural light are necessary.
21. The wall between the attached garage and the house should be fireproofed. Metal lath and plaster or ⅝″ gypsum board should be used.
22. The garage floor should be several inches above grade, to prevent rain and snow from entering.
23. Concrete is the best material for garage floors.
24. The floor should slope to door, to permit drainage.
25. Lights and convenience outlets should be provided.
26. To cut costs, part of the basement can be used as garage space. This necessitates

a sloping lot that will enable part of the basement to be exposed.
27. In very cold climates, garages can be heated. This is also important if the garage is used for a laundry. Heat should be from the house furnace; open-flame heaters should never be used.
28. Basementless houses require that storage space be provided in garages. Consider making one wall a storage wall.
29. As a convenience, garage doors can be obtained which open from the house or car by electronic controls.

Planning the Basement

In warm climates or in areas with a high water table, basements are generally omitted. If a basement cannot be built, because of water or rock problems, a ground-level addition can be built, to compensate for this loss of space. If the money, ordinarily spent for the average basement, is used in this manner, an addition consisting of 500 to 550 square feet can be built. This is sufficient to make a fine recreation room, play area, extra bedroom, TV room or utility room. It does have the advantage of being entirely above the ground.

Many contemporary homes, in all climates, are built on a concrete slab. This enhances the

Fig. 111. An ample basement workshop. Note pegboard tool panels and the noise-deadening tile ceiling. (Wood Conversion Co.)

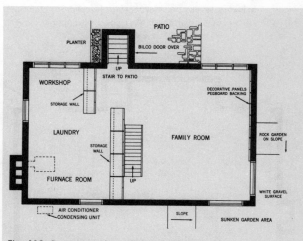

Fig. 112. Basement plans. (Bilco Company)
Interior stair running front to back. With a southeast sun exposure, the deep windows at the corners of the house catch the summer breezes. A storage partition dividing recreation room from workshop serves as an effective sound barrier, with doors providing easy access to basement entrance and the yard. Open planning insures excellent ventilation.

long, low appearance of a house, but necessitates elimination of the basement.

In cold climates, basements are popular, because so much of the year is spent indoors. The basement provides an excellent play space, recreation area, clothes drying area, and workshop or hobby area. See Fig. 111. The laundry, furnace, and garage can be located here. See Fig. 112.

On a sloping lot, a basement can be included with little extra cost. On a flat lot, a basement will add significantly to the cost of

Fig. 113. Good use is made of a sloping lot by exposing the basement to light and air. (Andersen Corp.)

a house. The big difference is that the house on the sloping lot requires less excavating and would require a high foundation anyway. This waste space beneath the house can be economically used for a basement. See Fig. 113.

As the basement is being planned, consider the following:

1. Interior stairs should be planned to give access to the basement. These are most satisfactory if they come down from the kitchen or family room on the first floor.

2. The stairs should be arranged so they do not spoil a large portion of the basement area by cutting into usable space. Refer again to Fig. 112.

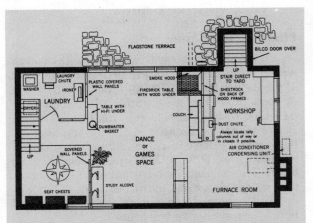

Interior stair at end of plan. The family room adjoining a flagstone terrace and the unusual basement fireplace-barbecue arrangement offer economical indoor-outdoor enjoyment at a luxury level. Outside access to workshop, cleanup room or dirt-associated areas makes good planning sense.

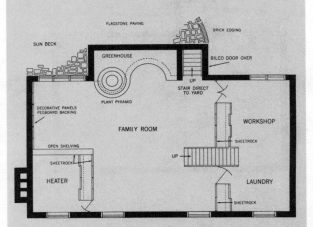

Interior stair running length of plan. Here, with installation of a longer window and centralized basement entrance, the homeowner can create a blend of indoor-outdoor pleasures: barbecue, greenhouse, spacious functional basement. Further partitioning for hobbies, food storage, etc., should be done with concern for traffic and ventilation.

Fig. 114. Direct access from outside is important to good utilization of the basement. (Bilco Co.)

3. It is of great importance to have an outside entrance to the basement, Fig. 114.

4. The furnace should be located near the chimney.

Fig. 115. A well located laundry area and laundry chute. Notice the convenient outside door. (Bilco Co.)

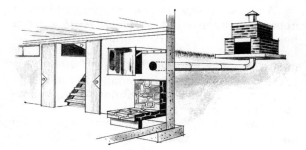

Fig. 116. Economy basement fireplace. (Bilco Co.)

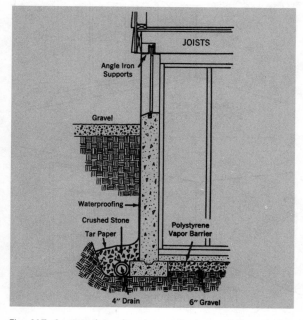

Fig. 117. Section through a large aluminum gliding window used in basement. (Bilco Co.)

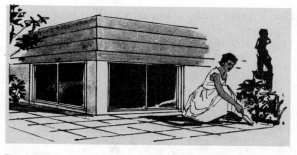

Fig. 118. Windows in series aid in lighting and ventilating a basement. (Bilco Co.)

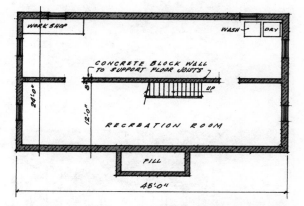

Fig. 119. A commonly used, but poor, basement plan. The 12' x 45' recreation room gives a tunnel-like appearance to the basement.

5. The laundry area should be separated by partitions and located near an outside door. The laundry chute should be in this area also. See Fig. 115.

6. The basement recreation room should be located so that one can reach it without going through the furnace or laundry room.

7. A fireplace in the basement should be below the fireplace on the first floor. The furnace flue and all fireplace flues should be in one chimney, for most economical construction. A variation of this is shown in Fig. 116.

8. Toilet facilities should be located near the laundry area. It is desirable to locate these below a first-floor bath or kitchen, for economy.

9. Plenty of windows for light and ventilation are a necessity. Basement windows need not be small and widely spaced. Grouping windows adds much to the brightness and ventilation. See Figs. 117 and 118.

10. Proper orientation can utilize breeze and sun.
11. A sloping lot will permit a large portion of the basement to be exposed. Refer again to Fig. 113.

12. Basement rooms should be kept in normal proportion. Long, tunnel-like rooms make a person feel he is in a cave. See Fig. 119.
13. Many homeowners plan to save money by finishing their own basements. However, any work that is difficult for the owner to do should be done by the builder. It is less expensive to have the builder do this while he is on the job than to have him come back later. See Fig. 120.

Window Planning

Windows are a very important part of both interior planning and exterior styling. Properly selected and located, they increase the usefulness of a room.

A pleasant view can be enjoyed or blocked depending upon window selection. If a room has a pleasant view, the window sill should be low enough to enable a seated person to look out without straining. Windows with large open glass areas are recommended for this purpose. Muntins across windows make viewing difficult. See Fig. 121.

Properly located windows can increase the possibilities for natural ventilation. Natural

Fig. 120. Steps in finishing a basement. Owner can have builder leave basement unfinished, frame it in or completely finish the job. (Bilco Co.)

LARGE GLASS AREAS
ENHANCE THE VIEW

SMALL GLASS PANES
TEND TO OBSCURE THE
VIEW

Fig. 121. Choice of windows is important in room planning.

ventilation can be limited to a single room or through windows in several rooms. See Fig. 122. The Federal Housing Administration requires a minimum of 4% of the floor area to be available in open window area. If a house will not have air conditioning, this should be greatly increased. Many homes have year around heating-cooling systems which keep the temperature comfortable at all times. Natural ventilation is not as important in this case as natural light and view.

Possibly the most important function performed by windows today is to relieve the close, boxed-in feeling a person has in a room having few or no windows. The smallness of the room is relieved by tying it into the outdoors through windows. The use of natural light greatly helps in making a room pleasant. While artificial lighting is well developed, natural lighting is still of great importance in designing a room that is pleasant to use. The Federal Housing Administration's minimum acceptable glass area in residential work is 10% of the floor area. In most cases it is necessary to greatly exceed this to get the results wanted. Actually, it is not unusual to have window glass area equal to 20% or 25% of the floor area.

Windows can be planned to achieve a sense of privacy. Typical of this are the high narrow windows often used in bedrooms. See Fig. 123. They permit natural light and ventilation, yet increase the sense of privacy. They also increase the amount of wall space upon which furniture can be placed.

The location and size of windows has a great influence upon the furniture that can be used in a room. Windows with a sill near the floor remove that portion of the wall as a place to locate a piece of furniture. As window sizes are selected, keep in mind the standard furniture sizes.

As windows are selected, the designer must always be aware of exterior design. Changes in window size influences the exterior appearance. The style of window must be in keeping with the style of house. For example, aluminum awning windows would be completely out of place on a colonial style house.

Even the location of a window in a wall is important. After deciding upon where a window should go to give the best interior use, the designer must see how the exterior appears with the window in that location.

Window Types

There are many types of windows available today. Those in most common use in residential construction are shown in Figs. 124 through 130. These are available in wood and metal.

The *double-hung window* is most commonly used. They can provide ventilation at the top or bottom of the window opening. However, only half of the window can be open at any time. Most double-hung windows are held open with spring-loaded balances or a friction holding device. See Fig. 124.

A horizontal *sliding window* is much like the double hung. The major difference is that the sash slides sideways rather than up and down. They run on nylon rollers. No spring balances are needed to hold them open.

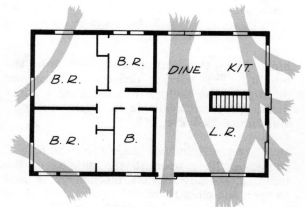

Fig. 122. Possible paths for natural ventilation.

Fig. 123. High windows give privacy and wall space for furniture.

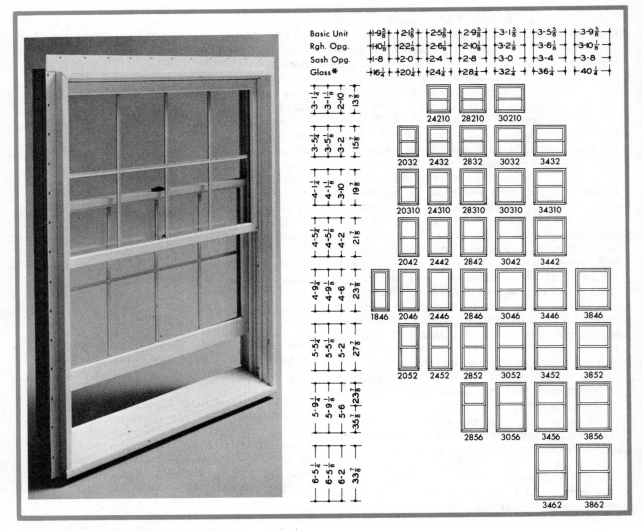

Fig. 124. Double hung windows. (Andersen Corporation)
   Note: Several windows may be placed side by side to form a large window area. To find the overall unit dimension for a multiple window unit with a nonsupporting mullion, add the basic unit dimensions plus ½″ to this overall basic unit dimension. Openings requiring a supporting mullion add 2″ for each supporting mullion. To find the rough opening, add ½″ to the overall basic unit size.

Sliding doors are also available. See Figs. 125 and 126.

The *awning window* hinges from the top of the sash. See Figs. 127, 128, and 129. It swings open to the outside of the house. Most types have a crank operating through gears and a lever to provide ventilation. It can be left open during a rain. They are sold in single units and multiple units. A multiple unit can be several windows high and wide.

Hopper windows are much like awning windows. The major differences are that they hinge from the bottom and open into the building. This window deflects the incoming air toward the ceiling, thus reducing a direct draft. They are available in single and multiple units. See Fig. 129.

Casement windows hinge from the side of the sash. They open to the outside of the building. Usually a crank mechanism is used to open and close them. When open, the entire window area provides ventilation. They are sold as single or multiple units. Some are

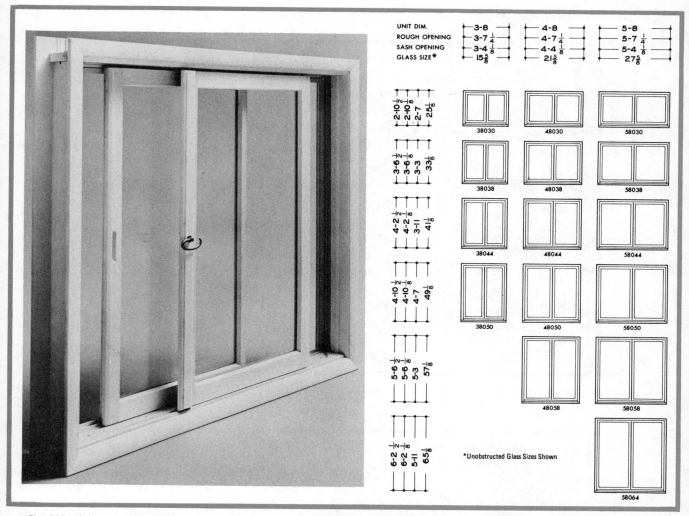

UNIT DIM.	⊢ 3-8 ⊣	⊢ 4-8 ⊣	⊢ 5-8 ⊣
ROUGH OPENING	⊢ 3-7¼ ⊣	⊢ 4-7¼ ⊣	⊢ 5-7¼ ⊣
SASH OPENING	⊢ 3-4⅛ ⊣	⊢ 4-4⅛ ⊣	⊢ 5-4⅛ ⊣
GLASS SIZE*	⊢ 15⅝ ⊣	⊢ 21⅝ ⊣	⊢ 27⅝ ⊣

2-10½ / 2-10⅛ / 2-7 / 25⅝	38030	48030	58030
3-6½ / 3-6⅛ / 3-3 / 33⅝	38038	48038	58038
4-2½ / 4-2⅛ / 3-11 / 41⅝	38044	48044	58044
4-10½ / 4-10⅛ / 4-7 / 49⅝	38050	48050	58050
5-6½ / 5-6⅛ / 5-3 / 57⅝		48058	58058
6-2½ / 6-2⅛ / 5-11 / 65⅝			58064

*Unobstructed Glass Sizes Shown

Fig. 125. Sliding windows. (Andersen Corporation)

Note: Multiple units of these sizes are available. To find the overall unit dimension which has a nonsupporting mullion, add the sum of the unit dimensions and subtract 2". The overall rough opening dimension is equal to ¾" less than the overall unit dimension.

available with a fixed window unit. See Figs. 129 and 130.

Picture windows are large, fixed windows. They provide no ventilation. The glass is usually ¼" plate glass or an insulating glass. The insulating glass is two sheets of glass with a dead air space between. If ventilation is desired, other types of windows are placed next to the picture window.

Class Activities

1. Make a drawing of the bathroom or kitchen in your home. List the ways it violates the principles of good planning.

2. Plan a new bath or kitchen for your home, using the existing space. Carefully apply the principles of good planning.

3. Make a notebook, using pictures of kitchens and bathrooms found in magazines and manufacturers' catalogs. Try to find examples that illustrate the principles of good planning. Devote one section to new ideas and new products for these areas.

4. Visit exhibit houses and write a report, analyzing the good and poor points in room planning. Explain what could be done to improve each item rated as poor.

5. Compute the cost of adding the following desirable features to a home: a foyer 4'-0" wide and 6'-0" long; a second bathroom; a separate surface-cooking unit and oven, instead of the usual stove; an outside exit to a basement of a house on a flat lot; enlarging the two-car garage from 18'-0" x 18'-0" to 20'-0" x 20'-0".

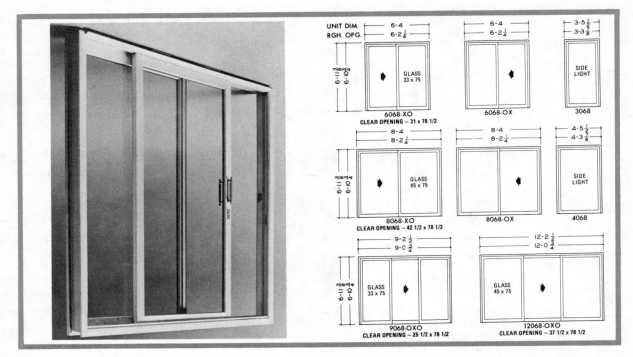

Fig. 126. Sliding doors. (Andersen Corporation)

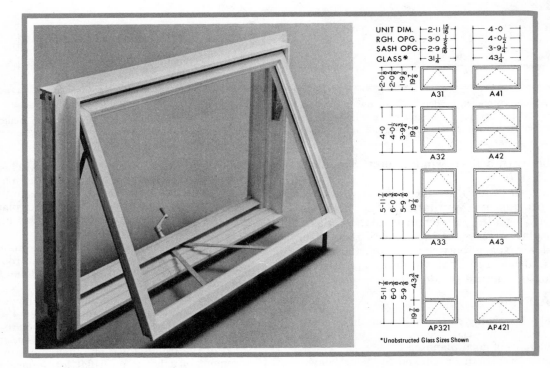

Fig. 127. Awning unit. (Andersen Corporation)
 Note: Multiple units of these sizes are available. See casement unit illustration for explanation.

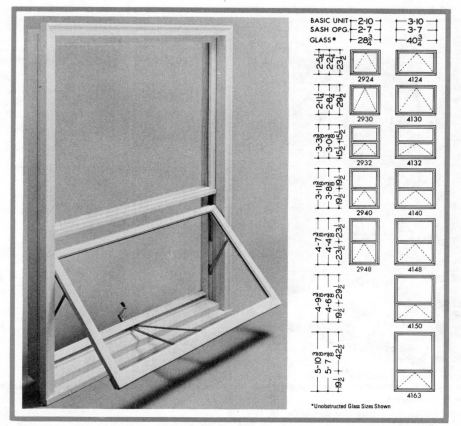

Fig. 128. Fixed sash with awning sash. (Andersen Corporation)

Note: Multiple units are available. To find the overall basic unit dimension, add the basic unit dimensions plus 2⅞". The rough opening size is the sum of the basic units plus ½".

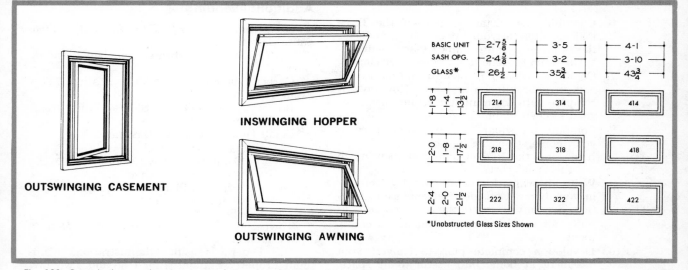

Fig. 129. Outswinging awning, inswinging hopper, and outswinging casement windows. (Andersen Corporation)

To find the overall basic unit width of multiple units, add the basic unit dimensions plus 2⅞" to the total. To find the rough opening width, add the basic unit width plus ½".

These units can be stacked vertically. The overall unit dimension for stacked units is the sum of the basic units plus ¾" for two units high, less ¼" for three units high, and less 1¼" for four units high.

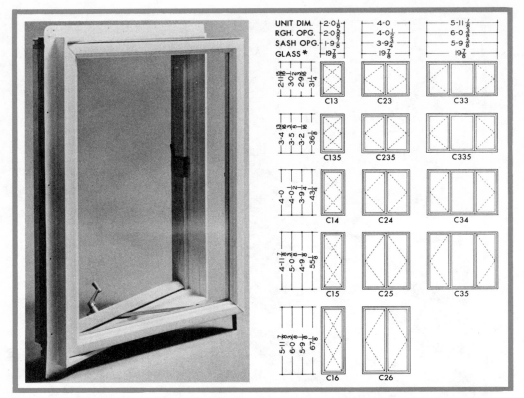

Fig. 130. Casement window. (Andersen Corporation)

Note: Multiple units of these sizes are available. To find the overall unit dimension for a combination unit, add the unit dimensions together plus $1/8''$ for each unit joining. To find the rough opening, add $1/2''$ to the overall unit dimension. Example: If 2 unit C23 windows are joined to form a 4-window opening, the unit dimension is $4\text{-}0'' + 4\text{-}0'' + 1/8'' = 8'\text{-}01/8'' + 1/2''$ or $8'\text{-}05/8''$.

6. Compute the distance between the three major centers in your kitchen at home. Does the kitchen require unnecessary walking? What could be done to improve its efficiency?

7. Compute the amount of wall and base cabinets in your kitchen at home. How does it compare with the minimum requirements for good kitchen planning?

8. Compute the square feet of closet space in your home. Considering the value of your home and the total square feet, how much did this space cost?

9. Write an evaluation of the laundry facilities in your home. Consider convenience of location, ease of working in the area and accessibility for repairs and adjustments of equipment.

10. Develop a complete plan to convert your basement at home into useful living space. In addition to drawing a floor plan, figure the cost of the additions (walls, ceiling, floors, expanded electrical systems, etc.).

Additional Reading

Architectural Record (Editorial Staff), *Time Saver Standards.*

Better Kitchens Institute, "Kitchen Planning Book."

Gerber Plumbing Fixtures Corporation, "Tips From Your Plumber."

Ramsey, Charles G., and Sleeper, H.R., *Architectural Graphic Standards.*

Small Homes Council, "Basements."

———, "Garages and Carports."

———, "Handbook of Kitchen Design."

———, "Household Storage Units."

———, "Kitchen Planning Standards."

———, "Laundry Areas."

———, "Separate Ovens."

Townsend, Gilbert, and Dalzell, J.R., *How to Plan a House.*

U.S. Federal Housing Administration, "Minimum Property Standards for One and Two Living Units."

U.S. Housing and Home Finance Agency, "Design for Livability."

CHAPTER THREE

DESIGNING THE EXTERIOR

Before a final set of plans can be drawn, the elevations must be planned and sketched. Even a simple freehand sketch to an approximate scale is very helpful. While certain construction problems may be involved, the primary problem is that of developing a suitable exterior for the plan.

Evaluating Designs

Everyone does not agree as to what is the most pleasing design or the best design. Certainly, each person is entitled to his own value judgments and to like things which seem pleasing to him. However, there are certain principles of design which must be carefully considered by designers and purchasers of buildings. These are reflective of good taste. The ability to examine and evaluate building designs is something that is intangible. It is developed through study and practice, much the same as an artist would study and work. Just because a person happens to like something does not mean it is good design or in good taste. As just mentioned, people do not agree as to what they like, and because of this variance, a building could be of good design and in good taste but a well trained designer might not like it. He may appreciate it, but not like it. The human element is always present in judging the esthetic.

For example, certain architectural designers will argue that there is only one way to design a house. The house should appear as though it belongs to the ground and the hills and trees surrounding it. In their exterior design, they try to achieve the feeling that the house was put there by nature and that it belongs, just as the rocks and hills belong. Frank Lloyd Wright did design work of this type.

Then there are other designers who try to give their houses the feeling of freedom from the earth. They feel the house is an independent creation and is unrelated to the earth. This type of house gives the impression that it is floating above the earth, near but separate.

Another group of designers might be classified as the traditionalists. They believe that the classical house styles are the best, and they reflect the design and details of the past in all their designs. The classical house must be modified so it is acceptable to modern society; yet, it must retain the flavor of the past as authentically as possible. Certainly, a genuine 1800 New England Colonial with its primitive kitchen, outside toilet, and poorly operating windows would not sell today. People who like traditional design demand modern conveniences such as central heat, plumbing, and a garage. It is possible to blend the best of the past with the conveniences of the present into an excellent, well styled house.

Whatever feeling toward design appeals to the designer should be clearly reflected in the styling of a house. A house should never be "no style" or just a house. Neither should it be a mixture of styles, borrowing a part of one style and mixing it with parts of others. The end result is reflective of nothing; it is simply

a nondescript hodgepodge. If a style is desired, it should be honestly reflected.

It is disappointing to view a house with an excellent front elevation of high-quality masonry, only to find that the sides and rear are framed in with wood siding. The "false face" is deceiving and disturbing. Let the exterior be genuine.

It is generally considered best practice today to design a functioning floor plan and then to design a shell for this plan. It is extremely difficult to force a plan to fit a preselected exterior design. However, as the plan is being developed, the designer constantly should keep in mind what is happening to the exterior. The plan and the elevations must be developed together.

Fig. 140. A symmetrical house exterior.

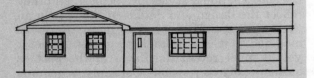

Fig. 141. An asymmetrical house. The long right-hand extension balances the gable end on the left.

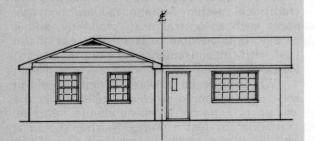

Fig. 142. A house out of balance. The heavy gable end overweighs the other half.

Basic Principles of Building Design

As the elevations are being designed, the composition, proportion, scale, contrast, rhythm and unity of the building must be considered.

The *principle of composition* refers to the combining of the parts of a house to achieve a harmonious whole. All the principles of building design influence the composition of a building.

Symmetrical and Asymmetrical Designs

A building is of either *symmetrical* or *asymmetrical* composition. The Georgian house is a good example of symmetrical structure. See Fig. 140. It is built on a centerline, with windows spaced an equal distance on each side of this line. Frequently, a slight variance in symmetry does not spoil the overall feeling of precision, balance and order. The plan of a house should not be forced to fit a predetermined, symmetrical exterior. The exterior should not control interior design.

Fig. 141 is an example of a pleasing house with an asymmetrical exterior. This type exterior gives a feeling of balance, by having portions of the structure of varying sizes and shapes grouped around a focal point, such as the front entrance. Although it is not mathematically symmetrical, the observer feels satisfied. The structure does not appear top-heavy or off balance. Fig. 142 illustrates a house that is the same length on each side of a centerline, but which gives a feeling of imbalance.

To achieve a feeling of balance, the larger portions of a building should be located nearer to the focal point than the lower or smaller portions. Such a feeling is difficult to achieve. Refer back to Fig. 141; the large mass is the gable end which is near the front entrance (the focal point of the house).

The parts of the structure should seem to belong together; yet, they should have some contrast, both in mass and proportion.

Proportion in Design

Proportion must be considered in designing exteriors also. This refers to the relation of the size of one thing to the size of another or to the whole. Various designers and artists through the years have set up rules of proportions which they felt were satisfactory or

most pleasing. However, the actual proportions that are pleasing vary with the individual and his culture. The proportions between the windows and the mass of the house which were pleasing in a Colonial house in 1700 certainly are not pleasing in today's contemporary homes with their glass walls. In this sense, proper proportion involves where a thing is used and with what it is associated. The entire effect can be altered by a simple change in the relationship of the size of associated elements. See Fig. 143.

A designer will consider the *scale* of the items involved in elevations. Such items as doors and stairs must be of such a size or scale as to permit easy use by the average person.

A frequent violation of the proper consideration of scale is a huge picture window placed in a small house. This window dominates the entire wall area and conflicts with the standard-size windows and door. It is *out of scale*, and a more pleasing exterior would result if the picture window were smaller or, in other words, on the same scale as the other windows. This does not mean that all windows have to be the same size. Size variation is common and acceptable. If a window appears to be somewhat out of scale, the appearance can be helped by keeping the glass panes approximately the same size.

The fireplace, together with its chimney, is an example of another common item that frequently gets out of scale. Some are too large for the size of the house, while others are so slender that they look weak and unimportant.

Contrast in Design

The monotony of an otherwise satisfactory exterior can be relieved by *contrast* in the design. A house may have contrast in the mass of the structure. For example, a small wing or ell can break the monotony, Fig. 144.

Various materials may be used in developing contrast. A house with a part brick and part frame or stone exterior is more interesting than one constructed entirely of one material. Contrast may be obtained by the use of color or glass.

It is difficult to obtain contrast by using various geometric shapes such as rectangular and semicircular masses and arches. In most cases, each should stand alone. It is usually

Fig. 143. A massive chimney that is out of proportion in relation to the house.

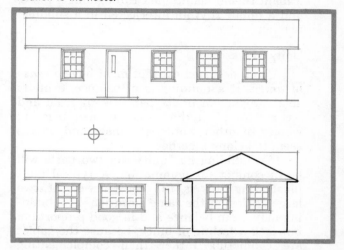

Fig. 144. The house at the top leaves a feeling of monotony. This is relieved by adding an ell.

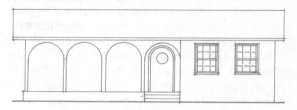

Fig. 145. Introduction of a conflicting geometric shape — the round arch — has violated the basic retangular mass of this house.

best to vary the proportions of each geometric mass, rather than to introduce another form. For example, if a structure is basically built on a rectangular mass, it is unsatisfactory to introduce semicircular or triangular forms such as an arch. See Fig. 145.

Even though a building is a stationary object, it can offer the viewer *a feeling of rhythm or movement*. A solid, unbroken wall does not offer this feeling. However, a wall that is broken by windows, shutters, trim and other details which describe a definite, repetitive pattern introduces a feeling of rhythm. Rhythm can be subdivided into *pronounced*

patterns and *secondary*, or more subtle *patterns*. To illustrate, a building may have an evenly spaced detail, such as columns, that is highly prominent. This detail sets the main theme or pattern of rhythm. A minor detail, such as a small amount of paneling, could also present a second pattern of rhythm, but be subservient to the main theme, the columns. This is much the same as writing music, with a main theme maintained throughout a piece, and a minor rhythm interjected in a subdued manner.

Unity of Design

A well designed exterior must have *a sense of unity*. If a building is in balance, exhibits good proportion of its parts, is to scale and has a sense of rhythm, it is a unified, pleasing whole. In other words, the mass and details seem to belong together.

If a building has unity, no two parts will be in conflict for domination. A typical fault illustrating this is the construction of two large gables on the same elevation. The building may be in balance and in good proportion, but lack a feeling of unity, because the gables are conflicting rather than complementing each other.

The violation of any of the principles of design will destroy the sense of unity. Dormers out of scale or the selection of conflicting geometric masses will damage the unity of the building. Certainly, an examination of the completed elevation with a consideration of the principles of design is a vital final step in the designing of elevations.

Identifying Characteristics

It is usually possible to guess what purpose a building was designed to serve by simply examining the exterior. Buildings have characteristics that, because of their function and association with the past, make them different from other buildings. It is easy to identify a school or a church without ever going inside. You know what they are because they look like a church or school. This is their character.

Some of today's buildings are quite different from their counterparts of 200 years ago, and yet there is still something about them that is characteristic. Churches have changed as drastically as any building. Nevertheless, even though clothed in new materials

which are assembled in radical manners, it is possible to tell that the building is a church.

Homes can have character too. A low, charming Cape Cod leaves the visitor with entirely different reactions than a flat-top, glass-wall, contemporary house. Even the building materials influence the character of a house. The designer should consider this as he plans his exterior designs.

Mass, Texture and Color

The designer cannot proceed to work on the elevations without considering the mass, surface texture and color of the exterior.

The *mass* is the large geometric bulk of the structure, usually a rectangular form. The overall appearance probably is influenced more by the mass of a building than any other one thing. Compare your reaction to the two-story Colonial in Fig. 140 with your reaction to the long, rambling ranch house in Fig. 141. Compare your reaction to the mass of a long, wide, low supermarket with that to a six-story office building. Your first impression or reaction is to the mass. Then the factors of surface texture and color are noted.

The exterior surface *texture* stimulates sensory reactions. The various exterior materials evoke varied reactions. Glass and aluminum panels leave a cold feeling when compared with the warmth of a brick or stone exterior. A wood exterior is warm and conventional. Other materials such as precast concrete, mosaic tile and porcelain panels have different textures and produce different feelings and reactions. As the character of a building is planned, consider its texture.

Anyone who has examined paintings knows the value of *color*. A feeling of warmth and friendliness can be engendered by using the warm colors. Other colors can provoke a feeling of coldness or loneliness. Interest can be excited, character spelled out and good taste reflected by proper and careful selection and use of color.

Factors Influencing Styling

Before the plans can be drafted, the design of the roof and its relationship to the house proper must be determined. This includes the type of roof suitable for the style of house, as well as the height and pitch of the roof. The cornice details and amount of overhang should be decided.

Another consideration is the exterior materials to be used. While cost and availability of materials are important factors involved in this decision, certainly appearance should be paramount. The material must be suitable for the style of the house. The monotony of a large wall of one material can be relieved by a skillful blending of several materials. For example, frame blends well with brick or stone, stone and brick look well together, and large areas of glass can be used with any of these materials.

As styling decisions are made, consider the appearance of the side and rear elevations. These are important to the overall effect created by the house. All sides of the house should be in character.

As indicated in the discussion of building sites in Chapter 1, the shape and slope of a lot influence the type of house best suited for the site, and this in turn influences the styling.

Styling is influenced by the neighborhood. It would be unwise to have a house that is drastically different from those in the immediate neighborhood.

The likes and dislikes of the owners should be reflected in the styling. While this may produce a satisfied homeowner, if the design is not tempered by the judgment of a trained designer, a "no style" house may very well be created.

The amount of money available certainly will affect styling. This will be reflected in many ways, such as in the choice of exterior materials or in the choice of a gable roof instead of a more expensive hipped roof, or a square plan instead of an *L*, *T*, or *U* plan.

Building codes and deed restrictions frequently limit the style and type of house that can be built.

Climate has a lot to do with styling. Consider the effect that mild winters have on the way people live. Warmer climates with long growing seasons encourage designers to bring the outside right into the living area, through the use of glass. Large patios and outdoor living are involved. Homes in areas of long, severe winters cannot use large glass areas, because of the great loss of heat.

The section of the country in which the house will be built frequently dictates its style. Various sections look with favor upon particular styles. For example, in Virginia, colonial styling reigns supreme. Some extreme contemporary houses are built, but they are at a minimum. The people have lived in this colonial atmosphere for generations, and this is what they desire when they build. Building a house which clashes with the local tastes could be a risky investment.

It is usually a mistake to build a house in one section of the country that was designed for another. For example, a New England Colonial house would be out of character in southern California. With its small windows, it would be difficult to ventilate and keep cool in the hot seasons. The many completely enclosed rooms and lack of contact with the outside give it a closed, restricted feeling. It would be difficult to live in such a house in an area with long, warm seasons.

Whether a house will have a basement influences its planning and styling. If a low appearance is desired, the basement could well be eliminated. This puts the finished floor almost on grade. If a basement is used on such a house, the windows are partially buried below the surface of the ground, permitting very little light and ventilation.

If a house is built on a slope, with a good portion of the basement wall exposed, the basement area is much more usable. However, this greatly affects the exterior styling since careful consideration must be given to making this foundation pleasing. A split-level house uses this foundation wall to good advantage, by permitting the use of windows and doors.

Common Roof Types

No study of styling would be complete without consideration of the types of roofs in common use. Fig. 146 illustrates some common roof types.

Probably the most frequently seen roof is the *gable* or, as it is sometimes called, the *A roof*. This is an economical, easy roof to construct. It handles rain and snow easily and is adaptable to many styles of homes. It is easily vented by louvers at the peak of the gable end.

An adaptation of the gable roof is the *hip roof*. This roof is more expensive to build, because of the labor involved in framing it. It tends to give a house a low appearance and does away with the gable end. This eliminates maintenance of the siding on the gable end.

Houses that are almost square can use a hipped roof to advantage, if all sides are brought to a common point in the center.

The *flat roof* is coming into more frequent use on contemporary homes. It requires the least cost for materials and labor, but demands special care in sealing against leaks. Some contemporary homes use a *shed roof* to provide some slope to facilitate drainage. This is also inexpensive to construct. Both the flat and shed roofs need special consideration of structural strength in areas of heavy snows; considerable extra weight can accumulate on such a roof.

A variety of the shed roof found on some of today's homes is the *monitor*. It is a combination of two shed roofs, with skylights between the two roof levels.

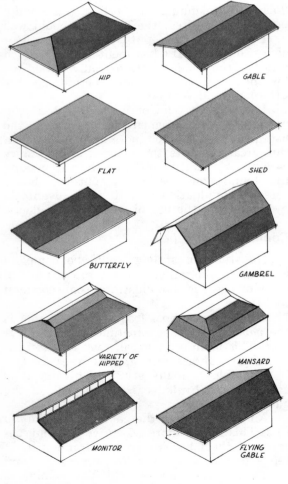

Fig. 146. Roof types.

Two roof styles seldom used today are the *gambrel* and the *mansard*. These are representative of some traditional house styles. The gambrel is characteristic of the Dutch Colonial house, while the mansard is found on French Provincial houses.

A roof style seen with increasing frequency on contemporary homes is the *butterfly roof*. Since all water is shed to the center of the house, good workmanship is required to prevent leakage. It is not an expensive roof to build.

A styling feature used on gable roofs is to build out the overhang at the ridge and slant it to the eave. Such a feature is called a *flying gable*. It gives a house a rakish appearance and a feeling of increased length.

The Development of Architectural Styles Influencing Residential Design

As a study of the development of the various architectural styles progresses, it can be seen that the story of the buildings cannot be separated from the story of the people who built them and lived in them.

The study of ancient architecture is a study of large buildings — cathedrals, palaces, tombs and public buildings. The people lived in huts of no particular style or description, and, therefore, the homes of men were not a part of the architectural heritage of the ancients. The following discussion is centered upon later events which did exert an influence upon the dwellings of man.

Old World Residential Architecture

Much of the influence on American residential architecture came from Europe. There were several periods in the history of Europe that produced architectural styles that eventually exerted a significant influence upon the houses built in America. These styles can be classified as:

English
　　Old English or Cotswold
　　Tudor
　　Elizabethan or Half-Timbered
　　Jacobean
　　Georgian
　　Regency
Mediterranean
　　Italian Renaissance Villas and Farm
　　　　Houses
　　Spanish Renaissance Farm Houses

From these European influences, there developed in America several architectural styles reflective of the European heritage of the people.

The American styles developed were:
> The Early 17th Century New England House
> The Southern Colonial House
> The Georgian Style
> The Cape Cod Style
> The Dutch Colonial
> The French Colonial
> The Federal House
> The Greek Revival Style
> The Victorian Style
> Spanish Architecture in Florida
> Spanish Architecture in the Southwest

English House Styles

The Norman conquest of England occurred in 1066. Following this episode of history, English country houses and farm houses developed distinguishing characteristics. These cottages became one of the more important influences upon early American architecture. They are commonly called Old English or Cotswold, since many were built in the Cotswold area of England. Sometimes this style is simply called Norman, because these houses closely resembled the houses of the Normans from Northern France. This type of house was popular until about 1500.

Old English Style or Cotswold

These cottages were built by the small merchants, farmers and country squires. See Fig. 147. They were low in appearance, with the roof line at the head of the window and sometimes lower. They were built from stone, brick, stucco and occasionally a bit of half timber was used. The roofs, generally, were tile or slate, while poorer families thatched their roofs. The roof had a very steep pitch to help shed snow and rain, and the thatch was rolled under at the eaves giving a rounded effect. The casement windows were few in number and quite small. They were made from many small pieces of glass, sometimes diamond shaped, because it was not yet possible to make glass in large pieces. They were placed at random in the exterior walls; their location depended upon the placement of interior partitions or where the owner happened to want a window.

Fig. 147. Old English, Cotswold or Norman farmhouse — The Ann Hathaway Cottage, Stratford on Avon, England.

Fig. 148. Old English Style, built near Plymouth, England.

Little planning of the interior was done. Rooms usually showed very poor relationship, and the kitchen was frequently a long way from the dining room. Such inconvenience would not be tolerated in today's functional houses.

The Old English house was very informal and rambling and exhibited no tendency toward symmetry. See Fig. 148. The fact that

these houses were occupied for centuries accounts for the rambling plan. Wings and gables were added by various occupants as room was needed. Frequently, the additions were from a material different from the original house. This accounts for Old English houses that are part stone, part brick and part half timber.

Fig. 149. A Tudor house — Hengrave Hall, Suffolk, 1538. (B. T. Batsford Ltd.)

Fig. 150. An Elizabethan House — Speke Hall, Lancashire. (B. T. Batsford Ltd.)

This low, rambling, rough-textured house with its large, high-pitched roof was very pleasing in appearance and quite picturesque. It is admired today for its quaintness. Its beauty comes from the aging of its rough-textured materials.

Tudor Style

Late in the fifteenth century, England was in the midst of civil wars, called the Wars of the Roses. Two great powers were fighting to claim the English throne. The House of Tudor came to power, and with the country at peace, home construction began again. Many of the wealthy had fled to Europe during the fighting. There they saw the beginning of the Renaissance, a period of culture. The architectural forms of France and Italy impressed these people, and they brought these ideas back with them when they returned to England. Workers were even brought from Italy to assist in building construction. Out of these influences came a style which was called Tudor, after the reigning power of the time. A large Tudor house is shown in Fig. 149.

Tudor houses were large houses. Characteristic of this style were large, prominent gables; large, high chimneys with high, decorative chimney pots; and walls of masonry (brick, stone) or stucco. The casement-type windows were tall and narrow and occasionally included stone mullions and transoms. They were made of many small panes of glass, frequently of leaded glass.

The Tudor house was usually a full two-story house and sometimes had a half-story in the attic. The roof was very high-pitched and steep, with the roof line generally on a level with the ceiling of the second floor. This style did not have the low, rambling appearance of Old English houses. It was not symmetrical, though it exhibited some formal planning and a semblance of symmetry.

Elizabethan or Half-Timbered

During the reign of Queen Elizabeth, the Tudor house underwent gradual styling changes until a new variety emerged to become a style of its own. The use of an exposed timber frame with stucco or brick filling between the timbers became popular. (Many Elizabethan houses had considerable stone on the exterior.) The exposed timber frame became

the outstanding characteristic of the Elizabethan style. See Fig. 150.

Most other characteristics were similar to the Tudor. The Elizabethan house had many prominent gables, was usually a full two stories and had tall, narrow casement windows. The windows were fitted between the structural timbers, and the sashes contained many small panes of glass.

Several large, prominent chimneys usually were a part of this style. Occasionally, the second floor would cantilever over the first floor, and the heavy corner timbers of the second floor would project down and be carved.

The exterior of the Elizabethan house was not symmetrical. It was an informal, rambling house. The rooms merely were placed where the owner wanted them.

Jacobean Period

After the reign of Queen Elizabeth, the House of Stuart ruled England. Few changes occurred in house styles for over one hundred years. No one style developed sufficiently to become recognized. This was the Jacobean Period. However, other things were happening that were to influence the house designs in America today. During the reign of the Stuarts, the American colonies were settled. The English Puritans settled in New England and Virginia; the Quakers settled in Pennsylvania, and the Dutch began settling in New York and Pennsylvania.

Finally the Stuart line ended, and a prince from Holland was invited to become the King of England. This was the beginning of the House of Hanover. During the reign of George III, a Hanover king, the Colonies gained their freedom and formed the United States of America.

Toward the end of the 15th century, the Renaissance was born. With this classical awakening came influences that led to the Tudor house. After several hundred years of development, the influence of the Renaissance brought about a new style of house on the Continent and in England. This was a house as had never been seen before. The style came to be known as the Georgian, since it evolved during the reign of the Georges of the House of Hanover. By 1700, it was a well established style.

Georgian Style

The Georgian house, a completely new style, was very formal and symmetrical. It was usually rectangular. Reflected in the details were direct copies of the classical architecture of early Italy. The cornice was usually of a classical design, and a pediment was frequently used.

Basically, the front entrance was exactly centered on the front elevation, and the windows were balanced on either side. The house was usually two full stories with a high-pitched gable roof providing attic rooms, if dormer windows were added. The second-floor windows were placed directly above those of the first floor.

The exterior was usually brick with stone quoins at the corners. Large chimneys, generally at the ends of the house, were prominent.

Since the Georgian style was so formal and fixed, little freedom was left for interior planning or room arrangement. Typical of a Georgian house was a large hall through the center of the building, with the stairs to the second floor directly in front of the main entrance. The living room was usually on one side of this hall, and a dining room was on the other. Upstairs, the two main bedrooms were placed with a bath or sewing room between, to enable the builder to preserve the exterior balance of windows on the front elevation. Other less important rooms such as the kitchen, pantry, or maid's room were placed in the rear, and little attempt was made to keep this part of the structure symmetrical.

The Georgian is a beautiful house and is still very popular. See illustrations of the Georgian houses built in the American Colonies in the next portion of this chapter.

Regency Style

At the time of the American Revolution, King George III became unfit to rule. His son was appointed as a Regent to act in his place. During this period of history the Georgian style was modified so that it was less formal and more refined. Much of the classical detail of the Italian Renaissance, which influenced the Georgian, was removed. Designers studied ancient Greek and Roman architecture for design ideas. Characteristic of a Regency house were a curved porch roof over the front entrance, octagonal windows, long shutters

Fig. 151. Regency Style Homes. (English Embassy)

on the first-floor windows and curved top edges of walls projecting from the corners of the house. The roof was usually hipped and rather steep. The house was a full two stories, and the windows were double-hung, with small panes of glass. See Fig. 151.

England had developed trade with the Far East, and some people believe the curved roof over the front porch or over the front, bay windows was the influence of the Chinese.

Wrought iron balconies and porch railings were frequently used.

The Mediterranean Styles

The architectural styles of Italy and Spain found acceptance in the southern parts of the United States. Both countries have warm climates similar to that of our Southern states. These houses were designed to ward off heat, rather than intense cold, as were the English and French styles. It may frequently be difficult to separate Italian and Spanish houses, although there are some distinguishing features.

The Italian Styles

The architecture of Italy was influenced by the Italian Renaissance. This awakening initiated a movement that sought out and copied the details of the classic buildings of ancient Rome. It was this style that was used in the designing of Italian villas. The Italian style had a low-pitched, tile roof and classical design features such as balustrades. It, generally, was a full two-story building, with a loggia having columns and arches. (A *loggia* is a roofed gallery which is within the body of a building; it is attached at the second floor and has three sides enclosed and one side open to the air.) The casement-type windows, generally, had a wide trim surrounding them. The exterior was usually stucco. See Figs. 152 and 153.

The Italian styles were brought to the United States by American tourists who visited the Italian villas, liked them and copied them upon returning home.

The Spanish Styles

The developments of the Spanish Renaissance influenced the architecture in Spain. However, Spain had been conquered and occupied by the Moors from Africa; therefore, Spanish architecture was influenced by both

Fig. 152. Grand Canal, Venice, Italy. Notice the loggia and characteristic trim around windows.

Fig. 153. The Villa Agostini a Cusignana in Italy. (Italian State Tourist Office)

factors. This style differed somewhat from the Italian. A low-pitched, gable roof was common, but it was not tile, as were Italian houses. Stucco was a common exterior material, and casement windows were used. The Spanish employed balconies with decorative railings, Fig. 154. They also built around a patio, frequently enclosing it on all four sides by the house. This provided a cool, private place to relax. In an attempt to keep the houses cool, the Spanish built the walls very thick. This made it necessary to locate the windows in a deep opening, which caused a dark shadowy effect.

The Spanish styles were brought to this country by Spanish settlers who lived in Florida and southern California.

Early American Residential Architecture

The first settlers in the New World lived in crude shelters. These, usually, were dugouts, cabins or wigwams. They were built from whatever material was close at hand and with no concern for style. None of these early houses were log cabins. Log cabin construction was not introduced in the colonies until 1638 by the Swedes in Delaware.

Early 17th Century New England Houses

As the settlers prospered and towns grew substantially, well finished houses were constructed. These were usually made from the common materials available locally. See Fig. 155. Sawyers cut lumber where it was plentiful. If the soil was right, bricks were made and burned in kilns.

These houses were much the same as those lived in by the settlers in their mother coun-

Fig. 155. An Early 17th Century New England House in Salem, Mass. (Essex Institute)

Fig. 156. A 17th Century Cottage — The Peake House, Medfield, Mass., 1680. (Arthur Haskell, photographer, Historic American Buildings Survey, Library of Congress)

Fig. 154. Spanish style house. Notice hipped tile roof and casement windows.

try. There is a striking resemblance between the medieval houses of Old England and the Early Colonial houses of New England.

The houses were predominantly timber-framed. Stone and brick were scarce and used only for the most expensive houses. The typical house used hewn oak posts and beams, joined with pegged joints. It was usually covered with clapboard siding.

Most houses were very simple. The people had to work to survive and did not have time to spend on ornate decorations. The houses, usually, were rectangular, with a large chimney in the center serving many fireplaces. See the Peake House, Fig. 156.

The rooms tended to be low, and the roofs were steeply pitched and often thatched. The doors and windows were placed where needed, with little consideration for exterior appearance. Windows were small, and if they contained glass, it was in small pieces, for glass was precious and expensive. See Fig. 157.

The second floor occasionally overhung the first floor. This overhang was an influence from the medieval towns of Europe where houses were crowded and ground was precious. This was an attempt to gain a larger space on the second floor without consuming more ground space.

Through the years, rooms were added on and roofed over. This led to a type of house referred to as the Lean-To or Saltbox. See the Richardson House, Fig. 158.

An example of a large farmhouse of the 1800's is shown in Fig. 159. Notice the gambrel roof and double-hung windows.

Southern Colonial Architecture

A great region running from Delaware Bay to the Savannah River and inland to the Piedmont region became what was called Virginia. This area was settled mainly by the English. Here developed a style of architecture commonly known as Southern Colonial.

The early homes here were much the same as those in other parts of the colonies — crude huts or dugouts. As more colonists arrived, frame houses were built. These were of hand-hewn timber frames covered by clapboards. See Fig. 160. Brick houses were built early

Fig. 158. Saltbox or Lean-To Style, built 1750. (Old Sturbridge Village, Mass.)

Fig. 159. A large New England farmhouse built in 1801. (Old Sturbridge Village, Mass.)

Fig. 157. Leaded windows of house built in 1698. (Library of Congress)

Fig. 160. Early Southern Colonial — the Blair House. (Colonial Williamsburg)

here, possibly in the early 1600's, but the frame house still predominated at this time. Construction methods were much the same as in the other colonies.

The 17th century houses in Virginia had thatched roofs and, later, wood shingles. Almost all roofs were of the gable type. The windows were small and of the medieval, casement type with leaded, diamond panes. A striking feature was a great exterior chimney. This was wide at the base, enabling a large fireplace to be built.

The soil in the South was suitable for brickmaking. With skilled brickmakers among the early settlers, brick fast became a popular building material. This was much more true in the South than in New England.

The typical Southern house was built on a central hall plan, with chimneys located at each end of the house. It was usually rectangular, with a small projecting porch, and was commonly one and one-half story. Dormers were used a great deal to increase the livability of the second floor, though some houses were built without dormers and relied only on small windows in the end walls for light and ventilation. See Fig. 161.

The Georgian Style in the Colonies

The Colonies looked to England for trade and fashions. As the Renaissance brought about the development of the Georgian house in England, eventually the English Georgian influenced house styling in the Colonies. The Georgian house became popular in the Colonies in the early 1700's.

This was a very formal style. The houses were usually rectangular, and the windows were placed in perfect symmetry. Interior rooms were arranged to permit a balanced exterior. The front entrance was placed in the exact center of the structure. The pediment of the Romans was used a great deal. Doorways were usually flanked with pilasters rising to a cornice or pediment.

Fig. 161. A brick Southern Colonial — the Red Lion Inn. (Colonial Williamsburg)

Fig. 162. Mount Vernon, the home of George Washington in Virginia. (Mount Vernon Ladies Association)

Fig. 163. A late Georgian House — the Governor's Palace, Williamsburg, Virginia. (Colonial Williamsburg)

Windows were almost universally of the double-hung type and were made up of many small panes of glass. Blinds of the louvered type were very common; some paneled blinds were used in the Middle Colonies.

Most Georgian houses were either frame or brick. Attempts were made to stucco over the brick or frame exterior and incise lines to make it resemble stone masonry, but this was esthetically unsuccessful. Mount Vernon is a classical example of a frame Georgian treated to resemble stone masonry, Fig. 162.

The roof was usually pitched about 30 degrees, which was lower than Colonial roofs. While many gable roofs were used, the hipped roof was the most popular. Some roofs were cut off below the ridge to form a flat deck which was enclosed with balustrades. See Fig. 163.

Many later Georgian houses had large pilasters extending the full height of the facade. Some used a small entrance portico with pilasters and a pediment above. See Fig. 164.

Georgian houses were built with one and one-half to two and one-half stories. They had gable, gambrel and hipped roofs. Dormer windows of many shapes were used; they were usually narrow, and frequently the gable end was treated as a pediment. See Fig. 165.

Georgian chimneys were usually simple, rectangular shapes with a small molded cornice at the top.

The early Georgian house was much simpler than those built after 1750. It was a large, impressive house with a bold appearance. The roof tended to be pitched steeper than the later styles. Usually, it had no entrance pilasters or portico. The windows were built in smaller panes than the later Georgian, sometimes having 18 to 24 lights per window. See Fig. 166. The dormers had rectangular windows, while the later Georgian frequently had arched dormer windows. Later Georgian houses, also, commonly had a balustraded roof deck, while these were seldom used on earlier styles. Refer back to Fig. 163.

The Georgian houses built in the Middle Colonies were much like those of New England and the Southern Colonies, except they were

Fig. 164. A variation of the Georgian style — Gunston Hall, built near Alexandria, Virginia. Notice the portico over the front entrance.

Fig. 165. The Adam Thoroughgood House, 1636, thought to be the oldest in the English-speaking colonies. Built in Princess Anne County, Virginia. (Frances Johnston, photographer, HABS, Library of Congress)

Fig. 166. Berkeley Plantation on James River, Virginia, built 1726. Architecture directly influenced by Georgian Style.

usually stone. Some were built of brick, but stone was a readily available material. Throughout Pennsylvania, Georgian houses can be found. Fig. 167 illustrates a house of this type.

As cities grew, row houses were built. They had common walls between them and were built right up to the front sidewalk. Sometimes, a small front yard was allowed. See Fig. 168. The styling was a direct influence of the homes of the time, and the Georgian influence was strong. The use of wrought iron railings and columns became common. See Fig. 169.

By the beginning of the 18th century, the deep South was beginning to build its system of large plantations. This, especially, was true in the Carolinas.

Rivers were the main method of transportation, because much of the land was swampy and unsuitable for roads. Since wealth was beginning to come to plantation owners, they began to build large houses. These were of the Georgian style. Many of the largest were facing rivers, since this was the "highway" of the day. They were built miles from the nearest neighbor.

Some plantation owners began adding a portico with two-story, slender columns. George Washington was among the first to do this at Mount Vernon. This portico permitted the exposure of all the windows on the second floor; yet it protected them from the hot sun

Fig. 168. Captain's Row on King Street, Alexandria, Virginia. Built just before the Revolution.

Fig. 169. Row houses with wrought iron and small front yards, typical of Virginia.

Fig. 167. Georgian house as built in Pennsylvania. Home of James Audubon, Audubon, Pennsylvania.

Fig. 170. Georgian House with portico on three sides, built in Louisiana.

and driving rain. Frequently, this portico was built facing the river; some built it on three sides. Fig. 170 illustrates a beautiful Southern house with columns on the front and sides.

While many call this "Southern Colonial," it is a Georgian house built during Colonial times. Porticos built in northern Colonies were definitely a Southern development.

Fig. 171. Peter Bronck stone house, 1663, and brick house built in 1738 (New York State Department of Commerce)

Fig. 172. Stepped gable of an early Dutch Colonial house of the 17th century.

Dutch Colonial Architecture

The Dutch and Flemish settled in Long Island and New Jersey. They brought with them the architectural style copied from the streets of Amsterdam, Leyden and Utrecht, and from the farmlands of the Dutch and Flemish lowlands. Although, in the New World, this style developed into one that was distinctly American, it retained a great deal of the flavor of its origin.

The first houses were much the same as those in New England. They were either dugouts or frames, covered with bark or other readily available material.

As more settlers arrived and the colony called New Amsterdam thrived, new houses were built. Usually these were wood, brick or stone. Occasionally, all three materials were used in one house. A large number of the very early houses were frame, since the settlers were familiar with wood, and it was easily worked.

In the Hudson Valley, settlers found ample supplies of stone and built many fine stone houses. The big problem was securing lime to develop a strong mortar. The walls, usually, were from one and one-half to three feet thick. See Fig. 171.

In early New Amsterdam, the houses were usually two and one-half or three stories. The outstanding architectural feature was the stepped gable rising to a chimney or ornamental finial at the ridge. The stepped gable was a carryover from the medieval architecture of

Fig. 173. Hendrick Bries House, built in 1723 in East Greenbush, New York. (HABS, Library of Congress)

the Low Countries and Germany. See Fig. 172. This was an early example of a Dutch Colonial.

By the 18th century, the styling had changed. See Fig. 173. The straight-lined gables were heavily used, instead of the earlier stepped gable. Roofs were steep and had chimneys on each end. Many of these houses were brick. These, as were the earlier Dutch Colonial, were from one and one-half to three stories high. Additions were frequently built during the years of occupancy.

Another style also developed during the 18th century in this area. It is most commonly known today as a Dutch Colonial, but it is more properly called a Flemish Colonial house. The most outstanding feature is the gambrel roof. The actual heritage of this roof cannot be traced to the Dutch or Flemish, since the English and Swedish also used the gambrel roof.

The roof was large, permitting almost a full second story, with the overhangs boxed in. Frequently, the overhang was large enough to cover a front porch. The roof was usually covered with wide wood shingles. Dormer windows were used to open up the living area on the second floor.

The chimney was always on the interior. See Fig. 174. This style of house was of frame and stone construction. Shutters on all windows were common. Frequently, wings were built as additional space was needed.

Cape Cod Colonial Cottage

This house style can now be seen throughout the country, but it seems to have originated in the Cape Cod area of Massachusetts.

They are one story or one and one-half story buildings. The roof is rather steep and is a simple, gable type. The eaves are plain and have little overhang. The eave line is near the top of the window, giving the house a low appearance. See Fig. 175.

The exterior siding is white, frame clapboard or brown (or gray), wood shingles. Shutters are used on all windows. The windows are the double-hung type and have many small panes. Dormer windows are not characteristic of this style, but many modern versions do add two single dormers on the front and, occasionally, a shed dormer at the rear. These should be small and in proportion to the house.

Fig. 174. Flemish (Dutch) Colonial, Lexington, Mass.

Fig. 175. A Cape Cod Cottage — the Elizabeth Kelley House, Mass. (Arthur Haskell, photographer, HABS, Library of Congress)

A large central chimney containing several flues is a distinct characteristic of the Cape Cod. Since it required several fireplaces, a large chimney was necessary.

French Colonial Architecture

The French Colonial empire in North America was immense. It extended from the Alleghenies to the Rocky Mountains and from the Gulf of Mexico to Labrador and Hudson's Bay. This remained under French control until the early 18th century. There were few towns in this vast area and only a few forts and Indian villages.

France lost this territory to England and Spain after the Seven Years War (1756-63). Before this time, French explorers, trappers,

missionaries and some settlers worked their way up the St. Lawrence River and across the Great Lakes. They established forts at strategic points such as Sault Sainte Marie, Frontenac and Duluth. They began establishing settlements along the Mississippi Valley. By 1682, French explorers had traveled south all the way to the Gulf of Mexico. Settlements were started at Mobile, Biloxi, Fort Toulouse, Natchez and Natchitoches. In 1718, New Orleans was founded; in 1764, St. Louis.

The division of this territory in 1763 gave all lands east of the Mississippi to England and all to the west to Spain. However, the territory remained culturally French, and strong elements of this can be found in places today.

The architecture of many of these cities became a blend of several cultures. The houses of New Orleans are an excellent example of this blending.

Fig. 176. An early French Colonial house, 1737 — a re-erected structure in Cahokia, Ill. (Lester Jones, photographer, HABS, Library of Congress)

Fig. 177. A two-story French Colonial as found on plantations — Poente Coupee Parish, La., 1750. (Richard Koch, photographer, HABS, Library of Congress)

The French Colonial Style

The early French Colonial house was usually of half-timber construction. However, it differed considerably from that of England. Heavy cedar and cypress logs were placed vertically on the ground and set much as fence posts. They were spaced a few inches apart, and the spaces were filled with a clay and grass mixture. Some builders used Spanish moss or deer hair instead of grass with the clay.

Later, the same type of construction was improved by the use of a stone foundation with a wood sill. The upright logs were placed on this sill. Such an arrangement prevented the rotting of the logs, as occurred with those buried in the ground. See Fig. 176.

This house was one story, with several rooms all in a line, and a stone chimney either in the center or at one end. Generally, this structure was surrounded by a "galerie" or porch, which gave access to the rooms. Many slender posts were used to support the roof of the galerie. The roof shape in Fig. 176 is characteristic of this style. Usually, the main house was covered with a steep, hipped roof, and a lower-pitched roof was placed over the galerie.

As plantations grew, larger houses were built. They, usually, were two stories with stucco-covered brick walls and columns on the ground floor, and wood construction on the second floor. The galerie was extended across the front on both levels; sometimes, it was also across the rear of the house, and a few houses had a galerie on all four sides. See Fig. 177.

The supporting posts for the first-floor galerie were also stucco-covered brick and were styled on classical lines. The second-floor posts, usually, were slender and wood.

Spanish Architecture in Florida

Spanish explorers penetrated the New World early. The first landing in Florida was in 1513 by Ponce de Leon. By 1528, Panfilo de Narvaez had landed in Tampa Bay and explored inland in the state of Florida. DeSoto left Tampa Bay in 1539 and traveled through Florida, Georgia, the Carolinas, Tennessee, Alabama and almost to Ohio. He then went south into Arkansas and Oklahoma, returning to the Mississippi River where he died. Remnants of his party reached Mexico in 1543.

In 1565, the Spanish sent about 2,000 persons to establish a defense outpost at St.

Augustine. They murdered a group of French settlers who had already made homes there.

A crude fort was built of earth and logs. In 1593 a group of Franciscan friars arrived and, over the years, established many Spanish missions in the area. The mission buildings were built of stone and wood.

Indian and pirate raids destroyed many of the forts. In 1672, the first stone fort, Castillo de San Marcos, was built at St. Augustine. It is one of the most impressive examples of Spanish architecture in Florida, Fig. 178.

Britain acquired control of Florida in 1763 and ceded it back to Spain in 1783. It remained Spanish until American occupation in 1821. Very few buildings of this early Spanish period now exist. The present Spanish influence is due to a revival of this influence in the twentieth century.

Spanish Architecture in the Southwest

In 1609, the Spanish were building La Villa Real de Santa Fe de San Francisco, the capitol of the province of New Mexico. This was only two years after the English landing at Jamestown, Virginia. Coronado explored the mountains and plains of Arizona, New Mexico, Colorado and Kansas. In 1542, Cabrillo sailed north beyond San Francisco. Mexico was by now settled by the Spanish, north of today's Mexico City. The Franciscan and Dominican friars were establishing missions which were the main examples of Spanish architecture. The friars were responsible for their construction and used what they knew about architecture from Spain. The mission was more than just a place of worship. It was an entire community, containing sleeping rooms, kitchen, storerooms and shops.

The missions, built by unskilled Indian labor at a time when tools were scarce, were rather crude. The walls were built of adobe bricks — a mixture of clay and straw, formed into blocks weighing about 50 pounds. These were dried in the sun and stacked to form the walls.

Roof beams were hewn logs laboriously lifted into place. The roof was of rough-hewn planks. Over the planks, 6 inches of adobe clay was spread to form a solid slab roof. An example of such a mission can be seen in Fig. 179.

When the Spanish settled the area now called Texas, missions were built as in New Mexico. The most famous of the missions is the Alamo, built in 1718 at San Antonio.

Another characteristic type of building is illustrated in Fig. 180. The walls were adobe, and flat logs were used as roof supports. This type house is still built today in New Mexico.

The first California Spanish mission was established at San Diego in 1769. From this

Fig. 178. The Castillo de San Marcos, St. Augustine, Fla., built 1672. (U. S. Dept. of Interior, National Park Service)

Fig. 179. The mission church of San Estevan at Acoma, New Mexico — completed about 1642. (Laura Gilpin, photographer)

Fig. 180. A modern residence styled after early adobe houses in New Mexico. (Laura Gilpin, photographer)

small, difficult beginning, the Spanish moved north, establishing many missions along their route. In 1776, as the thirteen English Colonies gained their independence, the Spanish established a mission at the Golden Gate.

The California missions were built mainly from adobe bricks, as in New Mexico. The walls were very thick and tapered to the top; they were coated with lime and sand to prevent erosion by rain. These missions differed from those in other areas in the Southwest because they used quite a lot of burned brick. This enabled the builders to reinforce arches and to build piers.

Red tiles formed into half cylinders were used for roofing, and wooden beams and planks made up the structure of the roof.

Since the builders had bricks, they could build arches. The arch is repeated in the long arcades of the missions, forming a major architectural motif.

Fig. 181 is an example of a splendid mission, Mission San Carlos Borromeo, built in 1793. This was one of the first structures to use stone as the basic material. The facade was covered with stucco. Arches were used a great deal. The dome on the tower was directly influenced by the Moorish tradition in Spain.

The houses built by the Spanish at this time in the Southwest were of the same materials as the missions — adobe walls and wood roof planking with a tile outer cover. The roofs were usually the shed type. Architecturally, the houses were very simple. They were commonly built in a "U" shape, with a patio open on the fourth side. The veranda facing the patio was usually supported by wooden posts and not by heavy pillars and arches, as were common on the missions. See Fig. 182. This veranda served as a covered corridor, giving access to each room, since the building was only one-room wide and had no inside halls. It also served as a lounging place.

In the northern part of the Spanish holdings in California, one of the most beautiful of all Spanish California houses developed. It was a two-story house with a long veranda on the ground level and a balcony above. Wood supporting posts were run from the ground to the roof. Since many of these houses were built in Monterey, the style is named after this town. See Fig. 183.

The ground level usually contained the living area, dining area, cooking and service areas and a stairway leading to the second floor. This stairway was on the outside of the building and ran up from the veranda. The balcony and veranda frequently were covered on the ends by a lattice.

The balcony railings were light and delicate. The roof was usually a gable style and was low-pitched. Frequently it was hipped at the ends. Wood shingles were used extensively as a roofing material.

Fig. 181. The Mission San Carlos Borromeo, built in 1793, located on the Monterey Peninsula, California.

Fig. 182. A Spanish Colonial house built in Southern California, 1819. (HABS, Library of Congress)

The house was rectangular in shape and, therefore, did not encircle a patio. Adobe walls were built around an area to the rear of the house, to form a private patio.

The exterior walls were mainly adobe, averaging three feet in thickness on the first story and two feet in thickness on the second story. The adobe exterior was covered with a mud plaster and whitewashed. Occasionally, the adobe walls were covered with wood planks placed horizontally as clapboards, or vertically as board and batten.

The windows were small and had small panes of glass. Since the walls were very thick, the windows were set deeply and the resulting window ledge formed window seats.

The Federal Style

After the Revolutionary War, houses began to change. The architecture of England had a great deal to do with these changes. By 1800, a style called the Federal Style was popular. The house was still a basic rectangle and usually two stories high. The symmetrical appearance of the English Georgian house was used. The detail of the house became delicate; smaller members replaced the heavy ornamentation of the earlier Georgian period. The hipped roof and the gable roof were used, but they were not pitched as steep as earlier styles. A roof style called the monitor was common, with small windows near the ridge on a hipped roof.

Another common characteristic of the Federal house was a delicate balustrade on the roof. Often, this was near the eave and practically concealed the roof. See the Longfellow House, Fig. 184.

Fig. 183. A Monterey style house — the Larkin House in Monterey, Calif. (HABS, Library of Congress)

Fig. 184. A Federal Style — Longfellow's House, Cambridge, Mass.

Fig. 185. Federal Style — Salem Towne House, 1796. (Old Sturbridge Village, Mass)

The main entrance usually had an overhead, fan-shaped light and glass side lights. If columns were used on the front, they were regularly spaced; each column tapered gradually to a narrow extremity. See the Salem Towne House, Fig. 185.

Greek Revival Style

In the early 1830's, interest in classical Roman and Greek architecture became great. This caused some abrupt styling changes in the houses of the time. Designers found in the early Greek buildings a masculine vigor that was a sharp contrast with the delicate, feminine Federal style. The revived interest took the country by storm.

Greek temples became examples of excellence. Massive columns supporting a portico were used to imitate these temples. The Doric order of Greek architecture was the most popular and was extensively copied. The building was comprised of large, plain surfaces and large mouldings dividing these surfaces into panels.

Full-length French windows were commonly used, and large panels of glass were installed.

Fig. 186. Greek Revival Style — Levi Lincoln House, 1836. (Old Sturbridge Village, Mass.)

The Greek Revival home had to be a large structure. The design was massive and entirely out of keeping for small houses. It was not popular long and by 1850 was being replaced by the Victorian style. See the Levi Lincoln house, Fig. 186.

Victorian Style

The Victorian period was one of confusion. Houses were large and very heavily ornamented. Carvings and turnings were fastened on porch roofs, eaves and gables. Porch balustrades were very ornately carved. It was a period of poor taste, when many large, irregular, two-story houses were built. The heavy, fancy trimming of this style was given the name *gingerbread*. See Fig. 187. Designers paid little attention to pleasing proportions, balance or a feeling of unity or harmony.

By 1900, the people reacted against this style, and a rapid change was made to a style that did away with all forms of ornament — the bungalow. The form and decoration of the house was supplied by the structure. If something was needed for structural purposes, it was used, but nothing extra was used simply for decoration.

These later styles — the Greek Revival, the Victorian and the bungalow — have had little influence on the American house of today. The earlier Colonial styles, however, have exerted considerable influence in the styling of today's house, and some are quite popular in a form closely resembling the original.

Fig. 187. A Victorian House.

Fig. 188. Savoye House, Poissy, France, built 1930. Entrance hall, garage, laundry and servants' rooms at ground level; living quarters on top level. (French Cultural Services)

One story house with traditional detailing. (The Garlinghouse Co., Inc.)

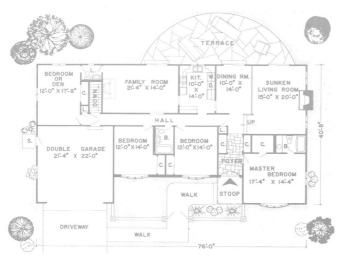

Flat roof contemporary design. (The Garlinghouse Co., Inc.)

Contemporary plank and beam house. (The Garlinghouse Co., Inc.)

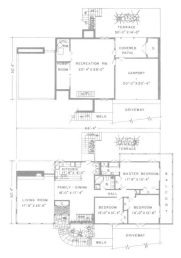

French Provencial styling. (The Garlinghouse Co., Inc.)

Split level design. (The Garlinghouse Co., Inc.)

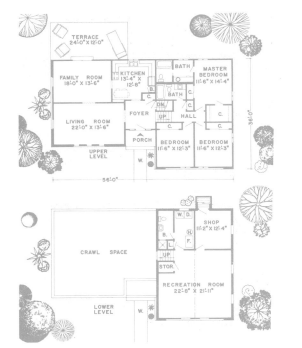

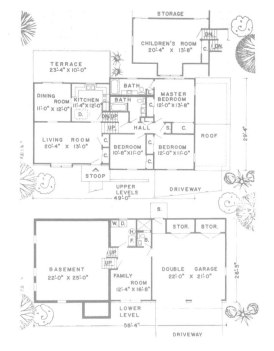

Split level design. (The Garlinghouse Co., Inc.)

Colonial styling. (The Garlinghouse Co., Inc.)

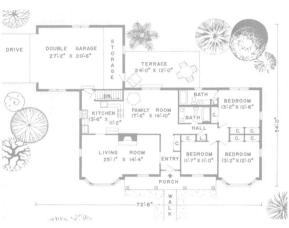

DRIVE

DOUBLE GARAGE
27'-2" X 20'-6"

STORAGE

TERRACE
24'-0" X 12'-0"

DN.

FAMILY ROOM
17'-6" X 14'-10"

BATH

BATH

C.

BEDROOM
13'-2" X 12'-6"

KITCHEN
13'-6" X 11'-2"

HALL

C.L.

C. C.

C. C.

LIVING ROOM
25'-1" X 14'-4"

ENTRY

C.

BEDROOM
11'-7" X 11'-0"

BEDROOM
13'-2" X 12'-0"

PORCH

WALK

72'-8"

54'-0"

BEDROOM
11'-0" X 11'-6"

B.

KIT.

UP.

C.

LIVING ROOM
20'-0" X 15'-6"

P.

20'-0"

36'-0"

LOWER FLOOR PLAN

BALCONY

SLEEPING LOFT
12'-0" X 9'-2"

C.

DN.

SLEEPING LOFT
12'-0" X 5'-0"

LIVING ROOM
BELOW

32'-0"

UPPER FLOOR PLAN

A-frame cottage. (The Garlinghouse Co., Inc.)

Residential Architecture in the United States Since 1900

Since the turn of the century, residential architecture has been experiencing a revolution. New concepts involving the function of a house and its relationship to the occupants have evolved. Experimentation with new forms and new building materials has contributed materially to this revolution.

Residential architecture has assumed characteristics completely new and unrelated to that of the past. It is difficult to classify some of the current work and to give it a permanent name. The following classifications are those currently popular, but only the test of time can identify and characterize a style.

Classifications of Residential Architecture Since 1900 in the U.S.:

> The Bungalow
> Modern Style
> The Ranch House
> The Contemporary Style
> The Japanese Modern
> Outstanding Area Styles
> > The California House
> > The Pacific Style
> > The Hawaiian House
> > The Florida House

The Bungalow

From 1900 to 1920, many houses were built and called bungalows. They were a revolt against the elaborate, highly decorative Victorian house. While they never developed into a style of their own, they were a new approach to house design. All decorative elements were eliminated. The structural elements were left visible, and simplicity was

Fig. 189. A house of the modern style built in France. (French Cultural Services)

the keynote. These houses were not attractive, yet thousands were built.

They were one-story homes, with a roofed porch extending across the front. Typically, they were two-rooms wide and quite long, with the narrow dimension facing the street. Both frame and brick construction were common. The gable roof was universally used.

During this time, the more popular, traditional styles were built as they are today. The Georgian and Cape Cod will always be built.

The Modern House

The style of house commonly referred to as "modern" or "modernistic" developed primarily in Europe during the early 1920's. Architects such as Le Corbusier, Gropius, Hoffmann and Neutra rejected the traditional way to plan and build a house. Their approach was to plan the interior to suit the needs and way of life of the occupants. Then they covered this plan with a simple shell, devoid of unnecessary decoration. Its function was to shelter the plan from the elements of nature. The exterior, then, became simply the result of the developed plan. See Figs. 188 and 189.

The outstanding feature of the modern house was not its exterior appearance, but the interior plan of rooms. The house was designed to be functional and to reflect the modern way of living. Considerable emphasis was placed on working out the best room arrangement and use of space.

Building costs were getting higher, so houses were becoming smaller. The modern house attempted to get a feeling of spaciousness in a small floor area, by combining several rooms. It was called an *open plan*.

The use of large, glass areas in the exterior walls also contributed a great deal to the open feeling. The windows were placed where needed, with little regard to what this did to the exterior. The emphasis was on a livable, open, floor plan.

The large glass areas were usually placed away from the street and toward the best view. Since automobiles were becoming common, garages were placed on the front of the house. Roofs were commonly used as sun decks and for outdoor living.

An influential factor was the development of new materials and new construction techniques. The exterior wall was no longer needed

to serve as the main support of the structure, because steel framing and columns could be used. Walls, then, became only thin skins to retard the elements. New materials began replacing brick and stone. Large glass panels, aluminum skins and plastic materials were new exterior materials coming into use at that time.

The exterior style of the modern house can be easily recognized because of its box-like shape. See Fig. 190 for an example of a small house of this style. Simplicity was demanded. Very little decoration was used. The roofs were flat, and the exterior walls presented large, plain, unbroken areas. Long expanses of glass broke the wall on occasion, and corner windows came into use. A pleasing architectural effect was created by skillful use of proportioned, rectangular solids. The entire house

Fig. 190. A small modern house.

Fig. 191. A modern version of the western ranch house. Notice the rambling plan, veranda and private patio. (Clifford May, designer and builder, Clifford May Associates)

portrayed simplicity and functionalism. Many people disliked it, and the style did not gain the acceptance in the United States that it did in Europe. However, the modern house did contribute much to residential architecture. Progress made in the planning and construction of houses had lagged far behind that made in such fields as transportation, communication and medicine. The modern house was a rich and genuine effort to enable man to live as he should in a modern society. While the style is now out of favor, the lessons it taught are reflected clearly in houses of today.

The Southwestern Ranch Style

On the open prairie in the Southwest, land was cheap and plentiful. Timber was scarce, the prairies flat and windy. It was hot in the summer and cold in the winter. The people settling the area could not build the two-story stone or frame Colonial that they were accustomed to seeing in the east coast colonies. Instead, they developed an entirely new style of house — the low, rambling, ranch house. See Fig. 191.

This house was built of adobe bricks and had a flat or low-pitched roof. Since it seldom rained in this area, the houses were built on the ground, and hard-packed, earth floors were common. If wood floors were used, they were built over a crawl space.

These houses were one-story high and had low ceilings. Since land was cheap and plentiful, it was more economical to add rooms on the ground level than to build a second story. All that was necessary to add a room was to mix adobe bricks and let the sun bake them. The walls could be built right to the ground.

These houses were designed for outdoor living and, frequently, were built around a patio, as were the Spanish houses. Since all rooms were on the ground floor, most of them had doors opening onto the patio.

The Midwest Ranch House

The ranch house did not become popular until the 1940's. As it spread to the midwest, it was modified by builders to fit a more restricted building site. The modified ranch house still retains many of the features of the early California and prairie ranch houses. They are now brick as well as frame, and tend to fit an *L* shape rather than a winding, rambling *U* shape.

The rooms in the modernized version of the rambling ranch house are smaller and fewer in number. Fireplaces are retained for decorative purposes, and garages have been added. The house, often, is built with a basement. A typical example is shown in Fig. 192. Other varieties of this style are shown in Figs. 193 through 195.

The Japanese Modern House

The style of house commonly called Japanese Modern has developed from the study and appreciation of Japanese architecture. The best way to understand what this is today is to go back a few hundred years and follow the story of the development of building in Japan. The Japanese had a strong culture and an architecture of their own. However, the architecture of China spread its influence into Korea, Indonesia and Japan. Therefore, what we think of as Japanese architecture is really an assimilation of the Chinese influence by the existing Japanese architecture. This Chinese influence was secondary in importance to the Japanese culture and architecture.

Climate is a big factor influencing the Japanese architecture, as is the rough landscape. Japan is a country of steep hills and mountains, rapidly falling valleys, and lakes, oceans, rivers and waterfalls. The Japanese people have always been sensitive to the esthetic, and they take advantage of these natural beauties in their architecture. The use of the picturesque and the close relationship of a building to a slope, to water, to a striking tree or to a hillside became a part of the architecture of Japan. The houses were not strictly symmetrical, as were the Chinese houses, and the Japanese design had more freedom and was not as formal and strict as the Chinese design. An American version is shown in Fig. 196.

The Japanese also try to make their houses part of the total landscape, by using trees to balance their typically asymmetrical houses and by relating the house and nature with stone lanterns, walls and shrines. This composes a complete architectural picture that is related not only to the immediate surroundings but to the distant landscape. To view a Japanese home is the same as viewing a completed painting. See Fig. 197.

The Japanese built their houses primarily from wood. They used wood so that the nat-

Fig. 192. A typical midwest ranch house. (Andersen Corp.)

Fig. 193. One variety of the midwest ranch house. (Andersen Corp.)

Fig. 194. A variety of the midwest ranch house. (Rowe Manufacturing Co.)

Fig. 195. A low-cost house, frequently called a midwest ranch. (*House and Home* magazine)

Fig. 196. Japanese modern home, built in Hawaii. (R. Wenkam, photographer, and *House and Home* magazine)

Fig. 197. A detail of a modern Japanese house in Tokyo, Japan. (Shokokusha Publishing Co.)

Fig. 198. Chinese influence on Hawaiian home. (R. Wenkam, photographer)

Fig. 199. Interior of Japanese modern house in Tokyo, Japan. Steel construction and new materials were used. (Shokokusha Publishing Co.)

ural beauty of the grain and color could be displayed. Usually, it was undecorated, but rubbed smooth. The houses were built on a rectangular framework of delicate appearing members, so that the entire effect was one of lightness and delicacy. Even the thatched roofs enhanced this effect. The Chinese house tended to portray solidity and formal dignity. See Fig. 198.

The interior and exterior of the Japanese Modern house are highly characteristic of the people. The interior partitions are sliding paper screens, and the exterior is composed of sliding wood shutters. The floors are covered with woven mattings. See Fig. 199. The wood panels are plain and unpretentious, as shown in Fig. 200 which illustrates their use in a Japanese Modern home.

Freedom of arrangement is great. The interior screen partitions can be moved, and the entire house can be opened into one large room. See Fig. 201.

Japanese houses are planned with freedom for expansion. As more space is needed, it is added on. Each addition is placed to take advantage of a view or is built with a private garden or court.

Fig. 200. Interior of Japanese modern house — notice sliding screen partitions and use of wood. (R. Wenkam, photographer and *House and Home* magazine)

Fig. 201. Interior of Japanese modern house — notice mats on floor and pads to sit upon. Wood walls and ceiling are typical. (R. Wenkam, photographer and *House and Home* magazine)

Fig. 202. A Hawaiian house — notice the open walls. (R. Wenkam, photographer)

The curved roofs, so often considered characteristic of Japan, were mainly used on temples. These temples were influenced by Chinese Buddhist monks who came to Japan. Through the years, Japanese architecture brought some change in this influence. The elaborate Chinese pailoo with complicated brackets and cornices developed into the simple Japanese tori with only two posts and crossbeams. The Japanese influence gradually caused the high roofs to become lower and substituted plain uncolored wood for the elaborate coloring of the Chinese.

By the 17th century, Japanese architecture (mainly temples and larger structures) had become more complex. More carving was used. Roofs took on complicated shapes. Dormer-like gables were added, sometimes one being placed above the other. This developed into the reduplicated roofs and dormers seen on shrines and castle towers. These fantastic shapes brought much acclaim to Japanese architecture.

However, the lasting values of Japanese architecture were those of an earlier period when the traditional Japanese house was developed with its open plan, simple design and use of natural materials. The beauty of a lovely

interior set against a lake or garden, with mountains in the distance and pines framing the view, is the contribution of the Japanese architecture.

In the United States, very successful attempts have been made to adapt the Japanese concepts of house planning and design to the American way of life. Through a skillful blending of cultures and customs, a style of house, called the Japanese Modern, is being built.

It attempts to capture the open floor plan and spacious rooms, the simple, undecorated, exterior styling, the honest use of materials and the use of large openings to take advan-

Fig. 203. A Hawaiian house. The exterior is more conventional, but interior shows Japanese influence. (R. Wenkam, photographer)

Fig. 204. A Hawaiian house utilizing a view. Notice large overhang and bamboo screen below floor level. (R. Wenkam, photographer)

Fig. 205. A break with tradition in Hawaii. (R. Wenkam, photographer)

tage of a view or a private courtyard. Sliding screens and low simple furniture are characteristic. These have been illustrated in Figs. 199 through 201.

The Hawaiian House

The architectural styles of the Japanese and Chinese, many of whom settled in Hawaii, appear predominately in the type of houses being built there. They all stress view and climate and try to make the most of these local advantages. While it is difficult to separate some Hawaiian houses from Japanese, modern examples of what is being built in Hawaii are shown in Figs. 202 through 204.

Architects in Hawaii experiment freely with new ideas in housing. Figs. 205 and 206 illustrate an exciting example of a rustic Hawaiian house.

The Pacific Style

The Pacific style is a design trend that is gaining acceptance. It tends to be a blend of the Traditional and the Contemporary styles. The predominant influencing style is Japanese architecture. The Pacific style tends

Fig. 206. Interior view of Hawaiian house in Fig. 205. (R. Wenkam, photographer)

to use Japanese ideas for house arrangement, but does not use their design details. These are more Traditional American. It is built on a 4'-0" x 8'-0" modular component.

Open room planning and outdoor living are part of this style. It establishes a pleasant, indoor-outdoor relationship through the use of glass and view; yet it retains some of the Traditional style in overall appearance. See Fig. 207.

The roof has considerable overhang and usually has a small gable at the ridge, with a change of pitch at the eave and exposed lookouts. It has been influenced by Japanese styling and has an Oriental appearance. The style makes use of sliding screens and natural materials. Stained wood exteriors and wood shingle roofs are characteristic. See Fig. 208.

Private patios with trellises, pools and gardens are used. Glass walls face this area, while the street side has few or no windows, thus insuring privacy.

Quarry tile is used on floors in some rooms, as well as on counter tops. This is an Oriental influence.

The Pacific style tries, as does the Japanese style, to recognize that a house affects the lives of the people who live in it even more than it reflects their taste and status. This includes the love of nature and outdoors, an appreciation of simplicity of design and an appreciation for the natural texture and color of materials.

The house is usually low, irregular in shape, without a basement. The delicate framing and rectangular shapes of the Japanese predominate.

The Contemporary House

The Contemporary house is designed for livability. It is designed and built to meet the needs of today's way of living and is a revolt against all of the past. It is an attempt to look to the present and future needs of man and his family. As the work day shortens and the three-day weekend becomes a reality, the home will play an increasingly important role in the satisfaction of man's leisure-time needs. It must include family recreation space for all kinds of activities, but must still provide a high degree of privacy for every member of the family. Such a house must be flexible so that rooms can be changed as needed.

Fig. 207. A Pacific style house. (Duenke Building Co.)

Fig. 208. A Pacific style house. (Duenke Building Co.)

The Contemporary house must provide a relaxed setting for a life of busy leisure. It is manifestly suburban and informal in character. It is less pretentious than the Traditional house and is an outward expression of our industrial age and the American way of living. Such a house could be a long, low, one-story structure, generally rambling and asymmetrical. See Figs. 209 and 210. It could be a two-story or even a split-level house. Generally, it does not have a basement and is built on a slab.

The living areas face private gardens or a distant view rather than the street. The design is a supreme attempt to secure a close relationship between indoor and outdoor living. It is

an attempt to bring the outdoors into the house. Considerable indoor planting is a part of the Contemporary house. This is not only attractive, but helps to maintain a healthy humidity level. Much of the exterior wall surface is put into glass, especially in the living areas. The picture window is obsolete, as entire walls are glass. The feeling desired is to be free from the enclosement of walls. The interior floor plan is an open plan with few partitions. Frequently the kitchen, dining and living areas are one large room with perhaps a screen or fireplace serving as a partial divider. See Figs. 211 and 212.

Exposed ceiling beams are common, and much emphasis is placed on the use of natural materials. The material is not painted, but is permitted to reflect its own characteristics of color and texture.

The Contemporary house and its lot are treated as a whole. Together they form a single unit and present a feeling of belonging together. The house may be anchored snugly to the ground or suspended above the site, depending upon the conditions found.

The exterior design is rather simple. Window sizes vary according to the needs of the occupants. Doors are placed where needed, rather than where they will produce a symmetrical appearance. The structural skeleton is not covered and becomes part of the character of the house. Materials requiring a minimum of maintenance are selected.

Fig. 211. A contemporary house — the Kirkpatrick house, Kalamazoo, Mich., Norman Carver, Jr., designer. (*The Secondary Treasury of Contemporary Houses*)

Fig. 209. A long, low contemporary house. (Jules Gregory, Architect)

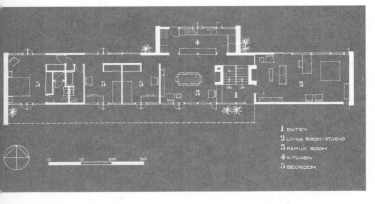

Fig. 210. Floor plan for the contemporary house in Fig. 209.

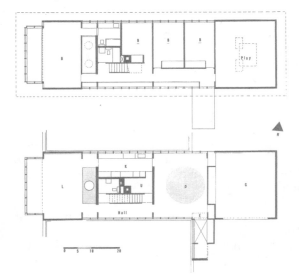

Fig. 212. Floor plan of Kirkpatrick house (*Architectural Record*)

The roof is usually supported in such a manner that no load is applied to the interior partitions and exterior walls. The roof framing is commonly wood or steel beams or trusses. The exterior wall panels simply hang on this skeleton. They can be glass, aluminum, brick or any desired material. Complete freedom of interior arrangement is thus available, with flexible room dividers such as large panels, cabinets, glass, etc. These partitions can be moved to new locations to permit rapid changes in the area of partially enclosed space. They sometimes extend to a height of 6 or 7 feet, which is just sufficient to break the lines of sight. Even the closets are designed for flexible rearrangement of hanging rods and shelf space.

The interior materials are also selected for freedom of maintenance. Tile floors commonly replace hardwood flooring. Walls of glass, wood paneling and plastic materials are common.

The Contemporary house utilizes labor-saving and automatic devices extensively. Temperature control, stereophonic phonographs and speakers, television, and many kitchen devices are among the services built in today's Contemporary house.

The basement is almost nonexistent, with the recreation room being built on ground level for convenience. The same is true for the heating unit and laundry facilities. The traditional family workshop is often being placed in the garage.

The Florida House

The new house being built in Florida is a sharp break with old styles. It is also a break with old ways of thinking, old ways of living and old ways of building. Since planning and design affect the everyday life of the occupant — physically and psychologically — the Florida house of today is structured differently than just a few years ago. It is open to the breeze, with many houses having every room with large screened openings. See Fig. 213. Some houses have screened areas off many rooms, Fig. 214. These areas are not porches, in the common sense of the word; they are screened areas of grass outside a house. See Fig. 215. Even swimming pools are screened as shown in Fig. 216. Though many houses are air conditioned, they still have large areas that can be opened to the air. Such a house has no definite boundary between indoors and out-

Fig. 214. A large, private screened area off a bedroom. (Philip Hess, photographer)

Fig. 213. A Florida house with all rooms opening upon a screened area. Walls behind screen are mostly glass. (*House and Home* magazine, Rudi Roda, photographer)

Fig. 215. A large screened yard area. (Philip Hess, photographer)

doors. The Japanese call this characteristic "engawa," meaning an uncluttered space belonging inside and outside. See Fig. 217.

This house was developed in an attempt to meet the special climate conditions and to suit a special way of life. It enables the occupants to get the most out of living in Florida. The design of the Florida house met the big problems of hot sun, steamy rain and insects; it also met the demand for outdoor and informal living. The houses have large overhangs to shield windows from the sun, and they use sun screens and shrubs for additional protection. The large overhang, lowered sun screens and awning-type windows enable the house to receive cooling breeze during the season of heavy rain. See Fig. 218. The large screened areas are necessary for protection from insects.

Fig. 218. Large overhang and louvered openings help weather condition a Florida house. (*House and Home* magazine, Rudi Roda, photographer)

Fig. 219. A brick Florida house built in Tampa, Florida — low maintenance is a feature, Betty Weld, designer. (William Amick, photographer)

Fig. 216. An indoor pool in a Florida house. Notice the informal atmosphere for relaxed indoor-outdoor living.

Fig. 217. A totally screened patio and pool on a Florida house. (Robert H. Ford, photographer)

Fig. 220. A typical Florida house.

Since the stress in Florida is on leisure and informal living, the Florida house is designed to be easily maintained. Much brick is used for exterior walls, with prefinished plywood popular for interior walls. Floors are commonly terrazo and need practically no care. Aluminum and plastic panels are used on the exterior and interior, and much glass is evident. See Figs. 219 and 220.

The California House

Out of the architectural revolution on the Pacific Coast developed a type of house commonly referred to as the California house. It grew out of an awareness of environment and a way of life. The main concept is that of outdoor-indoor living.

The California house is designed for an informal, relaxed way of life. It takes full advantage of California's bright sunshine and luxurious growth, but also provides shelter against the abundant rainfall. While outdoor living can take place year-round in much of California, provision is made for chilly evenings and nights.

The California house is related to its natural environment, as well as to the individual site, and is an attempt to provide a restful yet exciting experience. It uses natural materials in a natural setting. Stone, brick and wood are characteristic. Glass is widely used in an attempt to relate the outdoors to the interior setting. See Fig. 221.

Many California cities are located upon mountainous terrain. These sites provide full

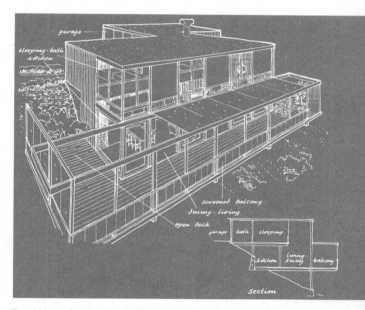

Fig. 222. A sketch of a California house showing its relationship to mountainous terrain, Gordon Drake, architect. (Reinhold Publishing Co.)

Fig. 221. An interior view of a California house — notice the use of wood and glass, Gordon Drake, architect, (Reinhold Publishing Co.)

Fig. 223. Notice the exposed structure of the California house — each part serves a useful function, Gordon Drake, architect. (Reinhold Publishing Co.)

and extended views, as well as opportunities to utilize the sun and wind. See Fig. 222. The site, as well as fences and walls, is used to insure privacy.

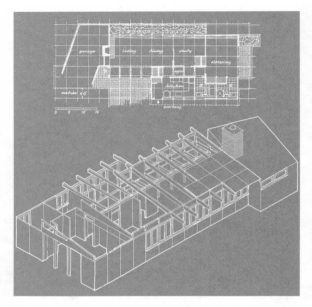

Fig. 224. A panelized California house with floor plan. Notice the simplicity of structure, Gordon Drake, architect. (Reinhold Publishing Co.)

Fig. 225. A California house with a shed roof and celestory windows, Gordon Drake, architect. (Reinhold Publishing Co.)

Fig. 226. A California house with a balcony relating the house to the surroundings, Gordon Drake, architect. (Reinhold Publishing Co.)

The California house is a simple house. The structure is prominently exposed and provides the character. Unnecessary embellishments are avoided. See Figs. 223 and 224.

The heat and glare of the sun are controlled by a large overhang. Natural light in each part of the house is controlled by clerestory windows, translucent panels and louvered screens.

Considerable planting (interior as well as exterior) is characteristic of this house. It is considered as an integral part of the overall design.

The roof is flat or the shed type. Interior walls are commonly wood, using the intrinsic color and grain to give a feeling of naturalness. See Fig. 225.

Large outdoor terraces that open to the sky are characteristic of the California house. These are usually paved with bricks, wood blocks or other suitable materials. Again, plantings tie the house and terrace together as a unified whole. See Figs. 226 and 227.

Houses Around the World

So often, the houses we see in our locality are accepted as being the usual or standard house. A trip around the United States indicates that even in one country the type of house being built varies. A trip around the world reveals even more differences.

In some countries, the houses closely resemble those in the United States. However, in less fortunate countries, this is not true. Their houses are very crude shelters. In other countries, home ownership is rare, except for the wealthy. In some parts of the world, large apartment units are being built to house a more privileged middle class. The poor have no hope of ever owning a house of any quality.

The following illustrations are an attempt to tell the story of houses in selected countries around the world.

Fig. 227. An outdoor terrace bringing nature indoors. Notice the use of natural materials, Gordon Drake, architect. (Reinhold Publishing Co.)

Fig. 228. Residence, British Columbia, Canada. (The Royal Architectural Institute of Canada)

Fig. 231. A private residence in Norway. (Norwegian Information Service)

Fig. 229. A private residence in Brazil. The middle class live in apartment houses, and only the wealthy can afford private houses. (Brazilian Embassy)

Fig. 232. Small cottages near Stockholm, Sweden. Cottages are prefabricated and erected by the owners. Instructors are available to supervise the building and give assistance. (Swedish Tourist Traffic Association)

Fig. 230. Only a small proportion of the Danish population own their own homes, which usually are terrace houses with 2 to 3 rooms on each floor, as these in Copenhagen. (Royal Danish Ministry for Foreign Affairs)

Fig. 233. A larger house in Sweden — notice the use of native materials. (Swedish Tourist Traffic Association, Jan Olsson, photographer)

Fig. 234. A small Swiss chateau.

Fig. 235. Houses near Innsbruck, Austria.

Fig. 236. Apartment type residences being built in Madrid, Spain. (Spanish Embassy)

Fig. 237. Houses in Athens, Greece.

Fig. 238. An example of today's architecture in expensive houses in Italy, Leonardo Ricci, architect. (Italian State Tourist Office)

Fig. 239. Another contemporary house built in Italy, Leonardo Ricci, architect. (Italian State Tourist Office)

Fig. 240. A view of houses in Bethlehem.

Fig. 243. A Moro House, Philippine Islands.

Fig. 241. Native houses, Addis Ababa, Ethiopia.

Fig. 244. Houses in India built in a community development. All villagers help when one decides to build a house. (Information Service of India)

Fig. 242. Native housing in Frigwagle, Guinea, West Africa.

Fig. 245. A Japanese house of today. Construction is steel. The design, however, reflects the traditional architecture of Japan. (Shokokusha Publishing Co.)

Fig. 246. A Korean house.

Architecture in Transition

As can be seen from the preceding pages, home styling has changed through the years, as have man's way of living and his outlook on life. This brings to mind the question, "What of the future — what new forms in home design and structure will arise?" The following homes are examples of designs that defy classification at the present time.

The home shown in Figs. 247 and 248 is an adventure in the use of new forms to divide space both inside and outside the house. Notice the floor plan is a quadrate cross, combining indoor and outdoor living. Each room has complete privacy; outdoor courts are tastefully used, yet no hall space is required.

Fig. 247. Use of new forms in space planning, Edward J. Seibert, architect (*House and Home* magazine)

Fig. 249. Use of new roof form, Robert E. Buchner, architect (*House and Home* magazine, Ben Newby, photographer)

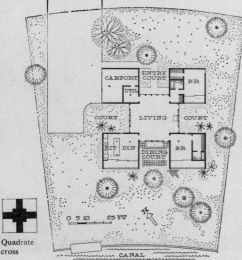

Quadrate cross

Arrangement of rooms establishes four courts, all of which relate to the central pavilion.

Fig. 248.

Fig. 250.

The horizontal lines of the structure are capped by the striking pyramid roof which covers the living area.

In an attempt to use new forms to shelter the house itself and screen it from the surrounding countryside, the architect used a huge sloping roof shell (Figs. 249-251). While the shape of the shell is interesting, of even more interest is the feeling of wonder about the world inside the shell. The translucent panels at the left shelter the pool and terrace.

Fig. 253.

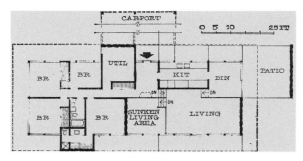

Fig. 254.

The home in Figs. 252-254 is an attempt to transform the basic rectangle, by application of a double-conoid roof. This brings a sense of motion to the usually static rectangle. The roof produces interesting effects, not only by its flowing motion, but by the changes in ceiling heights. The house takes advantage of a sloping lot and has three floor levels.

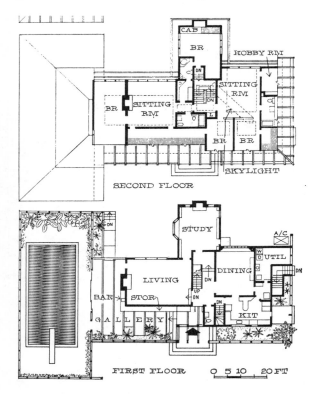

Fig. 251.

Fig. 252. Use of double-conoid roof, Jules Gregory, architect (*House and Home* magazine)

Fig. 255. Combination of Japanese and California influences, Campbell and Wong, architects (*House and Home* magazine)

The traditionally strong regional features of the California house are combined with the Japanese influence in the home in Figs. 255-257. However, the use of new forms tends to modify this structure. The sweeping roof and wide overhang are the most important elements of the design. Wide corner boards influence the vertical feeling of the house. It is really a two-story house, wisely utilizing a sloping site. Elements of nature abound in the design, as do the post and beam framing.

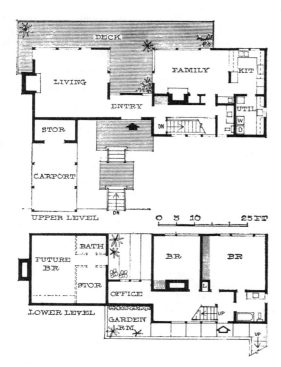

Fig. 256.

Fig. 257.

Fig. 258. Exposed structure becomes design feature, Penrose K. Spohn, architect (*House and Home* magazine)

This house displays the forms of structure and integrates them in the design of the building, Figs. 258 and 259. Each side of the house was designed as a truss. This enabled the house to span a wide distance such as over a ravine or stream. Support is needed only on the ends of the house. The engineering of the truss, including the bolt heads, becomes part of the design.

The alternating of wood and glass panels gives a rhythm that is actually derived from

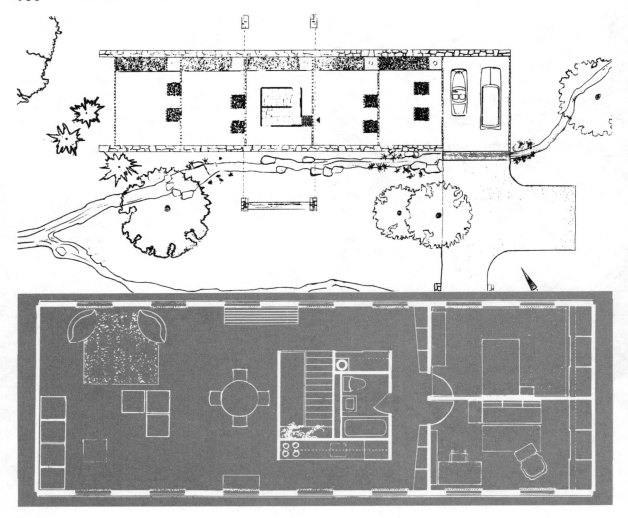

Fig. 259.

the vertical members of the truss. The architect says, "The first act of home-making is leveling an area; but too often the level area is lost by setting the house on it. So I set the house over the level at right angles. This becomes the basic design element." The house stresses the feeling of simplicity, clarity and order.

These are but a few of the houses being designed. They are one-of-a-kind houses and represent architecture in transition.

Class Activities

1. Sketch the floor plan of a house from a magazine devoted to house design and construction. Then sketch two different exteriors for this plan. Be certain to apply the principles of building design, composition, proportion, scale, contrast, rhythm, and unity.

2. Try to find houses in your neighborhood, which represent the basic styles listed below. Record the street address of each house.

   Elizabethan or Half-Timbered
   Georgian
   Spanish
   Southern Colonial
   Cape Cod Cottage
   Victorian
   Bungalow
   Southwestern Ranch
   Japanese Modern
   Florida House
   California House

3. On graph paper, make a freehand sketch of the front elevation of each of the above styles. Include sufficient detail to identify it.

4. Read in an encyclopedia or other source about how to make adobe bricks. Try to make a few, using a wood box as a mold. Perhaps, they could be baked in an oven or kiln in the art department. The art instructor might be able to direct you to a source of clay that would be satisfactory.

5. Construct from cardboard a small scale replica of one of the house styles. Windows, shingles, bricks and other parts can be drawn with black ink. Color can be added using water color or tempra paint. Clay could be used when building styles that utilized adobe or burned brick.

Additional Reading

Architectural Record (Editorial Staff), *Record Houses.*

————, *The Second Treasury of Contemporary Houses.*

————, *A Treasury of Contemporary Houses.*

Bayles, Douglas, and Perry, Joan, *California Houses of Gordon Drake.*

Ford, Katherine (Morrow), and Creighton, T. H., *Designs for Living.*

Forman, Henry C., *Architecture of the Old South.*

Harada, Jiro, *The Lesson of Japanese Architecture.*

Harling, Robert (ed.), *et. al., House and Garden Small Homes.*

Klaber, Eugene H., *Housing Design.*

May, Cliff, *Sunset. Western Ranch Houses.*

Newcomb, Rexford, *The Old Mission Churches and Historic Houses of California.*

Pagani, Carlo, *Italy's Architecture Today.*

Pilcher, Donald E., *The Regency Style.*

Richardson, Albert E., *Georgian Architecture.*

Summerson, Sir John N., *Architecture in Britain, 1530 to 1830.*

Waterman, Thomas T., *The Dwellings of Colonial America.*

Wright, Frank L., *The Natural House.*

Yorke, Francis R., *The Modern House.*

Yoshida, Tetsuro, *The Japanese House and Garden.*

CHAPTER FOUR

THE WORKING DRAWINGS
AND SPECIFICATIONS

After the process of planning the house is complete and scale sketches have been made and all ideas pertaining to the house have been recorded, the actual plans from which the house will be built can be drawn. These plans are called *working drawings*.

A set of working drawings for the average house will include roof and plot plan, floor plans for each level or story, a foundation or basement plan, elevations of all sides of the house, wall sections to illustrate the method of construction and details on which the builder will need special information.

No set of plans is complete without a set of specifications. *Specifications* detail all the points involved in the house construction that cannot be indicated on the working drawings.

As the working drawings are prepared, notes are made concerning the things that need to be clearly indicated. These are then written in a set form and become a part of the specifications for the house.

Preparing for Work

Before any drawing is started, several preliminary decisions must be made. First is the size of paper to use. If the house is to be small or average in size, usually *B* size (11" x 17") paper will be quite satisfactory. For larger houses, *C* size (17" x 22") will be needed. If the house is large and rambling, it may be necessary to cut the sheet from a roll of vellum. All drawings in a set should be the same size.

The number of details to be placed on one sheet also will influence the size paper to use.

Some prefer to place the floor plan, kitchen details and door and window schedule on one sheet; the foundation plan, wall sections and other details on a second sheet; and the elevations on third and fourth sheets, as required. Others prefer to use very large sheets of vellum and place the floor plan, foundation plan and details on one sheet and all the elevations on a second sheet. This is satisfactory; however, it is a little more difficult to keep the larger drawings clean, and a damaged tracing is a greater catastrophe.

Drawing to Scale

When the working drawings for a house are made, it is not possible to draw them full size. The drawings must be made using a small increment, such as ¼ inch, to represent one foot of the actual house dimension. This is called *drawing to scale*. A floor plan drawn to the scale ¼" = 1'-0" reduces the house 48 times, so it will fit on a standard sheet.

Two common instruments, called *scales*, are used to measure distances on architectural drawings — the triangular architect's scale and the flat architect's scale. See Fig. 280.

The triangular scale has three edges with eleven different scales located on them. The flat scale usually has four scales on its edges. Many architectural draftsmen prefer the flat scale, because it is easier to locate the scale being used. The triangular scale requires much turning to keep the scale being used in working position.

A ¼-inch to ½-inch border is commonly used on architectural drawings. This dresses

up the work and gives it a finished appearance.

It is necessary to decide to what scale each part of the working drawing will be drawn. Under normal conditions the following scales are used:

Floor plan	¼″ = 1′-0″
Foundation plan	¼″ = 1′-0″
Elevations	¼″ = 1′-0″
Construction details	¾″ = 1′-0″
Wall section	¾″ = 1′-0″
Plot plan	1/16″ = 1′-0″
Cabinet details	⅜″ = 1′-0″

Larger scales are used if they will increase the clarity of the drawing.

The *template* is a drafting device used to assist in architectural drafting. Fig. 281 illustrates one such tool. The more common symbols are cut in the template and need only be traced by the designer. Templates for use in house planning are made to the scale ¼″ = 1′-0″.

Reading the Architect's Scale

Examine the ¼-inch scale. Notice the end ¼″ is divided into twelve parts. This ¼″ space represents one foot and each of the twelve parts represents one inch.

The proper way to lay out or measure with a scale is indicated in Fig. 282. Assume that it is desired to lay out a distance of 14′-6″, at a scale ¼″ = 1′-0″. Find the ¼-inch scale. From the 0 (zero) on the end of the scale, move toward the center until the number 14 is found. See *B* in Fig. 282. This distance is fourteen of the ¼-inch increments and represents 14 feet. From the 0 on the scale, count off 6 inches on the finely divided scale at the end of the instrument. See *A* in Fig. 282. The total distance from *A* to *B* is then 14 feet, plus 6 inches, or 14′-6″.

Architectural Symbols

Since working drawings are made to a very small scale, it is not possible to indicate many parts of the house by actually drawing them as they appear to the eye. It is also not economical, considering the time it would take. Many parts of the house are, therefore, represented by standardized symbols.

Also, it is difficult to represent materials on a drawing, and symbols have been developed to indicate these. Fig. 283 presents the more frequently used symbols. For a complete listing, consult architectural standards books.

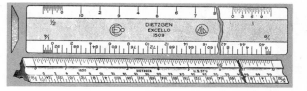

Fig. 280. Flat and triangular architect's scales. (Eugene Dietzgen Co.)

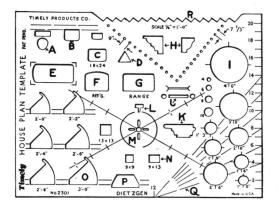

Fig. 281. Clear plastic house plan template contains cut-outs to make 18 different architectural outlines in several different sizes, all drawn to a scale of ¼″ = 1′. (Eugene Dietzgen Co.)

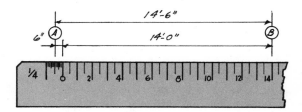

Fig. 282. Using the architect's scale.

Dimensioning a Working Drawing

Since the working drawings for a house are drawn to a very small scale, the actual sizes of the building and its many parts can be indicated accurately only by recording the actual size of the drawing. This process is called *dimensioning*.

A good way to study dimensioning is to examine carefully drawings made by trained architectural draftsmen. You will notice that there are some slight differences in the dimensioning technique, all of which are acceptable. When dimensioning, the primary consideration should be to show the information in a way most helpful to the men building the house. A knowledge of how a house is built assists the draftsman to decide where and how to

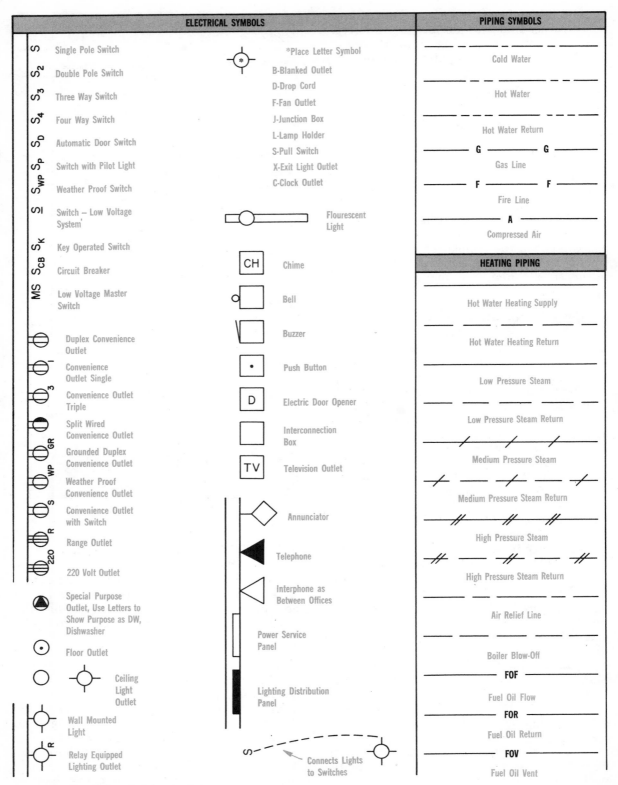

Fig. 283A. Electrical and piping symbols.

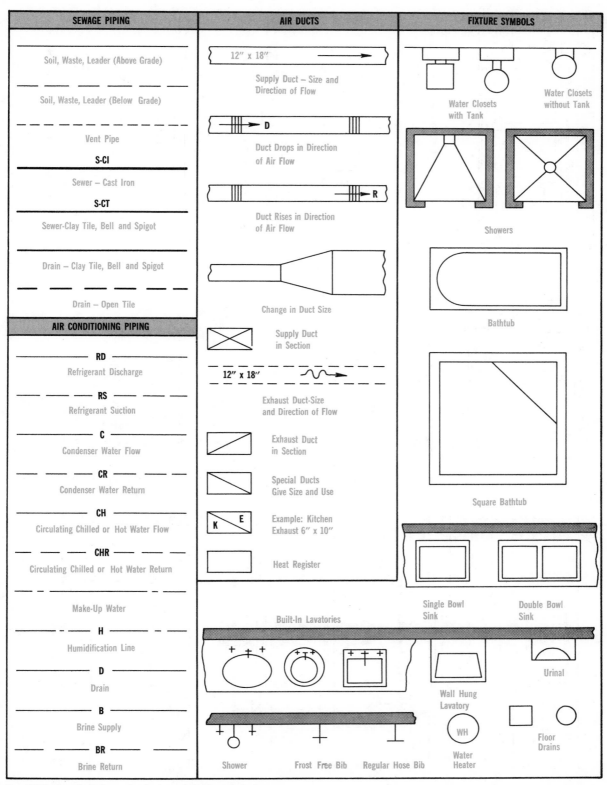

Fig. 283A. (cont) Piping, air duct, and fixture symbols.

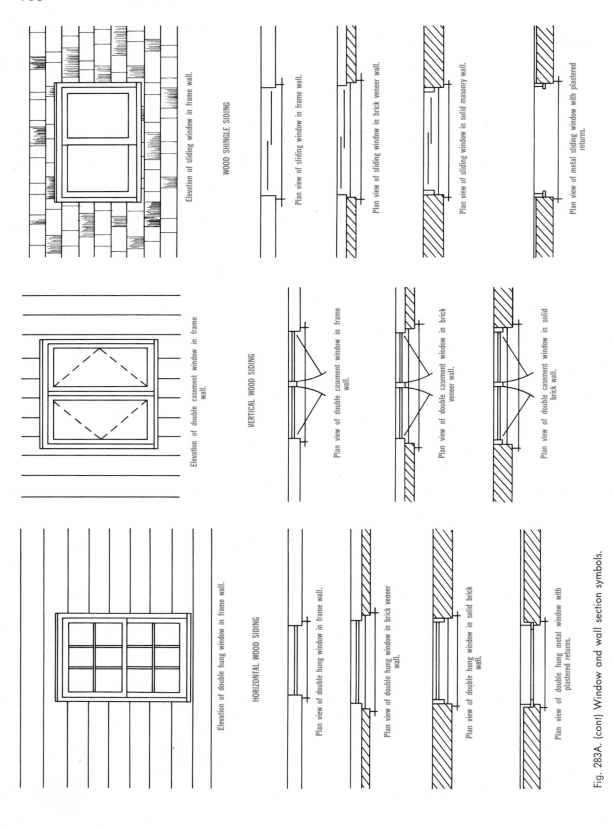

WOOD SHINGLE SIDING

Elevation of sliding window in frame wall.

Plan view of sliding window in frame wall.

Plan view of sliding window in brick veneer wall.

Plan view of sliding window in solid masonry wall.

Plan view of metal sliding window with plastered returns.

VERTICAL WOOD SIDING

Elevation of double casement window in frame wall.

Plan view of double casement window in frame wall.

Plan view of double casement window in brick veneer wall.

Plan view of double casement window in solid brick wall.

HORIZONTAL WOOD SIDING

Elevation of double hung window in frame wall.

Plan view of double hung window in frame wall.

Plan view of double hung window in brick veneer wall.

Plan view of double hung window in solid brick wall.

Plan view of double hung metal window with plastered returns.

Fig. 283A. (cont) Window and wall section symbols.

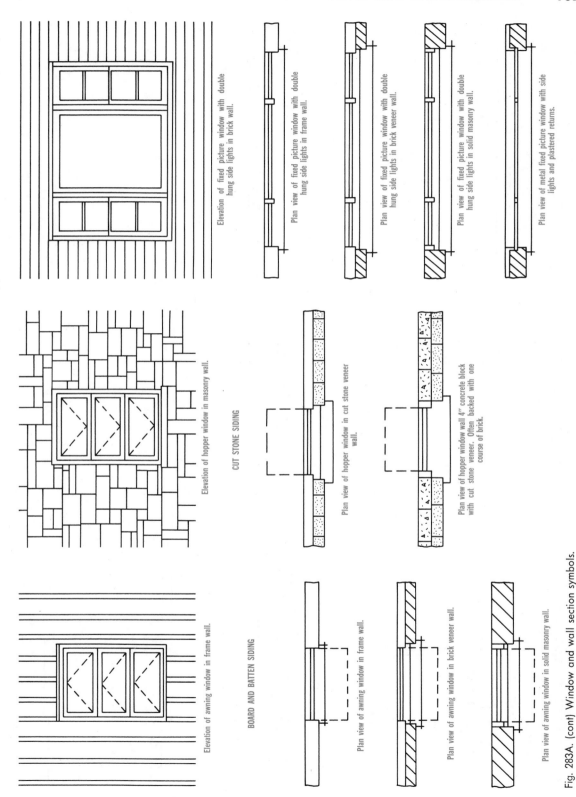

Elevation of fixed picture window with double hung side lights in brick wall.

Plan view of fixed picture window with double hung side lights in frame wall.

Plan view of fixed picture window with double hung side lights in brick veneer wall.

Plan view of fixed picture window with double hung side lights in solid masonry wall.

Plan view of metal fixed picture window with side lights and plastered returns.

Elevation of hopper window in masonry wall.

CUT STONE SIDING

Plan view of hopper window in cut stone veneer wall.

Plan view of hopper window wall 4" concrete block with cut stone veneer. Often backed with one course of brick.

Elevation of awning window in frame wall.

BOARD AND BATTEN SIDING

Plan view of awning window in frame wall.

Plan view of awning window in brick veneer wall.

Plan view of awning window in solid masonry wall.

Fig. 283A. (cont) Window and wall section symbols.

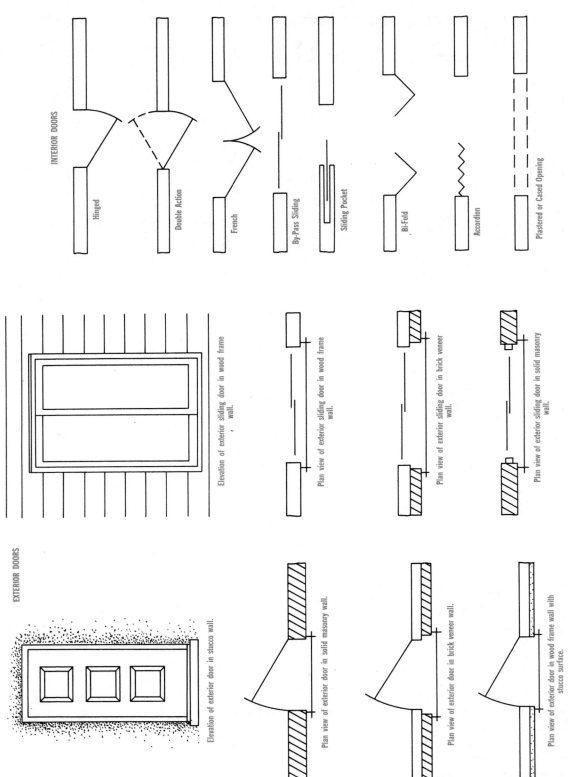

INTERIOR DOORS

Hinged

Double Action

French

By-Pass Sliding

Sliding Pocket

Bi-Fold

Accordion

Plastered or Cased Opening

Elevation of exterior sliding door in wood frame wall.

Plan view of exterior sliding door in wood frame wall.

Plan view of exterior sliding door in brick veneer wall.

Plan view of exterior sliding door in solid masonry wall.

EXTERIOR DOORS

Elevation of exterior door in stucco wall.

Plan view of exterior door in solid masonry wall.

Plan view of exterior door in brick veneer wall.

Plan view of exterior door in wood frame wall with stucco surface.

Fig. 283A. (cont) Door and wall section symbols.

ARCHITECTURAL SYMBOLS

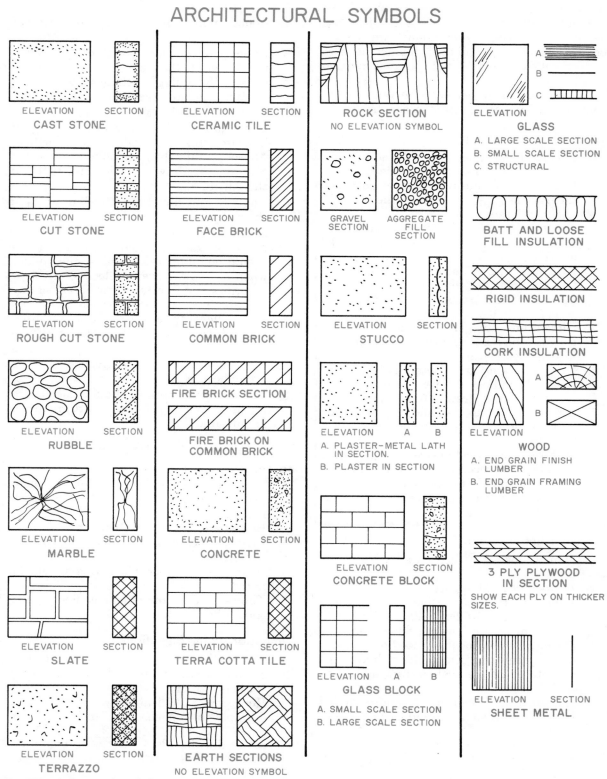

Fig. 283B. Architectural symbols.

place dimensions. Each drawing should be completely dimensioned. If it will help those using the drawings, dimensions can be repeated. At no time should a builder have to add or subtract to find the size of a portion of a house.

The following pages describe practices in general use though exceptions can be found.

General Dimensioning Techniques

1. Everything is dimensioned the actual size, even though it is drawn to scale.
2. Dimensions should not be crowded. Keep them at least ¼ inch from the drawing and each other.
3. An unbroken dimension line should be used; the dimension should be placed above it.
4. Distances over 12 inches are recorded as feet and inches. If the distance is an even number of feet, record the inches with a zero, *i.e.*, 12'-0".
5. Dimensions are placed on a drawing so they can be read from the bottom or right side of the drawing.
6. Every drawing and detail should have the scale indicated, even though on the same page and drawn to the same scale.
7. Anything unusual should be explained with a note. Notes are lettered horizontally.
8. Materials, electrical devices and plumbing fixtures are recorded by symbols. See pages 92 and 93 for common symbols.

Examine the working drawings in this chapter. These are complete.

Dimensioning the Floor Plan

1. Dimensions are placed on all sides of the plan.
2. Doors and windows are located by dimensioning to their centerline. These dimensions are placed off the plan.
3. All ells or projections are dimensioned.
4. Overall dimensions are placed on all sides of the drawing. The builder should not have to add to or scale a drawing to find a dimension.
5. Intermediate dimensions should be added to see that their total equals the overall dimension.
6. Notes are used to clarify things that cannot be clearly drawn, such as a clothes chute or dishwasher.

7. Interior partitions are commonly dimensioned from center of stud to center of stud.
8. Exterior dimensions are indicated from the edge of the foundation. In frame houses, the siding overhangs the foundation and is not included in the overall dimensions of the house.
9. Door and window sizes are commonly indicated in a door and window schedule. All such units that are alike are given a code on the drawing which ties them to the schedule.
10. The size and direction of ceiling joists is shown by a special symbol.
11. Rooms are identified by name, as living room or dining room. The bedrooms should be numbered, to assist the builder when he has the owner select colors, floor coverings and lighting fixtures. He simply records "bedroom #1 — walls pink, oak floors, light fixture No. 3517 Westinghouse." This reduces confusion and mistakes.
12. Size and number of stair treads and risers are indicated.
13. The size and depth of the fireplace opening are commonly shown. Hearth material is indicated.

Dimensioning the Foundation and Basement Plan

1. All techniques mentioned for the floor plan apply to the foundation or basement plan.
2. Beams are located by their centerline.
3. Piers are located by dimensioning to their centerline.
4. If an area is to be filled, this should be noted.
5. The size and direction of floor joists should be noted.

Dimensioning the Elevations

1. The ceiling line and finished floor line are indicated. The total distance between these is frequently shown.
2. Roof slope is indicated by a symbol. The example in the elevation of the sample set of drawings is 4⎓12. This indicates 4 inches of rise in the roof for every 12 inches of run.

3. Exterior materials are noted as brick, asphalt shingles or board and batten siding.
4. The overhang of the roof at the eaves is frequently dimensioned.
5. The finished grade is indicated with a note.
6. Window sizes are sometimes lettered on top of the window elevation, but the door and window schedule is preferred.

Dimensioning the Details

1. All parts of the typical wall section are identified by name and size.
2. Cabinets and other built-ins require only overall dimensions. Notes indicating other information, such as material and finish, are recorded in the specifications. If cabinets are stock units, the manufacturer's name and stock number can be recorded on the cabinet elevation.
3. Fireplace details should be completely dimensioned. Face material and hearth material should be indicated with a note.
4. Stair details should have tread and riser size indicated. Total stair rise and run should be noted.
5. Other built-ins are treated the same as the kitchen details. Anything unusual, such as a special planter, should be detailed to a larger scale and completely dimensioned. This would include dimensions on joints and other construction details.

Lettering

Much of the information supplied by architectural drawings is found in dimensions and notes placed on the working drawings. It can be seen, therefore, that the lettering used to record this information is of great importance. Above all other considerations, it must be legible.

Style of Lettering

Much of the lettering found on architectural drawings has an artistic character and reflects to some extent the individuality of the draftsman. Regardless of how skilled and artistic a draftsman may be, the lettering he uses should be simple and easily and rapidly executed. A beginning draftsman would do well to use the simple, vertical, gothic letters he learned in beginning drafting courses. He

can begin to develop his own flairs as he develops skill and a feeling for the work.

Fig. 284 illustrates a style of architectural lettering used by many architectural draftsmen. Notice that it is easily read and is comprised by simple, quickly made strokes.

A good draftsman will always use guidelines. These should be very light, so they will not reproduce when prints are made from the tracings.

Size of Lettering

Lettering for all dimensions and notes should be from ⅛" to 3/16" high. The draftsman should be consistent throughout a set of working drawings. If ⅛" lettering is used at the beginning of a job, it should be used throughout.

Main titles such as "Door Schedule" and "Window Schedule" or the room titles should be ¼" high. This makes them stand out. The *title block* should have the main title lettered 5/16" high and the other lettering ⅛" high. See Fig. 285.

These lettering heights are suggested as being good practice; with experience, a draftsman can begin to vary these to suit his desires.

Proficiency in Lettering

It is recommended that students study the shape and form of the suggested style of archi-

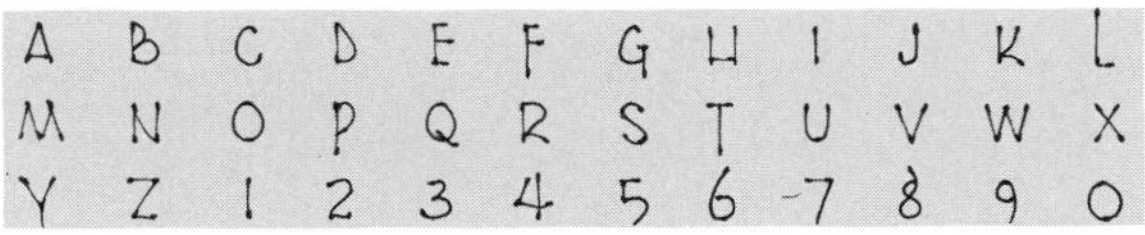

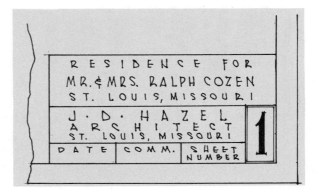

Fig. 284. A popular style of architectural lettering. Notice the letters are heavier at the ends of each line; the draftsman does this to give the lettering character and snap.

Fig. 285. Title block.

tectural lettering as shown in Fig. 284 and practice to master these. This mastery, however, is only the beginning. It is just as important to correctly space both letters in a word and words as it is to form each letter properly.

The effect desired with lettering is uniformity. The letters in any word should not appear more crowded than letters in any other word. This means that the space between some letters must be greater than that between others. The properly spaced word is an illusion to fool the eyes. Adjacent letters with straight sides should be placed farther apart than those with curved sides. More white space is needed to give the illusion that the letters are an equal distance apart.

In Fig. 286, notice the space between the letters *M* and *A* in the word at the left is about half as much as that between the *I* and *N*. Since both *I* and *N* present tall, vertical lines, they need more space between them. Also notice that, in the word at the right, the spacing is equal between all letters; it simply does not look right.

MAIN   MAIN

Fig. 286. Spacing between letters is visually equal.

The actual distance between the letters in a word is determined by the draftsman. He spaces them so they can be easily read and "look right."

The usual spacing between words is about the same as the height of the letters used.

The spacing between lines is determined by the draftsman. He uses a distance that is pleasing to the eye.

Drawing the Floor Plan

Since the entire set of working drawings is based upon what develops as a floor plan, it is customary to draw it first.

The floor plan represents a top view of a house that is cut about half way between the floor and ceiling. When the top half is removed, the view that remains represents the floor plan. It reveals the location of windows, stairs, fireplace, cabinets and many other items. See Fig. 287.

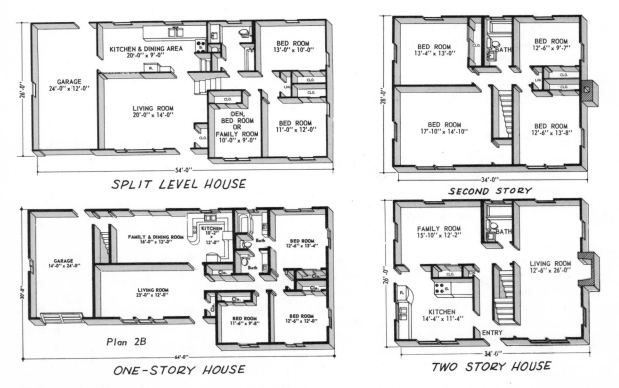

SPLIT LEVEL HOUSE

SECOND STORY

ONE-STORY HOUSE   Plan 2B

TWO STORY HOUSE

Fig. 287. Pictorial views of houses with cuts made through the windows. This illustrates how a draftsman looks at a house as he draws the floor plan. (Southern Homes, Inc.)

These items are located and their sizes are indicated by dimensioning this floor plan. Other details, such as location of electrical outlets, lights, stove and bathroom fixtures, are shown. Notes indicate the direction of floor joists and, sometimes, the type of material on the floor.

One-Story House

The preliminary layout should be very light. Remember to allow room on the paper for such things as porches, patios, and dimensions.

1. Lay out the overall width and length of the house.
2. Insert the interior partitions.
3. Draw in the fireplace, kitchen and bathroom fixtures, and stairs.
4. Locate windows and draw in symbols. If in doubt as to location, lay out front elevation, and locate windows on it so exterior is pleasing. Then record on floor plan.
5. Draw porches and patios.
6. Darken all lines.
7. Indicate material symbols on exterior walls.
8. Locate electrical fixtures and switches.
9. Draw in all doors.
10. Dimension interior of house.
11. Dimension exterior of house. Locate doors, windows and porches first; overall dimension last.
12. Place code for door and window schedule on plan.
13. Complete door and window schedule in a clear corner of the paper.
14. Label items needing identification, such as range and refrigerator.
15. Indicate with notes any other information, such as joist direction and floor materials.

Study the floor plan in this chapter, and note how items are located and dimensioned. Use this as a reference for good dimensioning practice.

Two-Story House

The procedure for a two-story house is exactly the same as that described for a one-story house, except a floor plan for the second floor is necessary. This is the only additional drawing required.

Split-Level House

A split-level house is a little more difficult to draw. Usually the rooms on level four and level three are placed together on one floor plan, and levels two and one form the basement plan. See Fig. 288. The actual layout and drawing are the same as for a one-story house.

Drawing the Foundation or Basement Plan

A *basement plan* shows the basement layout and the footings. When no basement is used, the drawing shows the footings and foundation wall and is called a *foundation plan*.

The same procedure for drawing the floor plan can be followed for the foundation or basement plan. Much time can be saved by laying a piece of vellum over the floor plan and lightly tracing the exterior walls of the house and locating such items as fireplaces and stairs. Remember this must be done lightly so not too much carbon is deposited on the back of the sheet from the pencil lines on the floor plan. If much pressure is used when tracing, the darkness of the pencil lines on the floor plan will be reduced, and traces of carbon will adhere to the rear of the sheet containing the foundation plan.

The basement plan includes windows and doors, columns and girders to support the house, a furnace, footings, perhaps laundry facilities, or a recreation room or garage. All these and other items are located and dimensioned in the same manner as the floor plan. The direction of floor joists is shown with a symbol and note.

Study the basement plan in this chapter and note items included and how they were dimensioned.

Drawing the Elevations

An *elevation* is a view looking directly at a house. Four elevations are required to de-

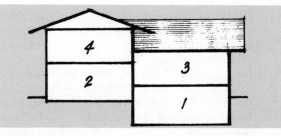

Fig. 288. Split-level house.

scribe satisfactorily the exterior of the average house. These are views from the front, rear, right and left sides.

The elevations, more than any other single factor, illustrate the taste of the owner and architect. They can be seen and understood by everyone. The designer must keep in mind constantly the style of house he is trying to develop and apply the principles of design, balance, proportion and color.

Many different elevations can be made from the same floor plan. Certainly, the designer should try many versions before he makes his final decision.

Suggested Procedure for Drawing Elevations

The preliminary layout must be made very lightly because it usually is necessary to make changes as the elevation develops.

It is quite possible that some preliminary work on the elevations has been finished at this point; generally, some of the elevations must be completed, at least partially, as the floor plan is developed, so the influence of such things as ells and window locations can be seen. When it becomes necessary to lay out the elevations, proceed as follows:

1. Lay out the finished floor line — most draftsmen start with the front elevation.
2. Decide on ceiling height, and lay out the finished ceiling line.
3. Decide how far above grade the finished floor is to be, and draw in the grade line. It may be necessary to refer to a freehand sketch of the typical wall section and to information concerning the slope of the lot upon which the house is to be built.
4. Draw a vertical line on one end, to represent the exterior extreme end.
5. Measure the length of the house, and draw in the other end.
6. Locate and record any ells or breaks in the exterior wall.
7. Block in the roof by locating the ridge and cornices. The pitch must be ascertained and drawn on an end elevation and the cornices located. This can then be transferred to the front elevation.
8. Locate doors and windows by their centerlines. Draw the head of the window the required distance from the finished floor. This is usually 6'-8". Block in the window, according to the decided dimen-

sions. Use the proper symbol to illustrate the type of window to be used. Scale drawings of windows are available in manufacturers' catalogs; these can be slid under the vellum and copied, thus saving much layout time.

9. Locate chimney, porches, flower boxes and other items.
10. Draw foundation and footings.
11. Indicate materials, by drawing proper symbols. Do not attempt to draw every brick or every shingle. The symbol indicates the material. It is common to finish the front elevation completely, but to record material symbols only partially on the other elevations. This saves time and is still quite effective.

Drawing the Sections

As mentioned in an earlier chapter, the type of construction and the method of assembling the parts of a house are decided during the planning stages. Actually, the wall section is sketched on graph paper during this planning stage and need only be drawn to scale at this point.

The procedure for drawing the wall section can vary to suit the draftsman. However, there are certain details that should be a part of a well-made wall section. The more important of these are as follows:

1. Label all parts.
2. Use symbols to help differentiate parts.
3. To reduce overall height, break section.
4. If stock windows are to be used, do not draw a window section, but locate the head of the window by a dimension from the finished floor.
5. Dimension footing and foundation, and show depth below grade.
6. Dimension overhang at the eave.
7. Show roof pitch.

An examination of the wall section in this chapter illustrates these and other pointers. In Chapter 5, other wall sections are illustrated and should be carefully studied.

Drawing the Details

Many parts of a house cannot be shown clearly on the floor plan, foundation plan and elevations because of the small scale. Anything needing clarification is drawn to a larger scale; this is called a *detail*.

The items most frequently needing detailing are stairs, fireplaces, cabinets and other built-ins, and special construction designs. Some parts of the structure may be assembled in an unconventional manner and need special drawings. Details of cornice construction seem to be needed most frequently.

Stair Details

A simple straight stairway can be indicated on the floor plan and dimensioned with a note. However, many designers prefer to draw a simple section through the stair as shown on the working drawings in this chapter. This clarifies most points and definitely checks to see if sufficient room is available to accommodate the stair. Headroom can also be checked with such a detail.

If a stair is open and has ornate balusters and newel posts, a more elaborate detail is necessary. This is especially true if the stair is to be a custom job. (A *custom job* is designed and built especially for one house.) If the stair is a manufactured, stock stair, a detail is unnecessary.

The dimensions required on the typical stair detail are the rise, run, tread and riser sizes, and headroom clearance. If balusters and newel posts are used, these sizes must also be indicated. Stairs are discussed in detail in Chapter 1.

Fireplace Details

A fireplace is only as good as its design. If improperly built or proportioned, it won't draw properly and will produce smoke inside the house. Detailing the fireplace assures that it will be built to proper dimensions, since this gives the mason a guide to follow.

Three views are needed in most cases. A *horizontal section*, showing the hearth, opening size and flue linings, is indicated on the floor plan. Under most conditions, it can be dimensioned there and need not be redrawn as a separate detail.

A *vertical section* is necessary. This is drawn as a special detail on one of the sheets. Usually, it is tied in with the third fireplace detail, a *front elevation*. Examine the fireplace detail in this chapter. It has all the required essentials. A more complete discussion of fireplaces can be found in Chapter 10.

Proven specifications for fireplace design can be found in standards publications such as *Architectural Graphic Standards* or *Time Saver Standards*.

A good detail will indicate the size of the fireplace opening, the depth, the splay and required masonry thicknesses. Also, it is wise to specify the flue size desired. On the elevation detail, materials are indicated by symbols and notes.

Cabinet Details

The various kitchen cabinets are located in plan view on the floor plan. This shows the base cabinets, bars and major appliances. Since the wall-hung cabinets were cut away with the upper half of the house, they are shown with dotted lines. See the kitchen on the working drawings in this chapter. It is not necessary to dimension these cabinets. Usually, the house is carefully measured after it is built, and cabinets are purchased to fit the existing space.

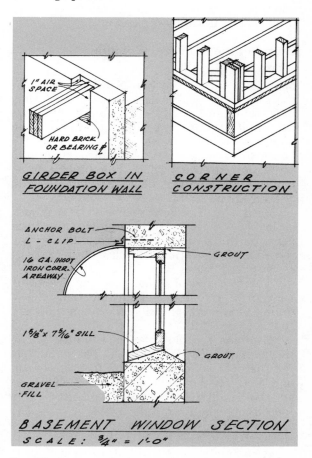

Fig. 289. Corner, girder box, and basement window details.

It is necessary to show an elevation of all walls with cabinets, but customary to dimension only the heights wanted.

A typical section through the cabinets is required. This can be one appearing at a corner of the room where the cabinets turn the corner or may be a separate drawing to a larger scale. The latter detail is especially necessary if the construction is unusual.

Other cabinets, such as bathroom lavatories, room dividers and built-in drawers in bedrooms, all need details. They are drawn in the same manner as the kitchen-cabinet details.

Other Details

Details should be included for any other part of the house that involves unusual construction or that the designer feels needs special consideration.

Typical of these are cornice details, girder and pier details, corner post details and special problems with windows. See Fig. 289.

Drawing the Roof and Plot Plan

The main purpose of a roof and plot plan is to locate the house upon the lot. If the owner has confidence in the builder, they may confer and decide where to put the house by simply walking over the lot. However, an architect usually draws such a plan so the house location is clearly specified. This is a protection to the owner. The builder must put the house on the lot as the plan specifies. See Fig. 27 in Chapter 1.

Such a plan is necessary whenever money is loaned on a house. Loaning institutions insist on this protection. They also insist upon recording the location of wells, septic tanks or sewer lines if these exist.

The roof and plot plan also shows the top view of the roof and indicates how it will drain. This is an aid in interpreting how the roof is to be built.

Examine the plot plan in Chapter 1. Notice that the lot size is given. The data from the surveyor is dimensioned in feet and tenths of a foot. The house is located from the street and both sides of the lot. Frequently, other identifying data are given. Driveways and sidewalks are indicated and, sometimes, large trees.

A complete survey will also reveal the elevations of the various corners of the lot and the finished elevations after the house is built and the grading completed. This indicates exactly how surplus water from rain and snow will be drained away from the house. It also tells the builder how the lot is to be graded.

Specifications

A house is made from many parts and many materials. The contractor purchases and assembles these into a finished house.

In order that no misunderstanding occurs between the contractor and the owner concerning what is to be built, how it is to be built and what materials are to be used, the house is described in working drawings. Items that cannot be clearly shown on the drawings are described in writing in a document called the specifications.

The kinds of materials used and the quality of these materials must be specified. For example, finished floors could be oak, maple, ceramic tile, asphalt tile or other materials. Flashing could be galvanized iron, aluminum or copper. Water pipes could be galvanized iron, copper or brass. The concrete mix desired should be indicated. These and many more material selections must be clearly specified.

The quality of materials is not uniform from product to product and should be indicated. There are many grades of construction lumber. Roofing materials, hardware and lighting fixtures vary in quality. The high-quality materials are more expensive, but the quality of materials directly influences the life of the house parts as well as the total price.

Another variable that cannot be shown on working drawings is the workmanship desired. For example, after concrete is poured, it should be kept moist for seven days, to secure the most satisfactory curing job. This should be specified. It protects the owners against the possibility of shoddy work.

Certain parts of the construction job are the responsibility of the contractor, such as providing electricity for construction purposes or hiring labor and paying the employment taxes. These and other responsibilities should be clearly indicated.

If the owner is to assume certain responsibilities, these should be recorded. Frequently, the owner chooses to do interior and exterior painting. This becomes a part of the specifications.

All accessories to be supplied by the contractor should be specified. Do the windows have screens and storm sash? Are sidewalks and driveways included? What shrubbery, if any, is in the contract? Are the stove, refrigerator and dishwasher included?

The architect occasionally will call for certain articles by their trade name. For example, a Westinghouse Range Platform Model PLB may be required. This means that the bidders must supply this exact range.

While such a procedure guarantees the exact item the owner desires, it does tend to increase the cost, because it removes all other range manufacturers from bidding. To overcome this disadvantage, architects frequently specify Westinghouse Range Platform Model PLB *or equal*. This permits any other company with a range of equal quality to submit a bid. Such competitive bidding will lower the cost of the unit.

Most houses are built on a *bid basis*. This means that the owner or architect contacts several contractors, and each indicates how much he will charge to build the house. In order for a contractor to make a bid, he must have an entire picture of the structure and everything to be included. This requires a complete set of working drawings, accompanied by detailed specifications.

If an item is not clearly recorded, disagreements can occur. Some such disputes lead to costly law suits. The contractor is not responsible for supplying any item not called for on the working drawings or in the specifications. Verbal promises are no stronger than the character of those making them.

Upon occasion, the working drawings will disagree with something recorded in the specifications. In these cases, the "General Conditions" of the specifications provide that the specifications will be held correct and have precedence over the working drawings.

When the owner decides to accept a bid from a contractor, a legal agreement binding on both parties is written and signed. This is called a *contract*. The working drawings and specifications become a part of this contract. The contractor, then, has agreed to build the house indicated by the drawings and specifications for a specific sum of money, and the owner has agreed to pay the contractor the sum indicated in the contract.

Writing the Specifications

The first portion of the specifications is called "General Conditions." These conditions record the relationships existing between the contractor and the owner. They also include items that are not part of any of the trades covered in other divisions of the specifications.

A very complete set of General Conditions has been published by the American Institute of Architects, and, usually, these are made a part of the General Conditions by referring to them with a statement such as "the latest edition of the 'General Conditions of the Contract' published by the American Institute of Architects shall be understood to be a part of this specification and shall be adhered to by this contractor." This is the same as if the architect has copied the General Conditions verbatim and attached it to the specifications. The remainder of the specifications is arranged by trades, as nearly as possible, in the order in which the work is to be performed. An examination of a set of specifications will reveal that the first division is that involving excavating, filling and grading. Of necessity, the excavation must come first, followed by concrete work in the footings and foundation on through the order of work.

The exact form of the specifications varies somewhat from architect to architect, and the degree of detail also varies according to his decisions. In general, the specifications for a residence will include the following divisions: General Conditions; Special Conditions; General Scope of Work; Excavating, Filling and Grading; Concrete; Masonry; Carpentry and Millwork; Lathing and Plastering; Sheet Metal and Roofing; Glass and Glazing; Painting; Finish Hardware; Heating and Hot Water; Plumbing; and Electrical.

The set of specifications following is a simple set. They were written for use with the working drawings in this chapter.

General Conditions

The latest edition of the standard form of "General Conditions of the Contract" published by the American Institute of Architects shall be understood to be a part of this specification and shall be adhered to by this contractor.

Special Conditions

Sec. 1. Examination of Site. It is understood that the contractor has examined the site and is familiar with all conditions which might affect the execution of this contract and has made provision therefor in his bid.

Sec. 2. Time of Completion. The work shall be completed within 90 calendar days after written Notice to Proceed is issued to the contractor.

Sec. 3. Existing Trees. Existing trees within 15 feet of the foundation line for the new structure shall be carefully protected by the general contractor from injury which might result from any operation connected with the execution of this contract.

Sec. 4. Cleaning. The general contractor shall periodically remove from the building and premises all rubbish and debris and at the completion of the work he shall leave the entire building and premises "broom clean," all glass washed clean and all wood and plaster work of walls and ceilings brushed clean and free from stains or discoloration.

Sec. 5. The acceptance of this contract carries with it a guarantee on the part of the general contractor to make good any defects in the work of the building arising or discovered within one year after completion and acceptance of same by the architects, whether from shrinkage, settlement or faults of labor or materials.

Sec. 6. House shall receive standard termite protection by reliable dealer.

General Scope of Work

Sec. 1. The work consists of the General Construction including mechanical and electrical work of a one-story, single-family residence as shown on the drawings.

Sec. 2. Responsibilities of Contractor. Except as otherwise specifically stated in the Contract, the contractor shall provide and pay for all materials, labor, tools, equipment, water, light, heat, power, transportation, superintendence, temporary construction of every nature, taxes legally collected because of the work, and all other services and facilities of every nature whatsoever necessary to execute the work to be done under this contract and deliver it complete in every respect within the specified time, all in accordance with the drawings and specifications.

Division 1: Excavating, Filling, and Grading

Sec. 1. Scope. This division includes excavating, removal of all obstructions, filling, grading, and related items required to complete this work as indicated on the drawings and/or specified.

Sec. 2. Finished Grades. The words **finished grades**, as used herein, mean the required final grade elevations indicated on the drawings.

Sec. 3. Excavation.

a. **Dimensions.** Excavate to elevations and dimensions indicated, plus ample space for construction operations and inspection of foundation.

b. **Drainage.** Keep excavation free from water. Do not conduct water from excavations onto private property.

c. **Footing trenches** may be excavated to the exact dimensions of the concrete, and side forms may be omitted if concrete is poured in clean-cut trenches without caving. Place footing and foundations upon undisturbed and firm bottoms. The contractor shall not pour foundation footings until the architect inspects and approves the bearing.

Sec. 4. Grading.

a. **Grading.** Do all cutting, backfilling, filling and grading necessary to bring all areas within property lines to the following subgrade levels:

(1) **For paving, walks and other paved areas** to the underside of the respective installation as fixed by the finished grades therefor.

(2) **For lawns and planted areas** to four (4) inches below finished grades.

b. **Materials for Backfill and Fill.** All material used for backfill and fill shall be free from deleterious materials subject to termite attack, rot, decay or corrosion, frozen lumps or objects which would prevent solid compaction.
Materials for backfill and fill in various locations shall be as follows:

(1) **For Interior of Building.** Use sand or an approved, properly graded mixture of sand and gravel. Foundry sand shall not be used.

(2) **For Exteriors, Under Paving.** Use excavated materials free from top soil, or other materials approved by the architect.

(3) **For Use Under Lawns and Planted Areas.** Use, after architect's approval, excavated materials with admixture of top soil or earth. Heavy clay shall not be used.

c. **Backfill Against Foundation Walls** shall:
Be deposited in six (6) inch layers, each to be solidly compacted by tamping and puddling.

d. **Subgrades for Lawn and Planted Areas.** Slope the subgrade evenly to provide drainage away from building in all directions at a grade of at least 1/4 inch per foot.

e. **Settlement of Fills.** Fill to required subgrade levels any areas where settlement occurs.

Division 2: Concrete

Sec. 1. Scope. This division includes all concrete and related items required to complete the work indicated on the drawings and/or specified.

Sec. 2. Materials.

a. **Portland cement** shall meet the requirements for Type I.

b. **Aggregates.**

(1) **Fine aggregates** shall be natural sand, or sand prepared from inert materials having similar characteristics, if approved by the architect.

(2) **Coarse aggregates** shall be crushed stone, ground clean and free from foreign matter. Size range for walls shall be designated, as "No. 4 to 3/4."

c. **Water.** Water used for concrete work shall be clean and free from injurious amounts of oils, acids, alkalies, organic or other deleterious substances.

d. **Metal Reinforcement.** Wire mesh reinforcing shall conform to A.S.T.M. Designation A82-34 and shall be free from excessive scale, rust or coatings which will reduce bond to the concrete.

Sec. 3. Depositing Concrete.

a. **Deposit concrete** as nearly as practicable in its final position to avoid segregation due to re-handling or flowing.

b. **Retempering.** No concrete that has partially hardened or has been retempered shall be used.

c. **Compaction.** Concrete shall be thoroughly compacted by vibrating during placement.

Sec 4. Curing. All concrete should be sealed with a standard concrete sealer.

Sec. 5. Cleaning. Clean all exposed concrete surfaces and all adjoining work which has been stained by the leakage of concrete.

Division 3: Masonry

Sec. 1. Scope. This division includes masonry and related items required to complete this work as indicated on the drawings and/or specified.

Sec. 2. Materials.

a. **Water** shall be clean and free from injurious amount of acids, alkalies, organic materials and other deleterious substances.

b. **Mortar** for brickwork shall be one-to-two lime mortar, except for terrace, fireplace hearths and chimney above roof where one-to-three cement mortar with 20 percent lime shall be used.

c. **Brick** to be selected by owner.

Sec. 3. Installation.

a. **All masonry work** shall be laid plumb, true to line and with level courses in common bond.

b. **Joints in masonry** shall be nominally ⅜-inch wide, and shall be cut flush and as the mortar takes its initial set shall be tooled with a ½-inch diameter round tool 6 inches longer than the masonry unit.

Sec. 4. Cleaning. Upon completion clean all brickwork from top down with solution of non-staining soap powder and clean water using stiff fiber brushes or a solution of one part muriatic acid in ten parts water. Wet thoroughly before applying acid solution and protect other work. Rinse surfaces with clean water immediately after cleaning.

Division 4: Carpentry and Millwork

Sec. 1. Scope. This division includes the furnishing and installation of all carpentry, millwork and related items required to complete this work as indicated on the drawings and/or hereinafter specified.

Sec. 2. Materials.

a. **Rough lumber** shall be Utility Grade Yellow Pine.

b. **Exterior Millwork.** Vertical Siding. **Battens and gable ends** shall be cypress, redwood or plastic-coated plywood.

c. **Sheathing** shall be ½" insulating type similar to "Insul-Board" by James Manning Co.

d. **Attic insulation** shall be rock-wool batts installed in accordance with manufacturer's instructions.

e. **Interior trim** shall be of pine. Pattern selected by owner.

f. **Interior doors** shall be as indicated on door schedule.

g. **Exterior door frames** shall be 1¾" thick, rabbeted with 1⅛" outside casings of white pine.

h. **Interior door frames** shall be ⅞" thick pine.

i. **Double hung sash** shall be Andersen or equal.

j. **Kitchen cabinets** shall be birch. Counter tops Formica or equal.

k. **Medicine cabinets** shall have three adjustable glass shelves, all furnished and set complete by the carpenter.

l. **Closets and wardrobes** shall have ⅞" by 12" shelving and one clothes pole running length of space.

m. **Living room, hall bedroom floors** to be straight line oak; select grade, finished natural; kitchen vinyl plastic tile over plywood underlayment; bathroom, ceramic tile set in rubber into squares, cemented to plywood sub-floor; entrance hall imitation slate; fireplace hearth to be ceramic tile cemented to plywood or hardboard underlay.

Division 5: Interior Walls

Sec. 1. Ceilings to be ½" dry wall, vertical walls to be ⅜" dry wall, all joints taped and coated according to manufacturer's specifications.

Sec. 2. Kitchen wall to have wood wainscoting 40" high, to be birch, ⅜" dry wall above.

Sec. 3. Stair walls to be ⅜" dry wall.

Sec. 4. Baths to be ceramic tile 4'-0" everywhere except at tub where it is ceiling height.

Division 6: Sheet Metal and Roofing

Sec. 1. Scope. This division includes furnishing and setting of all sheet metal, roofing and flashing and related items required to complete this work as indicated on the drawings and/or specified.

Sec. 2. Materials.

a. **All flashings, valleys,** and miscellaneous items of sheet metal work shall be 26 gauge galvanized iron extending 10 inches from valley or ridge.

b. **Wood shingles or shakes,** natural cedar installed according to manufacturer's specifications.

c. **Nails** for fastening shakes shall be zinc coated or aluminum.

d. **Bituminous-saturated roofing felt** shall be 15 lb. felt.

Sec. 3. Application.

a. Roofing shall not be laid until all sheet metal, valleys or work which extends under roofing material have been installed. Coordinate roofing work with flashing of intersections around vertical surfaces.

b. Roof and flashings shall be weathertight, free from leaks and other defects.

c. Cover roof surfaces with 15-lb. bituminous saturated roofing felt before laying wood shakes or shingles. Double felt not less than 36 inches wide at valleys, hips and ridges. Extend up vertical surfaces 6 inches. Lap joints 3 inches. Nail sheathing 12 inches on center in both directions through metal discs.

d. Application of shakes shall be according to manufacturer's specifications.

Sec. 4. Guarantee. Roofing shall be weather and water tight. The roof shall be guaranteed by the roofing contractor against leaks due to defects in material and workmanship for a period of 5 years.

Division 7: Painting

Sec. 1. Scope. This division includes all the painting, both exterior and interior for the structure. The intent is to paint walls, ceilings, wood doors and bucks, and all other items painted in usual practice.

Sec. 2. Materials.

a. The term paint used herein includes emulsions, latex paint, enamels, oil paints, sealers, stains, varnishes, shellacs and any other allied coating.

b. Latex Base Paint will be "Ludens Smooth-Spread" or equal.

c. Alkyd Flat Enamel shall be "Ludens Alkyd Flat Enamel" or equal.

d. Varnish shall be "Durox-Seal" or equal.

e. Exterior primer shall be synthetic by "Ludens" or equal.

f. Exterior paint shall be "Ludens" exterior oil paint or equal.

g. Stain shall be by G. Dulac Co. or equal.

Sec. 3. Preparation of Surfaces. Surfaces to be painted shall be clean, dry and free from dirt and frost. Cover knots and pitch streaks with orange shellac, aluminum paint or a resin sealer. Fill nail holes and minor imperfections with putty between first and second coats. All millwork and trim shall be back primed.

Sec. 4. Exterior Painting. Wood sash and doors shall be given one coat of exterior primer and two coats of exterior oil paint.

Sec. 5. Interior Painting.

a. Wood trim shall be stained to match birch doors.

b. Wood doors and plywood ceiling in living room shall be given two coats "Durox-Seal" or equal sanded between coats.

c. All walls and ceilings shall be given two coats Latex base paint.

Division 8: Finish Hardware

Sec. 1. Scope. This division includes builder's Finish Hardware and related items required to complete the work specified and/or indicated on the drawings.

Sec. 2. Materials.

a. Exterior swing doors shall have $1\frac{1}{2}$ pair bronze butts $4\frac{1}{2}$" x $4\frac{1}{2}$".

b. Interior swing doors shall have 1 pair bronze butts $3\frac{1}{2}$" x $3\frac{1}{2}$".

c. All knobs and spindles shall be brass or bronze type NM-I by Lock-Tite Co. or equal.

d. All exterior swing doors shall have bronze threshold No. 861 by Chalmers Co. or equal.

e. Cylinder locks and latches shall be by Lock-Tite Co. or equal.

f. Folding closet doors shall be Simpson or equal.

Sec. 3. Installation. All hardware items listed here and others required to complete the work shall be installed in a workmanlike manner.

Division 9: Heating and Hot Water

Sec. 1. Scope. This division includes furnishing and installing space heating equipment and equipment for generating and storing hot water.

Sec. 2. Description of system — gas forced air duct system.

Sec. 3. Furnace should be Arkla Gas Airconditioner, 3 ton cooling, 120,000 BTU heating or equal. Installed with evaporative cooler, necessary duct work and thermostat. Will operate on natural gas.

Sec. 4. Installation — as recommended by manufacturer. To be in basement. Ducts to be installed according to furnace supplier recommendations. Ducts to be kept between floor joists as much as possible.

Sec. 5. Tests and adjustments — furnace to be thoroughly tested and regulated.

Sec. 6. Hot water supply. Water heater to be 30 gallon unit, glass lined, with safety valve and outside vent. To be gas fired. To be American Standard or equal.

Sec. 7. Fireplace Unit to be Majestic Thulman Harthline model L36LS.

Division 10: Plumbing

Sec. 1. Scope. This division includes the furnishing and installation of all plumbing and related items as required to complete this work as indicated on the drawings and/or hereinafter specified.

a. Lavatories, 20" x 18", one brown, one yellow, cast iron, acid resisting enamel, built-in stopper, with stainless steel rim, to be built into Formica top, trap below sink.

b. Water closet bowls — one yellow, one brown, vitreous china.

c. Seats for water closets — color of water closet, one brown, one yellow, closed front, with cover and self-sustaining hinge.

d. Bath tubs, one brown, one yellow, exact shade to be selected by owner; cast iron, acid resisting enamel, 5'-0", stopper built-in, properly trapped.

e. Kitchen sink, white double compartment, cast iron with acid resisting enamel, swing type spout, trap below sink, 21" x 32" twin bowl.

f. Water pipe — galvanized wrought iron.

g. Pipe cleanouts — cast iron with brass plugs or screwed fittings with brass plugs.

h. Waste and vent piping — galvanized wrought iron pipe.

i. Soil pipe — cast iron with coated fittings.

j. Septic tank to be 1,000 gallon, installed with sufficient drain field to insure proper operation. Drains set in gravel beds. To meet county health standards.

Sec. 2. Installation.

a. Drainage and vent piping shall be installed extending through roof not less than one foot

with 4# lead flashing at least 24" square. Piping shall be assembled and installed without undue strains or stresses and provisions shall be made for expansion and contraction.

b. Erect soil, waste and vent stacks of sizes shown and extend above roof.

c. No change of direction in drainage piping shall be greater than 90 degrees.

d. **Prohibited Fittings:** No double hub, or double tee branch shall be used on soil or waste lines. The drilling and tapping of building drains, soil, waste, or vent pipes and the use of saddle hubs or bands are prohibited.

e. **Prohibited Connections:** No fixture or device shall be installed which will provide a back-flow connection between a distribution system of water for drinking and domestic purposes and a drainage system, soil or waste pipe so as to permit or make possible the backflow of sewage or waste into water supply system.

f. All joints and connections shall be made gas- and water-tight. All exposed threads on ferrous pipe shall be given a coat of acid-resisting paint.

g. All caulked joints shall be firmly packed with oakum and shall be secured with caulking lead, not less than 1" deep.

h. Cast iron pipe joints shall be caulked.

Sec. 3. Tests. Tests shall be made in accordance with City Authority or Utility company having jurisdiction.

Division 11: Electrical

Sec. 1. Scope. This division includes all interior electrical wiring, fixture installations and related items required to complete the work indicated on the drawings and specified.

a. The work under this division shall commence at the point of attachment at the service entrance equipment.

b. Electrical service supplied to the structure will be 208 volts, 3-phase, 60-cycle, 3 wire.

c. Allowance of $150.00 for selection of light fixtures by owner.

d. Bath #2 receives ceiling exhaust fan. Post light by driveway to be electric.

Sec. 2. General Requirements.

a. Electrical system layouts indicated on drawings are diagrammatic and locations of outlets and equipment are approximate; exact routing of raceways, location of outlets and equipment shall be governed by structural conditions.

b. The right is reserved to make any reasonable change in location of outlets and equipment prior to roughing-in, without additional expense to the owner.

Sec. 3. Materials and Appliances.

a. Materials and appliances of the types for which there are Underwriter's Laboratories Standard requirements, listings and labels, shall have listing of Underwriter's Laboratories and be so labeled, or shall conform to their requirements, in which case certified statements to the effect shall be furnished, if requested.

b. Materials other than those listed herein shall be the size, type and capacity indicated by the drawings and the specifications. Insofar as possible use one type and quality.

c. Hood over surface unit to be Nutone 1600, 30 inch, or equal.

d. Surface unit and oven to be General Electric or equal.

e. Dishwasher to be Hotpoint H47 or equal.

Sec. 4. Final Inspection and Tests. Test system free from short circuits and grounds with insulation resistances, not less than outlined in Section 1119, 1955 National Electrical Code.

Build Your Vocabulary

Following are words that you should understand and use as a part of your working vocabulary. Write out a brief explanation of what each means.

Working drawings
Vellum
Scale
Floor plan
Foundation plan
Elevations
Details
Plot plan
Specifications
Symbols

Reading a Working Drawing

The following questions are designed to see how well you can read working drawings. Read the question, find the answer on the set of drawings in this chapter and write the answer on a sheet of lined paper. Upon completion, your instructor will check these to see how well you have done.

Work rapidly. Remember that extra time spent by a workman looking for an answer on a set of working drawings is time and money wasted.

1. How many pairs of shutters are on the house?
2. How much does the roof overhang at the front porch?
3. The fireplace hearth is to be made from what material?
4. What are the dimensions of the large bath?
5. How many floodlights are required?
6. What kitchen appliances are specified?
7. What are the stair tread and riser sizes?
8. What size is the front door?
9. Where are pull-chain lights used?
10. What size ceiling joists are required?
11. How wide is the hall to the bedrooms?
12. What size and kind of windows are used in the kitchen?
13. What size steel beam is used to support floor joists?
14. How many stools are in the house?
15. Explain how the drier is to be vented.

16. How many sill cocks are shown?
17. What is the maximum length of the house?
18. What material is to be used to face the fireplace?
19. How much insulation is required in the ceiling?
20. What size footing is specified?
21. How thick is the front porch floor?
22. What material is to be used on the ceiling of all rooms?
23. What is the clear headroom in the basement from joist to finished basement floor?
24. What reinforcement is required in the front porch floor?
25. Where is the telephone located?

The following questions will see how familiar you are with the specifications.

1. What provision is made for termite protection?
2. Bathroom lavatories are to be what colors?
3. How long should poured concrete be allowed to cure?
4. What width masonry joint is specified?
5. How high above the floor is the ceramic tile around the tub to be placed?
6. What type of roofing felt is required?
7. What is the capacity of the water heater?
8. Where does the responsibility of the electrical contractor begin?
9. Who is responsible for cleaning up the building site after the job is completed?
10. Explain how the foundation should be back filled.
11. What size kitchen sink is required?
12. What type of water pipe is specified?
13. What restrictions are specified for the water to be used for concrete work?
14. How long must the contractor guarantee the work of the building?
15. What restrictions are placed on backfill materials?
16. What pattern of interior trim is specified?
17. What kind of nails are to be used to install the wood shakes on the roof?
18. What type of flooring is to be used in the bedrooms?
19. What type of flashing material should be used?
20. How many coats of paint are to be applied to the exterior?
21. What kind of hinges are required on interior doors?
22. What kind of guarantee is specified for the roof?
23. Explain how exterior wood surfaces are to be prepared for finishing.
24. What plumbing fittings are prohibited?
25. What type of fine aggregate is specified for use in concrete work?

Class Activities

1. Design a small storage building. It is to be used to store a riding lawn mower, garden tools, and lawn furniture. It should contain about 100 square feet of floor space. Each exterior wall should have a window. The door opening should be at least 5'-0" wide. The floor is a concrete slab. Electric lights and outlets are necessary. The inside surface of the walls is not finished. Assume it is to be built on a flat site. Use any building materials you desire. Keep the cost as low as possible. Use simple construction methods. Draw a complete set of plans for this building. Write what specifications are necessary to insure the use of proper materials.

2. Design a summer cottage that will comfortably sleep four people. It should have a kitchen with stove, sink, refrigerator, and some storage. A bath is required but use minimum space. Materials used should require little maintenance. The maximum size is 750 square feet. The lot upon which the cottage will be built slopes toward the lake with a one foot drop for every six feet of horizontal distance. It is level in the other direction. Draw a complete set of plans for the cottage. Write a set of specifications to insure the use of proper materials and construction techniques.

3. List the things you would like in a residence. For example, a workshop or family room may be important to you. Sketch a floor plan and preliminary elevations for a residence having all the things you included in this list. Calculate the number of square feet in the plan. Secure an estimate of the local cost per square foot to build this residence. Do you think you will ever be able to afford to build this building? If not, reduce the size of the plan until it is such that you believe someday you might be able to build it. Draw a complete set of plans assuming the building is to be built on a level site. Write a complete set of specifications.

Additional Reading

Architectural Record (Editorial Staff), *Time Saver Standards.*

Buss, Truman C., Jr., *Simplified Architectural Drawing*, pp. 61-128.

Dalzell, James R., *Blueprint Reading for Home Builders.*

Kenney, Joseph E., *Blueprint Reading for the Building Trades.*

Ramsey, Charles G., and Sleeper, H. R., *Architectural Graphic Standards.*

Small Homes Council. Various bulletins.

Townsend, Gilbert, and Dalzell, J. R., *How to Plan a House*, pp. 300-332.

U.S. Federal Housing Administration, "Minimum Property Standards for One and Two Living Units."

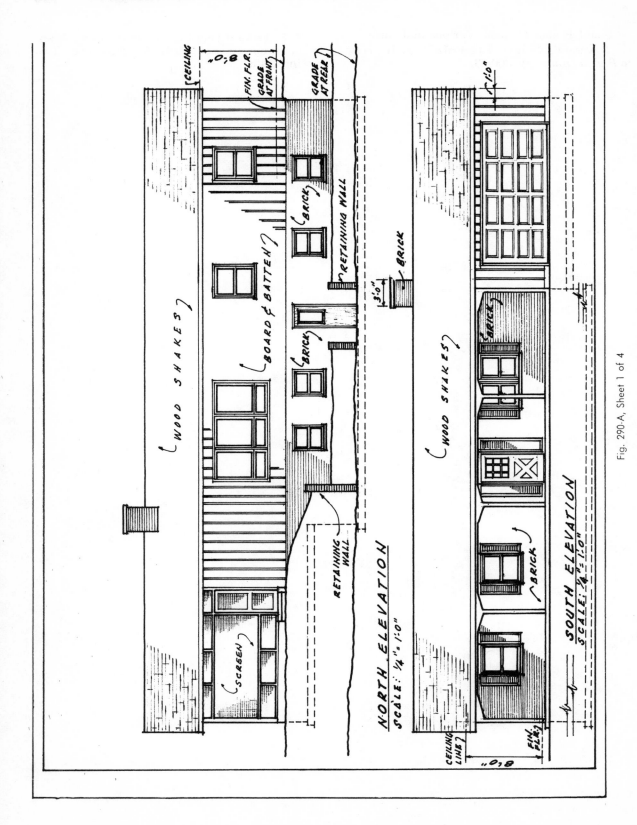

NORTH ELEVATION
SCALE: 1/4" = 1'-0"

SOUTH ELEVATION
SCALE: 1/4" = 1'-0"

Fig. 290-A, Sheet 1 of 4

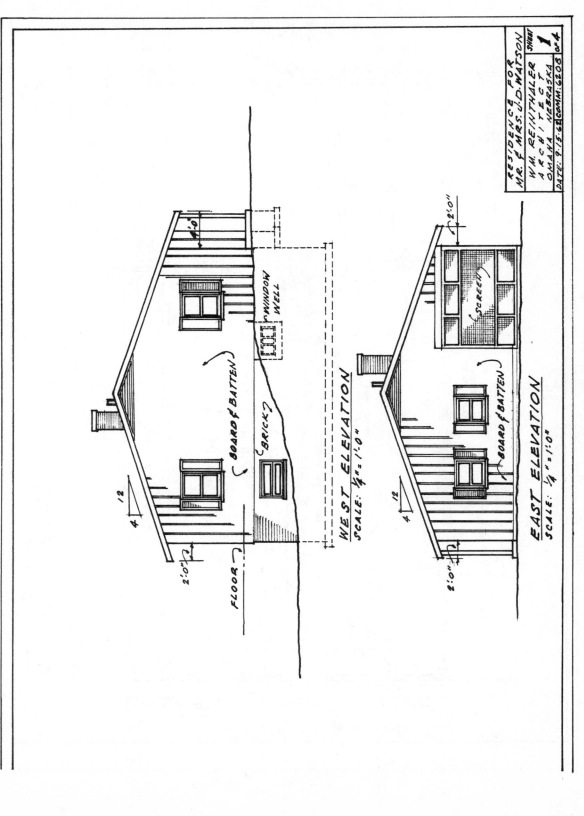

Fig. 290-B, Sheet 1 of 4

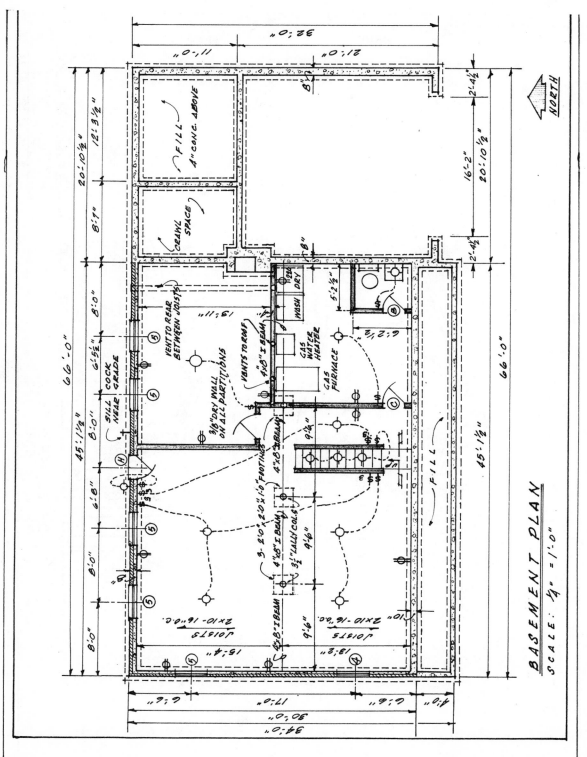

BASEMENT PLAN

SCALE: ¼" = 1'-0"

Fig. 290-C, Sheet 2 of 4

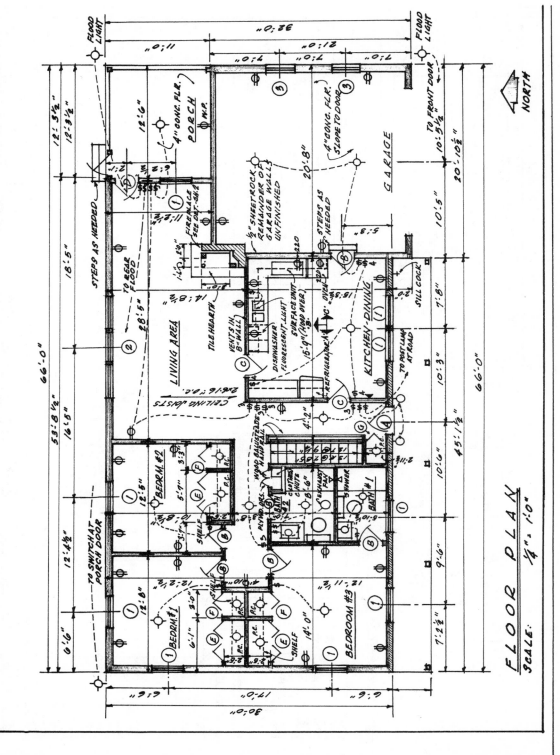

FLOOR PLAN

SCALE: ¼" = 1'-0"

Fig. 290-D, Sheet 2 of 4

DOOR SCHEDULE

MARK	QUANTITY	SIZE	TYPE	MATERIAL	REMARKS
A	1	1¾"x3'-0"x6'-8"	SEE ELEV.	PINE	PAINT
B	8	1⅜"x2'-6"x6'-8"	FLUSH	BIRCH	HOLLOW CORE
C	3	1⅜"x2'-6"x6'-8"	LOUVERED	PINE	
D	1	1¾"x2'-6"x6'-8"	10 LIGHTS	PINE	
E	3	1⅜"x5'-0"x6'-8"	FOLDING	PINE	LOUVERED
F	3	1⅜"x2'-6"x6'-8"	FOLDING	PINE	LOUVERED
G	1	1⅜"x2'-0"x6'-8"	FOLDING	PINE	LOUVERED
H	1	1¾"x2'-6"x6'-8"	9 LIGHTS	PINE	SEE REAR ELEVATION

WINDOW SCHEDULE

MARK	QUANTITY	SIZE	TYPE	REMARKS
1	8	3'-4"x4'-6"	D.H.	WITH SCREENS
2	2	11'-2"x6'-1"	FIXED AWNING	ANDERSEN J8633 OR EQUAL
3	2	3'-0"x3'-2"	D.H.	
4	2	1'-10"x2'-8"	HOPPER	STEEL-BASEMENT
5	5	3'-0"x3'-6"	D.H.	WITH SCREENS

RESIDENCE FOR
MR. & MRS. J.D. WATSON
WM. REINTHALER
ARCHITECT
OMAHA NEBRASKA
DATE: 9-15-62   COMM: 6208
SHEET 3 OF 4

TREADS: 9¼" WITH 1⅛ NOSING
RISERS: 7.85"
LINEN CLOSET
CLOTHES CHUTE THRU FLOOR TO BELOW STAIRS
BASEMENT FLR.
FIN. FLR.
CLOSET 9'-6"
CLOSET 2'-0"
2'-0"
3'-6" @ 1'-7.85" TREADS
2'-4" MIN.
LANDING
STAIRS TO BE ENCLOSED.
NOTE: TO BE NATURAL PINE OR OAK TREADS & RISERS

ELEV. OF LAV. - BATH #2
FORMICA
FLUORESCENT LIGHT
DISHWASHER   SINK   FORMICA
ELEV. "B"

FURRED PLASTER
FORMICA
REFRIG.
ELEV. "A"
CABINET DETAILS
SCALE: ¼" = 1'-0"

HOOD
OVEN
FORMICA   SURFACE UNIT
ELEV. "C"

STAIR DETAILS
SCALE: ⅜" = 1'-0"
2'-8"
IRON RAIL
HALL   FIN. FLR.
WOOD HANDRAIL
LANDING
BSMT. FLR.

Fig. 290-E, Sheet 3 of 4

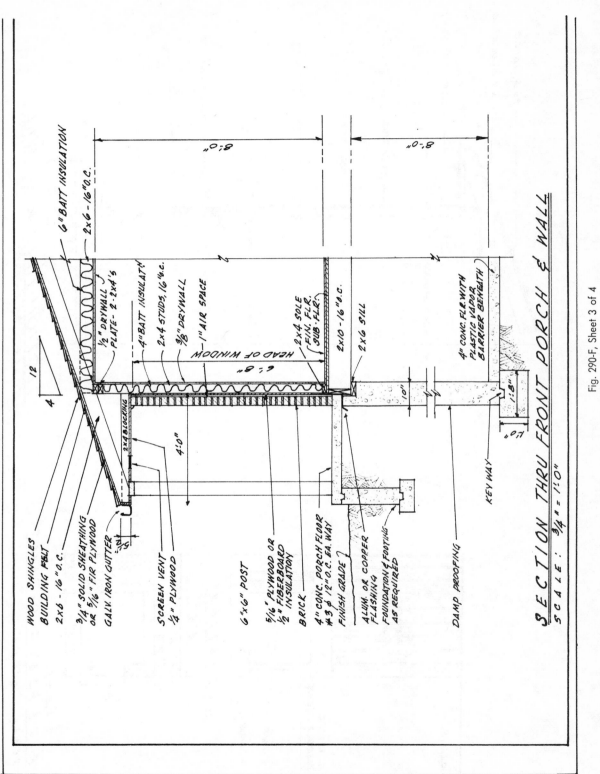

WOOD SHINGLES
BUILDING FELT
2×6 - 16" O.C.
3/4" SOLID SHEATHING OR 5/16" FIR PLYWOOD
GALV. IRON GUTTER

SCREEN VENT
1/4" PLYWOOD

6"×6" POST

5/16" PLYWOOD OR 1/2" FIBERBOARD 1/2" INSULATION
BRICK

4" CONC. PORCH FLOOR #3 φ 12" O.C. EA. WAY
FINISH GRADE

ALUM. OR COPPER FLASHING
FOUNDATION & FOOTING AS REQUIRED

DAMP PROOFING

6" BATT INSULATION
2×6 - 16" O.C.

1/2" DRYWALL
PLATE - 2 - 2×4's
4" BATT INSULATION
2×4 STUDS, 16" O.C.
5/8" DRYWALL
1" AIR SPACE

HEAD OF WINDOW

2×4 SOLE
FIN. FLR.
SUB. FLR.
2×10 - 16" O.C.
2×6 SILL

4" CONC. FLR. WITH PLASTIC VAPOR BARRIER BENEATH

KEY WAY

2×4 BLOCKING

4'-0"

8'-0"

8'-0"

6'-8"

12

4

SECTION THRU FRONT PORCH & WALL

SCALE: 3/4" = 1'-0"

Fig. 290-F, Sheet 3 of 4

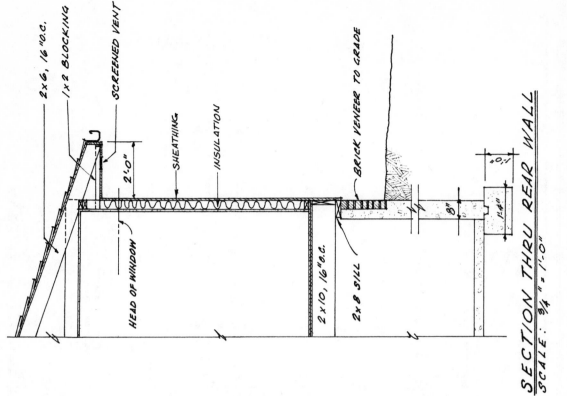

2 x 6, 16" O.C.

1 x 2 BLOCKING

SCREENED VENT

SHEATHING

INSULATION

BRICK VENEER TO GRADE

2'-0"

HEAD OF WINDOW

2 x 10, 16" O.C.

2 x 8 SILL

8"

1'-0"

1'-4"

SECTION THRU REAR WALL

SCALE: 3/4" = 1'-0"

Fig. 290-H, Sheet 4 of 4

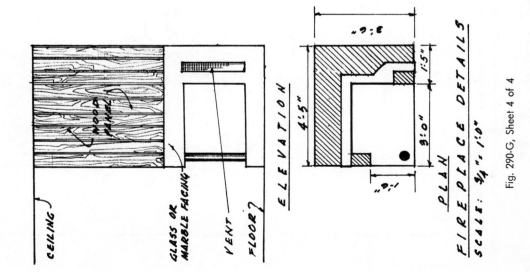

CEILING

WOOD PANEL

GLASS OR MARBLE FACING

VENT

FLOOR

ELEVATION

4'-5"

8'-3"

1'-5"

3'-0"

1'-9"

PLAN

FIRE PLACE DETAILS

SCALE: 3/4" = 1'-0"

Fig. 290-G, Sheet 4 of 4

METHODS OF HOUSE CONSTRUCTION

There are many ways to make a pot of soup. Many ingredients are available, from which the cook can choose those he wants to use. These ingredients can be combined in different proportions, with the resulting product, a pot of soup, being pleasing and tasty. Some soups are standard the country over; their ingredients are much the same. However, some cooks like to prepare new kinds of soup and to find better ways to make standard soups.

The same is true when a designer plans a house. A house can be built by one of several standard methods. Certain materials are commonly accepted and are used in a conventional manner, all over the country.

Some designers are not satisfied with conventional construction techniques and are trying new methods of construction.

This chapter discusses and illustrates the commonly accepted methods of house construction, as well as some newer approaches in use today.

How a Conventional House is Built

After the architect has considered the many factors involved in relating a house to the building site, a plot plan is drawn. This carefully locates the house on the site. The builder is responsible for laying out the exact location and for digging the foundation.

This layout is begun by measuring with a steel tape from the corner stakes of the site. At the corners of the foundation, batter boards are erected, with their posts set wider than the proposed foundation. By careful measuring, each side is located and marked on the

batter boards. Chalk lines are run to outline the foundation. These are sighted, the corners are squared and the chalk lines are leveled. Usually a transit is used for this job. See Fig. 310.

As soon as the foundation is laid out, the digging begins. This is most often done with a small bulldozer or a backhoe. If the house is to have a basement, the entire area is excavated until it is a little larger than the finished basement. This allows room for a footing and the basement walls. If the house is to be built without a basement, the trench for the footing is dug wide enough to permit erection of the foundation wall.

After the foundation trench has been dug, footings poured and foundation wall constructed, the sills, girders and floor joists are placed and the subfloor is applied. The sills are bolted in place.

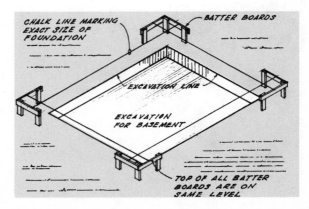

Fig. 310. Method for laying out the foundation of a building.

Once the subfloor is completed, the exterior walls are laid out on the subfloor; pieces are cut to size and nailed together to form a wall or part of a wall. This is then placed in a vertical position and nailed to the joists. Bracing is necessary to hold it in place.

Next, the interior partitions are assembled and erected, followed by installation of the ceiling joists. This considerably stiffens the structure. The exterior sheathing is applied, while other workers cut and erect the rafters. The roof is completed by the application of roof sheathing, builder's paper and shingles.

Then, windows are set in place and flashed. Builder's paper is nailed over wood sheathing. This is followed by the siding, which can be either wood, aluminum or masonry. The house is now weather tight.

Miscellaneous pieces of trim such as facia, frieze and soffit are installed. The prime coat of paint is applied to all exterior wood.

Inside the house, several tradesmen are at work. The electrician installs the wiring; the plumber, the pipes and fixtures; and the heating contractor, the furnace and air-conditioning unit.

Cabinetmakers build and install the kitchen counters, cabinets and other required items such as room dividers, built-in bedroom drawers and bathroom lavatory cabinets.

After all this is finished, the insulation is installed, and the interior walls are plastered, covered with drywall or panelled. See Fig. 311.

The flooring contractor then installs the hardwood floors. Before these floors are sanded and finished, painters and paperhangers decorate the interior. Then the electrician hangs the light fixtures. Finally the flooring contractor sands and finishes the hardwood floors and installs tile in the bath and kitchen. This completes the basic house.

Before leaving the job, the builder is responsible for cleaning away all debris and for landscaping the house. Any driveways and sidewalks are installed at this time.

Frame House Construction Details

There are several acceptable methods of framing a house. This discussion illustrates

Fig. 311. Insulation being installed in a conventionally framed house. Notice the composition sheathing, double plate and cut on the rafter. The rafters are placed directly above each stud. (National Gypsum Co.)

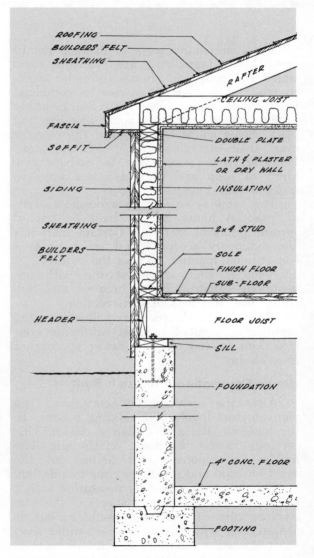

Fig. 312. Typical wall section through a frame house.

one conventional, widely accepted and used method. Fig. 312 shows a typical wall section for a frame house.

Sills

The sill, usually a 2 x 6, is bolted to the foundation. Between the sill and the foundation, a strip of sealer is installed. This sealer is usually about ½″ thick and is composed of an insulation material held between two layers of heavy, asphalt-impregnated paper. When the sill is bolted down, the sealer is squeezed tightly and fills any openings between the foundation and the sill. Sometimes a thin layer of fresh mortar is used both as a sealer and as a leveling device for the sill. See Fig. 313.

Fig. 314 illustrates common types of sill construction used on houses with wood floors. Fig. 315 illustrates a typical detail for a frame house with concrete floors.

The sills are bolted to concrete-block foundations with ½″ bolts, having 2″ washers on the head. These are embedded 15″ to 18″ into the foundation and fully grouted. The bolts are spaced not more than 8′ apart, with two bolts in each sill piece. If the foundation is poured concrete, ½″ bolts are embedded 6″ deep and are placed not over 4′ apart, with at least two bolts in each sill piece.

If building is done in areas with little wind, such anchorage may be omitted.

Floor joists are toenailed to the sill, and the header is nailed to the ends of the joists.

Termites are found in almost every section of the United States. If they are prevalent, the sill should be protected against attack. The lumber can be treated with chemicals that repel the termite, or a termite shield can be used. The most common shield is a layer of metal placed under the sill and projecting on each side of the foundation. This prevents termites from traveling up the foundation and attacking the wood sill. Termites can travel inside hollow masonry foundations and can penetrate poor mortar and porous concrete. Refer again to Fig. 313, which illustrates a typical termite shield.

Framing the Walls

Most builders choose either to cut all the studs to size or to buy precut ones. The exterior wall is laid out on the subfloor, and the studs are spaced and nailed to the sole and to a single, 2 x 4 plate. The normal spacing of studs is 16″ on center. Window openings

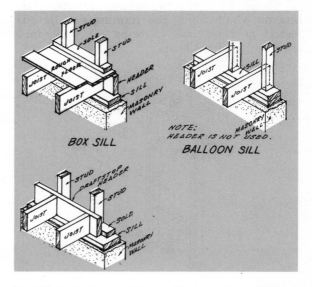

Fig. 314. Typical types of frame sill construction with wood floors.

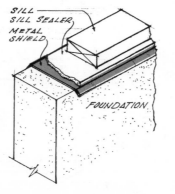

Fig. 313. Metal termite shield and sill sealer.

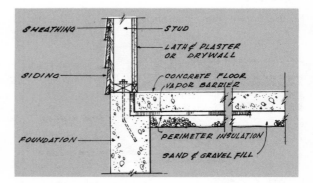

Fig. 315. Typical section through a frame house with a concrete slab on grade.

are located, and a rough opening is framed. The studs are doubled around any opening in a bearing partition. See Fig. 316.

The corners of the exterior wall are most often built up from three 2 x 4 studs. Fig. 317 illustrates one method. The small blocks at the sole are used for securing baseboards.

The wall is raised into position and is braced to hold it until other parts of the structure are in place. A frame wall is strengthened considerably if 1 x 4 members are let in the 2 x 4 studs on an angle. See Fig. 318.

After all exterior framing is up, the second 2 x 4 is added to the plate. This is used to increase the strength of the plate, since it has to help support the roof.

The building is measured across diagonals to check that the walls are square. The bracing which holds the framing can be adjusted at this time to bring all walls into their required positions.

Interior partitions are framed in the same way as the exterior structure. A special problem occurs where an interior partition meets an exterior wall. Fig. 319 illustrates a method for framing when the partition meets a stud. This requires that an extra stud be inserted in the exterior wall, to provide nailing space for lath or drywall sheets. If a partition does not meet a stud in the exterior wall, two extra studs must be inserted in the exterior wall.

Sheathing the Walls

Wall sheathing is placed next to the stud framing. It strengthens the wall by resisting lateral movement. It also has insulation values. The siding is placed over the sheathing.

The three types of sheathing in common use are solid lumber, plywood, and fiberboard. Lumber sheathing can be applied perpendicular to the studs or on a 45° diagonal. The diagonal application makes the wall more rigid. If diagonal sheathing is used, the let-in brace can usually be omitted. It is covered with building paper before the siding is applied.

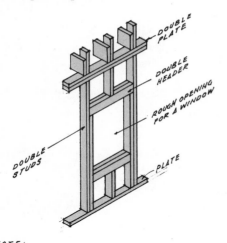

NOTE:
HEADER IS ALWAYS DOUBLED OVER ANY OPENING IN A BEARING PARTITION.

Fig. 316. Framing around opening.

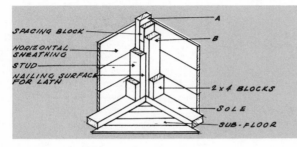

Fig. 317. A method for framing a corner. Studs A and B are spaced by nailing short lengths of 2 x 4 between them at 3'-0" intervals.

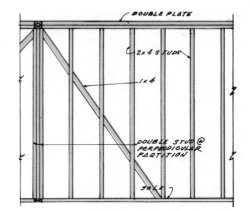

Fig. 318. A frame wall strengthened by a 1 x 4 let into studs.

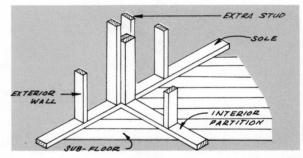

Fig. 319. An interior partition framed into the exterior wall.

Plywood and fiberboard sheathing are made in large sheets. The most common size sheet is 48″ x 96″.

Plywood is applied with face grain parallel with the studs. This gives maximum strength. It is covered with building paper before the siding is applied. Plywood sheathed walls have greater strength than lumber or fiberboard sheathed walls. Plywood also gives a solid base into which to nail the siding.

Fiberboard sheathing is coated with a bituminous coating. This gives it a degree of moisture resistance. It is not necessary to cover it with building paper. It will not hold nails. Wood siding must be nailed through the sheathing into the studs. See Fig. 320. Information on sheathing spans and thickness is in Chapter 7.

Siding

There are many types of exterior siding for frame construction. The most common are shingles, wood siding, plywood, hardboard, and stucco. The common sizes of these materials are shown in Table 2A, on following page.

Shingles are available in wood and cement-asbestos. *Wood shingles* (upper left) are applied in single and double course. The single course wall has two thicknesses of wood at the thinnest place. Much of the wall has three thicknesses. A double course wall uses a low grade shingle such as No. 3 for the undercourse. A No. 1 grade shingle is used for the outer course. Double coursing provides better wall coverage. It also gives the rows of shingles a deeper shadow line due to the extra thickness. A wider exposure is used with double coursed shingles. *Exposure* is the area of the shingle not covered by another shingle.

Cement-asbestos shingles (upper right) have a baked-on factory finish. They are made in many colors. The surface is made in a variety of textures. When placed over wood sheathing, a fiber shingle backer is used. The unit is nailed directly to the wood sheathing. When placed over composition sheathing wood nailing strips are needed. The composition sheathing will not hold nails. The shingle is nailed directly to the nailing strip.

There are many kinds of *horizontal wood siding* (lower left). Two of the most common are bevel and shiplap. There are several other patterns of shiplap siding in addition to the one shown.

Plywood siding is available in sheets 48″ wide and 8′, 9′, and 10′ long. It is made with a variety of surface textures. This siding is nailed directly to the studs. The panels are placed vertically so there are no horizontal joints. A variety of joints are used to join these panels (lower right). The joints should be sealed with caulking compound.

Horizontal plywood siding is applied in the same manner as bevel siding. The pieces are usually lapped 1½″.

Hardboard siding is available in sheets 48″ wide and 8′, 9′, and 10′ long. It is also made to resemble horizontal bevel siding. A variety of surface textures are available. Most panels have a factory applied prime coat. Hardboard panels are applied directly to studs or sheathing. The horizontal siding can be applied with a plain lap just like bevel siding, see figure on lower left. For additional shadow, it can have a wood nailing strip as shown for cement-asbestos siding, see figure on upper right.

Framing Joists

The typical method for framing joists onto the foundation was shown in Fig. 314.

A number of different methods are used when framing joists to a beam. The simplest method is shown in Fig. 321. The joist rests on top of the girder. If it is desired to increase headroom or clearance below, the joists can

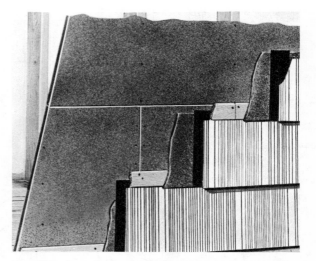

Fig. 320. A wall sheathed with fiberboard. Notice the method for installing shingles as the exterior siding. (National Gypsum Co.)

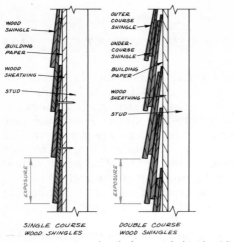

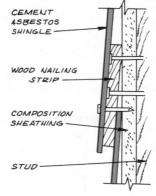

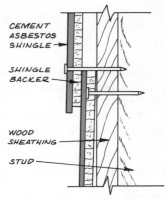

Typical construction details for wood shingle siding.

Typical construction details for cement-asbestos shingle siding.

Table 2A

Typical Frame Siding Materials

CEDAR SHAKES	Length	18″	24″	32″			
	Exposure	8½″	11½″	15″			
CEDAR SHINGLES	Length	16″	18″				
	Exposure	12″	14″				
CEMENT-ASBESTOS SHINGLES	SIZE	8¾″ x 48″	12″ x 24″				
	EXPOSURE	7¾″ x 48″	11″ x 24″				
BEVEL SIDING	ACTUAL WIDTH	3½″	4½″	5½″	7½″	9½″	11½″
	EXPOSURE	2½″	3½″	4½″	6¼″	8¼″	10¼″
SHIPLAP SIDING	ACTUAL WIDTH	5¼″	7¼″				
	EXPOSURE	5¼″	7¼″				
HARDBOARD PANELS	WIDTH	4′-0″	4′-0″	4′-0″			
	LENGTH	8′-0″	9′-0″	10′-0″			
HORIZONTAL HARDBOARD SIDING	WIDTH	10″	12″	16″	24″		
	EXPOSURE	8⅞″	10⅜″	14⅜″	22⅜″		
PLYWOOD PANELS	WIDTH	4′-0″	4′-0″	4′-0″			
	LENGTH	8′-0″	9′-0″	10′-0″			
HORIZONTAL PLYWOOD SIDING	WIDTH	10″	12″				
	EXPOSURE	8½″	10½″				

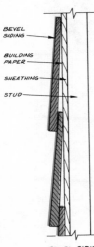

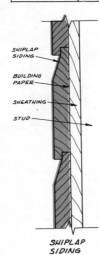

Horizontal wood siding.

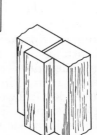

Plywood panel joints.

be cut to fit around the beam. If a flush ceiling is desired on the floor below the beam iron, stirrups can be used, or the joist can be cut to fit a metal beam and a steel plate fastened below. These methods are illustrated in Figs. 322 and 323. A method for framing a joist into a steel beam is illustrated in Fig. 324.

An opening in the floor, such as a stairway, requires that some joists be cut. Since this weakens the floor, a header is installed to support the cut joists. This header is doubled and sometimes tripled, if the distance is great. Frequently, iron stirrups are used in this situation. See Fig. 325.

If an interior partition runs parallel with the joists, the joist supporting the partition must be doubled to carry the weight.

Bridging

Bridging consists of rows of small diagonal braces, nailed between the joists. See Fig. 326. These distribute any load on the floor above over a wider area, thus putting the strain on many joists, rather than permitting one or two to carry the load. Besides this, bridging stiffens the floor and tends to keep the joists in line by preventing warping.

Bridging should be installed in rows from one side of a house to the other. Normally, these rows are spaced not over 10' apart. Typical bridging members are cut from 1 x 4 stock.

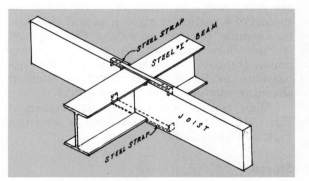

Fig. 324. Joist framed into steel I beam.

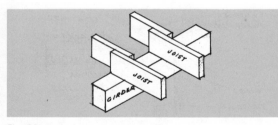

Fig. 321. Joist lapped on top of girder.

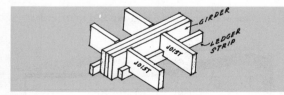

Fig. 322. Joist notched over ribband nailed to girder.

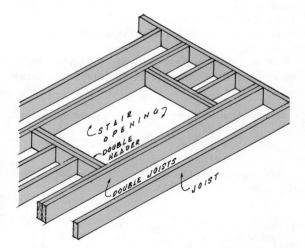

Fig. 325. An opening framed to receive a stairway. Notice the double joists and double headers.

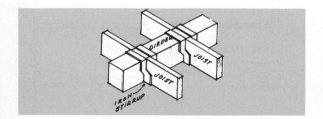

Fig. 323. Joists hung on girder with iron stirrups.

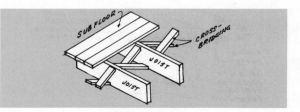

Fig. 326. Cross bridging in place between floor joists.

The subfloor should be installed before the bridging is nailed tightly. Usually, the top ends of the bridging are nailed in place before the subfloor is laid, but the lower ends are not fastened until the joists have adjusted to the subfloor. See Fig. 327.

Eaves

The eave is that portion of the rafters which extends beyond the exterior wall. There are many ways to frame an eave. Some are typical of a particular style or period of house; for example, the eave on a Cape Cod Cottage, is built only one way. On a contemporary house, the eave is designed for a desired appearance or for a special function, such as shielding windows from the sun's rays.

Some typical eave designs are detailed in Figs. 312, 333 and 342. Others are shown in Figs. 328 through 331.

Stucco

An exterior stucco finish is used a great deal in some parts of the United States. It is used in the warmer, dryer climates. In Fig. 331A are three commonly used types of wall construction utilizing stucco as the final exterior finish.

Wire lath is fastened to masonry walls with concrete nails. It is fastened to frame walls with a large-headed galvanized nail. The nail has a space ring on it. This keeps the head about 3/8″ above the surface of the sheathing or masonry. The head holds the wire lath to the wall. See Fig. 331B.

The exterior stucco is made of a portland cement base. Usually three coats are applied.

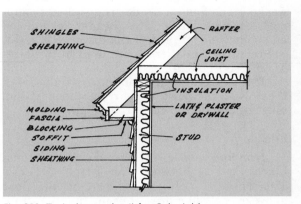

Fig. 329. Typical eave detail for Colonial house.

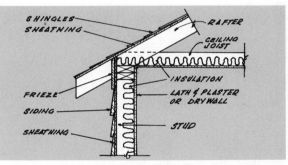

Fig. 330. Typical detail of eave with exposed rafter ends.

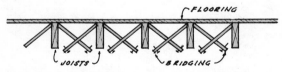

Fig. 327. Lower end of cross bridging is not nailed in place until subfloor is nailed to joists.

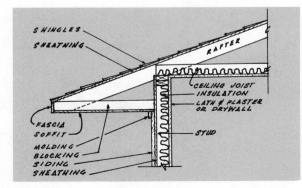

Fig. 328. Typical eave detail for wide overhang.

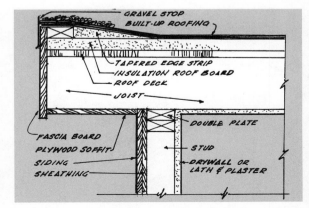

Fig. 331. Typical eave detail for flat roof.

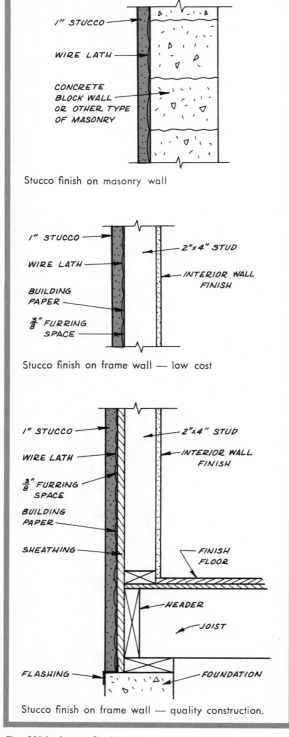

Stucco finish on masonry wall

Stucco finish on frame wall — low cost

Stucco finish on frame wall — quality construction.

Fig. 331A. Stucco finishes.

See Fig. 331C. The first coat is the scratch coat. It is worked into the wire mesh. The second coat is the brown coat. It builds up the thickness of the finish and smooths out many irregularities left in the scratch coat. Commonly these are made of one part portland cement to three parts sand. Some lime is also added. The final coat is the finish coat. The actual finished appearance of the house depends on this coat. It can be trowled smooth or brushed for a rougher texture. The finish coat can be tinted by adding coloring. Stucco can be painted with a paint suitable for this purpose.

A metal molding is applied on all edges and around all openings in a wall to be finished with stucco.

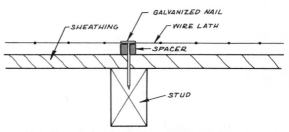

Fig. 331B. Wire lath is spaced out from sheathing so stucco can flow behind the lath.

Fig. 331C. The basic preparation for a stucco finish includes wire lath and a scratch coat of mortar. (Keystone Steel and Wire)

Solid Masonry Construction

While many methods and materials are used to construct solid masonry walls, only those commonly used are discussed. Refer to a standards book for additional information.

Most frequently, solid masonry walls are built entirely from one material — such as brick, stone or concrete block — or are constructed with a brick or stone veneer covering concrete blocks or tile backing.

Solid Brick or Stone

Exterior walls for one- and two-story houses may be constructed of 8 inches of solid brick or stone. Careful selection of the bricks and the pattern of laying them is essential to the appearance of the house. See Fig. 332 for frequently used bond patterns for brick walls.

Details of solid masonry wall construction are shown in Fig. 333. Notice the beveled cut on the end of the floor joists. Since the masonry wall is heavy, any movement in the ends of the floor joists tends to crack the wall. The bevel cut reduces this danger. Fig. 334 illustrates a solid masonry house with a concrete floor.

Furring strips are necessary for high-quality work. A *furring strip* is a 2 x 2 wood member fastened on the interior of a masonry wall, to insure that an air pocket is left between the wall and the interior of the house.

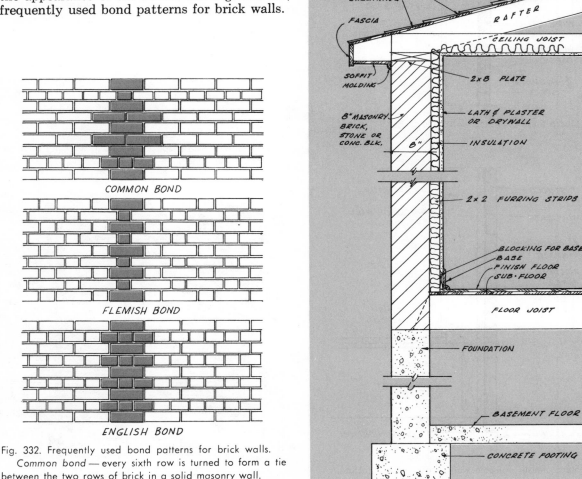

Fig. 332. Frequently used bond patterns for brick walls.
Common bond — every sixth row is turned to form a tie between the two rows of brick in a solid masonry wall.
Flemish bond — every other brick is turned to form a tie.
English bond — every other row is turned to form a tie.

Fig. 333. Section through solid masonry wall.

Solid masonry is a poor insulator, and the interior of the house would be very hot in summer and cold in winter without the air space provided by the furring strips. This space also permits installation of insulation, to further decrease heat loss through the wall. See Fig. 335.

If a solid masonry wall is not furred out, moisture will condense on the walls, due to interior, warm, moist air contacting the cold, exterior wall.

The solid masonry wall needs to be "tied together" into a solid mass. This is most often done by turning an occasional brick or an entire layer of bricks sideways, to form a tie. See Figs. 332 and 336.

Another variety of solid masonry wall has two thicknesses of brick, spaced 1 inch apart. This provides a dead air space and reduces some of the difficulties of the solid masonry wall. However, even with this type wall, it is still best to furr out the interior. See Fig. 338.

A low-cost, solid masonry wall can be constructed from 8-inch, concrete blocks. The wall can be erected quickly, and the holes in the block provide dead air space. Furring the interior surface is recommended. See Fig. 339. The standard concrete block is 8″ high, 8″ wide and 16″ long. Concrete blocks are manufactured in a variety of textures and faces, to break the monotony of the large block and to make an attractive wall.

Brick Veneer over Concrete Block or Tile

In an attempt to have a faster-built, less-expensive wall, a 4-inch, brick facing is used over 4-inch, concrete block or over terra-

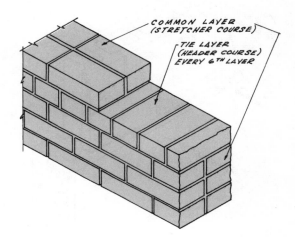

Fig. 336. Brick wall in common bond showing tie made with a header course.

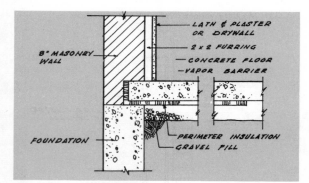

Fig. 334. Section through a solid masonry wall with concrete slab floor on grade.

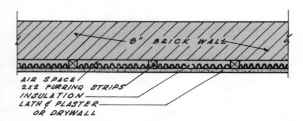

Fig. 335. Section through solid masonry wall with interior wall furred out.

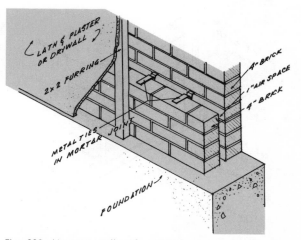

Fig. 338. Masonry wall with a 1-inch air space separating each unit; this is frequently called a cavity wall.

cotta tile. This method now is widely used instead of walls of solid brick or solid stone. See Fig. 340. These walls should be furred out for insulation purposes. Frequently, a 1-inch air space is left between the brick and the concrete block or tile.

Masonry Veneer over Frame Construction

A frame house with a masonry veneer has all the advantages of a frame house; yet, it has the low-maintenance qualities of a masonry house. An examination of Fig. 341 shows

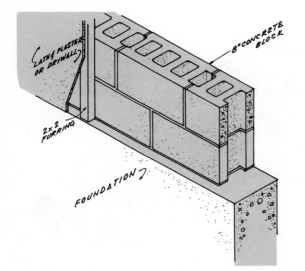

Fig. 339. Typical construction of an 8-inch concrete-block wall.

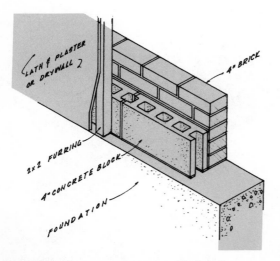

Fig. 340. Brick veneer over concrete-block wall.

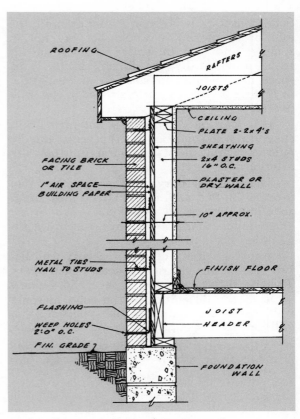

Fig. 341. Masonry veneer over frame construction.

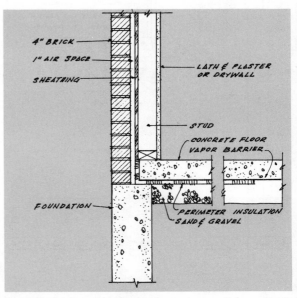

Fig. 342. Section through masonry veneer wall for a house with a concrete slab floor on grade.

that the conventional frame wall is used. This provides the fine insulation offered by a frame house. The high exterior-maintenance cost of the frame house is reduced by the use of the 4-inch brick or 6-inch stone veneer instead of wood siding. Fig. 342 illustrates a masonry-veneer house with a concrete floor.

The masonry veneer is placed one inch away from the sheathing. This dead air space serves as an insulator, but more importantly, as a space to carry away condensation that forms on the inside of the masonry wall. The interior frame wall is not touched by the moisture.

A house constructed with a masonry veneer over a frame wall must have a larger foundation than usual, not because of the extra weight, but because this construction is 10 inches thick, compared to 8 inches for solid masonry and 5 inches for a typical frame wall.

Framing the Roof

A conventionally framed roof is composed of rafters and a ridgepole. The *ridgepole* is a horizontal board upon which the rafters rest at their upper ends. It adds little to the strength of the structure, but aids in the erection and alignment of the rafters. Usually it is 1-inch lumber, about the same width as the rafters. The *rafters* support the sheathing, builder's felt and roofing material. Since there are various styles of conventionally-built roofs, different kinds of rafters are necessary. Fig. 343 indicates the common kinds of rafters used in roof construction.

Common rafters are straight-run rafters, extending without interruption from the ridge to the eave.

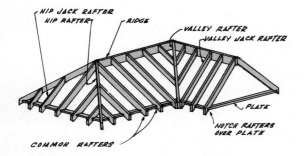

Fig. 343. Types of rafters used in roof framing.

Valley rafters run from the ridge to the eave, but are located at the point where two sections of a roof come together, forming a trough or valley.

Valley-jack rafters are short members, running from the ridge to the valley rafter.

Hip rafters run from the ridge to the eave, but are located where two sections of a roof come together to form a peak or ridge. Since hip rafters and valley rafters span longer distances than common rafters, frequently they must be larger to carry the additional load caused by the greater distance.

Hip-jack rafters run from a hip rafter to the eave. They are shorter than common rafters.

When a roof is framed by conventional methods, the rafters are cut on the ground and nailed into place one by one. Then the sheathing is applied followed by a covering of builder's felt. The roofing material, such as asphalt shingles, is nailed over the builder's felt.

The method for ascertaining the proper size rafters to use is explained in Chapter 7.

Frequently, a builder will use wood roof trusses, instead of conventional rafters. A *truss* is a preassembled unit, consisting of two rafters, a ceiling joist and all necessary members to strengthen the roof. See Fig. 344. A definite savings in materials and labor results through the use of trusses.

Small wood members can be used in truss construction, because of the truss design. It is braced similar to the framing on a bridge, enabling small members to span long distances, to support the necessary weight.

Another savings is in labor. Since trusses are assembled on the ground, they can be easily and quickly made. The time spent to install them is reduced considerably from that required for conventional roof framing.

Roof trusses also offer the advantage of increased flexibility for interior planning, since they span the entire width of a building and require no supporting wall inside the house.

Post, Plank, and Beam Construction

Post-and-beam construction lends itself well to the design and construction of contemporary houses. It permits an open interior

area, free from supporting walls. It also frees the exterior walls from supporting the roof, thus enabling the use of large areas of glass and lightweight materials in these walls. The need for large, long, heavy footings is eliminated.

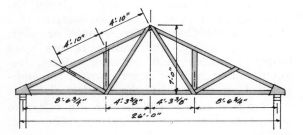

Fig. 344. Typical roof truss for a small house.

Post and beam construction is a simple framing system that can be rapidly erected. There are several framing systems that can be used. Figure 345 shows a system using beams as rafters and joists. The roof and floor decking are structural planks. Figure 346 shows a system using beams the length of the structure. The roof decking is applied transversely over the beams. The top of the beam is shaped to match the roof slope.

The spacing of these members varies with their size and the species of wood to be used. Tables for selecting these structural members are in Chapter 7.

A frequently used roof decking is 2- to 4-inch thick wood planking. See Fig. 347. This decking becomes the finished, interior ceiling. This utilizes the natural color and grain of the wood. See Fig. 348. Composition decking is also manufactured for this use. See Figs. 349 and 350. Tables for selecting decking are in

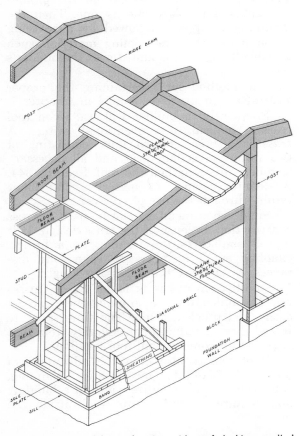

Fig. 345. Post and beam framing with roof decking applied transversely over the beams. Posts are required through the center of the house to support the ridge beam. The exterior wall can be typical frame wall construction with the roof beams resting on the double plate or on individual posts. (National Forest Products Association)

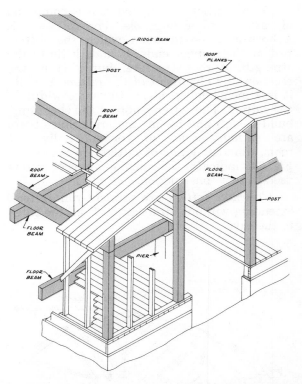

Fig. 346. Post and beam framing with roof decking applied transversely over the beams. Posts are required through the center of the house to support the ridge beam. The exterior wall can be typical frame wall construction with roof beams resting on the double plate.

Chapter 7. Stress skin panels, as in Fig. 398-400 and 478 can be used.

The two-inch roof and floor decking provides adequate insulation in moderate climates. In cold climates additional insulation is often needed. Sheets of rigid insulation can be applied to the bottom of the planks. This does hide the beauty of the natural wood interior ceiling. If this is undesirable, a rigid insulation can be applied on top of the roof decking and the roofing material over this. This is shown in Fig. 741.

Fig. 349. Composition roof decking being installed on house with open-beam ceiling. (National Gypsum Co.)

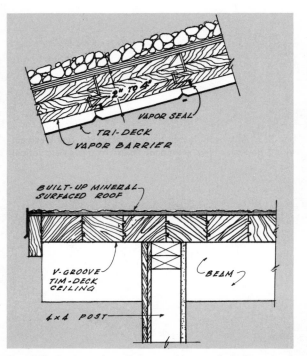

Fig. 347. Sections through composition roof decking (top) and wood roof decking.

Fig. 348. An interior view of a framed house with exterior walls in place. (Timber Structures, Inc.)

Fig. 350. Interior view of ceiling built with composition roof decking; see Fig. 349. (National Gypsum Co.)

The finished flooring is applied over the floor decking in the same manner as conventional construction.

Typical construction details are shown in Fig. 351 through 358C. The plank floors will carry normal uniform loads. If a load is to be concentrated in one area, as a bearing partition or bathtub, additional framing is needed. See Fig. 351. The extra support can be above or below the floor decking. Regardless of where they are placed they must transmit the load to the main structural members.

Non-bearing partitions that run parallel with the floor planking also need extra support. See Fig. 351.

Three types of beams are commonly used. These are solid, built-up cased, and spaced beams. See Fig. 352. The spaced beam permits electrical wiring and plumbing to run inside the beam. See Fig. 353.

Construction details at the sill are shown in Fig. 354 and 355. These will permit the

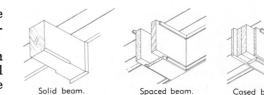
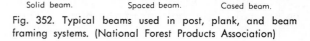

Fig. 352. Typical beams used in post, plank, and beam framing systems. (National Forest Products Association)

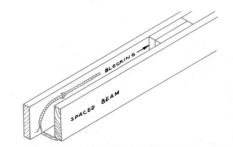

Fig. 353. A spaced beam gives a place to run electrical wiring and plumbing. (National Forest Products Association)

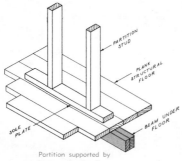

Partition supported by beam under the floor.

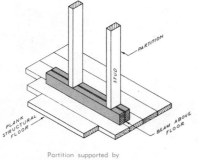

Partition supported by beam above the floor.

Support for non-bearing partition parallel to plank.

Fig. 351. Unusual floor loads require extra structural support. (National Forest Products Association)

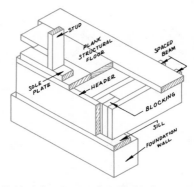

Fig. 354. Typical framing at the sill. Notice a spaced beam is shown. It could be a solid or built-up beam. (National Forest Products Association)

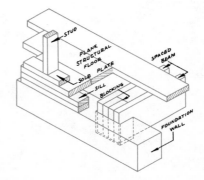

Fig. 355. Another way to set a beam and frame the building at the sill. (National Forest Products Association)

house to have a crawl space or basement. If a slab floor is to be used, construction could be as shown in Fig. 356.

The floor beams will be supported in the center of the house by a column or pier. If solid beams are used they would be joined as in Fig. 357. The column can be made wider by adding bearing blocks. This permits the bearing surface of the column to be increased.

Normally at least a 6″ width parallel to the beam is needed. If solid or built-up and spaced beams are used the construction would be as in Fig. 358. Another method of connecting columns and beams is in Fig. 358A.

Roof beams serving as rafters should be directly above the posts. Fig. 358B shows how

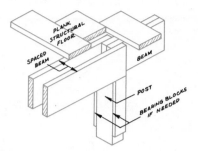

Fig. 358. Framing a spaced beam over a post. (National Forest Products Association)

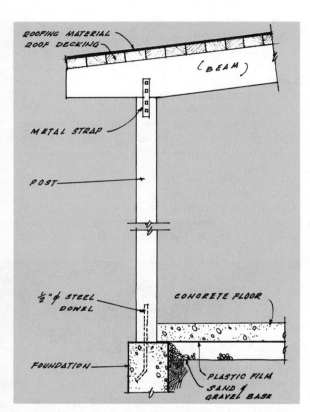

Fig. 356. Wall section through post-and-beam construction.

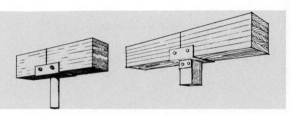
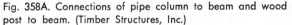

Fig. 358A. Connections of pipe column to beam and wood post to beam. (Timber Structures, Inc.)

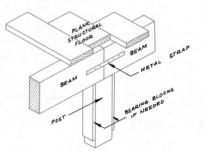

Fig. 357. Framing a solid beam over a post. (National Forest Products Association)

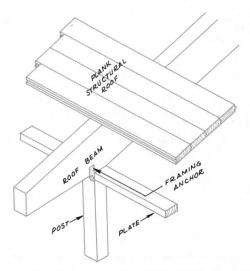

Fig. 358B. Each roof beam is above a post. Metal framing anchors join them together. (National Forest Products Association)

a roof beam could be joined to the exterior wall. Metal framing anchors or angle clips are used. There are several methods for joining the roof beam to the ridge beam. These use metal connectors. See Fig. 358C.

The areas between the posts on exterior walls are filled with windows, doors, or solid panels. The solid panel areas provide a place to frame in lateral bracing. These walls are usually framed with 2 x 4 studs as in conventional construction. Lateral bracing is accomplished by letting in a diagonal brace or using sheathing, as plywood or fiberboard. See Fig. 345.

Posts may be solid or built-up from 2" material. They must be of a size to carry the design load. Tables for this are in Chapter 7. Usually no posts under 4" x 4" are used.

Steel House Framing

The steel-framed house is becoming more common in many parts of the country. It can be framed with few members and can have long spans uninterrupted by columns. Spans of 30 feet and longer are common; this allows big open areas. See Fig. 359. All structural members can be slender, and these are pleasing to the eye when left exposed. Construction of overhangs, balconies and covered walkways is easily accomplished. See Fig. 360.

Since the steel frame carries all loads, the choice of wall panel material is unlimited. Metal, wood, plastic or glass panels may be used with equal ease. Interior planning is freed from the restrictions of supporting walls.

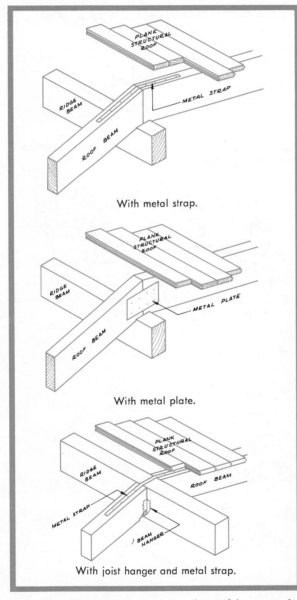

Fig. 358C. Typical ways to support the roof beam on the ridge beam. This absorbs horizontal thrust. (National Forest Products Association)

Fig. 359. Heat and light ducts carried in interior soffit. Notice balcony at tree-top height. (Bethlehem Steel)

Fig. 360. Patio of steel-framed house. Notice wide overhang and sun deck on roof. (Bethlehem Steel)

Fig. 362. Steel enables house to cantilever large sections. (Bethlehem Steel)

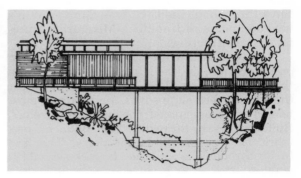

Fig. 363. A steel-framed house spanning a ravine.

With steel framing, a house can be built on the side of a steep hill or on top of a rock formation. The house can be cantilevered over a cliff or can span a ravine. See Figs. 361 through 363.

Steel framing is not affected by termites. It will not sag, burn, shrink or rot. Usually fabricated in a shop, the steel framing for an average residence can be erected on the site in less than one day. See Fig. 364.

Fig. 361. Entire floor area of house is supported by wide flange steel sections on four concrete pylons embedded in rock mass. (Bethlehem Steel)

Fig. 364. Erecting shop-fabricated steel framework. (Bethlehem Steel)

The Factory-Manufactured House

Throughout the centuries, man has searched for a better and easier way to build dwellings. Although the prefabricated structure was a natural development, it is not a current development. This technique has been used for centuries. The pyramids built in 3000 A.D. were prefabricated. The limestone blocks from which they were constructed were preformed, then hauled to the building site where they were placed in predetermined locations.

Roman armies carried prefabricated shelters. Prefabricated houses were shipped from the East to California during the Gold Rush. The Union Army used prefabricated structures throughout the Civil War. Mark Twain's boyhood home in Hannibal, Missouri is a prefabricated structure.

Up to World War II, the biggest step in prefabrication, in the United States, was in the precut house. The factory-cut parts for the house were shipped to the site and most homeowners assembled the parts themselves. Builders began to realize the value of prefabricating houses in larger parts. The first break-throughs were the factory-assembled window and the prefitted door and door frame. Kitchen cabinets are also factory made.

Since World War II, modern construction methods and new design approaches have made possible the construction of houses in factories. These are transported to the building site for final erection and finishing.

Special-purpose machines such as power nailers are used. Adhesives have been developed that speed construction. Large jigs are used to assemble sections of the house. They can turn sections over so both sides can be finished.

A large company can take advantage of mass purchases of material, thus lowering the cost of the house. Quality can be more closely controlled in a factory than on the site. The man hours required to build a house can be reduced. Bad weather does not stop construction.

Currently there are two approaches being used to construct houses in factories. One uses *modular components*. These are panels or sections of walls, roofs, and floors. The other approach is *modular units*. A modular unit is a room size or large portion of a house that is completely assembled in a factory. It is moved to the site much like a mobile home. These are discussed in detail in the following pages.

Buildings from Modular Components

A modular component is a factory-assembled part of a building. Typical examples are wall panels, floor panels, roof panels, and trusses.

The use of standardized building components enables a builder to construct a house in the fastest possible time with the least waste of materials. This helps reduce the cost of the house. It is applying the principles of mass production of standardized parts as used in the auto industry to building construction.

The system of modular components described in the following pages was developed by The National Lumber Manufacturers Association.

Standardization

Companies manufacturing building materials are making an effort to change their product sizes to fit a modular plan. All types of materials such as floor tile, plywood paneling, and sheathing panels are sized to fit the modular plan.

The standard module is a 4″ cube. This unit is used to build larger modules. A 4′-0″ cube is a major module. It is made of 4″ modules. Minor modules are 16″ and 24″ cubes. See Fig. 364A.

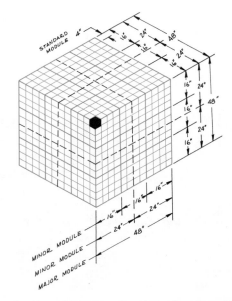

Fig. 364A. The modular system includes length, width, and height. It is based on a 4″ standard module. (National Forest Products Association)

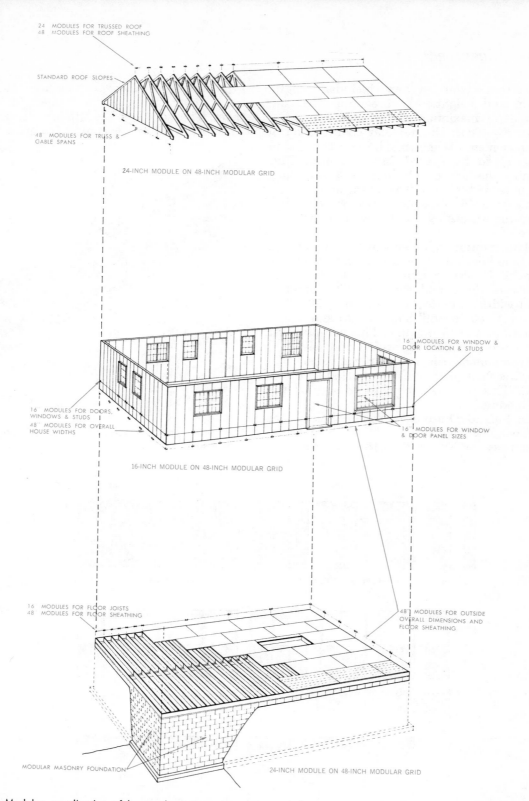

24 MODULES FOR TRUSSED ROOF
48 MODULES FOR ROOF SHEATHING

STANDARD ROOF SLOPES

48 MODULES FOR TRUSS &
GABLE SPANS

24-INCH MODULE ON 48-INCH MODULAR GRID

16 MODULES FOR WINDOW &
DOOR LOCATION & STUDS

16 MODULES FOR DOORS,
WINDOWS & STUDS

48 MODULES FOR OVERALL
HOUSE WIDTHS

16 MODULES FOR WINDOW
& DOOR PANEL SIZES

16-INCH MODULE ON 48-INCH MODULAR GRID

16 MODULES FOR FLOOR JOISTS
48 MODULES FOR FLOOR SHEATHING

48 MODULES FOR OUTSIDE
OVERALL DIMENSIONS AND
FLOOR SHEATHING

MODULAR MASONRY FOUNDATION

24-INCH MODULE ON 48-INCH MODULAR GRID

Fig. 364B. Modular coordination of house elements.

All structural and aesthetic elements of a house are related. Coordinated modular increments of the structural elements, in an example house on the 48-inch module, are shown in the diagrammatic drawings. Standard sizes of various existing materials will easily fit the modular increments of the example shown.

The modular system includes length, width, and height. All three must be considered for maximum effectiveness.

In Fig. 364B the modular coordination of house elements is shown. The roof trusses are designed to be spaced 24″ on-center. This permits the use of plywood roof sheathing which is 48″ x 96″. The sheathing has no waste. If a 16″ on-center spacing was used, the same sheathing would be used with no waste.

The exterior wall components are built on a 16″ module. This provides normal structural support. It also permits the use of a wide variety of doors and windows. The common panel widths are 16″, 32″, 48″, 64″, 80″, 96″, and 144″. The overall house width and length is based on the 48″ module. This permits most effective use of floor sheathing and joists.

When using the modular component design, the floor joists must be butted. See Fig. 364C. This permits each joist to stay on the 16″ module.

In Fig. 364D are examples of typical door and window components. There are many other possible designs than those shown. Any type of door or window can be used. However, the component must be framed to receive them. The height of the window sill will vary with the window selected. A company could

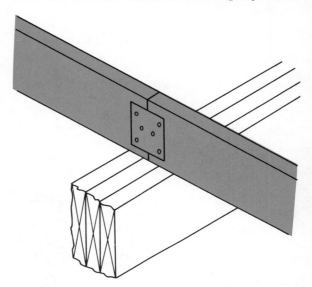

Fig. 364C. In modular construction, floor joists are butted end to end.

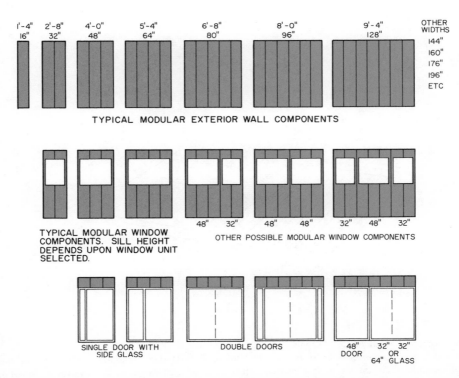

Fig. 364D. These are just a few examples of modular component designs. (National Forest Products Association)

manufacture several window components having the same widths but different window sill heights.

An example of how a typical component is framed is shown in Fig. 364E. It is framed using the same structural standards as conventional construction. The width is based on modular size. This example is 64″ wide. This is equal to four 16″ minor modules. The window opening is the rough opening size. The window unit is installed in this opening. Windows selected are those that fit the module. The finished unit has the window installed and sheathing, siding, and sometimes interior finished wall material in place.

Examples of how outside and inside corners are framed where exterior walls meet are in Fig. 364F and 364G. An outside corner requires that one component have the end stud set-in the thickness of the frame wall it will meet. The sheathing overhangs and is nailed to the second component forming the corner.

Two exterior walls forming an inside corner are shown in Fig. 364G. This requires an extra stud in the component to which the wall is perpendicular.

Application of Modular Components

In Fig. 364H is a plan for the exterior walls of a small house. It is based on a 48″ major module grid. The walls are made up of modular components. Some of the components contain the needed doors and windows. Others are simply solid wall sections. The individual components can be as small as 16″. They can be of any width that permits the use of the 16″ module. Reexamine Fig. 364D for examples.

Assembling a House with Modular Components

The foundation is located and constructed in the same manner as that for the conventional house. The floor joists, cut to the proper length and notched in the factory, are in-

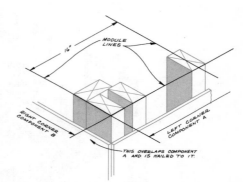

Fig. 364F. The size of the component is from stud to stud. This is typical framing at an outside corner of exterior wall. (National Forest Products Association)

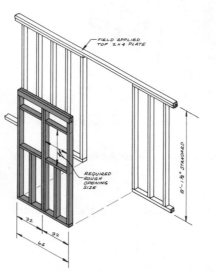

Fig. 364E. Typical framing for window component. This 64″ unit is framed for two windows to fit in the rough opening between studs. Notice that the studs are doubled where the components join. The factory-finished component will have the window installed, sheathing, siding, and often interior wall finish in place. (National Forest Products Association)

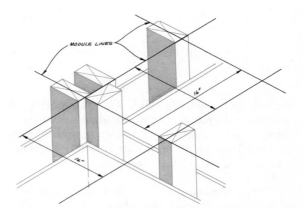

Fig. 364G. Typical framing at inside type corner formed when two exterior walls meet. (National Forest Products Association)

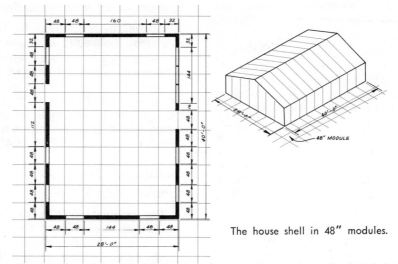

The house shell in 48" modules.

The plan on a grid of 48" modules. The dimensions refer to components, not the actual door or window size.

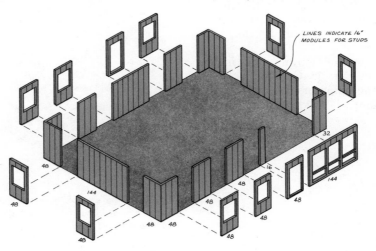

The actual modular components needed to form the exterior of the house plan above.

Fig. 364H. Plans and components for a 48" modular home. (National Forest Products Association)

stalled first. See Fig. 365. The subflooring of tongue-and-groove, plywood sheets covers a great area rapidly. The tongue-and-groove construction helps bind the subfloor together into a well supported, integral unit. See Fig. 366.

After the subfloor is installed, the wall panels are unloaded and placed. See Fig. 367. Usually, the first panels to be erected are those forming a corner, Fig. 368. These panels consist of the studs, sole, plate, sheathing, siding, insulation and the sheetrock on the interior of the panel.

Other exterior wall panels are unloaded and are joined to the corner panels. These panels may contain door openings and windows. Usually, the windows are already installed. Generally doors are installed after the panel is erected. See Fig. 369.

After the exterior wall panels are placed, the gable ends are unloaded and installed. See Figs. 370 and 371.

Next, factory-assembled roof trusses are raised in place, and plywood sheathing is applied. See Fig. 372.

While the roof is being shingled, the remaining exterior details are installed, such as the corner board illustrated in Fig. 373.

Fig. 365. Assembling factory-cut and notched floor joists. Notice the joists are numbered to speed installation. The notches are used to speed location of the joists. (National Homes Corp.)

Fig. 368. Corner panels in place. Notice how panel fits the 2 x 4 fastened to the joists and how siding overlaps at the foundation. The interior surfaces are covered with sheetrock that is factory installed. (National Homes Corp.)

Fig. 366. Installing tongue-and-groove, plywood subfloor. (National Homes Corp.)

Fig. 367. Completed subfloor on a house ready to receive wall panels. Notice panels on truck at left. (National Homes Corp.)

Fig. 369. Tongue-and-groove wall panels being joined. Notice the plate overlap that is used to secure the panels together. (National Homes Corp.)

On the interior, ceiling insulation is applied and sheetrock is installed in the conventional manner. See Fig. 374. The other trades such as plumbing and heating coordinate their work. Frequently, the plumbing is in factory-assembled sections, which are set into the house as a unit.

Fig. 375 shows craftsmen putting the finishing touches on a factory-manufactured house. This particular house was built on a concrete slab which contained the plumbing and heating ducts. The shell for such a house can be erected in a few days by a very small crew.

Fig. 372. Raising factory-assembled roof trusses. Notice that they span the entire dwelling and require no interior supporting wall. (National Homes, Corp.)

Fig. 370. A factory-assembled, gable end being unloaded. Notice that the last wall panel is left out to enable workers to carry in the gable ends and trusses. (National Homes Corp.)

Fig. 373. Installing finish pieces. (National Homes, Corp.)

Fig. 371. The gable end raised into place. Trusses are positioned and ready to be raised. (National Homes Corp.)

Fig. 374. Interior ceiling insulation and sheetrock are installed conventionally. Notice the long lengths of material used. (National Homes, Corp.)

Fig. 375. Nearly completed exterior. (National Homes Corp.)

Building from Modular Units

A *modular unit* is a factory-built, finished, room size or larger section of a building. See Fig. 375A. It usually contains in assembled form all the required parts of that section of the building. Commonly these include interior and exterior wall finish, roof, insulation, floor, wiring, heating, plumbing, and painting. The unit is ready for occupancy within a few days after it is set on the foundation. Generally the only on-site work is the joining of the modules, applying a few trim pieces, and connecting the utilities. The foundation is prepared before the module is delivered to the building site.

There is no standard modular unit design. The designs in use vary considerably. They are the result of research and experimentation of many individuals and companies. The following discussion shows how some companies have designed and put modular units into production.

Modular Units in Residential Design

Following are some general factors to be considered when designing a residence to be constructed with modular units. Various approaches are being used and new designs are being developed regularly.

A preliminary consideration is the overall width and length of the module. Since they are factory-built, they must be moved to the building site. State laws control the size of units that can be moved on highways. In this case they would actually be moved like a

trailer. Laws vary from state to state. In general, trailers over 10' wide require a special permit. Some states permit moving up to a 12' width with a special permit.

It is recommended that the 12' width be used whenever possible. The actual width of the module will vary depending on the eave overhang. A typical width is 11'-9" to the outside of the framing. The 3" remaining are used by roof overhang and trim. The 11'-9" width will normally give an interior room width of 11'-3".

When 12'-0" sections are used, the house can be divided into two equal modules. The division is made along the central bearing wall. See Fig. 375A.

If the width must be held to 10'-0" and a 3" eave is used, the module size will be 9'-9". If the overall 20'-0" width is inadequate, a field-built center section can be added. See Fig. 375B. Here two 10'-0" modules were built with the central hall section added on the job in the conventional manner.

The length of the module is also regulated by state law. The permissable length includes the module and the tractor pulling it. When length is a factor, the cab-over-engine tractor will permit longer modules to be moved.

Height is a third consideration. State laws govern the height of the truck and its load.

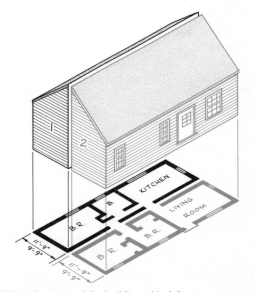

Fig. 375A. A two-module building. Modules are commonly 9'-9" or 11'-9" wide.

A normal maximum height is 14'-0". To meet this requirement, some modules are built with ceiling heights of 7'-6". Low sloped or flat roofs can be used. Low-bed trailers or special-built trailers can reduce the height of the shipment.

Height can be saved by using a thicker but lower floor joist. For example, a 3 x 8 floor joist might be used instead of a 2 x 10. The same adjustments could be made on ceiling joists and rafters.

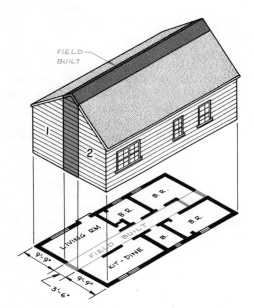

Fig. 375B. A two-module building with a field-built section to add width.

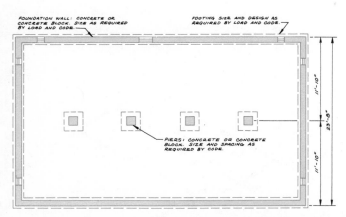

Fig. 376. Typical foundation plan for two-module building. (Small Homes Council, University of Illinois)

Foundation Design

A typical foundation design for modular residential design is shown in Fig. 376. It is built in a conventional manner before the modules are delivered to the building site. The two modules join over the piers. The foundation is designed to carry the live and dead loads exactly the same as a conventional house. In Fig. 376A are sectional views of typical foundation designs.

Floor Construction

Conventional wood framed floor construction is commonly used. The wood headers are doubled around the entire modular unit. See Fig. 376B. If the span is great enough, the headers must be tripled. A 2 x 8 floor joist spaced 16" O.C. would be satisfactory for most designs. Plywood subflooring is generally used. Any type of finished floor can be laid over it.

Wall Construction

The conventional 2 x 4 stud wall system is frequently used. The studs were placed conventionally except on the wall where the

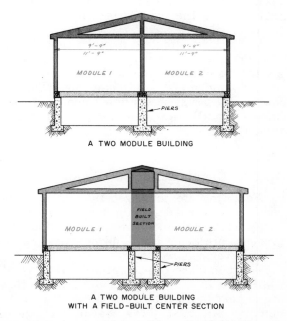

Fig. 376A. A two-module building with field-built center section. (Small Homes Council, University of Illinois)

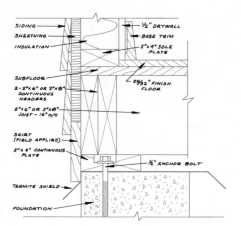

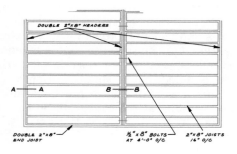

SECTION A-A

modules join. Here the studs were placed flat 16″ O.C. See Fig. 376C. Any type of sheathing or siding can be used. If masonry exterior walls are desired, the wall is sheathed in the factory. The brick is applied on the job. The wall is insulated in the factory in the conventional manner. Door frames in the wall where modules join have split frames.

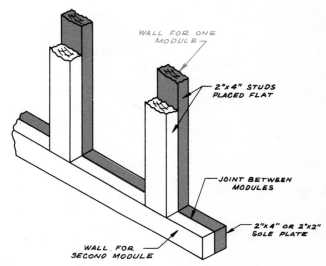

Fig. 376C. Typical design for interior wall joining modules.

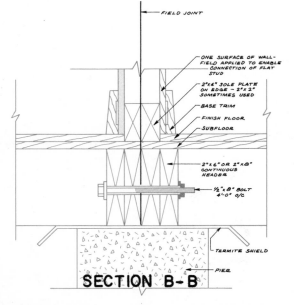

SECTION B-B

Fig. 376B. Typical floor framing plan and construction details. (Small Homes Council, University of Illinois)

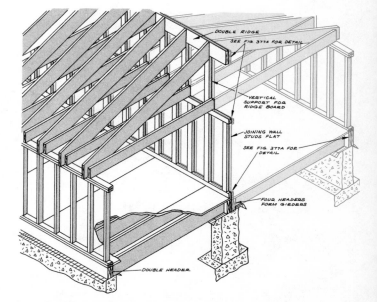

Fig. 377. Typical framing plan for residence made from two modules. (Small Homes Council, University of Illinois)

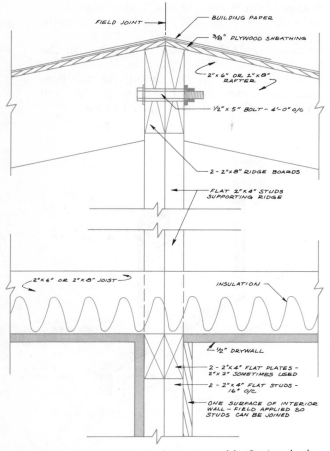

FIELD JOINT

BUILDING PAPER

⅜" PLYWOOD SHEATHING

2"x 6" OR 2"x 8" RAFTER

½"x 5" BOLT - 4'-0" O/C

2 - 2"x 8" RIDGE BOARDS

FLAT 2"x 4" STUDS SUPPORTING RIDGE

2"x 6" OR 2"x 8" JOIST

INSULATION

½" DRYWALL

2 - 2"x 4" FLAT PLATES - 2"x 2" SOMETIMES USED

2 - 2"x 4" FLAT STUDS - 16" O/C

ONE SURFACE OF INTERIOR WALL - FIELD APPLIED SO STUDS CAN BE JOINED

Fig. 377A. The ridge is often supported by 2 x 4 studs above the interior supporting wall. (Small Homes Council, University of Illinois)

Roof Construction

Typical roof construction for a two-module building is shown in Fig. 377. Each module has half the roof. Conventional rafters and ceiling joists are used. The ridge is supported by 2 x 4 studs resting on the interior supporting wall. See Fig. 377A. The ridge boards are bolted together. Conventional roof sheathing and shingles are factory-applied.

Framing for a two-module building with a field-built section is shown in Fig. 377B.

Instead of using rafters, half-section roof trusses could be used. It is designed like a full truss except a vertical member is placed at the end over the interior supporting wall. See Fig. 377C.

Still another approach to roof design is in Fig. 378. Here the roof is pivoted on bolts where the rafters meet the ceiling joists. The module is shipped with the roof in an almost flat position. On the site, the roof is lifted and a kneewall is used to support it. The ridge opening is filled by a small section set in place. This is supported by the kneewall.

The overhang at the eaves can be fastened to the roof in the factory if the extra width does not hinder shipping. It can be field-applied if necessary.

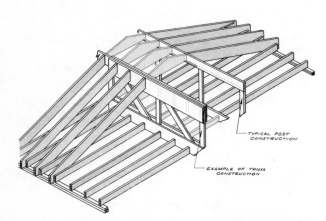

TYPICAL POST CONSTRUCTION

EXAMPLE OF TRUSS CONSTRUCTION

Fig. 377B. Roof construction detail for two-module building with a field-constructed center section. (Small Homes Council, University of Illinois)

Fig. 377C. A half truss used on a modular unit.

Preparation for Lifting

Included in the design is some means of lifting the completed module. The module is designed to be supported from below the floor. It must therefore be lifted from the same place. A common lifting system is to use a cable sling from a crane. These are attached to some type of ring in the top of the module. The ring must be part of a rod that carries through to the bottom of the module. The sling usually goes to the four corners. However, additional cables can be attached to other rings in the walls. See Fig. 378A. The lifting rods are usually removed after the module is set in place.

Mechanical Considerations

On most modular units all wiring, plumbing, heating, and air conditioning requirements are factory-installed. Whatever systems are used, the module must be carefully designed to accommodate them. The problems presented by having to move the unit must be carefully studied. The heating system that is easiest to use is electric. It requires no ducts or central heat generating plant. If central heat is used it appears easiest to run the ducts overhead.

No parts of the plumbing system should extend below the floor joists. Use lightweight plastic drain, waste, and vent piping where accepted. This reduces the weight of the module.

Finishing

Plan for as little on-the-site finishing as possible. Typically a house can be set and finished in three to seven days. The actual time will depend upon the extent of factory finishing. Some modules are completely finished in the factory. Even outside painting is complete. These require some exterior work to conceal the joint between the modules. A board and batten exterior is excellent for this purpose. If horizontal siding is used, a vertical strip can be used. A better appearance results

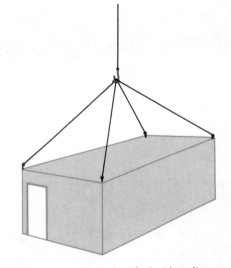

Fig. 378A. Modular units can be lifted with a sling-type hoist.

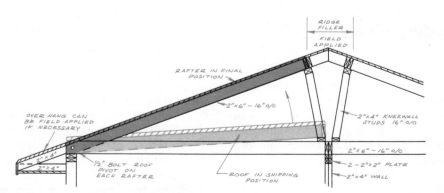

Fig. 378. Another roof framing plan. The roof is shipped in an almost flat position. This reduces the overall height during shipping. On the site, the roof is lifted and supported in place by the kneewall. The ridge filler is set in place. The overhang can be field-applied if the extra width causes shipping problems. (Paxton Prestige Homes)

Fig. 378B. A two-modular residence. This building is designed for a long, narrow lot. (Scholz Homes, Inc.)

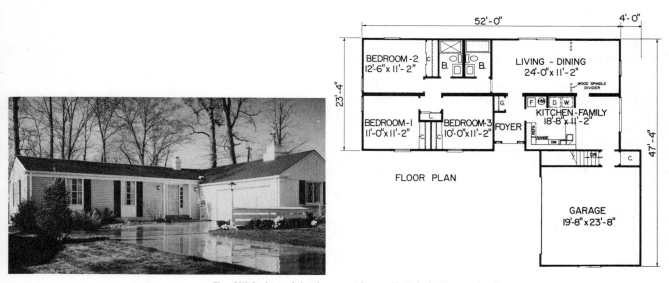

Fig. 378C. A modular house with an ell. (Scholz Homes, Inc.)

if the siding is field-applied over the joint. Masonry veneers are field-applied.

The joint in the floor usually needs field-finishing. If it has tile, the tile over the joint is field-applied. It is easier to cover the joint with carpeting.

Some Solutions

In Fig. 378B is a two-module residence designed for a narrow city lot. Nothing in the exterior apearance indicates it is a factory-built modular house.

A larger ell-shaped residence is shown in Fig. 378C. The house is made of two modules. The garage is field-built from factory-made wall panels.

Modules for Commercial Buildings

A modular building concept using a welded steel frame is shown in Fig. 379. The steel

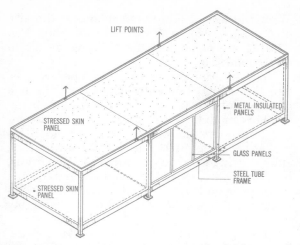

Fig. 379. This module system uses a steel tube frame and stressed skin panels. Notice the lift points built into the structure. They are located so the unit is balanced when it is lifted. (Insta-Buildings, Inc.)

framing provides the structural support for both live and dead loads. The siding, roofing, and flooring panels are attached to it.

In Fig. 379A is shown a bank building constructed from three modules each 12'-0" wide by 40'-0" long. The use of a standard module permitted the designer to plan a small drive-in bank with one module. See Fig. 379B.

Fig. 379A. This is a three-module building. (Insta-Buildings, Inc.)

One Module

Two Modules

Four Modules

Six Modules

Fig. 379B. Notice how the addition of modules enables the designer to expand the activities housed in this bank building. (Insta-Buildings, Inc.)

Fig. 379C. Interior showing the union of two modules. Notice the double steel posts at the line of union. (Insta-Buildings, Inc.)

With the use of additional modules, the size of the bank was expanded considerably. Fig. 379B shows plans for bank buildings using up to six modules.

The interior can have large, open spaces. See Fig. 379C. The only evidence of the line of union of the modules is the double post.

This module is constructed on an assembly line. First the steel frame is welded together. See Fig. 380. The frame has the roof, siding, windows, doors, utilities, partitions, interior siding, carpeting, and other required features installed. The unit is completely finished when it reaches the end of the assembly line.

The units are loaded on trucks for delivery to the building site. See Fig. 380A. At the site they are removed by a crane and set on the foundation. See Fig. 380B.

Fig. 380. The steel frame is welded together. Then the roof, siding, doors, and windows are installed. Interior work is completed next. (Insta-Buildings, Inc.)

Fig. 380B. Each unit is lifted by a crane from the truck and set on the foundation. (Insta-Buildings, Inc.)

Fig. 380A. The finished units are moved to the site. (Insta Buildings, Inc.)

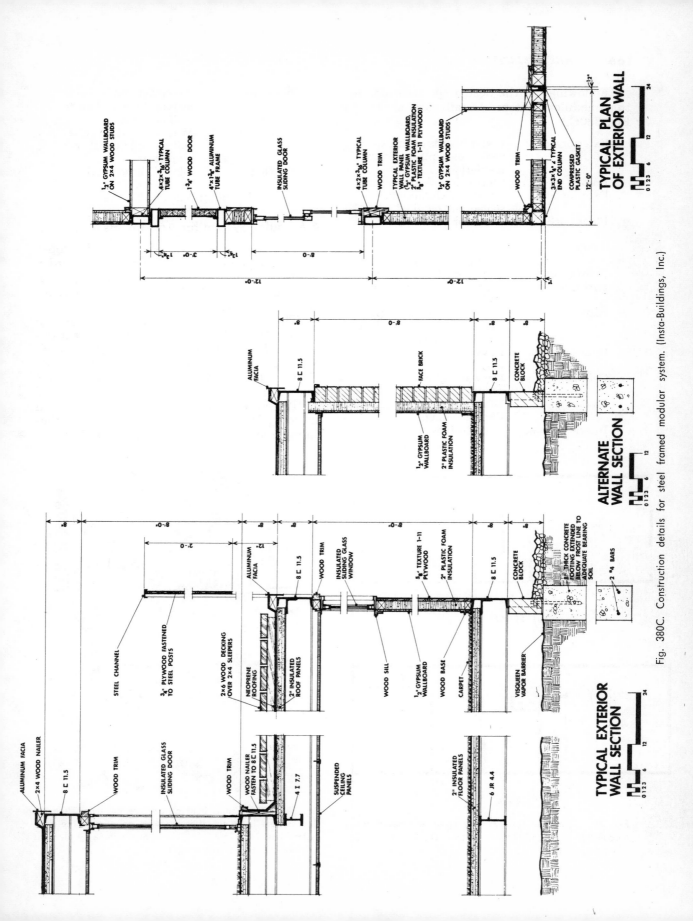

Fig. 380C. Construction details for steel framed modular system. (Insta-Buildings, Inc.)

Following are the design specifications for this modular system. Details are shown in Fig. 380C.

Exterior walls:	Cedar boards or brick veneer over plastic foam insulation.
Frame:	Steel columns and beams.
Exterior trim:	Anodized aluminum, sealed and caulked.
Floor purlins:	6″ junior 4.4 I beams 4′-0″ O.C.
Subfloor:	2″ insulated panel with ½″ plywood underlayment.
Ceiling purlins:	4″ I beam 17.7 4′-0″ O.C.
Partition studs:	2 x 4 construction grade Douglas fir, 16″ O.C.
Roofing:	2″ insulated panel, 5 ply asphalt with 15# felt layer plus vapor barrier.
Interior walls:	Drywall (glued) or wood paneling.
Ceilings:	Drywall (glued) or acoustical.
Floors:	Vinyl asbestos tile, ceramic tile, carpeting.
Interior doors:	1¾″ flush type, birch.
Windows:	Anodized aluminum, awning type or floor-to-ceiling glass.
Insulation:	Walls 1½″ rigid styrofoam, ceiling and floor 2″ rigid styrofoam.
Heating:	Electric baseboard perimeter.
Air conditioning:	Thru-wall units.

A Modular System for Apartments

The system to be described was developed by the Magnolia Homes Division of Guerdon Industries, Inc. as experimental housing under the Federal Housing Administration's Experimental Housing Program.

The basic technique used was to design the apartments in units that could be factory-built and stacked on top of each other on the building site. The final design had two modules; an upper and a lower to make up one apartment. See Fig. 381.

The lower floor module was 12′ wide and 32′ long. It contained a living room, kitchen-dining room, stairwell, and a pantry.

1ST FLOOR

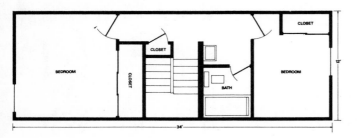

2ND FLOOR

Fig. 381. Floor plan for two-story apartment designed for modular construction. (Magnolia Homes Division of Guerdon Industries, Inc.)

Fig. 381A. The unit is built on an assembly line. Here the floor system is shown. It is mounted on a cart. The floor system has 2 x 6 joists, 16″ on center with ⅝″ plywood subfloor. (Guerdon Industries, Inc.)

The upper floor was a module 12′ wide and 34′ long. It contained two bedrooms with wardrobes, linen closet, complete bath, and stairwell.

The modules were designed using wood frame construction. The interior walls and ceilings were covered with fire-rated sheet rock. These were sprayed with a plaster veneer finish. When dry, this plaster develops a hardness of 3000 psi. This approaches concrete in hardness. The floor surfaces were ⅛″ vinyl asbestos black tile.

A total electric system was used. The heating system used was a baseboard convection radiant heat. There is no forced air system, no blower, no filter, and no register or heat ducts. The radiant heat system was placed on the outside walls. The water heater and cooking stove were electric. Air conditioning was not planned.

All kitchen cabinets had plastic veneer facing. In the bath area, a fiberglass surface pressure laminated to exterior grade plywood was used instead of tile. The exterior sufaces were exterior grade cedar plywood.

The process of constructing and erecting the apartments is shown in Figs. 381A through 383C.

Fig. 381C. Here the walls are being set in place on the floor. Notice the insulation in place on the walls in the background. (Guerdon Industries, Inc.)

Fig. 381B. The walls are assembled on jigs and moved to the floor system with overhead conveyors. The ceiling is also constructed on jigs and carried to the assembly area with an overhead crane. The wall and ceiling units are covered with dry wall and insulated before moving to the floor system. The walls are constructed of 2 x 4 studs 16″ on center. The ceiling has 2 x 6 joists 16″ on center. (Guerdon Industries, Inc.)

Fig. 382. This is a second floor unit on the production line. Notice the waste vent plumbing tree has been set in place. Factory-installed plumbing greatly speeds the erection time on the site. The bath fixtures are all installed in the factory. On the site sewer and water lines are connected to the public utilities. (Guerdon Industries, Inc.)

Fig. 382A. This photo shows the side of the production line where the walls are attached to the floor. Notice the finished wall on the jig ready to be lifted to the assembly line. (Guerdon Industries, Inc.)

Fig. 382C. After the units are assembled, the exterior siding is attached and the aluminum windows are installed. Above and below each window are painted panels. These are painted before they are installed. (Guerdon Industries, Inc.)

Fig. 382B. Plaster being sprayed over interior dry wall material. This eliminates the need to tape the seams between the dry wall sheets. Windows, floors, and appliances are covered with plastic sheets to protect them from the spray. (Guerdon Industries, Inc.)

Fig. 383. Completed units are placed on trailers for movement to the building site. (Guerdon Industries, Inc.)

Fig. 383A. On the site, a first floor module is lifted from its trailer. It will be set on a concrete foundation. Notice the completed units in the background. (Guerdon Industries, Inc.)

Fig. 383C. The second floor module is in place. Notice the crane used to handle the units. In the foreground is a trailer designed to transport the modules.

The roof used was a built-up type with gravel aggregate. It is performed on the site. In this way, the entire row of apartments can have a continuous roof installed at the same time.

There are a few pieces of exterior trim that were applied on the site. (Guerdon Industries, Inc.)

Fig. 383B. The first floor units are set on a masonry foundation. The second floor units are placed on top. The units are joined together with lag bolts. (Guerdon Industries, Inc.)

Fig. 384. The townhouses are bricked on the site as a custom-designed treatment. White antique brick extends to the second level. The top floor has exterior walls of brown cedar shingles. (Guerdon Industries, Inc.)

There are many approaches to modular construction. In Fig. 384 masons are shown installing a brick veneer on a modular-designed townhouse. In this case the lower module was sheathed in the factory. The foundation was designed to support the building and provide a footing for the brick veneer. The brick was installed on the site after the modules were erected.

The floor plan for this townhouse is shown in Fig. 384A. It was designed especially for mass production modular construction. The basic plan is flipped over as units are put together to form a long building. See Fig. 384C. Compare the floor plan in Fig. 384B with the exterior view in Fig. 384C.

Another modular design is shown in Fig. 385. It has four apartments on the first floor and two on the second. In Fig. 385A the five modules used are shown. Some trim and panels were installed on the site.

The factory-produced modules were 12′ wide, 56′ long, and 11′ high. The air condi-

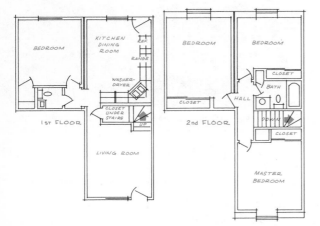

Fig. 384A. Floor plan of modular-designed townhouse. (Guerdon Industries, Inc.)

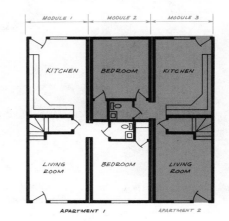

Fig. 384B. First floor, two townhouse units. (Guerdon Industries, Inc.)

Fig. 384C. Exterior of modular apartment building shown in Fig. 384B. (Guerdon Industries, Inc.)

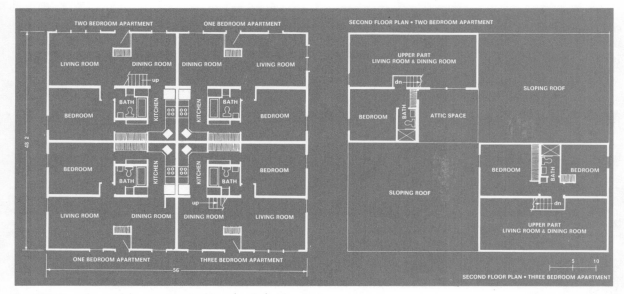

Fig. 385. Plans for modular apartments. (Guerdon Industries, Inc.)

Fig. 385A. Plans showing the five module units for the apartments in Fig. 385. (Guerdon Industries, Inc.)

Fig. 385B. This is a 16-unit modular-designed apartment building. It contains eight one-bedroom and eight two-bedroom apartments. (Scholz Homes, Inc.)

Fig. 386. A colonial exterior on the same apartment complex shown in Fig. 385B. (Scholz Homes, Inc.)

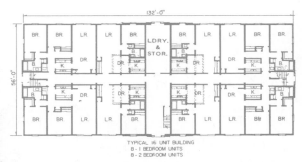

Fig. 385C. Apartment entrance and lobby detail. (Scholz Homes, Inc.)

Fig. 386A. Floor plan for the 16-apartment modular-constructed apartment building in Fig. 385B. Details of each apartment are in Fig. 386B. (Scholz Homes, Inc.)

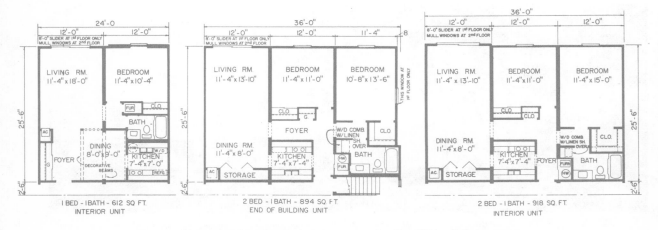

Fig. 386B. Planning details for apartments in Fig. 386A. (Scholz Homes, Inc.)

tioning, furnace, all kitchen equipment, and bath fixtures were installed at the factory. The modules are wood frame construction. The exterior siding is exterior grade cedar plywood. A metal roof was used. All windows are double-insulating glass. Interior walls and ceilings were sprayed-on plaster and grooved cedar plywood.

Another modular apartment complex is shown in Fig. 385B. The details of the entrance are seen in Fig. 385C. Another style exterior is in Fig. 386. The design details of the floor plan are shown in Fig. 386A. This particular building has eight one- and eight two-bedroom apartments.   Details for each apartment are shown in Fig. 386B. An interior view of the living room, dining room, and patio is in Fig. 386C.

It requires two modular units for a one-bedroom apartment. The two-bedroom apartment requires three modular units. The units are 11'-4" or 12'-0" wide depending upon the location. The first floor units are 25'-6" long. The units are stacked with a crane. See Fig. 387. Notice the special sling designed to lift the modular unit.

Steel and concrete is finding use in production line, factory-produced modules. An example is shown in Fig. 387A. This is an office building constructed from 16 steel and concrete modules. Eight modules were used for each level. See Fig. 387B. Any exterior siding can be used. In this example the exterior was a brick veneer.

Fig. 387. Each modular unit is lifted into place. (Scholz Homes, Inc.)

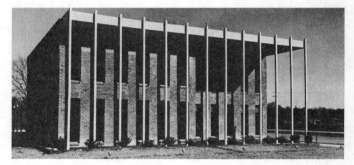

Fig. 387A. This office building was built from 16 rectangular steel and concrete modules. They were 12' wide and 40' long. Eight modules formed each floor. The building was erected in one day. The exterior was bricked after erection. (Guerdon Industries, Inc.)

Fig. 386C. The living room and dining room of a first-floor apartment. Notice the patio area made accessible by sliding glass doors. (Scholz Homes, Inc.)

Fig. 387B. The second floor steel and concrete modules were set in place with a crane. (Guerdon Industries, Inc.)

The structural load is carried in wall columns of structural steel. See Fig. 387C. The steel framed walls may be sheathed and finished with any exterior siding. Notice in Fig. 387C that wood blocking is used around

Fig. 387C. Steel framed walls are welded together. Wood blocking is used around window openings. (Guerdon Industries, Inc.)

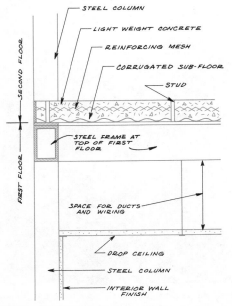

Fig. 388. Detail of union of two modules.

window openings. The wall is cross-braced with steel bars. The entire steel assembly is welded together. The use of steel columns in the wall gives sufficient strength to stack units five stories high.

The floor of the module has a steel perimeter frame. Inside this floor frame is a subflooring of corrugated metal. Steel studs are inserted into the corrugated metal to stretch the steel concrete reinforcing mesh. The studs also serve as a depth gage for pouring the concrete floor. A special lightweight concrete is used. See Fig. 388. In total weight, the modules are lighter, stronger, and more durable than wood frame modules. In cost, the two systems are about the same.

Another advantage to the steel and concrete module is the great reduction of combustible materials used.

In the module shown in Fig. 387B, a suspended ceiling was used. The space between the corrugated steel floor of the second floor unit and the suspended ceiling of the first floor unit was used for ducts and electrical wiring. See Fig. 388.

Mobile Homes

The mobile home today is much larger and more luxurious than the original trailer concept of a few years ago. Approximately 90% of all new single family houses built each year under $15,000.00 are mobile homes. Approximately 5 million people live in mobile homes. About 500,000 mobile homes are built each year. See Fig. 389.

There are about 22,000 mobile home parks. About 65% of all mobile homes are located in established parks. The park provides connections for utilities. They have many other features such as paved roads, swimming pools, a community building, and playgrounds.

Design Standards

The mobile home is a factory-built unit. It is often moved across state lines. The average mobile home buyer is not trained or qualified to recognize many of the technical details of construction. In order to promote a high quality of construction, national standards have been developed for mobile home design and construction. These are sponsored by the Mobile Homes Manufacturers Associ-

ation, National Fire Protection Association, and the Trailer Coach Association. This publication is titled, "Standard for Mobile Homes." It is published by the American National Standards Institute. It is Standard ANSI-A 119.1-1969.

The standard is divided into four parts:

Part I   Construction
Part II   Plumbing Systems
Part III   Heating Systems
Part IV   Electrical Systems

The basic principles set forth in Part I, Construction Standards are:

1. To provide safe, healthful, and comfortable living facilities with adequate storage space and economy of maintenance.
2. To provide adequate natural light and ventilation.
3. To provide structural strength and rigidity sufficient for design loads, both in transit and on site.
4. To provide adequate running gear and hitch for safe transportation of the mobile home.

5. To provide equipment designed and installed for safety of operation, ease of service, and adequate for the intended use.
6. To provide installed materials of adequate specifications to resist deterioration.

Fig. 389. A mobile home on a landscaped lot. (Champion Home Builders Co.)

This is a 12-wide mobile home plan. This unit is 12'-0" x 56'-0". It contains 672 square feet, two bedrooms, and two baths.

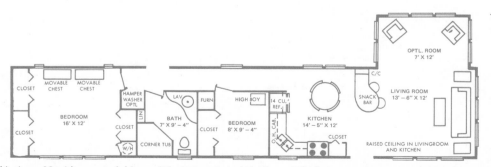

This is a 12-wide expandable mobile home. It is 12'-0" x 59'-0". It contains 792 square foot, one bath, two bedrooms, and an expandable living room.

Fig. 389A. Typical mobile home floor plans. (Mobile Homes Manufacturers Association)

7. To provide against the entrance of water and winds at all joints, connections, and openings in exterior surfaces.
8. To provide arrangement of habitable spaces for fire and health safety.

The *construction* section gives details on structural design requirements for windloads. This includes hurricane and windstorm resistive units.

Heat loss criteria are established. The insulation needed can vary with the climate for which the unit was designed.

The *plumbing system* section is designed to provide the proper functioning of all fixtures, supply lines, and drain lines. It includes traps, cleanouts, fixture connections, shower stalls, water distribution systems, safety devices on water supply tanks and heaters, drainage systems, and vent piping.

The *heating system* section includes LP gas fuel supply systems, gas piping design, oil piping systems, venting of heat-producing appliances, air ducts, air conditioning, and safety devices.

The *electrical system* section is based on the National Electrical Code. It includes material on receptical outlets, branch circuits, load calculations, disconnecting means, branch circuit protective equipment, power supply assemblies and methods of wiring.

Floor Plans

The design of a floor plan for a mobile home follows basically the same principles as for house planning. However, space is at a premium and every square foot requires more careful consideration.

Some typical floor plans for 12'-0" wide homes are in Fig. 389A. A plan for a 24'-0" wide unit is in Fig. 389B. This is called a double wide since it is made from two 12'-0" wide units placed together. In some areas a 14'-0" wide unit is built. Some as long as 70'-0" are available. State highway regulations must be observed when selecting the size of the unit since it must be moved on public highways.

In Fig. 389A notice that one plan has an expandable area to enlarge the living room. This type of home is called an expandable mobile home.

The plans in Fig. 389A and 389B show representative room sizes. The length shown is the actual length of the living area. The length listed by the manufacturer includes the 3'-0" hitch extending beyond the end wall of the mobile home.

Storage is an important aspect of planning. It is necessary to locate storage closets and cabinets carefully. They must be near the area in which the items to be stored are to be used.

A combination kitchen-dining area is used a great deal. See Fig. 389C. Standard size ranges and refrigerators are used. The bath is held to the minimum acceptable size, Fig. 390. Small shower units or corner bath tubs are used. A bath adjoining a bedroom is shown in Fig. 390A. The living area usually is given the largest number of square feet. See Fig. 390B.

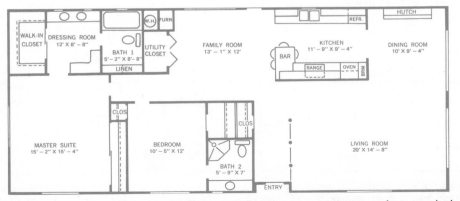

A double-wide mobile home. It is 24'-0" x 56'-0". It contains 1,344 square feet, two bedrooms, family room, two baths, and a utility room.

Fig. 389B. Plan for a double-wide mobile home. (Mobile Homes Manufacturers Association)

Mobile Home Parks

It takes a great deal of planning to design a functional mobile home park. Basically a successful park involves finding a good location, careful site planning, and competent management. The Mobile Homes Manufacturers Association gives these details in their publication, "How to Build and Operate a Mobile Home Park."

Some major factors involving location include:
1. Proper zoning for mobile homes.
2. Will the park fit into the community?
3. Near to community facilities, as shopping, churches.
4. Cost of land and improvements.
5. Availability of utilities.
6. Availability of public transportation.
7. Competition by other parks.

Fig. 389C. A kitchen-dining area with a Spanish influence. (Boise Cascade)

Fig. 390A. This bath is located off the bedroom. (Boise Cascade)

Fig. 390. This bath illustrates the principles of good planning. (Champion Home Builders Co.)

Fig. 390B. A living area with contemporary furnishings. (Boise Cascade)

8. In a developing growing area.

Some major factors to consider when planning the site include:

1. Each home needs a degree of privacy.
2. Mobile homes should form neighborhood clusters. This breaks a large group of homes into small, neighborly communities.
3. Landscaping is essential for privacy and appearance.
4. Provide paved roads to each home. It should be easy to move about the subdivision.
5. Provide parking for two cars for each mobile home. Off the street parking is most attractive.
6. Remember that the mobile homes have to be moved occasionally.
7. Locate utilities so homes can be easily connected and disconnected.
8. Surface water must be drained away.
9. Most parks provide a concrete entry patio on each lot.
10. Sidewalks are needed to move from the home to the parking area.

11. A refuse disposal system must be planned.
12. Locate the community building so it is easily reached by all living in the development.
13. Street lights are very beneficial.
14. Laundry facilities are needed.
15. Recreational facilities are valuable. Playgrounds and swimming pools are frequently built.

There are many ways to plan the mobile home lots. The most commonly used plans are shown in Figs. 390C through 392C.

Angled lots are shown in Fig. 390C. They are positioned so that the front side of the mobile home faces toward the street. Angle lots are usually 40′ to 45′ wide and 85′ to 100′ deep.

Rectangular lots are shown in Figs. 391 through 392C. They can be made perpendicular to the street, as in Fig. 391 or parallel with the street as in Fig. 391B. The perpendicular plan is most frequently used because it permits more lots per lineal foot of street. Notice how the mobile home is near the edge of the lot in Fig. 391A, Part A. This has the disadvantage that the rear door opens on the neighbor's lot. In Fig. 391A, Part B, the home is moved to leave a service area on this side. Notice how the auto parking area in Fig. 391A, Part B forms a part of the service area. This permits the rear side door to be used as a service entrance.

The mobile homes on the rectangular lots in Fig. 391B are near the back of the lot. This is a poor practice because it leaves no room for a patio or access to the rear door. Privacy is at a minimum since the full out door area

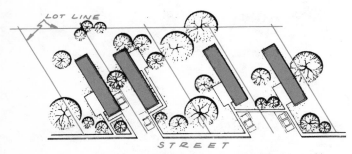

Fig. 390C. Angled mobile home lots. (Mobile Home Manufacturers Association)

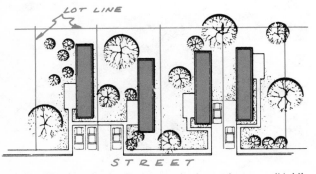

Fig. 391. Rectangular lots perpendicular to the street. (Mobile Home Manufacturers Association)

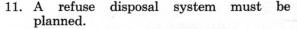
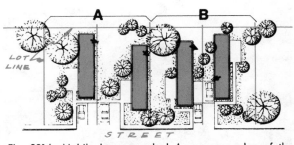

Fig. 391A. Mobile homes marked A are near edge of the lot. This is not a good practice. At B, they are moved to leave a service area. (Mobile Homes Manufacturers Association)

is exposed to the street. This is improved in Fig. 391C. Here the home was moved to the center of the lot.

Radial and cul-de-sac lots are shown in Fig. 392 and 392A. They show design possibilities from curved streets or a looped street end. These lots have the same planning characteristics as the rectangular lots perpendicular to the street. The angular relationship of one home to the other gives a feeling of greater lot size. They can help create small communities within a larger development. A plan for a total development is shown in Fig. 392B.

The community center building can serve many purposes. It can include things as a lounge, recreation facilities such as pool and table tennis, game and meeting rooms, a small kitchen, office for park manager, and laundry facilities. A typical building is in Fig. 392C.

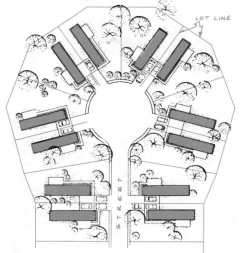

Fig. 392A. These are cul-de-sac lots. (Mobile Homes Manufacturers Association)

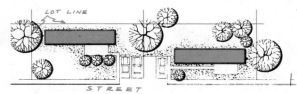

Fig. 391B. This is a rectangular lot parallel to the street. It is a poor practice to put the home near the rear of the lot. (Mobile Homes Manufacturers Association)

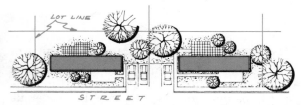

Fig. 391C. On lots parallel with the street, the mobile home should be in the center of the lot. (Mobile Homes Manufacturers Association)

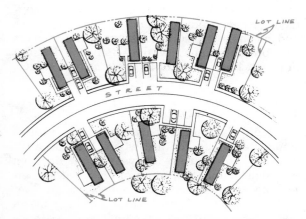

Fig. 392. These are curved street lots. (Mobile Homes Manufacturers Association)

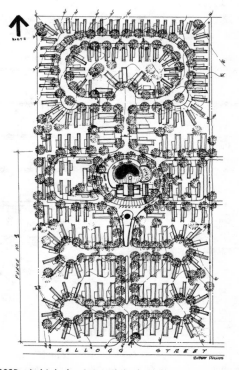

Fig. 392B. A high-density mobile home community. (Mobile Homes Manufacturers Association)

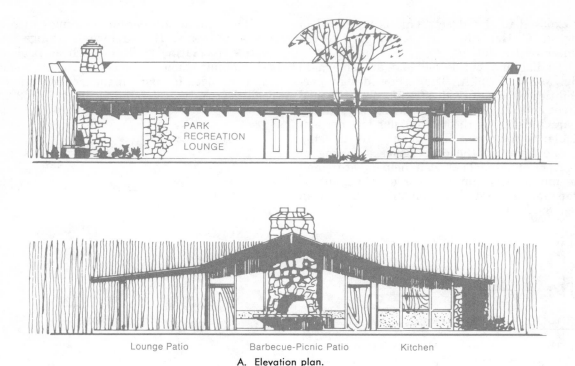

PARK
RECREATION
LOUNGE

Lounge Patio   Barbecue-Picnic Patio   Kitchen

A. Elevation plan.

GAME & MEETING ROOMS   MANAGER

GENERAL STORAGE

Folding Partitions

Telephone

Down

LOUNGE PATIO   RECREATION LOUNGE   FOYER

MEN

Dispensers

WOMEN

Double Fireplace   KITCHEN

BARBEQUE-PICNIC PATIO

B. Floor plan.

Fig. 392C. Elevations and floor plan for a mobile home park community center building. (Mobile Homes Manufacturers Association)

New Developments in House Construction

The field of building construction is one of tremendous importance and size. Hundreds of companies compete to supply materials for building construction. Part of the efforts of the companies is devoted to supplying the commonly accepted materials for conventional construction. However, research and development of new products to do jobs better, easier and cheaper is also a constant activity. This unit presents some new developments that are in recent production or in experimental stages.

Solid Laminated Partitions

Solid, laminated partitions are studless units, developed for use where interior walls are not load bearing. They are built up from a 1-inch, laminated, gypsum core, with interlocking joints where the panels meet. Over this is applied a ½-inch-thick finishing material. These partitions have high fire resistance and impact strength.

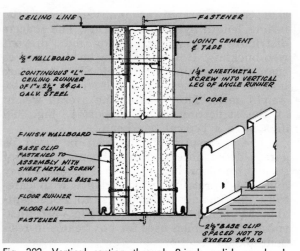

Fig. 393. Vertical section through 2-inch, solid, non-load-bearing, interior partition. (National Gypsum Co.)

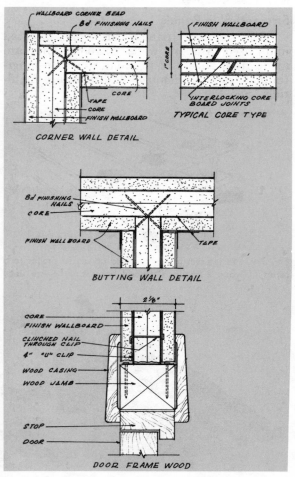

Fig. 394. Horizontal section through 2-inch, solid, non-load-bearing, interior partition. (National Gypsum Co.)

Such partitions save considerable labor cost, due to their rapid installation. Also, they are crack resistant; the finish board is in large sheets and is laminated to the 1-inch core with a special cement.

The exposed joints are taped and cemented in the same manner as in drywall construction. See Figs. 393 and 394 for details.

Box Beams

Box beams are simple in construction. They consist of one or more vertical plywood webs laminated to seasoned lumber flanges

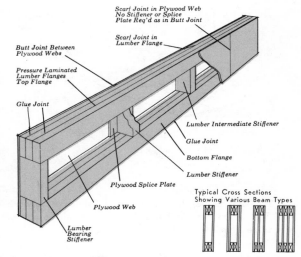

Fig. 395. Typical plywood box beam. (Plywood Fabricator Service, Inc.)

Fig. 396. A typical box beam installation. (Lumber Dealers Research Council)

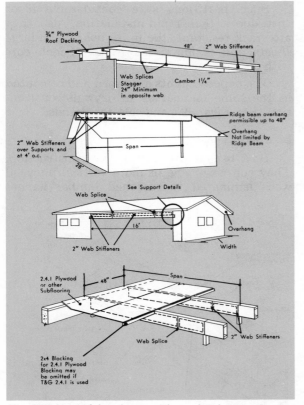

Fig. 397. Uses of box beams. (Plywood Fabricator Service, Inc.) Top to bottom: As flat-roof girders. As ridge beam. As garage lintel. As floor beam.

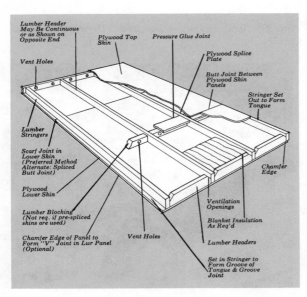

Fig. 398. A stressed-skin panel. (Plywood Fabricator Service, Inc.)

that are separated at intervals along the beam's length by vertical spacers. The spacers distribute concentrated loads and prevent web-buckling. Box beams can be designed to span distances up to 120 feet. Since they are hollow units, they have a high strength-to-weight ratio. This reduces the overall weight of the structure to be supported. Fig. 395 illustrates a typical box beam.

These structural units can be used as garage-door lintels, ridge beams, flat-roof girders, or floor beams as in Fig. 396. They must be fabricated in accordance with carefully developed specifications, to be acceptable for maximum span use. Fig. 397 illustrates the common uses for box beams in residential construction.

Structural data for box beams can be found in Chapter 7.

Stressed-Skin Panels

Stressed-skin panels are prefabricated units used in floors, walls, or roofs. They are made from sheets of plywood glued to longitudinal framing members or other core materials. See Fig. 398.

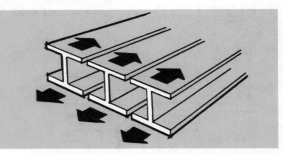

Fig. 399. Stressed-skin panels produce an action similar to a series of wood I beams. (Plywood Fabricator Service, Inc.)

Fig. 400. A typical installation of stressed-skin panels on a roof. (Lumber Dealers Research Council)

Fig. 401. A stressed-skin panel vault. Vaults have honeycomb core with plywood skins. (Douglas Plywood Association)

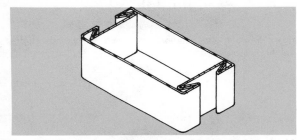

Fig. 402. The basic panel section — interior surface could have paneling or other material built into the assembled panel.

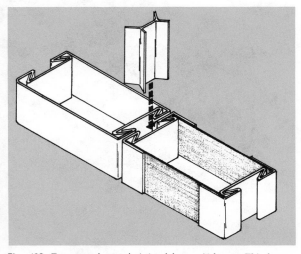

Fig. 403. Two metal panels joined by an X beam. This beam also supports roof weight.

The glue joint between the plywood cover skins and framing members enables the panel elements to act as one unit in resisting loads. The action is similar to a series of adjoining, built-up, wooden I beams. See Fig. 399.

Since these panels are fabricated and can be quickly installed, they save on-the-site labor costs and enable a builder to get a house "under roof" rapidly. They save additional time, because required insulation can be installed as they are manufactured.

These panels are dimensionally stable, light in weight, and have high strength. Fig. 400 shows flat panels, and Fig. 401 shows vaulted panels.

Structural design data for stressed-skin panels can be found in Chapter 7.

Panelized Metal Houses

All-metal, preformed panels have been developed, experimentally, to permit easy, rapid erection of exterior walls. They require no nails, screws, welding or riveting. The panels fit closely so that no adhesives or gaskets are needed.

Such a house is rodent-, termite-, and rot-resistant. It weighs considerably less than the conventionally paneled house and, therefore, requires a much lighter foundation. Insulation can be installed in the panels, before they are assembled.

These panels are designed to be formed in a rolling mill and could be manufactured cheaply in large quantities.

Some details of one experimental system are shown in Figs. 402 and 403.

Aluminum Sandwich Panels

Lightweight wall and roof panels with an aluminum outer skin and a hardboard interior skin are in use. The interior of the panel is made from a phenolic-impregnated honeycomb paper. Houses built with these factory-manufactured panels can be erected in one day. Aluminum channels and angles are used to assemble the panels. See Fig. 404.

Precast Concrete Panels

Houses are being built from lightweight, concrete panels. These panels are 20 inches wide and exhibit all the virtues of concrete. They are fireproof, resistant to vermin and are dimensionally stable. The panels are strong enough to span large distances.

Roofs are framed with wood beams, and the panels are nailed to them. A mastic is used to seal the joints in the roof before the finished roofing is applied.

All joints between the panels are joined with a *T*-shaped metal spline. The vertical joints on the walls are caulked. A system for framing such a house is illustrated in Fig. 405.

Other New Developments

Many new products are being tested in experimental houses. Plastic plumbing is a product receiving considerable interest. It can reduce plumbing costs considerably, and it requires fewer joints, since it comes in long rolls.

Plastic pipe can be joined to fittings rapidly, simply by coating the end of the pipe with a solvent and putting the two pieces together. This, in effect, welds the two pieces together.

Prefabricated wiring is another innovation coming into use. Wall panels are wired in the factory. The service-entrance panel (with appliance outlets, remote-control relays, and branch-circuit feeder boxes) is also made in the factory.

Surface-mounted wiring is available. With this system, a small metal conduit is fastened to the baseboard, with outlets placed where desired. The interior walls are completed, and this wiring is applied over the walls at the baseboard. It is quick and easy to install and can be changed readily. Some companies are experimenting with a special baseboard, with

the wiring built into it. This has the advantage of concealing the wiring and presenting a finished appearance.

Another new development in house construction is the use of power staplers in place of nails. Many parts of a house can be assembled rapidly with a stapler. The application of sheathing, underlayments, asphalt roof shingles, gypsum lath and drywall can be readily performed. See Fig. 406.

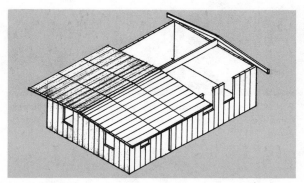

Fig. 405. Roof and exterior walls made of precast, lightweight, concrete panels.

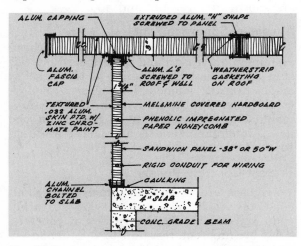

Fig. 404. Section through a house constructed with aluminum sandwich panels.

Fig. 406. Installing shingles with a stapling hammer. (Bostitch)

Build Your Vocabulary

Following are words that you should understand and use as a part of your working vocabulary. Write a brief explanation of what each means.

Conventional construction
Batter boards
Frame construction
Sill
Foundation
Footing
Joists
Studs
Header
Plate
Sole
Partition
Weep holes
Flashing
I beam
Girder
Box beam
Termite shield
Sheathing
Bridging
Subfloor
Perimeter insulation
Furring
Masonry construction
Brick veneer
Trusses
Ridgepole
Valley, valley jack, hip jack
    and common rafters
Caulking
Plancier
Frieze
Facia
Soffit
Eave
Post-and-beam construction
Steel framing
Factory-manufactured house
Prefabrication
Solid laminated partitions
Precast panels
Sandwich panels
Stressed-skin panels
Vapor barrier

Class Activities

1. Locate a house being built by conventional construction methods. Visit it regularly and photograph the various stages of construction. A suggested sequence of photos is given below.
    For a frame house:
    A. Building located on site with batter boards.
    B. Foundation excavated.
    C. Foundation completed.
    D. Floor joists in place.
    E. Exterior walls in place.
    F. Roof framing in place.
    G. All sheathing installed.
    H. Windows installed.
    I. Roofing and siding completed.
    J. Yard landscaped and walks and driveway finished.
    For a concrete-slab house:
    A. Building located on site with batter boards.
    B. Foundation ready to pour.
    C. Floor with plumbing, heating, and electrical wiring installed, before concrete is poured.
    D. Floor after concrete is poured.
    E. Walls erected.
    F. Roof framing in place.
    G. All sheathing in place.
    H. Windows installed.
    I. Roofing and siding completed.
    J. Yard landscaped and walks and driveway finished.

2. Build, to scale, the framing of a conventional house. Cut wood framing materials to a scale of $1'' = 1'-0''$. Tack or glue these together, using the proper house-framing methods. Include interior partitions. The completed project should represent the skeleton framing of a house. Several class members can work together on one house.

3. Using full-size framing members, build sections of a house frame. These should be nailed together. Suggested projects are listed below.
    A. Illustrate box sill construction for western framing. Include sill, header, joists, rough flooring, sole and studs.
    B. Illustrate a typical eave construction for frame house with $2'-0''$ overhang. Include stud, plate, rafter, ceiling joist, facia, blocking, soffit, wall sheathing and wood siding.
    C. Illustrate one method of framing an interior partition into a frame exterior wall. Include subfloor, sole and studs.
    D. Illustrate a common method of framing an exterior corner of a frame house. Include the sole, studs and sheathing.

4. Construct a scale model of a wood frame roof truss.

5. Using clay and wood, construct a scale model of a typical wall section through the sill of a frame house with a concrete slab floor. Use any scale desired. Include gravel fill, perimeter insulation, concrete slab floor, foundation, studs, sheathing, siding and sole.

6. Build, to scale, the framing for a house, using the post-and-beam method. Observe how this skeleton differs from the conventional house framing.

7. Bring samples of building-construction materials to class for examination. These could become a part of a permanent collection for the school drafting area.

8. Using your ingenuity, develop ways to test building materials. Some examples follow:

   A. Support a wood member (2 x 4 x 12′-0″) on each end, and apply a load to the center. This load could be bricks, concrete blocks or metal. Continue to load until the member fractures. Record the number of pounds needed to break the member. Repeat this with several members, and average the breaking load. Compare this average with that reported in a standard load table.

   B. Expose 1-inch wood sheathing and ½-inch sheetrock to the same source of heat. With a thermometer attached to the outer surface, keep a record of temperature changes every minute. After the temperature on the thermometer begins to change, what conclusion can you draw about the insulation qualities of these two materials?

   C. Measure the thickness of a piece of wood siding and a piece of masonite siding. Allow these materials to soak in water several days. Remove and observe the condition of the surface. Measure the thickness. What conclusion can you draw concerning the resistance of these materials to moisture?

9. Find a floor plan for a residence in a magazine or newspaper. Try to plan modular wall components for the exterior walls. If the design does not permit this, change it until modular components can be used. Show the size of each component on the revised floor plan.

10. Develop a design for a small one story residence that can be built as modular units. Draw the floor plan. Draw a section through the unit to show construction details.

Additional Reading

Architectural Record (Editorial Staff), *Time Saver Standards*, pp. 125-137, 147-149, 170-179, 188-197, and 683-685.

Canadian Wood Development Council, "Post and Beam Construction for Residential Buildings," Wood Data Manual No. 2.

Douglas Fir Plywood Association, "The Design of Built-Up Beams with Plywood Webs." *Fir Plywood Technical Data Handbook*, Section 9.

————, "The Design of Flat Panels with Stressed Covers." *Fir Plywood Technical Data Handbook*, Section 9.

Durbahn, Walter E., *Fundamentals of Carpentry*, pp. 49-214.

"Fabrication of Components," Manual No. 2, National Lumber Manufacturers Association, 1619 Massachusetts Avenue N.W., Washington, D. C.

"The Manufactured House," *House and Home*, December, 1960, pp. 106-139.

Michelson, L. C., and Behrend, Herbert, "How to Build and Operate a Mobile Home Park," Mobile Homes Manufacturers Association, 6650 North Northwest Highway, Chicago, Illinois 60631.

National Lumber Manufacturers Association, 1619 Massachusetts Avenue N.W., Washington, D. C. 20036, Technical Services Division publishes an extensive series of Wood Construction manuals.

Ramsey, Charles G., and Sleeper, H. R., *Architectural Graphic Standards*, pp. 8-13, 30-33, 36-38, 49-57, 97-107, 122-134, 198-201, 208-216, 224-228, 263, 276-277, and 279-281.

"Standard for Mobile Homes" ANSI A 119.1-1969, American National Standards Institute, 1430 Broadway, New York, New York 10018.

"The UNICOM Method of House Construction," Manual No. 1, National Lumber Manufacturers Association, 1619 Massachusetts Avenue N.W., Washington, D. C.

U.S. Department of Health, Education, and Welfare, "Wood Frame House Construction," pp. 47-141.

U.S. Federal Housing Administration, "Minimum Property Standards for One and Two Living Units," pp. 72-189.

FOOTING, FOUNDATION AND BASEMENT CONSTRUCTION

If a building has an inadequate foundation and footing, it will settle; the plaster and bathroom tile will crack; doors and windows will be forced out-of-square and not operate properly. It is, therefore, extremely important that the foundation and footings be properly designed.

Footings

A *footing* is a concrete pad upon which the foundation wall is built. It must provide support for the building, without excessive settlement or movement. A footing is to a house as snow shoes are to a person walking on snow. The snow shoes distribute the man's weight over a large surface, thus preventing him from sinking.

Conventional Rectangular Footings

The following factors should be considered when designing and constructing footings:

1. Footings should be made of poured concrete.
2. The concrete should be poured continuously. No load should be placed on a footing until the concrete has thoroughly set up.
3. If a footing trench is dug too deep, the excess space should be filled with concrete.
4. Footings can be poured in earth trenches without side forms if the soil is firm enough to retain its shape.
5. Footings should be protected from freezing.
6. Footing width should be designed to support with safety the load to be placed

upon it. This involves (1) bearing value of the soil, (2) stability of the soil, (3) earth pressure on the foundation and (4) the weight of the house on each lineal foot of footing.

7. In residential construction, a footing should never be less than 6 inches thick. The thickness should never be less than one and one-half times the projection of the footing from the foundation. A much used standard is to make the footing the same thickness as the foundation wall. See Fig. 410.
8. If it is necessary to increase the width of the footing to support the determined load, and if the footing projection exceeds one half the width of the foundation thickness, it is necessary to increase the thickness of the footing. The thickness-to-width ratio of a footing should be kept close to 2 to 1. For example, if a footing is 8″ thick, it should be 1′-4″ wide. If this width is not enough to support the load and must be increased to 1′-8″, then the footing thickness must be increased to one-half of this, or 10″.

Flared Footings

9. If flared footings are used, they should be poured at the same time that the foundation wall is poured.
10. The effective bearing area is figured in the same way as that for rectangular footings.
11. The slope of the flare should not be less than 60 degrees from the normal. See Fig. 411.

Stepped Footings

Stepped footings are a means of cutting the cost of basementless houses built on sloping lots. Stepping the footings down the hill removes the necessity of digging very deep into the hillside, thus eliminating the cost of extra foundation material. See Fig. 412.

12. Stepped footings have horizontal steps and vertical steps. The vertical step should not be *higher* than three-quarters of the horizontal distance between steps. The horizontal distance between steps should not be *less* than 2'-0". See Fig. 413.

13. The horizontal and vertical steps should be poured monolithically (at the same time). Their widths should be the same.

Pier and Column Footings

14. Pier footings and column footings support considerably more load per square foot than do footings under foundation walls. The load on each pier or column should be figured, and footings should be designed that are large enough to carry this load.

    The load per square foot calculated for exterior wall footings cannot be used for pier and column footings.

15. The minimum thickness for a pier or column footing is 8 inches, with a footing thickness of not more than one and one-half times the projection. The usual minimum size of a footing for typical residential construction is 2'-0" x 2'-0". See Fig. 414.

How to Ascertain Foundation Footing Sizes

For the average, single-family residence, footing sizes can be ascertained using the

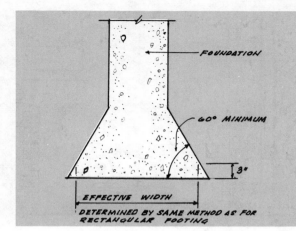

Fig. 411. A flared footing.

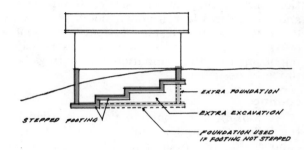

Fig. 412. Stepped footings save labor and materials.

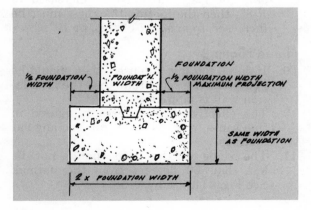

Fig. 410. A rectangular footing.

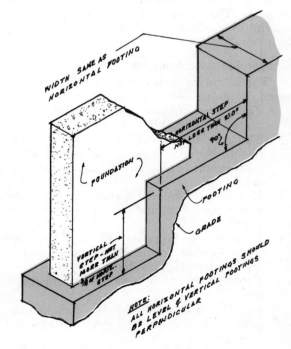

Fig. 413. Stepped footing design details.

Table 3
Standard Footing Sizes for Residential Construction

	FRAME HOUSE		MASONRY OR MASONRY VENEER HOUSE	
	Minimum Thickness in Inches	Projection Each Side of Foundation in Inches	Minimum Thickness in Inches	Projection Each Side of Foundation in Inches
One-Story				
No Basement	6	2	6	3
Basement	6	3	6	4
Two-Story				
No Basement	6	3	6	4
Basement	6	4	8	5

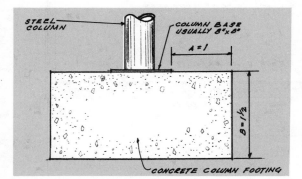

Fig. 414. Typical column footing proportions.

Fig. 415. Live loads bearing on roof.

Table 4
Common Design Loads for Live Loads

Design Factor	Live Load PSF[1]	Dead Load PSF[1]
Floors of rooms used for sleeping area	30	10
Floors of rooms other than sleeping	40	10
Floors with ceiling attached below	—	10
Ceiling joists with limited attic storage	20	10
Ceiling joists with no attic storage	5	10
Ceiling joists if attic rooms are used	30	10
Roof rafters with roof slope less than 3 in 12	20	see roof mat.
Roof rafters with roof slope over 3 in 12	15	see roof mat.

[1]Pounds per square foot

Live load is the weight, or force exerted, by items that are not a part of the building itself. Furniture is an example of a live load. It can be moved about and varied and is not an integral part of the structure.

The roof presents special live-load problems. It is subjected to two live-load forces — wind and snow. See Fig. 415. The actual wind and snow loads vary from one part of the country to another and can be ascertained best by examining local building codes. For sloped roofs in most parts of the United States, it is adequate to figure a combined wind and snow load of 30 pounds per square foot. Flat-roof, load requirements vary widely. Northern states, usually, will require a wind and snow allowance of 40 pounds per square foot; 30 pounds per square foot will suffice in Central states, and 20 pounds per square foot in Southern states. Again, local codes should be consulted. Common design loads for live loads are indicated in Table 4.

The weight to be placed on one lineal foot of footing is calculated by adding the weights of a strip of the house. This strip should be one foot wide, should run from the top of the footing to the ridge and should include all live- and dead-load design figures.

standard sizes indicated in Table 3. Another satisfactory, simple method was shown in Fig. 410.

If a house design may have foundation loads greater than normal, the footing sizes should be calculated. To figure footing loads, it is necessary to ascertain the total load that will be placed upon one lineal foot of footing. Such a load is comprised of two forces – dead-load and live load.

Dead and Live Loads

Dead load is the weight of the materials used to construct the building. This includes the foundation, exterior walls, floors, roof and partitions.

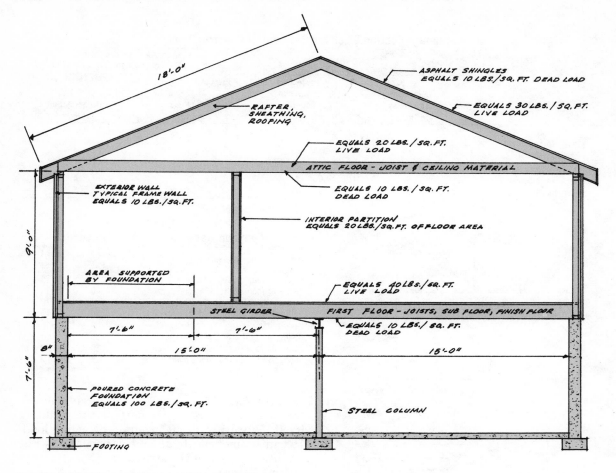

Fig. 416. Typical live and dead loads for a frame house.

The average weights of conventional materials are fairly standarized. Some of these are listed in Table 5.

Footing Design Problems

The following problem illustrates the calculation of weight on a footing and the size of the required footing.

Assume we are calculating the footing requirements for a one-story, frame house built by conventional methods and with standard materials. See Fig. 416. The bearing soil is hard clay. The roofing material is asphalt shingles.

The tabulation of both the live and dead weights of this house is shown in Table 6.

The foundation section is 7'-6" high and 8 inches thick. A 1'-0" section is cut from the house. This gives a foundation surface of 7.5 square feet. An 8-inch concrete wall weighs

Table 5
Average Weights of Conventional Construction Materials[1]

Material	Weight PSF
Concrete wall, 8″	100
Concrete wall, 10″	125
Concrete wall, 12″	150
Concrete block wall, 6″	40
Concrete block wall, 8″	55
Concrete block wall, 12″	80
Brick wall, 4″	35
Brick wall, 8″	74
Brick veneer (4″) over frame wall	45
Brick veneer (4″) over 4″ concrete block wall	65
Typical frame exterior wall with 4″ studs	10
Roof, wood or asphalt shingles	10
Roof, asbestos slate	12
Roof, 3/16″ slate	15
Roof, 3/8″ slate	22
Roof, tar and gravel	15
Interior partitions (per square foot of floor area)	20

[1]Other weights can be obtained from a standards book.

100 pounds per square foot, Table 5; therefore, this 7'-6" section weighs 750 pounds.

The first-floor area of the one-foot-wide slice runs from the foundation to the steel girder in the center of the house. The girder is supporting half of the weight of the first floor; the foundation wall supports the other half. Therefore, the area supported by the foundation is 1'-0" wide and 7'-6" long. This gives an area of 7.5 square feet. The dead weight of the first floor is 10 pounds per square foot, and the live weight is 40 pounds per square foot, giving a total of 50 pounds per square foot. Since the footage held by the foundation is 7.5 square feet, the total weight held is 375 pounds.

The ceiling joist load is computed in the same manner. It is assumed, for this problem, that the attic will have limited storage use.

The roof weight is found by figuring on a one-foot-wide slice of the roof. The roof area, then, is 1'-0" x 18'-0" (rafter length) or 18 square feet. Since the roof has asphalt shingles, the dead weight is 10 pounds per square foot. The average live load is 30 pounds per square foot, giving a total roof load of 40 pounds per square foot. The weight of the roof is then 18 square feet times 40 pounds per square foot or 720 pounds.

The entire length of the rafter is bearing on the foundation, so the entire weight of the roof is supported by the foundation. The steel girder, usually, does not assist in supporting the roof, so no roof load is figured into the load on the steel beam.

The exterior wall section is 1'-0" x 9'-0" or 9 square feet. A typical frame exterior wall weighs 10 pounds per square foot, so 90 pounds is added to the weight on the footing.

The actual load of the partition is bearing more on the steel beam than on the exterior foundation, but since these computations are rough averages it can be assumed to be bearing evenly. A one-foot strip of floor area equals 15 square feet; half of this amount is assumed to be bearing on the exterior foundation. The dead load for the partition is 20 pounds per square foot of floor area (7.5 square feet). This adds 150 pounds to the total load.

These figures show that approximately 2310 pounds is bearing on each lineal foot of footing. The house is built upon hard, dry clay which offers 3 tons or 6000 pounds of support to each square foot of footing bearing

upon it. See Table 7. The normal footing required for this house is 1'-4" wide. A one-foot slice of this offers 1.3 square feet of surface bearing on the soil. This will offer support to 6000 pounds per square foot times 1.3 square feet or 7800 pounds. Since support for only 2330 pounds per square foot is needed, the standard footings are more than ample.

If the soil were soft clay, it would support one ton or 2000 pounds per square foot. On this basis, the standard footing would offer support to 2000 times 1.3 square feet per lineal foot of footing or 2600 pounds; this, again, is quite adequate for the frame dwelling being constructed. If, however, the house were built with an 8-inch solid masonry wall, the one-foot slice of the house would weigh 2906 pounds, and the 1'-4" footing would be inadequate. Increasing the width of the footing to 1'-6" would give a footing surface of 1.5 square feet per lineal foot or a load bearing support of 3000 pounds, which is adequate. However, this increases the footing projections to 5 inches, instead of 4 inches. While this is somewhat beyond the desired 2 to 1 ratio between footing thickness and width, it is not enough to change the proportions. If the projection of the footing had to be increased

Table 6
Example of Load Calculation for a Residence

Part	Size	Square Feet	Weight PSF	Total Weight in Pounds
Foundation	8" x 1'-0" x 7'-6"	7.5	100	750
First Floor	1'-0" x 7'-6"	7.5	50	375
Attic Floor	1'-0" x 7'-6"	7.5	30	225
Roof	1'-0" x 18'-0"	18.0	40	720
Exterior Wall	1'-0" x 9'-0"	9.0	10	90
Partitions	1'-0" x 7'-6"	7.5	20	150
Total Load				**2310**

Table 7
Average Safe Loads of Soils

Soil Type	Safe Load (Tons PSF)[1]
Soft clay; sandy loam	1
Firm clay; sand and clay mix; fine sand, loose	2
Hard dry clay; fine sand, compact; sand and gravel mixtures; coarse sand, loose	3
Coarse sand, compact; stiff clay; gravel, loose	4
Gravel; sand and gravel mixtures, compact	6
Soft rock	8
Exceptionally compacted gravels and sands	10
Hardpan or hard shale; sillstones; sandstones	15
Medium hard rock	25
Hard, sound rock	40
Bedrocks, such as granite, gneiss, traprock	100

[1]Safe load in tons per square foot of bearing surface of the footing.

several inches, then the footing thickness would also have to be increased to maintain something near the 2 to 1 ratio desired.

Footing for Piers and Columns

The weight placed upon a pier or column is concentrated on a small area. It is important that this footing be designed properly, to prevent the house from settling and sagging. (The term *column* refers to a wood or metal post used to support a beam. A *pier* is a masonry unit, usually 12 to 16 inches square, that supports a beam.)

An examination of Fig. 417 indicates why a pier or column footing carries a greater, concentrated load than a foundation footing. The column supports all the floor load extending halfway from the column to the founda-tion wall or to another column. In Fig. 417, the distance from the column to the foundation wall on the width of the house is 15'-0". Half of this is supported by the column. The same is true for the opposite direction; so a total width of 15'-0" of floor is supported by the column.

The column in Fig. 417 is located 10'-0" from the foundation wall on the length of the house. It supports half of this or 5'-0". It is also 10'-0" from the next column. Since the second column supports half this load, the first column supports only an additional 5'-0". The *total area* supported by the column is 15'-0" x 10'-0" or 150 square feet.

Assuming this column is the one indicated in Fig. 416, the total load on the footing would be as shown in Table 8.

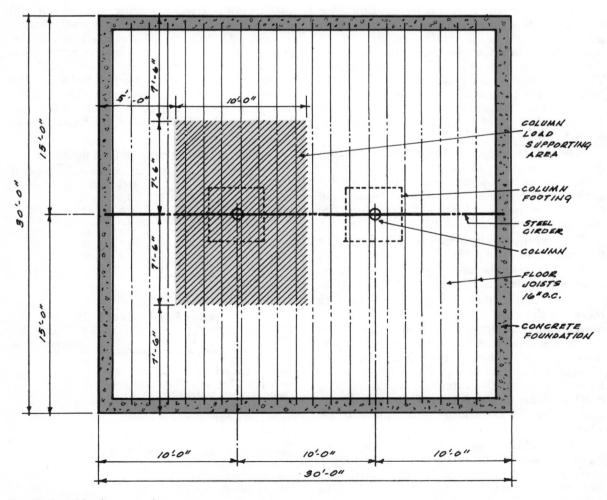

Fig. 417. A pier loading example.

Table 8
Example of Load Calculation on Pier Footing

Part	Square Feet	Weight PSF	Total Weight (Pounds)
Attic floor	150	30	4,500
First floor	150	50	7,500
Partition load	150	20	3,000
Total load on column			**15,000**

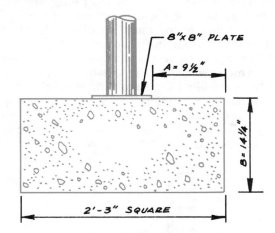

Fig. 418. Solution to typical column footing problem.

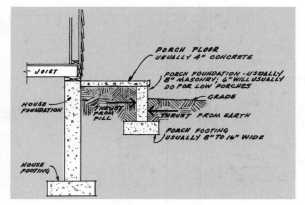

Fig. 419. Typical porch construction.

If a partition is directly over a column, it can be assumed that the column supports the entire weight. In such a case, the partition weight can be assumed to be 110 pounds per lineal foot of partition bearing on the column.

If this house is built upon hard clay soil, the soil will support 6000 pounds per square foot. The area of the footing required is ascertained by dividing 15,000 pounds by 6000 pounds per square foot; this equals 2.5 square feet. By taking the square root of the area, the length of the sides of the footing is found.

The sides of the footing should be approximately 2.23 feet or about 2'-3''. Fig. 418 indicates the solution to this problem. As the projection beyond the steel base lengthens, the footing must be made thicker. The proportion between projection *A* and thickness *B* should be close to a 1-to-1½ ratio.

Since, in this instance, the footing has to be 2'-3'' square to support the load properly, the projection is 2'-3'' minus the 8-inch base divided by 2. This gives a projection of 9½ inches on each side of the base. The thickness must be one and one-half times the projection or 14¼ inches.

If a footing has a large projection and the thickness is not increased, the projection may crack and break away.

Chimney Footings

A chimney is very heavy. It cannot be supported by the foundation footing, but must have a special footing poured for it. The procedure for calculating the proper footing size is the same as that for a pier or column, except the weight to be considered is the actual weight of the materials in the chimney.

Common brick weighs 120 pounds per cubic foot. The number of cubic feet of brick in the chimney should be ascertained, and then, this should be multiplied by 120 pounds.

Since most chimneys have a tile flue lining, the weight of this must be considered.

The base of most chimneys is quite large. Generally, it is as large as the size required for the footing. If this is the case, the footing is made approximately 6 inches larger than the chimney base, to increase the stability of the unit.

Porch and Stair Footings

The usual porches and stairs built are light enough that they require no footings. The end surface of a porch wall is sufficient to support the weight of the wall and the porch floor. However, it is a common practice to pour a footing about twice as wide as the foundation wall, to help stabilize the wall and to help overcome the thrust of earth up the foundation wall. See Fig. 419.

Depth of Footings

Footings must be below the frost line of the area in which the building is to be built. The *frost line* is the depth to which the soil

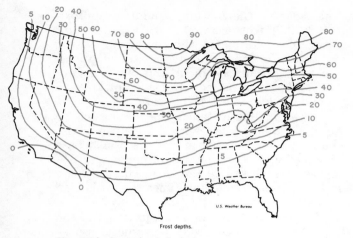

Fig. 419A. Frost depth in inches.

freezes. Freezing and thawing cause the soil to expand and contract. This generates great force. If the soil beneath a footing freezes it causes the foundation wall to move. This often causes cracks.

In Fig. 419A are the minimum footing depths for the United States based on the frost line of the area. This map only gives a general picture. Before designing a building, local building codes must be checked. They will specify minimum footing depths.

Footings must rest on natural, undisturbed soil which will provide adequate bearing. Footings on filled land must meet local codes for such construction. When the bearing capacity or stability of the soil is questionable, soil analysis, bearing tests, or special footing designs may be required.

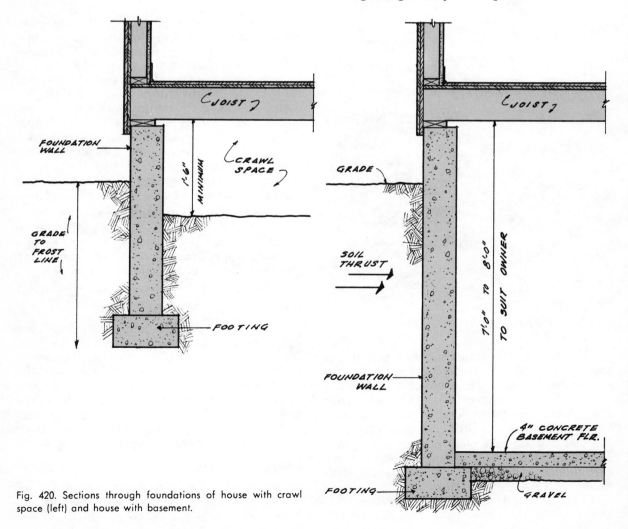

Fig. 420. Sections through foundations of house with crawl space (left) and house with basement.

Foundations

A foundation serves as the base upon which a house is built. It holds the house above the grade level and keeps the area under the house dry.

There are many kinds of foundations that can be used successfully. The type chosen depends upon many factors. If a basement is desired, the foundation forms the basement wall. If a house is to be built over a crawl space, the foundation may be a masonry wall or piers. A curtain wall may become part of a foundation. In areas where the soil does not offer sufficient support for usual foundations, pilings must be used to support the foundation wall.

Basement Construction

If a house is to have a basement, the foundation must be designed to serve also as the basement wall. It must withstand the thrust of the soil and repel surface and subsurface water. It also must resist the action of freezing and thawing, which can cause a building to rise and fall slightly and break in places. Fig. 420 illustrates a house with a basement wall as a foundation, as compared to the same house with a crawl space.

Poured concrete foundation walls are considered best for residential basement construction. The entire foundation is poured at one time, thus becoming a single, integral wall. It tends to crack less and leak less than other types. Unskilled labor can be used to place the forms and pour the walls, while walls built of concrete blocks and other masonry

units require highly paid masons to build them.

Concrete-block foundation walls are used widely for basement construction and are very satisfactory if carefully laid. Since the blocks are large, a foundation can be rapidly constructed. Blocks are very useful in areas where ready-mixed concrete is not easily available.

Foundations for Crawl Spaces

If a house is to be built over a crawl space, the foundation is made exactly the same as explained for the basement. The same materials and sizes are used. The only difference is the foundation for the house with the crawl space is dug only to the frost line or to a solid soil, whichever is the deeper. See Fig. 420.

The ground level should be at least 18 inches below the bottom of the floor joists and

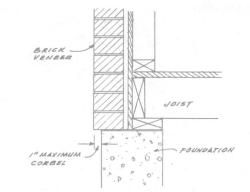

Fig. 421. Brick veneer corbelled over foundation.

Table 10
Standard Thicknesses of Residence Foundation Walls

TYPE OF FOUNDATION WALL CONSTRUCTION	MAXIMUM HEIGHT OF UNBALANCED FILL[1]	MINIMUM WALL THICKNESS (in Inches)	
		Frame	**Masonry or Masonry Veneer**
Hollow masonry, such as concrete block	3	8	8
	5	8	8
	7	12	10
Solid masonry	3	6	8
	5	8	8
	7	10	8
Poured concrete	3	6[2]	8
	5	6[2]	8
	7	8	8

[1]Height in feet of finish grade above basement floor.
[2]Provided forms are used on both sides for full height of wall.

12 inches below the bottom of the girders. Usually it is best to try to get 2'-0" or more. This permits easier access to plumbing, wiring and furnace connections that are below the floor. The larger space also allows more air to circulate below the joists, thus reducing moisture damage.

If moisture is a problem, the soil beneath the joists should be covered with a vapor barrier, with several inches of sand on top.

Foundations for Basements and Crawl Spaces

The thickness of the foundation wall should not be less than that of the exterior wall of the house supported, except that exterior walls of masonry veneer over frame construction may be corbelled one inch maximum. See Fig. 421.

Table 10 illustrates standard foundation wall thicknesses for residential construction. This table may be used for normal conditions.

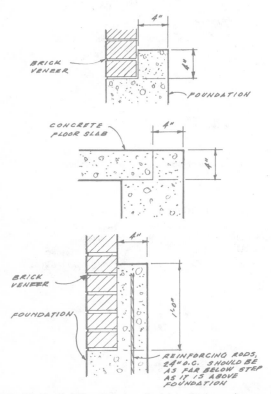

Fig. 422. Top of foundation reduced in thickness for special application.

The upper portion of the foundation can be reduced in thickness to 4 inches, to permit placement of brick veneer or to permit the edge of a concrete floor slab to rest on the foundation. This reduced 4-inch portion should not exceed 4 inches in height. If it does, reinforcing rods are required. Seldom should this height exceed 12 inches, even if reinforced. See Fig. 422.

Waterproofing Foundations

In order to perform its total function, the foundation should repel all water that runs against it. If a house does not have a basement, the foundation still should be expected to shed water and to keep the area under the house dry.

A number of things can be done to prevent water from penetrating a foundation. An easy thing to do is to bank the earth up against the foundation so the soil slopes away from it. This provides a natural drain away from the house for surface water.

Drain tiles are of great value in helping to carry away water found below the surface. These tiles are placed in a 2-inch thick, gravel bed just above the footing. They are placed ¼ inch apart, and this space is covered with building paper. The tiles are sloped so they drain to a storm sewer or dry well. See Fig. 423. About 6 inches of coarse gravel or crushed rock is placed over the tile.

Poured concrete foundations can be waterproofed by applying at least one coat of bituminous material to the wall. For severe conditions, several layers of bituminous ma-

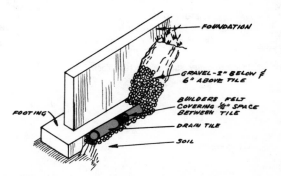

Fig. 423. Drain tiles used to carry away subsurface water.

Fig. 424. Polyethylene film being applied to basement wall. (Union Carbide Corp.)

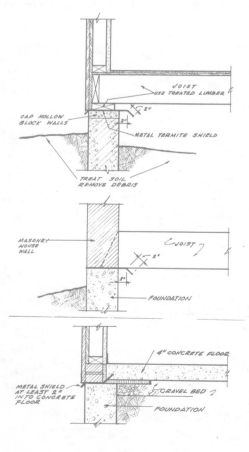

Fig. 425. Methods for installing metal termite shields.

terial can be applied or builder's felt can be adhered to the foundation. Polyethylene film (a plastic) is widely used as a waterproofing material. It comes in large sheets and is adhered to the exterior of the foundation wall. See Fig. 424.

Termite Protection

In almost every part of the United States a small, destructive insect called the termite exists. It lives in large colonies beneath the surface of the earth and thrives on the cellulose of wood.

Actually, two classes of termites exist — the subterranean and the nonsubterranean. The subterranean termites, who need moisture to live, do the greatest damage to buildings. They tunnel through the earth and consume any wood in their path.

These insects build mud tunnels up foundation walls and infest the wood portions of a house. They actually consume the wood, leaving only a thin shell to protect themselves. Any wood members thus damaged must be replaced, as they have little structural value.

The nonsubterranean termites are able to live in dry wood and without moisture or a colony in the ground. They are fewer in number and do less damage than the subterranean termite.

Several things can be done to reduce the danger of termite infestation. After a house is completed, all wood scraps should be removed. Any scraps buried in backfilling or grading become possible pockets for termite growth. From here they can tunnel into a house.

Poured concrete walls best resist penetration, since termites can get through the smallest crack in a foundation. If a foundation wall is built of hollow concrete block, these insects can crawl unobserved up the inside of the wall and attack the sill. To help prevent this, hollow walls should be capped with a solid masonry block, or they should have a metal termite shield installed, Fig 425. This tends to repel the insect, but is far from perfect protection. Termites can penetrate the masonry cap if it has a tiny crack, and they have been known to build their clay tunnels around metal shields.

The wood members likely to be infested can be treated with a chemical that repels

termites. The chemical can be brushed or sprayed on; however, it is much more effective to use lumber that has been treated under high pressure. By this method, the chemical is forced *into* the wood.

Another very effective preventative measure is to treat the soil with a termite-repellent chemical. Soil beneath concrete floors should be treated before they are poured and also the soil around footings and foundation walls. Termites cannot live in the treated soil around the house; yet plants and grass are not affected. The chemical usually is applied by trained exterminators who guarantee their work for many years.

As the house is being designed and built, some of these termite-repellent methods should be used. Usually no one method will suffice, and a combination of several will be necessary.

Piers, Columns and Curtain Walls

The purpose of a pier or column is to provide a foundation to support a load placed upon it. Usually piers are freestanding masonry units, while columns are usually steel or wood members. See Figs. 426 and 427. A *curtain wall* is a masonry wall built between piers. It is not as thick as a pier, but does help carry some load. However, the pier carries the main load. See Fig. 428.

Pier Design

Freestanding piers are divided into two classes — exterior piers and interior piers.

Exterior piers are subject to a load from above, as well as a horizontal load due to the wind. Such piers must be either poured concrete, solid masonry or hollow masonry with the cells filled with concrete to make a solid unit.

The freestanding exterior pier should not be built over three times its least dimension above grade, unless special reinforcement is added.

Interior piers usually are not subject to wind load. They can be poured concrete, solid masonry or hollow masonry. If hollow masonry, they should be topped with 4 inches of solid masonry, or the top masonry course should be filled with concrete.

An interior pier can be built above grade ten times its least dimension (if it is concrete or solid masonry) or four times its least dimension (if hollow masonry). See Fig. 429.

Piers supporting frame construction should extend at least 12 inches above finished grade.

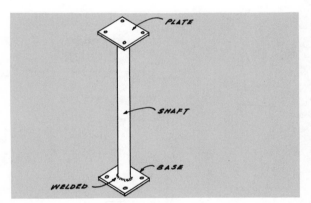

Fig. 427. Typical round steel column.

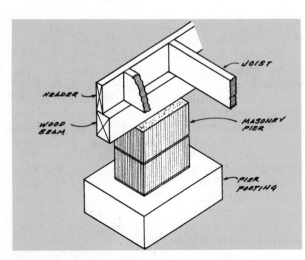

Fig. 426. Typical masonry pier.

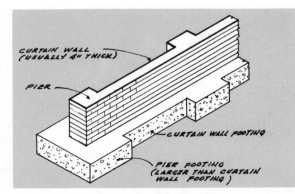

Fig. 428. Typical pier-and-curtain-wall foundation.

Table 11
Standard Pier Design Data for Single-Story Residences on Average Soil

PIER MATERIAL	MINIMUM PIER SIZE (in Inches)	MINIMUM FOOTING SIZE (in Inches)	PIER SPACING	
			Right Angle to Joists	Parallel to Joists
Solid or grouted masonry	8 x 12	12 x 24 x 8	8'-0" o.c.	12'-0" o.c.
Hollow masonry, interior pier	8 x 16	16 x 24 x 8	8'-0" o.c.	12'-0" o.c.
Plain concrete	10 x 10 or 12" dia.	20 x 20 x 8	8'-0" o.c.	12'-0" o.c.

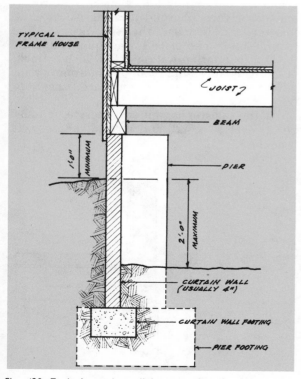

Fig. 429. Round, poured, interior concrete piers. (Lumber Dealers Research Council)

The actual size and spacing of piers should be determined by the load they must support. Table 11 gives pier design data usable for single-story residences built on average soil.

Pier with Curtain Wall

The use of a curtain wall with pier construction is limited to houses without basements. A basement requires a full foundation wall.

Since the curtain wall helps carry some of the load, braces the pier and helps resist the wind, an exterior pier can be built higher if it is combined with a curtain wall. See Fig. 430. A pier with a curtain wall can be

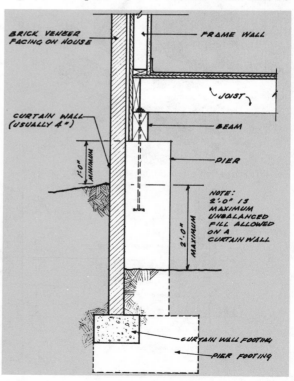

Fig. 430. Typical curtain wall between piers for frame construction.

Fig. 431. Typical curtain wall between piers for brick veneer over frame construction.

built ten times its least dimension above the footing, if it is concrete or solid masonry; it can be built four times its least dimension, if it is hollow masonry. Table 11 can be used as a guide for spacing piers with curtain walls. A curtain wall can be safely built above the footing to a height fourteen times the thickness of the curtain wall, if it is concrete or solid masonry; and ten times the thickness of the curtain wall, if it is hollow masonry.

Most curtain walls are made from one, 4-inch course of brick. The thrust of the earth against such a wall is great. Therefore, no 4-inch curtain wall should have more than 2'-0" unbalanced fill placed against it. See Fig. 431.

The curtain wall must be bonded or anchored to the pier so the two become a single unit. The pier and curtain-wall footing should also be a single, integral unit.

It is possible to support a brick veneer facing on a building up to one and one-half stories high on a curtain wall with sufficient footing to carry the weight. Refer to Fig. 431.

Pilasters

A *pilaster* is a masonry unit used to support the ends of beams or to stiffen a long foundation wall. See Fig. 432. The pilaster must be bonded to the foundation wall so the two become an integral unit.

If a foundation wall is very high or long, pilasters can be added about every 20 feet to help brace the wall against the soil pressure. In the typical residence this case seldom occurs.

More frequently, pilasters are used to provide the necessary support for the ends of beams on the foundation. A beam requires at least 4 inches of solid bearing surface. A pilaster can increase the thickness of the foundation at one place for adequate support.

If a foundation wall is only 6 inches thick, or if it is an 8-inch hollow masonry wall, pilasters are required for adequate beam support.

If the pilaster is poured concrete, it must be at least 2" x 12" and if solid masonry, it must be 4" x 12".

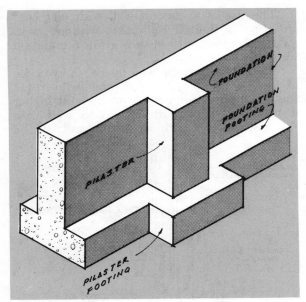

Fig. 432. Pilaster on a foundation wall.

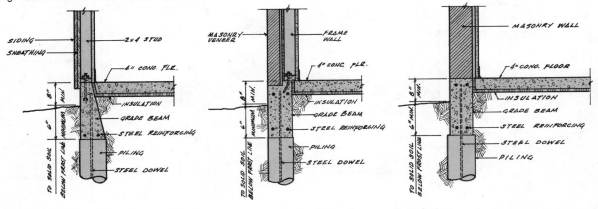

Fig. 433. Grade beam and piling construction for slab floor on grade.

Grade Beam on Piling Foundation

Upon occasion, a residence may be constructed upon pilings. A *piling*, as used in residential construction, usually is a concrete pier sunk into the ground. Frequently, it is cast in a hole dug in the ground or cast in a steel shell in the ground. The shell then is removed.

This type of construction can be used for normal residential construction and, generally, is used in areas where the soil cannot adequately support footings at the usual depths. The pilings are spaced in a manner similar to that discussed under piers. See Chapter 19 for more details.

On top of these pilings a poured concrete, grade beam is placed. This beam forms the foundation wall upon which the house is built. A house built this way does not have a basement. It can have a crawl space or a concrete slab on grade. The examples in Figs. 433 and 434 illustrate some common methods of construction of this type of foundation.

The following design factors are satisfactory for single-story residences built under normal conditions. If soil is of such a nature that it has unusually poor bearing qualities, pilings of larger diameters must be used.

1. Piling should be spaced 8'-0" o.c. maximum.
2. Piling should be at least 10 inches in diameter.
3. Piling should extend below frost line and have a bearing area of 2 square feet, for average soil.
4. Piling should have one, No. 5 bar running full length of piling and into grade beam.
5. Grade beam for frame construction should be at least 6 inches wide by 14 inches high.
6. Grade beam for masonry and masonry veneer construction should be 8 inches wide by 14 inches high.
7. Grade beam should have four, No. 4 steel bars for frame construction or four, No. 5 steel bars for masonry and masonry veneer construction.
8. The bottom of the grade beam should be below the frost line, unless provision

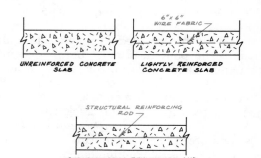

Fig. 435. Common concrete slabs.

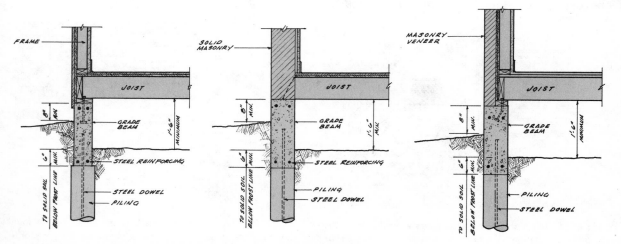

Fig. 434. Grade beam and piling construction for house with a crawl space.

is made so that moisture does not collect under the beam. Coarse rock or gravel should replace the soil under the grade beam, to enable moisture to drain away. If this is not done, freezing will cause the house to heave.

Slab Foundation and Floor

The design of the foundation and floor of a house to be built with a concrete slab requires consideration of the soil properties and size of the slab. There are four basic slab designs. The first is an *unreinforced* slab. See Fig. 435. It depends upon support from the fill below. This slab will crack when subjected to tension or warping. It may crack while drying due to shrinkage. The unreinforced slab must be in an area providing excellent drainage. It should be at least 4″ thick. Seldom are slabs larger than 32′-0″ in length poured. If a larger slab is needed, control joints should be provided. If a nonrectangular slab is to be poured, it must be divided into rectangular elements. Control joints are used at these places. Heating coils and pipes cannot be used in unreinforced slabs. The stresses generated by the heat will crack the slab.

A second slab is the *lightly reinforced* slab. It is reinforced over its entire area with a welded wire fabric reinforcement. See Fig. 435. The most common wire fabric used has a 6″ x 6″ square. The wire fabric resists stresses of drying shrinkage. It also helps resist cracking due to temperature change. This is required when heating pipes are embedded in the slab. The wire fabric helps the

slab resist some warpage and slab movement without cracking. This type of slab should be at least 4″ thick. It requires the support of the fill beneath the slab.

The lightly reinforced slab can have perimeter dimensions up to 75′-0″ without a control joint. Nonrectangular shapes are handled the same as stated for unreinforced slabs.

A third type of slab is the *structurally reinforced* slab. The slab is reinforced with steel reinforcing rods. While it still depends upon the fill beneath the slab for support, the

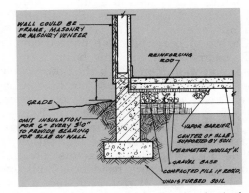

Fig. 435B. This slab is supported on the edges by the foundation. The compacted soil supports the remainder of the slab. This design is usually used for structurally reinforced slabs.

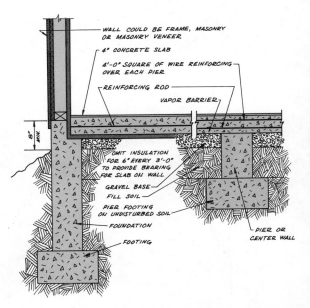

Fig. 435C. This slab is supported on the edges by the foundation. The center of the slab is supported by piers or a center wall.

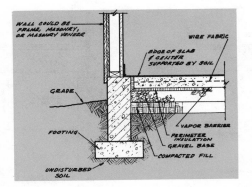

Fig. 435A. This slab is supported entirely by the soil underneath. This design is usually used with unreinforced and lightly reinforced slabs.

reinforcing enables the load to be distributed over a larger portion of the slab. See Fig. 435.

The *independently supported* slab is used where soil is very poor and will not support a ground-supported slab. The slab is reinforced to carry all the load to the foundation and piers. It has structural reinforcing rods. See Fig. 435. It does not depend on the soil to carry any of the load on the slab. It is designed much like a concrete beam or other structural member. The distance it must span and the load it must carry are used to calculate the reinforcing and thickness of the slab.

The three commonly used slab and foundation designs are shown in Figs. 435A, 435B, and 435C. If the slab is to be totally supported by the ground, it would be constructed as in Fig. 435A. This places no load on the foundation wall or footing. They carry the load of the walls and roof but not the floor. Usually the unreinforced and lightly reinforced slabs are constructed this way.

In Fig. 435B is the construction of a foundation in which the foundation carries part of the slab load. This construction is used with structurally reinforced and independently supported slabs. The structurally reinforced slab carries most of the load. The soil carries some but the load is spread over a wide area due to the strength of the reinforcing rods.

If the soil is poor, an independently reinforced slab is used. See Fig. 435C. Here the slab is supported by piers or supporting foundation walls. See Fig. 436. The area beneath the slab is filled to serve as support for the concrete when it is poured. Since this soil is not stable, it will eventually drop below the bottom of the slab. Table 12 gives design data for independently supported structural slab.

In Fig. 437 is a monolithically cast slab and grade beam. *Monolithically cast* means

Table 12
Design Data for Structural Slab on the Ground[1]

STRUCTURAL UNIT	MAXIMUM SPACING BETWEEN PIERS		
	6'-0" o.c.	7'-0" o.c.	8'-0" o.c.
Piers (Minimum)[2]			
Poured concrete (round)	10"	12"	14"
Concrete or masonry (square)	8" x 8"	10" x 10"	12" x 12"
Footing Area (Minimum)	115 sq. in.	130 sq. in.	175 sq. in.
Welded Wire Fabric Required	6 x 6—6/6	6 x 6—6/6	6 x 6—6/6

[1]Slab supported on edges by foundation and in center by piers.
[2]Piers are designed to support slab only; bearing walls must have separate footings designed to carry their load.

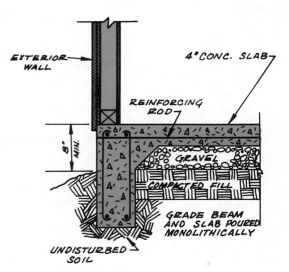

Fig. 437. Monolitically-cast slab and grade beam.

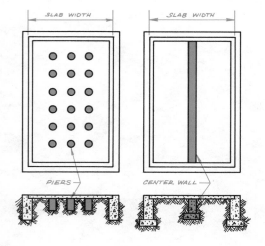

Fig. 436. Pier and center wall support for independently supported slab.

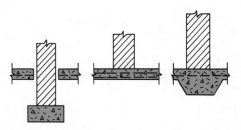

Fig. 438. Designs for carrying extra load of heavy interior partitions.

the slab and grade beam are cast at the same time. They are one solid concrete unit. This type of construction usually uses a structurally reinforced slab or an independently supported slab.

The means of designing load bearing partitions in slab construction are shown in Fig. 438. The unreinforced and lightly reinforced slab cannot support loads in excess of 500 pounds per lineal foot. If excess loads are to be placed on the slab, one of the designs shown in Fig. 438 must be used. In each case the reinforcement and concrete thickness must be determined by engineering analysis of the loads to be carried.

The exterior wall load should always be on a footing independent of the slab. In structurally reinforced and independently supported slabs, exterior wall loads are to be to a footing or grade beam. Interior load bearing partitions may be supported by the slab if they do not exceed the structural design capacity of the slab. Special reinforcing is needed if slab load carrying capacities will be exceeded.

Following are some additional factors related to concrete slab construction:

1. Slab on ground construction should not be attempted in areas having ground water or a hydrostatic pressure condition near the ground surface.

2. The site should be graded so water cannot collect beneath the slab.

3. Perimeter insulation should be used, except in areas where freezing weather seldom occurs. See Figs. 435A, 435B,

435C, and 439. Table 13 gives perimeter design data.

4. The slab should be poured continuously if possible. If a construction joint occurs, reinforcement should be provided for transfer of stress. See Fig. 440.

5. Concrete should be permitted to develop strength before being subjected to a load. It should be protected from freezing for at least two days after pouring.

6. The minimum floor slab should be 4 inches thick.

Fig. 439. Perimeter insulation being installed on slab floor edges. Plastic vapor barrier is being installed. (Dow Chemical Co.)

Table 13
Perimeter Insulation Design Data
for Heating Requirements[1]

Outside Design Temperature (° F.)	Distance Insulation Should Extend Under Slab (in Inches)	Thickness of Insulation (in Inches)
+31 and above	none; 12[2]	none; 1[2]
+21 to +30	Vertical edge of slab only	1
+11 to +20	12	1
+1 to +10	18	1
+0 to —9	24	1
—10 to —19	24	1½
—20 to —29	24	1½
—30 and lower	24	2

[1]These figures are for an unheated slab. If slab is heated, insulation thickness should be increased 50 percent.
[2]If house is air conditioned, install 12 inches of 1-inch thick insulation.

Fig. 440. Pouring the last of a continuous slab. Notice the radiant heating pipes in the slab. (Union Carbide Corp.)

7. Metal heating coils and reinforcement should be covered with at least 1 inch of concrete.

8. Hot air ducts in a slab should be completely encased in at least 2 inches of concrete, unless they are crush-resistant, noncorrodible, nonabsorbent and have tight-fitting joints. A two-inch coverage over the duct is required in all cases. See Fig. 441.

9. Slabs supported by compacted fill should not have more than 12 inches of earth fill or 24 inches of sand or gravel fill.

10. Slabs supported by foundation at the edges and piers in the center permit a maximum fill of 3 feet of earth or 6 feet of sand or gravel.

11. A vapor barrier should be placed below all slabs forming floors for habitable spaces. See Fig. 442.

12. The top of the floor slab should be at least 8 inches above finished grade.

13. The bottom of heat ducts in a slab should be at least 2 inches above finished grade.

14. Any wood sills should be 8 inches above finished grade.

15. All interior bearing partitions and non-bearing masonry partitions must be supported by footings resting on natural soil independent of the slab. It is possible to thicken the slab at such a point and provide special reinforcement to distribute this load. The 4-inch slab by itself can support only nonload-bearing, frame, interior partitions.

16. Structural slabs should be reinforced according to the design data in Table 12.

17. All piers should extend to natural, undisturbed soil.

18. Basement floor slabs and garage floor slabs should be designed according to the requirements set forth for house floor slabs.

19. Porch floor slabs should be reinforced, if they exceed 3'-6" in width.

Soil Investigation

The two factors affecting the design of a ground-supported slab are the soil properties and ground and surface water.

At least one test hole should be bored on the building site. The soil sample should be examined to see if it is suitable for ground-supported slabs. The boring should be at least 15' deep. Examine other buildings in the area to see if there is evidence of settlement or expansion of soil. This could indicate a problem exists.

The soil should be firm and be able to be compacted. Soils that are highly compressible,

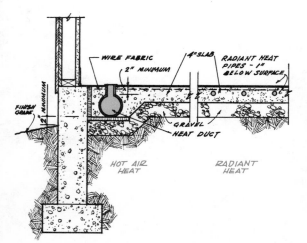

Fig. 441. Construction details for hot-air heating duct installation in concrete-slab floor.

Fig. 442. Forms ready for pouring of concrete-floor slab. Notice the polyethylene vapor barrier, wire reinforcing, heat ducts and plumbing. (Union Carbide Corp.)

highly expansive, or very loose are unsatisfactory.

Water causes problems with on-ground slabs. A high level of ground water or excess surface water will make it unwise to use a ground-supported slab.

If soil problems appear to be present, a soil engineer should be consulted to assist with the slab design and construction suggestions.

Build Your Vocabulary

Following are words that you should understand and use as part of your working vocabulary. Write out a brief explanation of what each means.

Footing	Pilaster
Dead load	Grade beam
Live load	Piling
Pier	Concrete slab
Column	Compacted fill
Prevailing temperature	Design loads
Frost line	Soil loads
Foundation	Monolithic cast concrete
Crawl space	Stepped footing
Unbalanced fill	Corbelled brick
Waterproofing	Grade
Drain tile	Column load area
Curtain wall	

Class Activities

1. Compute the total load on one lineal foot of footing and the footing size for your home.
2. Compute the weight upon one pier or column in your home, and design a footing to support this pier or column.
3. Compute the weight of a chimney or fireplace in your home, and design a footing to support it.
4. What is the frost line in your area? Explain why footings should be placed at this depth.
5. Ascertain the extent of termite activity in your area and the common preventive measures by local exterminators.

Additional Reading

Architectural Record (Editorial Staff), *Time Saver Standards*, pp. 22-23, 74-75, 131-132, 163-164, and 180-187.

Ramsey, Charles G., and Sleeper, H. R., *Architectural Graphic Standards*, pp. 1-4, 37, 70, 327, and 331.

U.S. Department of Health, Education and Welfare, "Wood-Frame House Construction," pp. 3-5.

U.S. Federal Housing Administration, "Minimum Property Standards for One and Two Living Units," pp. 41, 43, 75-99.

STRUCTURAL MEMBERS COMMONLY USED

The footing and foundation of a house must be designed to support the total weight of the structure and to provide a base upon which it can be built. The structural framework is assembled and secured in place, and the various materials that finish the house, such as siding, floors and roofing, are secured to this framework.

It is the purpose of this chapter to present design data to enable a residential builder to select the proper kind and size of structural members for this framework, to support the loads and stresses required of it.

Loads and Strength of Materials

Structural members are subject to the live and dead loads discussed in Chapter 6. A second consideration is the strength of the material from which they are made. These two factors — load and strength of materials — must be considered as structural members are selected.

Much of the work of ascertaining the strength of various structural members has been done by research groups and testing laboratories. For the typical house, the members can be selected from tables giving the load-carrying capabilities for various standard-sized members, according to the material from which they are made. No attempt will be made in this chapter to discuss how these load-bearing capacities were derived.

Selecting Joists

Joists are structural members that support a floor or ceiling. They are subject to live and dead loads. When selecting the proper joist size, one must consider total load, kind of material and distance the joist must span. Table 14 is typical of design data available in architectural standards books to assist with wood joist selection. In this table, the average live and dead loads, as discussed in Chapter 6, are included in the span tables.

This is but one of many tables. Such tables have been developed for all the common types of lumber used for construction purposes. Separate tables are available for each species of lumber, since they vary in their load-carrying capabilities. Detailed tables are available in the Federal Housing Administration publication "Minimum Property Standards for One and Two Living Units" and from the National Forest Products Association.

How to Read Table 14

The spans indicated in this table include the combined, uniformly distributed, live and dead loads. If a design load exceeds the normal figures for residences (as given in Chapter 6), maximum spans should be reduced to prevent overstressing.

The spans shown are maximum clear spans between the inner faces of supports.

The grades of lumber are indicated across the top of the table. The figures in the columns below are the maximum clear spans for the size of member indicated in the column at the left. For example, a 2 x 8 floor joist of No. 2, southern pine, if spaced 16 inches on center, will span 14'-9" if a live load of 30 pounds is upon it, and 13'-6" if a 40-pound live load is necessary. If these joists are placed

Table 14
Permissible Spans for Southern Pine Floor and Ceiling Joists

Floor Joists[1]

Nominal Size	Spacing C to C	40 LB. LIVE LOAD								30 LB. LIVE LOAD							
		No. 1 Dense No. 2 Dense KD or No. 1 Dense SR[2] 1750f		No. 1, No. 2 KD or No. 1 SR[2] 1500f		No. 2 Dense or No. 2 Dense SR[2] 1400f		No. 2 or No. 2 SR[2] 1200f		No. 1 Dense No. 2 Dense KD or No. 1 Dense SR[2] 1750f		No. 1, No. 2 KD or No. 1 SR[2] 1500f		No. 2 Dense or No. 2 Dense SR[2] 1400f		No. 2 or No. 2 SR[2] 1200f	
Inches	Inches	Ft.	In.	Ft.	In.	Ft.	In.	Ft.	In.	Ft.	In.	Ft.	In.	Ft.	In.	Ft.	In.
2 x 6	12	11	5	11	5	11	5	11	5	12	5	12	5	12	5	12	5
	16	10	5	10	5	10	5	10	1	11	4	11	4	11	4	11	4
	24	9	2	9	2	8	11	8	3	10	2	10	2	10	0	9	2
2 x 8	12	14	9	14	9	14	9	14	9	16	1	16	1	16	1	16	1
	16	13	6	13	6	13	6	13	6	14	9	14	9	14	9	14	9
	24	12	0	12	0	11	11	11	0	13	1	13	1	13	1	12	4
3 x 8	12	17	0	17	0	17	0	17	0	18	7	18	7	18	7	18	7
	16	15	7	15	7	15	7	15	7	17	0	17	0	17	0	17	0
	24	13	10	13	10	13	10	13	10	15	1	15	1	15	1	15	1
2 x 10	12	18	3	18	3	18	3	18	3	19	11	19	11	19	11	19	11
	16	16	9	16	9	16	9	16	9	18	3	18	3	18	3	18	3
	24	14	10	14	10	14	10	14	0	16	2	16	2	16	2	15	7
3 x 10	12	21	1	21	1	21	1	21	1	23	1	23	1	23	1	23	1
	16	19	4	19	4	19	4	19	4	21	2	21	2	21	2	21	2
	24	17	1	17	1	17	1	17	1	18	8	18	8	18	8	18	8
2 x 12	12	21	9	21	9	21	9	21	9	23	9	23	9	23	9	23	9
	16	19	11	19	11	19	11	19	11	21	9	21	9	21	9	21	9
	24	17	7	17	7	17	7	16	11	19	2	19	2	19	2	18	11

Ceiling Joists

Nominal Size	Spacing C to C	20 LB. ATTIC STORAGE								NO ATTIC STORAGE							
		No. 1 Dense No. 2 Dense KD or No. 1 Dense SR[2] 1750f		No. 1, No. 2 KD or No. 1 SR[2] 1500f		No. 2 Dense or No. 2 Dense SR[2] 1400f		No. 2 or No. 2 SR[2] 1200f		No. 1 Dense No. 2 Dense KD or No. 1 Dense SR[2] 1750f		No. 1, No. 2 KD or No. 1 SR[2] 1500f		No. 2 Dense or No. 2 Dense SR[2] 1400f		No. 2 or No. 2 SR[2] 1200f	
Inches	Inches	Ft.	In.	Ft.	In.	Ft.	In.	Ft.	In.	Ft.	In.	Ft.	In.	Ft.	In.	Ft.	In.
2 x 4	12	9	5	9	5	9	5	9	5	11	10	11	10	11	10	11	10
	16	8	7	8	7	8	7	8	5	10	9	10	9	10	9	10	9
	24	7	6	7	6	7	5	6	10	9	5	9	5	9	5	9	5
2 x 6[3]	12	14	7	14	7	14	7	14	7	18	5	18	5	18	5	18	5
	16	13	3	13	3	13	3	13	1	16	9	16	9	16	9	16	9
	24	11	7	11	7	11	6	10	7	14	7	14	7	14	7	14	6
2 x 8	12	19	6	19	6	19	6	19	6	24	7	24	7	24	7	24	7
	16	17	9	17	9	17	9	17	5	22	4	22	4	22	4	22	4
	24	15	6	15	6	15	5	14	3	19	6	19	6	19	6	19	6
2 x 10	12	24	9	24	9	24	9	24	9	31	2	31	2	31	2	31	2
	16	22	6	22	6	22	6	22	1	28	3	28	3	28	3	28	3
	24	19	7	19	7	19	6	18	0	24	9	24	9	24	9	24	9

[1]Assumed dead load 10 PSF.
[2]Grade designation for heavy joists (3" thick).
[3]Based on 5⅝" width.
Courtesy National Forest Products Association

closer together, 12 inches on center, they can span 16'-1" and 14'-9" respectively.

Ceiling joist spans are found the same way. The 2 x 8 joist above, if used as a ceiling joist with no attic storage and if placed 16 inches on center, will span 22'-4".

It should be pointed out that if these maximum spans are increased slightly, the member will not fail or break. However, it will be under excessive stress. This could cause a floor to sag somewhat or a ceiling to bow slightly.

Selecting Rafters

A rafter must be of such capabilities that it can carry the normal live loads imposed upon it, as well as the dead load of its own weight. As the span of the rafter increases, the total design load has more effect upon the member. The span of a rafter is the clear distance from the two points supporting the rafter. See Fig. 470. For an ordinary rafter, this is from the exterior wall plate to the ridgepole.

Roof Pitch

The selection of rafters is also influenced by the pitch of the roof. As can be seen from

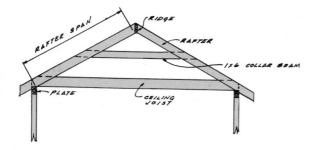

Fig. 470. Calculation of rafter span.

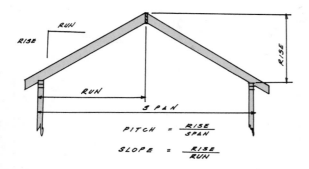

Fig. 471. Calculation of roof pitch.

Table 15, the pitch influences the span of the rafter.

Pitch is the angle of the roof from the ridgepole to the plate. It usually is expressed in the form of a ratio of the total rise to the total span of a building. Pitch $= \dfrac{\text{total rise}}{\text{total span}}$. See Fig. 471.

The angle of the roof is expressed on working drawings in terms of slope. *Slope* is a ratio between rise and run. The run is half the span. Refer again to Fig. 471. The symbol $4\overline{\big|^{12}}$ found on working drawings is an expression of slope. The numbers placed upon this symbol mean there is 4 inches of rise for every 12 inches of run. The pitch of such a roof is $\dfrac{\text{rise}}{\text{span}}$ or $\dfrac{4}{24}$ or $\frac{1}{6}$ pitch. The carpenter uses the expression of slope when he lays out the cuts on a rafter.

To clarify these concepts, follow the solution to this problem. Fig. 472 illustrates a house. The problem is to find the pitch of the roof and the slope for cutting the rafters. The computations in the figure should clarify the solution. The slope usually is indicated with a 12-inch run, while the rise, of course, varies. This roof can be said to have a one-quarter pitch or a slope of 6 inches rise for every 12 inches of run.

Table 15 is typical of design data available in architectural standards books to assist with rafter selection.

How to Read Table 15

The spans indicated in this table include the combined, uniformly distributed, live and dead loads. If the design exceeds this, special consideration must be given to the size of the member.

The grades of lumber are indicated across the top of the table. The figures in the columns below are the maximum clear spans of

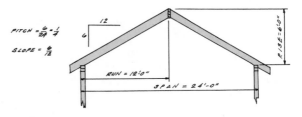

Fig. 472. Calculation of pitch and slope.

Table 15
Permissible Spans for Southern Pine Roof Joists and Rafters

Low Slope Roof Joists

Nominal Size	Spacing C to C	SUPPORTING FINISHED CEILING[1]				NOT SUPPORTING FINISHED CEILING[2]			
		No. 1 Dense No. 2 Dense KD or No. 1 Dense SR[5] 1750f	No. 1, No. 2 KD or No. 1 SR[5] 1500f	No. 2 Dense or No. 2 Dense SR[5] 1400f	No. 2 or No. 2 SR[5] 1200f	No. 1 Dense No. 2 Dense KD or No. 1 Dense SR[5] 1750f	No. 1, No. 2 KD or No. 1 SR[5] 1500f	No. 2, Dense or No. 2 Dense SR[5] 1400f	No. 2 or No. 2 SR[5] 1200f
Inches	Inches	Ft. In.	Ft. In.	Ft. In.	Ft. In.	Ft. In.	Ft. In.	Ft. In.	Ft. In.
2 x 6[6]	12	14 7	14 7	14 7	14 0	16 9	16 9	16 4	15 2
	16	13 3	13 3	13 1	12 2	15 3	14 7	14 2	13 1
	24	11 7	11 1	10 8	9 10	12 11	11 11	11 6	10 7
2 x 8	12	19 6	19 6	19 6	18 8	22 4	22 4	21 9	20 2
	16	17 9	17 9	17 5	16 2	20 3	19 6	18 10	17 5
	24	14 9	14 9	14 3	13 2	17 2	15 11	15 5	14 3
3 x 8	12	22 10	22 10	22 10	22 10	26 2	26 2	26 2	25 7
	16	20 9	20 9	20 9	20 6	23 9	23 9	23 9	22 2
	24	18 2	18 2	18 1	16 9	20 9	20 3	19 6	18 1
2 x 10	12	24 8	24 8	24 8	23 7	28 4	28 4	27 7	25 6
	16	22 6	22 6	22 1	20 5	25 8	24 9	23 10	22 1
	24	18 8	18 8	18 0	16 8	21 9	20 2	19 6	18 0
3 x 10	12	29 0	29 0	29 0	29 0	33 2	33 2	33 2	32 6
	16	26 4	26 4	26 4	26 0	30 2	30 2	30 2	28 1
	24	23 0	23 0	22 11	21 2	26 4	25 7	24 9	22 11
2 x 12	12	29 11	29 11	29 11	28 7	34 3	34 3	33 4	30 11
	16	27 2	27 2	26 9	24 9	31 1	29 11	28 11	26 9
	24	22 7	22 7	21 10	20 2	26 4	24 5	19 6	21 10

Rafters

Nominal Size	Spacing C to C	HEAVY ROOFING (OVER 5PSF)[3]				LIGHT ROOFING (LESS THAN 4PSF)[4]			
		No. 1 Dense No. 2 Dense KD or No. 1 Dense SR[5] 1750f	No. 1, No. 2 KD or No. 1 SR[5] 1500f	No. 2 Dense or No. 2 Dense SR[5] 1400f	No. 2 or No. 2 SR[5] 1200f	No. 1 Dense No. 2 Dense KD or No. 1 Dense SR[5] 1750f	No. 1, No. 2 KD or No. 1 SR[5] 1500f	No. 2 Dense or No. 2 Dense SR[5] 1400f	No. 2 or No. 2 SR[5] 1200f
Inches	Inches	Ft. In.	Ft. In.	Ft. In.	Ft. In.	Ft. In.	Ft. In.	Ft. In.	Ft. In.
2 x 4	12	11 9	10 10	10 6	9 9	13 9	12 9	12 3	11 5
	16	10 2	9 5	9 1	8 5	11 10	11 0	10 7	9 10
	24	8 3	7 8	7 5	6 10	9 8	9 0	8 8	8 0
2 x 6[6]	12	18 3	16 10	16 4	15 2	21 3	19 9	19 1	17 7
	16	15 9	14 7	14 2	13 1	18 5	17 1	16 6	15 4
	24	12 11	11 11	11 6	10 7	15 1	13 11	13 6	12 5
2 x 8	12	24 4	22 6	21 9	20 2	28 0	26 4	25 6	23 6
	16	21 1	19 6	18 10	17 5	24 7	22 9	22 0	20 4
	24	17 2	15 11	15 5	14 3	20 1	18 7	17 11	16 7
2 x 10	12	30 10	28 6	27 7	25 6	36 0	34 4	32 3	29 10
	16	26 8	24 9	23 10	22 1	31 2	28 10	27 10	25 9
	24	21 9	20 2	19 6	18 0	25 5	23 7	22 9	21 1

[1] Assumed dead load, 15 PSF.
[2] Assumed dead load, 10 PSF.
[3] Assumed live load, 30 PSF; dead load, 15 PSF.
[4] Assumed live load, 15 PSF; dead load, 7 PSF.
[5] Grade designation for heavy joists (3″ thick).
[6] Based on 5⅝″ width.
Courtesy National Forest Products Association

the rafters. The size and spacing of the member is indicated in the column at the left. For example, a 2 x 6 rafter of No. 2, yellow pine, spaced 16 inches on center, used to build a roof sloping over 3 in 12, will span 15'-4" for light roofing and 13'-1" for heavy roofing. This member will span 13'-1" for a roof that slopes less than 3 in 12 and does not support a finished ceiling.

Collar Beams

Collar beams, frequently, are used to stiffen a roof. A collar beam is a 1 x 6 tie placed between rafters on opposite sides of a roof. Refer again to Fig. 470. This member, usually, is placed on every second or third rafter and is most effective if placed midway between the ridge and the ceiling joist.

Some believe that the use of a collar beam reduces the required span of the rafter, but, in general practice, this is not accepted.

Roof Trusses

A number of organizations such as the Producers' Council, the National Retail Lumber Dealers Association and the Timber Engineering Company have given special attention to the design and use of trusses. The actual design of a truss is a job for someone trained in the engineering aspects of structural design, as an engineer or an architect. It is beyond the scope of this text to present such information.

Since trusses are widely used, they should be seriously considered by the house designer. Fig. 473 illustrates a truss design for roofs with a 4-in-12 slope. This design is suitable for spans from 20'-0" to 32'-0". The size of

the structural members required can be selected from the tables. The schematic drawing in the upper left corner of Fig. 473 indicates where the internal members of the truss meet the top cord and the ceiling joists. The lines on this schematic are the center lines of the structural members. These are indicated on the drawing of a truss at the bottom of Fig. 473.

The tail of the rafter can overhang the supporting wall without changing the design of the truss.

Other truss designs can be obtained from the publications of the companies mentioned above.

The structural members of the truss in Fig. 473 are held together with bolts. A split ring is installed between the two members. This is a circular ring of carbon steel which is inserted in round grooves cut in the structural members. The split ring is set halfway into each member. The bolt then pulls the members together, closing them over the ring. See Fig. 474.

Sheathing Spans

The spacing of joists and rafters directly influences the thickness of sheathing required. One-inch (¾" actual) solid wood sheathing can satisfactorily span up to 24 inches on roof construction.

Plywood used as roof sheathing should conform to the data in Table 16. It should be structural-interior type or exterior type.

Floor construction permits one-inch (¾" actual) wood sheathing to span not over 16 inches.

Table 16
Joist Spacing Standards for Plywood Sheathing

PLYWOOD SPECIES	MAXIMUM THICKNESS (INCHES)	MAXIMUM RAFTER OR JOIST SPACING (INCHES O.C.)					
		Asphalt or Wood Shingles or Shakes		Built-up Roofing		Slate, Clay Tile or Asbestos-Com. Shingles	
		Edges Blocked[1]	Unblocked	Edges Blocked[1]	Unblocked	Edges Unblocked	
Douglas Fir	⁵⁄₁₆	16	16	16	....	....	
	⅜	24	20	24	16	....	
	½	32	24	32	20	16	
	⅝	42	28	42	24	24	
	¾	48	32	48	28	32	
Western Softwoods	⅜	16	16	16	....	....	
	½	24	20	24	16	16	
	⅝	32	24	32	20	20	
	¾	42	28	42	24	28	

[1]Blocking of edges shall be by accurately cut wood blocking or by extruded aluminum clip designed for this purpose.

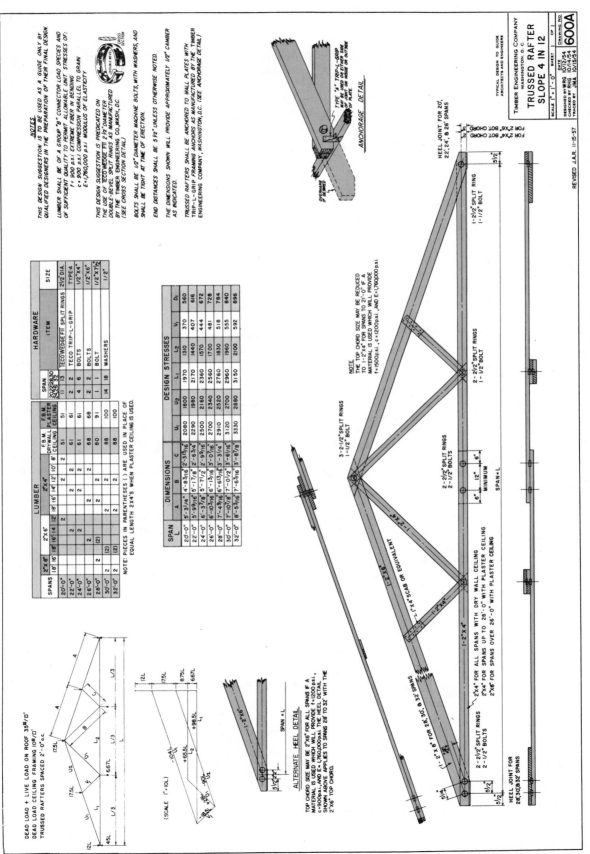

Fig. 473. Typical trussed rafter design. (Timber Engineering Co.)

Fig. 474. A split ring as used in truss construction. (Timber Engineering Co.)

If the finished floor is 25/32 strip material applied at right angles to the joists and if the ¾-inch wood subfloor is applied diagonally, the joist spacing can be a maximum of 24 inches on center.

If plywood is used as a subfloor, it should be 5-ply, structural-interior type or exterior type. The minimum thickness and maximum joist spacing are shown in Table 17. If plywood is used over a subfloor as a base for resilient flooring, it should be ¼ inch thick. If hardboard is used, it should be 3/16 inch.

Plywood subflooring used in the 2.4.1 system devised by the Douglas Fir Plywood Association is 1⅛ inches thick. The details of construction are discussed in Chapter 5. This flooring has a tongue-and-groove construction, and it is designed to span up to 48 inches.

Wall sheathing of one-inch (¾" actual) wood can span a maximum of 16 inches. If it is applied diagonally or if the stud wall framing is braced, it can be used over studs spaced 24 inches on center.

Plywood wall sheathing should be at least 5/16 inch thick for 16-inch spans and ⅜ inch thick for 24-inch spans. The material should be structural-interior type.

Fiberboard sheathing should be at least ½ inch thick. It also is available in 25/32-inch thickness. If the studs are braced, this sheathing can be placed over studs spaced 24 inches on center. If bracing is omitted, studs must be spaced 16 inches on center.

Gypsum sheathing must be at least ½ inch thick. Maximum stud spacing is 16 inches on center. If wall bracing is installed, the studs can be placed 24 inches on center.

Heavy Decking for Plank-and-Beam Roofs

Roof decking customarily is surfaced two sides, is tongue-and-groove and usually is run to a V-joint pattern. The 2-inch decking has a single tongue-and-groove; 3- and 4-inch decking have a double tongue-and-groove. See Fig. 475.

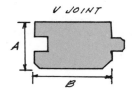

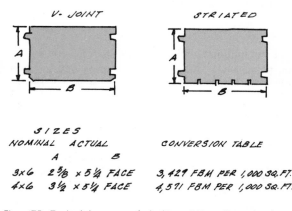

Fig. 475. Typical heavy roof decking. (West Coast Lumbermen's Association)

Table 17
Joist Spacing Standards for Plywood Subfloor

SPECIES OF PLYWOOD	PLYWOOD THICKNESS (INCHES)	MAXIMUM JOIST SPACING (INCHES O.C.)	
		Wood Strip Flooring	Wood Block or Resilient Flooring[1]
Douglas Fir	½	16[2]	16
	⅝	20[2]	20
	¾	24	24
	2 • 4 • 1	48	48
Western Softwoods	⅝	16[2]	16
	¾	20[2]	20
	⅞	24	24

[1]Solid blocking shall be installed under all edges at right angles to joists except when a separate underlayment material is installed over subfloor.
[2]May be 24 inches o.c., if 25/32 inch wood strip flooring is installed at right angles to joists.

Table 18
Maximum Spans for Decking Used in Plank and Beam Roofs
(As determined by allowable unit stress in bending and maximum deflection of 1/240th of the span length.)

Subject to local building codes, these spans are suitable for nominal 6″ and wider material. The computations for spans determined by bending stress include dead load allowance of 15 lbs. per square foot for decking, 3 ply roofing and gravel topping. Spans limited by deflection are computed on the basis of live load only. 2″ is for single tongue and groove; 3″ and 4″ are for double tongue and groove.

Simple Spans
The arrangement of a simple span has planks bearing on two supports. The end joints between the decking pieces, when the roof is of two or more spans, are in line over each intermediate support making the decking pieces uniform in length.

WEST COAST DOUGLAS FIR

Nominal Thickness	Grade	Live Load (lbs. per sq. ft.) 20	30	40	50
2″	Construction	9′-5″	8′-3″	7′-6″	6′-11″
2″	Standard	9′-5″	8′-3″	7′-6″	6′-11″
2″	Utility	7′-2″	6′-3″	5′-8″	5′-3″
3″	Select Dex	15′-3″	13′-3″	12′-0″	11′-3″
3″	Coml. Dex	15′-3″	13′-3″	12′-0″	11′-3″
4″	Select Dex	20′-3″	17′-9″	16′-0″	15′-0″
4″	Coml. Dex	20′-3″	17′-9″	16′-0″	15′-0″

WESTERN RED CEDAR

Nominal Thickness	Grade	Live Load (lbs. per sq. ft.) 20	30	40	50
2″	Select Merch.	8′-1″	7′-1″	6′-5″	5′-11″
2″	Construction	8′-1″	7′-1″	6′-5″	5′-11″
2″	Standard	6′-9″	6′-0″	5′-5″	5′-0″
3″	Select Dex	13′-0″	11′-3″	10′-3″	9′-6″
3″	Coml. Dex	13′-0″	11′-3″	10′-3″	9′-6″
4″	Select Dex	17′-3″	15′-3″	13′-9″	12′-9″
4″	Coml. Dex	17′-3″	15′-3″	13′-9″	12′-9″

Random Length Decking
Economical, random lengths of plank having well scattered joints, and each plank bearing on at least one support, is the basic arrangement for this type. The pieces should be end matched or end splined when of 2″ nominal thickness.

WEST COAST DOUGLAS FIR

Nominal Thickness	Grade	Live Load (lbs. per sq. ft.) 20	30	40	50
2″	Construction	10′-3″	9′-0″	8′-2″	7′-7″
2″	Standard	10′-3″	9′-0″	8′-2″	7′-7″
2″	Utility	7′-2″	6′-3″	5′-8″	5′-3″
3″	Select Dex	16′-9″	14′-6″	13′-3″	12′-3″
3″	Coml. Dex	16′-9″	14′-6″	13′-3″	12′-3″
4″	Select Dex	22′-0″	19′-3″	17′-6″	16′-3″
4″	Coml. Dex	22′-0″	19′-3″	17′-6″	16′-3″

WESTERN RED CEDAR

Nominal Thickness	Grade	Live Load (lbs. per sq. ft.) 20	30	40	50
2″	Select Merch.	8′-10″	7′-9″	7′-0″	6′-6″
2″	Construction	8′-10″	7′-9″	7′-0″	6′-6″
2″	Standard	6′-9″	6′-0″	5′-5″	5′-0″
3″	Select Dex	14′-3″	12′-3″	11′-3″	10′-6″
3″	Coml. Dex	13′-6″	12′-0″	10′-9″	10′-0″
4″	Select Dex	19′-0″	16′-3″	15′-0″	14′-0″
4″	Coml. Dex	18′-0″	16′-0″	14′-9″	13′-3″

Combination Simple and Two-Span Continuous
With the exception that every other piece in the end span is of single span length, all other decking pieces are two spans in length. End joints are over intermediate supports and are staggered in adjacent lines of deck pieces. This arrangement is best suited to three spans or any greater odd number of spans.

WEST COAST DOUGLAS FIR

Nominal Thickness	Grade	Live Load (lbs. per sq. ft.) 20	30	40	50
2″	Construction	10′-7″	9′-4″	8′-6″	7′-10″
2″	Standard	10′-7″	9′-4″	8′-6″	7′-10″
2″	Utility	7′-2″	6′-3″	5′-8″	5′-3″
3″	Select Dex	17′-3″	15′-0″	13′-6″	12′-6″
3″	Coml. Dex	17′-3″	15′-0″	13′-6″	12′-6″
4″	Select Dex	22′-9″	20′-0″	18′-3″	16′-9″
4″	Coml. Dex	22′-9″	20′-0″	18′-3″	16′-9″

WESTERN RED CEDAR

Nominal Thickness	Grade	Live Load (lbs. per sq. ft.) 20	30	40	50
2″	Select Merch.	9′-2″	8′-0″	7′-3″	6′-8″
2″	Construction	8′-9″	7′-8″	7′-0″	6′-4″
2″	Standard	6′-9″	6′-0″	5′-5″	5′-0″
3″	Select Dex	14′-9″	12′-9″	11′-9″	10′-9″
3″	Coml. Dex	13′-6″	12′-0″	10′-9″	10′-0″
4″	Select Dex	19′-6″	17′-0″	15′-6″	14′-3″
4″	Coml. Dex	18′-0″	16′-0″	14′-3″	13′-3″

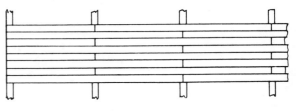

Courtesy West Coast Lumbermen's Association

This decking is installed by spiking each course to the preceding course at regular intervals through factory-drilled holes and toenailing to each beam.

Where there is a combination of warmth and high humidity inside a building and low temperature outside, the moisture vapor inside tends to move outward through walls and ceilings. In extreme cases, a vapor barrier and 1-inch, rigid insulation should be placed above the deck to prevent condensation on top of the decking. This is purely a provision for moisture control, since wood is a good insulating material. Decking 3 and 4 inches thick provides adequate thermal insulation.

The following coefficients of heat transmission or K values have been determined: Douglas fir, 1.0 BTU; hemlock, .89 BTU; and red cedar, .74 BTU per inch of net thickness at 12% moisture content.

Table 18 illustrates maximum spans for decking used on roofs. The span is influenced not only by the species and grade of lumber, but by the method of installing the decking. Three common methods are the simple span, random length, and combination simple and two-span continuous. Table 18 illustrates

Table 19
Allowable Spans for Fiberboard Decking

Roof Deck Thickness	Maximum Distance Between Supports
1½″	2'-0″ O.C.
2″	2'-8″ O.C.
3″	4'-0″ O.C.

Courtesy Wood Conversion Co.

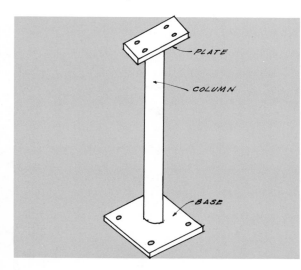

Fig. 476. Typical steel column.

these and gives some design considerations.

Other types of decking are available. For example, a fiberboard material is available in 1½-, 2- and 3-inch thicknesses, in sheets 2'-0″ by 8'-0″. It has the same construction advantages as thick wood decking and is available with a vapor barrier built-in. Table 19 gives design data for this type of roof decking.

The heat transmission U values for fiberboard roof decks are 0.18 for 1½ inch; 0.15 for 2 inch; and 0.10 for 3 inch thickness.

This product is manufactured with a vapor barrier for conditions where moisture is a problem.

Columns

Steel columns used in residential construction are manufactured in standard sizes. The load-bearing qualities of these members have been ascertained through actual load tests.

These columns are made from a steel shell filled with a special concrete mix that is carefully vibrated in place to fill all voids. A steel plate is welded to the top of the column to provide a bearing surface for the beam, and another steel plate is welded to the bottom of the column to form a base. See Fig. 476.

These structural members are available in many sizes. Table 20 records design data for those commonly used in residences.

Columns are subject to two forces — concentric loading and eccentric loading. A column is considered concentrically loaded if the vertical load bearing upon it is directly on top of the column. This is the case in the usual residential construction.

Eccentric loading is a load bearing on a column that is unbalanced by another load opposite it. See Fig. 477. If such a case exists,

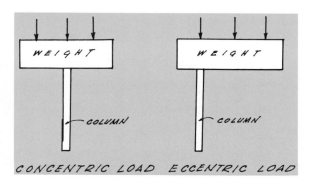

Fig. 477. Concentric and eccentric loading.

Table 20
Maximum Loads for Steel Columns

	Outside Diameter of Column (Inches)	Weight Per Foot of Column (Pounds)	Area of Steel (Square Inches)	Area of Concrete (Square Inches)	Maximum Load for Length of Column (Feet)[1]						
					6	7	8	9	10	12	13
Lightweight Steel Columns	3½	12	1.01	8.61	23	21	19	17			
	4	15	1.17	11.40	30	28	26	24			
Standard Weight Steel Columns	3½	15	2.23	7.39	38		32		27		
	4	20	2.68	9.89	49		43		37	31	28

[1]Safe concentric load in thousands of pounds
Courtesy The Lally Co.

the equivalent concentric load must be calculated. This is beyond the scope of this study.

Table 21 indicates the common sizes of the bases of steel columns. This is useful information when designing column footings.

Wood columns are used frequently in residential construction. The weight upon these columns is applied in a vertical direction. The load that a wood column can carry depends upon the compressive strength of the species of lumber from which the column is made. Table 22 gives the total load, in pounds, which wood columns of various sizes and lengths can carry. Remember that the longer the column, the less load it can carry.

The following example illustrates how to select a wood column. Assume a wood column must be 7'-0" long and must support a load of 12,500 pounds. An examination of Table 22

reveals that a square 3⅝-inch post of a material with a compressive strength of 1150 to 1400 pounds per square inch, if 7'-0" long, will support only 12,170 pounds. Southern pine, dense No. 1 structural, is an example of such material. This will not be a satisfactory column.

However, dense, structural Southern pine has a compressive strength of 1400 pounds per square inch. A 3⅝-inch square member of this material can carry up to 13,060 pounds safely and would be a satisfactory choice. The compressive strengths of common structural lumber are shown in Table 23.

Stressed-Skin Panels

The actual design of stressed-skin panels is beyond the scope of this text. The Plywood Fabricator Service, Inc., Chicago, Illinois has developed design methods and fabrication specifications for these panels.

The examples in Fig. 478 are panel sizes frequently used in residential construction. They are only a few of many possible designs.

Girders

Several computations must be made before girder size can be selected. First, the dis-

Table 21
Steel Column Base Dimensions

Column Diameter	Base in Inches
3½	8 x 8
4	9 x 9

Courtesy The Lally Co.

Table 22
Maximum Loads for Wood Columns
(in pounds)

Column Size (Inches)	Compressive Strength (Lbs. per sq. in.)	Height of Column						
		6'-0"	7'-0"	8'-0"	9'-0"	10'-0"	11'-0"	12'-0"
3⅝ x 3⅝	1150 to 1400	13,460	12,170	10,280	7,700	5,670	4,340	
	1400 to 1750	15,370	13,060					
	1750	17,000	13,130					
5⅝ x 5⅝	1150 to 1400	33,800		32,800	31,500	27,800	23,500	
	1400 to 1750	40,800		38,700	35,300	30,000		
	1750	49,700		45,850	39,000	30,500		

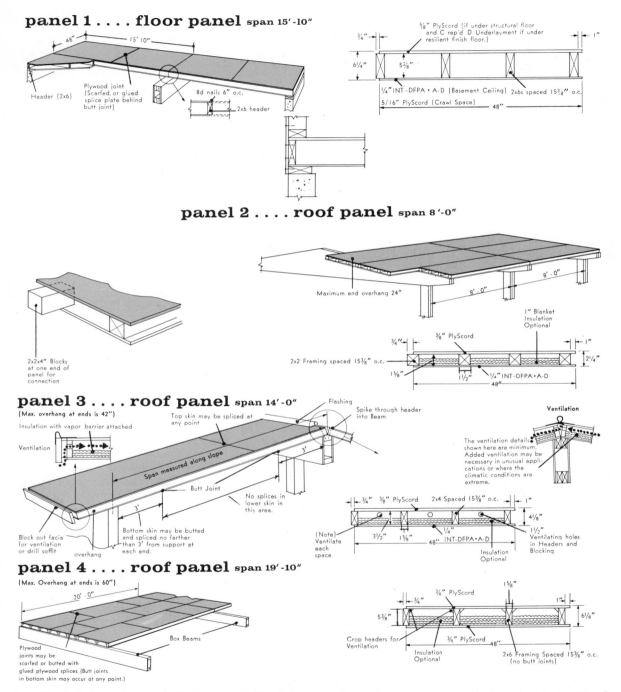

panel 1 .... floor panel span 15'-10"

panel 2 .... roof panel span 8'-0"

panel 3 .... roof panel span 14'-0"

panel 4 .... roof panel span 19'-10"

Fig. 478. The plywood stressed-skin floor panel No. 1 is designed to carry a permanent floor load of 50 pounds per square foot (10 psf dead load and 40 psf live load). Deflection under live load is limited to 1/360th of the span. No provision is made for load-bearing partitions.

Plywood stressed-skin panels 2, 3 and 4 are designed on a normal loading basis to carry a total uniform roof load of 40 pounds per square foot of horizontal projection (10 psf dead load and 30 psf live load). Deflection under live load is limited to 1/240th of the span.

The maximum permissible span may be taken as the clear distance between supports plus the distance required at each end for bearing or approximately the center-to-center distance between supports. (Douglas Fir Plywood Association)

Table 23
Compressive Strengths of Various Types of Wood Used for Columns

Compressive Strength (Lbs. per sq. in.)	Wood	Type	Grade
1150	Pine	Southern Long Leaf	#1 Structural Long Leaf
		Southern	Dense #1 Structural
1200	Douglas Fir	Coast Region	#1
	Oak	Red & White	1200 C—Grade
1250	Douglas Fir	Inland Region	Common Structural
1300	Pine	Southern	Dense Structural S. E. & S.
		Southern Long Leaf	Merchantable Structural Long Leaf
			Structural S. E. & S. Long Leaf
1325	Oak	Red & White	1325 C—Grade
1400	Douglas Fir	Coast Region	Dense #1
		Inland Region	Structural
	Pine	Southern	Dense Structural
		Southern Long Leaf	Prime Structural Long Leaf
1450	Douglas Fir	Coast Region	Select Structural
	Redwood		Dense Structural
1550	Douglas Fir	Coast Region	Dense Select Structural
1750	Douglas Fir	Inland Region	Select Structural
	Pine	Southern	Select Structural
		Southern Long Leaf	Select Structural Long Leaf

Reprinted with permission from Architectural Graphic Standards, John Wiley and Sons, Inc.

tance the girder must span must be ascertained. Then, the girder load area must be computed; this gives the area of the building the girder is to support. Next, the weight of one square foot of the house bearing on the girder must be ascertained. The total load on the girder can then be found by multiplying the girder load area by the weight per square foot of the house.

Once the total load is known, the material from which the girder is to be made must be decided. Finally, from safe load tables, a girder is chosen, which will span the specified distance and carry the determined load.

Girder Length

The length of a girder is the section spanning the distance between two supports. The determination of this length is a decision of the designer. The longer the span, the heavier the girder must be; the shorter the span, the more columns that must be used. The designer must reach a compromise between excessive girder weight and an overabundance of columns. If the span is excessive, the girder must be so large that it reduces the headroom in a basement. By using several columns, one can select a shallower beam, thus increasing the headroom.

How to Compute Girder Load Area

The girder in a typical house must support itself, the live and dead loads of the first floor, any partitions and the live and dead loads of the ceiling. For a two-story house, the weight of the second floor must be considered. The roof usually is supported by the exterior walls.

A girder in residential construction is assumed to carry the load imposed upon it uniformly along its length. This principle is considered as the total load is computed.

An examination of Fig. 479 reveals how the load imposed by a house is distributed on a girder. Assume that a 50-pound load exists on each joist. Half of this load is supported by the foundation and half by the girder. Since the girder supports the ends of two

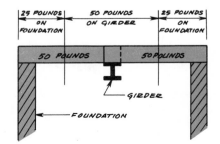

Fig. 479. Calculation of load on a girder.

joists, each with a 50-pound load, it supports a total of 50 pounds. Each foundation supports only one end of the joist and, therefore, supports 25 pounds.

To compute the load on a girder, the number of square feet of building supported by the girder must be multiplied by the weight of the house per square foot. The

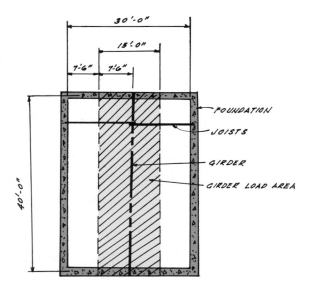

PLAN VIEW

Fig. 480. Visualization of load zone on a girder.

plan view in Fig. 480 shows a girder running through the center of a house. This girder helps support the load of half of the force applied downward by the joists and other load forces. In other words, half of the distance between the girder and the foundation is load upon the girder. The width of the girder load area is, therefore, 7½ feet on each side or a total width of 15 feet. The remainder of the load is supported by the foundation wall. The girder runs the entire length of the building, so the load area is 15 feet x 40 feet or 600 square feet. If the load were 90 pounds per square foot, the girder would have to support a total of 54,000 pounds, uniformly distributed along its length.

The weight per square foot can be ascertained by the method given in Chapter 6.

If a column is inserted in the plan view in Fig. 480, the situation changes. See Fig. 481.

In Fig. 481, the girder span is reduced. The span of each piece is 20'-0", and the width of the girder load area is still 15'-0". The total girder load area that each part of the girder must support is 300 square feet. If the load is 90 pounds per square foot, the total load is 27,000 pounds or just half of that in Fig. 480. It can be seen that the column reduces the girder span, and this reduces the load the girder must carry. Since the load is reduced, the girder can be a smaller structural member.

Sometimes a girder is not spaced in the center of a structure. See Fig. 482. Here the girder is 10'-0" from one foundation and 25'-0" from the other. The method of computing the girder load area is exactly the same as that

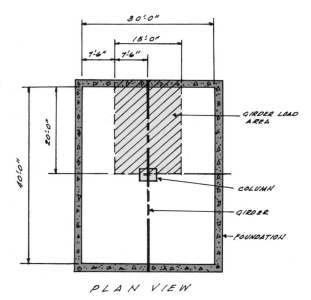

PLAN VIEW

Fig. 481. Visualization of girder load with supporting column.

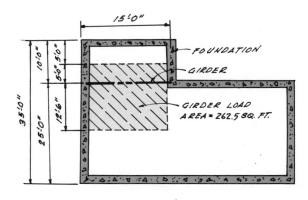

PLAN VIEW

Fig. 482. Load on girder placed off center.

described above. The girder supports half the load each way and has a total width of 5'-0" plus 12'-6" or 17'-6". The length of the girder is 15'-0" .The total girder load area is 262.5 square feet.

Solid and Nailed Wood Girders

Wood girders can be made from one solid piece of material or can be assembled from several 2-inch pieces, carefully nailed together so that the separate pieces act as a single member. The built-up girder is as satisfactory as a solid girder.

If the total load on the girder, the span and the strength or allowable working stress of the lumber to be used are known, it is possible to compute the necessary size of the girder. This information, however, is available in tables that show the maximum allowable loads on beams of different sizes and for various spans. The size needed will vary with the lumber species and grade used, since some lumber is stronger than others.

If the girder is built up of several pieces nailed together, care should be taken to use the percentage figures applying to built-up

Table 24
Permissible Spans of Solid Wood Girders
Allowable fiber stress 1,600 pounds per square inch; modulus of elasticity, E-1,600,000
(Allowable uniformly distributed loads for solid wood girders and beams in pounds computed for actual dressed sizes)

Solid dressed sizes	Span in Feet																
	4, 5, 6	7	8	9	10	11	12	13	14	15	16	17	18	19	20
3 by 6	2,435	2,078	1,812	1,602	1,434	1,296	1,180	1,080	995	921	855	796	744	696	654
4 by 6	3,366	2,875	2,505	2,213	1,981	1,791	1,630	1,493	1,375	1,272	1,183	1,101	1,030	965	905
6 by 6	4,885	4,165	3,633	3,211	2,873	2,596	2,363	2,166	1,995	1,845	1,714	1,595	1,492	1,396	1,310
2 by 8	2,145	2,145	2,016	1,785	1,600	1,446	1,320	1,213	1,119	1,038	967	902	846	795	749
3 by 8	3,460	3,460	3,233	2,864	2,567	2,322	2,118	1,944	1,794	1,663	1,549	1,445	1,354	1,263	1,197
4 by 8	4,770	4,770	4,470	3,960	3,549	3,212	2,930	2,690	2,484	2,304	2,145	2,002	1,878	1,765	1,662
6 by 8	7,260	7,260	6,783	6,008	5,386	4,875	4,446	4,082	3,768	3,495	3,255	3,039	2,850	2,678	2,522
8 by 8	9,880	9,880	9,247	8,193	7,344	6,646	6,063	5,566	5,139	4,766	4,437	4,143	3,886	3,651	3,438
2 by 10	2,700	2,700	2,700	2,700	2,564	2,323	2,120	1,949	1,802	1,672	1,561	1,459	1,371	1,290	1,217
3 by 10	4,370	4,370	4,370	4,370	4,139	3,749	3,424	3,146	2,908	2,699	2,517	2,353	2,210	2,079	1,961
4 by 10	6,035	6,035	6,035	6,035	5,719	5,177	4,731	3,348	4,019	3,732	3,480	3,255	3,057	3,878	2,715
6 by 10	9,160	9,160	9,160	9,160	8,680	7,862	7,179	6,598	6,100	5,664	5,283	4,940	4,641	4,368	4,121
8 by 10	12,500	12,500	12,500	12,500	11,835	10,720	9,790	9,000	8,318	7,724	7,205	6,738	6,329	5,957	5,620
10 by 10	15,805	15,805	15,805	15,805	14,992	13,581	12,401	11,399	10,536	9,785	9,126	8,535	8,017	7,546	7,120
2 by 12	3,265	3,265	3,265	3,265	3,265	3,265	3,122	2,871	2,657	2,469	2,305	2,158	2,028	1,911	1,806
3 by 12	5,260	5,260	5,260	5,260	5,260	5,260	5,037	4,633	4,285	3,982	3,716	3,478	3,270	3,081	2,909
4 by 12	7,270	7,270	7,270	7,270	7,270	7,270	6,963	6,404	5,925	5,507	5,140	4,813	4,525	4,265	4,029
6 by 12	11,050	11,050	11,050	11,050	11,050	11,050	10,566	9,718	8,991	8,357	7,802	7,303	6,869	6,472	6,115
8 by 12	15,050	15,050	15,050	15,050	15,050	15,050	14,408	13,252	12,260	11,396	10,638	9,959	9,366	8,826	8,337
10 by 12	19,080	19,080	19,080	19,080	19,080	19,080	18,249	16,786	15,529	14,435	13,475	12,615	11,863	11,180	10,560
12 by 12	23,130	23,130	23,130	23,130	23,130	23,130	22,090	20,320	18,797	17,474	16,311	15,270	14,360	13,533	12,783
2 by 14	4,115	4,115	4,115	4,115	4,115	4,115	4,115	4,115	3,669	3,412	3,186	2,885	2,808	2,587	2,502
3 by 14	6,165	6,165	6,165	6,165	6,165	6,165	6,165	6,165	5,931	5,515	5,150	4,825	4,540	4,281	4,046
4 by 14	8,510	8,510	8,510	8,510	8,510	8,510	8,510	8,510	8,200	7,626	7,123	6,674	6,280	5,923	5,600
6 by 14	12,930	12,930	12,930	12,930	12,930	12,930	12,930	12,930	12,440	11,571	10,810	10,125	9,530	8,987	8,498
8 by 14	17,630	17,630	17,630	17,630	17,630	17,630	17,630	17,630	16,964	15,780	14,740	13,809	12,996	12,258	11,590
10 by 14	22,335	22,335	22,335	22,335	22,335	22,335	22,335	22,335	21,487	19,986	18,670	17,490	16,460	15,524	14,676
12 by 14	27,040	27,040	27,040	27,040	27,040	27,040	27,040	27,040	26,010	24,194	22,600	21,171	19,925	18,192	17,766
14 by 14	31,760	31,760	31,760	31,760	31,760	31,760	31,760	31,760	30,512	28,390	26,530	24,860	23,390	22,040	20,838

Built-up girders

Multiply above figures by 0.897 when 4-inch girder is made up of two 2-inch pieces.
.887 when 6-inch girder is made up of three 2-inch pieces.
.867 when 8-inch girder is made up of four 2-inch pieces.
.856 when 10-inch girder is made up of five 2-inch pieces.

Loads to the right of the zigzag line will cause a deflection greater than 1/360 of the span.

NOTE.—Built-up girders of dressed lumber will carry somewhat smaller loads than solid girders; that is, two 2-inch dressed planks will equal only 3¼, whereas dressed 4-inch lumber will equal 3⅝. It is, therefore, necessary to multiply by the above figures in order to compute the loads for built-up girders.

Reprinted with permission from Light-Frame House Construction, U. S. Department of Health, Education and Welfare.

girders, as shown in the footnotes in Tables 24 through 27. This is necessary because the built-up girder, with each piece surfaced two sides, is slightly smaller than a solid girder.

Selecting a Wood Girder

The first consideration is the total load that the girder must support. This girder load for residential construction is assumed to be distributed uniformly along the length of the girder. These calculations are discussed earlier in this chapter.

Lumber Species

Once the load is known, the species of lumber from which the girder is to be made must be decided. Table 28 gives the allowable working stresses per unit for some of the comon species of lumber. The allowable working-stress unit is in pounds per square inch.

Under the heading "extreme fiber in bending," the first column gives working stresses in bending for members up to 4 inches in

Table 25
Permissible Spans of Solid Wood Girders
Allowable fiber stress, 1,400 pounds per square inch
(Allowable uniformly distributed loads for solid wood girders and beams in pounds computed for actual dressed sizes)

Solid dressed sizes	Span in Feet														
	4, 5, 6	7	8	9	10	11	12	13	14	15	16	17	18	19	20
2 by 6	1,318	1,124	979	865	774	699	636	582	536	495	459	427	399	372	349
3 by 6	2,127	1,816	1,581	1,397	1,249	1,128	1,026	938	863	798	740	688	641	599	561
4 by 6	2,938	2,507	2,184	1,930	1,726	1,559	1,418	1,297	1,194	1,102	1,023	952	888	831	777
6 by 6	4,263	3,638	3,168	2,800	2,504	2,260	2,055	1,881	1,731	1,599	1,483	1,379	1,286	1,202	1,126
2 by 8	1,865	1,865	1,760	1,558	1,395	1,260	1,150	1,055	973	902	839	783	733	687	646
3 by 8	3,020	3,020	2,824	2,500	2,238	2,024	1,845	1,692	1,560	1,444	1,343	1,253	1,172	1,100	1,034
4 by 8	4,165	4,165	3,904	3,456	3,906	2,800	2,552	2,342	2,160	2,002	1,862	1,737	1,626	1,528	1,435
6 by 8	6,330	6,330	5,924	5,244	4,698	4,250	3,873	3,553	3,277	3,037	2,825	2,636	2,468	2,315	2,178
8 by 8	8,630	8,630	8,078	7,151	6,406	5,793	5,281	4,845	4,469	4,141	3,851	3,595	3,365	3,157	2,969
2 by 10	2,360	2,360	2,360	2,360	2,237	2,026	1,848	1,699	1,569	1,455	1,356	1,268	1,190	1,118	1,054
3 by 10	3,810	3,810	3,810	3,810	3,612	3,271	2,984	2,740	2,531	2,348	2,267	2,045	1,917	1,803	1,698
4 by 10	5,265	5,265	5,265	5,265	4,992	4,520	4,125	3,788	3,500	3,248	3,026	2,830	2,653	2,496	2,352
6 by 10	7,990	7,990	7,990	7,990	7,576	6,860	6,261	5,751	5,312	4,929	4,593	4,294	4,029	3,787	3,571
8 by 10	10,920	10,920	10,920	10,920	10,330	9,351	8,537	7,841	7,244	6,922	6,264	5,857	5,493	5,165	4,868
10 by 10	13,825	13,825	13,825	13,825	13,085	11,849	10,813	9,933	9,176	8,815	7,934	7,419	6,958	6,543	6,168
2 by 12	2,845	2,845	2,845	2,845	2,845	2,845	2,724	2,503	2,315	2,150	2,006	1,878	1,763	1,660	1,567
3 by 12	4,590	4,590	4,590	4,590	4,590	4,590	4,394	4,039	3,734	3,468	3,234	3,026	2,842	2,675	2,524
4 by 12	6,350	6,350	6,350	6,350	6,350	6,350	6,075	5,585	5,165	4,797	4,474	4,189	3,933	3,705	3,496
6 by 12	9,640	9,640	9,640	9,640	9,640	9,640	9,220	8,475	7,837	7,280	6,791	6,357	5,970	5,622	5,307
8 by 12	13,160	13,160	13,160	13,160	13,160	13,160	12,570	11,556	10,685	9,926	9,260	8,669	8,141	7,666	7,237
10 by 12	16,670	16,670	16,670	16,670	16,670	16,670	15,923	14,638	13,536	12,573	11,728	10,980	10,311	9,710	9,166
12 by 12	20,170	20,170	20,170	20,170	20,170	20,170	19,274	17,709	16,384	15,220	14,197	13,291	12,482	11,753	11,096
2 by 14	3,595	3,595	3,595	3,595	3,595	3,595	3,595	3,595	3,199	2,973	2,776	2,490	2,443	2,301	2,173
3 by 14	5,365	5,365	5,365	5,365	5,365	5,365	5,365	5,365	5,171	4,805	4,485	4,202	3,949	3,721	3,514
4 by 14	7,420	7,420	7,420	7,420	7,420	7,420	7,420	7,420	7,151	6,646	6,225	5,814	5,465	5,150	4,876
6 by 14	11,290	11,290	11,290	11,290	11,290	11,290	11,290	11,290	10,849	10,086	9,415	8,821	8,292	7,814	7,384
8 by 14	15,360	15,360	15,360	15,360	15,360	15,360	15,360	15,360	14,796	13,754	12,840	12,030	11,307	10,658	10,071
10 by 14	19,465	19,465	19,465	19,465	19,465	19,465	19,465	19,465	18,740	17,420	16,261	15,236	14,321	13,498	12,755
12 by 14	23,590	23,590	23,590	23,590	23,590	23,590	23,590	23,590	22,685	21,088	19,685	18,445	17,236	16,340	15,440
14 by 14	27,690	27,690	27,690	27,690	27,690	27,690	27,690	27,690	26,630	24,754	23,108	21,652	20,350	20,142	18,125

Built-up girders

Multiply above figures by 0.897 when 4-inch girder is made up of two 2-inch pieces.
.887 when 6-inch girder is made up of three 2-inch pieces.
.867 when 8-inch girder is made up of four 2-inch pieces.
.856 when 10-inch girder is made up of five 2-inch pieces.

Loads to the right of the zigzag line will cause a deflection greater than 1/360 of the span.

NOTE.—Built-up girders of dressed lumber will carry somewhat smaller loads than solid girders; that is, two 2-inch dressed planks will equal only 3¼, whereas dressed 4-inch lumber will equal 3⅝. It is, therefore, necessary to multiply by the above figures in order to compute the loads for built-up girders.

Reprinted with permission from Light-Frame House Construction, U. S. Department of Health, Education and Welfare.

thickness. The second column shows stresses for timbers 5 inches and over in thickness.

Once the species has been decided, the corresponding bending stress can be selected. For example, if No. 1 common yellow pine is used for a girder, the extreme fiber in bending is 1,200 pounds per square inch. To ascertain the actual girder size, it is necessary to refer to a table of spans for wood girders with an allowable fiber stress of 1,200 pounds per square inch. See Table 26.

If this member had to support 2,000

pounds over a span of 10 feet, the wood girder would have to be 4 x 8, 3 x 10, or 2 x 12.

If a species such as Redwood, heart structural, with an allowable unit stress of 1,024 pounds per square inch, is selected, it is necessary to refer to Table 27 with a unit stress of 900 pounds per square inch.

In Tables 24 through 27 the stair-stepped, dark line sets the limits on deflection in the timbers. (*Deflection* refers to bending of the structural member.) Loads above the line will cause a deflection greater than 1/360 of the

Table 26
Permissible Spans of Solid Wood Girders
Allowable fiber stress 1,200 pounds per square inch
(Allowable uniformly distributed loads for wood girders and beams in pounds computed for actual dressed sizes)

Solid dressed sizes	4, 5, 6	7	8	9	10	11	12	13	14	15	16	17	18	19	20
2 by 6	1,127	961	837	738	660	595	541	494	454	419	388	360	335	312	292
3 by 6	1,820	1,552	1,351	1,192	1,065	960	872	796	731	675	625	580	539	502	469
4 by 6	2,514	2,144	1,866	1,647	1,471	1,327	1,206	1,102	1,012	933	864	802	747	697	650
6 by 6	3,650	3,111	2,708	2,389	2,134	1,924	1,747	1,597	1,467	1,352	1,252	1,161	1,081	1,007	941
2 by 8	1,605	1,605	1,503	1,331	1,191	1,075	980	898	827	766	712	662	619	580	544
3 by 8	2,580	2,580	2,414	2,135	1,911	1,726	1,572	1,439	1,325	1,225	1,139	1,060	990	927	870
4 by 8	3,570	3,570	3,340	2,953	2,643	2,388	2,175	1,993	1,836	1,700	1,590	1,472	1,375	1,288	1,210
6 by 8	5,420	5,420	5,064	4,481	4,011	3,625	3,300	3,025	2,786	2,579	2,396	2,232	2,086	1,953	1,834
8 by 8	7,390	7,390	6,905	6,110	5,464	4,941	4,500	4,125	3,799	3,516	3,265	3,043	2,845	2,664	2,500
2 by 10	2,020	2,020	2,020	2,020	1,912	1,730	1,578	1,449	1,336	1,238	1,153	1,077	1,009	946	891
3 by 10	3,255	3,255	3,255	3,255	3,088	2,792	2,546	2,336	2,152	1,997	1,859	1,735	1,624	1,525	1,435
4 by 10	4,500	4,500	4,500	4,500	4,267	3,864	3,520	3,230	2,981	2,763	2,572	2,402	2,249	2,113	1,988
6 by 10	6,830	6,830	6,830	6,830	6,473	5,860	5,341	4,902	4,524	4,193	3,904	3,647	3,416	3,206	3,020
8 by 10	9,320	9,320	9,320	9,320	8,827	7,980	7,284	6,685	6,179	5,719	5,324	4,972	4,657	4,374	4,116
10 by 10	11,795	11,795	11,795	11,795	11,181	10,110	9,226	8,468	7,815	7,245	6,744	6,299	5,900	5,540	5,215
2 by 12	2,435	2,435	2,435	2,435	2,435	2,435	2,328	2,136	1,973	1,832	1,708	1,597	1,497	1,410	1,328
3 by 12	3,920	3,920	3,920	3,920	3,920	3,920	3,754	3,446	3,183	2,953	2,752	2,572	2,413	2,269	2,138
4 by 12	5,430	5,430	5,430	5,430	5,430	5,430	5,191	4,766	4,393	4,087	3,809	3,553	3,341	3,143	2,964
6 by 12	8,250	8,250	8,250	8,250	8,250	8,250	7,870	7,232	6,682	6,202	5,781	5,407	5,072	4,770	4,499
8 by 12	11,240	11,240	11,240	11,240	11,240	11,240	10,733	9,862	9,111	8,456	7,783	7,374	6,916	6,506	6,134
10 by 12	14,250	14,250	14,250	14,250	14,250	14,250	13,597	12,491	11,541	10,711	9,985	9,338	8,760	8,240	7,769
12 by 12	17,240	17,240	17,240	17,240	17,240	17,240	16,460	15,121	13,960	12,967	12,086	11,304	10,605	9,974	9,404
2 by 14	3,065	3,065	3,065	3,065	3,065	3,065	3,065	3,065	2,729	2,534	2,366	2,212	2,076	1,954	1,845
3 by 14	4,600	4,600	4,600	4,600	4,600	4,600	4,600	4,600	4,412	4,097	3,825	3,577	3,358	3,161	2,984
4 by 14	6,340	6,340	6,340	6,340	6,340	6,340	6,340	6,340	6,102	5,668	5,288	4,950	4,648	4,377	4,132
6 by 14	9,630	9,630	9,630	9,630	9,630	9,630	9,630	9,630	9,258	8,601	8,020	7,511	7,054	6,642	6,270
8 by 14	13,140	13,140	13,140	13,140	13,140	13,140	13,140	13,140	12,628	11,730	10,942	10,244	9,619	9,058	8,552
10 by 14	16,640	16,640	16,640	16,640	16,640	16,640	16,640	16,640	16,002	14,854	13,860	12,975	12,183	11,472	10,830
12 by 14	20,140	20,140	20,140	20,140	20,140	20,140	20,140	20,140	19,167	17,982	16,780	15,706	14,748	13,887	13,110
14 by 14	23,640	23,640	23,640	23,640	23,640	23,640	23,640	23,640	22,742	21,120	19,690	18,440	17,310	16,370	15,388

Built-up girders

Multiply above figures by 0.897 when 4-inch girder is made up of two 2-inch pieces.
.887 when 6-inch girder is made up of three 2-inch pieces.
.867 when 8-inch girder is made up of four 2-inch pieces.
.856 when 10-inch girder is made up of five 2-inch pieces.

Loads to the right of the zigzag line will cause a deflection greater than 1/360 of the span.

NOTE—Built-up girders of dressed lumber will carry somewhat smaller loads than solid girders, that is, two 2-inch dressed planks will equal only 3¼, whereas dressed 4-inch lumber will equal 3⅝. It is, therefore, necessary to multiply by the above figures in order to compute the loads for built-up girders.

Reprinted with permission from Light-Frame House Construction, U. S. Department of Health, Education and Welfare.

span. This is the limit usually set for deflection of girders and joists. Any deflection greater than this is likely to cause plaster cracks and sticking doors.

Box Beams

Figs. 483 through 485 illustrate typical designs for box beams which are part of, and support for, a roof. These are designed, on a normal loading basis, to carry a total uniform roof load of 40 pounds per square foot of horizontal load (10 psf. dead load and 30 psf. live load). Deflection under live load is limited to 1/240 of the span.

The box beams in Fig. 486 are designed, on a normal loading basis, to carry a total uniform floor load of 50 pounds per square foot (10 psf. dead load and 40 psf. live load).

These commonly used designs meet the requirements of normal residential construction. Box beams can be designed to carry a wide variety of loads over many different spans. Detailed design data can be obtained from the Plywood Fabricator Service, Inc. and the Douglas Fir Plywood Association.

Table 27
Permissible Spans of Solid Wood Girders
Allowable fiber stress 900 pounds
(Allowable uniformly distributed loads for solid wood girders and beams in pounds computed for actual dressed sizes)

Solid dressed sizes	Span in Feet															
	4, 5, 6	7	8	9	10	11	12	13	14	15	16	17	18	19	20
2 by 6	842	717	623	548	489	439	398	362	332	304	281	259	240	222	207
3 by 6	1,359	1,159	1,005	884	788	708	642	583	534	490	452	417	385	357	331
4 by 6	1,877	1,600	1,390	1,223	1,089	980	887	808	739	678	625	577	534	496	459
6 by 6	2,723	2,319	2,013	1,773	1,579	1,430	1,285	1,170	1,071	983	905	835	773	715	663
2 by 8	1,195	1,195	1,123	991	885	796	725	663	608	561	520	492	449	418	392
3 by 8	1,928	1,928	1,801	1,589	1,419	1,278	1,162	1,061	974	898	831	771	717	668	624
4 by 8	2,666	2,666	2,488	2,198	1,963	1,770	1,610	1,470	1,351	1,247	1,154	1,072	997	931	869
6 by 8	4,045	4,045	3,781	3,335	2,980	2,687	2,441	2,232	2,050	1,891	1,751	1,626	1,513	1,411	1,318
8 by 8	5,515	5,515	5,148	4,547	4,062	3,663	3,328	3,043	2,795	2,578	2,386	2,216	2,063	1,924	1,797
2 by 10	1,504	1,504	1,504	1,504	1,423	1,286	1,170	1,072	987	912	847	789	737	689	647
3 by 10	2,428	2,428	2,428	2,428	2,296	2,074	1,888	1,728	1,591	1,472	1,365	1,271	1,185	1,109	1,040
4 by 10	3,357	3,357	3,357	3,357	3,174	2,864	2,611	2,391	2,202	2,036	1,891	1,761	1,644	1,539	1,443
6 by 10	5,095	5,095	5,095	5,095	4,818	4,352	3,962	3,629	3,342	3,092	2,870	2,673	2,496	2,336	2,191
8 by 10	6,947	6,947	6,947	6,947	6,570	5,933	5,403	4,949	4,558	4,215	3,914	3,645	3,404	3,186	2,989
10 by 10	8,800	8,800	8,800	8,800	8,523	7,518	6,844	6,270	5,774	5,340	4,958	4,617	4,312	4,037	3,786
2 by 12	1,812	1,812	1,812	1,812	1,812	1,812	1,729	1,585	1,462	1,354	1,260	1,176	1,099	1,032	970
3 by 12	2,918	2,918	2,918	2,918	2,918	2,918	2,787	2,556	2,357	2,182	2,029	1,890	1,770	1,660	1,560
4 by 12	4,038	4,038	4,038	4,038	4,038	4,038	3,856	3,536	3,262	3,022	2,810	2,623	2,454	2,303	2,165
6 by 12	6,130	6,130	6,130	6,130	6,130	6,130	5,852	5,367	4,950	4,587	4,266	3,980	3,725	3,495	3,286
8 by 12	8,360	8,360	8,360	8,360	8,360	8,360	7,978	7,319	6,750	6,253	5,818	5,427	5,080	4,766	4,482
10 by 12	10,595	10,595	10,595	10,595	10,595	10,595	10,107	9,270	8,550	7,920	7,367	6,875	6,434	6,037	5,674
12 by 12	12,822	12,822	12,822	12,822	12,822	12,822	12,233	11,221	10,349	9,588	8,918	8,321	7,788	7,308	6,870
2 by 14	2,278	2,278	2,278	2,278	2,278	2,278	2,278	2,278	2,876	1,875	1,746	1,631	1,628	1,434	1,350
3 by 14	3,409	3,409	3,409	3,409	3,409	3,409	3,409	3,409	3,273	3,035	2,825	2,638	2,472	2,322	2,186
4 by 14	4,717	4,717	4,717	4,717	4,717	4,717	4,717	4,717	4,530	4,200	3,918	3,654	3,425	3,219	3,031
6 by 14	7,157	7,157	7,157	7,157	7,157	7,157	7,157	7,157	6,872	6,373	5,930	5,545	5,198	4,884	4,599
8 by 14	9,751	9,751	9,751	9,751	9,751	9,751	9,751	9,751	9,371	8,692	8,092	7,563	7,088	6,663	6,274
10 by 14	12,365	12,365	12,365	12,365	12,365	12,365	12,365	12,365	11,869	11,008	10,250	9,578	8,977	8,436	7,943
12 by 14	14,965	14,965	14,965	14,965	14,965	14,965	14,965	14,965	14,367	13,326	12,410	11,595	10,867	10,212	9,618
14 by 14	17,567	17,567	17,567	17,567	17,567	17,567	17,567	17,567	16,872	15,646	14,580	13,620	12,760	11,990	11,288

Built-up girders

Multiply above figures by 0.897 when 4-inch girder is made up of two 2-inch pieces.
.887 when 6-inch girder is made up of three 2-inch pieces.
.867 when 8-inch girder is made up of four 2-inch pieces.
.856 when 10-inch girder is made up of five 2-inch pieces.

NOTE—Built-up girders of dressed lumber will carry somewhat smaller loads than solid girders, that is, two 2-inch dressed planks will equal only 3¼, whereas dressed 4-inch lumber will equal 3⅝. It is, therefore, necessary to multiply by the above figures in order to compute the loads for built-up girders.

Reprinted with permission from Light-Frame House Construction, U. S. Department of Health, Education and Welfare.

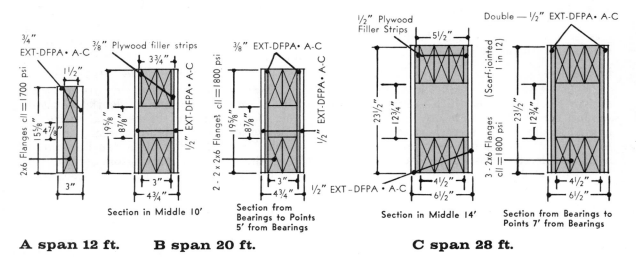

A span 12 ft.   **B span 20 ft.**   **C span 28 ft.**

Fig. 483. Box beam as ridge girder, designed for houses up to 28'-0" wide. The beam can overhang up to 4'-0" at gable end. (Plywood Fabricator Service, Inc.)

Table 28
Allowable Unit Stresses for Structural Lumber and Timber
(All sizes, dry locations)
Working Stresses for Manufacturers' Association Standard Commercial Grades

SPECIES OF TIMBER	GRADE	ALLOWABLE UNIT STRESS IN POUNDS PER SQUARE INCH; (EXTREME FIBER IN BENDING)	
		Joist and plank sizes; 4 inches and less in thickness	Beam and stringer sizes; 5 inches and thicker
Douglas fir, coast region	Dense superstructural	2,000	2,000
	Superstructural and dense structural	1,800	1,800
	Structural	1,600	1,600
	Common structural	1,200	1,400
Douglas fir, inland empire	Dense superstructural[a]	2,000	2,000
	Dense structural[a]	1,800	1,800
	No. 1 common dimension and timbers	1,135	1,135
Larch, western	No. 1 common dimension and timbers	1,135	1,135
Pine, southern yellow	Extra dense select structural	2,300	2,300
	Select structural	2,000	2,000
	Extra dense heart	2,000	2,000
	Dense heart	1,800	1,800
	Structural square edge and sound	1,600	1,600
	No. 1 common	1,200	1,200
Redwood	Superstructural	2,133	1,707
	Prime structural	1,707	1,494
	Select structural	1,280	1,322
	Heart structural	1,024	1,150

[a]When graded the same as corresponding grade of coast region Douglas fir.

Reprinted with permission from Light-Frame House Construction, U. S. Department of Health, Education and Welfare.

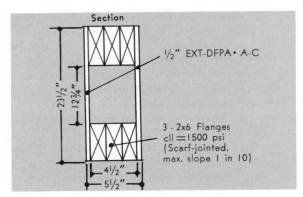

Fig. 484. Flat-roof box girder designed to span 48'-0" spaced 4'-0" o.c. (Plywood Fabricator Service, Inc.)

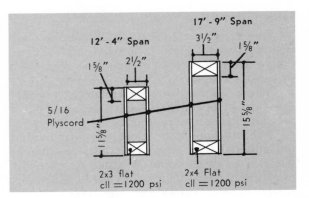

Fig. 485. Box beams designed as floor beams, to be spaced 4'-0" o.c. (Plywood Fabricator Service, Inc.)

Table 29
Typical Glued Laminated Beam and Purlin Sizes[1] (Small Spacing)

BEAM		TOTAL LOAD—POUNDS PER SQUARE FOOT			
Span	Spacing	30 Lbs.	40 Lbs.	50 Lbs.	60 Lbs.
16'	4'	3¼ x 8[2]	3¼ x 9⅝	3¼ x 9⅝	3¼ x11¼
	6'	3¼ x 9⅝	3¼ x11¼	3¼ x11¼	3¼ x12⅞
	8'	3¼ x 9⅝	3¼ x11¼	3¼ x12⅞	3¼ x14½
18'	4'	3¼ x 9⅝	3¼ x11¼	3¼ x11¼	3¼ x12⅞
	6'	3¼ x11¼	3¼ x12⅞	3¼ x12⅞	3¼ x14½
	8'	3¼ x11¼	3¼ x12⅞	3¼ x14½	3¼ x16⅛
20'	4'	3¼ x 9⅝	3¼ x11¼	3¼ x12⅞	3¼ x12⅞
	6'	3¼ x11¼	3¼ x12⅞	3¼ x14½	5¼ x12⅞
	8'	3¼ x12⅞	3¼ x14½	5¼ x12⅞	5¼ x14½
22'	4'	3¼ x11¼	3¼ x12⅞	3¼ x12⅞	3¼ x14½
	6'	3¼ x12⅞	3¼ x14½	5¼ x12⅞	5¼ x14½
	8'	3¼ x14½	5¼ x12⅞	5¼ x14½	5¼ x16⅛
24'	4'	3¼ x11¼	3¼ x14½	3¼ x14½	5¼ x14½
	6'	3¼ x14½	5¼ x12⅞	5¼ x14½	5¼ x16⅛
	8'	3¼ x14½	5¼ x14½	5¼ x16⅛	5¼ x17¾
26'	4'	3¼ x12⅞	3¼ x14½	5¼ x14½	5¼ x14½
	6'	3¼ x14½	5¼ x14½	5¼ x16⅛	5¼ x17¾
	8'	5¼ x14½	5¼ x16⅛	5¼ x17¾	5¼ x19⅜
28'	4'	3¼ x14½	5¼ x12⅞	5¼ x14½	5¼ x16⅛
	6'	5¼ x12⅞	5¼ x16⅛	5¼ x17¾	5¼ x17¾
	8'	5¼ x14½	5¼ x17¾	5¼ x19⅜	5¼ x21
30'	4'	5¼ x12⅞	5¼ x14½	5¼ x16⅛	5¼ x17¾
	6'	5¼ x14½	5¼ x16⅛	5¼ x17¾	5¼ x19⅜
	8'	5¼ x16⅛	5¼ x17¾	5¼ x19⅜	5¼ x21
32'	4'	5¼ x12⅞	5¼ x16⅛	5¼ x17¾	5¼ x17¾
	6'	5¼ x16⅛	5¼ x17¾	5¼ x19⅜	·5¼ x21
	8'	5¼ x16⅛	5¼ x19⅜	5¼ x21	5¼ x22⅝
34'	4'	5¼ x14½	5¼ x16⅛	5¼ x17¾	5¼ x19⅜
	6'	5¼ x16⅛	5¼ x19⅜	5¼ x21	5¼ x22⅝
	8'	5¼ x17¾	5¼ x21	5¼ x22⅝	5¼ x24¼

[1]Design based on roof loads applied to roof slope. Maximum live load deflection 1/360 of span. Assumed dead load 12 pounds per square foot.
[2]Cross section size of beam.
Courtesy Timber Structures, Inc.

Glued Laminated Wood Beams

Glued, laminated structural members are manufactured in stock lengths and shapes. These are engineered to carry specified loads of various spans.

These manufactured members are about one-third stronger than a sawn timber of equal section of seasoned material.

For interior applications, the laminations are adhered with water-resistant, casein-type glues. For exposure to weather or excessive moisture, special glues are used. These are made of waterproof, exterior-type phenol, resorcinol or melamine resin.

The structural members in Tables 29 and 30 are but a few of the many stock types available. Manufacturers' catalogs should be consulted for a more complete listing. These tables are for butterfly, peaked, peaked and cambered, slightly tapered and simple straight beams, as shown in Fig. 487.

To use these tables, the span and desired spacing must be decided. The total roof load must then be ascertained. The correct beam size can then be chosen from the table.

These members can also serve as purlins. A *purlin* is a small beam laid at right angles to the rafters and used to support the rafters

Table 30
Typical Sizes of Glued Laminated Beams and Purlins
(Wide spacing. 1/240 Deflection. f=2200+15% for Short Term Duration of Live Load)

BEAM OR PURLIN		TOTAL LOAD (P. S. F.)					
Span	Spacing	30	35	40	45	50	55
16'	6'	3¼x8¹	3¼x9⅝	3¼x9⅝	3¼x9⅝	3¼x9⅝	3¼x11¼
	8'	3¼x9⅝	3¼x9⅝	3¼x11¼	3¼x11¼	3¼x11¼	3¼x11¼
	10'	3¼x9⅝	3¼x11¼	3¼x11¼	3¼x11¼	3¼x12⅞	3¼x12⅞
	12'	3¼x11¼	3¼x11¼	3¼x12⅞	3¼x12⅞	3¼x14½	3¼x14½
	14'	3¼x11¼	3¼x12⅞	3¼x12⅞	3¼x14½	3¼x14½	5¼x12⅞
	16'	3¼x12⅞	3¼x12⅞	3¼x14½	3¼x14½	5¼x12⅞	5¼x12⅞
20'	8'	3¼x11¼	3¼x12⅞	3¼x12⅞	3¼x12⅞	3¼x14½	3¼x14½
	10'	3¼x12⅞	3¼x12⅞	3¼x14½	3¼x14½	5¼x12⅞	5¼x12⅞
	12'	3¼x12⅞	3¼x14½	5¼x12⅞	5¼x12⅞	5¼x14½	5¼x14½
	14'	3¼x14½	5¼x12⅞	5¼x12⅞	5¼x14½	5¼x14½	5¼x16⅛
	16'	3¼x14½	5¼x14½	5¼x14½	5¼x14½	5¼x16⅛	5¼x16⅛
	18'	5¼x12⅞	5¼x14½	5¼x14½	5¼x16⅛	5¼x16⅛	5¼x17¾
24'	8'	3¼x14½	3¼x14½	5¼x12⅞	5¼x14½	5¼x14½	5¼x14½
	10'	3¼x14½	5¼x14½	5¼x14½	5¼x14½	5¼x14½	5¼x16⅛
	12'	5¼x14½	5¼x14½	5¼x14½	5¼x16⅛	5¼x16⅛	5¼x16⅛
	14'	5¼x14½	5¼x14½	5¼x16⅛	5¼x16⅛	5¼x17¾	5¼x17¾
	16'	5¼x14½	5¼x16⅛	5¼x16⅛	5¼x17¾	5¼x17¾	5¼x19⅜
	18'	5¼x16⅛	5¼x16⅛	5¼x17¾	5¼x19⅜	5¼x19⅜	5¼x21
32'	8'	5¼x16⅛	5¼x16⅛	5¼x17¾	5¼x17¾	5¼x19⅜	5¼x19⅜
	10'	5¼x16⅛	5¼x17¾	5¼x19⅜	5¼x19⅜	5¼x19⅜	5¼x21
	12'	5¼x17¾	5¼x19⅜	5¼x19⅜	5¼x21	5¼x21	5¼x22⅝
	14'	5¼x19⅜	5¼x19⅜	5¼x21	5¼x21	5¼x22⅝	7x21
	16'	5¼x19⅜	5¼x21	5¼x21	5¼x22⅝	7x21	7x22⅝
	18'	5¼x21	5¼x21	5¼x22⅝	7x21	7x22⅝	7x24¼
40'	8'	5¼x19⅜	5¼x21	5¼x21	5¼x22⅝	7x21	7x21
	10'	5¼x21	5¼x22⅝	5¼x22⅝	7x21	7x22⅝	7x22⅝
	12'	5¼x22⅝	7x21	7x22⅝	7x22⅝	7x24¼	7x24¼
	14'	7x21	7x22⅝	7x22⅝	7x24¼	7x25⅞	7x25⅞
	16'	7x22⅝	7x22⅝	7x24¼	7x25⅞	7x25⅞	7x27½
	18'	7x22⅝	7x24¼	7x25⅞	7x25⅞	7x27½	7x29⅛
50'	8'	7x22⅝	7x22⅝	7x24¼	7x24¼	7x25⅞	7x27½
	10'	7x24¼	7x24¼	7x25⅞	7x27½	7x27½	7x29⅛
	12'	7x24¼	7x25⅞	7x27½	7x29⅛	7x29⅛	7x30¾
	14'	7x25⅞	7x27½	7x29⅛	7x30¾	7x30¾	9x29⅛
	16'	7x27½	7x29⅛	7x30¾	9x29⅛	9x29⅛	9x30¾
	18'	7x29⅛	7x30¾	9x29⅛	9x30¾	9x30¾	9x32⅜

¹Cross section of beam.
Courtesy Timber Structures, Inc.

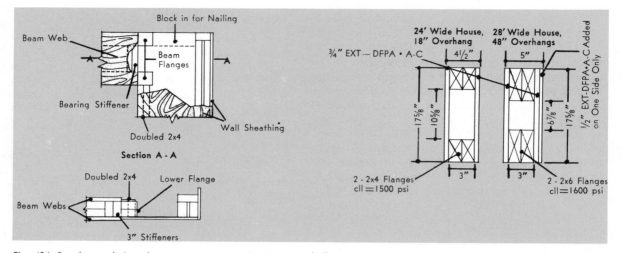

Fig. 486. Box beam designed to serve as garage lintel over 16'-0" span, for houses 24'-0" and 28'-0" wide. (Plywood Fabricator Service, Inc.)

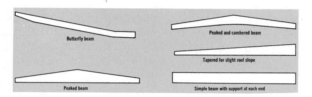

Fig. 487. Typical glued laminated roof beams. (Timber Structures, Inc.)

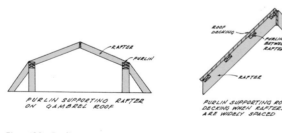

Fig. 488. Purlins.

Fig. 489. American Standard *I* beam (left) and a wide-flange beam. (Bethlehem Steel Co.)

or roof decking when rafters are widely spaced. See Fig. 488.

Steel Girders

The most common structural steel shapes used in residential construction as girders are the standard *I* beam and the wide-flange beam. See Fig. 489. The method for ascertaining the size of steel girders follows the same principle as that for wood girders. As wood girders vary in width for a given depth, so steel girders vary in weight, depth and thickness of web and flanges. The wide-flange beam has the advantage of presenting a wide bearing surface to rest upon the foundation wall. Frequently, the standard *I* beam must have a flange welded to it to distribute the load to the foundation.

Tables presenting the allowable loads on wide-flange and American Standard *I* beams can be found in Chapter 19. They assume the total load is uniformly distributed. The members are laterally supported. The loads include the weight of the beam, which should be added to the computed beam load to arrive at the total load upon the member.

If the beams in these tables have a single concentrated load at the center of the span, the allowable concentrated load is one-half the allowable uniformly distributed load for the same span.

An examination of the allowable load tables reveals that the vertical column on the left lists the span in feet. The figures in the

other vertical columns are the allowable loads on each beam in kips. (A *kip* is 1000 pounds.)

The size of the beam is indicated across the top of the table. These sizes are given by indicating the height of the beam, followed by the width. Directly beneath the beam size is the weight of one lineal foot of the beam.

Running through the actual load portion of the tables is a solid black line. This line indicates that the load just above it will produce maximum allowable sheer stress on the web of the beam. It is best to use the beam loads given just below the solid line to avoid the possibility of excessive deflection of the beam.

As a summary of these tables, follow this description of a beam as found in the tables. A wide-flange beam 8 inches high and 5¼ inches wide is available in two weights, 20 and 17 pounds per lineal foot. If a 20-pound beam is selected to span 15'-0", it will carry 18,100 pounds uniformly loaded. Since this includes the weight of the beam, the total allowable load the beam will carry, in addition to its own weight, is 17,800 pounds. The beam weighs 300 pounds or 20 pounds per foot x 15 feet of beam.

Light Open-Web Steel Joists

A steel-framed house may use steel I beams for roof framing or, if long spans are necessary, may use open-web joists, Fig. 490. This is especially true of houses with flat roofs and open planning, where interior partitions are not used for support and/or do not reach ceiling height.

Table 31 indicates allowable loads and spans for selected lightweight, open-web joists. Many other stock sizes and types are commercially available.

The figures in the left-hand vertical column indicate the joist type. For example, a 10-S-2 joist is 10 inches deep, S design; it uses a stock, steel angle for the cords. A 10-S-3 is the same design as a 10-S-2, but has a larger steel angle for cords.

Notice that there is some overlapping in the load-carrying capabilities of these joists. A 12-S-6, spaced 12 inches on center and spanning 20'-0", will carry 280 pounds per square foot, while a joist that is deeper but made from lighter angles, a 14-S-4, will carry 245 pounds per square foot under the same conditions.

Lintels

A *lintel* is a horizontal structural member which spans window and door openings and supports the wall above the opening. The wall area supported by a lintel is called a *spandrel*. See Fig. 491. Lintels may be made from wood, concrete or steel.

Computing Lintel Load

In order to select the proper lintel size, the weight of the material supported by the lintel must be computed. This usually involves computing the number of cubic feet in the spandrel and multiplying this by the weight of one cubic foot of the material used (generally brick). This gives the total load on the lintel. The span of the lintel is the width of the window opening. The proper lintel can then be selected from a table of safe loads.

If the wall space above an opening is built from masonry units, such as brick, the lintel does not support the weight of the entire area. See Fig. 492. Only the area within an isosceles triangle requires support. This tends to form

Fig. 490. Two types of open-web steel joists. (Bethlehem Steel Corp.)

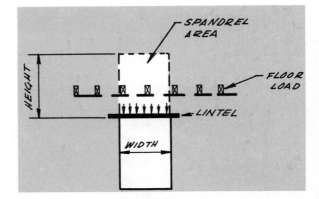

Fig. 491. Weight on lintel is weight of materials in spandrel plus floor load, if floor load height is less than width of window opening. Height of spandrel is same dimension as width of window opening.

Table 31
Safe Loads for Open-Web Steel Joists

Total safe loads consist of live loads plus dead load plus weight of joist.
Maximum deflection for tabulated spans and safe loads will not exceed 1/360th of the span. Tabulated safe loads are based on joists being properly braced laterally as required for standard joist construction.
Design Working Stress: 20,000 psi.

Joist Type No.	Clear Span	Total Safe Load Pounds	Total Safe Loads in Pounds Per Square Foot for Various Joist Spacings																			Joist Type No.
			[1]12"	14"	16"	17"	18"	19"	20"	21"	22"	23"	24"	2'-6"	3'-0"	3'-6"	4'-0"	5'-0"	6'-0"	7'-0"	
8 S 2	10'-0"	3500	350	300	263	247	233	221	210	200	191	183	175	140	117	100	88	70	58	50	8 S 2
10 S 2		3800	380	326	285	268	253	240	228	217	207	198	190	152	127	109	95	76	63	54	10 S 2
10 S 3		4000	400	343	300	282	267	253	240	229	218	209	200	160	133	114	100	80	67	57	10 S 3
10 S 4		4400	440	377	330	311	293	278	264	251	240	230	220	176	147	126	110	88	73	63	10 S 4
8 S 2	15'-0"	2333	156	134	117	110	104	99	94	89	85	81	78	62	52	45	39	31	—	—	8 S 2
10 S 2		2889	193	165	145	136	129	122	116	110	105	101	97	77	64	55	48	39	32	—	10 S 2
10 S 3		3689	246	211	185	174	164	155	148	141	134	128	123	98	82	70	62	49	41	35	10 S 3
10 S 4		4400	293	251	220	207	195	185	176	167	160	153	147	117	98	84	73	59	49	42	10 S 4
12 S 3		4400	293	251	220	207	195	185	176	167	160	153	147	117	98	84	73	59	49	42	12 S 3
12 S 4		4600	307	263	230	217	205	194	184	175	167	160	154	123	102	88	77	61	51	44	12 S 4
12 S 5		5000	333	285	250	235	222	210	200	190	182	174	167	133	111	95	83	67	55	48	12 S 5
12 S 6		5600	373	320	280	263	249	236	224	213	203	195	187	149	124	107	93	75	62	53	12 S 6
14 S 4		5200	347	297	260	245	231	219	208	198	189	181	174	139	116	99	87	69	58	50	14 S 4
14 S 5		5800	387	332	290	273	258	244	232	221	211	202	194	155	129	111	97	77	64	55	14 S 5
10 S 2	20'-0"	2167	108	93	81	76	72	68	65	62	59	56	54	43	36	31	—	—	—	—	10 S 2
10 S 3		2767	138	118	104	97	92	87	83	79	75	72	69	55	46	39	35	—	—	—	10 S 3
10 S 4		3433	172	147	129	121	115	109	103	98	94	90	86	69	57	49	43	34	—	—	10 S 4
12 S 3		3333	167	143	125	118	111	105	100	95	91	87	84	67	56	48	42	33	—	—	12 S 3
12 S 4		4167	208	178	156	147	139	131	125	119	113	109	104	83	69	59	52	42	35	30	12 S 4
12 S 5		4967	248	213	186	175	165	157	149	142	135	129	124	99	83	71	62	50	41	35	12 S 5
12 S 6		5600	280	240	210	198	187	177	168	160	153	146	140	112	93	80	70	56	47	40	12 S 6
14 S 4		4900	245	210	184	173	163	155	147	140	134	128	123	98	82	70	61	49	41	35	14 S 4
14 S 5		5800	290	249	218	205	193	183	174	166	158	151	145	116	97	83	73	58	48	41	14 S 5
14 S 6		6200	310	266	233	219	207	196	186	177	169	162	155	124	103	89	78	62	52	44	14 S 6
14 S 7		6800	340	291	255	240	227	215	204	194	185	177	170	136	113	97	85	68	57	49	14 S 7
16 S 5		6000	300	257	225	212	200	189	180	171	164	157	150	120	100	86	75	60	50	43	16 S 5
16 S 6		6600	330	283	248	233	220	208	198	189	180	172	165	132	110	94	83	66	55	47	16 S 6
16 S 7		7200	360	309	270	254	240	227	216	206	196	188	180	144	120	103	90	72	60	51	16 S 7
16 S 8		7800	390	334	293	275	260	246	234	223	213	203	195	156	130	111	98	78	65	56	16 S 8
18 S 6		7200	360	309	270	254	240	227	216	206	196	188	180	144	120	103	90	72	60	51	18 S 6
18 S 7		7600	380	326	285	268	253	240	228	217	207	198	190	152	127	109	95	76	63	54	18 S 7
18 S 8		8200	410	351	308	289	273	259	246	234	224	214	205	164	137	117	103	82	68	59	18 S 8
20 S 6		7400	370	317	278	261	247	234	222	211	202	193	185	148	123	106	93	74	62	53	20 S 6
20 S 7		7800	390	334	293	275	260	246	234	223	213	203	195	156	130	111	98	78	65	56	20 S 7
20 S 8		8400	420	360	315	296	280	265	252	240	229	219	210	168	140	120	105	84	70	60	20 S 8
14 S 4	25'-0"	3920	157	135	118	111	105	99	94	90	86	82	79	63	52	45	39	31	—	—	14 S 4
14 S 5		4667	187	160	140	132	125	118	112	107	102	98	94	75	62	53	47	37	31	—	14 S 5
14 S 6		5707	228	195	171	161	152	144	137	130	124	119	114	91	76	65	57	46	38	33	14 S 6
14 S 7		6693	268	230	201	189	179	169	161	153	146	140	134	107	89	77	67	54	45	38	14 S 7
16 S 5		5387	215	184	161	152	143	136	129	123	117	112	108	86	72	61	54	43	36	31	16 S 5
16 S 6		6453	258	221	194	182	172	163	155	147	141	135	129	103	86	74	65	52	43	37	16 S 6
16 S 7		7200	288	247	216	203	192	182	173	165	157	150	144	115	96	82	72	58	48	41	16 S 7
16 S 8		7800	312	267	234	220	208	197	187	178	170	163	156	125	104	89	78	62	52	45	16 S 8

(Continued)

[1]Allowable uniform total load per foot of joist.
Courtesy Bethlehem Steel Corporation.

Table 31 (con't.)
Safe Loads for Open-Web Steel Joists

Total safe loads consist of live loads plus dead load plus weight of joist.

Maximum deflection for tabulated spans and safe loads will not exceed 1/360th of the span. Tabulated safe loads are based on joists being properly braced laterally as required for standard joist construction.

Design Working Stress: 20,000 psi.

| Joist Type No. | Clear Span | Total Safe Load Pounds | Total Safe Loads in Pounds Per Square Foot for Various Joist Spacings | | | | | | | | | | | | | | | | | | Joist Type No. |
			[1]12"	14"	16"	17"	18"	19"	20"	21"	22"	23"	24"	2'-6"	3'-0"	3'-6"	4'-0"	5'-0"	6'-0"	7'-0"	
18 S 6	25'-0"	7200	288	247	216	203	192	182	173	165	157	150	144	115	96	82	72	58	48	41	18 S 6
18 S 7		7600	304	261	228	215	203	192	182	174	166	159	152	122	101	87	76	61	51	43	18 S 7
18 S 8		8200	328	281	246	232	219	207	197	187	179	171	164	131	109	94	82	66	55	47	18 S 8
20 S 6		7400	296	254	222	209	197	187	178	169	161	154	148	118	99	85	74	59	49	42	20 S 6
20 S 7		7800	312	267	234	220	208	197	187	178	170	163	156	125	104	89	78	62	52	45	20 S 7
20 S 8		8400	336	288	252	237	224	212	202	192	183	175	168	134	112	96	84	67	56	48	20 S 8
22 S 7		8000	320	274	240	226	213	202	192	183	175	167	160	128	107	91	80	64	53	46	22 S 7
22 S 8		8600	344	295	258	243	229	217	206	197	188	179	172	138	115	98	86	69	57	49	22 S 8
24 S 8		9000	360	309	270	254	240	227	216	206	196	188	180	144	120	103	90	72	60	51	24 S 8
16 S 5	30'-0"	4489	150	129	113	106	100	95	90	86	82	78	75	60	50	43	38	30	—	—	16 S 5
16 S 6		5378	179	153	134	126	119	113	107	102	98	93	90	72	60	51	45	36	30	—	16 S 6
16 S 7		6444	215	184	161	152	143	136	129	123	117	112	108	86	72	61	54	43	36	31	16 S 7
16 S 8		7467	249	213	187	176	166	157	149	142	136	130	125	100	83	71	62	50	41	36	16 S 8
18 S 6		6044	201	172	151	142	134	127	121	115	110	105	101	80	67	57	50	40	33	—	18 S 6
18 S 7		7289	243	208	182	172	162	153	146	139	133	127	122	97	81	69	61	49	40	35	18 S 7
18 S 8		8200	273	234	205	193	182	172	164	156	149	142	137	109	91	78	68	55	45	39	18 S 8
20 S 6		6556	219	188	164	155	146	138	131	125	119	114	110	88	73	63	55	44	36	31	20 S 6
20 S 7		7800	260	223	195	184	173	164	156	149	142	136	130	104	87	74	65	52	43	37	20 S 7
20 S 8		8400	280	240	210	198	187	177	168	160	153	146	140	112	93	80	70	56	47	40	20 S 8
22 S 7		8000	267	229	200	188	178	169	160	153	146	139	134	107	89	76	67	53	44	38	22 S 7
22 S 8		8600	287	246	215	203	191	181	172	164	157	150	144	115	96	82	72	57	48	41	22 S 8
24 S 8		9000	300	257	225	212	200	189	180	171	164	157	150	120	100	86	75	60	50	43	24 S 8
18 S 6	35'-0"	5181	148	127	111	104	99	93	89	85	81	77	74	59	49	42	37	30	—	—	18 S 6
18 S 7		6248	179	153	134	126	119	113	107	102	98	93	90	72	60	51	45	36	30	—	18 S 7
18 S 8		7238	207	177	155	146	138	131	124	118	113	108	104	83	69	59	52	41	34	30	18 S 8
20 S 6		5619	161	138	121	114	107	102	97	92	88	84	81	64	54	46	40	32	—	—	20 S 6
20 S 7		6819	195	167	146	138	130	123	117	111	106	102	98	78	65	56	49	39	32	—	20 S 7
20 S 8		8000	229	196	172	162	153	145	137	131	125	119	115	92	76	65	57	46	38	33	20 S 8
22 S 7		7333	210	180	158	148	140	133	126	120	115	110	105	84	70	60	53	42	35	30	22 S 7
22 S 8		8600	246	211	185	174	164	155	148	141	134	128	123	98	82	70	62	49	41	35	22 S 8
24 S 8		9000	257	220	193	181	171	162	154	147	140	134	129	103	86	73	64	51	43	37	24 S 8
20 S 6	40'-0"	4917	123	105	92	87	82	78	74	70	67	64	62	49	41	35	31	—	—	—	20 S 6
20 S 7		5967	149	128	112	105	99	94	89	85	81	78	75	60	50	43	37	30	—	—	20 S 7
20 S 8		7000	175	150	131	124	117	111	105	100	95	91	88	70	58	50	44	35	—	—	20 S 8
22 S 7		6417	160	137	120	113	107	101	96	91	87	83	80	64	53	46	40	32	—	—	22 S 7
22 S 8		7600	190	163	143	134	127	120	114	109	104	99	95	76	63	54	48	38	32	—	22 S 8
24 S 8		8333	208	178	156	147	139	131	125	119	113	109	104	83	69	59	52	42	35	30	24 S 8

[1]Allowable uniform total load per foot of joist.

an arch, and some of the weight is transmitted to the wall beside the window.

If the lintel also supports a floor load as in Fig. 491, the weight is considered to be uniformly distributed along the entire length of the lintel. The total load is the weight of the spandrel plus the floor load. The spandrel height is the same as the width of the opening.

If the window opening exceeds the maximum safe span for the typical steel angles used for lintels, an *I* beam or wide-flange beam must be used. If the lintel supports a floor load or roof load, this must be included with the weight of materials in the spandrel to arrive at a total load on the lintel.

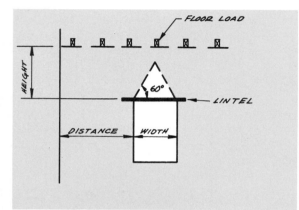

Fig. 492. Weight on lintel is weight of materials in isosceles triangle, if floor load above (height) is equal to or greater than window width and if distance from end of a wall is greater than width.

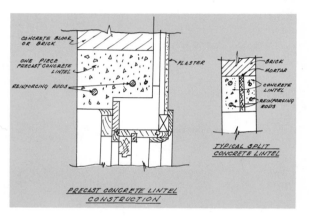

Fig. 493. Precast concrete lintel construction.

Table 32
Precast Reinforced Concrete Lintels in Masonry Walls

Lintels are tabulated per 4 in. thickness of wall; for 8 in. thickness, double the width and reinforcement; and for a 12 in. wall, triple it.

Lintels given have a capacity to carry only an equilateral triangle of 32 psf. masonry with a base of (L + 8 in.) on a clear span of L; no provisions are made for beams, purlins, or other concentrated loads.

Clear Span L	Total Length L + 1'-4"	Min. f'c (psi)	Height of Lintel (in.)	Reinforcement		Weight of Lintel (lb.)
				Bottom	Top	
4'-0	5'-4	2000	7⅝	1-#3	1-#2	170
5'-0	6'-4	2000	7⅝	1-#3	1-#2	203
6'-0	7'-4		7⅝	1-#3	1-#2	235
7'-0	8'-4	2500	7⅝	1-#4	1-#2	266
8'-0	9'-4		7⅝	1-#4	1-#2	299
9'-0	10'-4		7⅝	1-#6	1-#2	331
10'-0	11'-4	2000	11⅝	1-#5	1-#2	544
11'-0	12'-4		11⅝	1-#5	1-#2	592
12'-0	13'-4		11⅝	1-#6	1-#2	640
13'-0	14'-4	2500	11⅝	1-#8	1-#3	688

For wall to arch over opening and put only a triangular load on the lintel, there must be—(1) an unbroken, solid wall above the vertex of the triangle equal to about one-third the height of the triangle, and (2) no included concentrations of load.

Bottom bars only may be used if the lintel is plainly marked, properly handled, and always kept right side up. If plainly marked, but likely to be stressed by drooping in handling, use top bars for transportation purposes. If lintel is not marked and can be installed upside down, use same size bars in top as are scheduled for bottom.

Check texture of exposed surfaces of lintel to harmonize with exposed blocks. Either light weight or standard concrete may be used.

Courtesy Concrete Reinforcing Steel Institute.

Concrete Lintels

Precast concrete lintels are available in a variety of shapes and sizes. They are cast in standard shapes and reinforced with steel bars. Basically, they are made in two ways — as a single cast unit or as two separate pieces called a *split lintel*. See Fig. 493. A standards book should be consulted for a listing of concrete lintels and their load-carrying capabilities.

Table 32 presents data for standard, precast concrete lintels designed for carrying the load imposed by the weight of material in an equilateral triangle above the lintel.

Table 33 presents data for standard, precast, concrete lintels designed to carry uniformly loaded lintels.

Steel Lintels

Steel lintels are made from steel angles. Since steel is stronger than wood or concrete of the same thickness, it is most frequently used for lintel construction. A steel lintel can be much shallower than one of wood or concrete and can support as much or more load.

The typical use of steel lintels is illustrated for masonry veneer over frame and solid masonry walls in Fig. 494. Notice that a separate lintel is used for each 4 inches of masonry.

Table 33
Carrying Capacity of Reinforced Concrete Lintels

Table 32 gives lintel designs to carry an equilateral triangle of wall. This table gives the safe superimposed uniformly distributed load per lineal foot on 8 x 8 and 12 x 12 in. lintels on spans of 4'-0" to 12'-0".

8 x 8 In. Nominal Lintels (7⅝ x 7⅝)							
Clear Opening L	Reinforcement					Length of Lintel	Weight of Lintel (lb.)
	2-#3	#3 + #4	2-#4	#4 + #5	2-#5		
4'-0	697	1010	1320	1545	1870	5'-4"	340
5'-0	452	662	870	1130	1386	6'-4"	405
6'-0	309	460	612	800	980	7'-4"	469
7'-0	218	330	446	586	730	8'-4"	533
8'-0	157	247	336	446	556	9'-4"	597
9'-0	93	186	258	346	436	10'-4"	661
10'-0	78	136	192	264	338	11'-4"	725
11'-0	58	108	157	219	280	12'-4"	790
12'-0	40	82	124	176	228	13'-4"	854

To left of heavy line, f' c = 2500 or 3000 psi but to right of heavy line f' c $\overline{>}$ 3000 psi.

The reinforcement **must** be placed in the bottom of the lintel, and can be the only reinforcement if lintel is plainly marked, carefully handled and always kept right side up. If lintel is not marked and can be installed upside down, use same size bars in top as are scheduled for bottom.

8 WIDE X 12 IN. HIGH NOMINAL LINTELS (7⅝ X 11⅝)								
Clear Opening L	Reinforcement						Length of Lintel	Weight of Lintel (lb.)
	2-#4	#4 + #5	2-#5	#5 + #6	2-#6	#6 + #7		
4'-0"	2140	3020	3020	3020	3020	3020	5'-4"	513
5'-0"	1420	1830	2400	2400	2400	2400	6'-4"	609
6'-0"	995	1295	1445	1980	1980	1980	7'-4"	704
7'-0"	725	950	1065	1450	1690	1690	8'-4"	800
8'-0"	545	725	815	1115	1325	1460	9'-4"	896
9'-0"	420	565	635	880	1045	1255	10'-4"	992
10'-0"	315	430	490	680	815	980	11'-4"	1088
11'-0"	260	390	405	575	690	830	12'-4"	1184
12'-0"	205	290	330	470	570	690	13'-4"	1280

Below and to left of heavy line, f' c = 2500 or 3000 psi, but above and to right of heavy line, f' c $>$ 3000 psi. Either light weight or standard concrete may be used.

The above tables give uniformly distributed safe superimposed load per lineal foot; no allowance for beams, purlins, or other concentrations.

Courtesy Concrete Reinforcing Steel Institute.

The size of steel lintels is recorded on drawings by giving the length of the two legs first and then the thickness of the metal from which the lintel is made; for example — 4″ x 3″ x ¼″.

The safe load-carrying potential for the commonly used angles is indicated in Table 34. An examination of the heading of the table indicates that these angles are considered beams, since they are horizontal supporting members. The allowable uniform loads are in kips.

The proper angle size to use for a lintel is selected by first computing the total load on the lintel. Assume a load of 3,500 pounds is carried by a lintel spanning 5′-0″. This load could be the weight of brick as well as a floor load caused by the presence of floor joists resting on the lintel. This load will be supported by two lintels. As shown in Fig. 494,

the brick load on each is 1,900 pounds or 3,800 total for two.

An examination of Table 34 reveals that a 4 x 3 x 5/16 angle will support 1.9 kips over a distance of 5′-0″. This meets the demands of load.

Notice that angles are available with both legs the same length as well as with legs of unequal length. Usually, the longer leg is placed in a vertical position when the angle is used as a lintel. Frequently on a blueprint, the abbreviation *L.L.V.* (long leg vertical) is used.

An angle will carry a heavier load when the long leg is in a vertical position. An examination of Table 34 proves this. The extreme left-hand column, entitled "horizontal leg," indicates which of the legs of the member is in a horizontal position to carry the load indicated. For example, in the first grouping of

Table 34
Loads for Regular Series Angle Beams
(Allowable uniform loads in kips for angles laterally supported neutral axis parallel to horizontal leg.)

For angles laterally unsupported, allowable loads must be reduced.
For angles subject to torsion, make special investigation.

Horizontal Leg	Angle Size	Wt. per Ft.	Span in Feet											
			2	3	4	5	6	7	8	9	10	12	14
4″	7 x 4 x 7/16	15.8			17.0	13.6	11.3	9.7	8.5	7.6	6.8	5.7	4.9
	⅜	13.6			14.7	11.7	9.8	8.4	7.3	6.5	5.9	4.9	4.2
	6 x 4 x ⅜	12.3			11.0	8.8	7.3	6.3	5.5	4.9	4.4	3.7	
	4 x 4 x ⅜	9.8			5.0	4.0	3.3	2.9	2.5	2.2			
	5/16	8.2			4.3	3.5	2.9	2.5	2.2	1.9			
	4 x 3½ x 5/16	7.7			3.3	2.7	2.2	1.9	1.7				
	4 x 3 x 5/16	7.2			2.4	1.9	1.6	1.4					
	¼	5.8			2.0	1.6	1.3	1.1					
3½″	5 x 3½ x ½	13.6	20.0	13.3	10.0	8.0	6.7	5.7	5.0	4.4	4.0		
	⅜	10.4	15.3	10.2	7.7	6.1	5.1	4.4	3.8	3.4	3.1		
	5/16	8.7	12.7	8.4	6.3	5.1	4.2	3.6	3.2	2.8	2.5		
	4 x 3½ x 5/16	7.7	8.7	5.8	4.3	3.5	2.9	2.5	2.2	1.9			
	3½ x 3½ x 5/16	7.2	6.5	4.4	3.3	2.6	2.2	1.9	1.6				
	¼	5.8	5.3	3.5	2.6	2.1	1.8	1.5	1.3				
	3½ x 3 x ¼	5.4	3.9	2.6	1.9	1.5	1.3	1.1					
3″	4 x 3 x ½	11.1	12.7	8.4		5.1	4.2	3.6	3.2				
	⅜	8.5	10.0	6.7	5.0	4.0	3.3	2.9	2.5				
	5/16	7.2	8.0	5.3	4.0	3.2	2.7	2.3	2.0				
	⅛	5.8	6.7	4.4	3.3	2.7	2.2	1.9	1.7				
	3½ x 3 x ¼	5.4	5.2	3.5	2.6	2.1	1.7	1.5					
	3 x 3 x ¼	4.9	3.9	2.6	1.9	1.5	1.3						
	3 x 2½ x ¼	4.5	2.7	1.8	1.3	1.1							
2½″	3 x 2½ x ⅜	6.6	5.4	3.6	2.7	2.2	1.8						
	5/16	5.6	4.6	3.1	2.3	1.8	1.5						
	¼	4.5	3.7	2.5	1.9	1.5	1.2						
	2½ x 2½ x ¼	4.1	2.6	1.7	1.3	1.0							
	2½ x 2 x ¼	3.62	1.7	1.1	0.8								

Courtesy American Institute of Steel Construction.

angles, the horizontal leg is 4 inches. A 4 x 3 x 5/16 angle spanning 4'-0" will carry 2.4 kips. The third grouping of angles in the table has the 3-inch leg as the horizontal leg. A 3 x 4 x 5/16 angle spanning 4'-0" will carry 4.0 kips. The same angle, if placed with the 4-inch leg in the vertical position, will carry 1,600 pounds more than when placed with the 3-inch leg in the vertical position.

Wood Lintels

Wood lintels should be used where no joists or masonry spandrels are to be supported by the lintel. This lintel is used in the same way a concrete lintel is used. Refer again to Fig. 493.

The procedure for selecting the proper-sized wood lintel is the same as that for selecting a wood beam. The load to be carried by the lintel must be ascertained; the span must be decided and the proper lintel size selected from the wood beam tables in this chapter.

Lintels spanning the opening above a normal window in frame-house construction need only be a double 2 x 4.

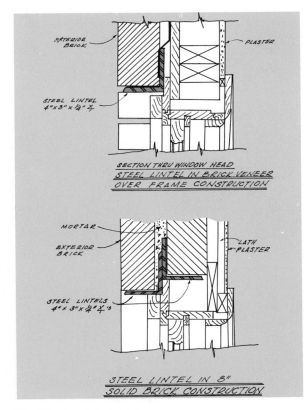

SECTION THRU WINDOW HEAD
STEEL LINTEL IN BRICK VENEER
OVER FRAME CONSTRUCTION

STEEL LINTEL IN 8"
SOLID BRICK CONSTRUCTION

Fig. 494. Use of steel lintels.

Build Your Vocabulary

Following are words that you should understand and use as a part of your working vocabulary. Write out a brief explanation of each.

Span
Lumber grade
Roof pitch
Roof slope
Collar beam
Trusses
Split ring
Stressed-skin panels
Coefficient of heat transmission
Concentric loading
Eccentric loading
Girder load area
Wide-span roof decking
Open-web joists
Wide-flange beams
American standard beams
Allowable unit working stress
Glued laminated beams
Box beams
Lintel

Class Activities

1. What is the maximum span for a Southern pine floor joist with a 40-pound live load, spaced 16 inches on center, if the joist is 2 x 8; 2 x 10; 2 x 12?
2. What is the maximum span for a Southern pine ceiling joist with a 20-pound attic load, spaced 16 inches on center, if the joist is 2 x 6; 2 x 8; 2 x 10?
3. What is the required size of a joist for a Southern pine, low-slope roof, supporting a finished ceiling, if the joists are spaced 24 inches on center and must span 18'-6"?
4. A roof rafter must span 19'-5". What size joist must be used to span this distance, if it is made of Southern pine, supports a heavy roofing, and is spaced 16 inches on center? If the rafter supports light roofing?
5. A roof has a total rise of 6'-0" and a total span of 24'-0". What are the pitch and slope of the roof?
6. If floor joists are spaced 16 inches on center, what thickness of solid wood sheathing should be used? What thickness of plywood sheathing should be used?
7. A roof having a span of 24 inches between rafters is to be decked with a fiberboard material. What is the minimum thickness that can be used?
8. A roof is to be decked with 2-inch Douglas fir, using a simple span decking plan. What is the maximum spacing for the rafters in this roof, if the live load is 40 pounds per square foot?

9. A round concrete-filled steel column must support 35,000 pounds with an unbraced column length of 8'-0". What size steel base is on this column? What size wood column would be necessary to support this load?

10. A post-and-beam house is to have the roof decked with stressed-skin panels. The panels must span 14'-0". What is the total thickness of the panel? What size solid stock framing material is required? How many pieces of framing are needed in a panel 4'-0" wide?

11. Compute the girder load area for your house, and ascertain load on the girder. Select the girder that would safely carry this load. Measure the girder installed in your house and see if it is the proper size.

12. A post-and beam house is to have the roof framed with a glued, laminated, peaked beam. If this beam is spaced 10 feet on center, must span 24'-0", and must support a total load of 40 pounds per square foot, what are the dimensions of the stock beam?

13. What size box beam is required if it is to serve as a floor beam and span 17'-0"?

14. What size open-web steel joist should be used to span 20'-0" and carry 40 pounds per square foot, if the joists are to be spaced 4'-0" on center? How many stock joists will economically carry this load?

15. A window in a brick house is 3'-6" wide. The lintel supports the brick, but no floor load. What is the total load on the lintel? What size concrete lintel would be required? What size steel lintel would be required?

Additional Reading

American Institute of Steel Construction, Inc., "AISC Specifications for the Design, Fabrication, and Erection of Steel for Buildings."

American Institute of Timber Construction. Numerous bulletins and design reports on wood products.

American Society of Civil Engineers, "Light Wood Trusses," Paper 1839.

Concrete Reinforcing Steel Institute, "Concrete Reinforcing Steel Institute Handbook."

Douglas Fir Plywood Association, *Fir Plywood Technical Data Handbook*. Also, bulletins on design use of plywood as a structural material.

Forest Products Laboratory, U.S. Department of Agriculture. Numerous bulletins and design reports on wood products.

National Bureau of Standards, U.S. Department of Commerce. Numerous standards bulletins.

National Forest Products Association, "Manual for House Framing."

———, "Maximum Spans for Joists and Rafters in Residential Construction."

———, "Plank and Beam Framing for Residential Buildings."

Plywood Fabricator Service, Inc., "Stressed Skin Panels."

Ramsey, Charles G., and Sleeper, H. R., *Architectural Graphic Standards*.

Timber Engineering Company. Numerous bulletins and design reports on wood products.

U.S. Department of Health, Education and Welfare, "Wood-Frame House Construction."

U.S. Federal Housing Administration, "Minimum Property Standards for One and Two Living Units."

U.S. Housing and Home Finance Agency, "Wood Roof Trusses for Small Buildings."

West Coast Lumbermen's Association. Numerous bulletins and design reports on wood products.

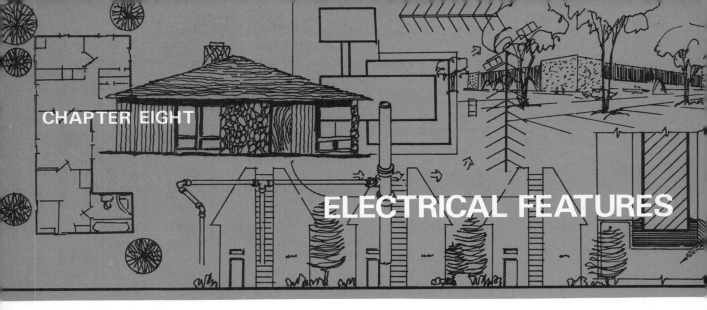

ELECTRICAL FEATURES

In today's home, electricity is used to perform so many tasks that a good wiring system is vital. The power company can make a full supply of electricity available, but the extent of its use in the home is determined by the house wiring. Every part of the system, from the service entrance to each circuit, should be planned to serve a specific purpose.

The expanded use of appliances, the rapid increase in air-conditioning installations and the revolution in house lighting — all increase the demands for electrical power. If the load requirements exceed the supply, operating efficiency suffers and the voltage drops. Lights operate poorly and appliances are inefficient or totally ineffective. A 5 percent voltage loss produces a 10 percent loss of heat in the heating appliance or a 17 percent loss of light from an incandescent lamp.

While designing a house, try to anticipate the future needs and allow extra circuits for future growth. Bring in enough current to handle the requirements of this demand.

Wiring should be done by a reputable electrical contractor. In most cities, an inspector checks the job while it is in progress and certifies that it meets the standard requirements for residential wiring.

Wiring Characteristics and Service Requirements

The planning of the electrical features of a home involves an understanding of voltage, wattage and amperes. They are defined as follows: a *volt* is the unit used in measuring electrical pressure (similar to pounds of pressure in a water system); an *ampere* is the unit used in measuring the electrical rate of flow (similar to gallons per minute in a water system); a *watt* is the unit of electrical power, which is composed of both voltage and amperage. For example, 1 ampere at a pressure of 1 volt equals 1 watt. If 1 watt is used for 1 hour, it is 1 watt-hour. One thousand watt-hours equals 1 kilowatt-hour.

The standards for electrical wiring and associated equipment are based on the National Electrical Code, prepared by the National Board of Fire Underwriters. The National Electrical Code is a basic minimum standard to safeguard persons and property from the hazards of misused electricity. It is not a design or specification manual. The National Electrical Code and the local electrical code always should be observed in engineering a home wiring system, to assure safety in operation. Maximum convenience and safety with load growth can be designed into a wiring system only by observance of sound and realistic standards.

Wiring System Characteristics

The major characteristics of a wiring system designed to carry the load demanded are:

1. *Accessibility* — Plug receptacles and switch facilities should be numerous, proper types and conveniently located.
2. *Capacity* — All parts of the electrical system should be capable of operating at rated voltage and supplying current in sufficient quantities to handle the full load. On a general-purpose circuit, the

normal load of lights and appliances should not exceed 50 percent of the rated circuit capacity.

3. *Isolation* — To assure efficiency of automatic operation, most automatic appliances should be served by individual circuits. Lights, television and other devices sensitive to voltage fluctuations should not be served by circuits to which motor-driven or automatic appliances are connected.

4. *Safety* — The system should comply with the provisions of the National Safety Code.

5. *Control* — The system should provide maximum operating convenience. Switches and other controls should be carefully positioned, with a sufficient number suited to family living habits.

Circuit Requirements

A sound approach to the design and layout of an electrical system is important. Probable loads of lighting, heating and appliances should be determined; then circuits and services to handle these loads should be installed. This prevents overloads, permits unrestricted use of electrical appliances and insures the attainment of the five major characteristics of a good wiring system — (1) accessibility, (2) capacity, (3) isolation, (4) safety and (5) control.

The designer should remember that a typical 20-ampere, 120-volt circuit carries 2400 watts. This can operate a 1000-watt iron and 1200-watt dishwasher, but would be overloaded if a 600-watt percolator were connected to the circuit.

Types of Residential Circuits

To provide all the requirements of functional wiring, several types of circuits are essential. The first type of 120-volt circuit serves two or more convenience outlets for appliance connection in the kitchen, pantry, dining, and laundry areas. This is classified as an *appliance circuit*. It should be of No. 12 wire and should be protected by a 20-ampere fuse or circuit breaker. Generally, two such circuits are needed in today's kitchens because of the large number of electrical appliances in use.

The second type of 120-volt circuit, called a *general-purpose circuit*, is also a 20-ampere

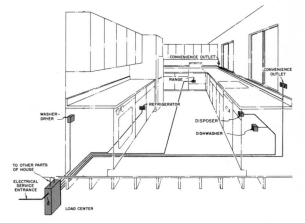

Fig. 535. Kitchen electrical circuits. (Kansas Gas and Electric Co.) Notice that the washer-dryer and range are on individual 240-volt circuits; the refrigerator is on a special-purpose, 120-volt circuit; the disposer and dishwasher share one special-purpose 120-volt circuit; and the convenience outlets share a 120-volt, appliance circuit.

circuit, but is used for lighting, convenience outlets, and small appliances such as lamps and radios. It serves all convenience outlets except those wired for appliances. Sometimes these circuits have only a 15-ampere capacity, but they should be 20 ampere. If they are 15 ampere, they will carry only 1800 watts.

The third type of 120-volt circuit is also a 20-ampere circuit, but operates a single outlet. It is called a *special-purpose circuit*. This circuit would operate a heavy-duty appliance such as a dishwasher or an air conditioner. These units operate on 120 volts, but have a high wattage rating, so each needs to be on a separate circuit.

Another type of circuit is used for such items as ranges, dryers, or central air conditioners which operate on 240 volts. See Fig. 535. The difference in the various 240-volt circuits is the size of wire used, the protective device incorporated, and the resultant capacity. The types of circuits used are: a No. 6 wire with a 60-ampere rating, 14,400 watts capacity; a No. 8 wire with a 40-ampere rating, 9600 watts capacity; a No. 10 wire with a 30-ampere rating, 7200 watts capacity; and a No. 12 wire with a 20-ampere rating, 4800 watts capacity. (The smaller the wire number, the larger the diameter of the wire.)

These various types of circuits are illustrated in Fig. 536.

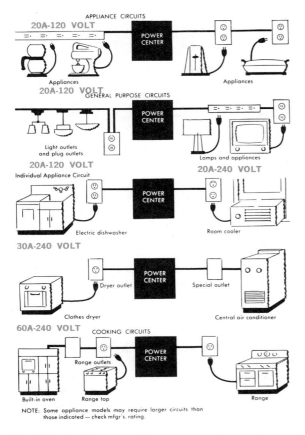

Fig. 536. Circuit types and typical uses. (Kansas Gas and Electric Co.)

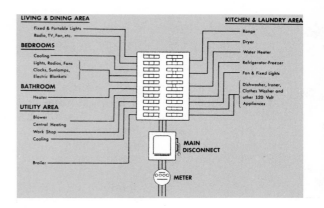

Fig. 537. Satisfactory electrical service for today's home demands. (Kansas Gas and Electric Co.)

The Number of Circuits Required

In a completely electrified, combination, kitchen-laundry area, it would not be unusual to find five single-outlet circuits, one to serve each the range, broiler, water heater, refrigerator-freezer, and dryer. A sixth circuit would serve fixed lights and an exhaust fan, while two appliance circuits would provide sufficient capacity to serve a dishwasher, ironer, clothes washer, toaster, radio, food mixer, iron, coffee maker and similar 120-volt appliances. So, with the appliances and services mentioned, eight circuits would be needed for this area.

In the utility area, an additional three circuits could be used to advantage; the first one could serve a blower and central heating unit; the second one, a summer cooling unit; and the third such loads as workshop motors or a soldering iron. General lighting could be connected to a lighting circuit serving other areas.

Three more circuits might also be used advantageously in the living-dining area, front entry and terrace, and for exterior lighting. For example, one circuit could serve both fixed and portable lights, and a second could serve the radio, television set, circulating fan, etc. Then, if central heating or cooling were not installed, were insufficient, or were not required for the entire house, local comfort could be obtained by operating a portable heating or cooling unit from the third circuit in this area.

Finally, three circuits could be used to advantage in the bedroom-bathroom section of the home; two circuits could serve all lights, radios, fans, clocks, sunlamps, electric blankets, etc., while the third circuit could be used to serve built-in bathroom heaters or a room air-conditioning unit.

In the house just cited, the wiring system calls for seventeen circuits. This is considerably more than most homes have today, yet it represents a conservative wiring plan. When one considers the estimates that the average homeowner will soon be using three times more current than that used today, it is apparent that less-expensive systems will not provide "housepower" for most convenient living 5, 10 and 15 years hence. Fig. 537 represents a satisfactory electrical service for an average home.

Service Entrance

The service entrance is that part of the wiring system that brings power from the pole to the house. The service entrance is the focal point of electrical adequacy in the home, for

it is the ultimate limit on the total energy which may be used. The size of this entrance should be decided only after a careful analysis of such factors as: number and types of electrical appliances and devices to be in the home; possible future additions; and trends toward the use of more than one unit of a particular device, such as adding several air conditioners. See Fig. 538.

As a guide to the selection of the proper size for a service entrance, the following sizes are outlined:

100 ampere — General-purpose circuits, electric cooking, water heater, electric laundry.

150 ampere — General-purpose circuits, electric cooking, water heater, electric laundry, air conditioning and electric heating (small homes). If house has total-resistance heating, amperage would have to be higher and should be computed to suit the load of the heating unit.

200 ampere — General-purpose circuits, electric cooking, water heater, electric laundry, air conditioning and electric home heating. If house has total-resistance heating, amperage would have to be higher and should be computed to suit the load of the heating unit.

Power Centers

In recent years, developments in service entrance equipment and residential panelboards have greatly influenced wiring-system layout. Almost any desired circuit array can be quickly assembled from inexpensive, mass-produced components in standardized cabinets. There has been marked improvement in

appearance, and most residential devices can be installed flush in the wall. They can be installed in the kitchen, laundry, utility room or front hall, wherever they are most readily accessible and close to the loads they serve. They need not be hidden away in the basement, garage or back hallway.

Location of the service entrance equipment is determined by the point of conductor entrance or meter location — usually a corner of the house. Subfeed load centers, supplied from the service entrance equipment, can be located in the kitchen, utility room, front hall or closet.

The code permits up to six circuits to be served directly from the service entrance conductors. Multiple mains can be conveniently arranged to serve heavy-duty appliance circuits — range, dryer, water heater — and feeders to branch-circuit distribution panels at power centers. On a main bus, typical equipment provides for up to six double-pole, fused switches or circuit breakers (or twelve single-poles operated by six handles). A

Fig. 539. A typical enclosed panel for indoor power centers. This is a 12-circuit center with circuit breakers. (Frank Adam Electric Co.)

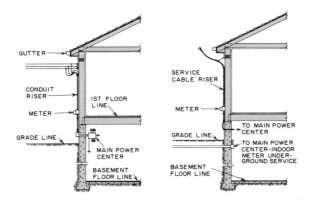

Fig. 538. Service installations for standard home service. (Kansas Gas and Electric Co.)

separate bus with a group of branch circuits in the same enclosure is fed from one of the mains.

A typical installation would provide the following circuits:

50-amp range
30-amp dryer
20-amp water heater
40-amp air conditioner (higher amperage required for large central air-conditioning units.)
40-amp kitchen panel to supply kitchen circuits
40-amp lighting panel for lighting requirements of entire house

When power centers are flush mounted in living areas, it is important that provisions be made for access to the spare circuits for future use. An empty 1-inch conduit, tubing or flex is extended to the basement or attic, terminating in a 4 11/16-inch box with blank cover. This provides ready access to the panel for connecting into the spare circuits. Fig. 539 illustrates a typical power center.

Electric heating and central, plant-type, electric cooling loads are usually fed from a separate panelboard served by one of the mains. The design of the wiring system for a central-type heating and cooling system is governed by the rating and application of the heating equipment. The system is a known electric load; consequently, relatively accurate circuit and feeder capacity design is entirely practical.

The rapidly developing trend toward built-in cooking appliances is easily and economically served by kitchen power centers. The conventional range circuit can become the feeder to the panel. Circuits to cooking appliances and other appliance outlets are short and efficient. Since average runs are little longer than runs between outlets, single-outlet circuits can be provided at little more than the cost of the panelboard overcurrent device.

For a typical all-electric kitchen with built-in cooking appliances, a standard 12-circuit (12 poles) panel provides a practical power center. The circuit schedule should have cooking appliances on individual circuits, automatic appliances on isolating circuits and portable appliance outlets on three-wire grounded circuits. For such a panel, the demand load should be calculated to get the size of the required feeder. This may be done as follows:

Small appliance load	1500 watts
Dishwasher	1200 watts
Disposal unit	300 watts
Refrigerator	300 watts
Freezer	300 watts
Cooking appliances	8000 watts (approx.)

Totaling these figures gives a load of 11,600 watts. Divide this by 240 volts, and the required current capacity of the feeder to the panel is found to be 48 amps. The 120-volt circuits should be divided between each side of the three-wire, 240-volt circuit.

It is necessary to select wire that will safely carry the demand load to be placed upon it. The greater the amount of current to be carried, the larger the diameter of wire necessary. Table 35 indicates the accepted ampere rating of selected standard wire sizes.

Calculating the Required Service Entrance Load

To ascertain the size of service entrance required, the electrical demands must be calculated. Most service entrances now are three-wire, single-phase, 120/240 volts. The calculation procedure follows.

1. Calculate the *lighting load* by multiplying the square feet of floor area by 4 watts per square foot. If the actual electrical layout is known, the number of circuits can be ascertained by examining the floor plan.

2. Add the total circuit capacity (in watts) allowed for small appliances in the kitchen, dining room, pantry, laundry and utility areas. To get this total, decide how many 20-ampere appliance circuits are needed, and multiply this by 2000 watts.

Table 35
Allowable Current Carrying Capacities (in Amperes) of Insulated Copper Conductors
(Thermoplastic Insulation)

Wire Size	Amperes
14	15
12	20
10	30
8	40
6	55
4	70
3	80
2	95
1	110
0	125

From National Electrical Code, 1962.

3. Add lighting load and small appliance load. Of this total take 3000 watts at 100 percent. Take 35 percent of the total load remaining after removing the 3000 watts. Add this to the 3000 watt load. This gives needed load for lighting and small appliance circuits. The entire load was not taken at 100 percent because all lights and appliances are never operated at the same time. *Note:* These calculations are for residential wiring only; consult Code for information on other types.

4. Add the wattage loads of the range and other fixed appliances, such as dryer, water heater and washer. Add 100 per-cent of this to the adjusted lighting and small appliance load (from Step 3).

5. **Divide this total wattage by 240 volts to find the required amperage for the service entrance.**

From these calculations can be found the size of the entrance wire required, so that sufficient current is admitted to the house to meet the electrical demands. See Fig. 540 for a sample problem in calculating the size of the service entrance.

Planning the Electrical System

General Planning Requirements

The choice of illuminating fixtures should be based upon the various visual tasks carried on in the home. Lighting must be planned for recreation, entertainment, reading, cooking, eating and the other activities in the home. In most cases, best results are achieved by a blend of lighting from both stationary fixtures and portable lamps. Some fixtures provide wide, general illumination, while others focus light in only one spot. The selection of the best fixture and the best location for this fixture to perform properly requires study and planning.

Convenience outlets should be located near the ends of wall space, rather than near the center, thus reducing the likelihood of being concealed behind large pieces of furniture. They should be placed so that no point along any usable wall space (in any room except a bathroom or utility room) is more than 6 feet from an outlet. Where windows extend to the floor, preventing use of ordinary convenience outlets, equivalent facilities should be installed using other appropriate means.

If a section of wall between two doors is 2 feet wide, a convenience outlet is needed.

In some rooms, it is desirable to install split-wired convenience outlets. A *split-wired outlet* is one in which each single receptacle in a box is on a separate circuit. For example, in a living room an outlet may be wired to a wall switch so the table lamp connected there can be turned on and off from the door. If this outlet has one receptacle wired to the switch and another receptacle on a separate circuit, it is said to be a split receptacle. Even though the lamp may be turned off, an appliance plugged into the second receptacle of this outlet can continue to operate.

For a 1500 sq. ft. home with electric range, electric water heater and electric home laundry

LIGHTING AND GENERAL PURPOSE LOAD:

    1500 sq. ft. x 4 watts/sq. ft. . . . . 6000 watts

SMALL APPLIANCE LOAD:

    Number of appliance circuits
    included in branch circuit
    layout — 4
    4 x 2000 watts/circ. . . . . 8000 watts

            total 14000 watts
        take 3000 at 100% . . . . 3000 watts
        and the remainder of 11000 at 35% . . . 3850 watts

RANGE DEMAND LOAD: . . . . 8000 watts

FIXED APPLIANCE LOAD:

    Water heater . . . . 3000 watts
    Clothes dryer . . . . 4500 watts
    Clothes washer . . . . 500 watts
    Ironer . . . . 1650 watts

            9650 watts at 100% . . 9650 watts

        Total watts of service capacity: 24500 watts

Required current carrying capacity of service entrance conductors (at 120/240 volts, 3 wire, single-phase):

$$\frac{24500}{240} = 102.8 \text{ amperes}$$

Service entrance conductors must be: No. 1's Type R in 1½" Conduit
                            or No. 1's Type TW in 1½" Conduit
                            or No. 2's Type RH in 1¼" Conduit

This service entrance can be described as a 25 kw service, the value obtained by multiplying the current rating of the service entrance by the voltage between the two ungrounded conductors (240 volts). A wide range of possible service entrance arrangements could be used to carry out the design set forth in this typical calculation. If a main disconnect switch is not required by local regulations, six or less circuit breakers can be used as protective subdivisions as set forth in Section 2351 a. of the National Electrical Code. If a main disconnect switch were required in this particular service entrance, either a 200-amp switch fused at 110-amps or, because the calculation contains spare capacity, a 100-amp switch fused at 100-amp or a 100-amp circuit breaker may be used as the main disconnect.

Fig. 540. Sample service entrance calculation. (Kansas Gas and Electric Co.)

Under normal conditions, convenience outlets should be placed 12 inches above the floor line. Exceptions to this might be found in baths and in kitchens with outlets above the counter top and with outlets above or built into fireplaces. There should be one convenience outlet for every 150 square feet (or major fraction thereof) in a room.

Wall switches should be located on the latch side of doors and on the traffic side of arches. They should be placed within the room for which the switch controls the light. Exceptions to this would be a switch controlling a yard light or stair lights for an adjoining area. Wall switches, normally, are located 48 inches above the floor line.

Frequently, a room will have two or more entrances, and it is necessary to control a light or a switch to a convenience outlet from these locations. Multiple switch control will accomplish this. If a light is controlled by two switches, it has a three-way switch. If controlled from three locations, it has a four-way switch.

It is especially important to have switch locations so placed that a person can enter the house from any door and progress to any other part of the house, having the way lighted before him. Also, it should be possible to turn off the lights in the area just vacated without retracing one's steps.

If a room is to serve several purposes, such as a kitchen-utility area, the wiring must serve both functions adequately. Special-purpose outlets may be necessary for a washer, a dryer or other high-current appliances.

The various electrical features of a plan are indicated on a drawing by symbols. These have been standardized and are common language in the construction industry. Fig. 541 lists these symbols.

Living Rooms

Lighting Provisions

Three types of lighting should be installed in the living room.

1. General illumination throughout the entire room may be provided by ceiling or wall fixtures or by lighting in valances, cornices or portable lamps. See Fig. 542.
2. Local lighting is needed at each furniture grouping or at each area where some specific activity (sewing, reading, card playing) is carried on.

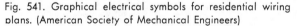

Fig. 541. Graphical electrical symbols for residential wiring plans. (American Society of Mechanical Engineers)

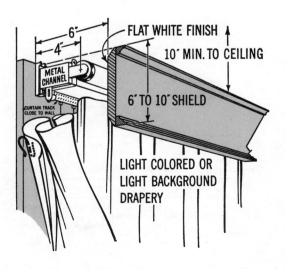

Fig. 542. Design considerations for valance construction. (Kansas Gas and Electric Co.)

3. Decorative lighting, such as picture illumination and bookcase lighting, creates focal points of attention.

Maximum use should be made of multiple switching and dimmer controls. This enables the lighting effects to be adjusted to suit requirements.

Convenience Outlets

Outlets should be spaced so no point along the floor is more than 6 feet from an outlet. If outlets are switch controlled, they should be split-receptacle outlets. Frequently, an outlet will be built flush with the mantle on a fireplace. A convenience outlet should be installed with each wall switch to facilitate use of vacuum cleaner or other portable appliances. See Fig. 543.

Special-Purpose Outlets

One outlet should be installed for a room air conditioner, if a central air-conditioning system is not planned.

Dining Areas

Lighting Provisions

For a combination living-dining room, the lighting system and fixtures in the dining area should harmonize with those in the living area. The types of lighting needed are:

1. General illumination, which is easily provided with a two-circuit fixture. This fixture requires two switches — one to operate the bulbs providing general illumination and another to operate the spotlights. See Fig. 544.
2. Accent lighting for the table, which can be provided by the spotlight in a two-circuit fixture, as just discussed, or spots can be built flush into the ceiling.
3. Supplementary and decorative lighting, should include any of a variety of perimeter lighting techniques. A china cabinet or an aquarium may be illuminated for a decorative feature.

Convenience Outlets

Outlets should be spaced so no point along the floor in a usable wall space is more than 6 feet from an outlet. If a table or counter is to be placed along a wall, an outlet should be provided above this height for use of portable appliances. This should be a split-receptacle outlet, for connection to appliance circuits. See Fig. 545.

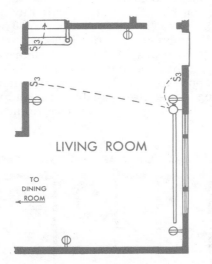

Fig. 543. General illumination of living room with a fluorescent strip in valance above window. Notice three-way switches. (Industry Committee on Interior Wiring Design)

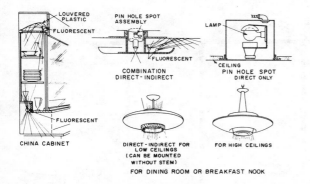

Fig. 544. Suggested means of general illumination, accent lighting and decorative lighting for dining areas. (Kansas Gas and Electric Co.)

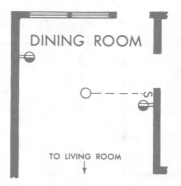

Fig. 545. General illumination in a dining room. Notice split-wired convenience outlets. (Industry Committee on Interior Wiring Design)

Bedrooms

Lighting Provisions

Two types of lighting should be provided in bedrooms.

1. General illumination can be provided by a ceiling fixture or cove or valance lighting. It should be switch controlled from the door to the bedroom. There are many styles of lights, from flush fixtures to hanging fixtures, that provide satisfactory general illumination.

2. Local lighting, such as bed lights for reading in bed, vanity lights or lights on full-length mirrors, should be considered.

Convenience Outlets

Convenience outlets should be placed so there is an outlet on each side and within 6 feet of the centerline of each probable individual bed location. No point on the floor line in any usable wall space should be more than 6 feet from an outlet. Outlets near beds should contain triple or quadruple receptacles to handle the clock, radio, lights, electric blankets and other appliances. See Fig. 546.

Special-Purpose Outlets

One single outlet is needed for a room air-conditioner in each bedroom, for houses in which central air conditioning is not planned. These may be used to operate electric heaters in cool weather.

Bathrooms

Lighting Provisions

The average bath should have a ceiling light for general illumination and wall lamps on each side of the mirror as supplemental lighting. If the mirror is large, side lighting is inadequate and overhead lighting must be used. A large bath should have a vapor-proof light installed over the tub or shower. A small bath can be satisfactorily lighted by only wall lamps on each side of the mirror. The use of large, luminous plastic panels provides an excellent means of general illumination.

If a bath has no exterior window, it is necessary to install a ventilating fan in the ceiling. These are available as a compact unit combining a light and an electric heater. See Fig. 547.

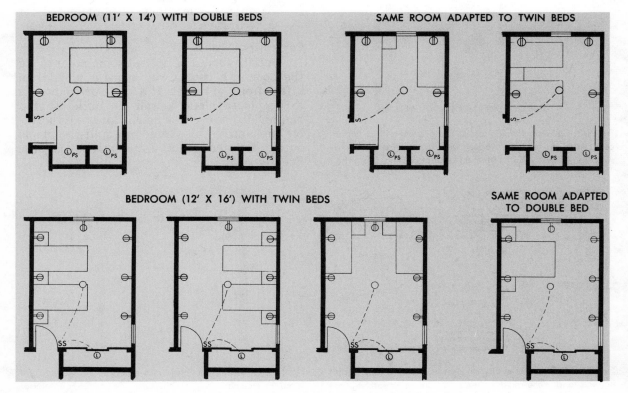

Fig. 546. Suggested outlet locations in bedrooms. (Industry Committee on Interior Wiring Design)

Convenience Outlets

Outlets generally are built into the wall lights installed on the sides of the mirror. An outlet should be installed at each mirror or vanity to accommodate electric razors and hair dryers. The receptacle which is a part of a lighting fixture will not satisfy this requirement, unless it is rated at 15 amperes and wired with at least 15-ampere-rated wires. See Fig. 548.

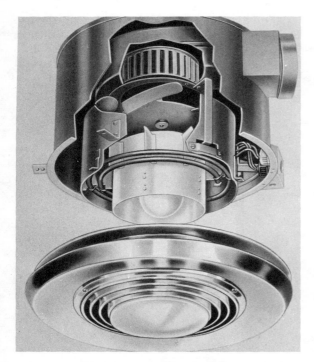

Fig. 547. This unit serves as a rapid electric heater, light and exhaust fan for bathroom use. (NuTone, Inc.)

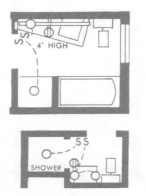

Fig. 548. Typical bath outlet layout. Notice the convenience outlet separate from the lights. (Industry Committee on Interior Wiring Design)

Special-Purpose Outlets

An outlet for a built-in, electric space heater should be provided, and a special outlet for a built-in ventilating fan that is switch controlled should be considered.

Kitchen

Lighting Provisions

Two types of lighting are required in the kitchen.

1. General illumination can be provided by a large ceiling fixture centered in the room. It may be mounted flush with the ceiling or it may be a pendant type. An excellent means of general illumination is provided by using luminous plastic ceiling panels that are lighted from above by fluorescent lamps. They create a skylight appearance. See Fig. 549.

2. Local lighting for work areas, such as the sink, surface unit, counter tops or inside cabinets, requires individual lamps. These should be controlled by a switch located on or near the area to be lighted. Fixtures frequently are built into the bottom of cabinets or hoods.

Convenience Outlets

Consider the location of such large appliances as a refrigerator, which requires one outlet. The counter requires one outlet for every 4 lineal feet of work surface frontage, with at least one outlet to serve each work surface. These outlets, usually, are 44 inches above the floor.

If a table is in the kitchen, one table-high outlet should be provided in that area. All

Fig. 549. An entire lighted ceiling of plastic panels over fluorescent lights. (Diffusa-Lite Co.)

convenience outlets should be split-wired, except the one for the refrigerator.

Special-Purpose Outlets

The range or surface unit and oven, ventilating fan, freezer, dishwasher, food disposal — all require consideration. The kitchen is the most demanding area of the house, when electrical needs are considered. See Fig. 550.

Laundry and Utility Areas

Lighting Provisions

Lighting fixtures should be placed to illuminate the work areas, such as laundry tubs, sorting area and ironing area. All lighting, especially in the laundry area, should be controlled by a wall switch. At least one large light, centered in the room, is needed. If the room is large, local lighting of work areas may be needed. Such things as a work bench or the furnace may require a local light.

Convenience Outlets

Convenience outlets should be placed in sufficient number to handle the activities. One should be in the ironing area, several near the work bench and one near the furnace. These convenience outlets should be split-wired for connection to appliance circuits.

Special-Purpose Outlets

The automatic washer, dryer, ironer, furnace and electric water heater require separate outlets and special consideration of their electrical demands. See Fig. 551.

Closets

Lighting Provisions

Each closet should have one light. Wall switches or door switches which automatically operate as the door is opened are recommended. A pull-chain light is satisfactory, but inconvenient to use.

Halls and Stairs

Lighting Provisions

Sufficient wall-controlled lights should be provided to illuminate the entire hall and stair areas. These may be ceiling or wall fixtures. Lights should have multiple-switch control at each end of the hall or the head and foot of the stair. Switches should be grouped together and never located so close to steps that a fall might result from a misstep while reaching for a switch.

Convenience Outlets

One outlet should be provided for each 15 lineal feet of hallway. If a hall contains over 25 square feet, it should contain one convenience outlet. Stairways require one outlet conveniently located for a vacuum cleaner or night light. This could be on an intermediate landing in a long stair.

Basement Area

Lighting Provisions

The lighting demands depend upon the use of the basement area. If it is simply a storage area, all that is needed are enough ceiling lights to provide general illumination and several

Fig. 550. A small kitchen outlet plan. Notice the split-wired outlets and the special-purpose outlet. (Industry Committee on Interior Wiring Design)

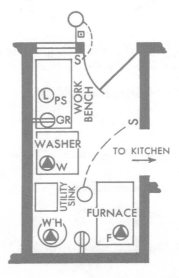

Fig. 551. A laundry-utility space with general illumination as well as local lighting. (Industry Committee on Interior Wiring Design)

convenience outlets located around the walls. Most often this area is to be used in the future for a recreation room, workshop, laundry or other activity. The considerations mentioned for these areas have been covered.

Garages and Carports
Lighting Provisions

At least one, 100-watt fixture should be provided in a one-car garage. However, it is preferred that two be used. These should be placed on each side of the car and 6 feet back from the front bumper. In a two-car garage, two lights will provide sufficient illumination. All fixtures should be controlled by wall switches located near the outside door of the house and on a convenient wall near the outside garage door.

If the garage is to contain a workshop or is to be used for other activities, these should receive additional attention and should be illuminated by local means.

Convenience Outlets

At least one outlet should be in a one- or two-car garage. It is much better if one outlet is provided in each wall of the garage.

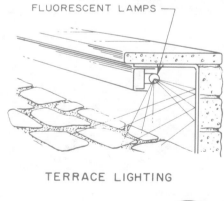

TERRACE LIGHTING

CENTER-STEM

Fig. 552. Various outdoor lighting devices. (Kansas Gas and Electric Co.)

Exterior Lighting
Lighting Provisions

All exterior entrances should have one or more light fixtures. Where a single light is attached to a house at the door, it should be on the latch side. Post lights set in the yard and lights along the driveway are of much value. They should all be switch controlled from within the house. Terraces and patios can be tastefully lighted by lights built into fences or walls or by freestanding luminaries. Large areas can be illuminated by floodlights. These are usually mounted under the eaves of the house and should be controlled by switches within the house. See Fig. 552.

Convenience Outlets

A weatherproof outlet near the front entrance is essential. It should be 18 inches above the grade. Many post lamps contain a weatherproof outlet built into the post. Such outlets are of great value on a patio or terrace for radios and electric cookers.

Porches
Lighting Provisions

Each porch, breezeway or other similar roofed area of more than 75 square feet in floor area should have one ceiling light, controlled by a wall switch within the house. If the porch is large or irregular in shape, additional lights may be needed. If it has more than one entrance, the light should be multiple switched to all entrances.

Convenience Outlets

One weatherproof outlet should be installed for each 15 lineal feet of porch or breezeway. It is recommended that such outlets be controlled by an inside wall switch.

Kinds of Light Fixtures

As lighting is planned, the kind and style of fixtures must be decided. The common kinds of fixtures are floor lamps, table lamps, tree lamps, lighted valances, interior spotlights, flush and cone lights, hanging fixtures, flush-with-the-ceiling fixtures, surface-mounted fixtures, cove lighting and luminous ceilings.

The examples that follow illustrate some of the units that are on the market. See Figs. 553 through 566. A careful study of manufacturers' catalogs is of great value when planning lighting and selecting fixtures.

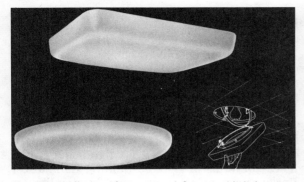

Fig. 553. Shallow, surface-mounted fixtures with light source and box above ceiling. (Prescolite Manufacturing Corp.)

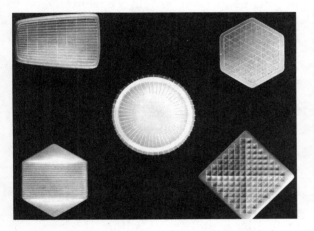

Fig. 554. Incandescent geometric thermopal glass light forms. Designed to be used in decorative patterns for a pleasing appearance in interior and exterior uses and placed in vertical and horizontal positions. (Prescolite Manufacturing Corp.)

Fig. 555. Wall-hung bathroom fixtures of bent glass. (Prescolite Manufacturing Corp.)

Fig. 556. Opal luminaries. (Prescolite Manufacturing Corp.)

Fig. 557. Pendant luminaries. (Prescolite Manufacturing Corp.)

Fig. 558. A hanging, metal cone spotlight used to highlight a special area. (Prescolite Corp.)

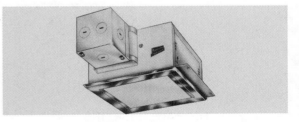

Fig. 559. A flush-with-the-ceiling fixture for general illumination. (Prescolite Manufacturing Corp.)

Fig. 560. An adjustable spotlight for highlighting an object of special importance, such as a fireplace. It is flush with the ceiling, and the box is above the ceiling. (Prescolite Manufacturing Corp.)

Fig. 561. A linear wall fixture available in 4'-0" lengths. Units can be butted to form a long light source for soft general illumination. (Prescolite Manufacturing Corp.)

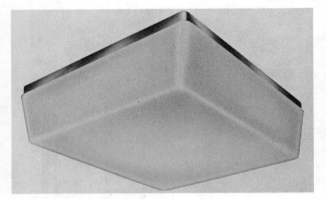

Fig. 562. A surface-mounted incandescent fixture for general illumination. (Prescolite Manufacturing Corp.)

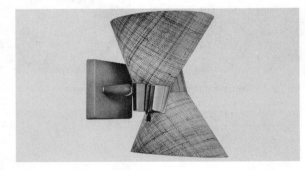

Fig. 563. Wall-mounted pin-up lamps with fiber glass shields. (Prescolite Manufacturing Corp.)

Fig. 564. A portable reading luminary. (Prescolite Manufacturing Corp.)

Fig. 565. A tree lamp, for dramatic lighting. (Prescolite Manufacturing Corp.)

Fig. 566. A floor-style tree lamp. (Prescolite Manufacturing Corp.)

Signal and Communication Systems

Signaling systems range from the minimum, a front doorbell, to elaborate chimes with multipoint control, to audible and visual annunciators in homes with servant accommodations.

The recommended minimum system is a chime with front and rear (trade) door controls which sound different tones or notes to identify each point of operation. If separate bells or buzzers are used, each unit should have a different tone to distinguish the front, rear or side door.

Flush-mounted loudspeaking telephone equipment installed at each commonly used exterior entrance, with an interior telephone station in basement, kitchen, and second-floor

hall (or master bedroom) saves steps and appeals to most housewives.

An annunciator may be installed in the kitchen with push-button stations in each bedroom, living room, recreation room, porch, etc., and is especially convenient in large, two-story houses. As an alternate, intercommunicating telephones may be substituted for the annunciator and push-button stations.

An automatic fire alarm system is recommended in every home, with detectors in critical areas, especially in the oil burner or furnace area and in the storage space and other areas not frequently visited by the family. An alarm bell and test button should be installed in the master bedroom or similar desirable area. This system should be powered by and should operate from a separate, independent transformer. Fire alarm systems are available with emergency power supply (rechargeable batteries) in case of power failure.

Wiring channels for telephone conductors should be planned when a new home is built. Service conduit, interior raceways, outlet boxes and telephone niches should be installed while the home is under construction. This allows telephone installations of greatly improved appearance. Conventional outlets may be used for permanently connected units, or the jack-plug receptacle for portable telephones. The local telephone company provides technical assistance, and it should be consulted regarding local service facilities, regulations, etc.

An intercommunicating telephone system is a highly desirable convenience for the larger home; manufacturers of the various systems should be consulted for specific features of equipment, installation details and required wiring.

Multistation television antennae systems provide outlets for operation of one or more TV sets from the same aerial, or for moving one set from room to room as occasion demands. Each television outlet should be served from a separate 120-volt circuit of two No. 12 wires.

Surface-Mounted Wiring

Many new homes are built of prefabricated sandwich or solid-core panels. This limits the use of wall cavities for wiring.

The surface-mounted wiring system is an economical solution to this problem and, also,

to the problem of rewiring an old house. See Fig. 567.

The main part of the system is a metal raceway. It serves as a baseboard, door trim or chair rail and provides a space for carrying wires. See Fig. 568. Specially designed outlets can be mounted where needed on the raceway, and switches are available for mounting on the raceway to control any of the outlets desired. See Fig. 569.

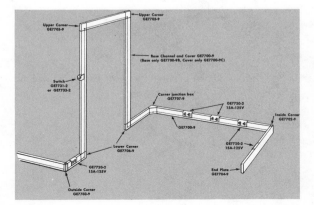

Fig. 567. Surface-mounted wiring system. (Wiremold Co.)

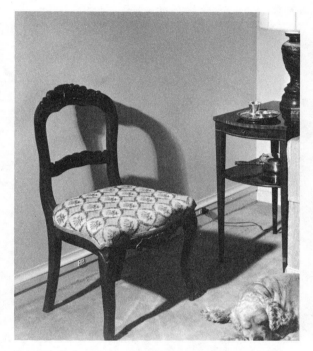

Fig. 568. The principal components of a surface-mounted wiring system. Notice the raceway forms the baseboard and door trim. The wires carry around the door opening inside the metal channel. (General Electric Co.)

Fig. 569. A surface-mounted wiring system framing a door, with a switch mounted on the raceway. (General Electric Co.)

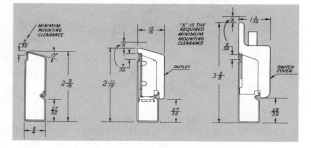

Fig. 570. Dimensions and clearances for a typical surface-mounted raceway wiring system. (General Electric Co.)

After the system is installed, the raceway cover can be easily removed for rearranging the outlets or for adding more outlets.

Fig. 570 gives the actual dimensions of the raceway for one such wiring system.

Low-Voltage, Remote-Control Wiring

Modern electrical living has created many demands on the wiring system of the home. One big problem is that of flexibility of control. The low-voltage, remote-control system* was designed to give the homeowner wider control of his electrical system; for example, all the lights in a house can be turned on or off from one point, such as the bedroom.

This system uses relays to perform the actual switching of the 120-volt line current. These relays are controlled by small switches

*Material on low-voltage, remote-control systems supplied by General Electric Company.

operating on 24 volts. This permits the use of inexpensive wiring similar to that used for door chimes. In addition, because these relays only require a momentary impluse to change from off to on (or on to off), the control switches are momentary-contact switches. This means that the low voltage causes a small current to flow only for the time the switch is pressed. See Fig. 571.

Since all switches used in this system are momentary-contact switches, as many as desired can be wired in parallel. They are not actually in the circuit, except during the short period that they are pressed. One type of switch performs the functions of a single-pole switch, a three-way switch or a four-way switch, with no complicated wiring. Even after installation, switches can be added to the system without changing the wiring.

Another outstanding feature of this system is that the heavy-gauge, current-carrying wires required for 120-volt service do not have to loop down to the switches or make several runs across a long distance to permit several switches to control one outlet. Instead, the current-carrying wires go straight to the outlet where the low-voltage relay is located. The control switches are looped to the relay with low-cost, small-gauge wire. This saves in the cost of expensive wire and prevents a voltage drop in the long runs of heavy-gauge wire, thus increasing the voltage at the outlet.

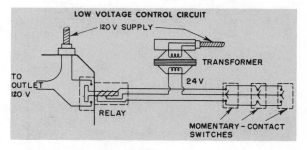

Fig. 571. A typical low-voltage circuit.

The 120-volt outlet is fed 120 volts and has a set of relay contacts connected in series with one side of the supply line. The relay coil is connected to three momentary-contact switches. These are operated by a transformer connected to a 120-volt line that steps the voltage down to 24 volts to operate the switches and relay. If a switch is touched, 24 volts flow to the relay. The relay actuates the outlet (which could be a light). This example is a 4-way switch, but special switches are not required such as in line voltage switching. Any number of other switches could be connected in to control this outlet.

By arranging switch points close together, a dial-type switch can rotate and make many contacts in a fraction of a second. In this way, master control of many circuits is possible. Switches of this type are available in nine-circuit and twelve-circuit controls. With this master control located in the bedroom, a person can turn on the coffeemaker or turn on the electric heaters in the driveway to melt off the snow, before arising from bed. See Fig. 572.

Planning a Low-Voltage Remote System

To realize the full advantage of this modern wiring system, proper planning is essential.

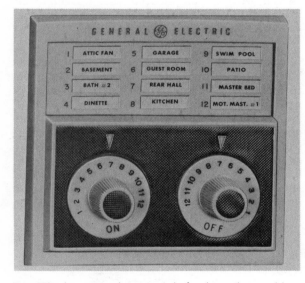

Fig. 572. A master-selector switch for low-voltage wiring. This one panel controls twelve lights. (General Electric Co.)

Fig. 573. Push-button switch used in low-voltage wiring systems. (General Electric Co.)

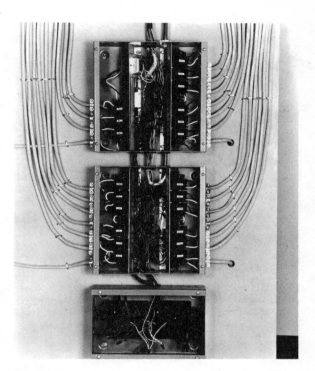

Fig. 574. A master relay-center box for a low-voltage wiring system. Each relay is located here and labeled for easy identification of the circuit. (General Electric Co.)

1. Decide on the kind of individual switches desired. Examine manufacturers' catalogs for the latest developments. Several types now in use are the dual, push-button switch, (lighted or non-illuminated), the locking-style switch, the trigger-style switch and the pilot-type switch. The push-button type is shown in Fig. 573. The locking style requires a key to operate, while the pilot-light style has a red light that glows, indicating that an unseen light is on.

2. Decide on the controls needed. It is necessary to study the electrical layout and to decide from how many locations each light or outlet should be controlled. Multiswitch control can greatly increase the convenience of living in a house.

The location of master-selector switches is important. A master-selector switch is, essentially, a console of individual switches mounted on a single plate for convenient selection of any of the individual circuits. Usually, the best locations for these master switches are beside the bed, garage door and other, frequently

used entrances. They should be located wherever it would be convenient to be able to operate all the circuits at once from a single location.

3. Decide on the type of installation needed. Manufacturers of low-voltage, remote-control, wiring systems recommend the use of the relay-center method of installation. This method has a master relay-center box (a large steel box as used for fuses or circuit breakers) in which are located the relays and master-selector switches. See Figs. 574 and 575. Any relays or switches that need to be added later are easily inserted in the box. It has the advantage of being easy to wire, and improper connections can be readily corrected. It also eliminates the slight buzz and click made by the relays as they operate.

The symbols in common use for low-voltage wiring are shown in Fig. 576.

Build Your Vocabulary

Following are words that you should understand and use as a part of your working vocabulary. Write a brief explanation of what each means.

Circuit
Convenience outlet
Light fixture
Wall switch

National Electrical Code
Electrical load
Ampere
Watt
Volt
Service entrance
Power center
Branch circuit distribution
   panel
Special-purpose outlet
General illumination
Accent lighting
Surface-mounted wiring
Low-voltage, remote-control wiring

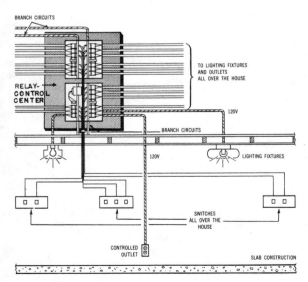

Fig. 575. A relay center for low-voltage remote control. Relays and master switches are located in this box. They are activated by individual switches located about the house. (General Electric Co.)

Symbol	Description
	Remote-Control Low-Voltage Wire
T	Low-Voltage Transformer
	Rectifier for Remote Control
B R	Box for Relays and Motor Master Controls
R	Remote-Control Relay
R P	Remote-Control Pilot-Light Relay
P 11	Separate Pilot Light, R.C. Plate
P 10	Separate Pilot Light, Inter. Plate
MS	Master-Selector Switch
MM R	Motor Master Control for ON
MM B	Motor Master Control for OFF
S M	Switch for Motor Master
S F6	R.C. Flush Switch
S F7	R.C. Locator-Light Switch
S F8	R.C. Pilot-Light Switch
S K6	R.C. Key Switch
S K7	R.C. Locator Light Key Switch
S K8	R.C. Pilot-Light Key Switch
S T6	R.C. Trigger Switch
S T7	R.C. Locator-Light Trigger Switch
S T8	R.C. Pilot-Light Trigger Switch
S T4	Interchangeable Trigger Switch, Brown
S T5	Interchangeable Trigger Switch, Ivory
O RO	Remote-Control Outlet for Extension Switch

Fig. 576. Wiring symbols for low-voltage, remote-control wiring. (General Electric Co.)

Class Activities

1. Trace the electrical circuits in your home. List the electrical units, such as refrigerator, connected to each circuit, plus the number of lights and convenience outlets. Ascertain the number of amperes each circuit can carry. Are any of the circuits overloaded?
2. Compute the size of the electrical service entrance needed for your home, for the home economics room or for the industrial arts shop in your school. In your report list each major appliance or machine and give its amperage rating.
3. **Make a freehand sketch of the home economics room or industrial arts shop in your school and indicate the location of each machine, 120-volt, and 240-volt electrical outlets and all lights. Ascertain the number of circuits needed, and list the equipment to be on each circuit.**
4. Invite, with the teacher's permission, a speaker from the electric company to talk to the class about the all-electric home.
5. Examine the location of convenience outlets in your home. Cite areas that have inadequate outlets.
6. Compile a list of all the special-purpose outlets in your home.
7. Make a freehand sketch of the plot plan of your home. Locate any sidewalks and driveways. Plan an adequate system of exterior lighting and show it on the plot plan with conventional symbols.
8. Make a modern telephone system for your home. Make a freehand sketch of the floor plan and locate the principally used telephone. Then indicate where other telephones or telephone jacks should be located.
9. Plan a communications system for your home. Make a freehand sketch of the floor plan; locate the master control unit and speakers on the plan.

Additional Reading

Architectural Record (Editorial Staff), *Time Saver Standards.*

Commery, Eugene W., and Stephenson, C. E., *How to Decorate and Light Your Home.*

Edison Electric Institute, "Handbook of Residential Wiring Design."

"Fixture Lighting Guide." Available from your local electric power company.

General Electric Company, "Remote Control Wiring."

———, "Wiring for Residential Outdoor Lighting."

"How to Help Homeowners Live Better Electrically." Available from your local power company.

Illuminating Engineering Society, "IES Lighting Handbook."

———, "Lighting Keyed to Today's Homes."

Industry Committee on Interior Wiring Design, "Residential Wiring Handbook."

National Board of Fire Underwriters, "The National Building Code."

Ramsey, Charles G., and Sleeper, H. R., *Architectural Graphic Standards.*

Sears, Roebuck and Company, "Simplified Electric Wiring Handbook."

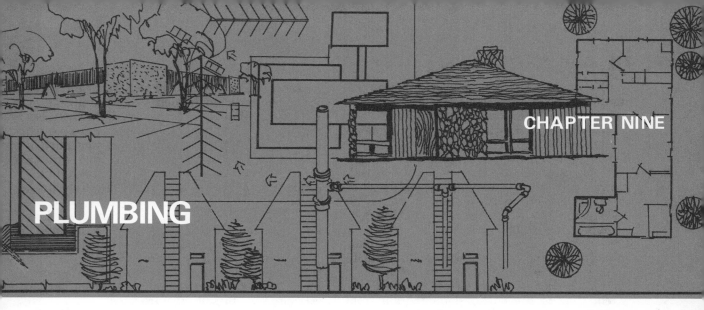

CHAPTER NINE

PLUMBING

A satisfactory plumbing system requires foresight on the part of the person planning the building. Also, it requires the services of a competent plumber to install the system correctly and to overcome unforeseen difficulties that always seem to arise after a building is under construction.

The plumbing system contains two major parts — the waste disposal system and the fresh water distribution system.

Waste Disposal System

The main parts of a waste disposal system are the soil pipes, waste pipes, house or building drain, and house or building sewer. The *soil pipe* is the part of the drainage system which receives the waste from water closets and carries it to the house or building drain. It may have other fixtures emptying into it. The *waste pipe* receives the waste from sinks, lavatories and bathtubs or other fixtures not receiving human excreta. It carries the waste to a soil pipe or to the house or building drain. The *house* or *building drain* receives the discharge from the soil pipe and waste pipes within the building and carries it to the house or building sewer. The *house* or *building sewer* begins just outside the foundation of the building and carries the waste to the sewer in the street or to the septic tank. Fig. 595 illustrates the parts of a typical residential waste disposal system, and Fig. 596 illustrates a multistory commercial system.

Parts of the Waste Disposal System

The following parts can be located in Fig. 596:

Branch interval — A section of soil pipe at least 8 feet long into which the waste from fixtures on the floor enters.

Branch vent — Any vent pipe connecting a branch of the drainage system with the vent stack.

Circuit vent — A group vent extending from in front of the last fixture connection of a horizontal branch to the vent stack.

Continuous waste and vent — A vent that is a continuation of and in straight line with the drain to which it connects.

Dry vent — A vent that does not carry water or water-borne wastes.

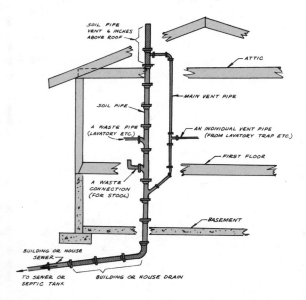

Fig. 595. Parts of a typical residential waste disposal system.

Dual vent — A group vent connecting at the junction of two fixtures branches and serving as a back vent for both branches.

Group vent — A branch vent that performs its function for two or more traps.

Leader — A pipe draining water from the roof to a storm sewer or other means of disposal.

Indirect waste — A waste pipe which does not connect directly with the building drainage system, but discharges into it through a properly trapped fixture.

Loop vent — Same as a circuit vent except it loops back and connects with a soil or waste stack vent instead of the vent stack.

Primary branch — A part of the drainage system that is the single sloping drain from the base of a soil stack or waste stack to its junction with the main building drain or with another branch thereof.

Relief vent — A branch from a vent stack, connected to a horizontal branch between the first fixture branch and the soil or waste stack. Its function is to provide for circulation of air between the vent stack and the soil or waste stack.

Secondary branch — Any branch of a building or house drain other than the primary branch.

Side vent — A vent connecting to the drain pipe through a 45-degree fitting.

Stack — A general term referring to any vertical pipe such as a soil pipe, waste pipe or vent pipe.

Vent stack — The main vertical vent pipe installed primarily to provide circulation of air to or from any part of the building drainage system.

Wet vent — A soil or waste pipe that serves also as a vent.

Yoke vent — A vertical or 45° relief vent of the continuous waste and vent type formed by the extension of an upright Y branch or 45° Y branch inlet of the horizontal branch to the stack.

Back vent — A branch vent installed primarily for the purpose of protecting fixture traps from self-siphonage.

General Design Considerations

The typical cast-iron soil pipe used for residential work usually is 4 inches in diameter. It has a large bell shape on one end of each length, and the largest outside dimension approaches 5½ inches. This bell shape is necessary for the joining of two pieces of pipe. When it must be hidden inside an interior wall, the wall must be framed with 2 x 6 studs to conceal the pipe. The designer must plan for this, as he plans room layouts and partition sizes. If a second-floor partition is not directly above a first-floor partition, with both concealing a soil pipe, great difficulties are encountered in running the soil pipe through the second floor to the roof. Because of the nature of the waste carried by a soil pipe and because of the large-diameter pipe required, it cannot turn sharp corners or make many turns. The designer should plan the waste disposal system so gradual bends and long straight runs of soil pipe are used.

Copper soil pipes have thin walls and small joints and can be placed inside the typical 4-inch interior partition. See Figs. 597 and 598.

For industrial buildings where heavy work is done or where temperatures vary or for buildings of multiple stories, steel or wrought-iron soil pipe is used.

Another major consideration is to design the waste disposal system so it can be installed with a minimum of cutting of structural mem-

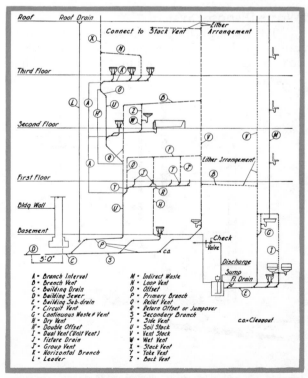

Fig. 596. A typical multistory waste disposal system. (U.S. Department of Commerce)

bers. Roof and floor joists should not be notched more than one-sixth of the joist depth, except when notched in the top only, where the notch can be a maximum of one-third of the joist depth and is no further from the face of support than the depth of the joist.

The soil pipe consists of the vertical stack which forms the central core of the waste disposal system. It runs from the house drain through the roof. Horizontal branches of soil pipe are run between floor joists, from the vertical stack to the water closets. These pipes have a slight slope from the water closets to the vertical soil pipe. Since the slope is small, they tend to clog easier than the vertical stack. The longer the horizontal pipe is, the more likely it is to clog. These pipes are usually 4 inches in diameter in residential work, but for large projects with many fixtures, the size is ascertained by the unit method. This is explained in the next section of this chapter.

The waste pipe, usually, is smaller in diameter than the soil pipe, because it carries a different type of waste. Waste pipes may be cast iron, galvanized steel, wrought iron or copper. A typical, waste-pipe layout is shown in Fig. 598. If a lavatory is to discharge unusual materials, such as chemicals, special consideration should be given to the material from which the pipe is made. A plan view of a bath showing a suggested layout for the waste pipe, vent pipe and hot-and-cold-water lines is shown in Fig. 599.

Waste disposal systems should have cleanout plugs located at convenient places. It is inevitable that a system will become clogged and will need rodding out. However, clogging can be decreased by making horizontal waste lines as short as possible and by avoiding sharp offsets. See Fig. 600. Fig. 601 illustrates the standard plumbing symbols used by draftsmen.

The house drain may be located below the basement floor, if the sewer or septic tank is below this level so waste will drain into it. If this condition does not exist, the house drain must be hung below the floor joists. The ideal situation, of course, is to locate it below the basement floor, so headroom is not reduced and unsightly pipes are hidden. This arrangement also permits satisfactory place-

Fig. 597. Copper waste pipe (left) and vent pipe. (Copper and Brass Research Assoc.)

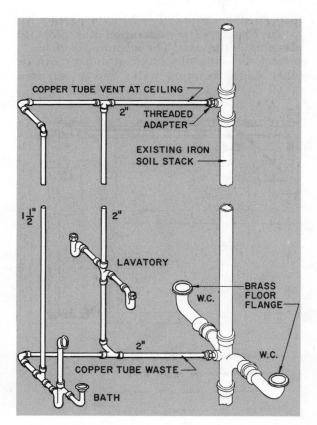

Fig. 598. Copper waste disposal system for two baths built back-to-back. (Copper and Brass Research Assoc.)

ment of fixtures in the basement. If a house drain is hung from the floor joists, all waste in the basement needs to be lifted up to it with a sump pump, which is a rather unsatisfactory arrangement.

Generally, the house drain is cast-iron pipe, but vitrified-clay pipe is acceptable. The average house drain carries the waste from the fixtures in the house only. For residential work, a 4-inch, cast-iron pipe or a 6-inch, clay-tile pipe usually will serve as a house drain. Occasionally, storm sewers are connected; this greatly increases the amount of water the pipe must carry.

The house sewer most frequently used is made of cast-iron pipe. It is suitable for installation on unstable soil, it resists clogging by tree roots and it withstands vibrations and heavy loads (such as trucks) passing over it. Vitrified, clay-tile pipe is satisfactory, if the above conditions do not exist. A cast-iron pipe buried in cinders or ashes will deteriorate due to chemical action, and clay pipe must be used under such conditions.

In Chapter 2 consideration was given to planning bathrooms. The advantages of back-to-back building of a kitchen and a bath or other areas requiring water and sewer were

Fig. 600. The large-diameter pipe on the right is a soil pipe. Notice the clean-out plug. Connecting into the soil pipe is a small-diameter vent pipe. Also shown are hot-and-cold-water lines and a waste pipe. (Copper and Brass Research Assoc.)

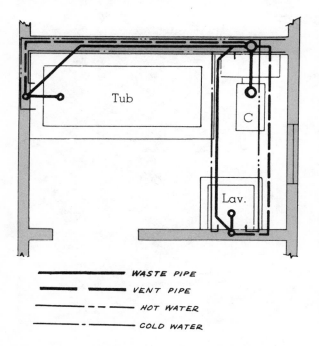

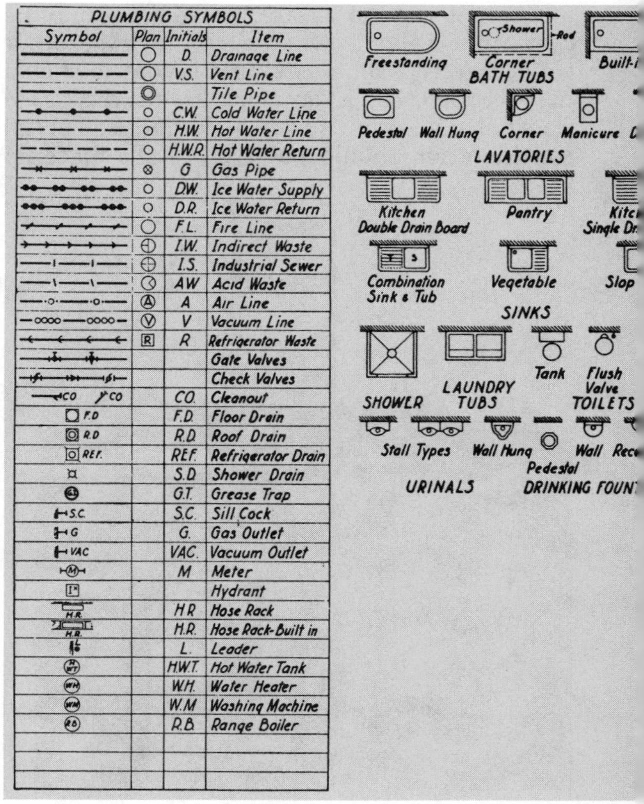

Fig. 599. Typical piping layout for a bathroom. (Housing and Home Finance Agency)

Fig. 601. Standard Plumbing Symbols. (U.S. Department of Commerce)

discussed. Fig. 602 illustrates the plumbing required to make this installation, while Fig. 603 indicates the extra expense involved if this principle is violated. The decision to be made is whether the owner considers the value of the split location to be worth the cost of the additional plumbing.

It is most economical to locate second-floor bathrooms directly above a kitchen or first-floor bath, so all fixtures can discharge into a common stack. Fig. 604 illustrates the drain and vent piping needed for such an installation. Remember that the common wall also reduces the cost of water piping.

Clothes washers and dishwashers should be located as near to the other plumbing in the house as is possible. If a washer is poorly placed, it can easily double the cost of plumbing a kitchen. Fig. 605 illustrates such planning.

Sizing Drains, Soil Pipes and Waste Pipes

Once the number and locations of fixtures have been decided, it is necessary to ascertain the size of the pipe used for the house or building drain, soil pipes and waste pipes. The

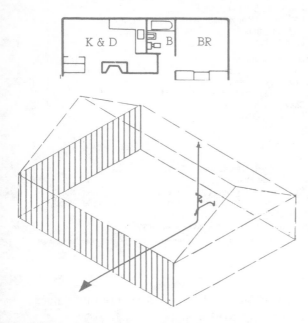

Fig. 602. Drain pipes required for back-to-back kitchen and bath installation. (Housing and Home Finance Agency)

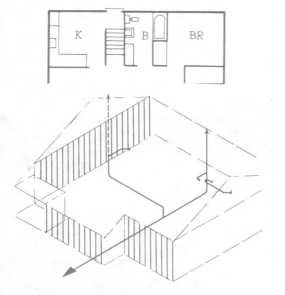

Fig. 603. Drain pipes required for separated bath and kitchen installation. Water piping is not shown, but would have to be extended also, thus increasing cost even more. (Housing and Home Finance Agency)

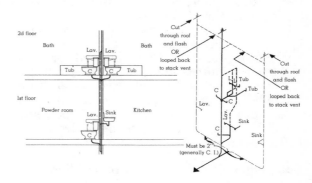
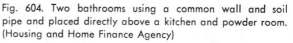

Fig. 604. Two bathrooms using a common wall and soil pipe and placed directly above a kitchen and powder room. (Housing and Home Finance Agency)

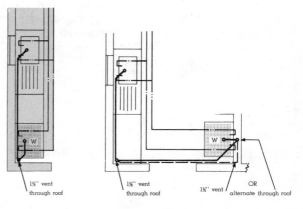

Fig. 605. Compare the differences in required plumbing for these two washer and sink locations. (Housing and Home Finance Agency)

size of pipe depends upon the number and kind of fixtures connected to each section. Each fixture discharges different volumes of waste. This flow of waste is measured in *fixture unit values* which were established by studies made by the Uniform Plumbing Code Committee.

A study of the volume of water discharged by various fixtures disclosed that a lavatory discharges about 7½ gallons of liquid per minute. This equals almost one cubic foot of water. The Committee established this as "one fixture unit" of discharge. Through studies of other fixtures, their values in units of discharge were established. Table 36 gives the established fixture unit values. For example, a bathtub adds 2 units or 15 gallons per minute to the needed waste-carrying capacity of the drain pipe.

To estimate fixture unit values not listed in Table 36, note the drain or trap size of the fixture in question and select the proper fixture unit value from Table 37.

For continuous or semicontinuous flow into a drainage system, such as from a pump, two fixture units should be allowed for each gallon per minute of flow.

The Committee's study also ascertained the pipe diameters required for building or house drains, horizontal branch pipes and vertical soil pipes. These standards are found in Tables 38 and 39.

Computing Size of Building Drain or Sewer

Assume a motel contains 30 water closets (tank type), 30 lavatories, 30 bathtubs, 6

Table 36
Unit Values of Plumbing Fixtures

Fixture	Units
Lavatory or washbasin	1
Lavatory—public, barber, beauty parlor	2
Kitchen sink	2
Kitchen sink with disposal	3
Bathtub, with or without overhead shower, private	2
Bathtub, public	4
Laundry tub	2
Drinking fountain	½
Combination fixture	3
Urinal wall or stall, public	4
Urinal, pedestal, public; syphon jet, blowout	8
Shower bath, private	2
Showers, per shower head	3
Floor drain	1
Dishwasher, domestic	2
Slop sink	3
Water closet, tank operated	4
Water closet, valve operated	8
One bathroom group (consisting of tank-type water closet, lavatory, bathtub and overhead shower; or water closet, lavatory, and shower compartment)	6
If bathroom uses flush-valve water closet	8

From National Plumbing Code, American Society of Mechanical Engineers.

Table 37
Trap Sizes and Estimated Fixture Unit Values

Fixture Drain or Trap Size (in Inches)	Fixture Unit Value
1¼ and smaller	1
1½	2
2	3
2½	4
3	5
4	6

Table 38
Capacities of Building Drains and Sewers

DIAMETER OF PIPE	MAXIMUM NUMBER OF FIXTURE UNITS THAT MAY BE CONNECTED TO ANY PORTION OF THE BUILDING DRAIN OR THE BUILDING SEWER[1]			
	Fall per Foot			
	1/16-Inch	1/8-Inch	1/4-Inch	1/2-Inch
Inches				
2			21	26
2½			24	31
3		20[2]	27[2]	36[2]
4		180	216	250
5		390	480	575
6		700	840	1,000
8	1,400	1,600	1,920	2,300
10	2,500	2,900	3,500	4,200
12	3,900	4,600	5,600	6,700
15	7,000	8,300	10,000	12,000

[1]Includes branches of the building drain.
[2]Not over two water closets.

From National Plumbing Code, American Society of Mechanical Engineers.

urinals, 5 slop sinks and 4 laundry tubs. What size drain pipe will be required to handle the entire flow, if the slope of the drain pipe is to be ⅛ inch to the foot?

Solution

The first step is to find the total fixture units that the pipe will carry. Examine Table 36 for the fixture units for each type of fixture in the motel. These are listed as follows:

30 bathroom groups x 6 units	180 units
6 wall urinals x 4 units	24 units
5 slop sinks x 3 units	15 units
4 laundry tubs x 2 units	8 units
	227 fixture units total flow

It can be seen that the building drain will have to carry 227 fixture units of flow. An examination of Table 38 reveals that a 4-inch pipe sloped ⅛ inch to the foot carries 180 units, while a 5-inch pipe carries 390 units. A 5-inch pipe, therefore, is required to carry the 227 units of waste from the building to the sewer in the street or to a septic tank.

A similar problem exists when the size of a soil pipe must be ascertained. Standards have been established on the unit flow basis; these are given in Table 39.

No soil or waste stack should be smaller than the largest horizontal branch connected to it. A 4 x 3 water closet connection is not considered a reduction in pipe size.

A stack vent should be carried full size through the roof; the vent should not be less than 3 inches in diameter or the size of the building drain, whichever is the smaller.

When provision is made for the future installation of fixtures, those to be added should be provided for in the calculation of required drain pipe sizes. Construction should provide for such fixture installation by terminating and plugging fittings at the stack where they eventually will be connected.

Computing Size of Horizontal Fixture Branch

If the motel were a one-story building and two baths were on a single, horizontal fixture branch, what diameter pipe would be required? (Assume that each bath contains a water closet, lavatory and bathtub with overhead shower.)

Solution

An examination of Table 36 reveals such a combination of fixtures has a unit value of 6. Since two baths feed into a single, horizontal branch, it must carry a total flow of 12 fixture units. An examination of Table 39 reveals that of "any horizontal fixture branch," a 2½-inch pipe carries 12 units; therefore, this would be a satisfactory pipe size for this fixture branch.

Table 39
Capacities of Horizontal Fixture Branches and Stacks

Pipe Diameter (Inches)	MAXIMUM NUMBER OF FIXTURE UNITS			
	Any Horizontal Fixture Branch[1]	One Stack Three Stories in Height or Not Over Three Branch Intervals	More Than Three Stories in Height	
			Total at One Story or Branch Interval	Total for Vertical Soil Pipe or Stack
1¼	1	2	1	2
1½	3	4	2	8
2	6	10	6	24
2½	12	20	9	42
3	20[2]	30[3]	16[3]	60[3]
4	160	240	90	500
5	360	540	200	1,100
6	620	960	350	1,900
8	1,400	2,200	660	3,600
10	2,500	3,800	1,000	5,600
12	3,900	6,000	1,500	8,400
15	7,000	....	....	....

[1]Does not include branches of the building drain.
[2]Not over two water closets.
[3]Not over six water closets.

From National Plumbing Code, American Society of Mechanical Engineers.

Computing Size of Soil Pipe or Stack

What size soil pipe or stack would be required for the motel, if the total flow were fed into the soil pipe by all horizontal branches?

Solution

The total flow of the motel was found to be 227 fixture units. Table 39 reveals that one stack, 3 stories in height (or less) and 3 inches in diameter, carries 30 fixture units; if 4 inches in diameter, it carries 240 units. Therefore, the 4-inch stack would serve adequately.

Traps

An important function of waste disposal is performed by the trapping devices. They must permit the passage of waste into the system; yet they must prevent offensive sewer gases from backing up in the waste pipes and entering the building. Each fixture should be separately trapped. The trap should be located as near the fixture as possible, and each trap should be provided with a clean-out plug.

There are many types of traps in use. Fig. 606 illustrates two common types. The water enters the trap and pushes the waste down the waste pipe. The last of the water enter-

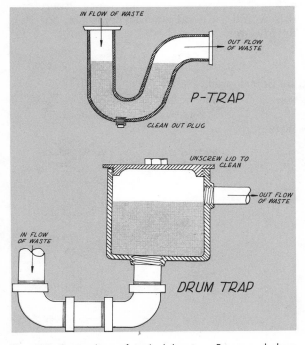

Fig. 606. Comparison of typical lavatory P-trap and drum trap used on bathtubs and showers.

ing remains in the trap, thus preventing sewer gas from backing up through the pipe. Trap sizes commonly used are given in Table 40. Usually, the trap should be the same diameter as the drain pipe to which it is connected.

Vents

It is necessary to vent a waste disposal system properly so that atmospheric pressure is maintained. Proper venting also prevents the loss of trap seals, enables the waste to flow normally and prevents deterioration of materials. Refer again to Figs. 595, 597 and 600 for examples of vents. Fig. 596 illustrates and defines vents commonly found in residential and commercial plumbing systems.

If a waste disposal system is not vented properly, the atmospheric pressure inside the waste pipe may become less (a partial vacuum) than the pressure in the room, and the water in the trap will be forced into the waste pipe, leaving the trap empty. The foul gases from the sewer system then can enter the building. Occasionally, the waste pipe will build up excessive pressure if not vented properly, and the waste in the trap will be sprayed into the room.

If the waste pipe is not vented properly, the flow of waste may compress the air in the pipe and seriously retard the flow of liquid. This is the same as having a waste pipe blocked by a physical obstruction, causing the waste to drain out slowly.

The gas in a waste system frequently contains acid-forming elements. If not vented,

Table 40
Commonly Used Trap Sizes

Fixture	Size of Trap and Fixture Drain (Inches)
Bathtubs	1½
Combination fixtures	1½
Drinking fountains	1¼
Floor drains	2
Laundry trays	1½
Lavatories	1¼
Shower stalls	2
Sinks, residence kitchen	1½
Sinks, hotel or public	2
Sinks, small (pantry or bar)	1¼
Sinks, dishwasher	1½
Sinks, service	2
Urinals, trough	2
Urinals, stall	2
Water closet	3

From Building Materials and Structures, United States Department of Commerce

these will attack the pipe and cause it to deteriorate and, eventually, to fail.

There are two main classifications of vents — (1) the pipes used to vent the soil and waste pipes and (2) individual vents to each fixture, designed to maintain atmospheric pressure in the disposal system.

The soil and waste pipe vent is obtained by extending the soil pipe up through the roof. It usually is the same diameter as the portion of the pipe that carries waste. Attached to this is the main vent pipe, which serves as the ventilation stack for the smaller fixture traps. This vent begins in the basement, at the bottom of the soil pipe, and runs the full height of the soil stack, connecting again in the attic, at least 3 feet above the highest fixture branch. See Figs. 595 and 600. The main vent must run straight up, with no offsets to slow the venting process.

The individual vents run from single traps and are connected into the main vent pipe above the overflow of the fixture vented. They are connected as near to the trap as possible, below and behind the fixture vented. If several fixtures are closely grouped, one individual vent can serve the group. The size of the vent pipe and the number of fixtures that can be vented with a pipe of a particular size can be found in Table 41.

It should be pointed out again that all residential piping must be hidden inside the walls of the building. In many industrial installations, the piping problems are very complex, and it is not possible or necessary to hide the piping.

Sizing Vent Piping

The nominal size of vent piping is determined by its necessary length and by the total of fixture units connected with it. Design data are reported in Table 41. *Note:* Only 20 percent of the total length of vent piping can be installed in a horizontal position.

The length of the vent stack or main vent should be its developed length from the low-

Table 41
Sizes and Lengths of Vents

Size of Soil or Waste Stack (Inches)	Fixture Units Connected	Diameter of Vent Required (Inches)								
		1¼	1½	2	2½	3	4	5	6	8
		Maximum Length of Vent (Feet)								
1¼	2	30								
1½	8	50	150							
1½	10	30	100							
2	12	30	75	200						
2	20	26	50	150						
2½	42	....	30	100	300					
3	10	....	30	100	200	600				
3	30	....	....	60	200	500				
3	60	....	....	50	80	400				
4	100	....	....	35	100	260	1000			
4	200	....	....	30	90	250	900			
4	500	....	....	20	70	180	700			
5	200	....	....	....	35	80	350	1000		
5	500	....	....	....	30	70	300	900		
5	1100	....	....	....	20	50	200	700		
6	350	....	....	....	25	50	200	400	1300	
6	620	....	....	....	15	30	125	300	1100	
6	960	....	....	....	....	24	100	250	1000	
6	1900	....	....	....	....	20	70	200	700	
8	600	....	....	....	....	....	50	150	500	1300
8	1400	....	....	....	....	....	40	100	400	1200
8	2200	....	....	....	....	....	30	80	350	1100
8	3600	....	....	....	....	....	25	60	250	800
10	1000	....	....	....	....	....	....	75	125	1000
10	2500	....	....	....	....	....	....	50	100	500
10	3800	....	....	....	....	....	....	30	80	350
10	5600	....	....	....	....	....	....	25	60	250

From National Plumbing Code, American Society of Mechanical Engineers

est connection of the vent system with the soil stack, waste stack or building drain to the vent terminal. It can terminate in the open air through the roof, or it can connect to the stack vent. In the latter case, the length includes the added length of the stack vent to its termination in open air.

Individual vents should be not less than one-half the diameter of the drain, and never less than $1\frac{1}{4}$ inches in diameter.

For residential use, the usual vent sizes are indicated in Table 42.

It is necessary to place vents away from traps, so the water in the trap will not be siphoned away, thus permitting sewer gas to enter the building. Table 43 lists the recommended distances that vents should be located from fixture traps to prevent seal loss.

The Septic Tank

In areas beyond the city sewer lines, a septic tank must be installed to treat and filter waste material. Factors to be considered in planning for such a unit include the type of soil and the size of the tank.

Liquid waste is purified in the tank and is then dispersed into drain tile which permits the liquid to drain into the soil. If the soil is sandy or if it contains gravel, this leaching into the soil is aided. However, soil that contains an abundance of clay does not absorb the liquid waste as well.

The contour of the land should be sufficient to permit a gravity flow of waste from the septic tank to the drain tile and thus to the soil. The slope also should permit the tank and drain lines to be installed close to the surface of the soil. The bacteria that act to purify the waste cannot exist deep in the ground.

The more fixtures that discharge waste into the tank, the larger the tank must be. Table 44 illustrates satisfactory tank sizes for residential use.

If a house draws its water supply from a well, the septic tank must be at least 50 feet from the well, and the drain field must be 100 feet away.

Fig. 607 shows a typical septic tank. The raw sewage enters through the inlet. It consists of heavy, solid matter that settles to the bottom, as well as liquid and materials that remain in solution. The heavy materials that settle to the bottom are called sludge. The

lighter organic materials rise to the surface to form scum. It is believed that the bacteria that thrive in the tank aid in the decomposition of the organic waste materials. A gas is produced which must be discharged to the atmosphere. This can be accomplished by equipping the tank with a vent above the ground or by inserting an inverted inlet pipe in the tank to permit the gas to be expelled through the soil pipe in the roof of the house. Fig. 607 illustrates the latter method.

Certain solids settle out and do not decompose. These must be removed periodically by pumping or dipping.

The liquid in the tank overflows into the outlet pipe and into the drain field pipe where it is percolated (filtered) into the soil.

If large volumes of water, such as rain from the roof, are run into the tank, solid matter cannot settle and is washed into the drain field pipes. Here the solids cannot be liquefied and purified, and consequently, they

Table 42
Usual Residential Vent Sizes

Fixture	Vent Pipe Diameter
Water closet	2″
Lavatory	$1\frac{1}{4}$″
Bathtub	$1\frac{1}{4}$″
Sink, kitchen	$1\frac{1}{4}$″
Laundry tray	$1\frac{1}{4}$″
Sink and tray combination	$1\frac{1}{4}$″
Shower	$1\frac{1}{4}$″
Dishwasher	$1\frac{1}{4}$″

From Capacities of Stacks in Sanitary Drainage Systems for Buildings, Federal Housing Administration.

Table 43
Recommended Distances from Fixture Traps to Vents

Size of Fixture Drain	Distance Trap to Vent
$1\frac{1}{4}$″	2 ft. 6 in.
$1\frac{1}{2}$″	3 ft. 6 in.
2″	5 ft. 0 in.
3″	6 ft. 0 in.
4″	10 ft. 0 in.

From National Plumbing Code. American Society of Mechanical Engineers

Table 44
Minimum Capacities for Septic Tanks

Number of Bedrooms	Minimum Liquid Capacity (Gallons)
2 or less	750
3	900
4	1,000
Each additional bedroom, add	250

From Septic Tanks, Their Use in Sewage Disposal, U. S. Housing and Home Finance Agency.

clog the pipes. This reduces the effectiveness of the system and, frequently, necessitates the replacement of the drain field.

The size of the drain field is best ascertained by the local health department. They will make percolation tests to see how well the soil will absorb water. The faster the water is absorbed, the smaller the drain field needs to be.

The Water System

The purpose of the water system is to provide a continuous supply of clean, pure water to the points of use within a building.

The water supply line from the water main to the house should be buried below the frost line, to protect it from freezing. This depth will vary from one section of the country to another.

The diameter of the pipe also will vary according to local conditions. If the water pressure on the city main is low, a large water service pipe must be run from the main to the house. This service pipe should be as short as possible, and turns and offsets should be avoided, since they retard the flow of water and reduce the amount of water flowing to the

building. Generally, two piping systems are used within a building — one for the cold water supply and one for the hot water supply.

Cold Water System

Usually the cold water system consists of a supply main suspended below the first floor. From this main, supply pipes are run to each fixture. The house service pipe should be ¾-inch diameter. The minimum pipe sizes to supply fixtures are indicated in Table 45.

All riser connections to the water main within a building should be made at a 45-degree angle to the main, and the riser connections to this branch from the main should be on a 90-degree angle. See Fig. 608.

The water system should be installed on a slight grade and should drain to one low point, if possible. This allows the entire sys-

Table 45
Minimum Sizes of Water Supply Pipes

Fixture or Device	Pipe Size (Inches)
Bathtubs	½
Combination sink and tray	½
Drinking fountain	⅜
Dishwasher (domestic)	½
Kitchen sink, residential	½
Kitchen sink, commercial	¾
Lavatory	⅜
Laundry tray, 1, 2 or 3 compartments	½
Shower (single head)	½
Sinks (service, slop)	½
Sinks (flushing rim)	¾
Urinal (flush tank)	½
Urinal (direct flush valve)	¾
Water closet (tank type)	⅜
Water closet (flush valve type)	1
Hose bibbs	½
Wall hydrant	½

From National Plumbing Code, American Society of Mechanical Engineers

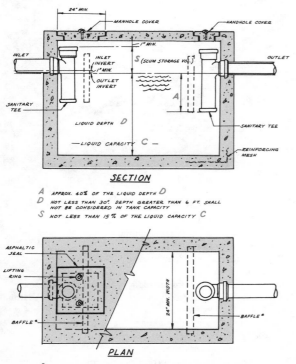

SECTION

A APPROX. 40% OF THE LIQUID DEPTH D
D NOT LESS THAN 30". DEPTH GREATER THAN 6 FT. SHALL NOT BE CONSIDERED IN TANK CAPACITY
S NOT LESS THAN 15% OF THE LIQUID CAPACITY C

PLAN

*BAFFLES OPTIONAL TO SUBMERGED INLET AND OUTLET SANITARY TEE

Fig. 607. Single-compartment septic tank.

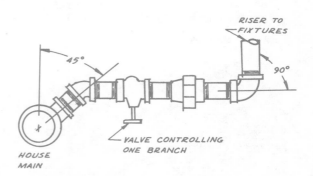

Fig. 608. Typical house main, branch and riser pipe in a water system.

tem to be drained by one valve located at the low end.

Valves should be located in the system so that service to various parts of the building can be shut off without turning off the entire system. Frequently, each fixture will have a separate shut-off valve, while other times, one valve may serve a branch and control several fixtures. These valves should be located so they are easily accessible. Fig. 609 illustrates a simple water system for a small house.

Hot Water System

The hot water system carries the water from the water heater to the various fixtures. One system of hot water distribution is a single pipe to each fixture as indicated in Fig. 609. A disadvantage to this system is that the water in the pipe must be run off before hot water reaches the fixture. This wastes water and is annoying, but the system is easier and less expensive to install.

A more satisfactory, but more costly, system is to have a gravity hot water return. Fig. 610 illustrates such a system. This permits a continuous flow of hot water to the fixture and provides instant service.

In residential building, water usually is heated by gas or electricity. These units heat the water to a predetermined temperature and

automatically shut off. When hot water is drained off and cold replaces it, they automatically turn on and again heat the water to the desired temperature. All water heaters must have a pressure relief valve to prevent explosions. If the heater should malfunction and continue to heat water beyond a safe level, great steam pressure is built up. This is bled off by the relief valve before the tank explodes, and it warns the user that something is wrong with the temperature control on the

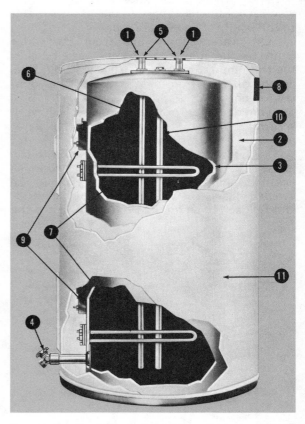

Fig. 611. Details of electric water heater. (Hotpoint Division, General Electric Co.)

1. Hot and cold water connections.
2. Fiber insulation.
3. Glass-lined, heavy-gauge steel tank.
4. Drain valve.
5. Pipe connections, threaded with 3/4-inch pipe thread.
6. Diffuse tube to stratify incoming cold water at bottom of tank.
7. High-intensity heating units.
8. Outlet box for electrical connections.
9. Automatic thermostats.
10. Magnesium rod to increase tank life in all kinds of water.
11. Metal exterior shell.

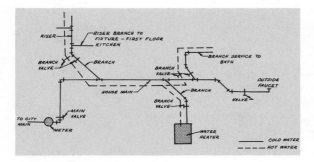

Fig. 609. A simple water-piping system.

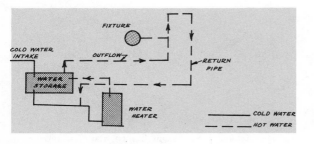

Fig. 610. Gravity-return, hot-water system.

heater. Fig. 611 illustrates the details of an electric water heater.

It is important to locate water heaters as close to the fixtures using hot water as possible. However, gas- and oil-fired units need a chimney to vent the gas from the burning of the fuel. This makes it more difficult to locate these types than it is to locate an electric water heater, since the electric heater does not need venting. Fig. 612 illustrates a satisfactory installation for a water heater needing venting.

Water pipe can be galvanized steel or iron, copper, or AAA lead pipe. Outside faucets should be of the frost-proof type or should have a shut-off valve so they can be drained in freezing weather.

It is a good practice to insulate hot and cold water pipes. Insulation on hot pipes retains the heat and thus saves money, while on cold pipes it keeps warm, moist air from causing them to sweat.

Build Your Vocabulary

Following are words that you should understand and use as a part of your working vocabulary. Write a brief explanation of what each means.

Septic tank
Cold water supply main
Valves
Water risers
Relief valve
Plumbing fixtures
Soil pipe

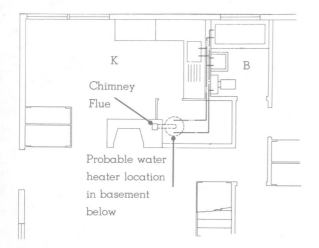

Fig. 612. A good, water-heater location, providing a vent and a short run to fixtures. (Housing and Home Finance Agency)

Waste pipe
House drain
House sewer
Primary branch
Secondary branch
Trap
Branch interval
Branch vent
Back vent
Circuit vent
Yoke vent
Continuous waste and vent
Side vent
Dry vent
Relief vent
Dual vent
Vent stack
Group vent
Loop vent
Leader
Indirect waste

Class Activities

1. Trace the plumbing system in your home. On graph paper, make a freehand sketch of the floor plan and locate all fixtures, hot and cold water pipes, and sewer lines. Be certain to indicate where the water and sewer lines leave the house.

2. Visit the local building inspector. Write a report giving the major requirements for the installation of a sewage system in the typical residence and small commercial building. Especially note any differences between these two types of buildings.

3. Using wooden dowel rods, construct a three-dimensional, scale model of a complete plumbing system for a residence. Be certain to include hot and cold water lines, sewer lines and vents. Fixtures and water heater can be molded from clay. Color hot water lines red, cold water lines green and sewer lines yellow.

4. Visit a house under construction when the plumbing is being installed. Notice how the pipes are placed through the walls and under the floor. Observe how the joints are sealed. Check the venting system. See if the pipes used meet minimum size standards.

5. Assume that the fixtures in one of the school rest rooms all flow into one sewer line. Compute the number of fixture units the line would have to carry. Ascertain the correct size sewer pipe, vent pipe and trap size for this job.

Additional Reading

American Society of Mechanical Engineers, "National Plumbing Code."

Architectural Record (Editorial Staff), *Time Saver Standards.*

Gerber Plumbing Fixtures Corporation, "Tips from Your Plumber."

Matthias, Arthur J., and Smith, E., *How to Design and Install Plumbing.*

National Bureau of Standards, U.S. Department of Commerce, "Plumbing Manual."

Ramsey, Charles G., and Sleeper, H. R., *Architectural Graphic Standards.*

U.S. Federal Housing Administration, "Minimum Property Standards for One and Two Living Units."

U.S. Housing and Home Finance Agency, "Capacities of Stacks in Sanitary Drainage Systems for Buildings."

———, "Manual of Individual Water Systems."

———, "Plumbing Fixture Arrangement."

———, "Septic Tanks, Their Use in Sewage Disposal."

CHAPTER TEN

HEATING, COOLING AND INSULATING

The all-year air-conditioning system is a well established means of heating and cooling. Houses without year-round temperature regulation are obsolete. Such systems supply heat when outside temperature drops and cool air when it rises. This makes living more healthful (especially for hay fever sufferers and heart cases), decreases the amount of housework since air is filtered the year around, and reduces family fatigue and irritation. It also reduces paint peeling, warped doors and furniture damage, by controlling the *humidity* (moisture content) of the air.

If air is too dry (low humidity), it drains moisture from wallpaper, furniture and woodwork; nose and throat membranes become dry and sore; lips become chapped; colds are frequent and bronchial ailments result. If air is too moist, the result is mildew, musty odors and warped doors and furniture. Humidity must be controlled all year.

A good all-year, air-conditioning system is on that is able to maintain an even, 75-degree temperature the year around. Such a system should give perfect circulation of air,

Fig. 640. Heat is drawn to cold outside wall, is chilled and settles to the floor.

with no feeling of air movement. During the winter, room temperatures should not vary more than 2 degrees throughout the day. From room to room, the temperature should not vary more than 4 degrees. When the outside temperature is 30 degrees, there should be no more than 3 degrees difference in temperature from the floor to sitting level or 4½ degrees from the floor to the ceiling. At zero degrees, the difference between the floor and sitting level should be no more than 5½ degrees; between floor and ceiling, a maximum of 8 degrees.

Placement of Heating and Cooling Units

Heat always flows from a warm object to a cold one. As a house loses heat to the colder outdoors, the human body feels cold because it is radiating its heat toward the cold walls, ceiling and floors. The heating system must supply heat as fast as it is lost. However, even if a furnace does this, a person still can feel cold. Comfort depends upon how heat is supplied, as well as how much heat is supplied. Older homes have heat registers placed on inside walls. The warm air rises to the ceiling and gradually descends to the floor as it cools. As the air passes cold windows, it is chilled rapidly and thus becomes heavier and descends faster. This causes a draft and a layer of cold air on the floor. The temperature inside the house may be 70 degrees on the thermometer, yet the occupants feel cold, because the exterior walls (being colder than the interior walls) draw away body heat. See Fig. 640.

Today's heating systems correct this by placing the heat outlets on the outside walls under windows. The heat enters the house on the outside perimeter and is, therefore, called *perimeter heating*. Perimeter heating sends a curtain of warm air up the outside wall; this reduces the loss of body heat to this wall. It also eliminates drafts and enables the heating system to maintain even heat. See Fig. 641.

Heat-emitting units should be low in height, but should be as large in area as possible, in order to maintain a low output per square foot, so that a concentration of heat is avoided. If care is exercised in the selection of heat emitters and their placement, along with correct calculation of heat losses, maximum comfort will be provided.

The unit heat emitter heats air, some of which is cooled by the cold wall on either side of it. This cooled air falls to the floor to be reheated by the unit. While this unit provides satisfactory heat, it does not provide the ultimate in correct heating effect.

The baseboard panel has the advantage of emitting heat along the entire cold wall. If baseboard panels are used, the cold wall and the cold air descending from a window are warmed, providing better distribution of radiant heat. Fig. 642 illustrates the difference between the two types of heat emitters.

In the summer, cool air is provided from forced-air cooling units, thus surrounding the warm outside walls with a protective curtain. This prevents the wall from radiating heat and absorbs heat from the body of the occupant, thus cooling him. Therefore, the all-year air-conditioning system provides heat in the winter and cool air in the summer — to the places in the house where it is needed the most.

It is imperative that air return to the circulating unit from every room except the bathroom and garage. A large hall should also have an air-return register. This aids in the circulation of air in the house and prevents "starving" the system for lack of air. It greatly increases the efficiency of the installation. Air returns located in crawl spaces and attics should be insulated to prevent excess loss of heat or coolness as the air returns. These returns are placed on inside walls in a perimeter system.

A wide range of devices is available for all-year air conditioning. Those in common use are forced-air, steam, hot water and electric units.

Forced-Air Heating Systems

In a forced-air heating system, air is heated by oil, natural gas, LP gas or electricity. In gas and oil systems, the fuel is burned in the furnace, and the heated air is forced through pipes to the outlets in the house. In electric systems, heating elements are located in the ducts or in a firebox. The blower forces air past the heating elements, thus warming the air.

There are three types of gas- and oil-fired, forced-air systems in common use — the up-

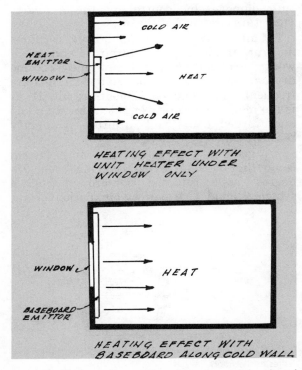

Fig. 642. Heating effects with unit heater and baseboard heat.

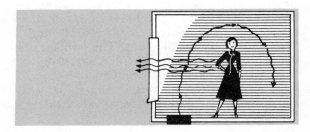

Fig. 641. Heat forms a protective curtain over outside wall.

flow, downflow and horizontal furnaces. These are illustrated in Fig. 643. In the *upflow system*, the furnace is installed in the basement, and the ductwork is placed between or below the floor joists. See Fig. 644. The *downflow furnace* forces air into ducts in the floor below it. It is ideal for perimeter heat in basementless houses, as the ducts can be placed in a concrete slab or in the crawl space beneath wood floors. The floors are kept warm through radiated heat from the ducts. The air in the house is warmed or cooled by the air forced through the ducts and blown into the rooms.

The *horizontal, forced-air furnace* is designed to hang in the crawl space below the floor in a basementless house or in the attic of a house with concrete floors. If installed below the floor, the ducts are hung below the floor joists; while in the attic, the ducts run above the ceiling joists.

There are two types of duct distribution systems in use for forced-air furnaces in houses with basements or crawl spaces. Both systems originate from the *plenum*, a metal box which is located at the top, side or bottom of the furnace. In the radial-distribution system, all the ducts radiate from the plenum to the outlets in the various rooms. In the extended-plenum distribution system, a long duct extends the plenum the length of the house, and smaller ducts lead from it to the various rooms. See Fig. 645.

The duct distribution system for a house built on a concrete slab can be either a loop perimeter or a radial perimeter. See Fig. 647. The ducts usually are transite or fiber that is lined with aluminum foil and wrapped with asphalt-filled, duplex kraft paper. It is used for supply and return lines in hot air furnaces. The series of pictures in Fig. 646 illustrate this installation.

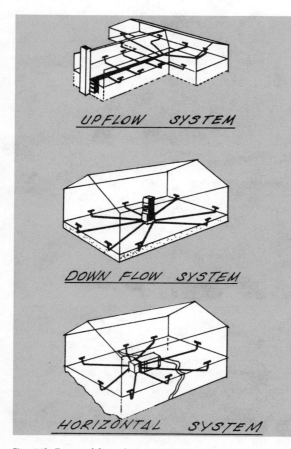

Fig. 643. Types of forced-air systems.

Fig. 644. An upflow gas-fired furnace and air-conditioning coil box on top. (Bryant Manufacturing Co.)

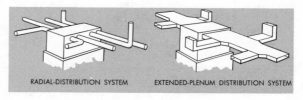

Fig. 645. Types of distribution systems.

Fig. 646. Installation of duct system in slab. (Sonoco Products Co.)
1. The foundation has been poured and the ditch dug for the duct.
2. Gravel fill has been made; moisture barrier is in place with joints sealed. Heat ducts go on top of vapor barrier. Note metal furnace plenum for downdraft furnace (left).
3. Metal is being fitted to duct to form T joint.
4. Duct is fitted to plenum chamber.
5. Mitered sections are in place to form elbows and T's.
6. Joints are covered with mastic tape.
7. Registers are fitted to perimeter section of duct.
8. Duct is installed, ready for concrete workers.
9. Reinforcing wire mesh is in place, ready for pouring of slab.

Forced-Air Cooling Units

There are many types of cooling units available for forced-air systems. Some furnaces are built with the heating and cooling system in two separate units, while other furnaces have the heating and cooling systems built into a single unit. Both types of cooling systems use the same ducts, blower and filters as the heating unit. Gas and electric cooling units are available.

Electric Cooling Units

When a liquid changes to a gas, it absorbs heat. This principle is utilized by the electric cooling unit. A liquid frequently used in electric cooling units is freon, which boils at 22 degrees below zero. The freon is pumped through coils placed in the furnace, and the blower forces air around these pipes; the freon absorbs large amounts of heat from the air in the furnace, thus cooling the air. The blower forces the cooled air through the ducts into the house. The freon, because it has absorbed heat, becomes a gas and is circulated to the compressor. This unit compresses the gas, thus concentrating the heat and raising the gas to an even higher temperature. The freon then is cooled by pumping it through an outside air unit called a condenser; it is circulated through tubes in water which absorbs the heat, thus cooling the freon and returning it to a liquid. The liquid freon is circulated back to the furnace cooling coil where it absorbs more heat from the air and repeats the cycle. The only electricity consumed is that needed to run the blower and the compressor. Fig. 648 illustrates this process for an air-cooled unit.

Water-cooled units must handle large quantities of water. Because of the great expense of water in many areas, they find

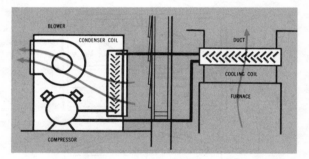

Fig. 648. Air-cooled systems. (United States Air Conditioning Corp.)

For areas where water supply is scarce or expensive and where water disposal is a problem, an "add-on" is available which uses outside air rather than water to cool the refrigerant in the condenser. This unit is also perfectly suited for homes where indoor space is very limited, because the refrigeration section can be located in almost any area where there is sufficient air circulation, indoors or out. Copper tubing carries the refrigerant from the refrigeration section to the housed cooling coil, usually installed on the outlet side of the air supply system.

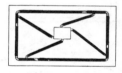

LOOP PERIMETER

In slab floor perimeter heating, the Loop System is generally preferred and should be used wherever practical because it produces more uniform temperatures. Duct extends completely around the perimeter of the building, and is supplied by feeder ducts.

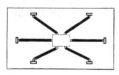

RADIAL PERIMETER

In the Radial System, air distribution consists of individual ducts running spoke-wise from the plenum chamber of a centrally located furnace to each perimeter warm air outlet.

Fig. 647. Types of perimeter distribution systems. (Sonoco Products Co.)

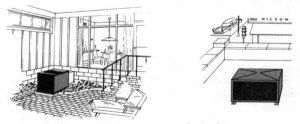

In The Yard

On Rooftops

Fig. 649. Residential condensers are usually placed in the yard, while in commercial buildings, they are placed on the roof. (Carrier Corp.)

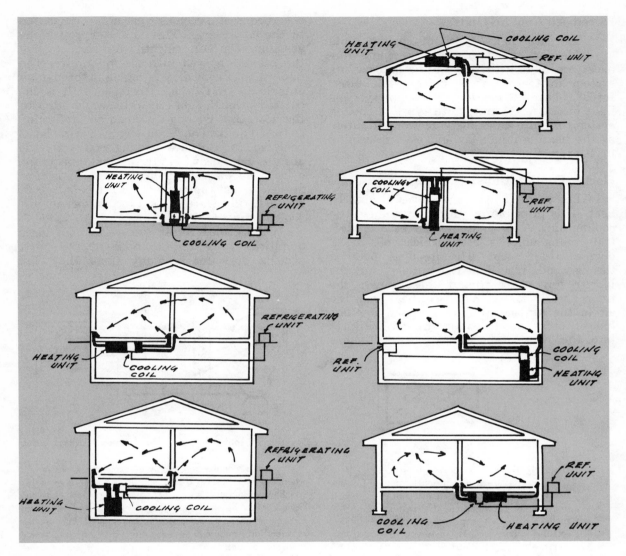

Fig. 650. Typical air-cooled installations. (United States Air Conditioning Corp.)

Top left: Counterflow furnace, located at the living level in a closet or equipment room. The cooling coil is placed under the furnace, and air is circulated by radial-duct distribution. The refrigerating unit is outside, with copper tubing running to the cooling unit.

Center left: The cooling coil placed in the ductwork next to the horizontal furnace suspended from the basement ceiling. Extended-plenum duct system distributes both warm and cool air. The refrigerating unit is outside, connected to the coil by copper tubing.

Bottom left: With a lo-boy furnace in the basement, the cooling unit is located in the main air supply duct of this extended-plenum distribution system. The refrigerating unit is located outside, connected to the coil by copper tubing.

Top right: In this home without a basement, the horizontal furnace is located in the attic with the cooling coil placed in the main supply air duct, between furnace outlet and the first duct branch. Extended-plenum duct distribution is used. Refrigerating unit is also located in the attic, next to a louvered vent.

Right, top center: The hi-boy furnace in this basementless home is recessed in closet or equipment room. The cooling coil is placed on top of the furnace with existing radial-duct distribution circulating air to all rooms. The refrigerating section is suspended from the breezeway ceiling.

Right, lower center: Another basement installation utilizes a hi-boy furnace with radial-duct distribution. The cooling unit is placed on top of the furnace, with the refrigerating unit located inside the basement, suspended from the ceiling, and vented through a window.

Bottom right: A horizontal furnace is located in the crawl space beneath this basementless house, with a cooling unit placed next to the furnace, and air distributed by the extended-plenum system. Refrigerating unit is outside.

limited use. Some units salvage some of the water and recirculate it, but the operating cost can still be high where water is scarce.

There are a number of different types of electric cooling units. One places the cooling coil in the furnace and the air-cooled condenser outside the building. The condenser can be located in the yard or on a rooftop. See Fig. 649. This system can be used on upflow, downflow and horizontal furnaces, as illustrated in Fig. 650.

Another type of system utilizes a furnace that contains the heating and cooling units in a single cabinet. Fig. 651 illustrates such a unit, with a water-cooled condenser. Also available are furnaces designed so that an air-conditioning unit can be added later. It operates in the same manner as the single unit, but occupies more floor space. Fig. 652 illustrates such a unit.

The exact method used to install water-cooled units is a problem for someone specializing in heating and cooling. Typical installations for various conditions are shown in Figs. 653 and 654.

The self-contained, electric air-cooling system is frequently used in homes in which the existing heating system cannot be easily converted to cooling. The ductwork of a hot-air system must be larger in cross section if it is to be used for cooling as well as heating. The self-contained system also is useful in homes with hot water or steam heat. The self-contained air conditioner contains all elements — refrigerator circuit, evaporator, compressor and condenser — in one sealed cabinet.

This type of air conditioner can be installed in the attic, with its own ducts leading to ceiling outlets, or it can be connected to the duct system of a horizontal furnace installed in the attic. It can be placed in a basement, crawl space, utility room, closet or attached garage. It can be installed through the exterior wall or can be located entirely outside the building on a roof, in a carport or on the ground. In these positions, it can tie into the existing duct system, or it can have

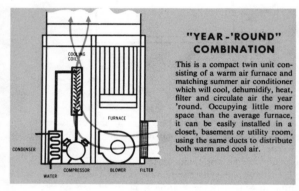

Fig. 651. Year-round combination furnace and air conditioner. (United States Air Conditioning Corp.)

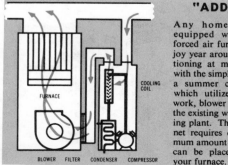

Fig. 652. Add-on air conditioning unit. (United States Air Conditioning Corp.)

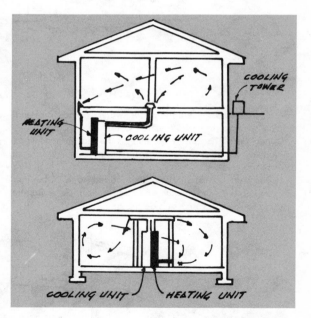

Fig. 653. Typical installations for single-unit, all-year, air-conditioning systems. (United States Air Conditioning Corp.)

Top: Located in the basement, this year-round combination circulates warm and cool air by extended-plenum distribution. A cooling tower outside the house cools water and returns it to the air-conditioning unit for reuse.

Bottom: Combination heating and cooling unit is neatly recessed in a centrally located closet, with radial-duct distribution circulating warm or cool air to all rooms.

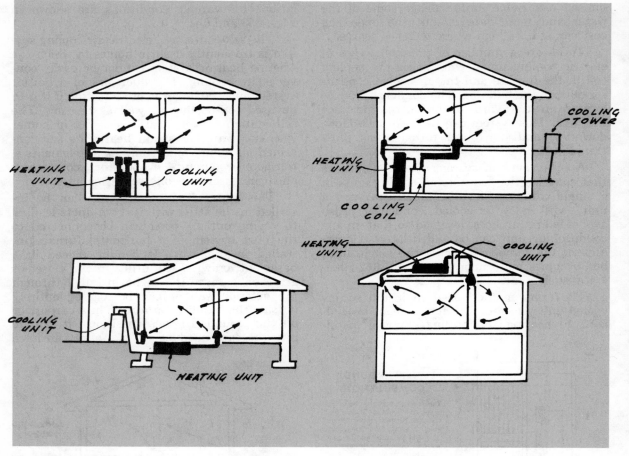

Fig. 654. Typical installations for water-cooled, air-conditioning systems. (United States Air Conditioning Corp.)

Upper Left: The lo-boy furnace is paired with a water-cooled air-conditioning unit, extended-plenum, distributing system.

Lower Left: A water-cooled unit added to a hi-boy furnace with extended-plenum, air distribution. A residential cooling tower is located outside the house.

Upper Right: Where there is not enough room in the crawl space to place a unit next to the horizontal furnace, it can be located in the attached garage, breezeway, or carport. Some additional ductwork will be necessary.

Lower Right: Where a horizontal furnace is located in the attic, a water-cooled add-on may be placed on the outlet side of the furnace in the extended-plenum distribution system.

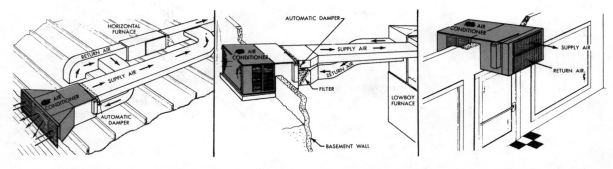

Fig. 655. Installation of self-contained air conditioner. (Frigidaire)

Left: Air conditioner ties into horizontal-furnace duct system.

Center: Air conditioner ties into upflow furnace in basement.

Right: Air conditioner in small commercial application.

a system of its own. In small commercial buildings, it can be installed through the wall and cool a large, open area. Fig. 655 illustrates several applications of this system as it ties into existing systems. Fig. 656 illustrates an

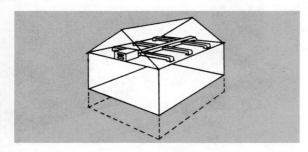

Fig. 656. Self-contained air conditioner with duct system separate from regular heating system.

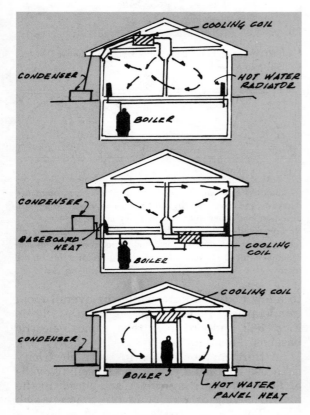

Fig. 657. Electric air conditioning with hot water heat. (United States Air Conditioning Corp.)
Top: Cooling unit (including blower, cooling coil and filter) located in the attic, with the refrigerating unit outdoors. Cooling coil is suspended from the joists in the basement ceiling, with refrigerating unit again outdoors.
Bottom: Cooling coil centrally located in a closet or under a stairway, with the refrigerating unit outside.

attic installation with a duct system separate from the regular heating system.

The electric, air-cooled air conditioner also is useful in cooling buildings having wet heat (hot water or steam). Such a building can be cooled in the summer by installing a chiller unit to send cold water through the pipe system or by installing a separate, forced-air cooling system using ducts and an electric air-conditioning unit. Fig. 657 illustrates three methods of installing electric air-cooled systems with the cooling coils inside the house and the condenser located outside.

A room air conditioner can be installed in a window or through the wall. This enables a house to be easily zoned for cooling, permitting some sections to be cooler than others or not cooled at all. Only electrical service to the unit is required. Since the unit blows air directly into the room, no ductwork is necessary. Fig. 658 illustrates such an installation in a frame wall. This type of installation frequently is found in motels and hotels, where

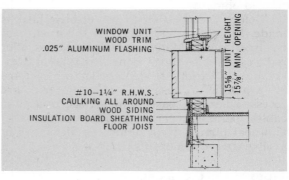

Fig. 658. A single-room air conditioner installed in a frame wall. (General Electric Co.)

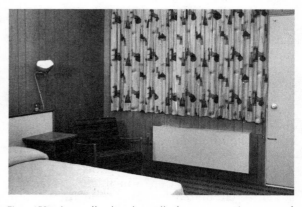

Fig. 659. A small, thru-the-wall, heat pump in a motel installation. (General Electric Co.)

room occupancy is irregular. Units are available that can heat in the winter as well as cool in the summer. As shown in Fig. 659, these units can be either small heat pumps or an electric air conditioner with built-in, resistance-heating elements.

Electric Heat

Electricity as a fuel to heat buildings has gained wide acceptance. It is quiet, convenient, clean and safe; it provides even heat, requires little maintenance, saves floor space and has a low installation cost. It enables a building to have zoned heat. Each room can be controlled by a separate thermostat, thus offering complete flexibility.

An important factor in electric heat is proper insulation of the building. Engineers recommend 6 inches of insulation in the ceiling, 4 inches in the walls, and 2 inches in the floor if the house is built over a crawl space. Doors and windows should be weather-stripped. Storm windows also are necessary in cold climates.

Before the decision to use electric heat is made, the cost of electricity in the area must be ascertained. Many power companies offer reduced rates to those using this type of heat.

A wide variety of electric heating systems is available. Those in common use are recessed heaters, baseboard panels, concealed cables, perimeter convectors, central furnaces and heat pumps. Heat pumps are discussed in a separate section of this chapter.

Types of Electric Heating Systems

Recessed, electric wall heaters are available in either the radiant or convection systems. See Fig. 660. The radiant heater delivers a high percentage of its heat in the form of direct radiation to a limited area. A bathroom heater is an example of this type. The convection-type heater distributes heat to a larger area, without any appreciable radiant heat. It usually has a small fan to assist in distributing the heat; the fan does not increase the amount of heat generated. Fig. 661 illustrates the difference between radiated heat and convected heat.

The electric baseboard panels use both radiant and convection principles. Heated air is gently circulated by convection throughout the room, thus assuring even heat distribution; heat also is radiated in sufficient amount

Fig. 660. A convection-type, recessed heater. (Hunter Division, Robbins and Meyers, Inc.)

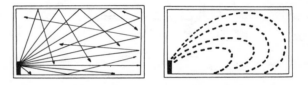

Fig. 661. Radiated heat (left) and convected heat.
Radiated heat: all surfaces and objects in the rooms are reached and warmed by radiant heat rays. Some are absorbed and some reflected to other cooler surfaces.
Convected heat: Convected heat is also provided by all radiant-heat distributors. Air coming in contact with the radiant surfaces is warmed and then circulates about the room with natural, gentle motion, without chilling drafts.

to allow body comfort, while the overall room temperature remains at a healthy level. Figs. 662 and 663 picture a typical electric baseboard heater.

A third method of heating with electricity is to use concealed cables in the ceiling, walls or floor. The heating cables are buried in the plaster ceiling or wall or in the concrete slab floor. This system tends to have slow heating response, because it must heat the wall or floor before it can heat the room. The ceiling heating cable should have at least a $3/8$-inch plaster coating over it. In concrete floors, the cable should have 4 inches of insulating concrete below and $1\frac{1}{2}$ inches of noninsulating concrete above. The recessed heater or base-

board heater tends to be more effective and efficient. Figs. 664 and 665 illustrate the installation of this cable. Also available are heating units suitable for installation in sidewalks and driveways to melt ice and snow. These are illustrated in Figs. 666 and 667.

Another effective means of electric heat is the floor-type perimeter convector. These are

Fig. 664. Concealed electric cable under plaster. (Electromode)

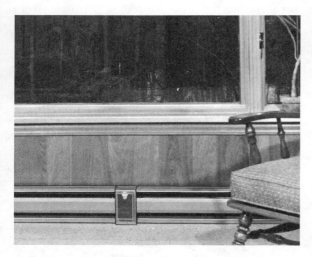

Fig. 662. An electric baseboard heater. (Electromode)

Fig. 665. Electric cable in floor ready for concrete cover. (Electromode)

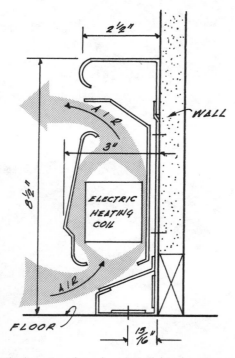

Fig. 663. A section through a typical baseboard convector. (Electromode)

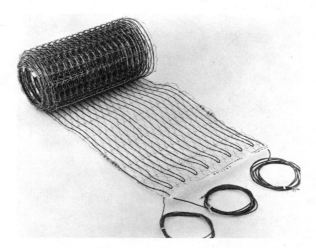

Fig. 666. Electric cable for outdoor installation in walks and driveways. (Electromode)

Fig. 667. Results of electric cable in driveway. (Electromode)

Fig. 668. A typical floor-type perimeter convector. (Electromode)

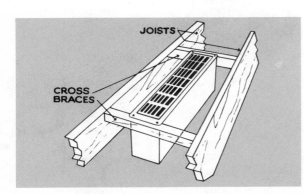

Fig. 669. Installation of floor-type individual-unit, perimeter convectors. (Electromode)

recessed in the floor, with a grill flush with the floor. Each unit is a separate heater. They can be located wherever a heat source is needed, such as under picture windows. Figs. 668 and 669 illustrate such a unit in a typical installation.

Central electric furnaces are available which operate exactly as a gas- or oil-fired furnace, except the source of heat is from resistance-type electric elements. The heat is distributed by a blower through ducts.

Many other types of electric heaters are available. Unit heaters as shown in Fig. 670 are used in industrial applications.

Infrared heaters are available for spot-heating, indoors and outdoors. This heater produces a heat similar to that of the sun, and it warms the person who steps under its rays. Industrial applications can be found at drive-in bank windows, at bus stops and at display windows of stores. Residentially, these heaters are used in baths, patios and swimming pools. Fig. 671 illustrates infrared heaters.

Fig. 670. Industrial application of electric unit heaters. (Electromode)

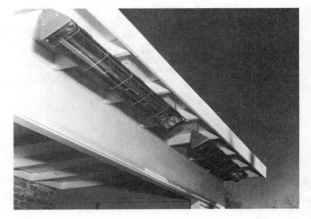

Fig. 671. Infrared electric heaters on a patio. (Electromode)

New forms of electric heat are under development. One new product is a decorative metal screen that heats when current is run through it one way and cools when current is run the opposite way. It uses two dissimilar metals. If current is passed through two dissimilar metals, one becomes hot and the other becomes cool. If the current is reversed, the opposite wires heat and cool.

A plywood heating panel that has graphite between the plys is being tested. When electric current is run through the graphite, its resistance to the current heats the plywood surface.

A paper that can be charged with electricity and which then radiates a low-temp-

erature heat is being developed. It can be applied to walls and ceilings or can be buried in walks and driveways.

A wall panel made of particle board, with a vinyl overlay and a thin, embedded, aluminum heating grid, is under study. These are exciting examples of possible developments in electric heating.

Various methods of solar heat have been developed and used under experimental conditions. While the efficiency of such a system needs improvement, it does hold promise for the future.

The Heat Pump

Another means of heating or cooling a building is to use a heat pump. See Figs. 672 and 673. The most commonly used heat pumps employ either air or water as their source of heat. This device literally pumps heat out of the air or water. Basically, it operates on much the same principle as a refrigerator. In the summer, the heat pump removes heat from inside the building and discharges it outside. In the winter, this cycle is reversed. Heat is removed from the outside air and discharged inside the building. Small heat pumps actually reverse their cycle, while large commercial units follow a slightly different system of reversing. The small heat pump is a single machine that uses the same components to provide heat or cooling. It requires no flue. Other types of furnaces, while they may be built into a single cabinet, have separate units for heating and cooling. Single-unit heat pumps are installed outside of buildings as shown in Fig. 674. Two-unit heat pumps have the compressor unit outside and cooling unit inside. Figs. 675 and 676 illustrate several applications of this type.

Water provides a greater amount of heat than air, in proportion to the electrical energy

Fig. 672. Residential or small commercial heat pump; outdoor section. (Carrier Corp.)

Fig. 673. A large heat pump for commercial construction. This unit provides 1,400 tons of cooling capacity in summer and in winter will transfer heat generated by people, lights and business machines in inner office spaces to offices on outside walls needing heat. (Carrier Corp.)

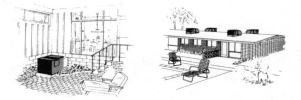

Fig. 674. Single-unit heat pump installed outside home on the ground or on the roof. Illustration shows four-family apartment with heat pumps on the roof. (Carrier Corp.)

put into the system. However, water is becoming less satisfactory in quantity and quality. In many areas, it is so scarce that it is prohibitive to use in large quantities. Water also creates scale and causes corrosion. Another problem is created when the large quantities of used water must be discharged.

An unlimited supply of air is available, and it does not damage the mechanical equipment. However, there are some disadvantages to the air system at the present time. It requires complex controls, and frost and ice form on the outdoor coils. More horsepower is required per BTU obtained, and the equipment has to be larger in size.

The earth is also used as a source of heat for small heat pumps. Coils buried below the frost line abstract heat from the earth. The initial cost is high, and good performance depends upon the quantity of moisture in the soil.

A fourth source of heat is found in large buildings that have areas that produce heat in the winter from the nature of the activity performed there. A heat pump can tap this source, thus keeping this area at a comfortable temperature and pumping the excess heat to another part of the building requiring heat. The applications of this heat source are more limited than the three others previously mentioned. Refer again to Fig. 673.

Heat pumps for residences and small commercial buildings usually supply heated or cooled air to the building by blowing it through a duct system. Larger commercial units, of the water-to-water or air-to-water type, send heated or chilled water to indoor room units, which then heat or cool the air in the room.

There are a number of ways air and water can be used to heat and cool buildings. These are explained in Figs. 678 through 681. The selection of the proper kind and size of unit requires the services of an engineer who understands the capabilities of the various systems.

Gas All-Year Air Conditioning

Gas can be used to heat and cool buildings. This discussion is concerned with a system suitable for residences and small commercial buildings. Larger units are available for larger installations. The gas-fired chiller-heater operates on the absorption principle.

Pure water is the refrigerant; a solution of water and lithium bromide, a harmless salt, is the absorbent. The refrigerant and absorbent do not deteriorate with use, and neither requires replenishing.

The unit operates under a vacuum at all times and has no moving parts. There are no valves to control flows or to separate chambers of differing pressure. Flows are induced by vapor-lift action, pressure difference and gravity. Fig. 677 illustrates the inside of a gas, air-conditioning unit.

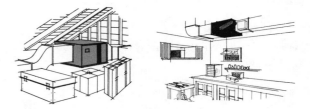

Fig. 675. A two-unit heat pump installed in attic and basement locations. The compressor unit is outside the house in a second cabinet. (Carrier Corp.)

Fig. 676. A two-unit heat pump in commercial installation. Ceiling-hung unit uses no floor space. Floor-mounted units provide zone control without ducts. Compressor unit located outside and usually on the roof. (Carrier Corp.)

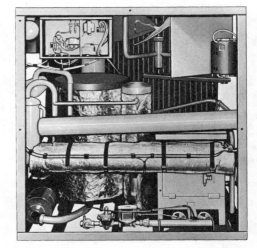

Fig. 677. Gas air conditioner. (Bryant Manufacturing Co.)

Fig. 678. Water-to-air heat pump. (Carrier Corp.)

Heating cycle operation: Outside water (1) is circulated through a condenser-chiller unit (2) which removes the water's low-temperature heat and transfers this heat to the system's refrigerant. Carried by refrigerant, the heat moves to a compressor (3) which elevates the heat to a high-temperature level. From the compressor, refrigerant moves the now-high-temperature heat to a coil in an indoor unit (4). Here the indoor unit circulates air through the coil, and heat from the refrigerant is transferred to the air. Ductwork (5) conducts the heated air to conditioned areas as desired.

Cooling cycle operation: Circulating inside air carries heat from conditioned areas to the indoor unit (1) which removes the heat from this air and transfers it to the system's refrigerant. Carried by refrigerant, the heat is moved then to the compressor (2) which elevates it to a high-temperature level. The refrigerant conveys this now-high-temperature heat to the condenser-chiller (3) where outside water extracts the heat from the refrigerant before carrying it outside (4).

Fig. 679. Water-to-water heat pump operation. (Carrier Corp.)

Heating cycle operation: Outside water (1) contains heat at low temperature which the system extracts by passing the water through a chiller unit (2). In the unit, the system's refrigerant takes heat from the water. Carried by refrigerant, the heat is moved to a compressor (3) which elevates the heat to a high-temperature level. From the compressor, the refrigerant conveys this now-high-temperature heat to a condenser (4) where heat is removed from the refrigerant by re-circulating water system. Through interior piping (5), this water carries the heat to indoor room units (6) or central-station indoor units which apply it to heating.

Cooling cycle operation: Air in conditioned spaces gives up heat to room units (1) which transfer it to the recirculating water system. Through piping (2), water carries the heat to the water chiller (3) where the system's refrigerant picks it up. By refrigerant, the heat is moved to the compressor (4) which elevates the heat to a high-temperature level. From compressor, refrigerant conveys this now-high-temperature heat to the condenser (5). Here, the heat is released to outside water (6) for disposal.

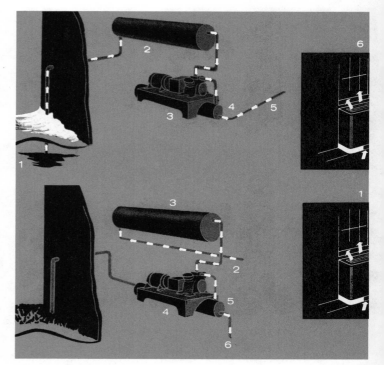

Fig. 680. Air-to-air heat pump operation. (Carrier Corp.)

Heating cycle operation: When passed through an outdoor unit (1), outside air gives up low-temperature heat to the system's refrigerant. Through a line (2), the refrigerant carries this low-temperature heat to a compressor (3) which elevates the heat to a desirable high-temperature level. From the compressor, the refrigerant moves the now-high-temperature heat to a coil in an indoor unit (4). Here the indoor unit moves air for conditioning through the coil, and heat from the refrigerant is transferred to the air. Ductwork (5) conducts the heated inside air to the conditioned areas where it is desired.

Cooling cycle operation: Circulating inside air carries heat from conditioned areas to the indoor unit (1) which transfers this heat to the system's refrigerant. Carried to the compressor (2) by the refrigerant, the heat is elevated to a high-temperature level. The refrigerant then moves this now-high-temperature heat to the outdoor unit (3) where it is discharged into outside air.

Fig. 681. Air-to-water, heat pump operation. (Carrier Corp.)

Heating cycle operation: Low-temperature heat from outside air is transferred to the system's refrigerant by an outdoor unit (1). The refrigerant carries this low-temperature heat to a compressor (2) which elevates the heat to a desirable high temperature. From the compressor, the now-high-temperature heat is moved by refrigerant to a condenser-chiller unit (3) in which the refrigerant gives up the heat to circulating water. Through the building's pipes (4), the circulating water carries this heat to room units (5) or central-station indoor units, which take the heat from circulating water and transfer it to the air in the building for comfort.

Cooling cycle operation: Air in the conditioned spaces gives up heat to room units (1) which transfer it to recirculating water. Through piping (2), the water carries this heat to the condenser-chiller (3) where the heat is transferred from the water to the system's refrigerant. Moved on to the compressor (4) by refrigerant, the heat is elevated to a high-temperature level. From the compressor, the refrigerant carries this now-high-temperature heat to the outdoor unit (5) which releases it to outside air.

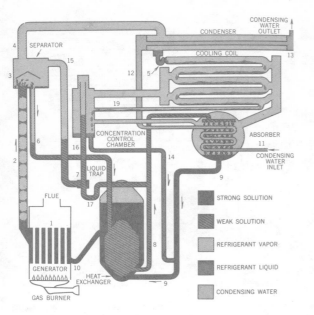

Fig. 682. Cooling cycle of gas-fired, single-coil, year-round, air-conditioning unit. (Arkla Air Conditioning Corp.)

The Cooling Cycle

Fig. 682 illustrates the cooling cycle of this type unit.

The generator contains a solution of lithium bromide in water. As heat is applied in the combustion chamber of the generator, it causes the refrigerant (water) to be boiled off. As this water vapor is driven off, the absorbent solution is raised by vapor-lift action through tube (2) into the separating chamber (3).

Here the refrigerant vapor and the absorbent solution are separated by baffles. The refrigerant vapor rises through tube (4) to the condenser, and the absorbent solution flows down by gravity through tube (6), through the heat exchanger and then to the absorber. A more detailed description of this circuit follows, with the refrigerant circuit being described first.

The refrigerant (water vapor) passes from the separating chamber to the condenser through tube (4), where it is condensed to a liquid by the action of cooling water flowing through the condenser tubes. The cooling water is brought from an external source, such as a cooling tower, city main or well.

The refrigerant vapor, thus condensed to water within the condenser, then flows through tube (5) into the cooling coil. Tube (5) con-

tains a restriction which offers a resistance, and therefore a pressure barrier, to separate the slightly higher absolute pressure in the condenser from the lower pressure within the cooling coil. The refrigerant (water) entering the cooling coil vaporizes, due to the lower absolute pressure (high vacuum) which exists within it. The high vacuum within the evaporator lowers the boiling temperature of water sufficiently to produce a refrigeration effect.

The evaporator or cooling coil is constructed with finned, horizontal tubes, and the air being cooled flows over the coil surface. Evaporation of the refrigerant takes place within the cooling coil. The heat of evaporation for the refrigerant is extracted from the air stream, and cooling and dehumidifying are accomplished.

In the absorber, the solution absorbs the refrigerant vapors which are formed in the evaporator directly adjacent.

To explain the presence of the absorbent at this point, it is necessary to divert attention back to the generator. The absorbent was separated from the refrigerant by boiling action. The absorbent then drains from the separator (3) down to the liquid heat exchanger and thence to the absorber through tube (8). The flow of solution in this circuit can actually exist by gravity action alone, because the absorber is slightly below the level of the separating chamber. It is also aided by the pressure difference existing between the separator and the absorber.

The absorber is a cylindrical shell which contains a coil through which cooling water is circulated. The solution flowing into the top of the absorber is distributed over the entire outside surfaces of the coil, so that a maximum area of absorbent solution is exposed to the refrigerant vapor which is flowing into this chamber from the evaporator.

It must be understood that cool lithium bromide in either dry or solution form has a very strong affinity for water vapor. Because of this, the refrigerant vapor is absorbed back into solution again. The rate of absorption is increased at lower temperatures; therefore, a cooling water coil has been provided within the absorber shell. The resultant of refrigerant and absorbent drains back through the heat exchanger through tube (9) to the refrigeration generator. Here again it is separated into

its two component parts by boiling action, to repeat the cycle.

Because of the slightly higher absolute pressure in the separator, as compared to the cooling coil or evaporator, absorbent solution rises through tube (17), through the liquid trap (7) and up into tube (16), thereby forming a liquid seal so that refrigerant vapor cannot flow through tube (15) from the separator chamber. In this manner, the cooling cycle is maintained.

The Heating Cycle

To convert this cycle of operation to the heating function, it is necessary only to cut off the supply of condensing water. With Fig. 683 as a reference, the cycle of operation is as follows: The solution of lithium bromide and water contained in the generator receives heat from the burner. The solution boils as in the cooling cycle and drives the water vapor up through tube (2), carrying with it droplets of lithium-bromide solution. The vapor and solution are separated in chamber (3). Since there is no flow of cooling water, the water vapor which rises to the condenser causes an increase in pressure. This vapor cannot escape, except in very small quantities, through the restriction (5). Only a small quantity of vapor passes through the condenser into the coil (which can now be called the heating coil).

Because of this increase in pressure, the water vapor can pass down through tube (15), through trap (7) and then up through tube (16) into what might be referred to as a second separating chamber, insofar as the heating cycle is concerned. The flow of water vapor through tube (16) continually carries droplets of the lithium-bromide solution which has drained from the separating chamber through tubes (6), (17) and into the trap (7). From this second separating chamber, the vapor flows through tube (18) to the heating coil where it condenses, thus transferring heat to the air passing over the coil. This liquid then flows through tube (19) back to the second separating chamber, where it mixes with the lithium-bromide solution formerly brought up tube (16) in droplet form. The mixture then goes through tubes (20) and (14) into tube (9) and back to the generator through tube (10).

There is no flow of lithium-bromide solution through tube (8) into the absorber, since

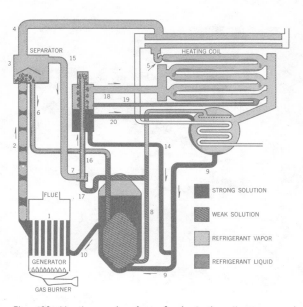

Fig. 683. Heating cycle of gas-fired, single-coil, year-round, air-conditioning unit. (Arkla Air Conditioning Corp.)

the pressure difference is not sufficient to force liquid up the tube into the top of the absorber.

The chamber which serves as a second separating chamber on the heating cycle also serves as a concentration control chamber on the cooling cycle. The purpose of this component is to maintain essentially constant capacity over the temperature range of the inlet condensing water. It operates as follows: As the incoming water temperature is increased, the outlet temperature also increases, thus assuming a constant temperature rise. The higher condensing temperature, which produces a higher condenser and generator pressure, causes small quantities of refrigerant to be stored in the concentration control chamber. This higher overall concentration of solution remaining in the cycle prevents the loss of capacity which would otherwise result from the higher inlet temperature. As the condensing water temperature decreases, the opposite reactions occur.

Hot-Water Heat

The typical hot-water heating system consists of a boiler, a burner (usually gas- or oil-fired), a flue to carry away waste fumes from the burner, a pump, a system of pipes to carry the hot water to the various rooms and heat emitting devices such as radiators. Also, a large number of control valves are used.

The typical boiler is very small and is housed in an attractive shell. It can be exposed to view and not detract from the room in which it is located. See Fig. 684. The boiler can be installed in a basement, a utility room or garage.

The types of heat-emitting devices used in hot-water heating systems include radiators, convectors, unit heaters, baseboards and panels. These units transfer heat for the circulating water to the space to be heated by radiation and convection. The design of the heat-emitting unit determines how much heat is supplied each way.

Radiators, radiant baseboards and panels supply a major proportion of their heat by radiation; while convectors, unit heaters, and finned-tube baseboards supply their greatest amount by convection.

The hot-water system may be designed as an open type, operating at atmospheric pressure, or it may be a closed type in which operation at higher pressures is made possible by confining and compressing the air in an expansion tank. The closed hot-water system, using mechanically applied energy to promote circulation, is called a *forced-circulation system*. The source of energy usually is a centrifugal pump driven by an electric motor.

Current design practice uses the closed system, because it operates satisfactorily at higher design temperatures.

Hot-water systems of the closed type have the advantage of requiring smaller distribu-tion mains and riser pipe sizes than atmospheric-pressure, gravity systems. They also permit greater flexibility in piping design. Better heat control is provided, since the system can vary the average water temperature to meet changes in outdoor temperature. This control holds fuel consumption to a minimum, since overheating of the water is prevented.

Tall and long buildings or a group of buildings are more easily heated with the forced-circulation system. If the proper pressure-temperature relationship is maintained in the system, water design temperatures approaching 400 degrees F. can be used in the transmission circuits and high temperatures, usually associated with steam, can be employed in the space-heating circuits. The temperature of the forced-circulation, hot-water system can be modulated between values of 80 degrees F. and 400 degrees F.

One- and Two-Pipe Systems

Hot-water systems are classified as one-pipe and two-pipe systems. A one-pipe system sends hot water from the boiler to the first radiator, through it to the second radiator and so on through all the radiators on the system and returns the water to the boiler through the same main. See Fig. 685.

A two-pipe system has one supply main carrying hot water to each radiator, which then discharges the water passed through it into a second main that returns the cooled water to the boiler. See Fig. 686.

The two-pipe system is preferred and generally used.

Fig. 684. Residential boiler. (Bryant Manufacturing Co.)

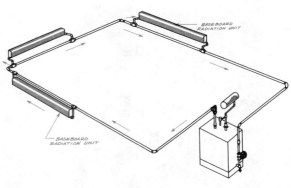

Fig. 685. Single-pipe, hot-water, heating system.

Types of Heat Emitters

The typical small-tube radiator is built with a spacing of 1¾ inches per section and is made of cast iron. See Fig. 687. It occupies less space than the older, column-type large-tube radiator. Generally, the small-tube radiator is installed in a wall recess.

Radiant baseboards are long, low units resembling the usual wood baseboards. See Fig. 688. They are installed along outside walls in place of wood baseboards. They are either hollow, cast-iron panels or finned tubing installed behind a metal enclosure. The hollow, cast-iron units depend almost entirely upon radiant heat, while the finned type depend more upon convection.

Widely used in industrial construction are wall-hung convectors, consisting of a finned heat emitter covered with a sheet-metal shield. The fins provide additional surface area for the release of heat to the air passing over the pipe. They may be recessed or surface mounted. See Fig. 689.

Unit heaters are also widely used in industrial heating. See Fig. 690. The hot water is forced through a coil in the unit, and an electric fan forces air through the coil, thus creating air circulation in the room and heating it by convection.

A convector is a space-heating device composed of a sheet-metal casing, with an outlet grill and a heating element of the fin-tube or cast-iron, fin type. The casing usually contains a damper to control air circulation. The air enters the casing near the floor line below

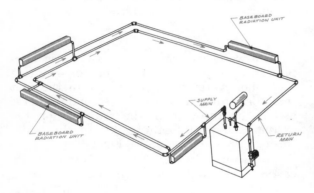

Fig. 686. Two-pipe, hot-water, heating system, reverse-return type.

Fig. 688. Hot-water, baseboard convectors. (Edwards Engineering Corp.)

Fig. 687. Small-tube, cast-iron radiator. (Crane Co.)

Fig. 689. Industrial, finned-type, wall convectors. (Edwards Engineering Corp.)

the heating element, is heated in passing through the element and is delivered to the room through the outlet grill located near the top of the enclosure. The room air movement thus established accomplishes a reduction in floor to ceiling temperature differential and tends to assure comfort in the living zone. See Fig. 691.

Fig. 690. Forced, hot-water, unit heaters. (Copper and Brass Research Association)

Fig. 691. Freestanding, convector, hot-water radiator, also available in semirecessed, recessed, wall-hung and long, low units. (Young Radiator Co.)

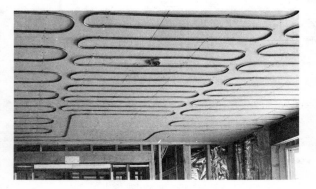

Fig. 692. Hot-water heating panel formed of 3/8" copper tubing. (Anaconda American Brass Co.)

Fig. 693. Hot-water, floor heating panel. (Copper and Brass Research Association)

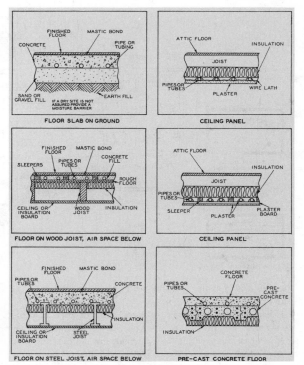

Fig. 694. Typical installations for floor and ceiling, hot-water panels. (Bell and Gossett Co.)

Panels are built either by securing copper tubing to the ceiling and plastering over it or by burying tubing in the concrete floor slab. Fig. 692 illustrates this installation for a ceiling before plaster was applied, and Fig. 693 illustrates a floor heating panel. These panels heat by radiant heat. While there are a number of ways to install these panels in the ceil-

ing and floor, Fig. 694 illustrates sound and proven installations.

Hot-water systems can provide zoned heating by regulating the flow of hot water to each room. Each room has a thermostat that controls a flow valve at the boiler. This controls the flow of hot water to each room. Fig. 695 illustrates such a zoned heating system.

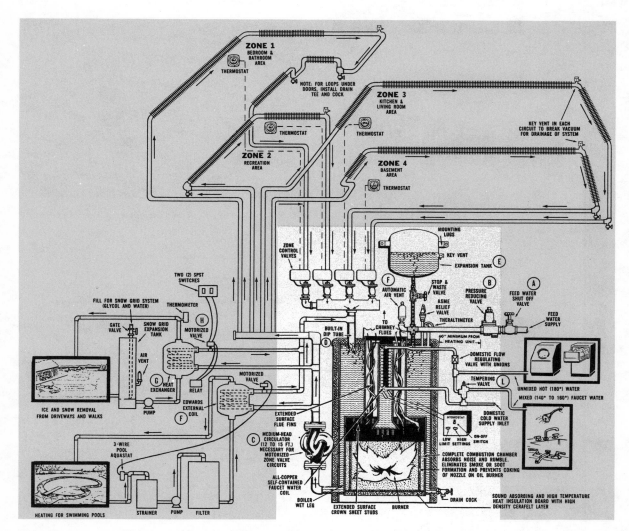

Fig. 695. Zone-controlled, hot-water, heating system. (Edwards Engineering Corp.)

When a zone thermostat calls for heat, its zone control-valve motor begins to run, opening the zone control valve slowly; when the valve is fully opened, the motor stops. The burner, either gas- or oil-fired, will now light and burn until the water in the boiler reaches the high limit (usually 220°F.). When the high limit is reached, the burner shuts off, but the water circulation to the zone calling for heat continues until

the zone reaches the temperature called for by the thermostat. If the zone removes enough heat to lower the water temperature to a preset low temperature (usually 180°F.), the burner ignites and heats the water up again. When the zone reaches the desired temperature, as called for by the thermostat, the zone, control-valve motor closes the valve, thus stopping the circulation of hot water to that area.

The boiler will keep the water between 180°F. and 220°F., even if the various zones do not call for heat.

Fig. 696. Hot-water coils of copper tubing used to melt snow from sidewalk. (Anaconda American Brass Co.)

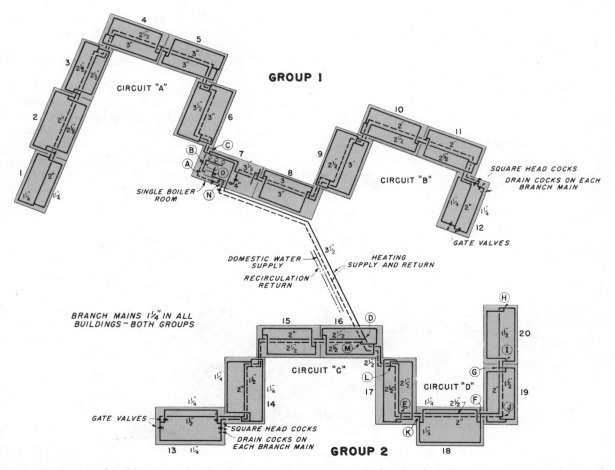

Fig. 697. A group of buildings heated with a hot-water system using one boiler. Supply and return mains are underground below the frost line. (Bell and Gossett Co.)

Copper coils for circulating hot water can be buried in driveways and sidewalks to melt ice and snow. Fig. 696 illustrates such a use, before the concrete was poured. These panels heat by conduction.

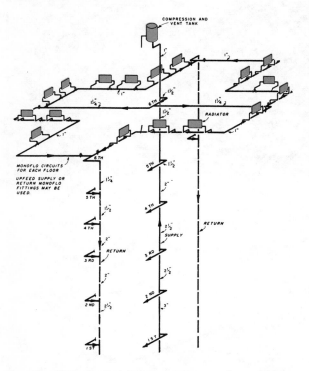

Fig. 698. Riser detail for hot-water system for multistory apartment building with individual apartment control of temperature. (Bell and Gossett Co.)

As indicated earlier, hot-water heat is a good system to use for long groups of buildings. Such a system with the size of mains is illustrated in Fig. 697.

A typical installation for a multistory building is shown in Figs. 698 and 699. This installation is even more difficult to design than a system for a long group of buildings. Special consideration of pumping, sizing of pipe and temperature control is necessary. All these systems should be designed by heating engineers.

Cold-Water Air-Cooling Systems

Some water chillers are designed to work in combination with a forced, hot-water heating system. However, they can be installed as a separate, space-cooling system, if another type of heat is in use. The chiller is a unit consisting of a compressor, condenser and evaporator tank. Basically this unit cools and circulates chilled water to the same units that emitted heat from hot water. There the cold is emitted to the air, and the water returns to the cooling unit to be rechilled and recirculated.

Another way to air-condition with a chilled-water system is to use an absorptive-type water chiller. Refrigeration is produced by the absorptive principle utilizing steam as the energy source. The cooling unit is a sealed refrigeration package; the unit operates under a vacuum at all times. The system is charged with lithium bromide and water.

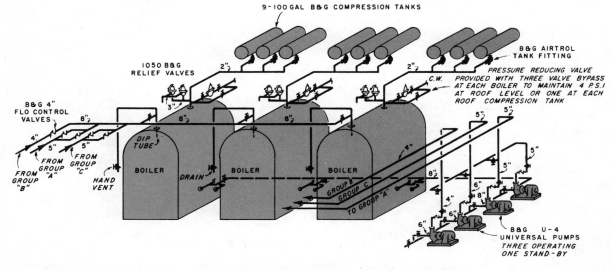

Fig. 699. Boiler room detail for apartment building in Fig. 698. (Bell and Gossett Co.)

There are many systems designed for producing chilled water for cooling purposes. Fig. 700 illustrates one type of water chiller. This type unit cools and does not heat. Fig. 701 provides a section through the unit, illustrating the components. Such a chiller can be used for cooling commercial buildings; it can also provide chilled water for industrial applications such as the manufacture of plastics.

A cold-water, space-cooling system that is not a part of a hot-water heating system, but is installed as a separate system, utilizes two types of units to emit the cold to the space. It uses cooling coils with air pulled through by fans and cooling coils with air pulled through by gravity. Fig. 702 illustrates a typical system with both types of units.

Steam Heat

Steam heat, generally, is used for large buildings. The system operates much the same as the hot-water system. The fuels commonly used are gas, oil and coal. The design of such systems requires the services of a heating specialist. As a steam system is considered, the type of fuel selected is important. Among the most important considerations for commercial installations are (1) the comparative cost of gas, oil and coal heating equipment, (2) cost of labor and supervision to operate the system, (3) fuel cost, based on heating value in BTU's, (4) maintenance, (5) efficiency of equipment, (6) cost of fuel storage and handling and (7) insurance.

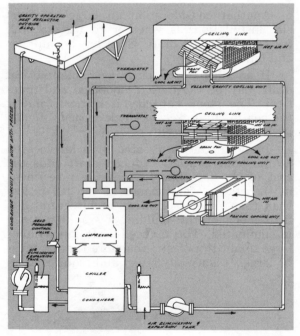

Fig. 702. Zone-controlled, chilled-water, cooling system. (Edwards Engineering Corp.)

The heat removed from the space by the refrigerant is rejected to the outside air through a gravity heat rejector located on a roof, under an overhang or other inconspicuous location. The gravity cooling units are hung from the ceiling. The hot air in the space rises, is cooled by the coils and descends, causing a gentle circulation of air. Each space can have a separate thermostat. Each thermostat controls a valve that regulates the flow of chilled water to that space, thus providing zoned cooling.

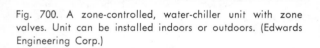

Fig. 700. A zone-controlled, water-chiller unit with zone valves. Unit can be installed indoors or outdoors. (Edwards Engineering Corp.)

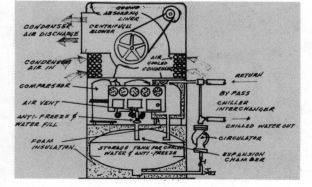

Fig. 701. Section through a water-chiller unit. (Edwards Engineering Corp.)

When considering oil as a possible fuel, pay particular attention to the grade of oil selected. It frequently is more economical to burn a lighter grade of oil in medium-sized and small plants, even where the price per gallon is higher than heavier, higher, BTU grades. Also, the dependability of local fuel sources should be considered.

In some areas where gas is the prevailing fuel, oil standby equipment is required by code or utility regulation. More advantageous gas rates are available if the heating plant can be switched to oil during times of peak gas demand. Dual-fuel burners are available for such installations. A dual-fuel burner uses either gas or oil within the same unit. See Figs. 703 and 704. In some areas, coal may produce as much as 50 percent more heat per dollar than other fuels. Fig. 705 illustrates an underfeed stoker system in a large heating installation.

Another consideration on large commercial installations is whether to use natural, forced or induced draft. Each has advantages and limitations.

If an adequate stack is available, natural draft may be the most economical and practical. The stack capacity is critical; and if the heating unit exceeds stack capacity, faulty performance will result.

Induced draft is created by a fan located at the boiler outlet. Induced draft adds the cost of the fan, but reduces the investment in the stack. Maintenance of the fan is less than that for a stack. Also, architectural disfigurement of the building by a high stack is eliminated. The induced-draft fan handles large quantities of air; therefore the fan must be large. It is usually bulky and requires extra

space. Since the exhaust atmosphere is corrosive, special materials are required in fan construction. Automatic draft controls, interlocked with burner controls, are essential.

A forced-draft fan is located at the inlet of the burner. It pushes combustion air into the furnace and through the boiler. Since the air handled is boiler room air rather than exhaust fumes, corrosion is not a problem. The forced-draft fan handles only half the volume of air handled by the induced-draft fan. Draft control is also eliminated. On new construction, forced draft generally is preferred over the other two methods, because it provides compactness, lower operating cost, lower maintenance and simplified controls.

Steam heat can provide thermostatic control of heat in each room by using individual room heaters, as shown in Fig. 706. An explanation of how this system works accompanies Fig. 707.

Fig. 704. A dual-fuel, forced-draft, burner-boiler complete for a new installation. (Iron Fireman Manufacturing Co.)

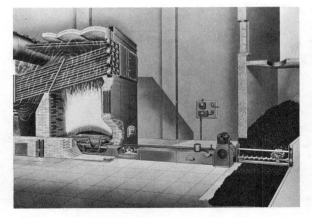

Fig. 705. A large commercial boiler with an underfeed coal stoker. (Iron Fireman Manufacturing Co.)

Fig. 703. A dual-fuel, forced-draft unit for converting an existing boiler unit. (Iron Fireman Manufacturing Co.)

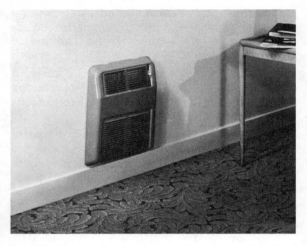

Fig. 706. A steam-heat unit controlled by an individual thermostat. (Iron Fireman Manufacturing Co.)

Heat Loss Calculations

Heat will flow from any heated space to any surrounding unheated space. When the outside temperature is lower than the temperature within, heat flows by transmission through the walls, partitions, ceilings, roofs, floor sections, doors and windows exposed to the outside. In addition, outside air will enter the heated space by infiltration through door and window cracks exposed to positive wind pressure.

Heat will flow through floor coverings and floors to the earth, when the floor is laid on the ground and the ground temperature is lower than the air temperature in the rooms. If the temperature outside the foundation walls is lower than that of the heated space, heat will be transmitted through covering, floor-slab edge insulation and foundation walls to the outside.

The estimated amount of heat loss per hour by transmission through walls, ceilings, floors, doors and windows, at the design conditions, is the *transmission heat loss* of the heated space, living unit or dwelling. The estimated amount of heat needed to warm infiltrated air to room design conditions is the *infiltration heat loss*. The sum of these is the total heat loss under design conditions.

Calculations of heat loss are made to determine whether the proposed heating system is adequate, *i.e.*, whether it is designed to supply the estimated heat required under design conditions. They also are made to estimate the annual heating cost of the system.

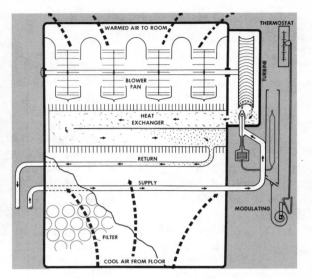

Fig. 707. A steam-heat unit with individual thermostatic control. (Iron Fireman Manufacturing Co.)

The steam enters the supply line and reaches the valve controlled by the thermostat. When the thermostat calls for heat, the valve opens, permitting steam to rush into the turbine. The steam turns the turbine which activates the blower. The steam passes into the heat exchanger and heats it. The blower pulls cool air from the floor over the heat exchanger, warming it, and blows it out the grill on the top of the unit. As the steam cools, it condenses and returns to the boiler through the return line.

The heat loss and the amount of heat needed to replace it are expressed in BTU's (British Thermal Units). One BTU is the amount of heat required to raise the temperature of one pound of water one degree Fahrenheit.

Coefficients of Heat Transmission — *k* and *U* Factors

The *coefficient of heat transmission* is an expression of the ability of a material or combination of materials to transmit heat from the hot to the cold side. The *k* factor is the BTU per hour, per square foot, per degree difference Fahrenheit, per inch of thickness for any homogeneous material, such as gypsum board. The *U* factor is a combination of *k* factors, expressing the combined heat flow capacity of materials. It is expressed in BTU per hour, per square foot, per degree difference Fahrenheit for the combination of materials, such as a ceiling which could be a combination of gypsum board and insulation of some kind. Each material has a *k* factor, but a combination of these gives a *U* factor for the ceiling.

Calculation of Heat Loss by Modified ASHRAE Guide Methods

The maximum hourly heat loss for each space to be heated should be calculated in accordance with the procedure described in the current edition of the *Guide* of the American Society of Heating, Refrigerating and Air-Conditioning Engineers. The loss also may be calculated by any recognized method which is suitable to local conditions, provided the results obtained are in substantial agreement with, and not less than, those obtained by using the procedure described in the ASHRAE *Guide*.

1. The outside design temperature used in the calculation must be established by FHA (Federal Housing Administration) for the locality in which the dwelling is built.

2. The inside design temperature used in the calculation must not be less than 70 degrees F., except that a lower inside design temperature acceptable to the Chief Underwriter may be used in calculating the heat loss from playrooms, laundry rooms, enclosed service porches, heated garages and similar spaces.

3. All conventionally constructed floors over basements or other warmed spaces are assumed to have no heat loss into these spaces.

4. Transmission coefficients used in the calculation must be those listed in the ASHRAE *Guide* or as established by acceptable tests. Selected coefficients are reproduced later in this chapter (Table 46).

5. The reduction in heat loss effected by storm windows and doors specified and furnished must be credited in the heat loss calculation.

Outside Design Temperature

The choice of an appropriate, outside design temperature is a necessary preliminary to the calculation of heat loss.

In establishing design temperatures for major population centers, it generally is necessary to depend upon experience, local heating practice or the ASHRAE *Guide*. The outside design temperatures so established are satisfactory, especially when adjusted for the lower temperatures normally experienced in the suburban areas surrounding the major population centers.

The following procedure may be used to establish an outside design temperature for a locality for which none has yet been established:

1. Determine the lowest recorded temperature in the locality for each of the six months, October through March. U.S. Weather Bureau figures should be used. If these figures are not available, reliable local sources may be used.

2. Average these figures and select the nearest five-degree multiple which should be used as the outside design temperature.

Inside Design Temperature

The choice of an appropriate inside temperature is also a necessary preliminary in the calculation of heat loss. The use of 70 degrees F. as the inside design temperature in habitable spaces is considered an appropriate minimum. Some areas such as enclosed porches and heated garages frequently are kept at lower temperatures than 70 degrees during the heating season. In selecting design temperatures for such spaces, it is important to consider the manner of use of the spaces by a typical homeowner.

Attic Space Design Temperature

The temperature in an attic space, ventilated in accordance with the FHA Minimum Property Requirements, usually is somewhat higher than the outside design temperature. However, in any heated room below, the air temperature at the ceiling usually is higher than the average for the room. Attic temperatures are affected by three major variables: (1) the amount of attic ventilating air, (2) the amount of ceiling insulation and (3) the air temperature gradient from the heated rooms below to the outside air.

Unless test data for the type of heat distribution system and construction used demonstrates that, at design conditions, the temperature of the air immediately below the ceiling is not significantly above 70 degrees F., ventilated attic spaces should be assumed to be at outside design temperature for the purpose of heat loss calculations because:

1. Specific data for more accurate determination of the conditions is not available.
2. The average temperature difference between room air and attic air will approach the difference between room air and outside air at design conditions as ceiling insulation is increased.

Unheated Crawl Space Design Temperature

The temperature of the air within a crawl space, ventilated in accordance with FHA Minimum Property Requirements, is somewhat higher than outside air temperatures at design conditions. The actual temperatures in the space depend upon a number of factors including (1) the amount of ventilating air, (2) the thermal conductance of the enclosing wall and floor sections and (3) pipe or duct insulation.

The more effective these factors are, the closer the temperature in the space approaches the outside temperature. Also, with uninsulated floors, homeowners tend to maintain higher room temperatures to overcome the cold-floor condition. This increases the actual heat loss through upper portions of the house over that ordinarily calculated.

An appropriate design temperature to use for unheated crawl spaces can be estimated by evaluating the factors indicated. This usually ranges from slightly above outside design temperature to a medium between inside and outside temperatures. Where crawl space vents can be adjusted to the closed position, the estimated temperature can be checked by the procedure in the ASHRAE *Guide*.

Heat Loss to Garage From
Adjacent Heated Spaces

In the calculation of heat loss from adjacent heated spaces to a garage, the temperature in the garage, whether heated or not, should be assumed to be outside temperature, based upon the supposition that the garage frequently may be left open to outside weather.

Floor Heat Loss to Basement

There should be no heat loss through conventionally constructed floors over basements, when heat from the heating unit or system is received by these spaces. It is assumed that the temperature of the air close to the ceiling of the basement will be nearly the same as the temperature of the air immediately above the floor over these spaces. When the heating unit is not located in the basement and no means for heating the basement is provided, the basement temperatures should be determined in the same manner as for an unventilated crawl space.

Infiltration Heat Loss

One air change per hour may be assumed a reasonable average for estimating the infiltration heat loss. Infiltration values calculated on the basis of the "crack method" are considered acceptable, provided the result is not less than the equivalent of one-half air change per hour.

Heat Transmission Coefficients for Windows and Doors

Appropriate heat transmission coefficients for windows and doors are contained in the ASHRAE *Guide*. Those most frequently used in the calculation of heat loss are:

Windows	Heat transmission coefficient
Single	1.13
Double	0.53
(1" air space)	

Wood doors	Heat transmission coefficient	Heat transmission coefficient with glass storm door
1" nominal	0.64	0.37
1¾" nominal	0.55	0.34
1½" nominal	0.49	0.32

Example of Heat Loss Calculation
by Modified ASHRAE Guide Method

The example which follows illustrates the ASHRAE *Guide* method of calculating the heat loss of a heated space, as modified by the basic data given herein. If the heat loss of each heated space in a living unit is needed to design or to review a heating system, the process illustrated in these examples is repeated for each heated space in the living unit. The total heat loss of the living unit is the sum of the heat losses of the individual spaces of the living unit.

Example. Calculate the heat loss of the room shown in Fig. 708, where: Ceiling is ½-inch plaster on ⅜-inch gyplath with ventilated attic over, and with 3-inch blanket insulation, $U = 0.08$.

Component	Dimensions	Area or volume	*U* or infiltration factor	x	Design temperature difference	=	Component heat loss BTU per hr.
Gross wall	11'-0" x 8'-0" + 11'-0" x 8'-0"	176	....		....		....
Glass	3'-0" x 4'-6"	27	1.13		70		2136
Net wall		149	.15		70		1564
Ceiling	11'-0" x 11'-0"	121	.08		70		678
Floor	11'-0" x 11'-0"	121	Basement below —no loss		....		....
Infiltration	11'-0" x 11'-0" x 8'-0"	968	.018		70		1220

Total heat loss from room in BTU per hour 5598

Walls are lap siding, 25/32-inch insulation board sheathing, 2 x 4 studs and ½-inch plaster on ⅜-inch foil-backed gyplath, $U=0.15$. Floor is located over heated basement.

Explanation of Example

An examination of the room in Fig. 708 reveals two outside walls capable of losing heat and having infiltration. The gross wall, 176 square feet, is the total surface area of these walls. Of this gross area some is window. This plan indicates two windows, each 3'-0" x 4'-6" or 13.5 square feet. This gives 27 square feet of glass. The *U* factor is 1.13 BTU per hour, per square foot, per degree difference Fahrenheit. The degree difference is indicated to be 70 degrees. The 1.13 x 70 equals 2136 BTU loss per hour.

The same procedure is followed for the other factors involved in heat loss — the net wall, ceiling, floor and infiltration.

The *U* factor is obtained from extended tables giving this factor for various materials and types of construction. Such tables are too lengthy to reproduce in this text. The ASHRAE *Guide* or other such publication should be consulted for these tables. As previously mentioned, selected coefficients of heat transmission are given in Table 46.

Fireplaces

A fireplace adds much to the attractiveness of a room and the joy of living in a house. Besides providing the pleasure of an open fire, a fireplace can serve as a source of heat when normal means of heating fail.

The design of fireplace elevations, has changed with the times. Many materials are in common use for facing the elevation, such as brick, marble, slate, stone, tile and glass. Wood trim and paneling commonly complete the elevation design.

The styling of the elevation should be in keeping with the house type. The fireplace designed for a formal living room should be entirely different in appearance than that designed for a colonial family room. See Figs. 709 and 710.

The size of the fireplace opening should be in proportion to the room in which it is to be located. A large fireplace in a small family room loses much of its appeal, because it is out-of-scale with its surroundings. The type of fire desired should also be considered. A large fireplace, if it is to project heat properly, must have a large fire. If too large a fireplace is built, it will produce too much heat for comfort in an average room. If a small fire is built in a large fireplace, the heat goes up the chimney. A satisfactory fire built in a 30-inch fireplace will produce more heat than the same size fire in a 48-inch fireplace.

Another consideration in planning a fireplace is its location. An attempt should be made to create an area of comfort and repose in the room, subject to the least disturbance from those moving about. Consideration

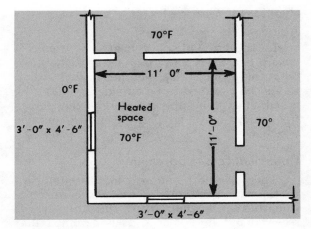

Fig. 708. Room for calculating heat loss.

Table 46
Selected Coefficients of Heat Transmission for Typical Wall, Ceiling and Floor Sections

Reference Illus.	Construction	Construction Variation	U Factor
	Frame Floor (Heat Flow Downward) $^{13}/_{16}$" hardwood floor building paper $^3/_8$" plywood subfloor 2 x 10 joists	No insulation between joists (open) $^1/_2$" rigid insulation board between joists 1" flexible insulation between joists 2" flexible insulation between joists	.29 .16 .12 .08
	Frame Ceiling (Heat Flow Upward) open joists	$^3/_8$" gypsum board ceiling $^1/_4$" plywood ceiling $^3/_8$" gypsum board and $^1/_2$" plaster ceiling $^1/_2$" composition board	.65 .66 .61 .45
	Frame Ceiling (Heat Flow Upward) 4" blanket insulation between joists	$^3/_8$" gypsum board ceiling $^1/_4$" plywood ceiling $^3/_8$" gypsum board and $^1/_2$" plaster ceiling $^1/_2$" composition board	.07 .07 .07 .06
	Frame Ceiling (Heat Flow Upward) Pine attic subfloor no insulation	$^3/_8$" gypsum board ceiling $^1/_4$" plywood ceiling $^3/_8$" gypsum board and $^1/_2$" plaster ceiling $^1/_2$" composition board	.29 .29 .28 .24
	Masonry Wall $^1/_2$" plaster	8" brick wall 4" brick, 4" concrete and gravel block wall	.39 .41
	Masonry Wall $1^5/_8$" furring $1^1/_2$" flexible insulation $^3/_8$" gypsum lath $^1/_2$" plaster	8" brick wall 4" brick, 4" concrete and gravel block wall	.13 .13
	Frame Wall, Brick Veneer 4" brick 4" stud $^{25}/_{32}$" fir sheathing building paper	$^3/_8$" gypsum board interior $^1/_4$" plywood interior $^3/_8$" gypsum board and $^1/_2$" plaster $^1/_2$" insulation board	.25 .25 .24 .19
	Frame Wall, Brick Veneer 4" brick 4" stud $^{25}/_{32}$" fir sheathing building paper gyplath plaster	1" flexible insulation 2" flexible insulation 4" flexible insulation	.13 .09 .06
	Frame Wall, 2 x 4 Studs yellow pine siding building paper $^{25}/_{32}$" fir sheathing no insulation	$^3/_8$" gypsum board interior $^1/_4$" plywood $^3/_8$" gypsum board and $^1/_2$" plaster $^1/_2$" insulation board	.25 .25 .25 .19
	Frame Wall, 2 x 4 Studs yellow pine siding building paper $^{25}/_{32}$" fir sheathing gyplath and plaster wall finish flexible insulation	1" flexible insulation 2" flexible insulation 4" flexible insulation	.13 .09 .06
	Frame Wall, 2 x 4 Studs yellow pine siding building paper insulation board sheathing no insulation	$^3/_8$" gypsum board interior $^1/_4$" plywood $^3/_8$" gypsum board and $^1/_2$" plaster $^1/_2$" insulation board	.16 .16 .16 .14
	Frame Wall, 2 x 4 Studs yellow pine siding building paper insulation board sheathing gyplath and plaster wall finish flexible insulation	1" flexible insulation 2" flexible insulation 4" flexible insulation	.10 .07 .06

(Continued)

Table 46 (con't)
Selected Coefficients of Heat Transmission for Typical Wall, Ceiling and Floor Sections

Reference Illus.	Construction	Construction Variation	U Factor
	**Frame Wall, 2 x 4 Studs** ⅜" exterior plywood siding no insulation	⅜" gypsum board interior ¼" plywood interior ⅜" gypsum board and ½" plaster ½" insulation board	.38 .38 .36 .26
	Frame Wall, 2 x 4 Studs ⅜" exterior plywood siding gyplath and plaster wall finish flexible insulation	1" flexible insulation 2" flexible insulation 4" flexible insulation	.15 .10 .07

Fig. 709. This fireplace is an example of excellent design. (Donley Brothers Co.)

The style is in keeping with the room and furniture. The materials used and the mantel are appropriate, and the size of the opening is in scale with the wall.

should be given to the location of comfortable chairs, books and other fireside comforts. Such roominess is most likely to be found at the side or end of a room. An end position is very likely to be preferable because of its seclusion. However, a side-wall position may allow more room for furniture to be grouped about the fireplace. A fireplace should not have doorways on either side, since this detracts from the sense of security and repose necessary for full enjoyment. Windows located very near a fireplace also intrude upon the atmosphere. See Fig. 711.

Fireplaces may be built flush with the interior wall or may project into the room to allow a mantel to be installed or to permit the fireplace to be flanked with bookshelves and cabinets.

Fig. 710. Character is added to this fireplace by inserting heavy timbers into the masonry and recessing a rustic mantel. (Donley Brothers Co.)

Fig. 711. This fireplace serves as the center of a cozy grouping of furniture, and is away from traffic patterns in the house. (Donley Brothers Co.)

It is considered best to locate a fireplace on an inside wall. This reduces heat loss to the outside and keeps the chimney warm, thus helping the fireplace to draw better.

Fireplace Design

While the design of fireplace elevations has varied with the times, the design of the interior portions has remained rather constant. Through experience, the proportions necessary to enable a fireplace to draw and burn properly have been established. If a fireplace is to be built conventionally (built brick-by-brick on the job), it is important that a proven design be followed. A type of fireplace gaining favor is the prefabricated metal unit.

Designing the Conventional Fireplace

Fig. 712 illustrates a proven, single-opening, conventional design for a fireplace. Table 47 gives the dimensions for fireplaces of different sizes based on this design.

The total thickness of the firebox wall, if it is lined with at least 2 inches of firebrick, should be a minimum of 8 inches. Where a firebrick liner is not provided, the firebox wall should be 12 inches thick.

The hearth should extend at least 16 inches in front of the fireplace opening and at least 8 inches on each side of the opening.

Combustible material should not be placed within 3½ inches of the edges of the fireplace opening. A distance of 8 inches is strongly recommended.

Occasionally, it is desired to build an ash dump, so that ashes can be cleaned out from a door in the basement, rather than from the hearth in the house. The dump is a metal door built in the floor of the firebox. This door pivots, permitting the ashes to drop inside the foundation walls of the fireplace to a clean-out door below in the basement. Fig. 712 illustrates this convenience.

The generally accepted method of constructing the conventional fireplace is to complete the rough brickwork of the fireplace from the footings to the chimney top before

Table 47
Dimensions for Conventionally Built, Single-Opening Fireplace

FINISHED FIREPLACE OPENING							ROUGH BRICKWORK AND FLUE SIZE										EQUIPMENT						
										New Flue Sizes[2]			Round	Old Flue Sizes			Hearth Assemblies	Damper Rotary No.	Damper Poker No.	Ash Dump	Ash-pit Door	Steel Angles[1]	
A	B	C	D	E	F	G	H	I	J	K	L	M		K	L	M						N	O
24	24	16	11	14	18	8¾	32	20	19	10	8	12	8	11¾	8½	8½	72	324	224	58	12 x 8	A-36	A-36
26	24	16	13	14	18	8¾	34	20	21	11	8	12	8	12¾	8½	8½	72	330	230	58	12 x 8	A-36	A-36
28	24	16	15	14	18	8¾	36	20	21	12	8	12	10	11½	8½	13	72	330	230	58	12 x 8	A-36	A-36
30	29	16	17	14	23	8¾	38	20	24	13	12	12	10	12½	8½	13	72 or 84	330	230	58	12 x 8	A-42	A-36
32	29	16	19	14	23	8¾	40	20	24	14	12	12	10	13½	8½	13	72 or 84	333	233	58	12 x 8	A-42	A-42
36	29	16	23	14	23	8¾	44	20	27	16	12	12	12	15½	13	13	72 or 84	336	236	70	12 x 8	A-48	A-42
40	29	16	27	14	23	8¾	48	20	29	16	12	16	12	17½	13	13	72 or 84	342	242	70	12 x 8	A-48	A-48
42	32	16	29	14	26	8¾	50	20	32	17	16	16	12	18½	13	13	72 or 84	342	242	70	12 x 8	B-54	A-48
48	32	18	33	14	26	8¾	56	22	37	20	16	16	15	21½	13	13	96	348	248	70	12 x 8	B-60	B-54
54	37	20	37	16	29	13	68	24	45	26	16	16	15	25	13	18	96		254	70	12 x 8	B-72	B-60
60	37	22	42	16	29	13	72	27	45	26	16	20	15	27	13	18	96		260	70	12 x 8	B-72	B-66
60	40	22	42	16	31	13	72	27	45	26	16	20	18	27	18	18	96		260	70	12 x 8	B-72	B-66
72	40	22	54	16	31	13	84	27	56	32	20	20	18	33	18	18	Special		272	70	12 x 8	C-84	C-84
84	40	24	64	20	28	13	96	29	61	36	20	24	20	36	20	20	Special	384	284	70	12 x 8	C-96	C-96
96	40	24	76	20	28	13	108	29	75	42	20	24	22	42	24	24	Special	396	296	70	12 x 8	C-108	C-108

Courtesy Donley Brothers Co.

[1]Angle Sizes: A—3 x 3 x ³⁄₁₆ ; B—3½ x 3 x ¼ ; C—5 x 3½ x ⁵⁄₁₆

[2]New Flue Sizes—Conform to new modular dimensional system. Sizes shown are nominal. Actual size is ½ in. less each dimension.

Note A—The back flange of the damper must be protected from intense heat by being fully supported by the masonry. At the same time, the damper should not be built in solidly at the ends, but given freedom to expand with heat.

Note B—The thickness of the fireplace front will vary with the material used—brick, marble, stone, tile, etc.

Note C—The hollow, triangular spaces behind the splayed sides of the inner brickwork should be filled to afford solid backing. If desired to locate a flue in either space, the outside dimensions of the rough brickwork should be increased.

Note D—A good way to build a smoke chamber is to erect a wooden form consisting of two sloping boards at the sides, held apart by spreaders at the top and bottom. Spreaders are nailed upward into cleats. The form boards should have the same width as the flue lining.

Note E—To use this table, select the number in the left-hand column that corresponds to the proposed width of fireplace opening and read the figures to the right on the same line.

Note F—Either rotary control damper or poker damper may be used.

undertaking the installation of the finished interior and front. See Fig. 713.

The entire hearth, including that portion outside the fire area, should be supported by the chimney footings and foundation. Notice in Fig. 712 that the hearth cantilevers over to meet the wood floor. This requires that steel reinforcing bars be placed in the 3½-inch concrete slab under the exposed hearth material. The floor joist does not support the end of the hearth.

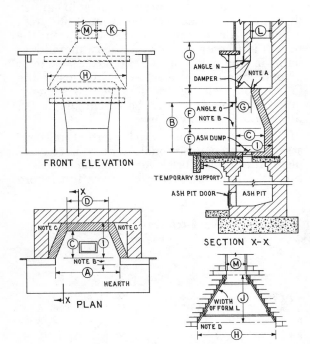

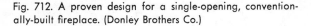

Fig. 712. A proven design for a single-opening, conventionally-built fireplace. (Donley Brothers Co.)

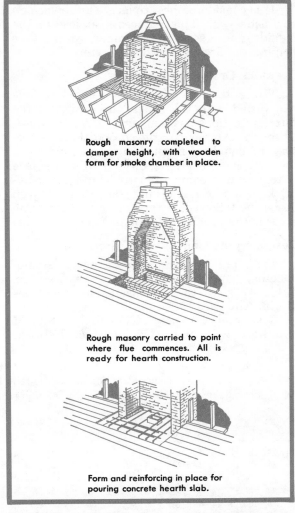

Rough masonry completed to damper height, with wooden form for smoke chamber in place.

Rough masonry carried to point where flue commences. All is ready for hearth construction.

Form and reinforcing in place for pouring concrete hearth slab.

Fig. 713. Conventional fireplace construction. (Donley Brothers Co.)

Table 48
Dimensions for Conventionally Built, Projecting Corner Fireplace

A	B	C	D	E	F	Old Flue Size		New Flue Size		L	M	Angle[1] 2 req'd	Plate Lintel	Corner Post Height
						G	H	G	H			J	K	
28	26½	16	14	20	29⅓	13	13	12	12	36	16	A-36	11 x 16	26½
32	26½	16	14	20	32	13	13	12	16	40	16	A-42	11 x 16	26½
36	26½	16	14	20	35	13	13	12	16	44	16	A-48	11 x 16	26½
40	29	16	14	20	35	13	18	16	16	48	16	B-54	11 x 16	29
48	29	20	14	24	43	13	18	16	16	56	20	B-60	11 x 16	29
54	29	20	14	23	45	13	18	16	16	62	20	B-72	11 x 16	29
60	29	20	14	23	51	13	18	16	20	68	20	B-78	11 x 16	29

Courtesy Donley Brothers Co.

[1]Angle Sizes: A—3 x 3 x 3/16; B—3½ x 3 x ¼.

Note A—The back flange of the damper must be protected from intense heat by being fully supported by the masonry. At the same time the damper should not be built in solidly at the ends but given freedom to expand with heat.

Note B—The thickness of the fireplace front will vary with the material used—brick, marble, stone, tile, etc.

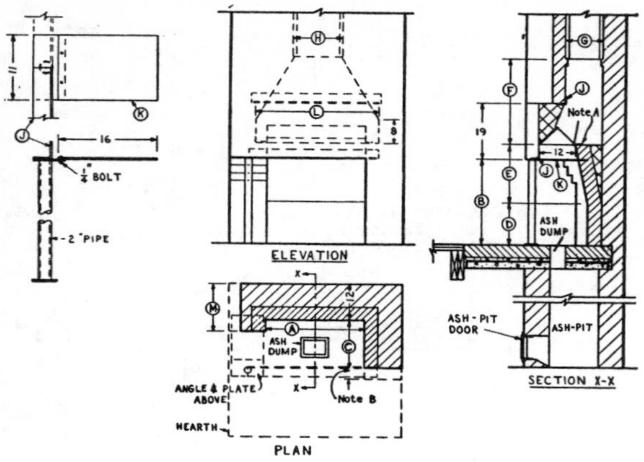

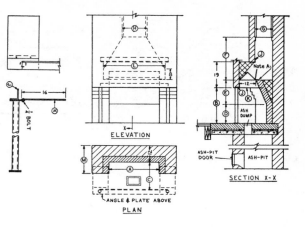

Fig. 714. A proven design for a conventionally-built, projecting-corner fireplace. (Donley Brothers Co.)

Fig. 715. Proven design for a three-way, conventionally-built fireplace. (Donley Brothers Co.)

Fig. 714 illustrates a proven design for a projecting-corner fireplace, and dimensions are shown in Table 48. This type of fireplace has two open faces. It can be built facing left or right.

A third type of conventionally built fireplace is the three-way fireplace. It affords the novelty of giving a profile view of the fire in rooms where there is no projecting corner

for the projecting-corner fireplace. Everyone within a room can see the fire, since the fireplace projects from the wall into the room. Fig. 715 gives the design of such a fireplace, and Table 49 gives the dimensions.

The double-opening fireplace is a fourth type in common use. These fireplaces open from one room to another and establish a sort of spiritual bond between persons in the two

Table 49
Dimensions for Conventionally Built, Three-Way Fireplace

A	B	C	D	E	F	Old Flue Size		New Flue Size		L	M	Angle[1] 2 req'd J	Plate Lintel 2 req'd K	Corner Post Height 2 req'd
						G	H	G	H					
28	26½	20	14	18	27	13	13	12	16	36	20	A-42	11 x 16	26½
32	26½	20	14	18	32	13	13	16	16	40	20	A-48	11 x 16	26½
36	26½	20	14	18	32	13	18	16	16	44	20	A-48	11 x 16	26½
40	29	20	14	21	35	13	18	16	16	48	20	B-54	11 x 16	29
48	29	20	14	21	40	13	18	16	20	56	20	B-60	11 x 16	29
54	29	20	14	23	45	18	18	16	20	62	20	B-72	11 x 16	29
60	29	20	14	23	51	18	18	16	20	68	20	B-78	11 x 16	29

Courtesy Donley Brothers Co.

[1]Angle Sizes: A—3 x 3 x 3/16 ; B—3½ x 3 x ¼

Note A—The back flange of the damper must be protected from intense heat by being fully supported by the masonry. At the same time, the damper should not be built in solidly at the ends but given freedom to expand with heat.

Table 50
Dimensions for Conventionally Built, Double-Opening Fireplace

Width of Opening A	Height of Opening B	Damper Height E	Smoke Chamber F	Old Flue Size		New Flue Size		Angle 2 req'd J[1]	L	Tee
				G	H	G	H			
28	24	30	19	13	13	12	16	A-36	36	35
32	29	35	21	13	18	16	16	A-40	40	39
36	29	35	21	13	18	16	20	A-42	44	43
40	29	35	27	18	18	16	20	A-48	48	47
48	32	37	32	18	18	20	20	B-54	56	55

Courtesy Donley Brothers Co.

[1]Angle Sizes: A—3 x 3 x 3/16 ; B—3½ x 3 x ¼

Note A—The damper and the steel Tee should not be built in solid at the ends but given freedom to expand with heat.

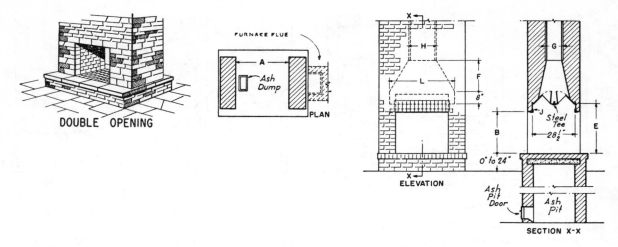

Fig. 716. Proven design for a double-opening, conventionally-built fireplace. (Donley Brothers Co.)

rooms. While there are varieties in design, the proven design shown in Fig. 716 uses two dampers mounted back-to-back. Table 50 gives the dimensions for the double-opening fireplace.

Welded Steel Prefabricated Fireplaces

There are a number of different types of welded steel fireplaces available. The steel heat-circulating unit increases the heat delivery of the fireplace. It also has the advantage of being carefully designed. All the mason has to do is to brick around the steel unit, build the chimney and install a finished face on the room side of the unit. See Figs. 717 and 723.

This unit heats the air in the space between the metal liners and ejects it into the room through grilles. See Figs. 718 and 719. Table 51 lists some common, available sizes for this unit.

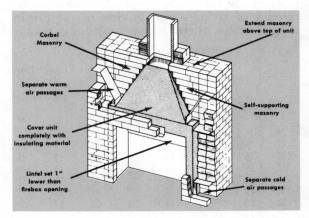

Fig. 718. A steel, prefabricated, heat-circulating fireplace with unit partially bricked up. Note cold-air intakes at the floor and the hot-air, ejection registers above them. (Donley Brothers Co.)

Fig. 717. A steel, prefabricated, heat-circulating, fireplace unit. (The Majestic Co., Inc.)

Table 51
Common Sizes of Prefabricated Steel Heat-Circulating Fireplaces

Finished Opening		Overall Dimensions			Approximate Flue Size
Wide	High	Wide	High	Deep	
28	22	34¾	44	18	8½ x 13
32	24	38½	48	19	8½ x 13
36	25	42½	51	20	13 x 13
40	27	47¾	55	21	13 x 13
46	29	55	60	22	13 x 13
54	31	63	65	23	13 x 18

Courtesy Majestic Co., Inc.

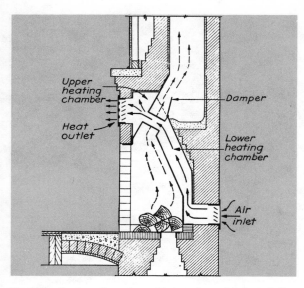

Fig. 719. Section through welded-steel, prefabricated fireplace. Fire warms air in lower heating chamber; warm air rises, drawing cool air in at air inlet and discharging warm air at heat outlet.

Fig. 721. Self-contained, steel, single-opening fireplace with prefabricated chimney. (The Majestic Co., Inc.)

Fig. 720. Self-contained steel fireplace. (The Majestic Co., Inc.)

Fig. 722. Welded steel fireplace with facing in place and plywood paneling above. (The Majestic Co., Inc.)

Another type of steel fireplace unit is a self-contained, all-metal unit. This unit requires no masonry. It has sufficient insulation below the hearth and behind the fire area so that it can be installed by placing it on a wood floor and backing it to a frame wall. The elevation can be faced with brick, glass or marble in the same manner as a conventional fireplace or a heat-circulating fireplace. Fig. 720 illustrates a projecting-corner fireplace of this type. This unit uses a steel, prefabricated chimney, built of corrosion-resistant alloys and stainless steel. It is comprised of three pipes, one inside the other, with Tyrex insulation between each set. Fig. 721 illustrates a single-opening welded steel fireplace with a prefabricated chimney. Fig. 722 illustrates a finished installation.

A combination of the all-metal chimney and the prefabricated steel, heat-circulating fireplace is shown in Fig. 723.

Fig. 723. Steel, prefabricated, heat-circulating fireplace with an all-metal chimney. (Vega Industries, Inc.)

Fig. 725. Wall-hung metal fireplace. (Vega Industries, Inc.)

Fig. 724. Freestanding metal fireplace. (Vega Industries, Inc.)

Fig. 726. Freestanding, welded, steel fireplace. (The Majestic Co., Inc.)

Placement of Fireplaces

Frequently, it is necessary to place two fireplaces back-to-back or in a corner. While the exact solution may vary, Fig. 727 illustrates some commonly accepted solutions. These are heat-circulating fireplaces. Notice the location of the cool-air inlets and warm-air outlets.

Chimneys

The use of prefabricated metal chimneys has already been discussed. This discussion will confine itself to the usual masonry chimney.

Still another type of all-metal fireplace is illustrated in Figs. 724 through 726. These units can be added easily after a house is built. They are lightweight and require no footing, since they are wall-hung or free-standing and use a metal chimney.

Fig. 727. Solutions to back-to-back and corner fireplace requirements.

Top: Foundation plan for corner fireplace showing location of intake grilles.

Center: Foundation plan for back-to-back fireplaces with grilles in sides or face.

Bottom: Foundation plan for two fireplaces with intake grilles in face, installed side-by-side.

Fig. 728. Solutions to chimney problems.

Left: Vary height of flue tile to prevent smoke of one flue from coming down other flue.

Right: Hood flues to help discharge smoke and shed rain.

The chimney should have a fireclay flue lining. When more than two flues are located in the same chimney, a 4-inch masonry division is necessary. The chimney wall should be at least 4 inches thick; it should be separated from the framing members of the building by a 2-inch air space and from flooring and sheathing by a ¾-inch air space. The top of the chimney should be 2'-0" above the ridge of the roof or any other obstruction nearby. If more than one flue is in a chimney, the flue tile should be projected unequally, as a safeguard against smoke pouring out of one flue and down the other.

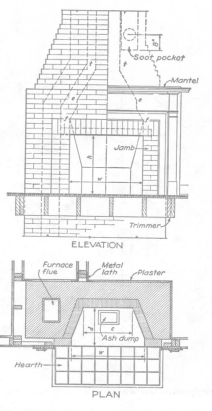

Fig. 729. Elevation and section through a conventionally-built fireplace illustrating flue location.

If a high building or trees interfere with the free discharge of smoke, the chimney can be hooded. This also protects the flue from rain. See Fig. 728.

A summary of chimney design is presented in Fig. 730.

A fireplace chimney is a good place to locate other flues for furnaces and for other units needing venting. Fig. 729 illustrates a section through a fireplace above the hearth, showing a second flue for a furnace; it also illustrates the elevation, showing how these flues are located. The furnace flue should be surrounded by at least 4 inches of masonry, if a fireclay flue lining is used or at least 8 inches, if no lining is used.

Mantels

Period-style wood mantels are fairly standardized. Certain types produced by millwork companies are available as stock items. These usually are attractive and well designed. For contemporary homes, the mantel as it is com-

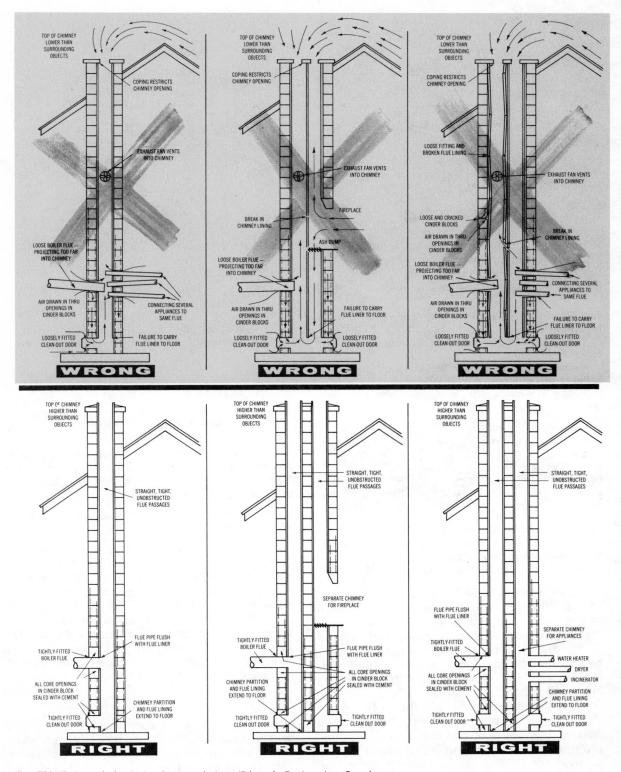

Fig. 730. Do's and dont's in chimney design. (Edwards Engineering Corp.)

monly conceived, frequently is omitted, and the design is produced through the use of the facing materials. Simplicity is an important factor. Fig. 731 illustrates some stock designs.

Fig. 731. Stock fireplace mantels and mantel surrounds. (Morgan Co.)

Insulation
Thermal Insulation

The major purpose of thermal insulation is to retard the passage of heat and cold. Practically all insulations are made of lightweight materials, having thousands of tiny air pockets. Each pocket provides resistance to the passage of heat. Since much heat in building materials is transmitted by conduction, these pockets reduce the rate of conduction.

Reflective materials retard the flow of heat by reflecting the radiant heat. A dead air space of at least ¾-inch must be in back of these materials in order for them to reflect radiant heat adequately.

A dead air space, such as that found in a frame wall between the sheathing and interior wall material, has some insulation value. However, it is equivalent to only ¼-inch of average insulation.

Types of Insulation

Many types of materials are available as building insulation. Following are descriptions of the common types.

Structural insulation board is made primarily from wood and cane fibers, formed into large sheets. Some types are asphalt coated. It is available as roof decking, sheathing and finish panels for interior walls. Descriptions of these applications follow.

Insulating roof-deck slab is used in the roof construction of open-beam ceilings in homes and commercial buildings. It can be applied to roofs of any pitch, and it provides (in addition to ceiling insulation) a structural roof deck and interior ceiling. It is composed of multiple layers, laminated together with a water-resistant adhesive. It is available in

Fig. 732. Insulating roof-deck slabs. (Tectum Corp.)

sheets of 2-inch and 3-inch thicknesses. A built-up roof or any type of shingle can be applied to this deck. See Fig. 732.

Roof insulation board is a structural insulation board designed primarily for flat-roof construction. It can be adhered to the roof sheathing. A built-up roof can be applied over it, or it can serve as sheathing and insulation. See Fig. 733.

Interior insulation board usually is ½-inch thick and is applied as the finished, inside-wall material. It has a factory-applied paint finish. It is used on walls in large sheets and on ceilings in the form of 12-inch-square tiles. See Fig. 734.

Insulation board sheathing is used for wall sheathing in frame construction. It not only insulates, but adds to the structural strength of the wall. It is treated with a waterproof coating that usually is asphalt. Any of the various siding materials (wood, brick, shingles or aluminum siding) can be applied over this material. See Fig. 735.

Insulating formboard is a structural insulating board designed for use as a permanent form for roof construction of reinforced gypsum or lightweight aggregate concrete that is poured in place. The formboard is placed on roof framing members, and the roof deck is poured on top of this. It thus serves as a form for supporting the poured deck material as it hardens and, after construction is completed, it insulates the roof deck. See Fig. 736.

There are many kinds of materials used in *blanket insulations*. These usually are mineral wool (rock, glass and slag) and vegetable fibers (wood and cotton). These are fire-retardant, moisture-resistant and vermin-repellent. They are available either with no backing or adhered to a paper backing or reflecting foil. Some are encased with a paper or reflective foil. They are available in long rolls and are stapled in place. See Fig. 737.

Batt insulation is similar to blanket insulation, except it is made in 4'-0" lengths. It serves the same purpose as blanket insulation.

Loose-fill insulations are bulk materials normally used for insulating existing build-

Fig. 734. Room finished with insulation board. (Homasote Co.)

Fig. 735. Insulation board sheathing. (Lumber Dealers Research Council)

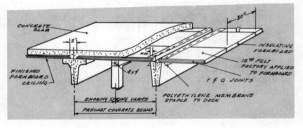

Fig. 736. Detail illustrating the use of insulating formboard. (Tectum Corp.)

Fig. 733. Roof insulation board being laid prior to application of a built-up roof. (Tectum Corp.)

ings. The fill is poured or blown between studs in the wall or is poured between ceiling joists. It is available in the same materials as blanket insulation, as well as in perlite and vermiculite.

Perlite is a white, inert, lightweight, granular material made from volcanic, siliceous rock. It is crushed and heated to 1800 degrees F. It then pops like corn, creating countless tiny air bubbles.

Vermiculite is a lightweight granular material manufactured by exploding an aluminummagnesium, silicate mineral. This mineral is made up of approximately one million separate layers per inch, with a minute amount of water between each layer. When heated to 1800 degrees F., the water changes to steam, causing the vermiculite to expand into cellular granules. Perlite and vermiculite are especially good for pouring into cavities in concreteblock walls.

A lightweight, *insulating concrete* is prepared by mixing perlite or vermiculite with Portland cement and water. This lightweight insulating material is used as roof decks. It also is used as a layer below concrete floor slabs on grade. A layer of insulating concrete is poured and topped with a layer of regular concrete.

Reflective insulations are composed of metallic surfaces, which either are paperbacked or have no backing. Aluminum foil is commonly used as reflective foil. It is adhered to batts, blankets and gypsum board. It also forms an effective vapor barrier.

Cellular glass slabs also provide effective insulation. The slabs are lightweight and easy to cut. Each cell in the slab is closed and impervious to air and water. It is excellent for perimeter insulation on concrete-slab houses, but also finds use as roof and floor insulation.

Polystyrene plastic slabs provide another insulation material. They are suitable for below-grade installation, such as for perimeter insulation for concrete-slab houses, for cavity-wall insulation and solid masonry insulation. See Figs. 738 through 740. They also are used for insulation of flat roofs, with a built-up roof laid over the top. See Fig. 741.

Fig. 738. Polystyrene insulation slabs adhered to foundation to reduce heat loss through edge of concrete-slab floor. (Sonoco Products Co.)

Fig. 737. Blanket-type, paper-backed insulation being stapled in place. (Bostitch)

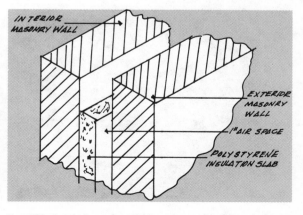

Fig. 739. Insulation of typical cavity wall with polystyrene slabs.

Polystyrene insulation slabs are bonded directly to solid-masonry walls. This not only provides insulation, but forms a base to which gypsum board can be adhered or plaster can be applied. Fig. 740 illustrates a basement wall with this slab insulation applied.

Insulation of Electrically Heated Living Units

Buildings heated with electricity should be very well insulated to minimize heat loss. Storm sash, weather stripping and storm doors are vital. The cost of heating a poorly constructed and insulated building with electricity is prohibitive.

The recommended maximum heat loss for an electrically heated building is 0.048 BTU (*U* value) for ceilings with cable heating panels and 0.072 BTU for other types of electric heat.

The walls in such a building should have a maximum *U* value of 0.082.

Floors over unheated basements should have a maximum *U* value of 0.099; over ventilated crawl spaces, 0.072; and between stories, 0.089.

General standards for electric heat require 6 inches of insulation in ceilings, $3\frac{5}{8}$ inches in walls and 2 inches in floors.

Insulation of Living Units Other Than Electrically Heated

The calculated heat loss of the living unit, according to recommended FHA minimums, should not exceed 50 BTU per square foot of total floor area, measured to the outside of exterior walls. This is computed for all floor area of spaces to be heated to 70 degrees F.

Ceilings below an unheated space or between different living units should have a maximum coefficient of heat transfer (*U* value) of 0.06 for ceilings with heating panels and 0.15 for ceilings without heating panels.

Heat loss through all exterior walls, doors and windows should not exceed 30 BTU per square foot of total floor area.

Heat loss through floors over unheated basements and crawl spaces should not exceed 15 BTU per square foot of floor area.

Perimeter insulation on concrete-slab floors, heated or unheated, should limit heat loss to not more than 5 BTU per square foot of floor area.

Where to Insulate

Any heated area should be surrounded by insulation. This normally places insulation in the ceiling, walls and floor. If an attic is not used, the insulation should be in the attic floor rather than in the roof. Exterior walls of a building always should be insulated.

Any rooms built in an attic should be insulated in the walls and ceiling, thus following the outline of the room.

Homes built over a crawl space require that the space be ventilated and the floors insulated. A polyethylene vapor barrier should also be placed on top of the soil and held in place with several inches of sand.

Slab houses require that rigid insulation be placed around the perimeter and under the slab. See Fig. 742.

Fig. 740. Polystyrene insulation slab applied to basement walls. (Dow Chemical Co.)

Fig. 741. Polystyrene slabs used to insulate a roof deck. Hot asphalt adheres slab to deck and built-up roof is applied over slab. (Dow Chemical Co.)

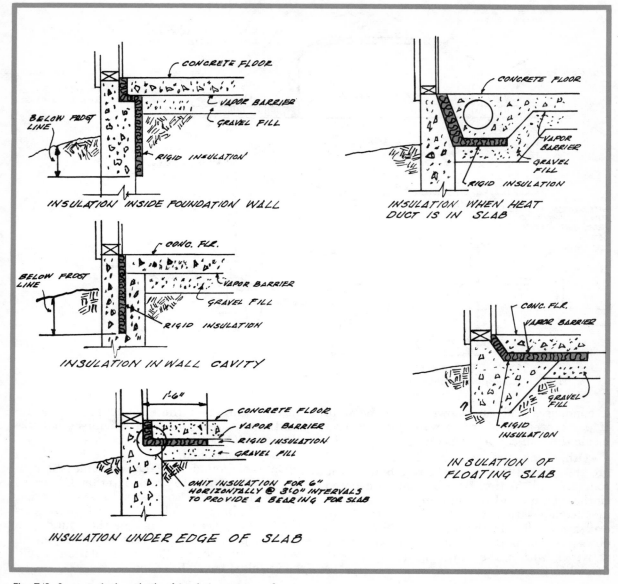

Fig. 742. Some typical methods of insulating concrete floors.

The floors of rooms over porches or unheated garages should be insulated. Water pipes in these floors also need insulation, to prevent their freezing and breaking.

Floors over a heated basement require no insulation. Fig. 743 illustrates the proper placement of insulation in a home.

Condensation Control

Moisture damage in buildings can be caused by leaks from the outside, such as around improperly installed flashing or poorly fitted windows. It also can be caused from the condensation of water vapor produced inside the building by such activities as cooking and bathing or by manufacturing processes giving off moisture to the air. Condensation can occur in summer or winter. It can be seen when windows sweat, but it also occurs inside the walls, unseen but damaging. Excess moisture inside a building can penetrate the interior wall. When it strikes the cold sheathing,

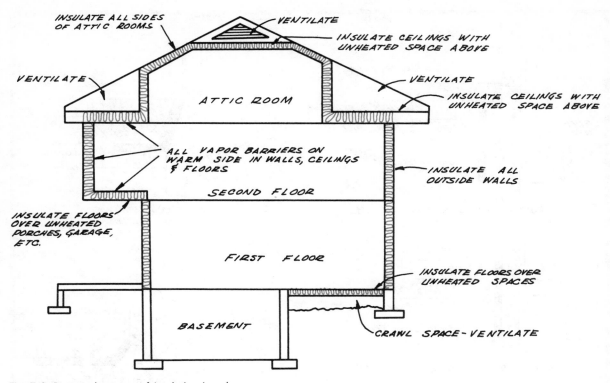

Fig. 743. Proper placement of insulation in a home.

it condenses and runs down inside the wall. If paint peels off a frame wall, condensation inside the wall can be suspected.

Other common sources of condensation are the ground under crawl-space houses, the concrete slab in this type building, unvented clothes dryers and fuel-burning devices. Summer condensation usually is the result of excess humidity in the air or soil. Since windows are open, the moisture caused by the activities within the house generally is dispersed to the outside.

Condensation can be controlled by providing exhaust fans in areas of high humidity, such as baths and kitchens, and by venting other devices, such as clothes dryers and heaters. A vapor barrier should be applied behind the interior wall finish, on the warm side of the insulation. This usually is adhered to the insulation which already has been installed in the wall. Such mechanical devices as dehumidifiers and such absorbent materials as calcium chloride or silica gel also help remove moisture from the air.

Crawl spaces require at least four ventilators in the foundation wall (one located close to each corner of the space). The aggregate ventilating area (net free) should be not less than 1/150 of the area of the space. As previously mentioned, a vapor barrier placed upon the ground is of considerable value in preventing moisture from entering the crawl space. It usually is covered with several inches of sand to hold it in place. The wall ventilators should be placed as high in the foundation wall as possible and should remain open all year. To prevent cold floors, insulation should be installed below the floor.

A concrete-slab house should have a vapor barrier placed below the slab before it is poured. If this is not done, the floors will sweat whenever the outside temperature changes very much. As a result, carpets will be wet and considerable moisture will be released to the air. The permeance of the vapor barrier should not exceed 1 perm (1 grain of vapor transmission per square foot, per hour, per inch of mercury vapor pressure difference). See Fig. 744.

A basement should have windows or other means of ventilation totaling not less than 1 percent of the basement floor area.

Natural ventilation of unheated attic spaces helps remove water vapor before it can cause damage. Attics and other spaces between roofs and ceilings should have a minimum ratio of net free ventilating area to the area of the ceiling of not less than 1:150. At least 50 percent of this ventilating area should be 3'-0" or more above the eave. The remainder could be in eave vents.

Flat roofs should have vents offering not less than ½ square foot of net free air area for every 150 square feet of roof area.

Sound Control

As a designer considers sound control, he is confronted with technical terms used by acoustical engineers. When an engineer calculates the *reverberation characteristics* of a room, he is attempting, through the use of established formulas, to ascertain the amount of absorption of sound in the room. A standard measure called *reverberation time* has been established to do this. This is the time required for a specified sound to die away to one thousandth of its initial pressure. If the calculated reverberation time is too long, the engineer must increase the amount of acoustical treatment. Fig. 745 illustrates how acoustical treatment influences reverberation time.

As a designer decides which acoustical material to select, he must consider the *coefficient of noise reduction* for the material. The coefficient is the percentage of the energy of a sound wave that is absorbed at each reflection. The coefficient of noise reduction to use for a particular situation has been ascertained by research. For example, in living rooms, bedrooms, libraries and dens, an acoustical material should have a coefficient of 0.40 to 0.50. Detailed tables of coefficients are available in architectural standards books. Manufacturers of acoustical materials list the coefficient of noise reduction for each type of material.

Noise causes definite human reactions. Tests have established suggested comfortable levels for various situations. For example, the noise level of a home, hotel room or apartment should be about 10 to 20 decibels. A *decibel* is a measure of noise intensity or loudness. By definition, a decibel is the amount of vibrational energy transmitted per second per cycle of vibration. It is the smallest change in energy that the human ear can hear. The human voice in normal conversation will range from 35 to 65 decibels.

Suggested decibel levels for various types of locations can be found in architectural standards books.

The two basic concepts of sound control involve (1) providing a quieter or more satisfactory acoustical environment and (2) providing good hearing or listening conditions. There are many things that can be done to improve the acoustical environment. Some treatments are rather simple, while others require the services of an acoustical engineer.

Three types of noise or sound must be considered when providing a quieter acoustical environment—direct noise, sound transmission and vibration. Direct noise is sound reaching the ear without being reflected, such as a traffic noise through an open window. Acoustical materials can help reduce the reflections of sound reaching the room, but they will have no effect on direct noise until it strikes the absorbing surface. This noise is one type of airborne sound. Outside airborne noises penetrate through open doors and windows, as well

Fig. 744. Vapor barrier being installed before pouring a concrete floor. It is important that no open places are left in the barrier. (Union Carbide Corp.)

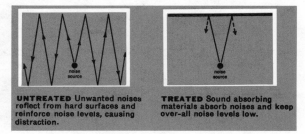

UNTREATED Unwanted noises reflect from hard surfaces and reinforce noise levels, causing distraction.

TREATED Sound absorbing materials absorb noises and keep over-all noise levels low.

Fig. 745. Hard, untreated surfaces reflect sound. (Owens-Corning Fiberglas Corp.)

as through cracks around these openings and through glass and thin doors. Storm windows, double-glazed sash and weather stripping help reduce this problem. Also, objects outside the building, such as trees, fences and balconies, can deflect the sound, thus reducing the amount permitted to penetrate the building.

Airborne noises developed within the building can be reduced by treating ceilings with acoustical materials, by hanging curtains or by laying carpeting. (Wall surfaces are treated only in extreme cases.) However, the muffling of sound within a space does not prevent it from being transmitted to other spaces.

Airborne noise control also involves reducing noise flow from one space to another. This frequently is reduced by separating the spaces with a double-stud wall, with no connections between the independent wall faces. Extra reduction can be obtained by adding sound-deadening material, flexible or rigid, between the studs. See Fig. 746. Airborne sound is also transmitted through floors to living spaces below. To overcome airborne noise transmission in wood floors, this same method can be used. Another method of reducing noise is to place nailing strips on the

subfloor and then to lay another subfloor, with the finish floor on top of these. An economical way to reduce much sound transmission through floors is to install ½-inch insulating lath and ½-inch gypsum board below the floor joists. Concrete floors have sufficient density to reduce sound transmission effectively. However, this effectiveness can be increased by adding ceiling and flooring materials. Fig. 747 illustrates details for reducing noise transmission through floors. There are many other methods to further reduce sound transmission in concrete floors. An architectural standards book should be consulted for design data. These construction techniques help reduce airborne and conducted noise.

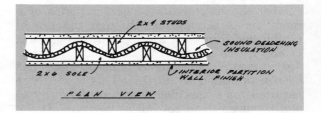

Fig. 746. Staggered stud wall reduces noise transmission to next space.

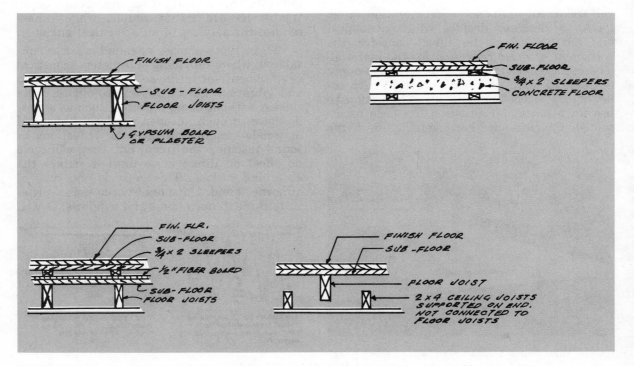

Fig. 747. Methods of reducing transmission of airborne noise and conducted noise through floors.

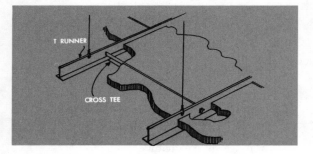

Fig. 748. Suspended ceiling with removable acoustical panels provides access to mechanical systems above ceiling. (Owens-Corning Fiberglas Corp.)

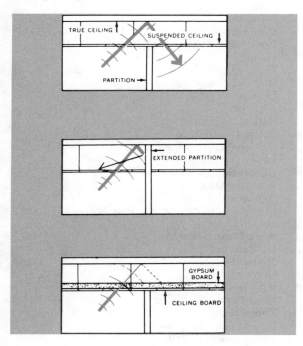

Fig. 749. Cautions in using acoustical materials. (Owen Corning Fiberglas Corp.)

Top: Sound can enter another space through ceiling.

Center: Partition blocks sound transmission.

Bottom: A solid mass, such as gypsum board, in a ceiling prevents sound transmission.

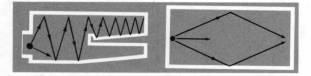

Fig. 750. Sound patterns in auditoriums with and without acoustical treatment. (Owens-Corning Fiberglas Corp.)

Left: Without treatment, sound bounces around auditorium and garbles performance.

Right: Treated auditorium reduces reverberation times to give improved hearing conditions.

A room with airborne noises that are objectionable, such as bathroom noises, can be surrounded with closets. The extra wall, plus the clothing in the closet, greatly reduces noise transmission.

The most effective barrier to sound transmission is a wall of solid mass, such as a solid-masonry wall. The thicker the wall, the more effective the barrier. Dead air space, as found in the typical interior partition, is rather ineffective. It takes solid mass to stop sound transmission.

There are a number of stock ceiling systems that provide for a dropped ceiling, with sound deadening panels as the finished surface. These usually are suspended by wires from the floor above, so that little sound is transferred by conduction. See Fig. 748. One caution is illustrated by Fig. 749. Sound can easily penetrate acoustical materials. These materials deaden sound within a space, but do little to stop it from passing through them to another space; therefore, sound could enter another space by going through an acoustical ceiling, bouncing off the floor overhead, and entering the next space. The only way to stop this is to put a solid barrier, such as masonry, through the ceiling to the floor overhead or put a sound-deadening mass directly above the acoustical ceiling.

Sound can be conducted through the framing members of a building. Suspended ceilings and double floors help reduce this somewhat. The most effective corrective procedure is to isolate the sound-producing device, so that it is not in direct contact with the structure. This can be done by placing machinery on sound-deadening pads or on a foundation that is entirely independent of the building foundation. Other noises are conducted by water, sewer and heating systems. If the plumbing system can be hung with hangers lined with rubber or other sound-deadening material, sound transmission will be reduced materially.

A significant amount of noise can be reduced if the mechanical equipment is carefully selected. Some types of such devices as furnaces and attic fans run quieter than others. Quiet operation should be one criterion for selecting such units.

Good hearing or listening conditions are important in auditoriums, music rooms and theaters. The major factors in design for good

hearing and listening include the cubic capacity of the space, the basic proportions of the space and the shape of the surfaces of ceilings and walls in relation to a stage or platform. The proper design of such facilities requires the services of an acoustical engineer. Fig. 750 illustrates what happens when an auditorium is not acoustically treated.

Acoustical Materials

There are many acoustical materials commonly used to dampen sound within a space. Curtains and carpeting are two in general use. Many types of wall panels and ceiling tiles are available. These are made from fiber glass, wood fibers, mineral wool and aluminum. Sound-absorptive plaster is available. It requires careful installation if it is to be effective.

These acoustical materials typically have many small openings, some of which are interconnected while others are not connected. The sound waves strike these openings and "get lost," thus dissipating their energy. Some surfaces absorb sound by vibrating, similar to a diaphragm when struck, and thus use up the sound energy.

When selecting acoustical materials, consider the following factors:

1. Appearance — A wide selection of textures, shapes and colors is available.
2. Performance — The coefficient of noise reduction should be ascertained.
3. Thermal insulation value — Most acoustical materials offer some insulation value.
4. Permanence — The product should be dimensionally stable and free from rot and vermin; it should resist moisture and withstand normal impact.
5. Maintenance cost — The material should be easily cleaned.
6. Fire resistance — The product should meet building code requirements for fire resistance.
7. Sanitary requirements — The material should not absorb or give off odors and should offer no sustenance to vermin.
8. Cost — Consider the cost of the material plus the cost of installation.

Build Your Vocabulary

Following are words that you should understand and use as a part of your working vocabulary. Write a brief explanation of what each means.

One-pipe, hot-water heating system
Two-pipe, hot-water heating system
Chilled-water cooling system
Steam heat
Hot-air heat
Boiler
Hearth
Mantel
Fireplace smoke shelf
Damper
Fireplace smoke chamber
Chimney
Perimeter heating
Duct
Plenum chamber
Radiator
Cooling coil
Compressor
Heat loss
Rigid insulation
Blanket insulation
U value
k factor
Reflective insulation
Poured insulation
British Thermal Unit
Design temperature
Infiltration heat loss
Reverberation time
Acoustical material
Coefficient of noise reduction
Decibel
Sound transmission
Radiant heat
Radiant baseboard
Convectors
Unit heated
Heat panels
Zoned heat control
Radial heat distribution
Plenum heat distribution
Heat pump
Convected heat
Radiant heat
Humidity
Upflow furnace
Downflow furnace
Horizontal-flow furnace
Freon
Flue

Class Activities

1. Make a study of the effectiveness of the heating plant in your home or classroom. Set the thermostat on 72 degrees. Place a series of thermometers on a wall, starting with one at the ceiling and then 2'-0" apart to the floor. Record the temperatures indicated by each, every hour for eight hours.

This will give the floor to ceiling difference. Record the outside temperature. Repeat this on days when the outside temperature is 30 degrees, 20 degrees, 10 degrees and 0 degrees. Does the heating system keep the room within acceptable limits?

2. Compute the heat loss for one room in your home. Explain what could be done to reduce this heat loss.

3. Using an architectural standards book, ascertain the insulating values for a frame exterior wall of a house with no insulation. Compare this with the insulating value of this wall when 2 inches of blanket insulation is added.

4. From local gas, electric and oil companies, ascertain the relative costs for the use of each fuel for heating. Prepare a report giving the advantages and disadvantages for using gas, electricity and oil for heating purposes in your community.

Additional Reading

Air Conditioning and Refrigeration Institute, "Air Conditioning and Refrigeration Institute Standards."

American Society of Heating, Refrigerating and Air-Conditioning Engineers, "Heating, Ventilating and Air Conditioning Guide."

Architectural Record (Editorial Staff), *Time Saver Standards.*

Bell and Gossett Company, "Engineering Manual."

Close, Paul D., *Building Insulation.*

Electrical Information Publication, Inc., "Fact Book, Electric Heating and Cooling."

Institute of Boiler and Radiator Manufacturers. Numerous bulletins.

Insulation Board Institute, "Fundamentals of Building Insulation."

National Bureau of Standards, Building Technology Division. Numerous publications relating to building construction and maintenance.

National Warm Air Heating and Air Conditioning Association. Numerous bulletins.

Ramsey, Charles G., and Sleeper, H. R., *Architectural Graphic Standards.*

Small Homes Council, "Moisture Condensation."

Sweets' Catalog Service, "Sweets' Architectural Catalog File."

U.S. Department of Agriculture, "Fireplaces and Chimneys."

U.S. Federal Housing Administration, Heat Loss Calculations."

———, "Minimum Property Standards for One and Two Living Units."

U.S. Housing and Home Finance Agency, "Condensation Control in Dwelling Construction."

———, "Crawl Spaces."

———, "Insulation, Where and How Much."

GETTING THE HOUSE BUILT

This chapter discusses the factors involved with getting the house built. The important task of selecting the lot must be completed. As this is done, some consideration should be given to locating the house on the lot. An architect or designer must develop the plans, the cost of the house must be estimated, a contractor must be selected and financing must be arranged. Certainly important is a consideration of the insurance needs.

The designing and building of a house is one of the largest business transactions which the average family ever undertakes. If properly handled, the building of a house can be a pleasant experience. If poorly handled, it can lead to displeasure, disappointment and actual financial loss.

Basically, designing and building a house involves (1) obtaining a set of working drawings and specifications, (2) getting bids and signing a contract, (3) checking the work as the house is constructed, accepting it and making final payment according to the contract.

Plans and Specifications

The most reliable source of plans and specifications is a qualified architect. He should study your housing needs and your financial status and then design a house to meet these requirements. Before making a final decision to contract with an architect, talk to his former clients to get their opinions concerning his performance. Be certain the ideas and styles emphasized by the architect are in keeping with your own. Ask him to show you plans he has completed. Remember that a fee is charged for designing the house and for drawing the plans, and the fee will be larger if the architect is employed to oversee the construction of the house. Be certain to ask the amount of the fee, before you contract with him to design a house.

Another source of plans and specifications is local building supply dealers. Large establishments frequently employ draftsmen with experience in small house construction. These men will design a house for a customer and give him the plans and specifications, free of charge, if the customer will buy his materials from the company. While this saves the architect's fees, frequently much more can be lost through poor planning and error.

Before entering such an agreement, talk with people who have had business dealings with the company. The desirability of the offer rests heavily upon the individual designing the plans. A well-trained architectural draftsman can provide a very satisfactory set of plans.

Many magazines offer to sell the plans of homes featured in the publication. Some of these are good, well planned and accurate. Frequently, however, changes must be made to meet requirements of local building codes. Also, a family frequently desires changes in the floor plan or elevations. These must be made by a person trained and competent in small home construction. Upon occasion, the entire plan must be redrawn to secure approval of the FHA or local financing agencies. Before a contract is let, all changes from the original

plans should be clearly set down, either in a redrawn plan or in revised specifications.

Some builders have stock plans of houses they have built. A buyer can select the plan he desires to have built. The builder can give an accurate cost figure, and he knows the exact construction time. However, such a procedure does limit the choice of plans and styles. It is wise to try to see some of the houses already built. If changes are desired in the builder's stock plan, these should be clearly noted and be made a part of the argeement. If a builder has a plan to suit your desires, this is a good way to select your home.

A large number of companies manufacture various types of prefabricated houses. Most companies have catalogs showing the houses available. The customer selects the house he wants from the catalog. It is possible that he may never see a set of plans. Changes can be made in these plans, but if this is done, they should be clearly noted and be made a part of the final contract. Since these changes also change the price of the house, each expense should be noted and recorded.

Still another source of house plans is a person trained as an architectural draftsman or one who has learned the trade through high school, junior college or trade experience. Many of these people draw plans as a sideline to their regular employment. Some have even gone full time into the business.

It would be wise to approach such a situation with caution. Many of these people do a fine job and develop a fine set of plans; others are not very good. Mistakes and inaccuracies cause loss of time and money. Ask those who have employed the person you are considering hiring. Their experience may save you money.

Getting Bids and Selecting a Contractor

After the plans and specifications have been developed, they must be approved by the agency loaning the money to build the house. Now the plans can be put out to several reliable contractors for firm bids. If you have employed an architect, he will solicit bids from reliable contractors and help select the best bid. If you have no architect, choose only contractors presenting recommendations from loaning agencies or who are bonded by the local home-builder association.

Usually a date is set as a deadline for contractors to return their plans and specifi-

cations, along with their bid. If all bidders are reliable and if their bids are based on materials of equal quality, the lowest bid is usually accepted. Occasionally, the lowest bid is not accepted because of a prolonged completion date. Bids should be examined for substitutions of materials for those in the plans and specifications. The low bid is not always the best bid. If all bids are too high, it is not unusual to confer with the low bidder to cut the plan and make substitutions until his price is acceptable.

Once the price is accepted, a contract must be drawn. If you have employed an architect, he will supply the information for contracts to be drawn up by the owner and his attorney. Without an architect, you must select the contractor and draw up the necessary contracts with his help.

A written agreement or contract between the owner and contractor is essential. Each party should have a signed copy of the contract.

A contract usually contains all points agreed upon by the owner and the contractor. Such items as method of payment and time of completion are included. It also includes a statement of general conditions and lists the duties of the contractor, the obligations of the owner to the contractor and the duties of the architect if one is employed. The plans and specifications are also a legal part of the contract.

Before signing a contract, have your loaning agency make a routine check on the contractor's financial position. He should be able to finance the materials for construction and should cause no delays in construction by taking time to raise money to continue operating.

Owner-Architect Relationships

If an architect is employed, the owner should have a written agreement with him, clearly detailing his duties and responsibilities, the method of payment and the responsibilities of construction left to the owner.

Usually the architect designs a house to suit the family's needs and budget. He helps decide how to locate it on the lot and even advises on the choice of a lot. The drafting of preliminary plans and making an estimate of cost are part of his duties. Under his supervision, the plans are revised, working drawings

are made and specifications are written. In most cases, the architect selects contractors and collects and analyzes their bids for the owner. He also provides the information necessary for writing the contract between the owner and the selected contractor.

If the owner desires to supervise the construction personally, the architect ends his responsibility with the signing of the contract to build. On the other hand, if the owner desires the assistance of the architect during construction, agreement between the architect and the owner should state that the architect will see that all work is carried out according to the plans and specifications and that he will examine proposals for substitutions and will make recommendations to the owner concerning the desirability of these changes. He will issue orders pertaining to the changes. In addition, he should make a final inspection of the finished dwelling, along with a check to be certain the dwelling is free of liens. If all is according to plan, the architect gives orders for the owner or loaning agency to make the final payment to the general contractor.

Usually the owner is responsible for finding out about such things as easements, lot boundaries, utilities and streets.

Owner-Contractor Relationships

As stated earlier, the owner and contractor sign an agreement which states clearly what the contractor will do for the price of his bid. The contractor is responsible for furnishing all materials and seeing that all work is satisfactorily performed. He employs and supervises all subcontractors, orders and pays for building materials and labor, schedules delivery of materials to the job and serves as general supervisor.

The owner usually has no direct responsibility for construction. He is morally obligated to select light fixtures, hardware, bath fixtures and other such items, so that construction will not be delayed. He should also see that the contractor is paid according to the contract. Usually this payment is in four parts: one-fourth when the foundation is laid; one-fourth when the building is enclosed and when plumbing, wiring and heating are roughed in; one-fourth when plastering is completed; and the final one-fourth when the building is inspected and accepted.

Occasionally a contract is drawn to permit the owner to do some of the work such as painting. This reduces the cost, but must be clearly stated in the owner-contractor agreement.

Estimating the Cost of a House

Before a house is built or before it even goes out for bids, it is best to secure an estimate of costs to determine if the house is within your price range as a prospective owner.

Several schemes have been used through the years for quick estimates of costs. These are called preliminary estimates.

Preliminary Estimates

One such scheme is to compute the number of square feet in the building by multiplying the outside dimensions — width x length. Nothing is subtracted for wall thickness. For example, a house 20'-0" x 60'-0" has 1,200 square feet. From past experience, many builders can estimate what they think it will cost per square foot to build the house in question. If this estimate were $10.00 a square foot, then the above house would cost approximately $12,000. Garages and porches frequently are figured at half the cost per square foot of the house.

Other builders prefer to estimate costs on a cubic foot basis. This is computed by multiplying the outside length by the outside width by the height from the basement floor to the eave line. The cubic footage of the attic is found by multiplying the length of the house by the width by the rise (from the eave to the top of the ridge) and dividing this figure by two. This takes into consideration the cubic footage lost by the sloping roof. Porches usually are figured at one-half their total cubic footage. Space occupied by footings is not included. Again, the builder's experience would enable him to make some estimate of the building cost per cubic foot. A house of 12,000 cubic feet built at a rate of $.90 per cubic foot would cost $10,800.

These are approximate methods for estimating the cost of a proposed house. The estimated cost per square foot or cubic foot will vary from city to city and from state to state. Only an experienced builder, familiar with local building costs, can give a reasonably accurate estimate.

Securing an Accurate Cost
by Regular Estimates

After a complete set of working drawings and specifications has been developed, the house is ready to be put out for bids. Interested contractors secure a set of the drawings and specifications and make a detailed analysis of materials and labor. If a contractor sets his price too high, he probably will not get the job, because someone will agree to do it for less. If he bids too low and gets the job, he actually could lose money.

Figuring the actual cost is an important task. It is done by a process builders call "taking off." Many large contractors employ an estimator whose sole job is to figure the cost of buildings. Small contractors may do this themselves or have their superintendent do it.

These estimates are made by carefully examining the plans and specifications, listing the amount of all materials needed and computing the cost of each. The labor involved in construction of the building is also figured. Standard printed forms for estimating are available, although some estimators prefer to use large ruled pads or printed estimating sheets of their own design.

The estimate usually is divided according to the types of work required. The estimator divides this in such a way as to simplify his estimating process. There is no standard way of dividing the estimates.

The process of estimating is too complex to explain in detail. Those desiring to undertake such a project should secure a text on estimating and follow the procedure suggested.

Available to contractors is a yearly publication[1], giving detailed, up-to-date figures on labor and other construction costs.

Fitting the House into Your Budget

An important question for the average family is: "How much can we afford to spend on a house?" Funds may be available in the form of cash savings, equity in a house and/or from a loan agency.

A "rule of thumb" to follow when considering how much can be spent for a house is to base your estimates upon your income. Most families can afford a house costing be-

[1]*Building Construction Cost Data*, Robert S. Means (ed.).

tween one and one-half to two and one-half times their annual income after taxes. The actual figure will vary depending upon the purchaser, his family and the type of life they lead. Two families with the same income cannot necessarily afford the same price house. One family may live in a conservative manner or may have only one or two children. They could probably afford a more expensive house than the family desiring an active social life and the best of cars or a family having a large number of dependents. These and other factors influence the amount of money available for a house.

About 20% to 25% of the monthly paycheck of the average family can be used to provide shelter. This includes rent or house payments, taxes, insurance, utilities, and repairs. Therefore, a family with an income of $800 a month after taxes can afford to spend up to $200 a month on shelter. The portion of this that can be spent directly on a house payment will vary with the family and where they live.

The above family will have a yearly income of $9,600 after taxes. They can afford a house in the $14,400 to $24,000 price range. Assuming they purchase a house for $24,000 and make a $4,000 down payment, they will have to finance $20,000. The monthly charges to be paid will approximate the following:

Loan $20,000 for 20 years at 7% interest monthly interest and payment	
toward principle	$ 77.50
mortgage insurance $20,000	
plain life insurance	8.00
taxes (estimated)	50.00
fire insurance (estimated)	12.00
utilities (estimated)	40.00
Total monthly payment:	$187.50

It can be seen from the preceding figures that this family is living to the limit of their potential. Also, it should be remembered that a house has certain maintenance and repair expenses. Even new houses require upkeep. The yard requires seed, fertilizer, a fence or a patio and puts extra demands upon the one-fourth of the monthly check allotted to shelter. These items should be acknowledged and allowances should be made for them.

In summary, do not buy a house you cannot afford. It will make living there most unpleasant. It will take away from your family

many things they enjoy, such as a nice vacation, music lessons, or that new bike. Remember you will need a newer car in a few years, and a new house calls for new furniture, carpets and draperies. Consider total cost carefully, not just the monthly payment.

Insurance

When a family owns a home, they assume obligations and undertake risks not applicable to a renting family.

First of all, when selecting a contractor, be certain the one you choose is reliable and will be able to finish the job. It is not uncommon for a general contractor to stop construction of the house before it is finished. As a prospective owner, you can protect yourself from such a loss by being certain that the contractor is bonded. This certifies that an insurance company is convinced that the contractor can and will complete the job. If he should fail to do so, the insurance company will employ another contractor to finish the work. The owner, therefore, is protected from loss.

The matter of liability for accident during construction is of great importance. Be certain the general contractor carries a manufacturer's and contractor liability policy. This will cover all types of accidents on the job, including mishaps involving curious children who like to explore buildings under construction.

If you are serving as your own general contractor and are employing workmen in the various trades to work for you, liability insurance is absolutely essential. Without it, you risk losing everything if an accident occurs on your property.

It also is necessary to carry insurance on the house and materials, to cover loss by fire or storm during construction.

After the house is completed, the owner must reexamine his insurance needs. Before a mortgage company will approve a loan, the house must be insured against loss by fire and lightning and, usually, against loss by windstorm, hail, explosion, smoke, vandalism, riot, falling aircraft and vehicles.

An additional *extended coverage* can be bought to include damage by falling objects, glass breakage, collapse and landslide, theft and burglary, water or steam, rupture of hot-water appliances, ice and snow, and freezing of plumbing.

It is important to consider detached garages. Usually the policy on the house will cover out-buildings up to 10% of the policy value. For example, a $12,000 policy will provide $1,200 coverage on a detached garage. If this building is worth more, then additional coverage should be obtained.

Insurance is necessary for the contents of the house. This will include loss from fire and, occasionally, theft on articles such as furniture, clothing, sports and hobby equipment and other personal property.

Another type of insurance needed by the property owner is liability insurance. This coverage protects the owner and his family against claims for damages which may result from accidents taking place on their home property.

The insurance coverages mentioned as available for the homeowner — the house, personal property, theft, and liability — are provided in some states as a "package policy." One policy provides coverage for all four perils.

Mortgage insurance is another valuable protection. Briefly, this life insurance policy is taken out on the breadwinner of the family for an amount equal to that of the mortgage. If the breadwinner dies, the insurance company pays off the mortgage, and the dependents live in a house clear of debt.

Certainly the homeowner should examine his insurance program carefully.

Financing a House

As a house is being planned, the prospective owner should carefully consider how he will finance it. Usually the purchase of a house is the largest and most important investment made by the average family. Much money can be lost through careless or unfortunate mortgage arrangements.

A mortgage is a contract. It requires that a loan be repaid, and it specifies the terms. If the homeowner fails to meet his obligation, the mortgage holder can then foreclose and resell the house.

State laws set limits on the kinds of mortgages that can be issued and their terms. Mortgage practices are fairly well standardized, but a person intent on financing a home

would do well to investigate a number of agencies and to compare their mortgage terms.

One method of financing is through government insured loaning agencies such as the Federal Housing Administration or the Veterans Administration G.I. Loans.

The Federal Housing Administration was set up by the National Housing Act for the purpose of "encouraging improvement in housing standards and conditions, to provide a system of mutual mortgage insurance, and for other purposes." This agency does not loan money, but insures the loan so the loaning agency is protected in case of a foreclosure.

The government limits the interest rates on these loans; it also sets up construction specifications which must be met before the agency will insure a loan on a house. The FHA will insure loans made to the general public, while the G.I. Loan is restricted to veterans. The G.I. Loan usually has a lower down payment and a lower interest rate than the FHA loan.

A second source of money, the largest source, is through conventional loans. These are made by savings and loan associations, mortgage companies, banks, insurance companies and individuals. These loans are not insured by the government. The interest rate and down payment on conventional loans usually is higher than on government-insured loans.

A third means for financing the purchase of a house is a *land contract*. This is an agreement between the present owner and the buyer. The buyer agrees to make a specified down payment and to make monthly payments to the seller. The owner is really providing the financing due to his equity in the building. It is possible for the first owner to have a loan against the property. He pays on his loan on the house from the monthly payments made by the buyer. Interest rates usually are a little higher than on conventional loans. Also, the price of the house tends to be inflated. A $12,000 house may sell for $12,500 or $13,000 under a land contract, because of the easy terms of purchase. It is an expensive way to purchase a house.

As a means for financing a house is sought, consider the following provisions:

1. In case of your death, what will happen to the mortgage? Will your family be evicted? Insurance on the breadwinner is a vital part of a good loan. If the breadwinner dies, the mortgage is then paid up in full.

2. Consider a plan which enables the purchaser to build up dividends which can apply to the mortgage if he becomes unemployed.

3. Check the payment plan in the loan agreement. It should permit the purchaser to pay off the mortgage before expiration of the full period, should he so desire. This should be accomplished with a minimum of penalty. The faster a loan can be repaid, the less the house will actually cost you.

Amount of loan $10,000.00 Interest rate — 7%		
Term of loan	Monthly payments (Int + Principle)	Interest paid
5 years	$198.02	$ 1,881.20
10 years	116.11	3,933.20
15 years	89.89	6,180.20
20 years	77.53	8,607.20
25 years	70.68	11,204.00

4. Compare rates of interest charged by various loaning agencies. Even ½ of 1% over 20 years amounts to a large sum to be paid. Suppose you purchased a house for $24,000 and made a down payment of $4,000. You would have to borrow $20,000. If you could afford payments of $145.00 a month, you could assume a 20-year loan. If the interest rate were 7%, you would pay $17,214 interest for the use of $20,000. The $24,000 house would cost you $41,214 over 20 years.

5. Check the method of computing interest on loan. A good loan arrangement should provide for monthly reduction of the principal, rather than a quarterly credit for payments. Under the quarterly plan, interest is charged on a fixed principal for each three-month period. Payments during a quarter do not reduce the interest charge until the next quarter. This quarterly plan increases the actual interest paid. Considerable savings in interest can be made with monthly reduction of the principal.

6. Consider the rate of amortization. *Amortization* means the gradual elimination of an obligation by periodic payments. Some

mortgages provide for regular payments for a term, such as five years, but must be renewed at the end of that time or the remaining principal must be paid in full at that time. A good loan should have a specific maturity date that permits complete repayment (amortization) of the principal and interest through regular monthly payments.

7. How large a monthly payment will be made? The size of the loan, plus interest, spread over a period of years, determines the monthly payment. Provide for payments as large as your budget will handle. The sooner the loan is paid, the less interest is required. However, be sure to allow for taxes and insurance charges. The addition of these to the loan payment could make your total monthly payment so large it becomes a burden.

8. Secure a statement of the costs of closing the loan. Certain items of expense are inevitable, such as appraisals, surveys, title search and recording the deed. The purchaser must bear these expenses. These can sometimes amount to several hundred dollars. An efficient loan agency often can cut these costs considerably.

9. Check that you are obtaining the most economical loan. The loan with the lowest down payment and smallest monthly payments usually is not the most economical or best. It calls for a longer term of payment, frequently at a higher interest rate. This increases the total interest paid and thus increases the actual cost of the house.

10. Consider the financing of "extras" in a loan. Some conventional loans permit the financing of appliances as part of the mortgage.

11. Consider the "open-end" provisions included in some mortgages, which permit borrowing additional funds at a later date, at the interest rate of the original mortgage. This may enable you to expand or improve the property.

12. Examine the loan for an *automatic grace period*, which enables you to lapse payments for as long as six months without being evicted. Usually this clause will become effective after you have paid on your loan for a specified period of years.

Trade-In House Sales

More and more builders and realtors are offering to accept the present house of a prospective buyer as part payment on a new house. This has been done for years in the automobile industry — the old auto is traded for a new one and the cash difference is paid. It is now becoming an accepted practice in the real estate business.

There are three trade-in plans in frequent use today: the straight trade; the guarantee trade and the conditional trade.

Straight Trades

In the straight trade, prices are fixed on both the old and new houses. The equity the customer has in the old house is applied toward the purchase of the new house. The builder assumes the loan on the old house and tries to sell it. The customer assumes the loan on the new house and moves in. This is a simple procedure. However, the customer may have had an opportunity to secure a higher price for his old house by placing it on the open market.

Guarantee Trades

In the guarantee trade, the customer signs a contract to buy a new house from a builder. The builder promises to buy the customer's old house at an established price, if the customer has been unable to sell it by a date specified in the contract. Frequently, the customer is required to put up a small cash advance to indicate his sincerity.

This plan is very flexible and gives the customer his best advantage to get "top dollar" from his old house.

Conditional Trades

In a conditional trade, the builder agrees to save a new house for a customer while the customer tries to sell his old house. It is quite simple and requires little capital investment from the builder. However, it does require the builder to remove his new house from the market for a set period of time, usually 15 to 90 days. Under such a plan, neither the builder or customer is assured of a completed sale. Basically, this plan has little to offer either party.

When a trade is being considered, careful appraisals of both the old and the new property are in order. Certainly, differences of

opinion arise when a customer learns the price of the new house or the proposed allowance for his old house. The builder is taking a risk trading and, occasionally, overprices his house or undervalues the trade-in.

Another difficulty when trading is the trading fee, which runs from 5 to 15 percent. This can change a person's mind about trading, when he sees what he must pay to conclude the agreement.

A well planned and fair trade can be beneficial to the builder and customer; however, each party must carefully weigh the advantages and disadvantages of the trade.

Build Your Vocabulary

Following are words that you should understand and use as a part of your working vocabulary. Write a brief explanation of what each means.

Architect
Bid
Contractor
Contract
Estimating
Interest
Mortgage insurance
Loans
Amortization
Loan closing costs
Down payment

Class Activities

1. Visit the office of a local architect. Secure information from him concerning the services he performs for the prospective homeowner. Write a paper detailing these services. Include information about the type of owner-contractor contract he uses when awarding a construction job.
2. Visit a local bank or home finance agency. Secure information about the requirements an owner must meet to secure a loan. Write a paper detailing these requirements.
3. From local architects, loan agencies or contractors, ascertain the local cost per square foot and cost per cubic foot to build a brick veneer residence.
4. Invite a local contractor or architect to visit the class. Ask him to explain how he estimates the cost of a house by computing the materials needed and the labor to be used.
5. A typical family with a salary of $7,500 after taxes can build a house in what price range?
6. From a local bank or a home finance agency, ascertain the following information concerning a $15,000 house loan:
   A. Interest rate currently used.
   B. Total monthly payment if loan is for 20 years.
   C. Total interest for 20-year period.
   D. The actual cost of the house after 20 years.
   E. Cost of insurance for 20 years.
   F. Estimated taxes for 20 years.
7. Visit an insurance agency and prepare a report detailing the types of insurance coverage available on residences and small commercial buildings.
8. Visit with a local realtor and ascertain his policy regarding trade-in house sales. Report on the advantages and disadvantages he cites for this means of house sales.

Additional Reading

Means, Robert S. (ed.), *Building Construction Cost Data.*

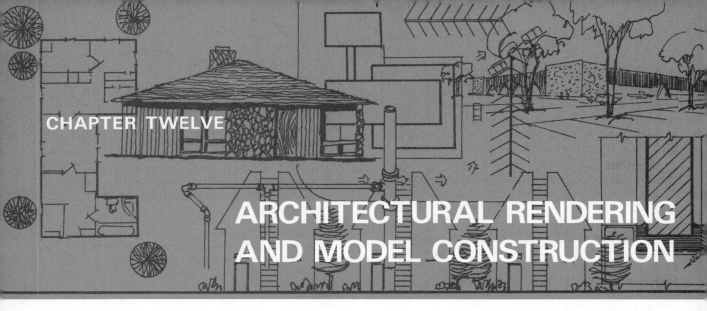

ARCHITECTURAL RENDERING AND MODEL CONSTRUCTION

Frequently it is advantageous to present a planned building in a way that relates it to its intended surroundings, so that others can visualize its finished appearance. Several methods of presentation are in common use. Presented in this chapter are perspectives, display drawings, models and architectural renderings.

Pictorial drawings and models help the client visualize the finished building. Many people cannot look at a set of plans and picture the end product. Pictorial drawings help the architect "sell" the customer on the design of the structure. They are used with sales literature and other advertising campaigns. They help rent apartments before they are built, and they sell prefabricated houses. A rendering of a proposed church building will help in its fund-raising campaign. Renderings influence the directors of corporations in their decisions concerning new plants and retail outlets.

Architectural Perspective

While there are many different types of perspective drawings, the procedure most frequently used is a two-point perspective. This can be a rather simple line drawing, or it can be shaded in pencil, drawn and shaded in ink or produced in color with the use of watercolors.

Architects and architectural draftsmen spend most of their time working on plans and details, and very little, if any, time is spent on perspectives. A small architectural office provides them more opportunity for drawing perspectives than a large office, since the large office usually employs someone with art training to do only this type of work.

Two-Point Perspective

Perspective drawings illustrate the theory that the further away an object is from the eye, the smaller it appears, Fig. 775. This is noticed when one drives an automobile; the road ahead appears to narrow and diminish

Fig. 775. The greater the distance an object is from the eye, the smaller it appears. This building is the same height at the rear but it appears lower. (Andersen Corp.)

to a point on the horizon. The same phenomenon occurs when one observes telephone poles or a long building. The portion of the building nearest the viewer appears larger.

It should be pointed out, therefore, that throughout the drawing process as explained in the following paragraphs, *any portion of a building touching the picture plane is true length*, while those portions behind the picture plane are smaller than normal. See Fig. 775.

The steps to follow when drawing a two-point perspective are given in the next paragraphs. For purposes of clarification, the total top view is kept clear of the front view, showing the actual perspective. In practice these usually are overlapped by permitting the *station point* (S.P.) to drop down over the front view, reducing the size of paper needed.

Layout for Top View

1. Near the top of the drawing paper locate a line called the *picture plane*. This is an edge view of the plane (drawing paper) upon which the perspective will be projected (Fig. 776).

2. Draw the outline of the floor plan, with door and window locations as shown in Fig. 776. It is not necessary to draw interior details or details of the back and the unseen end of the house. Time can be saved by making a print of the floor plan and taping it in position, thus removing the necessity to redraw it. Place one corner of the floor plan so that it touches the picture plane. Draw the house away from the plane on any angle desired; usually, an angle from 15 to 45 degrees is best. The angle chosen depends upon the details to be shown. The scale used to draw the floor plan usually is the same as that used on the working drawings; however, it may be changed, if a smaller or larger perspective is desired.

3. Draw a line from the intersection of the floor plan and the picture plane to the station point (S.P.). This usually is dropped perpendicular to the picture plane, but it can be on any angle desired. Consider how this angle will influence the perspective. If the station point is at the place such as S.P.$_B$, very little of the end of the building will be shown; while if it is at S.P.$_A$, very little of the front will be shown.

The distance the station point should be located from the building varies with the structure and the desired appearance of the rendering. If it is too close, the perspective will appear distorted. For most residences and small buildings, this distance is about 100 feet. Most commonly, the station point is placed back far enough so the entire structure and its immediate surroundings can be included in a cone of 60 degrees. The cone is constructed with its tip at the station point and its central axis on a line of sight to the corner of the building touching the picture plane. Experience will help ascertain satisfactory distances. The beginner probably will have to try several distances before he achieves the desired appearance.

4. From the station point, draw lines parallel to the sides of the floor plan, until they cross the picture plane at *C* and *D*. From these points, drop perpendiculars into the front view, until they cross the horizon at C^1 and D^1. These points are called the *vanishing points*. All horizontal lines run to these points. They are referred to as *vanishing point right* (VPR) and *vanishing point left* (VPL).

Layout for Front View

5. Fig. 776 also shows the *front view* of the picture plane, upon which the perspective is to be drawn. First, locate the *ground line* upon which the building rests. This can be anywhere near the bottom of the page.

6. Next locate the *horizon*, which represents the height of the viewer's eyes above the ground line. If the horizon is very low, 1 or 2 feet, little of the roof of the building is shown, and the walls loom large above the viewer. If the horizon is 6 to 8 feet above the ground line, the building appears as the viewer normally would see it. If the horizon is high, such as 15 to 20 feet or more, a bird's-eye view is given, and considerable roof and little wall are shown. A decision must be made as to the view desired.

Procedure for Projecting into Front View

7. Draw projectors from the corners of the building, (*X*, *Y*, *Z*) to the station point. See Fig. 777.

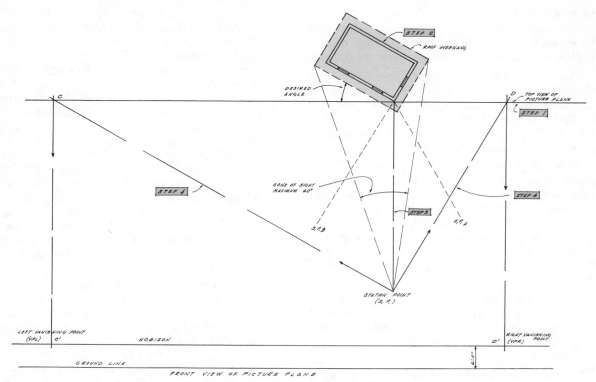

Fig. 776. Preliminary layout necessary before projecting points to draw perspective on picture plane.

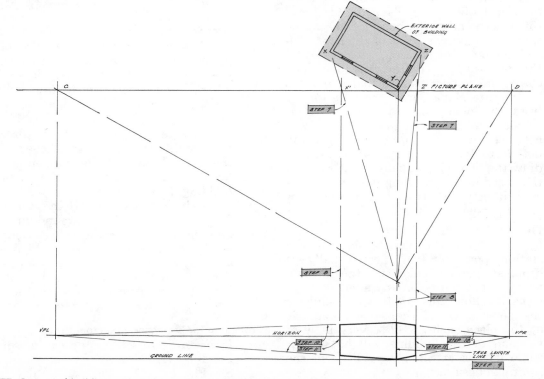

Fig. 777. Corners of building projected onto the picture plane, true height measured and edges extended to vanishing points.

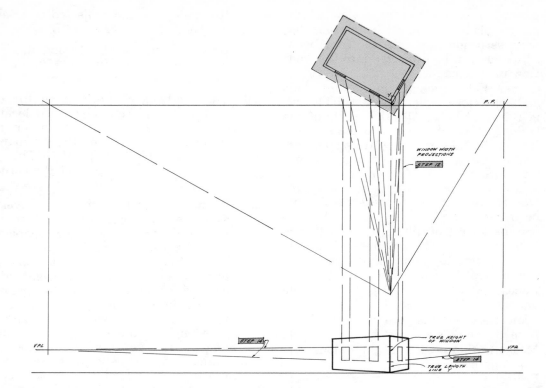

Fig. 778. Window widths projected onto picture plane, true height measured and edges extended to vanishing points.

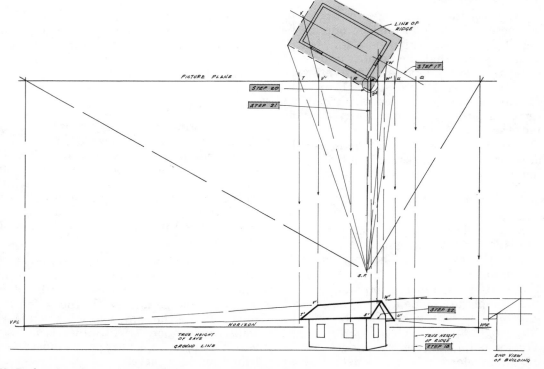

Fig. 779. Roof projected onto the picture plane and the overhang drawn.

8. Where these cut the edge view of the picture plane (X', Y, Z') in the top view, drop perpendiculars into the front view. All points can be projected into the front view in this manner.

9. Corner Y is touching the picture plane and, therefore, will appear true length in the front view. All other parts of the building (except the roof overhang projecting beyond the picture plane) are behind the picture plane and are, therefore, foreshortened. *All vertical measurements must be made on a true-length line.* In the front view, measure the true height of corner Y.

10. Run projectors of the horizontal edges to VPL and VPR. The junctions of lines X' and Y' with these vanishing lines locate the corners of the building.

11. Repeat Steps 6 and 7 to locate the doors and windows. See Fig. 778.

12. Project the widths into the front view from the top view.

13. Measure the actual heights along the true-length line.

14. Project these heights to the proper vanishing point (depending upon the side of the house). Locate any other parts in a similar manner.

When actually drawing a perspective, all these points are located on one drawing. They are separated here for clarity. It can be seen that the number of lines of projection are many, and the drawing rapidly becomes crowded. Projectors should be very light lines which may be removed after they have served their purpose.

15. Details such as window mullions usually are not carefully measured, but are estimated and drawn rapidly.

Roofs in Perspective

16. The drawing of roofs other than flat roofs presents special problems. One problem is locating the height; another problem is the overhang. This procedure is shown in Fig. 779.

17. Project the ridge in the top view until it cuts the picture plane at Q. Then project it into the front view. This becomes a *true-length line* in the front view.

18. The actual height of the ridge can be measured along this true-length line in the front view and projected to a vanishing point, in this case, VPL.

19. Repeat Steps 6 and 7 to find the length of the ridge $V'W'$. In Fig. 779, note projections of V and W to V' and W'.

20. The overhang S^2 projects on the other side of the picture plane. To locate it, project it back from the station point through the corner of the overhang to the picture plane at point S. This gives the point to use to project the corner of the overhang into the front view.

21. To find the true height of the overhang at the eave, project the point at which the overhang cuts the picture plane R into the front view. Measure the true height here, since this is a *true-length line*. Ascertain the true height of the eave by making a skeleton drawing of the end of the building to the scale used in the drawing. Project, horizontally, the true height of the eave to the true-height line on the perspective drawing. Then project this true-height point to the proper vanishing point. Draw the perspective where these cut the projections of the corners of the overhang, T' and S' front eave.

22. From corner S', run a line to VPR. The point where the projection of corner U cuts this line (U') is the corner of this rear eave. The rear eave is vanished to VPL.

Perspectives of Interiors

The principles of two-point perspective discussed for exterior views of buildings apply to interior perspectives. The top view of the room, with furniture located, should be drawn to the angle that seems to show the interior to best advantage. The horizon usually should be 6'-0" above the floor or ground line. This can be varied if a higher or lower view shows the room better.

The easiest beginning procedure is to draw the room in perspective as if it were a box. Then the furniture can be located. All furniture that is parallel with the sides of the room can use the same vanishing points as the walls of the room. If furniture is not square with the room, vanishing points must be established for each piece.

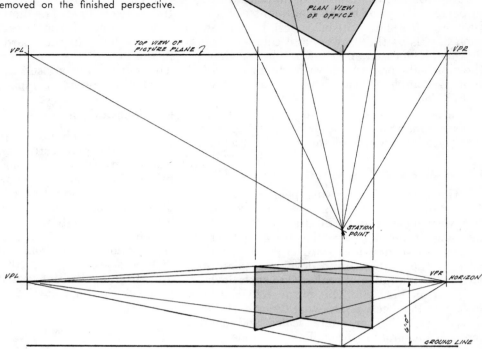

Fig. 780. The office walls are drawn in perspective as though the room were a box. The front walls are needed only for construction and are removed on the finished perspective.

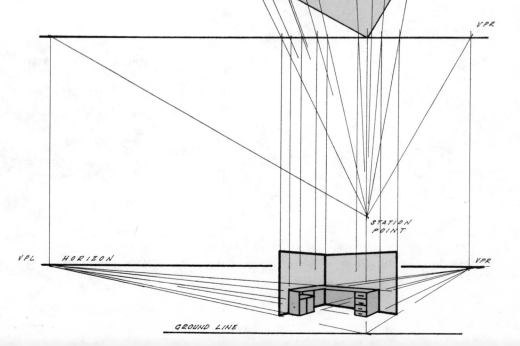

Fig. 781. The furniture is located in the room and drawn in perspective. Details can be as elaborate as desired. This drawing shows the office desk simply blocked in.

Fig. 780 shows the walls of an office drawn in perspective prior to the placement of furniture. Fig. 781 shows the office desk blocked in; such details as the drawers and cabinet doors now can be located and drawn. Fig. 782 shows the finished perspective, with chairs in position. A complete room perspective is shown in Fig. 783.

Interior perspectives can be rendered in the same manner as exterior perspectives. Fig. 784 gives an example of this type of drawing.

Perspective Drawing Boards

The system for drawing perspectives described on the preceding pages is accurate, but very slow. Industrial draftsmen usually use some type of perspective drawing board. A perspective drawing board is a device that permits the draftsman to develop a perspective in a wide range of scales. One such device is shown in Fig. 785. This is the KLOK Professional Perspective Drawing Board. It has a wide range of graduate scales and eight main vanishing points. The extreme left vanishing point is represented by the concave curve. A special T-square head slides along

this curve. There are five vanishing points on the horizon line. The horizon line is in the exact center of the board. The points are actually holes in the board. A pin is inserted in the hole of the vanishing point to be used. This device can be used to rapidly draw one-point or two-point perspectives.

Perspective Charts

Perspective charts are printed sheets with lines in true perspective. See Fig. 785A. The chart is placed under a sheet of vellum. The printed lines show through, giving the draftsman the direction to each vanishing point. The charts are available in various sheet sizes. They are ordered by giving the scale of the drawing, as $\frac{1}{4}'' = 1'-0''$, and the distance of the station point from the object. Typical distances are 50′, 75′, 100′, and 150′. There are several different perspective chart and grid systems in use.

Presentation Drawings

Presentation drawings are made to give the basic information about a building in an attractive form. They omit almost all details, such as dimensions, heating, and plumbing. They usually consist of the floor plan, site planting details, and a front and side elevation drawn in great detail, with shrubs and walks artistically presented. The building could be presented in perspective. Occasion-

Fig. 782. A detailed two-point perspective of the office. (General Electric Co.)

Fig. 783. Two-point perspective of kitchen and adjoining family room. (Revco, Inc.)

Fig. 784. Rendered interior perspective of kitchen and family area. (Better Kitchens Institute)

ally, a section through the building is required. Presentation drawings may give some data in table form, such as square feet or cubic feet in each room and for the total building. Some drawings show furniture on the floor plan.

The exterior and interior walls of the floor plan usually are drawn as solid lines. The lines for exterior walls are drawn thicker than those for interior walls. Other lines on the floor plan are thinner so they do not compete with the room layout.

The elevation or perspective is rendered in color, and all the drawings commonly are placed on one sheet. The paper usually is of heavy, high-quality, white stock that will take pencil, ink, or watercolors. Neat lettering is vital to an attractive presentation drawing.

Before the final drawing is made, careful consideration must be given to the placement of the various items on the page. The final arrangement should be balanced and attractive. The floor plan and perspective are the most important parts and should receive first consideration. Time should be spent deciding where to locate the lettering. Again, balance is necessary.

A common planning practice is to draw, in blocked-out form on separate sheets, the various parts to be included and, then, to arrange these in various ways on the display sheets. When a balanced, pleasing arrangement is reached, the final drawing can be done. A typical presentation drawing is shown in Fig. 786.

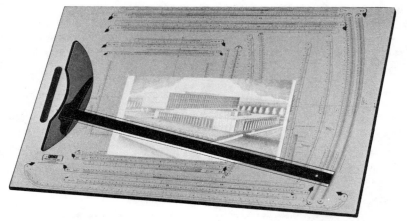

Fig. 785. A perspective drawing board. (John H. Klok and Bruning Division, Addressograph Multigraph Corp.)

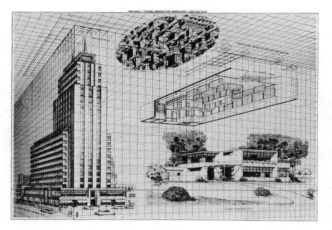

Fig. 785A. A perspective chart with several perspective drawings. (Graphic Indicator Co., Inc.)

Architectural Models

Scale models are the best means for presenting a proposed building or group of buildings to those who must approve the project. Models are also very useful in advertising and fund-raising campaigns. The effectiveness of the exterior design can be better determined from a three-dimensional, colored model.

The following discussion presents some of the common techniques used in model construction. In actual practice, the model builder is limited only by his skill and imagination. Companies that specialize in architectural model building face the problem of constructing high-quality models at a competitive price.

Of first consideration is the base upon which the model is to be built. Plywood and hardboard sheets are good. If the building site slopes, sheets of insulation board can be glued together, and the contours can be cut with a power disc sander. This material is easily shaped and painted. Since it has a rough texture, it represents grass very nicely when painted green. Felt flocking and blotter material also are used for grass.

The models are made to scale, and special attention must be given to details such as post lamps, cars, trees and shrubs, so they are in the same scale as the building. Most residential models are built to the scale $\frac{1}{4}'' = 1'\text{-}0''$ or $\frac{1}{8}'' = 1'\text{-}0''$. Commercial buildings are built to the scale $\frac{1}{8}'' = 1'\text{-}0''$, though very large projects frequently use $1/16'' = 1'\text{-}0''$ or $1/32'' = 1'\text{-}0''$. The designer must ascertain the size. Obviously, the larger the scale, the greater the amount of detail that can be included.

The building shell can be constructed of almost any convenient material. Heavy cardboard and thin balsa sheets are most frequently used. These are glued together or taped on the inside.

Exterior details such as siding and windows can be represented in a number of ways. Paper sheets are available, with bricks,

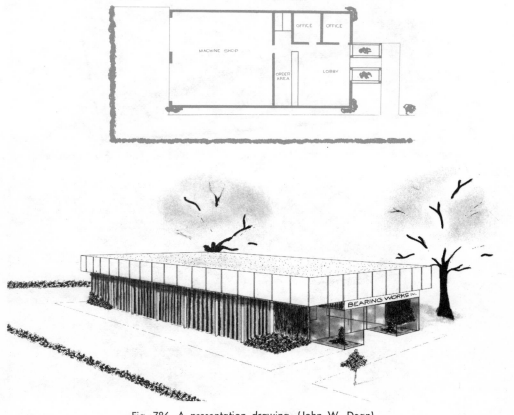

Fig. 786. A presentation drawing. (John W. Dean)

Apartment house rendering. (Garlinghouse Co., Inc.)

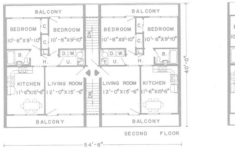 

Apartment floor plan. (Garlinghouse Co., Inc.)

A-frame rendering. (Home Planners, Inc.)

An architectural model of a large apartment building. (Joseph M. Seiler)

An architectural model of a portion of the Chicago, Illinois lake front. (Joseph M. Seiler)

An architectural model of a residence. (Joseph M. Seiler)

An office building exhibiting a natural character that relates it to its setting. (Western Wood Products Association)

A view of the office and warehouse of a building products supply company. (Butler Manufacturing Co.)

A massive roof and strong vertical support gives this bank a substantial appearance. (Butler Manufacturing Co.)

The office portion of a building products supply company. (Butler Manufacturing Co.)

Architectural sculpture is used to identify this medical building. (Feathercock, Inc.)

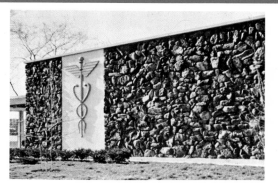

Attractive building for studio and merchandising area for interior design. (Butler Manufacturing Co.)

A steel framed office building with native stone exterior. (Butler Manufacturing Co.)

A manufacturing company office and plant. (Butler Manufacturing Co.)

stone and other siding materials printed upon them. Also, printed, paper or plastic sheets with windows, doors and roof shingles are sold. These are simply cut out and glued on. They are available from model shops supplying materials to model-railroad enthusiasts.

The siding materials and windows also can be indicated by simply drawing them on cardboard walls in black ink, much the same as the building elevations are drawn. These can be colored with watercolors to add realism.

Balsa sheets can be lightly scored with a knife, to give a feeling of depth to siding. Small strips can be glued on to form batten strips, and shutters can be drawn and glued on to add shadow lines.

Thin, opaque plastic can be used to represent porcelain enamel or colored-glass panels, and clear plastic can be used for windows and plate-glass, window walls.

Sheets of sandpaper make a good roofing material. For tar-and-gravel roofs, the entire sheet can be cemented in place. If a shingle roof is to be represented, the sandpaper sheet works well; however, some persons prefer to cut it into strips and glue it on, overlapping it to give the shadow-line appearance of shingles. Either balsa or wood veneer can be cut and glued on to represent wood shingles effectively, but it is a tedious task. Tar-and-gravel roofs can be further formed by gluing on finely crushed gravel or seeds, such as bird seed.

Wood can be stained with oil stain to represent redwood or other natural siding. Sidewalks and driveways can be painted on the base material. Gravel walks and patios can be made by gluing seeds or other such materials to the base.

Trees and shrubs can be purchased from model shops, or they can be hand made. Trees can be easily and economically made from dried twigs and weeds. The bare twigs can represent trees in winter, or they can be covered with sponge material or yarn to represent leaves. Small shrubs can be made from sponges. Thin wire stems with steel wool foliage painted green also can form attractive shrubs and small trees.

Wire can be used for railings and post lamps. Again, the thickness of the wire should be in scale with the entire building.

Plaster of paris is useful for walks, patios, stone walls and pools.

The coloring of models should be carefully considered. Watercolors and tempera paints frequently are used. Care should be taken that the colors used are not so intense that they appear unnatural. Few buildings are fire-engine red or sky blue. Very light tints are more lifelike and do not obscure other details that may be drawn on the walls.

Figs. 787 through 791 illustrate models of projects of varying sizes.

Fig. 787. A model of an urban renewal project for the Central Englewood District, Chicago, Illinois. Notice that most of the details of the buildings are omitted. The scale is 1″ =50″. (Solomon and Cordwell, Architects; Model by Callaghan-Seiler, South Haven, Michigan.

Fig. 788. A model of a one-story building designed to house an auto sales and service company. Notice the use of scale autos to enhance the overall scene. The scale is 1″=8′-0″. (J. G. Doverman, Architect; Model by Callaghan-Seiler, South Haven, Michigan)

Rendering Architectural Drawings

Architectural renderings are attempts to express the concepts of the architect in a form that people can understand and accept. Their purpose is to make clear to the viewer the ideas and plans that only the architect visualizes. They are more effective in imparting his ideas than are models or black-and-white elevations, because they relate the building not only to the site but to the areas surrounding the site. Color is vital to expressing the complete experience.

Fig. 789. A model of the Education Building, Western Michigan University, Kalamazoo, Michigan. Notice the use of trees and shrubs to place the building in its natural surroundings. Scale 1″=32′-0″. (Louis C. Kingscott and Associates, Architects; Model by Callaghan-Seiler, South Haven, Michigan)

The rendering provides the viewer with an honest representation of the building in its environment. This usually involves mature plantings and activities that are consistent with the building and its purpose.

The view represented is three dimensional, and shapes, masses and voids must be expressed to achieve this result. The use of texture, light, shadows and color is essential to the expression.

Buildings are composed of masses. Usually one large mass represents the basic structure, and smaller secondary masses contribute to the design. These must be recognized in a rendering and properly represented.

All surfaces have texture. These must be properly represented to give honest expression to the ideas of the architect. The more complex the surface treatment, the more attention attracted. Various methods are used to represent materials and textures. See Fig. 792. Textures must be represented in three-dimensional form, as are the masses of the building. Voids, such as windows and doors, also influence the representation of the structure. They can be made an important feature of design, or they can be minimized to be unimportant openings in the mass of the building. Methods of drawing are shown in Fig. 793.

The composition of a rendering is much like that used in painting composition. It serves to control eye movement. The primary function is to arrange the parts of the picture so as to direct the attention upon the build-

Fig. 790. A model of the Riksha Inn, Chun King Corp. The outstanding feature is the great detail involved. Scale 1″=4′-0″. (C. Everett Thorsen, Architect; Model by Callaghan-Seiler, South Haven, Michigan)

Fig. 791. A model of a contemporary home with fine detail. Notice the chimney, plastic bubble skylights, window mullions and stair details. Scale 1″=8′-0″. (Fred and William Keck, Architects; Model by Callaghan-Seiler, South Haven, Michigan)

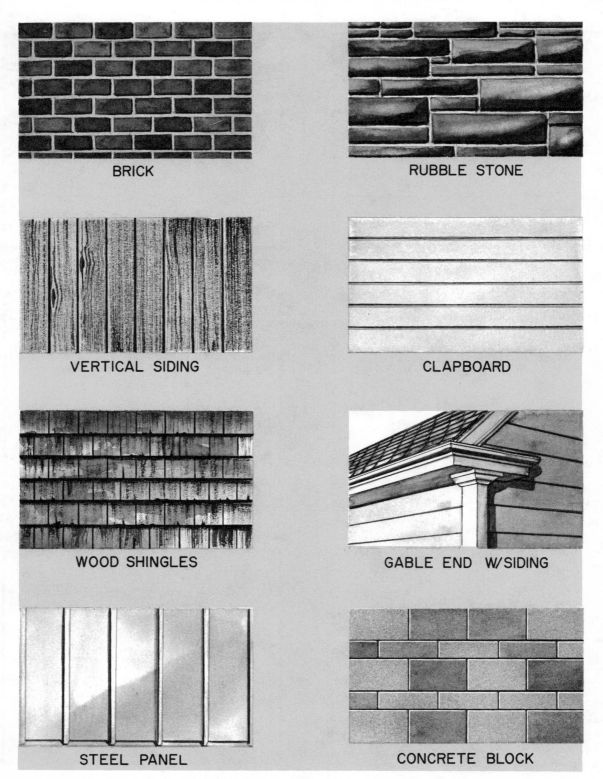

Fig. 792. Methods of representing material texture. Notice how the shading creates the illusion of roughness or smoothness.

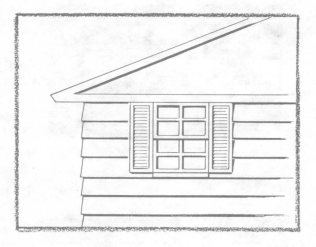
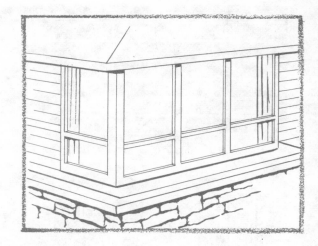
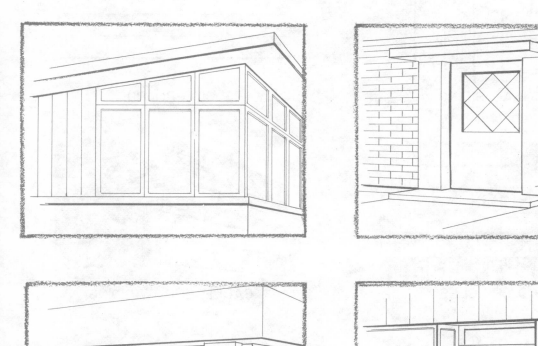

Fig. 793. Typical ways of drawing doors and windows on renderings. Notice the feeling of depth developed.

ELM

PINE

MAPLE

OAK

POPLAR

WILLOW

BIRCH

FIR

CEDAR

SHRUBBERY

Fig. 794. Methods of representing selected trees and shrubs.

ing. This is done by using shapes and lines of various weights and colors. The degree of darkness or lightness (value) of the color determines the strength of the stimulus that attracts the eye.

The trained illustrator, when he relates the elements of an architectural rendering, uses repetition, continuity, direction, rhythm, phrasing, balance, counterpoint, harmony, contrast, dynamic placement, tension and transition to develop meaning in the rendering and to give emphasis or direction.

The effectiveness of a rendering can be increased by the use of shadows. This is a rather difficult subject, and entire books have been devoted to the topic. A satisfactory approach is to estimate the extent and location of the shadows. To do this, a decision must be made concerning the location and direction of the sun. Usually the sun's rays are assumed to be coming from the right front of the building at a 45-degree angle; however, they can come from any direction. The suggested angle enables roof overhangs and porches to cast a shadow on the walls of the house. Practice in achieving a realistic appearance is necessary. Again, a study of finished renderings is helpful as a guide.

Colors must be carefully used. One frequent failing is to use colors that are too brilliant or that are abnormal for a building. The building should draw the attention of the viewer, and the colors on grass, trees and sky should be such that they do not dominate the scene.

Trees and shrubs should be used only to provide a normal and proper setting for the building and should be secondary to the building itself. They should not be drawn in careful detail, nor should an attempt be made to show the thousands of branches and leaves. For best results, trees and shrubs should be grouped. Most landscape gardeners do this as they design the plantings. Examine finished renderings or specialized books for methods of representing trees and shrubs. Selected examples are shown in Fig. 794.

Preliminary Layout

While there are numerous ways to make architectural renderings, the most successful for the beginner is to make the perspective of just the building on tracing paper. When this is completed, a second sheet of tracing paper can be placed over the perspective, and the details of the foreground, middle ground and background (such as trees, shrubs, parking areas and mountains) can be drawn. In this way, the details can be erased and changed without damaging the perspective sketch. It is also possible to draw many settings for the building, each on a separate sheet, without disturbing the building perspective. The importance of making many preliminary sketches cannot be overemphasized. After satisfactory drawings have been sketched, they are traced upon illustration board. This is a heavy cardboard upon which the final rendering is drawn and colored.

When the perspective is drawn on the tracing paper, most details should be made freehand. Renderings should not have a mechanical appearance. This especially is important on details, such as windows and shutters.

Careful consideration must be given to the overall picture to be presented. Basic to this is the placement of the objects on the sheet. While most perspectives of small buildings are drawn from eye level (Fig. 795), some buildings appear well from other positions. A rendering can be made from any position desired. Large buildings or groups of buildings, as in a shopping center, frequently are more attractive and descriptive if viewed from above and far away. This enables the artist to show the parking area, streets and other items of importance. It also gives a better picture of the entire plan. The final decision is up to the artist. See Figs. 796 and 797.

Fig. 795. This rendering makes effective use of shadows including that of the flag pole cast on the building. Human figures assist in establishing the size of the building. (American Institute of Architects, Kansas City Chapter)

Placement on the sheet involves consideration of three areas — the foreground, middle ground and background. The building should be placed so each of these areas is pleasing and related to the others. If one area is more important to explaining the building, it should receive a larger proportion of the drawing. At all times the building should be the center of importance. See Fig. 798.

The eye level should always be into the background. The sky should never be the eye level.

The building should be drawn large enough to fill the sheet, yet space should be allowed around it for the foreground, middle ground and background. The building should not appear cramped on the sheet. Usually a low view requires more space at the sides than a high view does. The building should be placed above or below the center of the sheet. Most artists prefer to place large buildings below center and small ones above center. Remember the building is between the foreground and the background; therefore, these should appear to relate to the structure.

As the surroundings are rendered, they appear more spacious than usually is expected. It is suggested that the surroundings be fully rendered and their extent be reduced by matting the rendering exactly the same as a painting.

The rendering should give a feeling of balance, but should not be symmetrical. Seldom are building surroundings symmetrical, and such a rendering appears unnatural.

Matting a Rendering

Matting involves framing the rendering in a heavy cardboard frame. The material used is matt board, and it is available in white and pastel colors. The matt frame should be kept a constant width at the top, left and right sides of the rendering, but slightly wider at the bottom. This tends to give the rendering a base.

Black and White Illustrations

As a preliminary to the use of color in architectural renderings, work with black and white. These shades produce striking illustrations that can be varied considerably in effect. Black is used for all dark values and white

Fig. 797. An architectural rendering of an apartment complex. Notice how the high viewpoint enables the artist to relate the project with the surrounding area. (American Institute of Architects, Kansas City Chapter)

Fig. 796. A rendering of a school showing the relationship between buildings, parking areas, tennis courts and athletic fields. Notice that background shows no sky. (American Institute of Architects, Kansas City Chapter)

Fig. 798. In this rendering, the building is located below the center of the page and is framed with trees on each side. The street plus the trees directs the eye upon the building. (American Institute of Architects, Kansas City Chapter)

for all light. Any of several mediums can be used, including pencil, ink, charcoal, pastels, watercolors and acrylic polymer emulsion paints. The grading of the values on the surfaces further increases the variety of effects possible. See Fig. 799 for selected examples.

Principles of Light and Shade

When an object is subjected to rays of light, that portion receiving the light is highlighted and tends to reflect the light, while the shaded portion tends to be darker. The farther the surface from the light, the darker it is because it reflects less light.

Fig. 799. Black and white illustrations — notice the different visual reaction to each, caused by varying the values of the black.

The shape of the surface influences the amount of light reflected and the shape of the reflected area. Fig. 800 illustrates this for selected basic shapes. On the sphere, notice that the reflected area is round and the shade becomes darker as the edges are approached.

The size of the reflected area is influenced by the shape of the object. Notice the cone. The base reflects a greater amount of light than any other part because it is larger in diameter; on the cylinder, the reflected area is approximately the same for the entire length. These simple observations are of great value in increasing the effectiveness of architectural renderings. Details such as shrubs and windows should be highlighted to give a natural appearance.

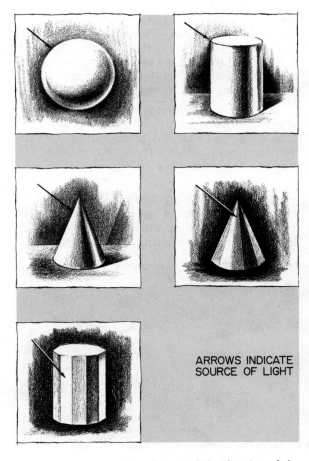

ARROWS INDICATE
SOURCE OF LIGHT

Fig. 800. The shape of an object and the direction of the light source influence the areas that are highlighted and shaded. As the light source (indicated by the arrow) moves, the area highlighted also moves.

Color Media

The most successful renderings are made by using a variety of media. The most used have been *watercolors*. Watercolors are easily diluted for varying value and intensity, and they can be intermixed to change the hue.

Colored inks are also useful. Because they dry fast, they are more difficult to use for large areas of color. However, they are especially useful for small details and can be used under or over watercolors.

Pastel sticks (similar to chalk) are extremely useful for coloring large areas. The sticks can be sharpened to a point for drawing lines of various widths. To color large areas, rub the stick over sandpaper and pick up the powder on a piece of cotton. Rub the cotton over the area to be colored. Graduations in value are easily obtained in this way.

A rough-surfaced, heavy paper is best for pastels, but a surface such as common artist's tracing paper accepts the pastel very well. Interesting effects can be achieved on rough-textured materials.

When the rendering is colored with pastel sticks, it should be sprayed with a clear fixative after it is completed, to prevent smearing. If watercolor and pastel sticks are to be used on the same rendering, apply the watercolor first, then the pastel, then the fixative.

If a grayed-color tone is desired, the pastel stick can be used on the reverse side of the tracing sheet. The tracing paper tends to gray the intensity of the color.

A kneaded eraser (eraser material that is similar to a putty) is an indispensible tool when using pastels. It can be shaped to a point, and small areas can be removed from the rendering to add "life" to the finished job. Examples of this are mortar joints, reflections, and highlights in a window. For straight lines, draw the eraser along the edge of a ruler.

Water-soluble paints of an *Acrylic polymer emulsion* type are excellent for rendering. They dry fast and will not smudge and wash off with water. They can be diluted with water for variations in value and are applied with a brush, as are watercolors.

The beginner can probably achieve the most satisfactory results using pastel sticks. They are easily handled and are available in sets representing the entire spectrum of colors.

It is advisable to consult art instructors for assistance in handling these materials.

The Use of Values

One major problem in rendering is to make the building stand out from the surroundings, so it can be seen and understood at a glance. The use of *value* (light and dark) or color is the means for doing this. In Fig. 801, the use of value is illustrated. At *A* the outline of the building is shown. Notice that this has little to attract attention. If the building is made of a light-colored material, it should remain light, and the surroundings should be darkened, as shown at *B*. A dark building usually is contrasted against a light background, as shown at *C*. If the end of the building is in the shade, it will appear as at *D*, and if the front is in the shade, it will appear as at *E*. The shaded portion immediately stands out against the light background, and the other portion loses prominence. None of these is sufficient to stand alone and must be combined to give the desired attention. At *F* the light front is against a dark background. Immediately, the light front attracts attention. At *G* the light end becomes prominent.

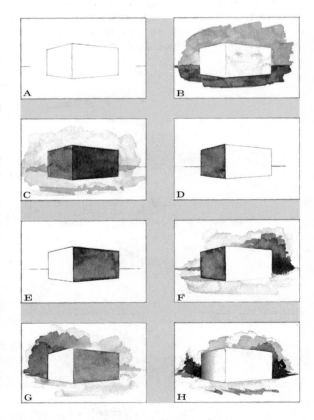

Fig. 801. Several of many possible uses of value.

The surfaces of the building to be darkened can be graded rather than simply dark or light. At *H* the end of the building is graded and the front is light. There are unlimited variations of value, and the artist must decide upon the value that does the best job.

An expansion of the use of value is shown in Fig. 802. At *A* the building outline is shown. At *B* the roof is dark, thus becoming the center of attention. At *C* an end has been graded; the roof is still prominent. At *D* a darkened foliage and foreground direct attention to the light front. The variations of this are many, but the principles of the use of value apply as seen at *E* and *F*. The artist must try to represent the building as clearly and as advantageously as possible.

As an excellent practice piece, obtain a photograph of a building, lay tracing paper over it and sketch the major outlines. Then experiment by using light and dark tones and graded shading. See Fig. 803.

The Use of Hue and Intensity

Hue refers to the quality of a color that enables the viewer to distinguish it from other colors. It is the name we give to a color, such as blue hue or red hue. Hue can be changed by adding another color; for example, yellow can be added to red to produce an orange hue.

If one hue is brought against another, even if they are similar hues, contrast exists. The more dissimilar these hues are, the greater the contrast. The farther apart the hues are on the color wheel in Fig. 804, the more dissimilar they appear. *Analogous colors* (colors near each other on the color wheel) are less useful to the artist making a rendering than *complementary colors* (colors opposite each other on the color wheel), because he is trying to build contrasts as a means of emphasizing a building. For example, a red-brick building can be brought into prominence by making a background of green trees, shrubs and lawn. The green is complementary to the red (opposite it on the

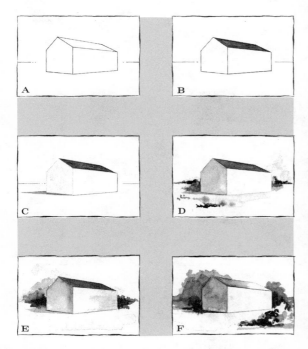

Fig. 802. The use of color value is expanded as a rendering is developed.

Fig. 803. Use of shading and value to vary building rendering. The photograph shows the actual appearance of the building. The drawing illustrates how the artist can vary the shading and value to present the building at a different time of day.

color wheel). If the same building were surrounded with a yellow-orange sky and brown foreground, it would lose much of its prominence.

An architectural rendering can accommodate very little color of full intensity. (*Intensity* refers to the strength of the color.) Intensity can be changed without changing value or hue by adding neutral gray of equal value. Intense color may be used on small portions of a rendering to call attention to a particular detail.

Complementary Color Schemes

While architectural renderings sometimes are done in analogous color schemes, the most used are the complementary schemes. They greatly aid in developing contrast and are more natural. Nature uses complements such as the red rose on the green bush. The proper use of complementary colors produces a harmonious picture. If contrast is uncontrolled, harmony is destroyed.

When a color scheme for a rendering is selected, one color should dominate. Never should a color scheme be based on complementary colors used in equal areas and full strengths. If an area is to be one color, such as red, then its complement, green, should be used in a smaller area or should be neutralized so it is not the same strength as the red.

A simple, yet effective, use of complementary colors is to use two — one warm and one cool. These usually are not used in full intensity. For example, portions could be done in orange with combinations of yellow and brown, while other areas could be in blue with green and violet indications. The cool colors complement the warm and are less assertive.

A person trained in the use of color can successfully use color schemes of a complementary nature in which the colors used are not exact opposites on the color wheel, but are near opposites. For example, green is the true opposite of red, but yellow-green and blue-green are near opposites and can be used effectively in complementary schemes.

Build Your Vocabulary

Following are words that you should understand and use as a part of your working vocabulary. Write a brief explanation of what each means.

Color value
Color wheel
Rendering
Matting
Perspective
Station point
Vanishing point
Horizon
Model
Hue
Intensity
Analogous colors
Complementary colors

Class Activities

1. Secure pictures of houses and small commercial buildings which show the front elevation. Catalogs of manufacturers of precut and factory-built homes are excellent sources. Draw, in two-point perspective, several of these houses. Draw one with the station point 6'-0" above the horizon and the house at an angle of 30 degrees to the picture plane. Lay a piece of paper over this perspective and draw another perspective with the station point 30 feet above the ground line. Notice the difference in appearance.

2. Try shading one of these perspectives in black and white. Use ink or a black pastel stick.

3. On another perspective try color. Use watercolors, followed by pastel sticks; then spray a fixative over this.

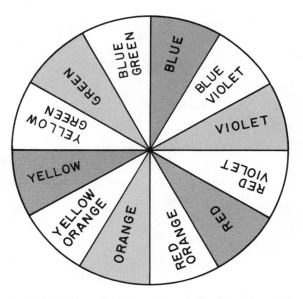

Fig. 804. A color wheel from which analogous and complementary colors can be chosen.

4. Practice drawing trees and shrubs. On another perspective drawing, attempt to place these to frame the building and direct attention to it.

5. Construct a model of a house or small commercial building. Include as much detail as you have time and skill to include. Since this is time-consuming, much of it could be done after school and at home.

6. Secure a photograph of a building. Place a sheet of tracing paper over it and copy the outline and details. With a soft pencil or pastel stick, render it to give an appearance different from the photo. Vary the amount of light on the building or the direction of the sun. Vary the degree of darkness of the surroundings (value). This could be repeated on other sheets until you have several different sketches of the same house. Notice how the variance of light and dark changes the atmosphere and character of the house.

7. Make a color wheel by mixing watercolors and painting these in the proper places. Secure an art book with a color wheel in it and use it for a guide. Consult your art instructor or an art book for proportions. Perhaps the art instructor could demonstrate this process for your class.

8. Prepare a report on the use of color on buildings in your neighborhood. Cite examples of buildings making good use of color in relating the walls, roof and trim. Explain why these are good. Cite examples of misuse of color and what could be done to improve the appearance of these buildings. Learn to look at your surroundings critically.

9. Make a display drawing of a building. Make the perspective in color and the remainder in black ink.

10. Mat your best rendering by framing it with a heavy, white or pastel matt board.

11. Try a group project. If your class is designing a shopping center or cluster of homes, prepare models of these and place them on a large base, showing roads, sidewalks and trees. Model automobiles and figures enhance such a display. This could be a project for the entire class, with each person completing a portion of it. Arrange to have this displayed in your school lobby and in show windows of local stores.

12. With the permission of your instructor, invite an architect or illustrator to speak to your class concerning renderings and to show examples of his work.

Additional Reading

Birren, Faber, *Color, Form and Space.*

———, *Creative Color.*

———, *The Story of Color.*

Choate, Chris, *Architectural Presentation in Opaque Watercolor.*

Guptill, Arthur, *Color in Sketching and Rendering.*

Hollis, Harold F., *Teach Yourself Perspective Drawing.*

Kautzky, Theodore, *Pencil Broadsides.*

Limback, Russell T., *American Trees.*

Norling, Ernest, *Perspective Made Easy.*

Salwey, Jasper, *Sketching in Lead-Pencil; for Architects and Others.*

Turner, William W., *Shades and Shadows: Their Use in Architectural Rendering.*

Watson, Ernest W., *How to Use Creative Perspective.*

PLANNING SMALL COMMERCIAL BUILDINGS

The planning of a commercial building requires the services of someone who is thoroughly familiar with the many demands of the business or industry involved as well as with the structural design of commercial buildings. Some of the basic planning considerations are introduced here.

As a beginning, the designer should carefully study and record all the activities that must take place in a building. These space needs can be rather simple, as in a barber shop, or extremely complex, as in a retail merchandising facility. For example, the latter establishment could require a receiving area, shipping area, sales area, display area, office area, lounge and rest room area and eating area. Each of these areas, in turn, requires many planning considerations.

Establishing the proper relationship between activities in the building is very important. Much time, effort and money can be saved if a proper relationship is obtained. For example, if a clerk is to check invoices for merchandise received and is to transfer these to another clerk who prepares them for payment, certainly these employees should have adjacent work areas. If the receiving clerk must walk across the office to consult the paying clerk, the company is losing money due to wasted time.

The designer must determine what equipment will be housed in the building so that he can plan for this in his design. This involves load on the building structure, space in which to place the equipment so it functions properly, utility connections and a means for

servicing any machines. Equipment could vary from a barber chair to an electronic data processing unit.

Other considerations may involve materials receiving, product shipping, flow of work through the establishment, customers' reactions as they enter a store, getting the most usable floor space for the least money, reduction of interior and exterior maintenance, reasonable operating costs for such items as heating and cooling, and space considerations for aisles, work stations, display and sales.

The newest developments and trends in the business should be considered. For example, are more stores using self-service? Do more people want larger apartments? Has data processing equipment changed office practices and office planning?

The structural design of the building influences interior design and planning. For example, the placement of columns definitely limits the interior planning. If wide, unbroken spaces are essential, as in a warehouse or bowling alley, the designer must consider structure along with interior design.

Exterior appearance definitely influences those who approach a building, and this effect must be considered. An exclusive retail establishment such as a jewelry shop, of necessity, must present a different exterior than a warehouse. An increase in the amount spent on the exterior is justified, for it is a necessary part of attracting customers and influencing business.

Interior appearance and materials used vary widely, depending upon the type of business. A theater requires materials for acoustical control. On the other hand, a warehouse requires tough, durable interior walls; frequently, the interior surface of the exterior wall is all that is needed for such a building. The designer should be familiar with interior finish materials and their applications. A gypsum-board wall would not last very long in a warehouse, but would serve adequately in an apartment or motel.

The designer must do much reading and studying of books and articles pertaining to the type of business to be housed. Visits to such establishments are helpful for client and architect. Business managers can tell what they like and dislike about their present building and what they would do "if they could build again."

It is important for anyone designing buildings that will be occupied by the public to check state laws pertaining to liability of the designer. In general, such buildings must have an architectural "stamp of approval."

One other important planning factor is the local building code for commercial buildings. This varies considerably from area to area and sometimes may limit design and construction. Often the use of certain materials is barred from use in buildings occupied by the public. For example, open-web steel trusses have been used successfully for years in multistory structures, but are still prohibited in some cities. The following major divisions are commonly found in building codes: special occupancy requirements, height; floor area restrictions and street encroachments; light and ventilation; means of egress; types of construction; design loads; chimneys, flues and vents; heating, ventilating, air conditioning, blower and exhaust systems; safeguards during construction; elevators, dumbwaiters, moving stairways and amusement devices; gas piping and plumbing; electrical installations; and signs and outdoor display structures.

Chapters 13 through 18 present some planning details for a selected variety of small commercial buildings. These suggestions are in no way complete, but should be of some assistance to the designer.

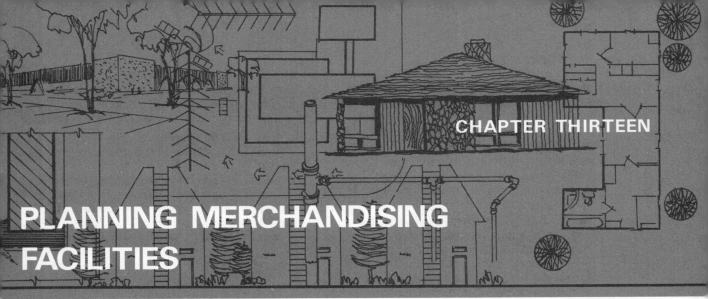

PLANNING MERCHANDISING FACILITIES

Each type of retail merchandising facility has special requirements that must be considered during the planning and designing phase. The planner should visit with those experienced in operating such a store and find out how the business is carried on, the best ways to display merchandise and the details of store operation. A study of the customer should be made to ascertain his buying habits and desired services, what attracts attention and lures him into the store and what things help close a sale. The planner is interested not only in the inside of the store, but in the outside as well. The entire facility should be planned as an integral unit.

A successful store requires careful consideration of three major elements: (1) a sales area that is efficient and attractive, (2) service areas, such as a storage area for merchandise or an area in which to move items to the sales area and (3) an exterior design that will attract customers into the store.

Following are general principles of planning which should be considered when planning retail merchandising outlets. Special planning considerations for selected types of stores then follow the general principles.

An Efficient and Attractive Sales Area

Since the major measure of effectiveness of store planning is the sales record, the area in which goods are displayed and sales are concluded is the heart of the merchandising facility. All other areas exist only to facilitate the sale. The following general principles apply to planning the sales area:

1. The merchandise to be sold must be known before planning can begin. Merchandise is grouped into three types — impulse, convenience and demand. *Impulse merchandise* usually consists of luxury items or items dependent upon good display for sale. Such items usually are not sought after, but are bought by those who, upon seeing them, suddenly decide they want one. Scarves, jewelry and cosmetics are impulse items.

   Convenience merchandise consists of standard items that are popular and much used, such as sheets, food or medicine.

   Demand merchandise involves necessities that bring many people shopping. Customers look especially for these items. Men's suits, furniture and appliances are demand items.

2. Some stores specialize in one type of item; for instance, a novelty shop mainly carries impulse items. In general, most stores predominately stock demand merchandise, with some impulse and convenience items. A person experienced in merchandising should classify items into their sales types for the person planning the store layout.

3. Demand merchandise usually is located far away from the entrance, since customers generally will persist until they find it.

4. Convenience merchandise usually is located midway between the entrance and the demand merchandise.

351

5. Impulse items are located near the store entrances. Here all customers pass them when they enter and leave the store. Much impulse merchandise is sold to demand and convenience buyers.

6. Customer traffic in the store must be carefully planned. Easy access from the store entrance to all sales sections is necessary.

7. Usually the store is divided into shopping areas, with each area, in actuality, becoming a small specialty shop. For example, one area in a department store may be devoted to men's clothing while another may display jewelry. These areas are reached by aisles. See Fig. 825.

8. Each specialty area should be planned as a separate shop, and the entire store plan should be developed by attractively grouping these areas.

9. The size and location of shopping aisles depends upon the size of the store and the type of merchandise. Most small retail outlets use one single, straight, center aisle extending the length of the store. If the store is fairly large, minor aisles should branch from the main aisle. In very large stores, several main shopping aisles may be used, with many minor aisles. In stores with heavy traffic in the main aisle, the minor aisles become the sales aisles, and the main aisle simply carries traffic.

10. The two patterns frequently used for placing aisles are the block system (or some variation) and the free-flow system.

The *block system* is illustrated in Fig. 826, top. It fits well with the columns in the structural system and frequently is used, but it has many disadvantages. Often it forces the customer to go out of his way to the elevator or stairs. More importantly, it provides little flexibility. Some sales areas need more floor space

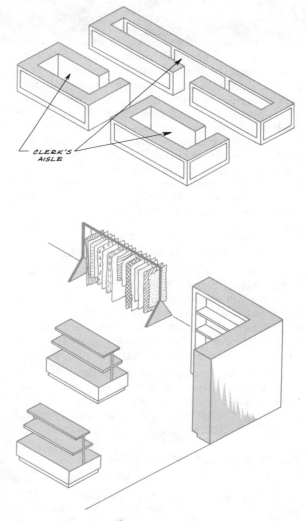

CLERK'S AISLE

Fig. 826. Block and free-flow arrangements of fixtures.

Top: Block plan. Arrangement is frozen, since standard fixture is used to display all types of merchandise. Considerable space is consumed by the clerks' aisle inside the fixture.

Bottom: Free-flow arrangement. Rearrangement of displays is easily accomplished. Fixtures are designed to display merchandise. No space is devoted to a clerks' aisle.

Fig. 825. Observe the division of merchandise into small departments or specialty areas. In the foreground is a seasonal display, with the steady demand items to the side and rear of the store.

than others. This is difficult to arrange with the block system. It also is difficult to rearrange fixtures and display seasonal merchandise.

11. The *free-flow system* also is illustrated in Fig. 826. Almost all trace of the block system of aisles is gone. Traffic can flow easily from area to area. Fixture design can be highly imaginative and flexible. Displays can be changed easily, and particular sales areas can receive more floor space during their sales season. Certainly, the space devoted to swimming suits in the summer should be adaptable to another use in the winter. Gloves and scarves can be displayed in this area merely by removing, adding or rearranging fixtures. This system is recommended for most effective and economical use of space.

12. Aisle width should be determined by the capacity of the store entrances and the flow of people to them from elevators and stairs. The width of a main aisle usually is from 6'-0'' to 11'-0'', and minor aisles from 3'-0'' to 4'-0''. Aisles for clerks need be only 2'-0'' wide, unless additional space is needed for opening deep drawers or other display or storage devices.

13. If a store has more than one level, stairs and elevators or escalators are necessary. If the store has only two levels, stairs usually are satisfactory; however, some mechanical means of vertical transportation is necessary for three or more stories.

14. Stairs, escalators and elevators must be carefully planned as a part of the traffic system. They must be easily accessible. Their width usually is determined by local building codes. In addition, they influence the placement of certain types of merchandise, so it may be viewed by the customer as he ascends or descends.

15. Stairs in small stores usually are located at the end of the building away from the entrance. This forces the customer to pass many sales areas, thus exposing him to considerable merchandise.

16. Escalators and stairs in large stores usually are located in the center of the sales area. This draws the customer to the center of the store, regardless of the entrance he may use.

17. Escalators are installed in pairs. One unit handles the upward traffic and the other the down traffic. The number of units and their width depend upon the anticipated number of people expected to use them.

18. To insure even traffic flow and to get maximum use from the units, only one bank of elevators or escalators should be provided. Second sections located in another part of the store usually do not carry an equal share of the load.

19. The interior of a store should reflect the type of merchandise for sale. A food store should give this impression rather than the impression that it is a hardware store. Some food stores handle a considerable variety of merchandise, but it should be so displayed that it does not change the customer's reaction when he enters. If many things are sold in a store, such as a department store, each sales area should clearly reflect what it has for sale.

20. The atmosphere desired for the various sales areas should be considered. An area devoted to toys frequently has a carnival air, while expensive silver or furs require a quiet, restful atmosphere. This influences the location of the sales areas on the floor plan. Bargain areas or noisy sales areas should be carefully located so they do not disturb those areas requiring quieter surroundings.

21. Sales areas that feature related merchandise should be conveniently near one another. Men's ties should be close to the shirt area, and paint brushes near the paint. Again, merchandising experience is valuable in making decisions pertaining to relationship.

22. If sales areas are on more than one floor, special attention should be given to the needs and demands of customers. For example, if lamps are sold with furniture on the second floor, the shades should not be on the first floor.

23. A good view over the entire store from any point is necessary. This increases the store's attractiveness and helps the customer locate the area he desires. High fixtures tend to block the overall view of the store.

24. Merchandising research has shown that most people turn to the right when they enter a store. This should be considered

when planning sales areas. Attractive aisles to the left should be planned to pull some people that way.

25. The planning of each sales area on the total sales floor includes not only a consideration of the area in which to contact the customer and make the sale, but also a consideration of how much merchandise will be on display before the public and how much will be kept in reserve stock on the floor. The section of this discussion on service areas considers this in detail.

Merchandise Display Equipment

The sales areas also need effective means of displaying merchandise. This can be counters, racks, platforms or any other similar device. Display fixtures can be used to store, protect and display merchandise; however, few fixtures ever are able to serve all three functions at the same time. The merchandise to be handled determines which function will be emphasized. Jewelry cases usually combine all three, while less expensive merchandise is stored and displayed, but not protected.

26. A decision must be made concerning means of display. For example, what merchandise should be left open for customers to handle and serve themselves and what should be kept out of sight in storage rooms? In exclusive clothing stores, the clerk selects the items to be shown the customer. In contrast, other stores may display the entire selection on open racks, permitting the customer to personally go through the entire stock on the floor.

27. Display fixtures should enable the maximum amount of merchandise to be available and seen, yet should not appear overcrowded.

28. Fixtures should be simple and unobtrusive. Their purpose is to display the merchandise. If the fixture attracts attention to itself, it detracts from the merchandise and reduces sales. The design of fixtures is a full-time occupation in itself.

29. Fixtures should be flexible in use and easily moved to permit rearrangement of the sales floor. They should occupy a minimum of space, yet display a maximum of merchandise.

30. Some fixtures are used entirely for storage purposes. The top of the fixture serves as a counter, and the merchandise is removed from the fixture by the clerk. Racks usually are used to store and display hanging items such as coats; a top over the rack protects the items from dust. Other items, such as lawnmowers or large appliances, are displayed without fixtures.

31. Every display fixture should be designed to serve a particular type of merchandise. A store should not adopt a standard fixture of uniform size and height and then force merchandise to fit it.

32. Several types of fixtures are in common use — the island fixture, the wall fixture and the freestanding fixture. The *island fixture* is a counter completely surrounding an area; the clerk serves from inside the island. A section of storage units also may be inside. See Fig. 827. The *wall fixture* is placed against a wall or partition. It may have shelves to the floor or have a base cabinet for storage, with display shelves above. The *freestanding fixture* provides customer access from all sides. It may have storage in the lower section or have open display shelves to the floor.

33. As fixtures are being planned, the need for chairs, mirrors or tables should be considered. Such areas as shoe departments and millinery departments need these items.

34. Combined with fixtures and displays is the need for special utilities. A lamp department needs ample electrical outlets, while an appliance department needs water and sewer facilities.

35. Special facilities are needed to house the cash register and merchandise wrapping systems. Credit departments need a separate area. The type of fixtures used depends upon the system adopted.

36. After determining the size of the sales area needed for each specialty to be handled, the areas are related one to another, and aisles are planned to carry the customer traffic. Then the details of each specialty area must be planned. The merchandise in each area must be carefully related to facilitate sales. In a jewelry area, the location of watch sales and watch repair must be considered. The

planner must decide where to locate the sterling items, necklaces and rings. Again, a knowledge of sales techniques for the particular merchandise is important.

37. Some specialty departments are large enough to warrant consideration of aisle usage within the one department. Also, each specialty department should consider the impulse, convenience and demand items it has to display. Each sales area must be planned as carefully as is the entire sales floor and in more detail.

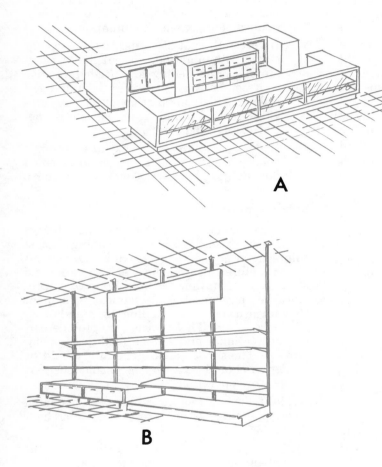

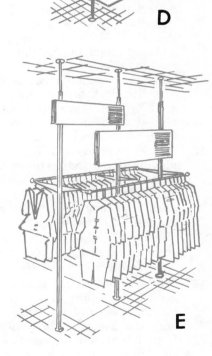

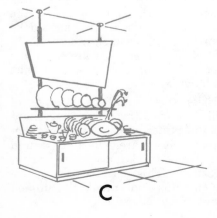

Fig. 827-A. An island fixture with a stock storage cabinet inside the island. The customer sales counter can have display below or be used for storage.

    B — A wall fixture with the display to the floor.

    C — A freestanding fixture with storage below.

    D — A freestanding fixture with no provision for storage.

    E — An open rack for clothing display.

Courtesy *Reflector Hardware Corp.*

Lighting

38. The type of lighting used in the sales area varies with the type of merchandise displayed. The lighting in a clothing area is quite different from that in a jewelry area. Since the placement of merchandise in the sales area varies from season to season, the lighting system must be highly flexible.

39. The primary purpose of lighting is to improve the display of merchandise. Lighting fixtures should not attract attention, since this detracts from the items displayed and reduces sales.

40. The sales area requires sufficient overall illumination to provide normal visibility in the store. More intense, special lighting should be used on displays to call attention to the merchandise.

41. Colors influence lighting practices. The material used behind dark-colored merchandise should be light, but not so light that there is a severe contrast between it and the merchandise. Since light-colored merchandise has a high value of light reflection, it should be displayed against a rather dark background. For example, a white enamel washer would not be displayed to maximum advantage against a light-colored wall.

42. Special lighting is built into fixtures displaying items that require high-intensity illumination. Jewelry shows up best in well-lighted display cases. It might be drab and unattractive if shown under general illumination.

43. For merchandise needing natural light, such as fabrics, daylight fluorescent fixtures frequently are used.

44. While the recommended footcandles needed for selling varies with the type of merchandise and the colors used, in general, the overall illumination should run from 25 to 100 footcandles. High-intensity, display lighting may be as much as 200 footcandles. Recommended footcandles can be obtained from architectural standards or lighting engineers' handbooks. Artificial light usually is preferred to natural light, since it is uniform and can be controlled easily.

45. The general illumination should be such that when the customer enters the store from the daylight, his eyes quickly and easily adjust to the light level inside the store.

46. The most effective and economical method of general illumination for a sales area is *direct illumination* from shielded or recessed light fixtures. This is a low-cost system. *Indirect lighting* is good for supplementary illumination, but is not economical for general illumination.

47. If recessed, spot-style lights are used for general illumination, special lights to illuminate the ceiling are needed to give contrast between the sales floor and the ceiling. This combination effectively provides general illumination as well as special display lighting.

48. Recessed fluorescent fixtures provide good general illumination, as do recessed floodlights. These are economical systems.

Service Areas

Service areas provide facilities for storage of merchandise, receiving incoming stock, shipping outgoing items, moving stock about in the store, behind-the-scene's work and store administration. In addition, they provide the space for the mechanical equipment that furnishes heating, cooling, light and other needed utilities. These areas also provide eating, recreational and lounge facilities for employees. The service areas generally should be hidden or should be a very inconspicuous part of the store operation.

The following factors should be considered when planning service areas for a merchandising facility.

1. A decision must be made early in the planning pertaining to the amount of reserve stock to be stored in the sales area to quickly replenish that sold from the display racks. Along with this should be a decision as to how much stock should be stored in larger storage areas on the same floor, but in storerooms hidden from public view.

2. The decision pertaining to storage of stock will vary with the type of merchandise and the philosophy of the merchandiser. Reserve stock areas located around the perimeter of the large sales floor generally are used. This permits easy access to stock and does not break the unified appearance of the sales floor.

3. The moving of merchandise to the sales floor should not interfere with the customer traffic patterns. The employee traffic patterns should be planned as carefully as those of the customers.

4. Outgoing merchandise also should be handled so it does not hamper sales.

5. Most merchandise is brought to and shipped from a store by truck. Facilities for docking, loading and unloading are necessary. This area should be completely separate from the entrances used by customers and from the customer parking areas. The service area for merchandise should be adjacent to this docking area. Large stores frequently have ramps into basement areas for trucks. Trucks should not have to extend into public streets when being unloaded.

6. It is advantageous if docking facilities can be under a roof to provide protection during inclement weather.

7. A conveyor belt is a good way to transfer items from the receiving dock to the service area where they are marked and put into stock.

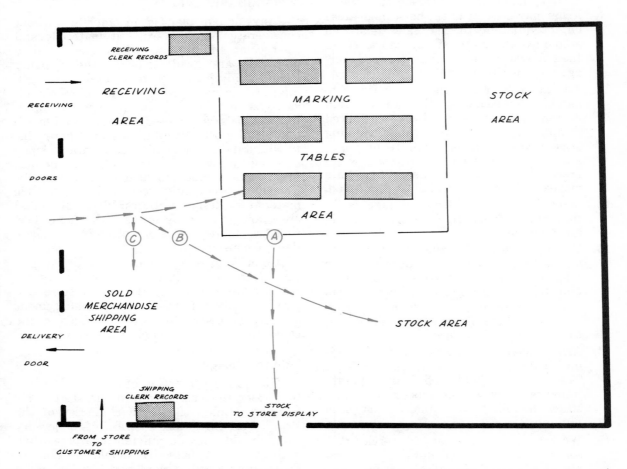

Fig. 828. This stock receiving, marking, storage and shipping area is only a suggested plan to show the activities normally carried on in such an area. The exact layout will vary considerably from store to store, depending upon the specific type of merchandise handled and the size of the store.

A — The merchandise is received and uncrated if it is to be put on display or sent to storage areas on the sales floor; it is marked and sent to the sales floor.

B — Other items might be received and placed in stock for future uncrating and marking.

C — Items may be received and immediately placed in the sold-merchandise, shipping area for delivery to waiting customers.

Various types of carts are used to move the merchandise. In large department stores, conveyor systems are used to transport items through this area. If the store is on several floors, freight elevators should be located in this area.

8. After merchandise is unloaded at the receiving dock, it should follow a predetermined traffic pattern as it is checked and marked, and then sent to storage, to the sales floor or to a customer. The receiving department needs tables, bins, racks and carts to facilitate this process. Fig. 828 illustrates a suggested receiving, marking, storage and shipping area.

9. If the store is on more than one level, freight elevators are needed to move merchandise.

10. Consideration should be given to having a large, supplemental storage area where items may be kept until the storage areas on, or adjacent to, the sales floor can accommodate more stock. Stock could then be transferred to these forward storage areas when needed.

11. Additional storage areas are needed to handle off-season stock that was not sold during the season or that is acquired during the off-season. Stores handling large items, such as furniture or appliances, frequently have a separate warehouse for remote storage; items are moved to the sales building as needed.

12. Some items need special storage facilities. Frozen foods, fresh flowers and furs are examples.

13. Usually merchandise that has been sold and is to be delivered is wrapped on the sales floor and then travels by some system to a shipping room. Large stores have a system of conveyors or chutes to transport these items. In small stores, carts frequently are used.

14. Arrangements are necessary for providing space for delivery trucks to load. This usually should be kept separate from the receiving area, especially in large stores handling merchandise that sells rapidly.

15. Workrooms are necessary for service personnel to perform their duties. For example, if a store does alterations or if displays and posters are made by store employees, work space must be provided for these operations. The office and executive staff require space to handle the store accounts and purchasing. Maintenance men need space for their equipment and supplies. Large stores frequently have lounges, sick wards and cafeterias for their many employees. Rest rooms are always a necessity.

16. Room is needed for the mechanical equipment used in heating, cooling and operating the store. The amount of space needed varies with the systems used and the size of the store. This area is vital, however, and cannot be neglected in overall planning.

17. Mechanical equipment in small stores usually is located in a basement area or at the rear of the ground floor.

Materials and Color

Any design plan is incomplete without consideration of the exposed materials and their color and texture. Many new building materials are available, and the designer should study manufacturers' catalogs to keep informed on new developments and their advantages and limitations. All types of building materials can be used in commercial buildings. The most advantageous are those able to withstand considerable wear. Various kinds of stone are widely used, as are numerous, fired, earthen products such as brick and tile. Cement is frequently used and is a flexible material for design purposes. Wood and metal are available in many forms. Other materials, such as fabrics, plaster, plastic and glass, deserve consideration.

Color is an integral part of the design picture. Here the architect usually secures assistance from men experienced in store display. Decisions from the store management are also necessary, since color influences the character and atmosphere of the store.

Exterior Design

The primary function of exterior design is to attract the customer into the store. This exterior should reflect the character of the store. Certainly, the exterior of a jewelry store should reflect a different character than a drugstore. A passerby should be able to know, from the exterior, what type of store it is. Some store fronts are so well designed that a sign is considered unnecessary. These are exceptions, however, and most stores use attractive signs as part of the front, to identify the store. Basically, a store front is an advertising medium.

1. The show window is a major part of the exterior design and is used to display mer-

chandise. The front may have floor-to-ceiling windows (open front) or smaller, framed windows, with backs blocking the customer's view into the store (closed fronts). Since "window shopping" is very popular, special attention should be given to the show window. It reveals the type of merchandise carried. In addition, it is a major "attention getter"; it promotes considerable impulse buying and accounts for a large percentage of the total store sales.

2. The size and construction of the show window depend upon the merchandise handled. A music store displaying pianos or television sets requires large open areas. A jewelry store usually needs smaller windows at such a height that viewing is easy.

3. Since many small stores carry merchandise of all sizes, consideration should be given to designing show windows that have great flexibility. For example, a window displaying major appliances should be easily converted to properly display small appliances such as irons or toasters.

4. The show window is an integral part of the store front and should be designed so it blends architecturally with the exterior.

5. Provision should be made for control of sunlight on a show window. Because the window is so important to the sales program, it never should be blocked out by reflections. A properly designed canopy provides a satisfactory solution when glare is a problem. The canopy not only provides light and reflection control, but

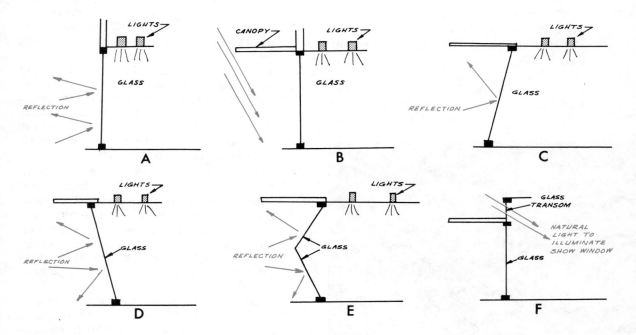

Fig. 829. Show windows are of many types. These sketches indicate those in common use. Of great importance is the reduction of glare and reflections which obscure the view of items in the window. If reflections can be diverted so they do not return to the eyes of the viewer, merchandise can be easily seen.

A. Vertical window has considerable reflection. Lights usually do not have intensity to exceed that of the sunlight.

B. A canopy reduces glare by cutting rays of the sun, thus permitting window lights to illuminate display at greater intensity than outside light.

C. Glass tilted backward is effective in reducing glare when the lower part of the building is usually in the shade. A canopy is helpful. Reflected rays are thrown up to be absorbed by ceiling material.

D. Glass tilted forward.

E. Another design to reduce reflected light from bouncing back into eyes of customers.

F. A show window with a transom.

protects the prospective customer from inclement weather. It frequently is used to carry a sign identifying the store. A canopy, to be effective, should shade the sidewalk so the viewer stands in the darkened area; if the show window area has a higher light intensity, reflection will be reduced. If a canopy is too high, it will be ineffective. Frequently, a transom is built over a low canopy, thus permitting light to enter the show window. This provides natural lighting for the display area, yet shades the viewer.

6. Another way to reduce glare on a show window is to tilt the glass or to use curved glass. Glass surfaces reflect light at the same angle at which the rays strike the glass. Light reflected off the tilted glass can be directed away from the viewer's eyes and toward a light-absorbing surface. Fig. 829 illustrates common solutions to reflection control on show windows.

7. An easy access to the show window area is essential, so that displays can be set up.

8. Some stores use large front windows (open front) for display purposes, with no special, built-in show window. The interior of the store extends up to the exterior window. This enables the floor

space occupied by window display to be converted easily to sales space whenever needed. It also permits flexibility in the use of display space.

9. Flexible lighting is necessary in show windows. Seldom is a display effective without dramatic lighting. It must be of greater intensity than interior lighting and must be more intense in the daytime than at night. The principles of lighting are the same as interior store lighting, in that general illumination is necessary, along with special display lighting on certain items. Light sources should be shielded to avoid blinding the viewer and should be inconspicuous. For some displays, up to 500 footcandles is necessary. Lighting should be placed so as to avoid casting shadows inside the display area.

10. The color of interior materials lining a show window or other display areas is important. A white background reflects the light in the area, thus making it easier to view the merchandise. Dark colors absorb light and make viewing more difficult.

11. Show windows should be easily viewed by all passersby, including those in automobiles. The more directions and greater the distance the display can be seen, the more valuable it is. Since automobiles pass rapidly, the store front must be able to attract attention instantly.

12. Many small stores can be built advantageously with an all-glass front, thus turning the entire store into a large show window. This is excellent planning, but the interior fixtures should be such that the view is not obstructed. Frequently, display cases and shelves are glass, to reduce obstructions to view and to passage of light.

13. Consideration should be given to orienting a store to the weather. In northern latitudes, show windows which can receive most of the sun's rays are most effective. In areas of high winds, some provision must be made to protect the customer. A recessed entrance sometimes provides effective protection.

14. The heavy ornamentation of store fronts, which was common a few years ago, has been completely abandoned in favor of simplicity. Excess ornamentation is ex-

Fig. 830. This commercial building illustrates effective use of the glass wall. It has character and appeal. The design is simple and uncluttered. Notice the ceiling spotlights providing general illumination. (Libbey-Owens-Ford Glass Co.)

pensive and detracts from the exterior display of merchandise. Fig. 830 illustrates an attractive exterior.

15. If a store is on a thoroughfare with heavy pedestrian traffic, room must be allowed along the front for those desiring to stop and view the merchandise. This could be provided by a recessed or slanted entrance. While this reduces inside floor space, the exterior display is of sufficient importance to warrant the loss. This entrance also serves as an aisle for customers. This aisle is needed even if the store is built to the front property line.

16. The recessed store front increases the amount of window display space available. Since the volume of sales is influenced heavily by the show windows, this usually justifies the expense of using this type of front.

17. While the show window is the most important consideration when planning a store front, the exterior space above the window also holds advertising possibilities. This space is only effective for those viewing the store from a distance, since those carefully viewing the show windows seldom look above eye level. Because of this, the upper portion usually is a flat billboard, with signs or slogans affixed. If this upper area also is devoted to show windows, they will compete with the street-level displays and be distracting. See Fig. 831.

18. A store on a corner has the advantage of having more room for display windows and more upper space for advertising. This space should be fully utilized in the exterior design.

19. The entrance doors are the final invitation to a customer to enter the store. They should appear to extend a welcome by allowing the person to see what is inside. Commonly used are full-length glass doors. All entrance doors should be easy to operate, and automatic doors are necessary in some stores.

20. Most stores should have double-entrance doors. Only extremely small stores can use a single door.

21. The door should fit into the interior customer traffic patterns. However, it usually is poor planning to place the door of a small store exactly on center. This creates an equal-size display window on each side, thus limiting their flexibility. Generally, one large window creates a better impression. This can be accomplished by placing the entrance off-center.

22. If at all possible, the level of the sales floor and the sidewalk should be the same. Ramps should be used if a difference exists. Steps should be avoided.

23. The design of signs identifying the store is a critical factor in overall exterior design. Generally, a simple sign is most effective and in best taste. The sign always should be lighted at night and should be easily read. The type of sign and the lettering used should be in keeping with the character of the store.

24. Since most stores now have year-round air conditioning and carefully controlled lighting systems, outside windows to admit light or air are unnecessary.

Fig. 831. Notice the recessed entrance located off-center to provide a large show window. The second floor front has been converted into a simple billboard to provide a mounting place for the sign, which has large and easily read lettering. A hood protects the show windows from excess glare and the customer from the weather. (Kawneer Co.)

Shoe Stores

1. Most shoe stores must operate at a high sales volume. This requires both an exterior that attracts attention and displays to pull the customer into the store. For this reason, most shoe stores use the all-glass, open-front exterior. The entire store interior, then, helps lure the customer inside. See Fig. 832.

2. Since high volume means many customers and a number of salesmen, careful planning of interior traffic is necessary. The customer should be able to enter and leave without conflicting with salesmen moving about to obtain merchandise.

3. A maximum number of chairs should be used. These should be attractive, durable and as small as possible, yet they should have arms and should comfortably seat the customer.

4. The floor should be carpeted, since it is necessary to protect the merchandise and customers may be walking in stocking feet.

5. If an open front is used, the chairs can be arranged in rows parallel to the windows, with aisles between. This gives the customer some privacy from those outside.

6. It is good practice to have open displays of shoes inside the store. This gives the customer a chance to examine the merchandise. It also offers an opportunity to display additional merchandise.

7. The storage of shoes on the sales floor is difficult. Usually, open shelving is built along the walls, and the boxes of shoes are arranged on these. While this is unattractive, it is convenient. This shelving should be no higher than the salesmen can reach from the floor. The monotony should be broken by inserting attractive displays of shoes at various points along the wall shelves. See Fig. 833.

8. A large portion of the stock is kept in the open shelving on the sales floor. Reserve stock is best stored in a stock room off the sales floor. This makes it readily available. Some storage could be in a basement area; however, care must be taken to prevent mildew damage.

9. Shoe stores tend to specialize in men's or women's shoes.

10. Impulse items are important to the financial success of shoe stores. Items such as hose, shoe polish, belts and ties are located near the entrance and sales desk. Here everyone is exposed to this merchandise.

Fig. 832. Display windows designed to attract attention and lure the customer inside. This is located off the mall in a large shopping center in Houston, Texas. The entire store and mall is air-conditioned. (Libbey-Owens-Ford Glass Co.)

Fig. 833. The interior of a shoe store. Notice the means for storing merchandise, the comfortable seating and the displays.

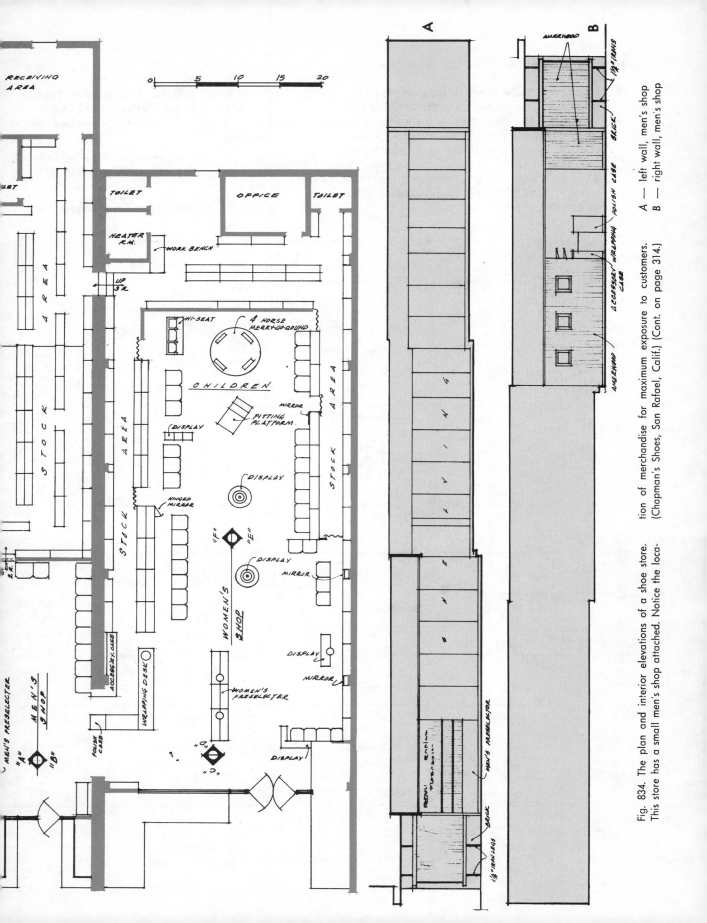

Fig. 834. The plan and interior elevations of a shoe store. This store has a small men's shop attached. Notice the location of merchandise for maximum exposure to customers. (Chapman's Shoes, San Rafael, Calif.) (Cont. on page 314.)

A — left wall, men's shop
B — right wall, men's shop

11. Usually a sales desk is located near the entrance. The salesman completes his sale and takes the customer and merchandise to the sales desk. Here a clerk makes change, wraps the items and asks about the purchase of impulse items nearby. The customer, upon conclusion of the sale, is near the exit and leaves with a minimum of confusion.

12. High-intensity lighting is very important. Shoes tend to be rather unobtrusive items, and special lighting is needed to make them shine.

13. Mirrors are necessary for viewing the footware. Some full-length mirrors also are necessary.

14. Fig. 834 illustrates a plan for a shoe store.

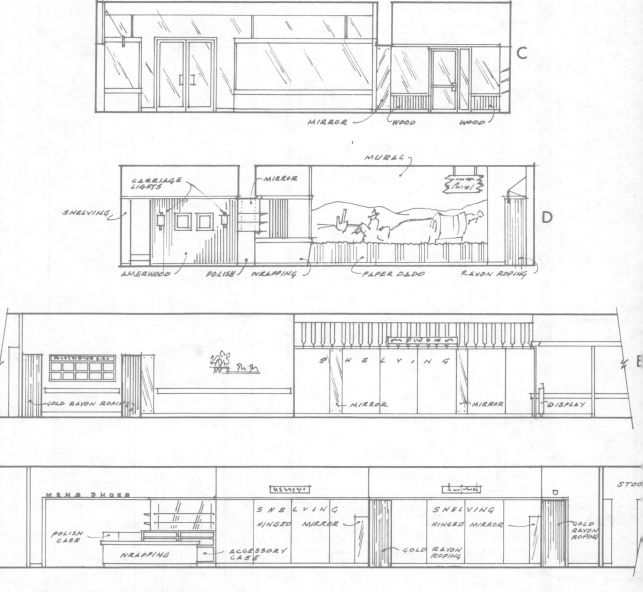

Fig. 834 (Cont.) Elevations of a shoe store.
   C — front
   D — back
   E — right wall, women's shop
   F — left wall, women's shop

Jewelry Stores

1. Most jewelry stores are built with an all-glass, open front. Fig. 835 illustrates such a store.

2. Merchandise usually is displayed in the lobby entrance.

3. Considerable impulse buying is characteristic and should be given emphasis in developing the layout of the sales floor.

4. Luxury and dignity should be strived for, in both interior and exterior design. Everything should be in good taste. Walls should be subtle and rich in appearance. Ornate designs detract from the merchandise, which is usually small and delicate.

5. Since most merchandise is small, the reserve stock area need not be large. Much can be kept in the display fixtures, yet out of sight.

6. Security from theft during the day and night is a major consideration. A vault and burglar alarm system are necessary.

7. Merchandise must be displayed with consideration to its security and protection. Self-service features are not useful, except for costume jewelry.

8. Usually the jewelry store is departmentalized. Watch and jewelry repair, gem display, silver, china, fountain pens, rings and bracelets and other items make logical groupings of merchandise. Notice the departments in Fig. 836. Fig. 837 illustrates a gift department.

9. Small items of jewelry are displayed in glass counters, while silver, china and other larger items are displayed on open shelving and tables. See Fig. 838.

10. The repair area usually is located in the rear of the store. This is a demand function, and this location forces the customer to pass by a great many impulse items on his way to and from the repair area.

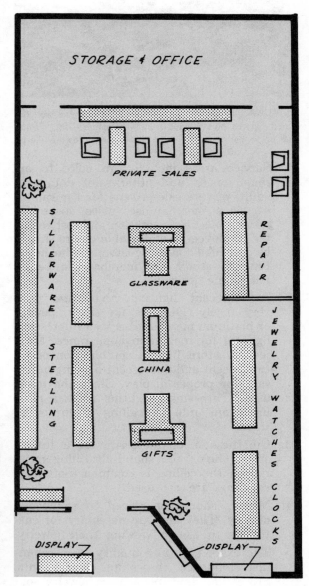

Fig. 836. A plan for a small jewelry store. Notice the location of the repair area which is a demand service. Impulse items as gifts, china and glassware are exposed to all customers. Tables and chairs provide for customer comfort.

Fig. 835. This store makes use of an open glass front and excellent lighting. The interior of the store helps attract the customer. The design is simple and does not compete with the merchandise. (Libbey-Owens-Ford Glass Co.)

Fig. 837. A gift department in a jewelry store. The well designed fixtures plus adequate lighting enhance the display and invite customers to enter. (Reflector Hardware Corp.)

Fig. 838. Open-shelving, glass display. Notice the effective use of the drape and glass shelves to bring attention to the merchandise. (Reflector Hardware Corp.)

11. Service areas include: an office to arrange credit and other sales details, a vault, private sales rooms for the sale of exclusive merchandise, office space for normal business operation and rest rooms for employees. Comfortable chairs should be provided for the customer who needs time to study the merchandise before reaching a decision.

12. Incandescent lighting highlights gems very nicely. Displays for silver, pewter or platinum merchandise need fluorescent lighting for maximum appearance. Most jewelry stores find a combination of incandescent and fluorescent lighting necessary for proper display. Since the items usually are small, lighting plays a most important role in calling attention to them.

13. Quietness is characteristic of a luxury store. The use of a sound-absorbing material on the ceiling is common. Soft floor coverings are also used.

14. Mirrors should be placed to enhance a display. They also are necessary for customers to use in viewing their jewelry.

15. The exact type and quality of merchandise influence the store departments. Stores handling inexpensive jewelry sold on a high-volume, bargain-sale basis usually have more display counters, and they eliminate private display rooms in order to get maximum merchandise on

display. Also, comfortable furniture for the convenience of the customer is not used, since this type of customer usually reaches a decision quickly and the space is needed for display.

Furniture Stores

Some furniture stores offer very specialized merchandise, while others offer a complete line of home furnishings. Specialized stores might sell only contemporary furniture or Early American styles. Some such stores do not even handle beds and kitchen items.

Furniture stores offering a broader line of merchandise stock all styles of furniture, as well as appliances, rugs, curtains, radios, television sets, bedding, lamps, china and glassware. Sometimes an interior decorating service is offered.

When planning a furniture store, consider the following general principles.

1. Window display space is a vital part of the planning. Some of the store frontage should be devoted to show windows that are large enough to display entire rooms completely furnished. The entrance should be open wide enough to permit a view of the interior. Some provision should be made for display of small items such as lamps and radios. Window lighting is essential. See Fig. 840.

2. Consideration should be given to placement of impulse, convenience and de-

mand items. Large furniture pieces and rugs should be in the rear of the store. Radios, television sets and appliances are convenience items and should be located between the demand and impulse items. Lamps and mirrors, as impulse items, are near the entrance, Fig. 839.

3. Fixtures are few. A large, open, floor area is needed. Furniture should be arranged in natural groupings, rather than simply lining up a long row of chairs or sofas. End tables and floor lamps can be arranged in normal settings with the larger pieces of furniture.

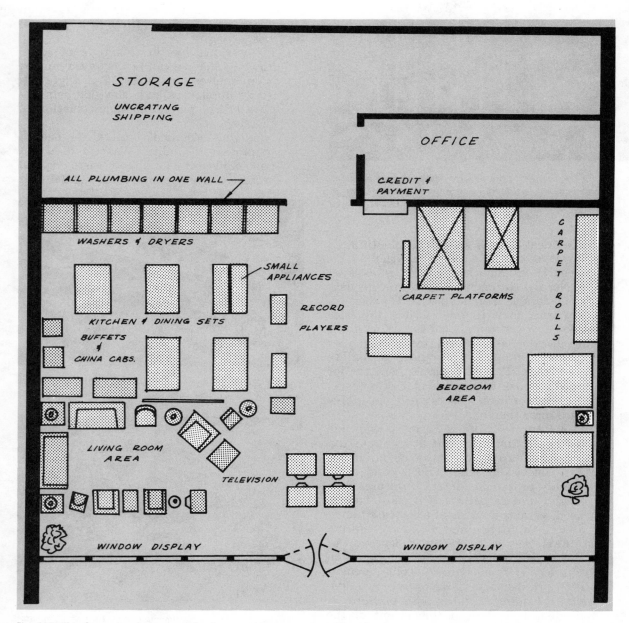

Fig. 839. This floor plan for a small furniture store suggests good locations for selected merchandise. The actual placement of individual items varies from day to day as they are sold and new stock is placed on the sales floor. Flexibility is needed to accommodate seasonal merchandise such as porch and lawn furniture.

Fig. 840. A furniture store utilizing the open-front merchandising trend. The main store and adjoining show rooms all are open to public view. (Libbey-Owens-Ford Glass Co., and Arthur Beck, Architect)

4. Electrical outlets should be plentiful, so furniture can be easily rearranged.
5. General illumination usually is assisted by local lighting from lamps on display.
6. Considerable merchandise is displayed on the sales floor. In small stores, the sales floor may contain almost the entire stock on hand. Large stores may use upper floors for storage or may have a separate warehouse. Provision should be made for moving stock without danger of damage. A freight elevator is essential in stores with more than one level.
7. If a furniture store is on more than one level, the first floor usually contains living room furniture, lamps, china, radios and television sets. The second floor usually contains bedroom furniture, mattresses and carpeting. If a third floor is used, various appliances are located here, as well as kitchen and outdoor furniture. An easy means for customer movement to these areas is necessary.
8. Space to store and prepare sold merchandise for delivery is necessary. An adequate loading and shipping platform is needed. It is best if this is out of the customer's sight.
9. Space is needed to receive and uncrate merchandise for display on the sales floor.

Appliance Stores

The typical appliance store usually departmentalizes. Kitchen items frequently are grouped together, such as ranges, refrigerators, freezers, dishwashers and kitchen cabinets. A second department is centered around laundry facilities such as washers, dryers and ironers, while a third grouping includes radios, record players and television sets. If small appliances are handled, these are grouped together.

1. Fixtures are few in this type of store. Small appliances can be displayed on low, open shelves or tables. See Fig. 841. Major appliances and television sets frequently are placed upon low platforms, Fig. 842.
2. Numerous electrical outlets are needed to provide flexibility. Washers need hot and cold water as well as a waste disposal system. Some appliances require 240-volt

Fig. 841. Small appliances can be effectively displayed on low, open fixtures. (Reflector Hardware Corp.)

Fig. 842. Notice the departmentalization existing in this appliance store. Each department is identified by easily visible signs. The floor is of durable material that will withstand the movement of heavy appliances. (Flintkote Co.)

The lobby of a savings and loan company. Notice the stone wall that serves as the focal point of the lobby. (Feathercock, Inc.)

A pleasant waiting room in an office. (Cole Steel Equipment Co.)

The lobby of a bank building with prestressed concrete members. Notice the ceiling structure. (Prestressed Concrete Institute)

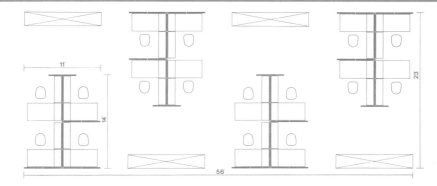

A panel system providing semi-private work stations. The rectangular units permit expansion as the size of the office area increases. (Herman Miller, Inc.)

A durable, light colored floor, warm colors on fixtures and walls, and good general lighting create a pleasant shopping atmosphere. (Azrock Floor Products)

Merchandising area for interior design business.

This cafeteria unit provides self-service merchandising. The food is placed in the unit from the rear. (The Bastian-Blessing Company)

A cafeteria serving line and dining area. (The Bastian-Blessing Company)

Striking furniture, warm colors, and soft lighting create a relaxed dining atmosphere. (Lee Woodward and Sons, Inc.)

current. Gas service is necessary to operate gas ranges and dryers. Television antennas are needed.

3. The small appliances usually are located near the entrance, with television sets and radios next. Major appliances generally are in the rear of the store.

4. If repair services are offered, a work space is needed with room for disassembly work. This takes considerable space and may be located in an adjacent building or in the rear of the retail store. Space is also needed for parts storage and parking for service trucks.

5. The repair area needs all utilities to check the operation of repaired fixtures.

6. A major repair center could be departmentalized into appliance repair and radio and television repair. The planning of each of these areas is a separate study in itself.

7. Durable floors and walls are needed, especially in the major appliance demonstration area.

8. Usually only one of each model of refrigerator, stove, etc., is displayed, and the remainder of the merchandise is stored in the crate in which it was shipped. This

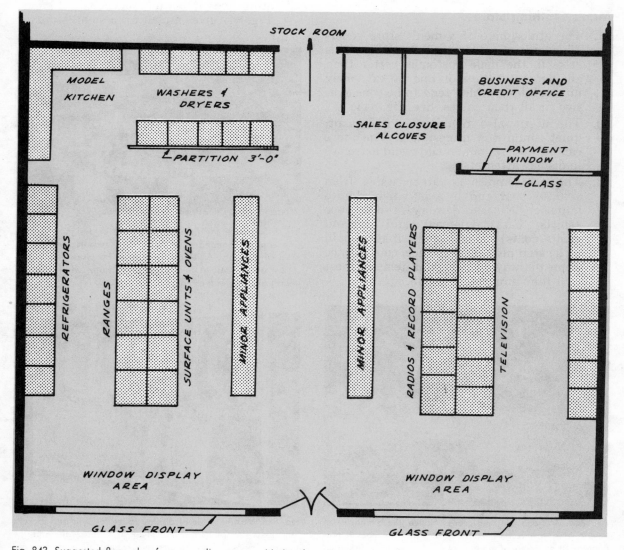

Fig. 843. Suggested floor plan for an appliance store. Notice that minor appliances must be passed by most customers.

calls for adequate storage for many large items.

9. Stores selling kitchen cabinets frequently build a model kitchen in the rear of the store.

10. Since many purchases are on credit, suitable office space and a place for customers to be interviewed and to make payments must be provided. This should be a part of the sales floor, yet should enable business transactions to be handled with a feeling of privacy.

11. Fig. 843 illustrates a plan for a typical appliance store.

Men's Clothing Stores

1. The atmosphere of a men's store generally is one of reserve and simplicity. This attracts the male customer better than an elaborate store or one of extremely unusual design. Men tend to be conservative in all their tastes. See Fig. 844.

2. The interior also should reflect a pleasant, quiet, unhurried atmosphere. The store can be modern, but should avoid extremes in display attempts.

3. The merchandise is rather stable from year to year and is easily divided into impulse (belts, ties, jewelry), convenience (shirts, hats, pajamas) and demand (suits, coats) items. Impulse items should be located near the entrance, convenience items midway and demand items farthest into the store. See Fig. 845.

4. The merchandise is seasonal, and plans should be made for easy rearrangement of fixtures, although this is not as important as for women's clothing. Most men simply change summer suits for winter suits or summer shirts for winter shirts. The same fixtures suffice for both. See Fig. 846.

5. Good lighting on merchandise displayed on mannequins helps sales. General illumination should be adequate.

6. It is a mistake to crowd fixtures together, since men prefer more space.

7. Dressing rooms and mirrors are necessary.

8. Workrooms for tailors are needed, if the store does its own alterations.

Fig. 847 gives a plan for a small store.

Fig. 845. Notice the fixtures are simple in design. Merchandise can be changed according to the season with a minimum of difficulty. Aisles are wide, and impulse items (accessories) are placed in the front of the store, while demand items (suits) are in the rear.

Fig. 844. A men's clothing store. Notice the simplicity of exterior design and the uncluttered display. The special spotlights in the ceiling along the glass display front highlight the window merchandise. (Libbey-Owens-Ford Glass Co.)

Fig. 846. Maximum use of display space for suits and jackets. This fixture is placed several feet from the wall, and the space behind is used for dressing rooms. They are entered from the ends of the display. (Reflector Hardware Corp.)

Women's Clothing Stores

1. A women's clothing store contains a wide variety of items which can be logically grouped, such as hosiery, blouses and lingerie. The entire store should observe the general principles of store planning as described earlier in this chapter. Each department should be carefully planned as a separate sales area. Planning the entire store, then, is the putting together of these smaller areas.

2. Impulse, convenience and demand items all occur in abundance. As usual, the demand merchandise (coats, dresses, suits) should be well inside the store; the convenience items (gloves, hosiery, sweaters) should be located between the demand items and the impulse items which are near the entrance. Typical impulse items are costume jewelry, pocketbooks and cosmetics.

3. Most women's clothing stores rely heavily on personal service. However, some items could be somewhat self-service.

4. Flexibility in display fixtures is vital, since most items are seasonal and fashions change rapidly. See Figs. 848 and 849.

5. A striking exterior with a dramatic display area is necessary. Since mannequins are used, large display windows are neces-

Fig. 848. These fixtures provide a high degree of flexibility. They can be raised and lowered or removed and replaced with other types of hanging rods, shelves or cabinets. Even the mirrors can be easily moved to facilitate a rapid rearrangement of merchandise. (Reflector Hardware Corp.)

Fig. 849. Fixtures rearranged to accommodate a two-level display. Notice the simplicity of design that makes the merchandise the focal point of attention. (Reflector Hardware Corp.)

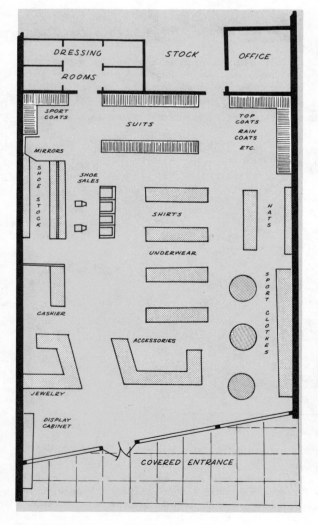

Fig. 847. Plan for a small men's store.

sary. The front should appear like a theatrical stage, with exciting sets and effective lighting. Generally, this calls for open fronts. Exclusive shops can use a closed front with a few, framed, display windows, but this is not effective for stores relying on volume sales. Figs. 850 and 851 illustrate two attractive exteriors.

6. Dressing rooms are needed for customers to try on clothing. Full-length mirrors also are necessary; these usually are grouped in threes.
7. Comfortable chairs are necessary in areas where expensive garments are shown.
8. If the store does alterations, a workroom is needed.

Fig. 850. A women's clothing store with a center entrance. Notice the recessed display windows providing sidewalk space for customers viewing the display. (Natcor Corp.)

Fig. 851. An attractive corner entrance to a women's store. The display windows are large and permit a view of the interior of the store. (Friedes, Inc.)

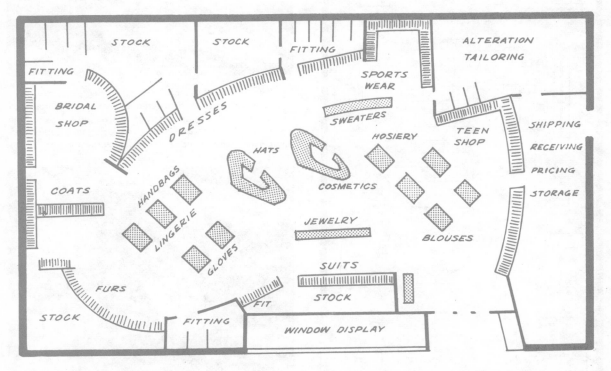

Fig. 852. A plan for a women's clothing store. Notice the demand items, such as furs and coats and the bridal shop, are located deep within the store to pull customers past impulse items, such as blouses, cosmetics and jewelry. Provision is made to maintain considerable stock readily available on the sales floor. An adequate number of fitting rooms are provided in several locations. Small items such as handbags and gloves (which require maximum exposure) are displayed on island-type fixtures that can be rearranged easily.

9. The usual offices, credit desk, sales desks and rest rooms are required.

An illustrative plan is shown in Fig. 852.

Hardware and Building Supply Stores

The typical hardware store handles a considerable variety of items, many of which are very small and difficult to display to advantage. Other items, such as power tools, are large and require considerable floor space. Some stores also handle housewares, small appliances, sporting goods, garden tools, auto supplies, radios and television sets. Such a store must be carefully departmentalized.

The typical building supply store carries a full line of hardware items, plus items needed for building construction, such as plywood, lumber, lighting fixtures, doors, windows, and

Fig. 853. A hardware and building supply store planned on two levels. The all-glass front transforms the store interior into a vast display. The interior lighting is especially effective.

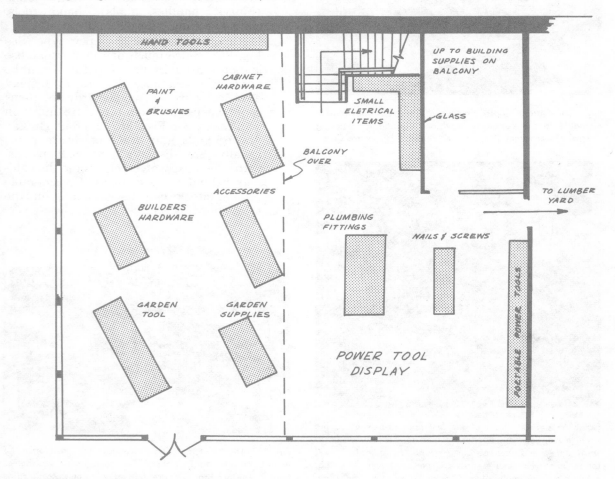

Fig. 854. Floor plan for a hardware and building supply store.

ceiling and wall materials. It seldom handles appliances and sporting goods. Figs. 853 and 854 illustrate hardware and building supply stores.

Fig. 855. Garden tools effectively displayed and readily available to the customer. Provision is made for stocking several of each item on the floor. (Reflector Hardware Corp.)

Fig. 856. A partial view of the first floor sales area of the store in Fig. 853. This floor is devoted to the common hardware store items such as garden tools, hand tools, power tools, paint and small hardware items. The second floor exhibits building materials such as doors, windows, paneling, kitchen fixtures, cabinets and light fixtures.

When planning a store to merchandise hardware, consider the following general principles.

1. Display impulse items near the entrance. Such items include small electrical appliances, sporting goods and garden tools and supplies. See Fig. 855. They also can be effectively displayed along the main aisle carrying customer traffic.
2. Demand items, usually placed at the rear of the store, are paints, wallpaper, large electrical appliances and large hardware items such as ladders.

    If the hardware store being planned will place considerable emphasis on minor and major appliances, refer to "Appliance Stores" in this chapter.
3. Convenience items placed between the entrance and the rear of the store include such things as small hardware items (hinges, handles, nails), hand tools, china, cooking utensils and cutlery.
4. Fixtures usually are the open type. See Fig. 856. Since much of the merchandise is not seasonal, special fixtures can be used. For example, fixtures to display electrical parts or small hardware items could be used. Tools often are hung on wall racks. See Figs. 857 and 858. Hinges, drawer pulls and other hardware items usually are displayed on wall panels, with the boxes of stock stored in cabinets behind these displays. Considerable reserve stock can be available on the sales floor this way.

Fig. 857. The hand tool and power tool section. Notice the wall panels for tool display, with stock stored on shelves below. The wall panels are lighted with fluorescent strips hidden behind a facia strip.

5. Open shelving along the exterior walls provides excellent display space for small appliances, cooking utensils and paint. See Fig. 859. This shelving should be adjustable to accommodate items of various heights.

6. Open floor area is needed for seasonal items that are frequently handled, such as sleds and bicycles. These frequently are placed in front of the all-glass, open front as a window display. Other seasonal items such as picnic equipment require simple, open shelves that can be converted easily to the display of other merchandise.

7. Auto tires are displayed on special racks. If tire mounting and balancing are offered, a connecting garage must be planned. Some auto items can be displayed in the garage area, to give exposure to additional merchandise. Most auto supplies can be displayed on open fixtures as shown in Fig. 860.

8. Floors should be attractive, yet should be able to withstand hard wear.

9. General illumination should be excellent, since most merchandise on display usually is not specially lighted.

10. Colors should be kept light so as to set off the merchandise.

11. Show windows can be of value in a hardware store, but should not obstruct a view of the interior. Most stores use the all-glass front and arrange items that are to be displayed in front of the window. Displays should reflect the character of the store.

12. A receiving and stock room is necessary. It should be large enough for items to be unpacked and for storage of merchandise.

Fig. 859. A wall display for paints, brushes, solvents and other painting supplies. Such a fixture makes maximum use of store walls for display and storage. (Reflector Hardware Corp.)

Fig. 858. A hand-tool display area arranged for maximum display, plus storage of a quantity of tools on the sales floor. (Reflector Hardware Co.)

Fig. 860. Auto supplies displayed on open fixtures. Considerable stock can be maintained on the sales floor. (Reflector Hardware Corp.)

Retail Cleaning Shops

Many cleaning establishments have a central facility for doing the actual dry cleaning or laundry. They establish retail stores in many locations in an area. These outlying stores collect the clothing, identify it and send it to the central facility. When cleaned, the clothing is returned to the retail outlet for customer pick-up.

When planning a customer pick-up facility, consider the following requirements.

1. The store front should be attractive. The all-glass front is commonly used. See Fig. 861.
2. Large, attractive signs calling attention to the store are vital, since such a facility usually is small.
3. A counter separating the customer area and the storage area is necessary. This accommodates the cash register and serves to hold the clothing as items are tagged and prepared to be sent to the cleaning facility.
4. A storage area behind the counter for cleaned clothing comprises the largest part of the store. It should contain racks for clothing on hangers and shelves for packages of laundry.

Fig. 861. A retail cleaning and laundry store. Notice the hooded drive-in window and large sign. (Natcor Store Fronts)

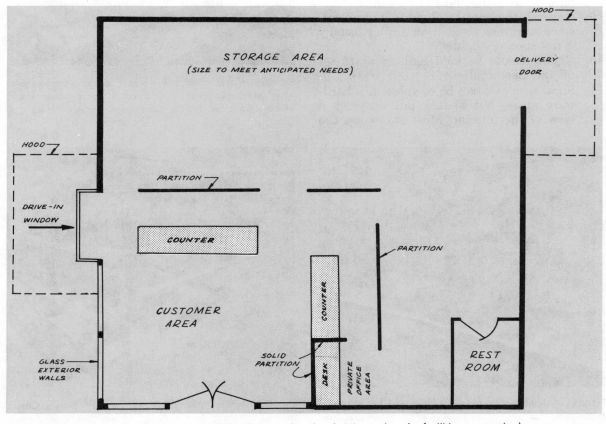

Fig. 862. The floor plan for the cleaning and laundry store (no dry cleaning or laundry facilities on premises).

5. A station should be provided for the loading and unloading of delivery trucks directly at the storage area. Provision should be made for a hood to shelter the trucks, so clothing can be protected during inclement weather.

6. It is desirable to screen off the customer's view of the storage and unloading area.

7. If drive-in service is planned, the drive-in window should be located so the counter clerks can see the window at all times and have easy access to it.

8. The drive-in window should have a hood over it.

9. Provision should be made for a small office area.

10. A rest room for employees is needed.

11. If dry cleaning is to be done at the retail facility, additional space is needed. Equipment manufacturers should be consulted for size and capacity of equipment.

12. Fig. 862 illustrates a typical floor plan.

Florist and Nursery Shops

1. Because of the nature of merchandise handled, a florist shop should use the all-glass, open-front exterior. Since the merchandise is perishable, very little stock storage is needed. The available merchandise should be in full view.

2. A large, well-lighted refrigerator case for cut flowers is the major permanent fixture. All details having to do with the sale of cut flowers should be located near this fixture.

3. Work space and tables for cutting, arranging and wrapping cut flowers are necessary.

4. Desks, chairs and writing materials are necessary for those desiring to enclose a card with the flowers.

5. The fixtures needed are very simple. Tables or simple shelves adequately display potted plants.

6. Some shops handle seeds, garden tools and planters, and provision for display and storage is needed.

7. Merchandise usually is not of the impulse, convenience and demand types. If specialty items are handled, they should be located near the entrance.

8. Usually merchandise is departmentalized with cut flowers and potted plants in separate sales areas. Fig. 863 illustrates one such facility.

9. The interior walls should not compete with the flowers for attention. Subdued colors and textures are favored.

10. Lighting is of extreme importance. Unless properly highlighted, flowers will not be shown to maximum advantage. Over-

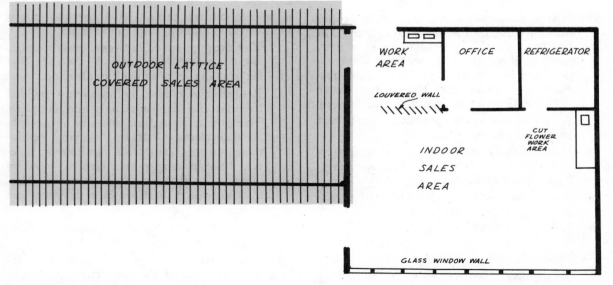

Fig. 863. Florist and nursery shop.

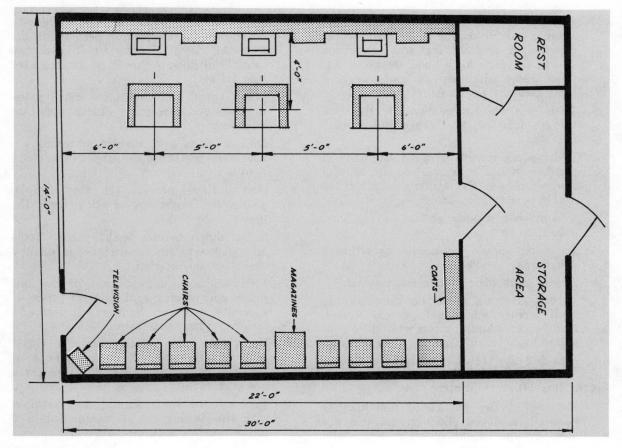

Fig. 864. Barber shop.

head spotlights and floodlights are necessary, as well as hidden lights.

11. Special attention must be given to proper humidity regulation. This and room temperature should be controlled at a level providing maximum protection. The temperature is usually kept lower than normal room temperature. Harsh or excessive lighting also can be damaging to flowers.

12. A manager's office and employees' rest room facilities are needed.

13. If potting is done in the store, work space and work benches are necessary. Sinks and water are vital.

14. The walls and floor should be of a material that is easily cleaned and unaffected by soil and water.

Barber Shops

The typical barber shop is relatively simple to plan because of the limited variety of services offered. Many shops only provide services that can be done while the customer is in the barber chair. Other services might include shoe shining and manicuring.

1. The average space between barber chairs should be from 4'-6'' to 5'-0''. See Fig. 864 for spacing in a typical small shop.

2. Behind the chairs, cabinets are needed to hold the barber's tools and supplies. These usually include scissors and comb, several electric cutters, shaving equipment, towels, sanitation equipment, electric hair massager and electric vacuum cleaner for removing hair particles. Also, it is necessary to store hair dressing and tonics. See Fig. 865.

3. An ample number of electrical outlets must be provided for each chair.

4. A sink equipped for washing hair is frequently located by each chair. In shops where hair shampooing is infrequent, one

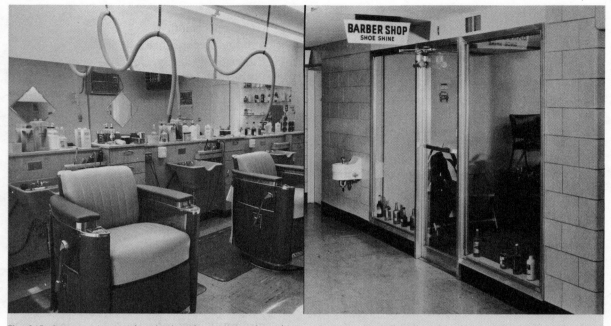

Fig. 865. An attractive, modern barber shop. Notice the cabinets for holding the barber's tools and needed supplies. Each barber in this shop has a shampoo sink. The vacuum system comes from overhead. (Geifer Barber Shop)

Fig. 866. A small barber shop located on the mall of a large shopping center. Notice the simple, attractive, glass front and the appearance of efficiency and cleanliness. (Burns and Russel Co.)

large washbasin could be located conveniently to all chairs, and small sinks could be located behind each chair for shaves and personal cleanliness of the barber.

5. Storage is a minor problem. Usually a number of cabinets located inside the customer area is adequate.

6. Containers for soiled linens should be near each barber's station.

7. Sufficient room to seat waiting customers comfortably and facilities for coats and hats are necessary.

8. Mirrors behind the barber and on the opposite wall are helpful.

9. A manicure area need not be over 5 or 6 feet square. Only a table and two chairs are needed. The supplies usually are kept on top of the table and in drawers below.

10. The shoe shine area is usually in the rear of the customer area. It is a demand service and a convenience for the customer.

11. The barbers need a rest room and space to change clothes.

12. Provision should be made for magazines and newspapers. Television for the customers is common.

13. Since most barber shops receive fresh linens from a laundry service, few have their own laundry equipment.

14. The cash register should be located so all barbers can have access to it without hindering another barber at work.

15. Some shops provide a soft drink machine.

16. Air conditioning is essential.

17. The all-glass, open-front store, exposing a clean, attractive interior, is excellent advertising to attract customers. See Fig. 866.

18. The exterior should be simple, yet it should clearly indicate it is a barber shop. The typical "barber pole" is generally used. An attractive sign is of value.

Service Stations

A service station is a building built solely as a profit-making, sales outlet for a petroleum company's products. Any services or accommodations provided are for the purpose of increasing sales and contributing to profits from the business.

Construction and equipment costs, plus expensive real estate, make the present-day service station a costly investment. To realize

the most from this investment, careful planning is necessary.

The design should fulfill the functional needs of a contemplated operation. A design can be no better than the analysis of the functions to be performed. An accurate service projection establishes the basis for a profitable operation which must be supported by good design. A good design in itself will not assure a profitable business.

The services offered by stations vary considerably. Some simply sell gas and oil and handle a few accessories. Others include lubrication, car washing, tire and battery sales, and offer accessories such as seat covers, lights and horns. Still others perform such minor repairs as tune-up and brake replacement. When a service station is being designed, the services to be offered must be clearly known. Following are some planning principles to consider.

Basic Essentials to a
Successful Service Station

In order of their importance, the following are vital to a successful operation:

1. Good location.
2. Good operation.
3. Product acceptance.
4. Functional design for the service to be performed.

It may be surprising to learn that the station itself is not the most important factor. However, this does not minimize the need for good planning and design. This discussion covers the site layout, building and equipment.

Site Planning

Ingress and egress are vital to a good service station. These involve the approaches and driveways.

1. Maximum approach widths and their minimum distances from property lines are usually governed by city or state rulings. Average approach width is 30 feet at the property line, with 10 to 15 feet a usual minimum distance from the edge of the approach to the property lines (at side and corner). Location of the approaches should give easy access to the islands, with no sharp turns necessary, Fig. 867.

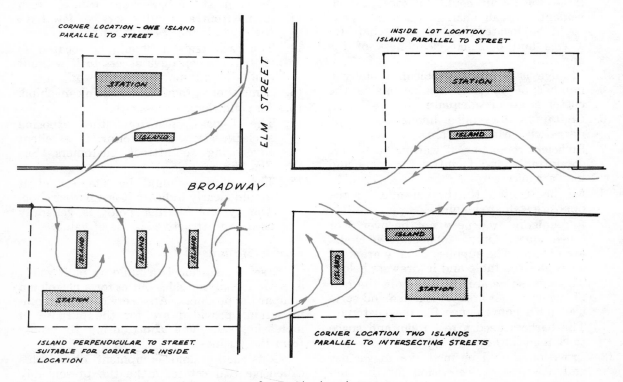

Fig. 867. Typical traffic patterns relating customer flow to islands and street.

2. Many codes require 15 feet from the property line to the center of the gasoline dispenser, so that the distance of 14 feet from property line to the face of the island is common. This allows sufficient room for a pedestal sign (if desired) to be set at the property line across from the island. An inner drive width of 16 to 18 feet is common. (This is the distance from the island's inside face to the building step.)

3. An outside parking area should be planned for customers' autos.

4. Grades are of the utmost importance. The service area around the islands should be nearly level to permit gasoline tanks to be filled completely, and yet should still allow enough slope on the slab for drainage. A common slope is ⅛ inch per foot in the direction of the island and ¼ inch per foot across the drives. Other driveway areas may slope more, if necessary, provided the grades are not excessive. Normally, maximum slopes should not exceed 10 percent.

5. Surfacing adjacent to the islands where gasoline is dispensed should be concrete. Asphalt will be damaged by gasoline, since the gasoline acts as a solvent. Approaches and other areas of the drive may be asphalt. Parking areas may be gravel.

6. Island width is commonly 3'-6". The length depends upon the number of dispensers, light poles and air and water facilities provided. Minimum center-to-center spacing of gasoline dispensers is 5'-0". This dimension is necessary because of the size of the dual dispensers which handle two grades of gasoline.

7. Large stations need several separate islands. These should be spaced so autos can be accommodated on both sides without blocking incoming or outgoing traffic. An architectural standards book should be consulted for various, recommended turning radii.

8. The island should provide water, compressed air and window cleaning facilities. Some provide vacuum cleaning facilities for cleaning the interior of customers' autos.

9. Identification signs should be provided on the streets the station serves. Normally a 6'-0" or 8'-0" pedestal sign is provided at the property lines or at the corner. Building signs may also be used along with letters on the building.

10. It is essential that the approaches receive floodlighting so that they can be seen clearly by the approaching motorist. Perimeter lighting (a term applied to floodlighting at the property line) is usually accomplished by fluorescent fixtures mounted on poles. Floodlighting for parking areas and additional areas of the driveway may also be desired.

11. Those areas not receiving light from island lights or canopy lights, such as the front and sides of the building, should receive face lighting. This may be a continuous strip of fluorescent fixtures on the soffit of the overhang at the roof line.

The Building

The service station building should be attractive and should provide adequate facilities for operation. Fig. 868 illustrates selected plans. Normal elements to be considered in the building planning are:

1. Sales office.
2. Service stalls.
3. Work area.

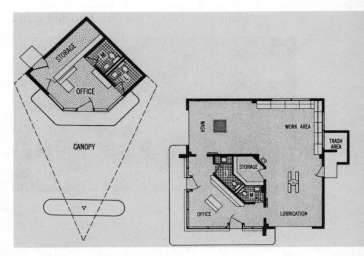

Fig. 868. Suggested plans for contemporary service station buildings. (Phillips Petroleum Co.)

4. Storage room.
5. Rest rooms.
6. Vending area.
7. Canopies.
8. Building utilities.
   a. Heating.
   b. Plumbing.
   c. Electrical.
9. Exterior color schemes.

12. The sales office should provide space for operator's desk, display and traffic. Maximum visibility to and from the office is essential both for display of items in the office and for clear view of the driveway areas by the operator. The display may feature tire racks, shelving or pegboard display. Average office area required is 300 square feet.

13. Service stalls usually are provided for car washing, lubrication and (in the large stations) maintenance.

14. The wash stall is provided with a mud sump to keep mud and oil from entering the sewers. Mud enters through grating on the top and settles to the bottom, whereas oil scum floats on the top. Sump outlet is between these two elevations. Floor should slope from the perimeter of the stall a total of 2 or 3 inches to the sump for proper drainage.

15. A splash wall between the wash stall and lube stall may be provided if desired, or the wall may be omitted for a more open operation. This wall usually is about 5'-0" high.

16. The ceiling should be high enough to accommodate a car on the hydraulic lift

at full height. Thirteen feet from floor to ceiling is recommended. If trucks are serviced, the ceiling should be even higher.

17. The lubrication stall has a hoist to elevate the automobile, thus making lubrication fittings accessible. The most popular type of hoist is the frame contact. Instead of raising the car by its wheels on a platform, the superstructure of the frame hoist makes contact directly with the car frame. Lubricating equipment may be either the portable type which rolls on the floor or the overhead type which is suspended from the ceiling. The overhead type has retractable hoses and is air operated.

18. Tire racks and shelving can be mounted on the walls of the stalls, usually across the rear. Also a work bench should be provided in the work area.

19. Service stalls are usually 15'-0" wide by 27'-0" long. Their entrances have 10' x 10' overhead doors. Larger doors are necessary if trucks are to be serviced.

20. If considerable trade is done in tires and batteries, an area without a hoist in the station should be provided. In a small station, the wash area can be used for this purpose.

21. The work area is essential for miscellaneous repair work and can be an area adjoining the stalls, either on the side or rear. There is no particular size connected with this area, since it may vary with the operations.

22. A locked storage area is necessary for merchandise items and should be large enough to carry stock for several days' operations. One hundred square feet is an average size.

23. Rest rooms should be given special consideration. Every effort should be made to provide attractive, easily maintained rest rooms. Tile floors and walls and good quality plumbing fixtures are best. Floor drains encourage frequent cleaning.

24. Formerly, rest rooms opened to the outside to provide privacy. However, some of the newer stations have inside rest rooms, which the public has accepted.

For the operator, maintenance and inspection of the inside rest room is easier, and their use can be more easily limited essentially to the station customers.

Fig. 869. A service station with a canopy over the service area. The canopy not only provides shelter, but attracts considerable attention, thus tending to lure the potential customer. Notice the use of stone and glass in the building as well as large, prominently placed signs that can be seen from a great distance. (Phillips Petroleum Co.)

25. Average rest room size is 50 square feet for ladies and 40 square feet for men.

26. Nearly all stations now have vending machines for bottled drinks, cigarettes, candy, etc. The popularity of vending is increasing. Some large stations have coffee, sandwiches, etc. in dispensers. Space should be provided in the larger stations for the vending machines and related activity.

27. Canopies are popular and are being installed on many stations. They afford shade and protection from rain and snow and are a definite asset to appearance. They also provide an effective means to light the island area. See Figs. 869 and 870.

28. Building utilities required are heat, plumbing and electricity.

Heating

Most codes require that any flame in the service stall area be 8 feet above the floor to avoid igniting any gasoline vapors present. Gasoline vapors are heavier than air and settle to the floor area. Thus water heaters and furnaces (both oil- and gas-fired) are suspended from the ceiling or mounted on the wall above the 8-foot level. In the case of the furnace, the need for a furnace room is eliminated.

Plumbing

No special requirements other than a mud sump or (in some cases) a grease trap apply. (National Plumbing Code Standards)

Electricity

Electrical service installed in accordance with the National Electrical Code fulfills normal operational needs. Special services require special consideration.

29. Petroleum companies recognize the importance of color and engage color experts and industrial designers to select colors which will appeal to the public. A light color (especially white) is popular because of its acceptance and its adaptability to floodlighting. Any trim or "modifying" colors are carefully selected, since these become part of the company image in the eyes of the public.

Equipment

Service station operating equipment for handling gasoline usually consists of the following.

30. *Underground storage tanks* are provided for regular and premium gasoline, and an additional tank also is installed for a possible future product. Tanks should be of sufficient size to receive the full delivery of a transport. Tank capacity is usually 4000 or 6000 gallons.

31. *Submerged pumps* are actually located in the tanks. The gasoline is pushed from the tanks. This purging method eliminates any chance of vapor lock. Previously, pumps were located on the islands, and the gasoline was pulled from the tanks by suction. Present-day gasoline is more volatile than formerly and has a greater tendency to vaporize (or vapor lock) when subject to suction pumping.

32. *Gasoline dispensers* on the islands meter the gasoline as it is pumped from the storage tanks to the automobile.

33. An *air compressor* provides air for service at the islands and operates the hoist and lubrication equipment.

Drugstores

The typical drugstore is much more complex than the name implies. Commonly these stores offer food service, cigars and cigarettes, stationery, gifts, cosmetics, cameras, books and magazines, household items, school supplies, prescription service and a wide variety of nonprescription medications. The exact items handled will vary from store to store.

Fig. 870. A service station designed to sell gasoline and oil only. The canopy attracts attention as well as sheltering the customer and attendant. (Butler Manufacturing Co.)

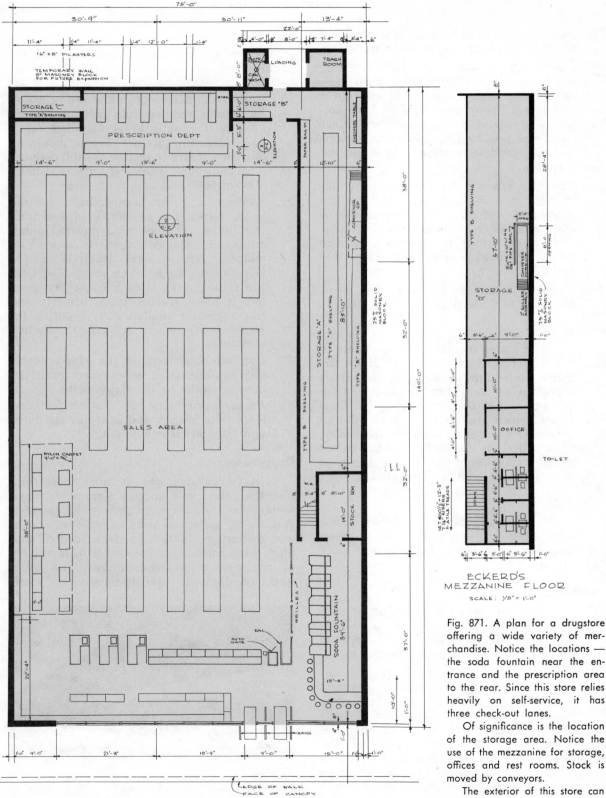

Fig. 871. A plan for a drugstore offering a wide variety of merchandise. Notice the locations — the soda fountain near the entrance and the prescription area to the rear. Since this store relies heavily on self-service, it has three check-out lanes.

Of significance is the location of the storage area. Notice the use of the mezzanine for storage, offices and rest rooms. Stock is moved by conveyors.

The exterior of this store can be found in Chapter 17. (Eckerd's Drugs and Alley, Williams, Carmen and King, Inc., Engineers and Architects)

Most drugstores rely heavily on self-service for most items; clerks merely help customers find items, give advice and show items housed in protective cases, such as cameras.

Following are some general principles to be considered when planning a drugstore.

1. Since drugstores are highly competitive and rely on a large volume of trade to make a profit, strict adherence to placing impulse items near the entrance, demand items in the rear and convenience items in between is necessary.

2. Most stores are arranged by departments. The prescription department, a demand department, should be located in the rear. The cashier, books and magazines, cigarettes and other demand items should be away from the entrance. See Fig. 871 for a typical plan.

3. The food service should be near the entrance and easily seen from the street. This attracts many customers.

4. Cosmetics tend to be impulse items and should be near the entrance. It is advantageous if they can be located opposite the food service.

5. Convenience items such as drugs, household items and sundries should be located between the prescription department and the entrance. Figs. 872 and 873 illustrate methods for displaying the many items found in a drugstore.

6. The food service area should be planned so that any congestion in this area will not block customer traffic aisles to other areas or to the cashier.

7. If extensive food service is planned, a study of restaurant fixtures is necessary. A decision will have to be made whether to have only counter service or to include booths. For extensive food service, a separate food preparation area is needed. This is best if it is located out of sight, in a room behind the counter area or in a basement area. The latter location would necessitate moving food and dishes with a dumbwaiter. See Chapter 15, "Planning Food Stores, Restaurants and Cafeterias."

8. Extensive utilities are needed for the food service area. These could include hot and cold water, large sewers and extra electrical power to operate the many food preparation appliances. Natural gas may be needed if much cooking is planned.

9. Considerable area is needed for stock storage. This could be on a lower level or in the extreme rear, since the usual open shelving used in the sales area can carry a good reserve supply of most items on display.

10. The prescription area should be open to public view and should be attractively arranged. This increases the confidence of the customer. Frequently this area is protected by glass partitions. Special shelving is necessary to accommodate the many items needed by the pharmacist. See Fig. 874 for interior elevation of a prescription area.

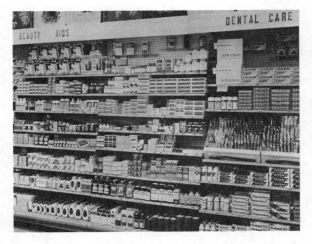

Fig. 872. Open wall shelving that is adjustable provides effective display and stock storage. (Reflector Hardware Corp.)

Fig. 873. Open island fixtures are commonly used to display merchandise in a drugstore. Notice the prescription center at the rear of the store. (Reflector Hardware Corp.)

11. Some drugstores use a closed or partially closed display window to advantage. The displays exhibited are simple and uncluttered. It is of advantage to be able to see over the display into the store proper. Many stores use the all-glass, open front so that the entire interior is the store's "face." See Fig. 875.

12. Good general illumination is necessary. In display areas where merchandise is protected, each display case is lighted separately.

Build Your Vocabulary

Following are words that you should understand and use as a part of your working vocabulary. Write a brief explanation of what each means.

Sales area
Service area
Impulse merchandise
Convenience merchandise
Demand merchandise
Block aisle system
Free-flow aisle system
Escalator
Elevator
Island fixtures
Wall fixtures
Open fixtures
Show window

Fig. 875. An open-front drugstore designed to attract the customer by presenting the entire contents of the store as a display. (Libbey-Owens-Ford Glass Co.)

Canopy
Reserve stock

Class Activities

1. Make a checklist of the principles that should be observed in planning one store, of a type discussed in this chapter. Select such a store in your community and secure permission to visit it. Then evaluate it by marking each item on the checklist as good, satisfactory or poor. The checklist should include exterior design, as well as interior design and planning.

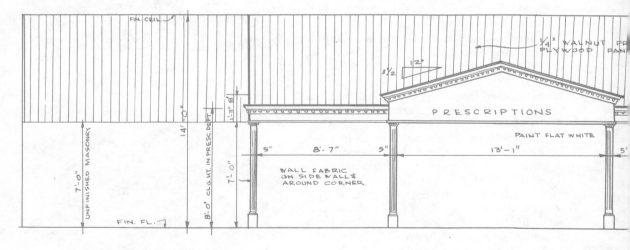

Fig. 874. Elevation of a prescription area. The attractive design calls attention to the service. (Eckerd's Drug Store and Alley, Williams, Carmen and King, Inc., Engineers and Architects)

2. Visit one store of a type discussed in this chapter and make a freehand, scale sketch of the interior arrangement. In class, revise this to improve the overall operation of the store, and draw the revised floor plan.

3. Build a cardboard model of a store interior (the building with the roof, and possibly, one or two walls removed). Build scale models of typical store fixtures. Arrange these on the floor to develop the most satisfactory plan.

4. Visit a shopping area near the school. Report on the exterior details of one store that truly reflect the character of the store. Explain why this exterior design is good. A photograph of the store would be useful in making your report.

5. Build scale models of store fronts, illustrating the more frequently used types of display windows. Include provision for sun control and for customer protection from bad weather. Finish the project by adding a store sign that is in keeping with the exterior design and the type of merchandise handled.

6. Visit stores of the type covered in this chapter and examine their service areas, until you find one that is well planned. Sketch a plan of this area and build a cardboard scale model, including storage shelves, bins and conveyors. Prepare a report calling attention to the outstanding features of this service area.

7. Work with several other class members, as a design team, to research the data for a particular type of store. Make preliminary drawings, revise these, and draw a complete set of plans. The material in Chapters 19-21 concerning structure will need to be studied as this planning proceeds.

Additional Reading

Ketchum, Morris, *Shops and Stores.*
Parnes, Louis, *Planning Stores That Pay.*

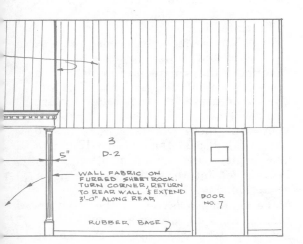

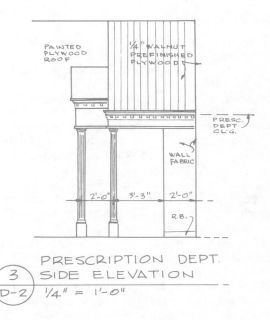

PRESCRIPTION DEPT.
SIDE ELEVATION
3/D-2   1/4" = 1'-0"

PLANNING OFFICES, BANKS AND MEDICAL OFFICES AND CLINICS

The increasing costs of construction have caused designers of offices, banks and medical buildings to focus attention upon the efficient use of space. Careful study of the activities to take place in an area has enabled designers to reduce the amount of space needed and, at the same time, to increase the efficiency of the workers.

This chapter discusses the principles to follow when designing office, banking and medical facilities.

Office Planning

Industry has long accepted the fact that it is necessary to make a careful study of all the factors involved when planning a manufacturing installation. On the other hand, office planning generally has been neglected. However, the high cost of unused space and inefficient operation has emphasized the values of, and need for, careful consideration of the use of space allotted to office functions.

It is unrealistic to allot a standard, set amount of space per employee in an office. Instead, the job of each employee should be studied, and he should be given sufficient space to perform his duties.

The use of private offices has been re-examined by planners and has been found to be costly and, in many cases, unjustifiable.

The effective utilization of office space can be accomplished only through careful planning. The planner must have a thorough knowledge of office operations and how they are performed, office personnel, and equipment.

An Approach to Office Planning

The proper approach to office planning is to survey the needs, to analyze these needs and, then, to apply the principles of planning to develop an effective layout. While exact procedures vary from company to company, the following steps suggest a logical approach.

1. Ascertain the personnel to be accommodated and what duties they perform.
2. List all needed equipment.
3. Develop an organizational chart of the workers, and chart the flow of work. This is illustrated in Fig. 890.
4. List all service facilities needed such as rest rooms and storage rooms.
5. Determine the square feet of floor area needed by each office activity. This will give a measure of the total footage needed.
6. Visit with those who will work in the office, and discuss their needs. If it is a new facility, visit similar facilities.
7. Provide for future, anticipated needs or expansion.
8. Make a detailed layout of the office arrangement. Templates are useful.
9. Let those who will work in the facility review the plan.

Office Planning Principles

The following factors must be considered when planning office layouts.

1. A supervisor who is working with his employees generally should be in the same

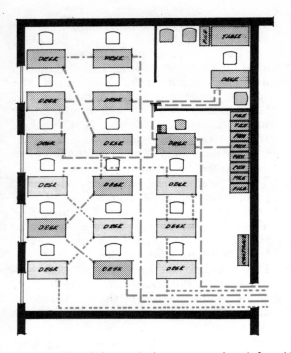 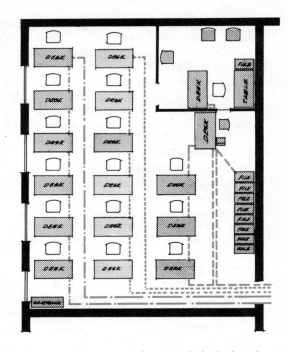

Fig. 890. Office before and after a survey of work flow. (An *Approach to Office Planning*, Engineering Services, General Electric Co.)

Left: Office before work flow survey was made. Consider-

able time was being wasted because clerks had to leave work stations to forward work.

Right: Office after survey established flow of work and clerks were seated to form straight-line flow.

room with them. His desk should be located at the rear of the workers' desks.

2. Employees within a unit doing the same type of work should be in the same room. Interrelated units of an office should be near each other. Transportation distance of work should be held to a minimum. If possible, work surfaces should be arranged so that each worker receives his work from the person adjacent to him. Refer again to Fig. 890.

3. Work in an office should follow a straight-line flow, to minimize backtracking. *The locations of work stations should be dictated by work relationships.* This principle is most important, and all other considerations should be subordinate to it.

4. A large, open office area generally is better than the same space divided into smaller offices. The open office makes control and communication easier, provides better light and ventilation, reduces space requirements, facilitates a better flow of work, simplifies supervision and eliminates partition costs. See Fig. 891.

5. Each employee should be allowed sufficient space to perform his function efficiently, yet this space should be held to the minimum needed.

6. Desks should face in the same direction, not back-to-back, unless there is some

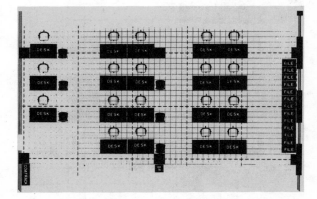

Fig. 891. A general clerical office arranged to accommodate sixteen clerks and three administrative employees. Notice the wide main aisles and the extra wide aisle in front of the file section. Space has been saved by placing the desks end to end with an aisle on each side. (*An Approach to Office Planning*, Engineering Services, General Electric Co.)

specific reason. Placing desks back-to-back does not save space and often stimulates conversations and other time-consuming practices.

7. Large offices should be partitioned into related activities by file cabinets or low dividers. This helps control noise, increases morale and reduces distraction by aisle traffic.

8. Noisy operations such as duplication or bookkeeping machines should be separated from quieter clerical areas. Special acoustical treatment may be necessary.

9. All clerical desks should be the same size and color. This gives the office a more pleasant appearance and facilitates rearrangement, because all units are the same size.

10. Desks are best arranged in straight lines, to facilitate straight-line flow of work.

11. Clerical desks should be at least 30 inches apart, to allow sufficient space for the worker's chair. Maximum space is 48 inches. The ideal spacing is 36 inches.

12. Primary aisles in a general clerical office should be at least 4'-0". Crossover aisles should be 3'-0", and secondary aisles between desks should be 2'-0". These should be wider if heavy traffic is anticipated.

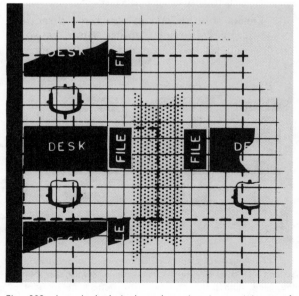

Fig. 892. A typical clerical work station in a minimum of space. (*An Approach to Office Planning*, Engineering Services, General Electric Co.)

13. The most efficient arrangement of desks in a general clerical office is to place two desks side by side. This provides an aisle on each side. When more than two desks are arranged in this fashion, the spacing between the rows of desks should be increased to a 33-inch minimum. A more satisfactory spacing is 42 inches. In any case, when such desks are placed end to end, each employee should have easy access to secondary aisles.

14. The typical clerical work station can be accommodated in 60 square feet of floor area. This figure includes 7 square feet allotted to an aisle beside the work station. If special equipment is needed, extra space must be allowed. See Fig. 892.

15. Desks should be arranged so that employees do not face the natural light. Light should come over the left shoulder. Rows of files may serve to block glare from windows.

16. Heavy equipment should be placed against walls or columns whenever possible, in order to avoid floor overloading.

17. It is poor practice to locate private offices on the outside walls and clerical work stations in an inside area. This gives a boxed-in feeling. Clerical areas need some outside window area.

18. A row of file cases makes an effective separation between office units.

19. The size of office furniture varies considerably. That selected should be large enough to meet the needs of the worker. Anything larger is waste.

20. Each office worker should have only the furniture needed to do his job. Excess furniture results in poor space utilization.

21. Employees having considerable public contact should be near entrances to the office. Employees doing confidential work should be away from entrances.

22. The employee work station should be located near the equipment he must regularly use.

23. The cost of office labor is greater than the cost of space, so anything that increases efficiency is to be preferred over something that may save space but reduce efficiency.

24. Attractive, comfortable working conditions increase the efficiency of personnel.

25. Future needs for expansion or added services should be considered. It should be possible to reorganize space with a minimum of rebuilding. Consideration should be given to the utilization of seasonal employees during peak business periods.

26. Clothes lockers in an office layout are obsolete and waste space. In large rooms, doorless or open coat and package areas should be provided, with hanging rods for coats and shelves for hats and other personal belongings. These areas should be located in the space least desirable for work to be done.

27. Very few employees, including top executives, need private offices. The primary consideration is the need for privacy in the conduct of the job, such as a job requiring frequent visitors or one in which a majority of the time is spent in conversation.

28. If a private office seems necessary, consider the furniture and equipment needed for the occupant to perform his duties, and plan to accommodate these.

29. A person having few visitors usually can be accommodated in an 8'-0" x 9'-0" office, while one who has frequent visitors needs a 9'-0" x 12'-0" office. An executive who holds conferences in his office may require 300 or 400 square feet. See Fig. 893.

30. The space allotted to a secretary depends upon her duties. She may perform duties other than dictation and typing, such as filing or greeting visitors.

31. An intercommunication system between the secretary and the executives she serves is desirable.

32. The secretary's office should be designed so she has an unobstructed view of the doorways, adequate file space, storage for office supplies and seats for visitors. See Fig. 894.

33. Where frequent interviews with the public are required, such as in personnel offices, the use of interview cubicles should be considered. Such cubicles need only be large enough for the interviewer, the applicant and a small desk or table. The partitions should be limited to a 7'-0" height, with acoustical treatment on the walls if necessary.

34. If some employees are away from the office most of the workday, returning only occasionally to file reports, consideration should be given to assigning two or more employees to each desk. This system is particularly effective if the hours the employees report to the office can be staggered. Other suggestions in the housing of such operations are the provision of 50-inch desks for the employees or the use of common work tables, with single drawers in file cabinets

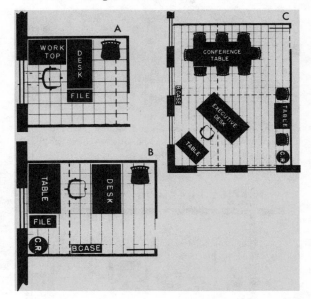

Fig. 893. A — A small private office 8'-0" x 9'-0".

B — A private office 9'-0" x 12'-0".

C — A large executive office with a small conference table requiring a room 16'-0" x 20'-0". (*An Approach to Office Planning*, Engineering Services, General Electric Co.)

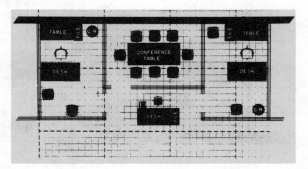

Fig. 894. Notice the location of the secretary. She is in a position to meet all visitors and is closely related to the two private offices she serves. The third space could serve as a conference room or another office. (*An Approach to Office Planning*, Engineering Service, General Electric Co.)

assigned for the storage of each employee's work papers and supplies.

35. The reception area should be pleasant and should favorably impress the visitor. Music, plants, paintings, drapes and comfortable furniture contribute to this atmosphere. See Figs. 895 and 896.

36. The location of rest rooms near the reception area should be considered, Fig. 897.

Fig. 895. An attractive reception and waiting area. Notice the light appearance provided by the obscure glass partitions. (Libbey-Owens-Ford Glass Co.)

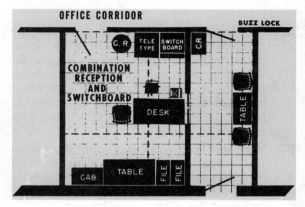

Fig. 896. A small reception and waiting room. (*An Approach to Office Planning*, Engineering Service, General Electric Co.)

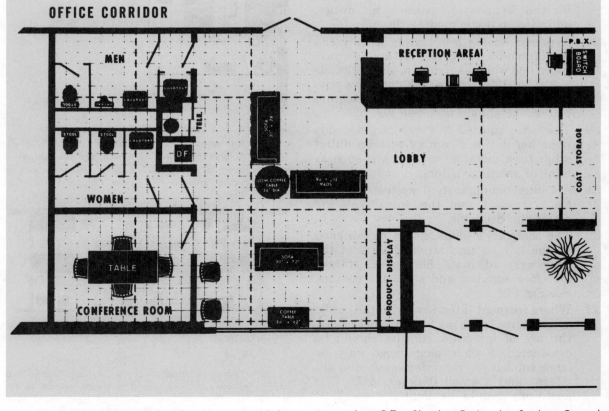

Fig. 897. An elaborate reception and waiting room. Notice the conference room, rest rooms and product display. (*An Approach to Office Planning*, Engineering Services, General Electric Co.)

37. If company products are to be displayed in the reception area, provision must be made for this. Refer again to Fig. 897.

38. The receptionist should have telephone connections to the various departments within the office. Outside connections are necessary also.

39. Small conference or interview rooms frequently eliminate the need for private offices. Another approach is to divide a space with 7-foot partitions. This provides considerable privacy, yet the space can be air conditioned and lighted with the same system used in the larger, general office spaces.

40. Allow 20 to 25 square feet per person in conference rooms accommodating up to thirty people. Allow 10 to 15 square feet per person for rooms accommodating thirty to two hundred people. This does not allow for tables, but assumes chairs will be set in rows facing a rostrum. If tables are to be used, ascertain the table size and allow clearance for side chairs and an aisle behind the chairs. Selected plans are shown in Fig. 898.

41. Conference rooms can be located off the reception room, if it is desired to reduce traffic in the office area.

42. Careful study should be made of files. Inactive files should be removed from the general office to warehouse or storage space. Files should be used for filing and not for storage of office supplies.

43. Active files should be located as near to those using them as possible. Some businesses prefer to use a central file room, Fig. 899.

44. The aisle space between files should be held to a minimum. Suggested aisle spacing by the General Service Administration, Washington, D. C. follows:

File Room	Drawers Per Person Working Therein	Aisle Space Suggested	
		Min.	Max.
Very Active	20 to 49	42"	45"
Active	50 to 74	36"	41"
Semi-Active	75 to 150	31"	35"
Inactive	Over 150	24"	30"

45. Standard files require an allowance of 5 to 7 square feet, and legal files require 6 to 8 square feet.

46. Office supplies on hand should be kept to a minimum. The bulk of the supplies should be kept in nonoffice space.

47. Employees doing detailed, close work should be in the best lighted areas. Glaring surfaces which affect vision should be corrected.

48. Lighting requirements vary with the activity. Corridors need about 20 footcandles, conference rooms and reception rooms about 35 to 40 footcandles, general offices and secretarial areas from

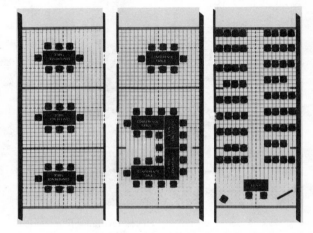

Fig. 898. A conference room 20'-0" x 45'-0". The use of folding doors enables this area to be used for three small conference rooms, one small and one large room, or the entire area may be opened for large meetings. The elimination of tables greatly increases the capacity of the room. (*An Approach to Office Planning*, Engineering Services, General Electric Co.)

Fig. 899. A centralized file room. (*An Approach to Office Planning*, Engineering Services, General Electric Co.)

50 to 75 footcandles and drafting and business machine sections from 75 to 100 footcandles. See Fig. 900.

49. Glare and reflected light should be avoided, since they increase eye fatigue. Uniformity of light distribution in clerical areas is vital.

Fig. 900. A series of private offices located off a clerical area. Simplicity and pleasant lighting add to the quiet, subdued atmosphere. (Libbey-Owens-Ford Glass Co.)

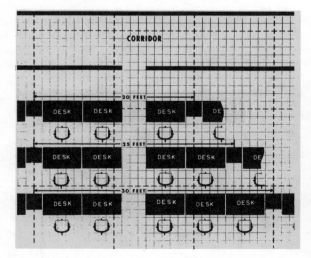

Fig. 901. Columns should be spaced to enable area to be used to the maximum. This requires them to be on 5-foot increments with 20'-0" a minimum span. The above drawing shows how standard desks can be spaced if columns are on the 5-foot module. (*An Approach to Office Planning*, Engineering Services, General Electric Co.)

50. Consideration should be given to the use of color. Color can reduce fatigue brought on by clerical duties. Bright colors or sharp contrasts should be used in halls, while a reception room should be painted in warm, inviting tones. In large, general clerical offices, the wall faced by the employees should be painted a light, cool color, while the other three walls should be a warm pastel such as yellow or tan.

51. Year-round air conditioning is widely used and tends to increase employee efficiency.

52. Stairways and exits should be planned so the distance from any employee to the nearest exit is not over 150 feet.

53. Rest rooms and drinking fountains should not be over 150 feet from offices.

54. Doors must be wide enough to permit easy movement of furniture.

55. In many offices, provision must be made for handling large quantities of mail.

56. Floors must be able to carry the load of special equipment.

57. If a large office is planned, column spacing must be considered. A minimum of 20'-0" between columns is recommended. See Fig. 901.

58. Special considerations are necessary to accommodate data processing equipment. These are discussed in the next section of this chapter.

59. Fig. 902 illustrates an office building plan, showing needed work areas and offices for a group of lawyers.

Fig. 902-A. Law offices. (See also next page.)

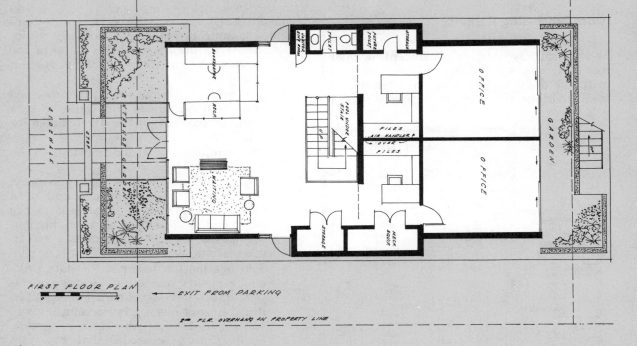

2ᴺᴰ FLR OVERHANG ON PROPERTY LINE

→ ENTRANCE TO PARKING

FIRST FLOOR PLAN   ← EXIT FROM PARKING

2ᴺᴰ FLR. OVERHANG ON PROPERTY LINE

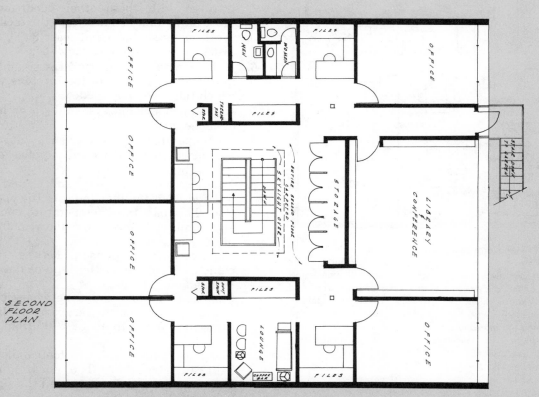

SECOND FLOOR PLAN

Fig. 902-B and C. Law office building in Sarasota, Florida. This building was designed to accommodate eight attorneys, with adjacent secretarial offices for each attorney. It is completely air conditioned. The structure is steel-framed, with the second floor cantilevered to the property line. The first floor was set back to allow access to a parking area in the rear. (Libbey-Owens-Ford Glass Co., and Frank Folsom Smith, Architect)

Data Processing Centers

The planning of a data processing center is an extremely complex assignment, involving the services of many people. Those concerned with the daily operation of the office or business divisions of a store or company must be consulted constantly. Experts from companies manufacturing data processing equipment must be deeply involved. Some of the factors to consider when planning such a facility follow.

1. The type of information to be processed must be ascertained. This could be data such as payrolls, materials handled or invoices.
2. The equipment needed must then be ascertained.
3. A plan for the flow of work is necessary. Work usually begins at one end of a facility and is carried in process to the other end. It is set up on a production-line basis. Fig. 903 illustrates such an installation.
4. The relationship between the data processing facility and other business operations must be ascertained. For example, if a company has a large accounting and statistical division, the data processing facility must be located so that employees involved with these other departments are a minimum distance from the facility.
5. Work aisles should be at least 3'-0", and aisles to carry heavy traffic 4'-0".
6. Units providing work surfaces should be located within 4 feet of the machine with which they are to be used.
7. Key punch machines should be at least 30 inches apart.
8. Each operator should have sufficient storage space to keep needed supplies near his machine.
9. The key punch department should be isolated from the remainder of the operation. This facilitates temperature control and eliminates noise from the remainder of the installation.
10. The working relationship between machines depends upon the type of data to be handled.
11. Ceilings and walls should be acoustically treated. Walls usually are treated from the ceiling down to about 5'-0" from the floor.
12. Machine rooms require 40 footcandles of light at table level. Too much illumination makes it difficult to read the signal lights on the machines.
13. Lighting should be installed so various sections can be turned off or on when needed.

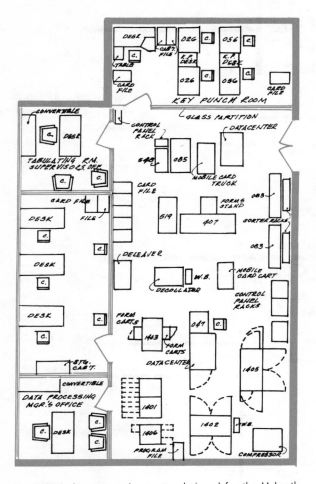

Fig. 903. A data processing center designed for the McLouth Steel Company. It handles payroll, tax information, check writing, labor distribution for cost analysis, mill order information, billing and invoicing, and sales analysis. The solid lines indicate machines and racks; the dotted lines indicate spaces needed for servicing the machine. This installation has equipment manufactured by the International Business Machines Corp. The machines, as identified by number are:

1401 Data Processing System
1402 Card Read Punch
1403 Printer
1405 Disk Storage Unit
1406 Storage
047 Tape to Card Printing Punch
083 Sorter
407 Accounting Machine
519 Document Originating Machine
548 Interpreter
085 Collator
026 Printing Card Punch
056 Verifier

14. Electrical power requirements must be ascertained. A constant rate of power must be available in order for the machines to perform the high-speed computations accurately. A tremendous amount of power is required. A separate feeder line for the computers should be considered. Usually transformers, separate from those supplying the building, are used for the facility.

15. Room temperature and humidity control is vital. The machines must be operated at the specific temperature recommended by the manufacturer.

16. Dust control is necessary. The room should be as "dust proof" as possible. Fig. 904 pictures a typical installation.

17. Storage space is needed for extra materials and parts.

18. Machines should have sufficient space surrounding them to permit repairs and adjustments.

19. The tabulating room supervisor's office should be adjacent to that area. It is necessary to design the facility so the supervisors have visual contact with the entire area.

20. Data processing equipment is heavy. Special consideration should be given to design the structure to carry the extra weight.

Planning Banks

Bank planning varies considerably, depending upon the size of the bank and the services it offers. Areas must be planned for each activity, and attention must be given to the relationships that exist between these activities.

An experimental banking system for small banks is being tried. These banks do not perform their bookkeeping in their building, but transmit information to a banking center. Here electronic equipment does the recording and transmits data back to the banks. This is done in a matter of seconds.

Planning Small Banks

The following planning principles should be considered when planning small banks.

1. The first consideration is to examine the site and locate the building, parking area and drive-in facilities to best advantage. Then it is necessary to study the plan of operation of the bank and to ascertain the traffic patterns of the various employees and customers.

2. Adequate customer parking is vital. Easy entrance to the bank from the parking area is necessary. A covered entrance is of value for inclement weather.

3. In a small bank, each employee usually performs several functions. These must be considered when locating work areas. It is customary for tellers to work in the bookkeeping area during lull periods; therefore, the teller area and the bookkeeping area should be adjacent, permitting employees to move between the two quickly and with a minimum of steps. Fig. 905 illustrates a small banking facility.

4. If a drive-in window is used, generally only one window can be staffed. Small banks cannot afford to operate more than one. Usually someone in the bookkeeping or teller area must handle these customers; therefore, the drive-in window should be visible from these areas.

5. The tellers and employees in the bookkeeping and machine area should have visual contact with the vault area, so they may control access to the vault.

6. The vault in a small bank serves the dual purpose of money and record storage and safe-deposit box location. Some control of customer traffic to this area is necessary. Usually a low partition with a gate is used to separate the lobby from the vault. The employee responsible for over-

Fig. 904. A data processing system. Notice the soft general illumination and clean conditions. (International Business Machines Corp.)

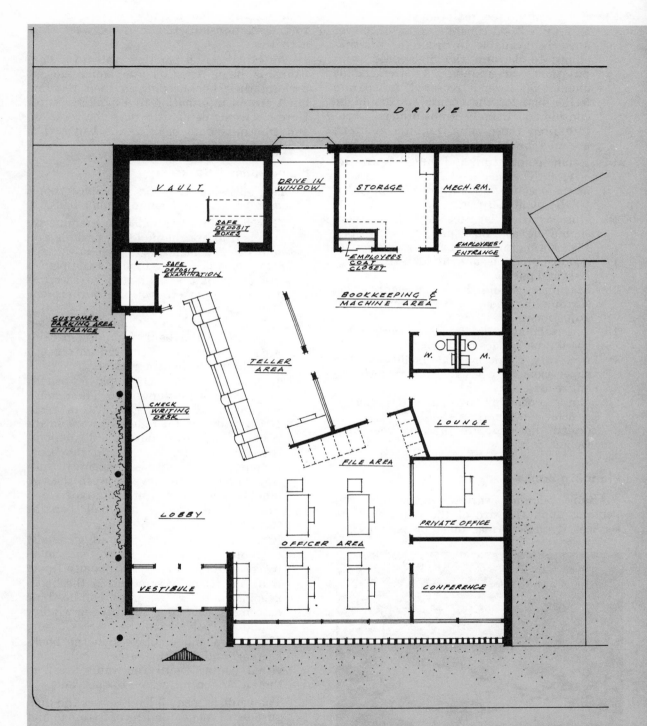

Fig. 905-A. This plan was developed to house an existing small bank. (William Hankammer, Bank Designer and Contractor, Jack Hankammer, Architect, Pittsburg, Kansas)

Since a primary consideration in planning is the cost of the facility, the designer is limited to a building of a size the bank can afford. Within this floor area, the designer attempted to embody all of the desirable characteristics of bank planning that could be obtained within the cost limitations. Notice the relationships established between work areas, vault location and control and the auto traffic.

Fig. 905-B and C. Front and side elevations of bank on page 348.

seeing activities in the vault should have his work station near this entrance.

7. Vault design varies considerably. The wall thickness varies with the type of vault door chosen. Frequently, a door that is 1½ to 2½ inches thick is used.

8. The vault should have a ventilator to supply oxygen to the area, in case someone inadvertently is locked inside.

9. An alarm system is important and should be planned by experts. Provision for installation should be made when the building is constructed. An alarm system reduces the need for a heavy vault.

10. A private area near the vault, but outside it, is needed for customers to examine their safe-deposit boxes. This usually is a partitioned cubicle containing a small table.

11. A hidden telephone should be installed in the vault.

12. The number of safe-deposit boxes needed and their size must be determined. They are available in a variety of sizes.

13. The interior ceiling height of the vault is usually 8'-0".

14. The small bank generally has three types of customers — those seeing the general teller, those writing checks and making deposits and those seeing bank officers concerning loans and notes. To reduce customer congestion, the check-writing and deposit-slip desk should be apart from the bank officers' area. Fig. 906 illustrates the relationship between the teller windows, writing desk and bank officers' area.

15. The bank officers' desks should be located away from the main lobby. This increases privacy for those discussing loans and notes.

16. Private offices for bank officials are nice, but require considerable floor area that usually is not available in a small bank. Offices frequently are clustered in a semi-private area. Desks may be separated by 6'-0" high partitions if desired.

Fig. 906. The writing desks in this bank are located to avoid congestion with the tellers' windows. The bank officials have a small office area in the lobby and a private office opening to the rear of this area. Materials used require a minimum of maintenance.

17. The bank president frequently desires a private office.

18. Several chairs near the bank officers' area are needed to seat waiting customers.

19. A small conference room is desirable. This can serve as a meeting place for bank directors and for private functions such as the disposition of wills. A telephone should be in this area.

20. In some banks, officers also serve at the tellers' windows. In this case, the officers' area and tellers' area should be closely related. Frequently, officers serve the window handling notes. When this is the case, this window should be nearest the officers' area, with the general tellers' windows located near the lobby area.

21. The tellers need drawers, shelves and cabinet space for storage of supplies used in their work. These should have locks for security.

22. The location of telephones varies with the floor layout and plan of work. A carefully planned, intercommunication system is necessary. It should be designed so conversations can be private. Especially important is a connection between the bank officials' area and the bookkeeping area.

23. Rest room facilities for employees are needed. These should be located so they are not in general view of the customer.

24. A small, employee's lounge is desirable. If space is at a premium, this area also could serve as a director's room or an extra office.

25. A storage room near the bookkeeping and machine area is needed. Tellers can store several days' supply of needed items at their stations.

26. A mechanical room for office machines and equipment is best if it can be centrally located. However, this location usually is not possible, because it interferes with the business traffic pattern.

27. Year-round air conditioning is vital.

28. Heating cables in the walk and parking area, to melt snow and ice, are good for customer relations.

29. Drive-in windows are improved if infrared lights are installed above them.

30. Exterior doors should swing out from the lobby. A double set of doors reduces uncomfortable drafts. If the doors are on the edge of the sidewalks, they will have to swing inward so as not to interfere with pedestrian traffic. Since this is undesirable, usually the entrance vestibule is recessed to allow the doors to swing out. Double doors are desirable.

31. An area for files should be planned. This should be near the department using the files.

32. A small bank usually cannot afford personnel to operate an exterior walk-up, customer-service window.

Fig. 908. A stock drive-in window equipped with a microphone for communicating with the customer. (Diebold, Inc.)

Fig. 907. Notice the outside entrance to the loan office at the right of this photo. This small bank provides double entrance doors and a single drive-in window. (Natcor Store Fronts)

33. The equipment to be accommodated in the bookkeeping and mechanical room must be determined so these areas can be planned. The typical, small bank has posting machines, microfilm equipment, adding machines, check-cancelling equipment, typewriters and filing equipment.

34. The bookkeeping equipment and machines should be placed so the operators can see the teller area clearly, since some employees work in both areas.

35. Closets are needed for employees' coats and personal belongings.

36. Working areas, such as the teller area, bookkeeping and machine area and bank officers' area, require 100 footcandles of light. The lobby needs only a minimum of general illumination. Other areas such as the check-writing table can use accent lighting.

37. Acoustical treatment is vital, especially in the machine area. Ceiling and wall treatment is needed to contain the noise within this area. The machine area may be separated with ceiling-high partitions.

38. If the bank operates a small-loan office, provision should be made for easy access to this by customers after regular closing hours, since this area operates the full day. See Fig. 907.

Additional Considerations for Larger Banks

39. Larger banks face different problems in relating areas. They employ full-time tellers and bookkeepers, so easy access between these areas is not important. A good intercommunication system serves well here.

40. Drive-in banking windows offer special planning problems. Fig. 908 illustrates a stock unit. Customers should be able to reach these windows easily from the street, without cutting across lanes of traffic or heavily traveled sidewalks. The window should be on the driver's side of the auto. See Figs. 909 and 910.

41. If several drive-in windows are used, space should be provided for automobiles to pass one another to reach alternate windows or to leave immediately upon completion of the business transaction. See Figs. 911 and 912.

42. Well placed signs are necessary to give drivers directions on traffic patterns to windows. Electric signs are available to tell a waiting customer when a window is empty. See Fig. 913.

Fig. 909. A two-window drive-in facility. Notice the traffic flow permits customers to enter from both streets, thus increasing the accessibility of the facility. The parking area serves a walk-up window at rear of the island. (Diebold, Inc.)

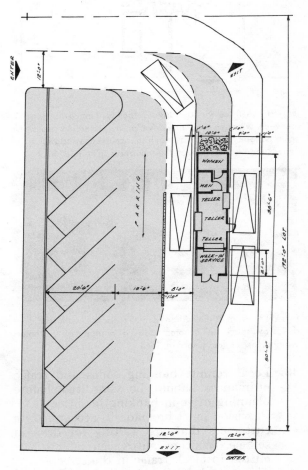

Fig. 910. Plan of a two-station drive-in banking facility. Notice the walk-up window off a small lobby. (Diebold, Inc.)

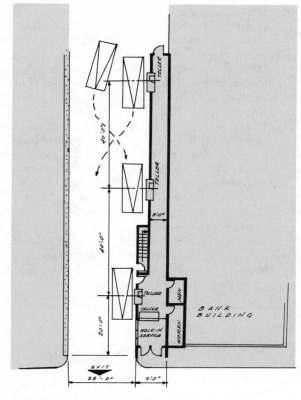

Fig. 911. A three-window drive-in facility. Notice the spacing between windows and the drive area, permitting customers to pass one another to reach unoccupied windows or to leave upon conclusion of their business. (Diebold, Inc.)

Fig. 912. A multiple-station drive-in facility with sufficient driveway space to accommodate a number of customers waiting for service. (Diebold, Inc.)

43. Local zoning, building codes and traffic ordinances should be consulted before planning drive-in banking facilities.
44. Provision must be made to accommodate customers that are waiting for drive-in service. Waiting autos cannot be permitted to block traffic in the street.
45. The outside, drive-in teller's room need only be large enough to accommodate the

Fig. 913. Electric, teller-operated signs notify waiting customers when a window is open. (Diebold, Inc.)

Top: Customer arrives; sign tells him to wait as all windows are busy.

Second: Teller finishes with a customer and actuates sign to signal her window is open.

Third: Sign tells customer to move to window 1.

Fourth: Next customer is told to wait until a window is open.

Fig. 914. A double walk-up window facing onto a sidewalk. (Diebold, Inc.)

Fig. 915. A remote banking station utilizing closed-circuit television and pneumatic tube for transferring materials to a teller in the bank building. (Diebold, Inc.)

Fig. 916. A pleasing bank entrance. Notice the sun screen and the extensive use of draperies. (Northrup Architectural Systems)

Fig. 917. A contemporary bank building of simple form. The interior furnishings provide the "face" to the public. Note the accent lighting over the writing tables and the lighting strips in the ceiling for general illumination. (Libbey-Owens-Ford Glass Co.)

one banking function. Frequently, a water closet is installed for the convenience of the teller.

46. A walk-up banking window serves customers who do not want to take time to enter the bank. Nearby parking is needed. See Fig. 914.

47. A drive-in banking unit located in a remote area can be installed, where space does not permit the usual drive-in banking with teller service. This unit has closed-circuit television for contact with a teller, and the materials are transferred from the unit to a teller via a pneumatic tube. The teller can operate this unit from inside the bank building. See Fig. 915.

48. State banking laws regulate the distance that drive-in stations can be located from the bank building.

49. A night-deposit window should be considered. It should be easily accessible and well lighted.

50. The exterior styling of banks varies considerably. It usually reflects the geographic location of the bank and the attitude of the management. There is no one best style, and colonial as well as contemporary styling is successfully used. See Figs. 916 and 917.

Medical and Dental Offices and Clinics

A clinic is a building designed to provide facilities for two or more doctors or dentists. Patients are treated here, but usually are not kept overnight as is the practice in a hospital.

The development of small clinics is a relatively new trend. The general procedure for years has been for medical doctors and dentists to set up practice in a remodeled residence or in a larger building in a downtown location. The trend now is for a group of doctors to use a building especially designed to meet their professional needs. This clinic frequently is located in residential areas. It is common for medical doctors and dentists to join together in one clinic. Figs. 918 and 919 illustrate two clinics and their floor plans.

Medical Offices and Clinics

As medical offices and clinics are being planned, the following principles should be considered.

1. The size of the waiting room depends upon the type of medical activity housed and the number of doctors using the room for their patients. Some medical activities, such as psychiatry, schedule

patients rather carefully and, therefore, require only a small waiting room. However, a general practitioner frequently sees large numbers of people, many for only a very brief time, and, therefore,

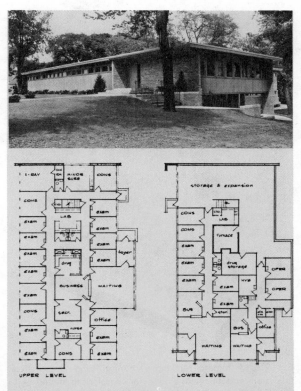

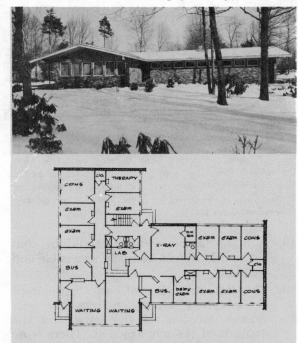

Fig. 919. A medical clinic designed on two levels to take advantage of a sloping site. (Marshall Erdman and Associates, Inc., Madison, Wisconsin, Designers and Builders of Medical Office Buildings)

Fig. 918. An L-shaped medical clinic on one level. (Marshall Erdman and Associates, Inc., Madison, Wisconsin, Designers and Builders of Medical Office Buildings)

Fig. 920. An attractive waiting room. Notice the provision for reading and the relaxed atmosphere of the room. Lighting is soft with no "medical atmosphere." (Flintkote Co.)

requires a large waiting room. A pleasant waiting room is illustrated in Fig. 920.

2. The duties of the receptionist must be known. In small clinics, she often serves the dual role of receptionist and business office clerk. In this case, the receptionist and business areas should be combined in one room. Larger clinics have a separate business staff and require a special business office. This should be near the waiting room and reception area. Fig. 921 illustrates a small clinic in which the receptionist serves as the business office clerk. Fig. 922 illustrates a plan with these duties separate.

3. In large clinics, provision should be made for a lounge for employees, such as the nurses and medical technologists. Small clinics cannot afford space for this.

4. Rest rooms for staff and patients are necessary. Easy access from the waiting room is desirable.

5. The equipment in a medical examination room varies according to the desires and the practice of the doctor. The equipment normally includes an examination table, scale, lavatory, waste container, desk, two chairs and a dressing booth. If a room is used for special examinations, space must be allowed for the needed equipment. It is common practice to use such a room for consultation as well as examination. In a room used only for examination, the desk and chairs could be omitted. Fig. 923 illustrates typical examination and consultation rooms, while Fig. 924 illustrates office suites for medical specialists.

6. If space is at a premium, the consultation-examination room can be enlarged, and the doctor also can use this as his office. The additional space is needed for files and books. Another possibility is to have

small examination rooms and separate consultation rooms which also serve as doctors' offices.

7. The walls of consultation and examination rooms should be soundproof.

8. In a very small clinic, one nurse frequently serves as a laboratory technician and receptionist, as well as the nurse. In such a situation, a combination business office and reception room is used, with the laboratory adjoining this area.

9. In clinics of moderate size, one person may serve as receptionist and handle the business functions, so that the nurse is

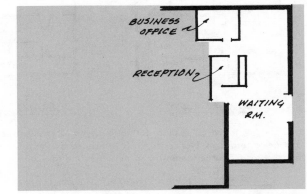

Fig. 922. A partial plan for a large clinic, showing separate business and receptionist areas.

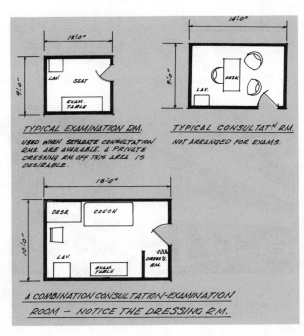

Fig. 923. Examination and consultation rooms.

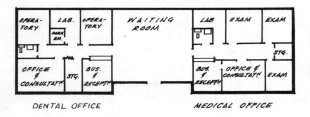

Fig. 921. A clinic housing one dentist and one medical doctor.

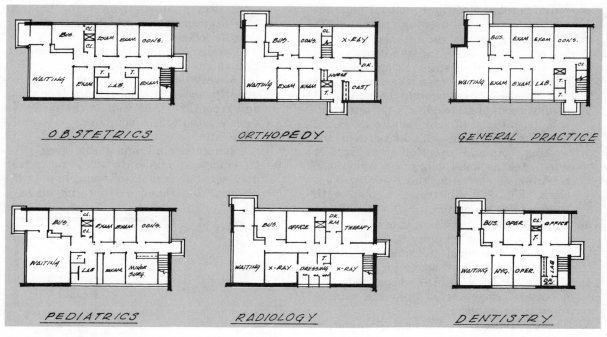

Fig. 924. Suggested office plans for various types of medical and dental practices. Notice the facilities needed by specialists, such as the large laboratory in obstetrics, the cast room in orthopedy and X-ray and therapy facilities in radiology. (Marshall Erdman and Associates, Inc., Madison, Wisconsin, Designers and Builders of Medical Office Buildings)

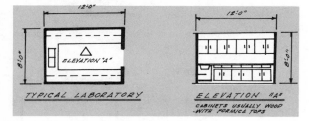

Fig. 925. Typical medical clinic laboratory.

Fig. 926. A large commercial laboratory serving many doctors. With such a facility in the area, doctors offices and medical clinics can be planned with a minimum of space allotted to a laboratory because they can send their work to the large concern. (Libbey-Owens-Ford Glass Co.)

freed for medical duties. In this case, the nurse's station and the laboratory could be combined so the nurse also can serve as a laboratory technician. Fig. 918 illustrates a combined laboratory and nurse's station. Fig. 919 has these duties separated.

10. The nurse's station should be located so it is close to the area used by the doctors served.

11. The nurse's station should be as near the waiting room as possible, since she must meet the patient and take him to a consultation or examination room.

12. The size of a laboratory and the equipment located there varies with the size of the clinic and the availability of commercial laboratories in the area. Fig. 925 illustrates a typical medical clinic laboratory. Fig. 926 is a large commercial laboratory.

13. If blood samples are taken and injections are given in a laboratory, a chair and couch are needed for the patient's comfort.

14. A rest room adjoining the laboratory is helpful for taking specimens.

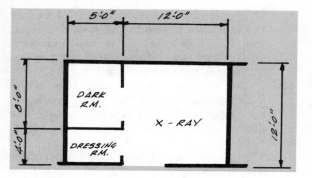

Fig. 927. Typical X-ray laboratory as found in a medical clinic.

Table 55

Typical Medical and Dental Space Requirements

Space requirements were developed by examining existing facilities. Requirements vary considerably, depending on type of practice and personal preference.

Room	Square Feet
Waiting room - medical (to seat 20 patients)	400
Waiting room - dental (to seat 6-8 patients)	100
Examining rooms - medical	100-140
Consultation rooms	100-140
Toilets	30
Nurse's station and workroom	80
Laboratory - medical (to handle EKG, BMR and X-ray)	100-300
Laboratory - dental	75-100
Recovery room - medical	140
Recovery room - dental	40-50
X-ray room - medical	120-180
Darkroom - medical	50
Darkroom - dental	15-25
X-ray storage and viewing room	100-120
Patient dressing rooms	30-40
Minor surgery room - medical	130
Operatory - dental	80
Supply room (sterilized supplies, sterilizers, autoclave, utensil washing)	80-120
Employee lounge	150-175
Kitchen (for patients in recovery rooms and personnel lunches)	65
Linen storage	100-120
Janitor room	80-120
Furnace room	As Req.
Library	100-120
Private doctor's office	100
Receptionist area	80-150
Business office	100-150

15. In large clinics, a full-time laboratory technician may be employed. If this person also handles X-ray work, this room should adjoin the laboratory. Fig. 927 illustrates a typical X-ray laboratory, darkroom and dressing room as found in medical clinics.

16. The X-ray room should be large enough to accommodate the equipment desired. Specialists should plan the layout, so maximum safety is afforded the patient and technician.

17. The darkroom is used as a place to develop X-ray plates and, sometimes, as a viewing room. It should be designed to accommodate all equipment.

18. All sterilization should take place in one area. This sometimes is a part of the laboratory. Provision should be made to vent the area to remove moisture.

19. Very little surgery is performed in a clinic. If minor surgery, such as a tonsillectomy, is contemplated, the surgical room should receive special consideration. Anesthesia facilities are necessary, as is provision for the complete removal of airborne bacteria. The latter condition is difficult to obtain without extensive facilities.

20. Suggested space requirements for medical and dental clinics are shown in Table 55.

21. Provision must be made for storage of janitorial supplies. This can be in the least desirable portions of the building.

22. The parking area required can be ascertained by establishing the average number of patients each doctor handles per hour. This varies with type of practice.

23. The atmosphere of clinics should be one of friendliness and warmth. This relaxes the patient and makes the visit more enjoyable. The selection of materials and colors is important.

24. Year-round air conditioning is very important. Chapter 10, "Heating, Cooling and Insulating," should prove helpful. It is necessary that the air in each room be changed frequently and that the fresh-air supply be considerable. Odors must be removed. Patients must be comfortable at all times. Certain rooms, as those in medical and dental surgery, require a 100 percent fresh-air supply.

25. Special plumbing fixtures are available for medical use. Manufacturers' catalogs should be studied to ascertain what is available and the advantages of each.

Dental Offices and Clinics

Many of the planning factors discussed for the medical clinic apply as well to the dental clinic. Following are considerations unique to dental clinic planning.

1. The waiting room can be considerably smaller than that required for medical clinics. Seldom does a dentist have over four people waiting at one time.
2. The receptionist should be able to talk with a patient without being overheard by those waiting. Usually this is accomplished by separating the reception area from the waiting room.
3. A rest room should be conveniently located near the reception room.
4. The reception area may be used for business office duties.
5. Provision should be made for hanging patients' coats. It is best if the patient can remove his coat before he enters the waiting room.
6. The darkroom can be very small, since X-ray work is limited.
7. The dentist should have a private office.
8. Three operatories usually are desired for a single dentist. The dentist, with his assistant, can use two, while a dental hygienist can use the third for X-ray, scaling, cleaning and tissue examinations. Fig. 924 illustrates a plan for an office for one dentist. Some dentists use four to six operatories.

9. It is desirable if the operatories can face the north, to take advantage of this light. Fig. 928 illustrates a typical operatory.
10. Operatories used for dental surgery require 100 percent fresh-air supply.
11. If two or more dentists work together in a clinic, they could share the operatory used by the dental technician, since one dentist seldom has enough work to keep her busy.
12. The operatories should be adjacent. Since the dentist and his assistant move from one to the other, many steps are saved.
13. Many desire to have one wall of the operatory glass, so that the patient looks out upon a private garden.
14. The operatory walls should be soundproof.
15. If space is available, a small room with a chair and couch is desirable for patients who need time to recover before leaving the building.
16. A small area is needed for a sterilizer. This usually is not much larger than a closet.
17. The patient upon leaving should have easy access to the exit. He should be able to arrange another appointment with some privacy.
18. Dental offices and clinics require less parking space than medical clinics, since they schedule patients rather rapidly.
19. Suggested space requirements are shown in Table 55.
20. A plan for a larger dental clinic is shown in Fig. 929. Notice the relationship the architect established between operatories and other facilities.

Doctors' Parks

With the rapid growth of suburban areas, the problem of providing convenient medical facilities has become a growing concern. One solution developed is the doctors' park. It is designed to furnish medical facilities for doctors specializing in various types of practice. The park is composed of a series of small buildings, each usually housing two to four doctors. Each doctor can practice individually, yet, he has the consultation services of others readily available.

Parking areas and approaches to each building are individualized and the patient can recognize his doctor's office and location.

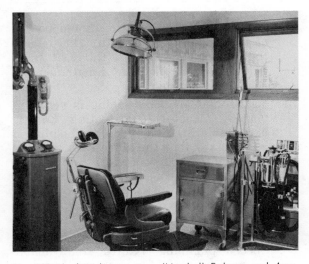

Fig. 928. A dental operatory. (Marshall Erdman and Associates, Inc., Madison, Wisconsin, Designers and Builders of Medical Office Buildings)

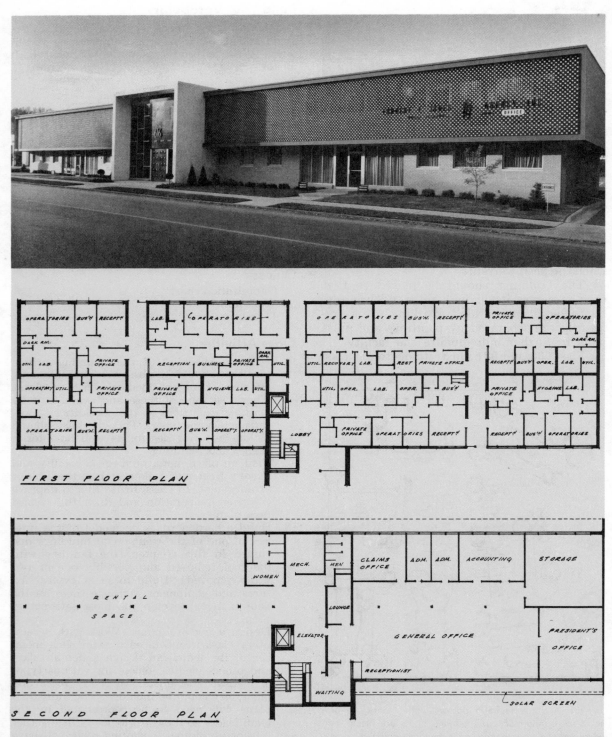

FIRST FLOOR PLAN

SECOND FLOOR PLAN

Fig. 929. A multipurpose office building. (Don Gumerson, AIA, Architect)

The first floor is devoted entirely to dental offices. The second floor houses an insurance company and has additional rental office space. It is built on a steel frame with floors and roof concrete. The second-floor windows are shielded by an anodized aluminum sun screen. The building is heated and cooled with air-cooled heat pumps.

Fig. 930. A doctors' park. Note the individual buildings and convenient parking. (Marshall Erdman and Associates, Madison, Wisconsin, Designers and Builders of Medical Office Buildings)

The office does not become just another room in a large, impersonal building.

Doctors' parks usually are developed in residential areas. Facilities can be expanded easily by the addition of other small buildings when the need warrants.

The buildings should be placed so that each preserves its individuality and has adequate, adjacent parking. Parking areas frequently are separated by plantings and grass plots to further individualize the facility.

Figs. 930 and 931 illustrate doctors' parks.

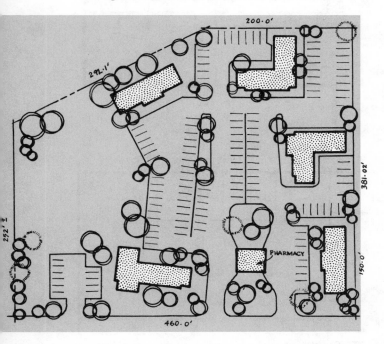

Fig. 931. A site plan for a doctors park. Notice the provision for a pharmacy. The parking areas are nicely individualized, helping to give each building and the doctors practicing there an individual identity. (Marshall Erdman and Associates, Inc., Madison, Wisconsin, Designers and Builders of Medical Office Buildings)

Build Your Vocabulary

Following are words that you should understand and use as a part of your working vocabulary. Write a brief explanation of what each means.

Medical Section

Dental operatory
Dental office
Laboratory
Examination room
Reception area
Doctors' park
Medical clinic
Medical office

Banks

Vault
Drive-in window

Offices

Organization chart
Work flow
Data processing

Class Activities

1. Make a checklist of the planning principles that should be observed when planning an office, bank, or medical office or clinic. Then visit one of these and evaluate it by marking each item on the checklist as good, satisfactory or poor. The checklist should include exterior design, as well as interior design and planning.

2. Visit an office, bank or medical facility and make a freehand, scale sketch of the interior arrangement. In class, revise this to improve the overall operation and draw the revised floor plan.

3. Build a cardboard, scale model of the interior of one of the commercial buildings discussed in this chapter (the building with the roof removed and possibly one or two walls removed). Build to scale, typical fixtures and equipment. Arrange these on the floor plan to develop the most satisfactory plan.

4. Design a doctors' clinic. Work with several other class members as a team. One member of the team can design a dental office, and others medical offices for various types of medical specialists. An X-ray room and laboratory could be included. The individual plans will need to be coordinated by the team leader so they will logically fit together into one building. A waiting room will have to be planned. After the preliminary planning is finished, a set of working drawings should be completed. It will be necessary to

consult later chapters concerning structure and exterior design.

5. If several teams have developed medical buildings, with each building accommodating several doctors, develop a plan to work these into a doctors' park. The buildings could be cut from blocks of pine (at a very small scale), and roads, parking and shrubbery could be arranged on a three-dimensional model.

6. Design a small, branch bank office. Provide two drive-in windows and space for two walk-up teller's windows. Select a lot in a desirable location, and plan the building to fit the site. Give special consideration to parking and to traffic flow to the drive-in windows.

Additional Reading

Offices

General Electric Company, "An Approach to Office Building."

Green, Lois W. (ed.), *Interiors Book of Offices.*

Manasseh, Leonard, and Cunliffe, Roger, *Office Buildings.*

Data Processing Centers

International Business Machines Corporation, "Planning for an IBM Data Processing System."

Medical Offices and Clinics

Kirk, Paul H., and Sternberg, E. D., *Doctors' Offices and Clinics.*

PLANNING FOOD STORES, RESTAURANTS AND CAFETERIAS

When planning either retail food stores or food service facilities, the designer faces a number of problems common to both. The exact solutions to these problems vary with the type of facility. In both facilities, food must be received, prepared and stored. Refuse must be removed. Customers must be received, and money must be collected.

Some problems facing the designer are peculiar to the particular type of business. A food store must display its items. A restaurant must cook its food and keep it in readiness to be served. Restaurants also must handle dishes and soiled linens.

This chapter presents points to consider when solving the common problems and the special problems of each facility.

Food Stores

The typical food store must stock and display thousands of items. Some are perishable and others are fragile. Some foods are received in bulk and require preparation and packaging. Considerable effort is required in stocking the sales area, and the location of various products influences the sales of these items. The following principles must be considered when planning a food store.

1. Before planning a store, the architect must thoroughly understand the objectives of those who will own and operate the facility.
2. The store front is of supreme importance and is due every consideration to make it attractive and inviting. Nothing is more important in the success of a food store.

Figs. 950 through 953 illustrate contemporary trends in food store design.

3. The store front usually is the all-glass, open type. This helps attract customers, since they can see the entire inside display.
4. Food store owners have found that pylons increase a market's attraction. See Fig. 954.
5. Customer traffic control is necessary from the time the customer enters until he leaves. The entrance and exit should be

Fig. 950. This illustrates a modern style rapidly becoming popular. (National Association of Retail Grocers)

The front of the building does not have ornamental brick or stone, so decorative grillwork is placed forward for "glamour." In this design, the grill screen is supported with I-beams that carry up to the roof line and extend back, forming a protective covering over the walk. Grill screen serves as windbreak and creates interesting shadow panels on the building. Instead of grillwork, brick or color tiles may be used, but thinner grill discourages birds nesting and is preferred over brick or tile.

Letters in store identification should be individual, boxed and illuminated. Those selected should carry out the modern theme of the design.

separate, even in the small food store. They should open on a lobby space.

6. The entrance and exit should be closely related to the parking area. Provision should be made for ease in moving sold merchandise to the customer's car.

7. Adequate parking is a must. The size of the parking area depends upon the location of the store. If located in a residential area enabling many customers to walk to the store, one parking space for every 2 square feet of sales area is sufficient. Some stores need to use a 1 : 1 or 2 : 1 ratio. A discussion of parking space is included in Chapters 16 and 17 pertaining to motels and shopping centers.

Fig. 952. This food store is located in Fort Worth, Texas. The interior of the store is the show window. The glass panels are 8 feet high and 7 feet wide, stacked three tiers high 24 feet to the roof. (Libbey-Owens-Ford Glass Co.)

Fig. 951. An elevation for a small store (4600 square feet), designed by architects of the National Association of Retail Grocers. The front window is recessed, thus providing a planting area to create interest. The carport gives the entrance protection and adds to the appearance of width.

Fig. 953. This food store is completely open to prospective customers. The open-front concept turns the entire store interior into a showcase, open and inviting to customers day and night. This supermarket is located in San Francisco, California. (Libbey-Owens-Ford Glass Co.)

Fig. 954. Pylons. (National Association of Retail Grocers)

Left: A simple type of truss faced with corrugated asbestos makes this "eye catcher." The support for the overhang is continued above and serves as the frame for the pylon. It is easily illuminated with a minimum of fixtures and expense. The lighting is interesting and effective because of the highlights and shadows created by the corrugations.

Center: The inexpensive, quonset-type building gets a

fine architectural lift by the addition of the dynamic entrance highlighted by this pylon.

Right: Colored, corrugated aluminum creates an interesting pylon here. This material requires a minimum of maintenance, and the original cost is not too high. The material used above the sign canopy is repeated in the facing of the pylon. This ties the pylon in architecturally with the building. The strong vertical lines make the pylon appear taller.

8. Any parking lot with a capacity of fifty or more autos should have at least two entrances.

9. Parking lot entrances should be at least 25 feet wide.

10. The parking lot should be designed so that 250 feet is the maximum distance a customer must walk to reach the store.

11. Since the customer has free access to almost all merchandise, good general illumination is needed over the entire store. Fluorescent fixtures usually are used to reduce the heat damage to perishable merchandise.

12. A store must be attractive and must be arranged so that it allows ease in shopping and efficiency in stocking.

13. A study of the traffic flow of customers and employees is necessary.

14. Food stores should be completely air conditioned.

15. The colors selected for walls, ceiling and fixtures should be light or neutral. Most food items are attractively packaged in colorful containers, and excess color in the building will detract from this merchandise.

16. Noise is a problem usually combatted with acoustical ceilings. Piped-in music helps to reduce attention to store noises and creates a pleasant atmosphere.

17. The interior walls should be made of a durable material that can be washed. Floors should be easy to clean and resilient enough for noise reduction and comfort in walking.

18. Economy of operation should be considered. This includes providing for a smooth work flow, allowing sufficient room for employees to work and operating the store with a minimum number of employees.

19. Equipment selected must be dependable and must have sufficient capacity.

Steps in Food Store Planning

20. The first step in planning the store layout is to select the basic equipment for each department. The proper amount of equipment is based upon the estimated sales.

21. The building itself should not be planned until the floor layout is completed. The building is a shell to house the store and attract customers and should not influence the layout of the store. An exception would be limitations caused by the shape of the lot.

22. Each department should be planned to handle the anticipated sales. Based on averages, the following percentages serve as a guide for planning a balanced store:

	Percent of store volume
Meats	25
Produce	10
Dairy	10
Bakery	6
Frozen foods	6
Ice cream	2
Groceries	36
Nonfoods	5 (will vary depending upon desires of owner)

23. The total estimated sales volume should then be proportioned to each area, according to the determined percentages. For example, if a store anticipates a $10,000 a week volume, the dollar volume expected of each department would be:

Meat	$ 2,500
Produce	1,000
Dairy	1,000
Bakery	600
Frozen foods	600
Ice cream	200
Groceries	3,600
Nonfoods	500
	$10,000

24. It is now necessary to select the equipment in each department. This involves first a study of equipment offered by manufacturers and then the selection of that to be used. The capacity of this equipment must be known, and the sales capacity per week per lineal foot of the equipment selected must be ascertained. This information is available from manufacturers, since they employ staffs competent in merchandising. To illustrate this, some sales capacities might be:

	Dollar sales per lineal foot of display cabinet per week
Meat display	$90.00
Produce	35.00
Dairy	60.00
Bakery	40.00
Frozen foods	25.00
Ice cream	20.00
Groceries	13.00
Nonfoods	13.00

25. If the estimated weekly dollar sales in each department is divided by the sales capacity of the equipment selected, the number of lineal feet of equipment needed in each department can be found. To illustrate:

	Weekly $ sales	$ Volume per lineal foot	Lineal feet of display needed
Meats	$2,500	$90	26
Produce	1,000	35	30
Dairy	1,000	60	16
Bakery	600	40	15
Frozen foods	600	25	24
Ice cream	200	20	10
Groceries	3,600	13	278
Nonfoods	500	13	38

26. Lineal feet of display refers to single-face cabinets as found along a wall. Island-type fixtures provide display area on both sides, and each side counts separately in computations.

27. Each department should then be analyzed to ascertain how much of the total lineal feet allowed is to be put into certain products. The grocery area is the most difficult. A suggested plan follows.

	Percent of total linear feet of shelving to each product
Breads and pastry	5
Coffee and tea	5
Glass goods	6
Canned vegetables	6
Canned fruits	3.5
All juices	2.5
Baby foods	3.5
Prepared foods	8
Packaged foods	4.5
Breakfast foods	5
Crackers and cookies	6
Baking and cooking supplies	8.5
Paper products	4.5
Household supplies	13
Housewares	7
Snacks	1.5
Candy and gum	3
Pet foods	1.5
Dietetic food	1.5
Health and beauty aids	3
Magazines	1.5

28. Each of the areas within a department can be subdivided into the products included in the area. Since this does not influence basic store layout, they will not be discussed.

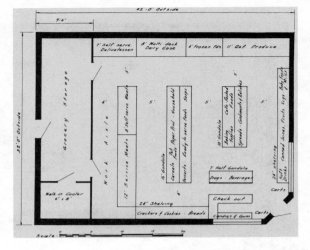

Fig. 955. A small food store covering 1344 square feet. Notice some meats are self-service. The service meat counter could become self-service if this were desired. The customer follows a counterclockwise shopping route. The refrigerated products are located in the rear of the store to pull customers onto the sales floor. (National Association of Retail Grocers)

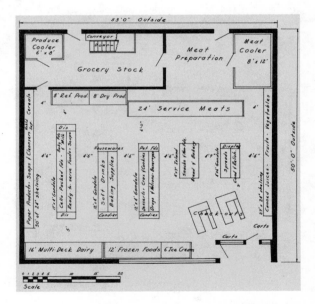

Fig. 956. A store of 2650 square feet. (National Association of Retail Grocers)

The traffic pattern is based on the premise that customers want to select meat first, produce second and then groceries. Notice the dairy is in the front corner, drawing customers to this area.

The check-out stands are placed on an angle because this provides more room. Notice that drugs, notions and candies are in view of the checker. A basement area is used for grocery storage, thus increasing space available for sales.

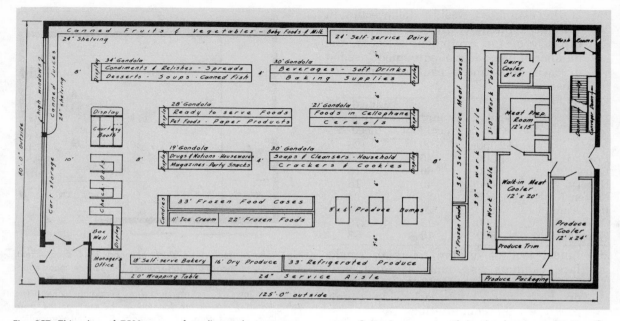

Fig. 957. This plan of 7500 square feet directs the customer traffic in a clockwise pattern. The produce and frozen foods are near the end of the shopper route. This plan has excellent meat and produce receiving, storing and preparation areas. Groceries are stored in the basement. Notice the conveyor near the receiving doors. The manager's office is conveniently located. (National Association of Retail Grocers)

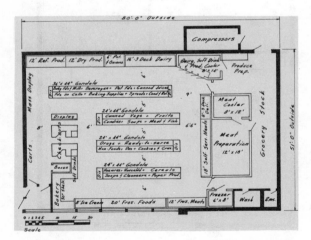

Fig. 958. This plan is for a store of 4808 square feet. (National Association of Retail Grocers)

Notice the compressor room located outside the building. This reduces building costs, removes noise and heat from the store and makes servicing easy.

A separate storage freezer is in the stock area, near the frozen food display areas. There is room to add a third check-out station by removing the box storage container.

29.   A commonly used guide for a sales objective is to plan for a minimum weekly sale of $3.00 per square foot of selling area. Therefore, a food store expecting to do

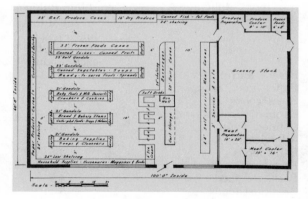

Fig. 959. This plan contains 6000 square feet. It devotes considerable area to grocery storage. The storage is located on the end of the building to make the building longer and appear more impressive.

Meat service is available first to the customer, who then follows a counterclockwise traffic pattern. (National Association of Retail Grocers)

$10,000 per week would have to have approximately 3,335 square feet of selling area, plus storage and preparation areas.

Figs. 955 through 959 illustrate well engineered food store layouts. These were planned by engineers of the National Association of Retail Grocers.

Fig. 960. An attractive, well-lighted produce department. Notice the use of mirrors to enhance the display. The department is attractively identified by a large sign and enhanced by a cluster of palm trees.

Two- and three-deck produce fixtures are available, for both refrigerated and dry produce. (Tyler Refrigeration Corp.)

Other General Planning Considerations

30. More merchandise per lineal foot can be displayed on multideck racks. Items such as frozen foods, cold cuts, smoked meats, chickens, produce and dairy products can be displayed in two- and three-deck fixtures. These can be refrigerated if needed.

31. Some food retailers use high gondolas in the center of the store. This increases display area per lineal foot. The height of these should never block the overall view of the store.

    Examples of selected types of sales cases are shown in Figs. 960 through 969. Manufacturers' catalogs should be consulted for details as to size, electrical power, drains, refrigerants and other needs to be planned for in the consideration of the mechanical needs of the building.

32. A nonmechanical check-out station should be provided for each $4,000 weekly volume. If mechanical check-out stations are used, a $6,000 weekly volume is needed for each station.

33. Aisles between gondolas should be about 4'-6" to 6'-0". The longer the aisle, the wider it should be.

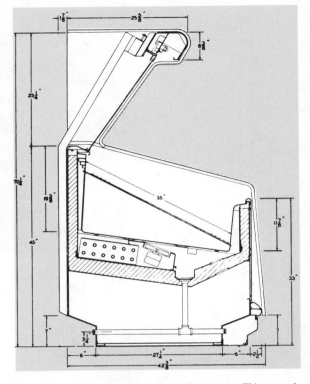

Fig. 961. A section through a produce case. This case is refrigerated, fluorescent lighted and has a drain to remove moisture. It is insulated with fiber glass and uses fans to establish forced-air circulation throughout the display area. (Tyler Refrigeration Corp.)

Fig. 962. A multideck dairy bar. This fixture displays considerably more merchandise per lineal foot of cabinet than the single-deck type. This increases the sales capacity of the store without expanding the building. (Tyler Refrigeration Corp.)

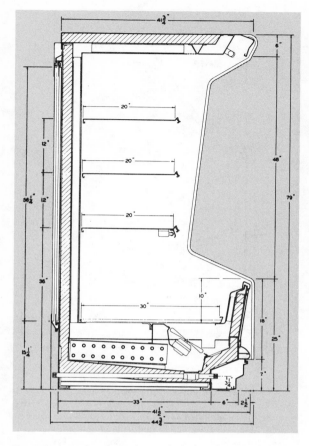

Fig. 963. A section through a multideck, refrigerated display case, used for display of dairy products and meats such as cold cuts. Merchandise is protected from room temperature by a cold screen of air across the entire display area. Shelves are adjustable in height and pitch. (Tyler Refrigeration Corp.)

Fig. 964. A multideck, refrigerated meat display for cold cuts and smoked meats. (Tyler Refrigeration Corp.)

Fig. 965. Frozen food and ice cream cases assembled in an island installation. These are available in many forms and provide for multilevel display if desired. (Tyler Refrigeration Corp.)

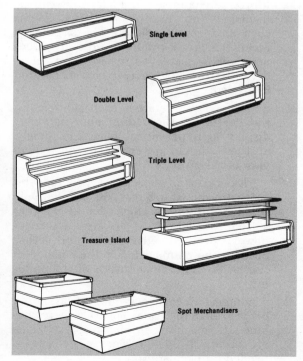

Fig. 966. Variations of frozen food and ice cream sales cases. These provide flexibility in merchandising display. (Tyler Refrigeration Corp.)

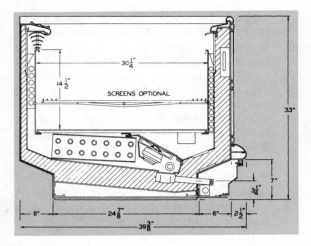

Fig. 967. A section through a frozen-food sales case. This unit has forced-air circulation of zero-degree air. The dry cold prevents frosting of packages. It has an automatic defrost system and a drain. (Tyler Refrigeration Corp.)

Fig. 968. A service-type, fresh meat display. This unit requires personnel to wait upon each customer. Notice the durable, easily cleaned walls. (Mirawal, Birdsboro Corp.)

Fig. 969. A grocery display section. Notice the special sales displays at the end of each gondola and the wide aisles to permit easy traffic flow. The floors are a durable tile. (Tile-Tex Division, The Flintkote Co.)

34. Customers select groceries comparatively rapidly. Aisles here tend to clear rapidly. Dairy and frozen food customers take more time; therefore, wider aisles are needed. Meat and produce customers take considerable time to make selections. Since this causes congestion, the widest aisles should be in the meat and produce departments. In very small stores, a 4'-6" aisle in meat and produce is adequate. Average-sized stores usually allow at least an 8'-0" aisle.

35. Sufficient space should be allowed behind check-out stations to accommodate waiting customers and to permit normal traffic flow for shopping customers. This might be 6'-0" in a very small store. Average stores should have 8'-0" to 10'-0".

36. As the layout is developed, consideration must be given to technical problems such as refrigerant lines, electrical power, plumbing needs and heating and air conditioning. For example, refrigerated cases require drains, electricity and refrigerant lines.

37. Rest rooms for employees are necessary.

38. The store manager needs space for an office. Usually this is located so he has an overall view of the store. Frequently, it is placed at the front of the store.

39. Attractive interior signs should be planned, to identify the various departments.

Location of Departments

40. The location of the numerous departments varies, depending upon the desires and experience of the manager.

41. Most food stores are departmentalized. Common groupings are: fresh fruits and vegetables, dairy products, baked items wrapped for self-service, meats, canned and packaged goods, sometimes a bakery and a delicatessen, liquor and frozen foods. Some large stores include other merchandise areas such as household items (dishes, pots, can openers), books and potted plants.

42. The meat department usually is located near the rear of the store. It requires a refrigerated storage area and a work area in which to prepare meat for display in

self-service counters. Since some customers prefer special cuts of meat or wish to discuss their selection of meat with a butcher, the work area should be located near the sales area. Seafood and poultry are included with the meat display.

43. Fresh fruit and vegetables usually are located on an outer wall near a storage area for the items not on display. This storage area should have a ready access to an outside receiving area. Since these items are perishable, deliveries are frequent. Provision is also necessary for disposing of spoiled products. All of this should be located away from the view and traffic pattern of the customer. Refer again to Fig. 959.

44. Baked items for self-service have a rapid turnover and need to be replenished frequently. These often are located on or near the traffic aisle first entered by the incoming customer. This location is also helpful for deliveries, since many stores stock their shelves with fresh items off the delivery truck at least daily.

45. Since the natural sequence of menu planning is to choose meat first, some retailers prefer to direct customer traffic to this area first, then past frozen foods, produce and into the grocery area. Refer again to Fig. 958.

46. Groceries occupy the center section of the building and use island-type gondolas for display.

47. The customer traffic pattern should lead customers past items of an impulse nature. Bakery goods and items on special sale often are purchased by customers who come to purchase something else. For example, if people coming to purchase meat, produce or canned goods can be led past other areas, they tend to purchase these impulse items even though they were not looking for them.

48. Frozen foods and ice cream usually are located near the end of the customer traffic pattern. See Fig. 959.

49. Small items such as tobacco, notions, drugs and candies should be in view of the check-out lanes.

50. Provision must be made for storage of carts near the check-out lanes. The checker should be able to dispose of the cart quickly to the storage area, making it ready for incoming customers.

51. It is very important to provide proper facilities for storing stock needed to replenish shelves in the sales area. The average supermarket handles about 6,300 items, and reserve stock could be considerable. It should be readily available for distribution to the sales area. Fig. 959 illustrates an excellent storage and preparation area.

52. The size of storerooms depends somewhat upon the nearness of supply houses. A store near a grocery supply house does not need as much space for stock as one with a distant supply.

53. Delivery doors should be located at the various stock areas, if possible. For example, produce should be delivered near the storage and preparation area.

54. If a basement is used for stock storage, a conveyor must be provided to move stock to the sales floor. The conveyor room on the sales floor must be located near the areas to be supplied. Items can be priced here. See Fig. 970.

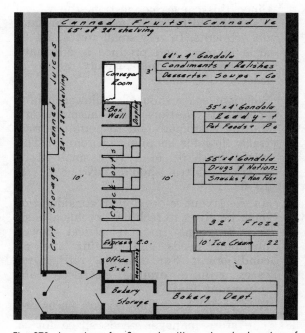

Fig. 970. A section of a floor plan illustrating the location of a conveyor room for moving groceries from basement storage to the sales floor. Especially important is the fact that it is located near the area where these items must be shelved. (National Association of Retail Grocers)

55. Meat and produce storage each require a cooler. These should be near an outside delivery door and next to the area in which these items are prepared for display.

56. Frequently, a second floor is located over the storage and preparation areas. General offices and an employees' lounge can be located here.

57. Some stores provide a small space furnished as a children's room. Television and comic books are provided for their entertainment while parents shop. This should be near the check-out lanes.

58. A customer pick-up or parcel room is desirable, Fig. 971. The customer can leave his purchases here while he moves his auto to the exterior door, thus eliminating his carrying heavy packages a long distance to his car. This space should be near the check-out area and should open onto the parking area. Small stores usually cannot afford to give space from the sales area for this convenience.

59. The stock storage for frozen foods, meat and produce should be near the display areas, to facilitate restocking the display fixtures.

60. The mechanical equipment, such as compressors and heating and air-conditioning equipment, should be accessible for

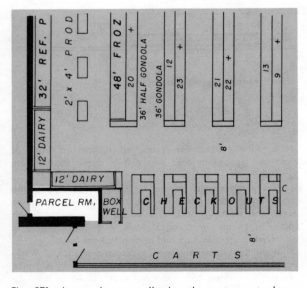

Fig. 971. A parcel room, allowing the customer to leave purchases here while he moves his car to the door to load. (National Association of Retail Grocers)

servicing without disrupting customer traffic. An outside door to this area is helpful. See Fig. 957.

61. Demand items should be displayed across the aisle from produce or meat areas, since the customer tends to concentrate on the produce or meat purchases and ignores items across the aisle from them.

62. If space permits, an aisle can be planned behind meat and produce displays, so they may be restocked from the rear. This completely frees the front side for customer traffic. See Fig. 959.

Preparation Areas

The preparation areas should be planned to process the meat and produce in the form and quantity it is expected to be received.

Produce Preparation

63. If produce items, such as potatoes, are received already packaged, they need only to be stored and delivered to the sales area. If received in bulk, they must be sorted, packaged and priced. The relation of the receiving door to the storage and preparation areas must be considered. Space and facilities must be provided for perishables requiring immediate attention and for merchandise to be unloaded and moved to storage, preparation and display areas.

64. Produce cooler rooms are more useful if they are rectangular. They need a vaporproof light. The cooling system should be designed to maintain 32 degrees under normal conditions and 45 degrees when being used by personnel. Figs. 972 and 973 (on the following page) illustrate engineered plans for produce preparation areas.

Meat Preparation Area

The basic layout of the meat preparation area varies with the shape and amount of space available, as well as with the volume of meat sales. Some managers prefer separate meat cutting and wrapping rooms. The following principles should be considered when planning this area.

65. The meat cutting blocks form the heart of the cutting room. They should be located so meat from the cooler is near and readily available to the cutters.

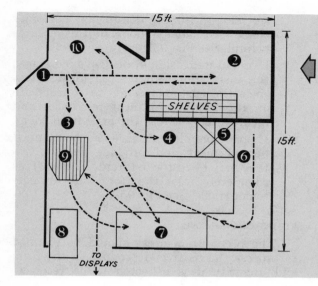

Fig. 972. A produce-preparation area for a store with sales of $1500 per week in produce. (National Association of Retail Grocers)

Notice that the receiving entrance (1) and cooler entrance (2) face each other. Perishable produce can be moved directly into the cooler, with no conveyor needed. Produce needing immediate inspection, such as out-of-season fruit, is placed in temporary storage (3). Banana storage is provided at the left of entrance (10). Potatoes and onions not taken directly to the sales floor are stored (7) beside the door to the produce display area. Bulk potatoes and onions can be easily moved from storage (7) to the sifter table (9) for sorting and bagging. Produce stored in the cooler is easily moved to waste facilities (4) where it is trimmed, washed at sink (5) if necessary, and drained at counter (6) from which it goes to the sales floor. Cart storage (8) is near the door to the display area. These carts transport produce to the display area. In this plan, produce is weighed and priced on the sales floor. Provision could be made for pricing in the preparation area if desired.

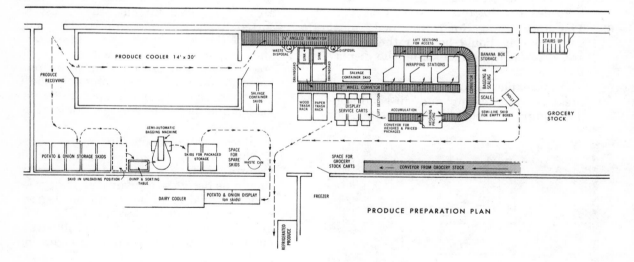

PRODUCE PREPARATION PLAN

Fig. 973. This is an assembly line, produce-preparation area designed for large-volume trade in produce. (National Association of Retail Grocers)

Bananas are received at a separate door and have their own storage box and work area, as indicated on the plan.

There are three assembly lines involved. One handles packaged dry produce, one wet produce and the third bananas. In actual operation, produce is received and directed into the produce cooler on skids or stacked on semi-live skids. Skids are moved into position next to the dumping and sorting table when ready for packaging. This is a wire-topped table with canvas catch bags below. Here dirt, peels, etc., drop into the bag. One end of the table has a gate to allow dumping into semiautomatic bagging ma-

chines. After merchandise is bagged, it goes on the skids and into the selling area where it is displayed on these same skids.

Wet produce, also placed on skids and stored in the cooler, proceeds directly to the angle trimveyor, moves across the washing sinks, and on to the conveyor which carries it to the wrapping stations. After wrapping, it is conveyed to the weighing and pricing stations.

In all three assembly lines, a proper sequence of working operation is planned for and effort is made to minimize amount of walking involved for workers. However, they do not work at any operation continuously. As a crew, they work on dry produce, then move to wet produce, and on to other tasks.

66. Sufficient space should be allowed around meat cutting blocks, so the cutters can work without interference from passing employees.

67. The meat wrapping area should be located so the cut meat is readily accessible.

68. The grinder and steak cutter should be near the wrapping area. They need not be near each other, since their functions are unrelated.

69. Power saws should be near the meat cutting blocks.

70. A sink is necessary in the cutting area.

71. Large operations might have a blooming cooler in which to store unwrapped meat after cutting. Blooming occurs when the meat surface absorbs oxygen, giving the meat a bright, red color. This process takes 30 minutes. For small operations, the cuts are put back into the main cooler for this period.

72. The use of conveyors helps in handling meat from cooler to cutting, to blooming, to wrapping.

73. The cooler should have controls to regulate temperature and humidity. Temperature should be low and constant.

74. The cooler requires electric lights, but they should provide a minimum of illumination and should have controls so that they are shut off when the cooler door is closed.

75. The wrapping area should be well lighted.

76. Provision should be made for moving cut meat to the wrappers and for removing the wrapped packages.

77. Temperature and humidity should be controlled in the wrapping room. The temperature should be as low as possible, usually 50 degrees, while also insuring the comfort of the workers.

78. Wrapped packages usually are stored on trays and are moved to the display area on portable racks.

79. The wrapping tables should have electrical outlets for the package-sealing irons.

80. The wrapping table, as the center of the packaging area, should be designed to handle the meat and supplies. Items such as labels, wrapping materials and scales are a part of this unit.

81. Some store managers prefer to have a glass window between the customer area and the wrapping area, so the operations can be viewed by all. Fig. 974 illustrates a meat preparation room plan.

Restaurants

A restaurant is an establishment where food and refreshments are served to the public. There are numerous varieties of restaurants, each serving special functions. This discussion is limited to the restaurant providing waiter service, the self-service cafeteria, the luncheonette and the drive-in restaurant.

Initial planning of any food service requires the following decisions be made:

1. What type and number of customers are to be served? Are customers repeat or transient? How many must be seated at peak demand hours?

2. What type of service is to be offered? Will this be cafeteria service or waiter service? Will it be counter service and/or table service?

3. What hours of operation are planned? Will all three daily meals be available?

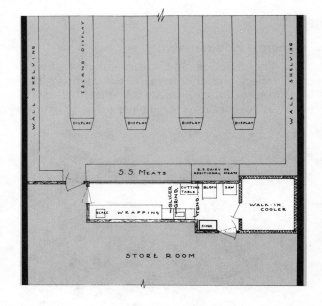

Fig. 974. A well-designed meat cutting and wrapping area. (National Association of Retail Grocers)

Notice the relationship of the cooler and cutting area. The cutting table and saw are convenient for the meat cutter. The wrapping section has a slicer, grinder, and tenderizer next to it. The wrapped packages are passed to the scale, then placed on carts for delivery to the display case.

4. What type of menu is planned? How elaborate will be the offerings and quality of food? What price meals are planned?

5. What type of interior atmosphere is desired?

6. What type of service areas are planned? Will private and public dining areas be needed?

7. What facilities are needed for food preparation? What food receiving, storage, preparation, cooking and service areas are needed?

8. What provisions are needed for dishwashing and waste disposal?

9. How large a staff is planned?

10. What is the total area needed to accommodate all these services?

It should be remembered that there are many types of food serving facilities, each having special requirements. The planning of a commercial cafeteria differs in many respects from that of a school cafeteria. A restaurant catering to transient trade differs from one serving luxury meals to repeat customers. The type of facility to be designed must be carefully studied, and decisions must be made to enable it to serve its function effectively.

General Considerations

11. The exterior and entrance area should reflect the character of the facility. The restaurant catering to a transient clientele frequently uses large glass areas to expose

Fig. 975. A small restaurant using glass walls to expose the attractive interior. (Northrup Architectural Systems)

the busy, attractive interior, thus inducing people to enter. See Fig. 975. An exclusive, expensive restaurant is better characterized by less interior exposure, thus reflecting a private, more fashionable atmosphere.

12. The entrance doors should be inviting and easily opened.

13. The entrance lobby in restaurants handling a large volume of trade is usually a simple, open area designed to accommodate incoming and outgoing traffic with a minimum of congestion. In more exclusive restaurants, it can be attractively furnished to provide a place for customers to wait before they are seated in the dining area.

14. Provision should be made for customers' coats. This could vary from an attendant-operated checkroom to a self-service rack.

15. The customer must be able to move easily from the entrance to the dining area.

16. Rest rooms, coat rooms and bars should be located near the entrance, to facilitate customer use.

17. The cashier's counter is located near the exit. It should be readily apparent, but not a dominant feature.

18. The materials used on the floor and walls should be extremely durable and easy to clean. The ceiling should absorb sounds and reduce the noise level. Furniture should be strong and durable.

19. Year-round air conditioning is vital.

20. Rest rooms provided for the employees should be separate from those for customers.

21. Rest rooms for customers are commonly located near the entrance lobby and should be easily accessible from the dining area.

22. Subtle, indirect lighting enhances the atmosphere and relaxed mood for dining. The level of illumination should be low, with general illumination of the dining area being from 5 to 20 footcandles. Incandescent and fluorescent lighting generally is used; neon lighting usually is reserved for exterior purposes. Any hazard the customer must face upon entry, such as a step up or down, must be specially lighted.

Dining Area

23. The seating in the dining area should be highly flexible. A facility designed entirely with booths is rigid and permits no rearrangement to accommodate groups or to readjust the traffic pattern. The use of a variety of means of seating is recommended.

24. The seating capacity of the dining area must be related to the kitchen production capacity.

25. Dining tables should be located so that they seat as many persons as possible, without interfering with traffic flow. Fig. 976 illustrates a pleasant dining room.

26. Round tables occupy less space than square tables. Since many people eat alone, quite a few tables should be for two persons. These can easily be moved together for larger gatherings. For those in a big hurry, stand-up tables should be available.

27. Customer and service aisles should be at least 3'-0" wide — more desirably, 5'-0".

28. Rectangular tables should be spaced from 3'-0" to 4'-0" apart, to permit customers to be seated or to leave with a minimum of interference. A table should be at least 2'-0" from the wall, if its chairs are backed against the wall. Circular tables should be at least 2'-6" apart.

29. While booths vary in size, the typical booth designed to accommodate four persons, seated two on each side, measures 4'-0" long and 5'-4" wide. A booth to accommodate two persons facing each other commonly measures 2'-6" long and 5'-4" wide. The aisle between a row of booths should be at least 3'-0". The backs of booths seldom should be higher than 4'-0" or lower than 3'-6".

30. Dining furniture should be comfortable, should be easily cleaned and should be able to withstand hard wear.

31. Pedestal tables are being used increasingly. They are more convenient than the conventional type, and they make it easier for the floors to be cleaned.

32. In restaurants with waiter service, the customer traffic and service traffic use the same aisles. The service entrance to the dining area should be located well away from the customers' entrance.

33. It is common to allow 10 to 12 square feet per table seat, when the dining area is planned.

Kitchen Area

The proper planning of the kitchen area is vital to the successful operation of a restaurant. It is highly complex and requires the

Fig. 976. A dining room designed for easy traffic flow. Notice that the pleasant view has been used to advantage. (Alsynite Division of Reichhold Chemicals, Inc.)

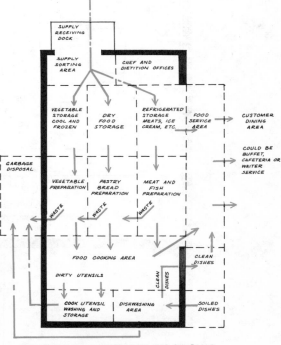

A SCHEMATIC PLAN ILLUSTRATING THE DESIRABLE KITCHEN WORK CIRCULATION PATTERN

Fig. 977. Desirable flow of kitchen work.

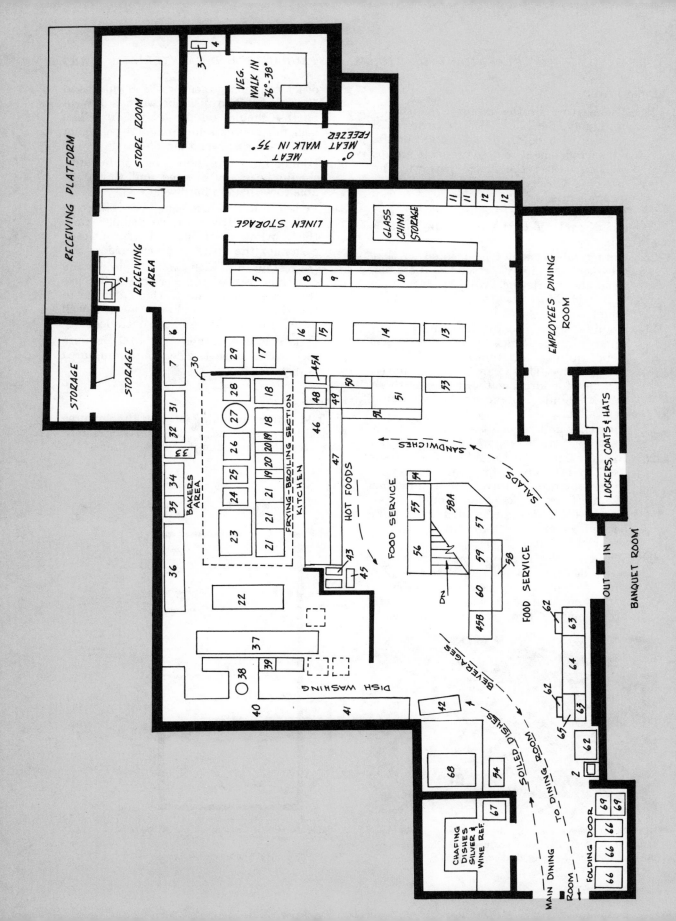

services of a food service consultant. Some planning principles follow.

34. The kitchen area involves the receiving of supplies, the storage of food, the preparation, cooking and serving of this food and the washing of dishes and utensils. Fig. 977 presents a theoretical floor plan.

35. The size of the food preparation area and the equipment located there varies a great deal. A small establishment specializing in short orders has a very simple layout and receives many items, such as bread and pastry, from an outside supplier. Large restaurants and cafeterias have extensive facilities. The planner must know what types of foods are to be served and how the preparation is to be undertaken.

— LIST OF EQUIPMENT

NO.	QUAN	NAME	NO.	QUAN	NAME
1	1	RECEIVING TABLE	37	1	CONVEYOR DISHWASHER
2	1	LAVATORY	38	1	PRE-WASHER DISPOSAL
3	1	MEAT CHOPPER	39	1	GLASS WASHER
4	1	WORK TABLE	40	1	SET OF SOILED AND CLEAN DISH TABLES
5	1	SALAD REFRIGERATOR	41	1	CONVEYOR
6	1	VEG. PEELER	42	1	SOILED DISH TRUCK
7	1	VEG. SINK	43	1	SOUP WARMER
8	1	SALAD CUTTER & SHREDDER	44		
9	1	DISPOSAL UNIT WITH SPRAY	45	1	LOWERATOR BOWL
10	1	SALAD PREPARATION TABLE	45a	1	LOWERATOR PLATE
11	1	CLOSED DISH TRUCK	45b	1	LOWERATOR CUP & SAUCER
12	1	TRAY TRUCK	46	1	CHEF'S COUNTER
13	1	ICE CREAM CABINET WITH DIPPER WELL	47	1	HOT FOOD SERVICE
14	1	PASS THRU REFRIGERATOR	48	1	RADARANGE
15	1	SLICER	49	2	TOASTERS
16	1	TABLE	50	1	SANDWICH UNIT
17	1	COOK'S REFRIGERATOR	51	1	SALAD TABLE WITH OVERSHELVES
18	2	BROILERS	52	1	TRAY SLIDE AND SHELVING UNIT
19	2	SPREADERS	53	1	SALAD REFRIGERATOR
20	2	FRYERS	54	1	PORTABLE ICE TRUCK
21	3	RANGES	55	1	ROLL WARMER
22	1	POT AND PAN STORAGE CABINET	56	1	TRAY TABLE
23	1	ROAST & BAKE OVEN	57	1	BEVERAGE COOLER
24	1	PAN RACK	58	1	URN STAND, ICE BIN AND SHELF
25	1	PYRA STOVE	58a	1	STAIRWELL COVER
26	1	PORTABLE WORK TABLE	59	1	ICE TEA URN
27	1	STEAM KETTLE	60	1	COFFEE URN
28	1	STEAMER	61		
29	1	BAKER'S REFRIGERATOR	62	1	GLASS TRUCK
30	1	CANOPY	63	1	WATER FILLER
31	1	FOOD CUTTER	64	1	ICE CUBE MACHINE
32	1	WORK TABLE	65	1	WATER STATION WITH BINS
33	1	MIXER	66	1	HOT & COLD FOOD TRUCK
34	2	PORTABLE CANS	67	1	WINE REFRIGERATOR
35	1	BAKER'S TABLE	68	1	ICE FLAKER
36	1	POT AND PAN SINK	69	1	DISH TRUCK

Fig. 978. (above and opposite) A food preparation area for a large restaurant. (Progressive Metal Equipment, Inc.)

Notice the dishwashing area is fairly close to the entrances from the dining room and banquet hall. Soiled dishes are put on large carts in dining room and moved to dishwasher. The extensive storage area is located adjacent to the receiving platform.

The sandwich preparation area is near the sandwich serving area (52) and the salad preparation is near the salad service area (51). Note the traffic flow through the food service area from salads (51) to sandwiches (52) to hot foods (47) to beverages (58).

Of special value is the relationship established in the kitchen area between the ranges (21), fryers (20) and broilers (18). The baking area is small, but a close relationship exists between the oven (23), pan rack (24), baker's table (35) and mixer (33). Notice that the entire cooking facility is covered with a huge hood (30). The pot and pan storage (22) is adjacent to the washing area and the kitchen.

36. The storage of food supplies should be as near to the preparation area as possible.

37. Some foods require refrigeration or freezing, while others require dry storage. Food storage should be near the supply entrance.

38. The food preparation area is between the food storage and serving areas.

39. Each kitchen area should be distinctly separate, yet all must be closely related for efficient operation.

40. In a kitchen used with waiter service, the prepared food ready to be served should be in the following order: salads near the incoming waiters' door, then sandwiches and cold meats, followed by the hot foods. Desserts and pastry should be next, with beverages last, near the door opening into the dining area. See Fig. 978.

41. The serving area for the salads and cold meats needs mechanical cooling units.

42. The serving area for the hot foods needs heating units. Various types of ovens, steam tables and heat lights are manufactured.

43. Clean dishes should be stored near the food serving area. It should require only a minimum of handling to get them here from the washing area.

44. In large kitchens, separate areas should be provided for the preparation of the various kinds of food. Usually meat, fish, vegetables, bread and pastry are separated.

45. Doors to the kitchen should be located so that incoming waiters are clear of those going out. Usually two separate doors are provided; these sometimes are automatic.

46. The dietition and chef should have office space near the kitchen and should be a part of any intercommunication system.

47. A kitchen ventilating system should be provided to remove odors and fumes. Hoods are frequently used. This system often is separate from that used for the dining area.

48. The kitchen should have about 20 foot-candles of light at the working level.

49. Floor drains are necessary, since the kitchen is completely washed down every day.

50. The floor should be on one level; differences in level are dangerous.

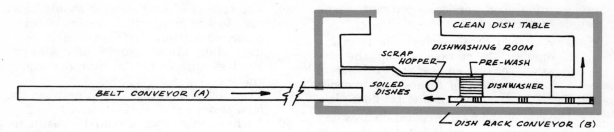

Fig. 979. Belt conveyor (A) transports soiled dishes from the cafeteria dining area to the soiled-dish table in the dishwashing room. Conveyor (B) carries the empty dish racks back to the soiled-dish table after they have passed through the dishwashing machine and the clean dishes have been removed. (Samuel Olson Mfg. Co., Inc.)

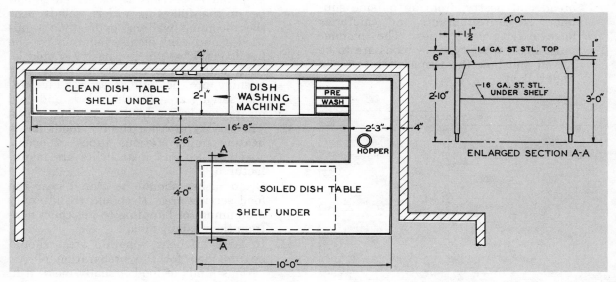

Fig. 980. This facility will clean 198 racks (4950 dishes) per hour. Note work flow from soiled-dish table, to scrap hopper, to prewash, through dishwasher and to clean-dish table. (Champion Dish Washing Machine Co.)

51. Kitchen walls, from ceiling to floor, should be washable. Tile is usually used. Floors are also tile.

52. Kitchen equipment should be such that it can be cleaned easily. Stainless steel equipment commonly is used. It should be located so the floor under and the walls behind it also can be cleaned easily.

Dishwashing Area

A dishwashing area should be provided in the kitchen, separate from the cooking-serving areas. Consideration should be given to setting up a production-line washing facility.

53. The dishwashing section should be very near the door used by those bringing soiled dishes into the kitchen.

54. This area usually includes: shelves for holding trays of soiled dishes while they are unloaded onto a table; sinks for soaking; preflushing equipment to dispose of food particles; a dishwashing machine; clean-dish table; and racks for dish storage. If dishes are moved to storage nearer the entrance to the dining area, trucks are necessary by the clean-dish table. Fig. 979 illustrates a small dishwashing area.

55. Glass-washing and silver-washing machines are available.

56. The design capacity of the dishwashing facility depends upon the serving capacity of the restaurant. Fig. 980 illustrates a dishwashing facility with waiter service. The dishes are brought to the facility on carts.

Fig. 981. A conveyor along the wall of a cafeteria. It carries soiled dishes into the dishwashing area. (Samuel Olson Mfg. Co., Inc.)

Fig. 982. A restaurant providing waiter service. (Samuel Olson Mfg. Co., Inc.)

Notice the use of a continental settee along the left wall in connection with movable tables and chairs. This provides flexibility in accommodating groups of various sizes. Behind the settee is a soiled-dish conveyor. The waiter places the trays of soiled dishes on the conveyor through the openings provided. The conveyor carries the dishes to the dishwashing area, out of sight of the customer.

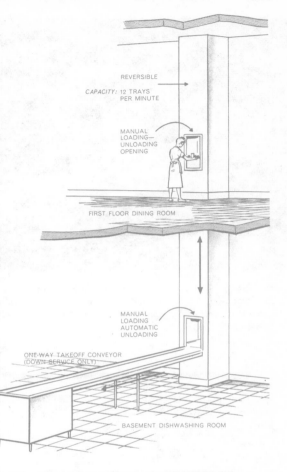

Fig. 983. An elevator moves trays of soiled dishes to a lower-level, dishwashing area. It can be reversed to return clean dishes to the first-floor dining room. (Samuel Olson Mfg. Co., Inc.)

57. If the dishwashing room is on the same level as the dining area, a conveyor can be built along a wall of the dining area to carry dishes directly into the dishwashing area. See Figs. 981 and 982.

58. If the dishwashing area is on another level, a combination elevator-conveyor can be used to move the dishes. See Fig. 983.

Cafeterias

A cafeteria is a restaurant designed to be almost entirely self-service. It usually caters to those desiring an inexpensive meal; therefore, the interior furnishings generally are not luxurious nor expensive. Such a food service needs a large volume of trade to succeed. Following are some factors to consider when planning a cafeteria.

59. The cafeteria should be as nearly self-service as possible.

60. The food service counter should be attractive and well lighted to display food to best advantage. Some areas need units to keep foods hot, and other foods must be kept cool. See Fig. 984.

61. Food in the service counter should be protected, yet should be readily available to the customer. In some cafeterias, hot foods are served, while salads, desserts and drinks are self-service. Self-service also is used for many small items such as silver, butter, bread and salad dressing.

Fig. 984. A food service counter designed to display the food to advantage. The clean lines of the installation plus effective use of lighting enhance the service considerably. (Bastian-Blessing Co.)

Fig. 985. A cafeteria service providing self-service on foods and drinks, including malted milkshakes. The cashier is located at the end of the line, so the customer pays as he leaves the line. Notice the flush ceiling lights above the counter and the durable, easily-cleaned fixtures and walls. (Bastian-Blessing Co.)

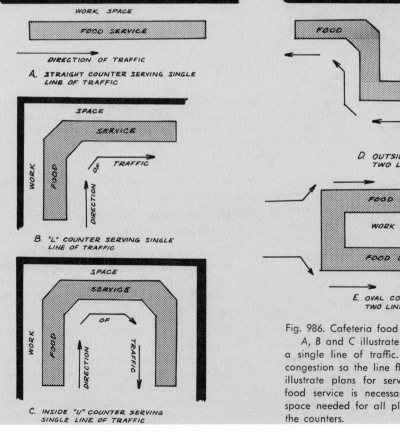

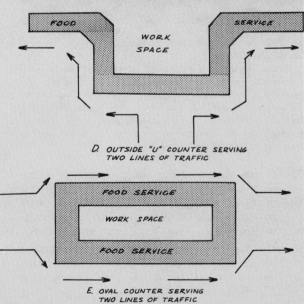

Fig. 986. Cafeteria food service patterns.

A, B and C illustrate commonly used plans for service to a single line of traffic. The important factor is to reduce congestion so the line flows smoothly and quickly. D and E illustrate plans for serving two lines of traffic. Duplicate food service is necessary for each line. Notice the work space needed for all plans, to permit attendants to service the counters.

62. Two systems for paying checks are in use. In one system, the customer pays as he leaves the food service counter. This slows service. In the second plan, the customer receives a check at the end of the line and pays the cashier as he leaves the cafeteria. Obviously, this reduces the bottleneck at the end of the food service counter.

63. Six to eight persons per minute can pass through a single serving line and pay for their meals at a cashier's stand at the end of the line. If a checker is used and the cashier is located elsewhere, ten or eleven persons per minute can be handled in a single line. If greater capacity is needed, a second line must be planned. Fig. 985 illustrates a food service line with the cashier at the end of the line. It also offers self-service on drinks.

64. Many plans are acceptable for the design of food service lines. Fig. 986 illustrates those in common use. Of great importance is a free flow of customers along the line, so congestion is avoided.

65. A long food counter can be divided into sections. Usually beverages and desserts are in a center section, with hot foods at one end and salads, sandwiches and cold meats at the other end. This, in effect, serves as two lines. Those desiring a hot meal go to the end serving hot foods and progress to the beverages and desserts in the center and to a cashier. Those wanting a cold meal enter from the end displaying cold foods. See Fig. 987 for a split line serving hot meals and short orders. (See page 382.)

66. Provision must be made for food preparation and delivery to the food counter. Frequently, the food preparation is in the basement, and food is moved up by dumbwaiters. If the food preparation is on the same floor as the service, provision must be made to replenish the food service counters without interfering with the flow of customer traffic. This usually means that some work space is needed behind the food service counter.

67. The removal of dishes is a big problem. A conveyor frequently is used. In some cafeterias, the customer is expected to carry his dishes to a conveyor for removal to the washing area. In others, employees do this. See the section on dishwashing for more information on conveyors.

68. Adequate means for the removal of food odors is necessary. Usually hoods are placed over areas producing odors and steam.

69. A smooth traffic flow must be maintained from the cafeteria entrance to the food service line, to the table and to the cashier.

70. Most cafeterias have cold-water dispensing units placed at intervals in the dining area, with a supply of glasses conveniently available.

71. Atmosphere is very important. The cafeteria should be attractively decorated and pleasantly lighted. General illumination need not be of high intensity. Music can be used to overcome some of the serving and eating noises.

Luncheonette and Short-Order Facilities

The luncheonette provides facilities planned for rapid service to large numbers of customers. It usually has a counter at which the customer sits, rather than tables and chairs. As a luncheonette is planned, the following principles deserve consideration.

72. Since speed is important, the system for securing food and carrying away soiled dishes is important. Conveyors are frequently used.

73. Generally the counter is either straight or *U*-shaped; the latter type seats more people per square foot. Fig. 988 illustrates suggested spacing for luncheonette counters and stools. (See Page 383.)

74. The counters should have a shelf below the top, upon which the customers may place items they are carrying.

75. On the serving side of the counter, another shelf must be provided, on which to store such service items as silver, napkins, condiments, water and water glasses, ice and coffee. The prepared food usually is brought from the kitchen by conveyor or is placed on a window-like shelf between the kitchen and the dining areas.

76. Counters vary in height. The trend is toward a low counter, about table height of 28 to 30 inches. This requires a stool of chair height of 18 inches. The typical high counter (usually 2'-6" to 3'-6") re-

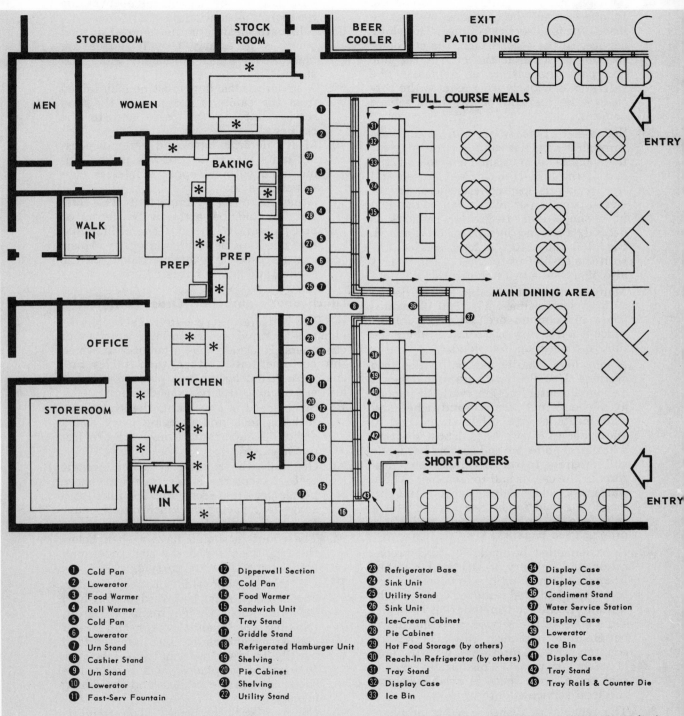

Fig. 987. Cafeteria serving layout for meals and short orders. From receiving, to preparation, to serving, this shows efficiency. There is one main serving line for full-course meals and one short-order line. Customers help themselves to cold drinks from shelves near serving counters.

Total area is 7,509 sq. ft.; seating capacity is 250; 10 food serving employees suggested; 7 food preparation employees suggested; 7 table cleaning and dishwashing employees suggested; average number of people served is 7 per line per minute. (Bastian-Blessing Co.)

1 Cold Pan
2 Lowerator
3 Food Warmer
4 Roll Warmer
5 Cold Pan
6 Lowerator
7 Urn Stand
8 Cashier Stand
9 Urn Stand
10 Lowerator
11 Fast-Serv Fountain
12 Dipperwell Section
13 Cold Pan
14 Food Warmer
15 Sandwich Unit
16 Tray Stand
17 Griddle Stand
18 Refrigerated Hamburger Unit
19 Shelving
20 Pie Cabinet
21 Shelving
22 Utility Stand
23 Refrigerator Base
24 Sink Unit
25 Utility Stand
26 Sink Unit
27 Ice-Cream Cabinet
28 Pie Cabinet
29 Hot Food Storage (by others)
30 Reach-In Refrigerator (by others)
31 Tray Stand
32 Display Case
33 Ice Bin
34 Display Case
35 Display Case
36 Condiment Stand
37 Water Service Station
38 Display Case
39 Lowerator
40 Ice Bin
41 Display Case
42 Tray Stand
43 Tray Rails & Counter Die

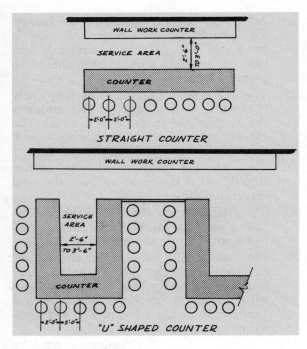

Fig. 988. Typical luncheonette counters.

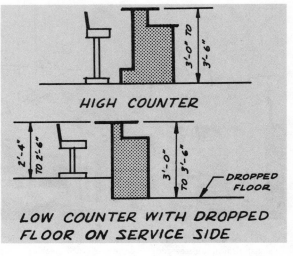

Fig. 989. High and low counters for food service.

quires the customer to climb up on a high stool and brace his feet against a footrest. The low counter is safer and more comfortable. See Fig. 989. The floor level behind a low counter frequently is dropped, to make serving easier and to provide more counter storage area.

77. Restaurants with a small floor area have a limited menu, offering only light meals and short-order foods. They depend upon high-volume and rapid turnover of customers. The food is prepared as the customer watches. Fig. 990 illustrates a typical plan for such a restaurant. Usually it is located on a busy thoroughfare and is a small, separate building or a small area of the street-level floor of a large building.

Drive-In Restaurants

The term *drive-in restaurant* refers to a wide variety of eating establishments. Some are very small and serve a limited menu, while others are elaborate and provide car service

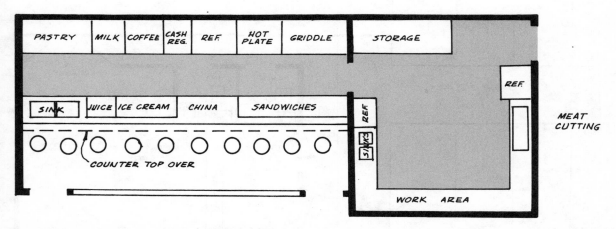

Fig. 990. A suggested plan for a small short-order restaurant. Notice the food is prepared in the dining area and all customers eat at the counter. The aisle behind the counter should be at least 3'-0". If the restaurant is in a busy loca-tion, the aisle should be wider to accommodate customers waiting for a seat. Special attention should be given to hooding the food-preparation area to remove fumes and odors.

Fig. 991. A canopy protecting the carhop and the customer. This installation utilizes plastic panels as roof decking. This permits natural light to come through yet provides some shade on sunny days. (Alsynite Division of Reichhold Chemicals, Inc.)

as well as an inside dining area. It is necessary to clearly decide what services are to be offered, before attempting to plan such a facility.

The planning of the kitchen and inside dining areas involves the same principles as found in restaurant and cafeteria planning. Special planning considerations for drive-in restaurants follow.

78. Adequate parking space is necessary. This should be quite large and easy to enter and leave. If inside service is provided, a separate parking area should be planned for these customers.

79. The car service parking area frequently is covered with a canopy. This protects the carhops and shades the customer. The canopy usually is a column-supported, lightweight roof. See Fig. 991.

80. The parking area should be sloped slightly, so it drains away from the food service building.

81. The kitchen forms the core of the facility. It can serve an inside dining area as well as an outside, car service area.

82. Provision should be made for easy access by carhops to the kitchen to fill their orders. Frequently this is a small room with an outside entrance and pass-thru windows from the kitchen. Fig. 992 illustrates a plan for such a facility.

83. Food service to the carhops should be separate from that offered to inside diners.

84. The pick-up counter should be large enough to accommodate about half of the carhops at one time. A single carhop usually can serve six or seven automobiles.

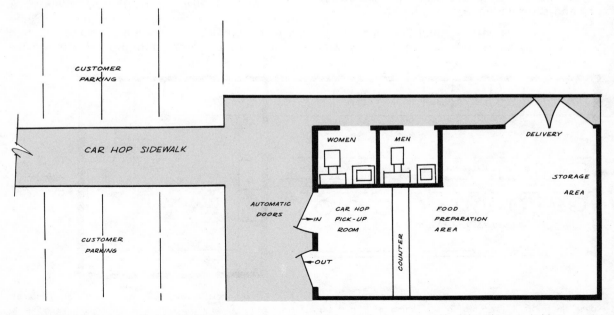

Fig. 992. A plan for a small drive-in. Notice the area used by the carhop to fill the order and return trays. Since paper plates and cups are used, dishwashing is held to a minimum. The customer parking could be covered with a canopy.

85. The dishwashing area should be convenient to carhops, inside service and the cooking areas of the kitchen.
86. Beverage dispensers should be near the pick-up counter.
87. Before the cashier's desk can be located, the procedures for handling payment must be determined. Frequently, the desk is located in the carhop pick-up area. If inside food service is available, one cashier could serve both activities, if properly located.
88. Suitable and sufficient storage is needed for food and supplies.
89. Rest rooms for employees and customers should be available.
90. Provision should be made to receive supplies without interfering with the normal flow of business.
91. The exterior of a drive-in restaurant should reflect the type of service offered. One with rather elaborate inside food service should present a different "face" than the typical short-order facility. The exterior should attract attention, yet should not be gaudy.

Class Activities

1. Make a checklist of the planning principles that should be observed when planning a food store, restaurant or cafeteria. Visit one of these and evaluate it by marking each item on the checklist as good, satisfactory or poor. The checklist should include exterior design as well as interior design and planning.
2. Visit a food store, restaurant or cafeteria and make a freehand, scale sketch of the interior arrangement. In class, revise this to improve the overall operation, and draw the revised floor plan.
3. Build a cardboard scale model of the interior of one of the commercial buildings discussed in this chapter (the building with the roof removed and possibly one or two walls removed). Build, to scale, typical fixtures and equipment. Arrange these on the floor plan to develop the most satisfactory plan.
4. Design a complete food store, restaurant or cafeteria. Work with several other class members, as a team. In a food store, one team member could design the receiving and storage area, another the meat preparation and sales area and others the general sales area. In a restaurant or cafeteria, one could design the food receiving and storage area, another the food preparation area and others could work on the serving and dining area. Both facilities need careful planning to provide adequate parking. The team leader will need to coordinate the efforts of his individual team members. It will be necessary to consult later chapters concerning structure and exterior design.

Additional Reading

Food Stores

National Association of Retail Grocers of the U.S. Various bulletins and other detailed information books. *Also*: "Exterior Designs and Interior Arrangements for 17 Food Stores;" "Modern Food Stores;" "Self-Service Meats;" and "Super Markets and Shopping Centers."

U.S. Department of Agriculture. Various bulletins.

Restaurants and Cafeterias

Bastian-Blessing Company, "Cafeteria Planning."

Champion Dish Washing Machine Company, "Dish Pantry Layouts."

Dana, Arthur W., *Kitchen Planning for Quantity Food Service*.

Kotschevar, Lendal H., and Terrell, M. E., *Food Service Planning: Layout and Equipment*.

Little, R. Keith, *Kitchen Layout Logic*.

Stokes, John W., *Food Service in Industry and Institutions*.

CHAPTER SIXTEEN

PLANNING MOTELS AND PARKING FACILITIES

Providing accommodations for travelers and parking facilities for shoppers has become a big business. The demand for these services is great. Nationwide companies have been formed, and they have invested large sums of money in building construction. Separate little "houses" no longer attract the tourist, and the gravelled lot does not adequately accommodate the shopper. Architects have devoted considerable study to the problems of providing motel units that offer the comfort demanded and the attractiveness expected. The corner parking lot has given way to multistory structures costing thousands of dollars. Both of these facilities must be carefully planned to efficiently accommodate the largest number of customers, at the lowest per-unit cost.

Motel Planning

The term *motel* has many different meanings. Generally speaking, it refers to one-story, rental units, usually for overnight guests. Most often, it is a long, low building. However, some motels are on two or more levels. See Fig. 1010. Traditionally, the motel is located next to a busy highway or at the outskirts of a city.

A trend is toward the use of *urban motor hotels*. These are multistory buildings designed to receive the casually dressed traveler. His automobile is parked in the garage located below the ground. He can drive into the garage, register and take an elevator directly to the floor upon which his room is located. This avoids the necessity of his making an unwanted appearance in the hotel lobby.

Fig. 1010. A courtyard view of multistory motel. (Motel/Motor Inn Journal)

Fig. 1011. A large, downtown, multistory motor inn. Notice the plastic panels used to separate the balcony spaces by units. (Alsynite Division of Reichhold Chemicals, Inc.)

The motor hotel frequently is located in a downtown location and combines the informality of a motel with the downtown location of a hotel. See Figs. 1011 and 1012.

The planning of a motel involves the consideration of many factors. The location and size of the building site are of primary importance. Other factors include: parking space, access roads, attractive appearance and living units designed to meet the needs of the prospective guests. Demands upon motels vary from locations accommodating only overnight guests to those where guests may spend a week or more.

Following is a discussion of factors important to consider when planning motels. This list is not intended to be complete, though it is extensive. No motel can ever meet all the standards set forth. Conditions such as location or climate generally require that a choice be made between desirable characteristics and that some features be included, which may be satisfactory but are not excellent.

Site Utilization

Of primary importance is the selection of a building site so located that the motel will prosper. This consideration is beyond the

scope of this study. The designer, however, must make the most of the site selected. Some factors to consider in site utilization follow.

1. Guests must be shielded from noise. A motel located close to a highway must

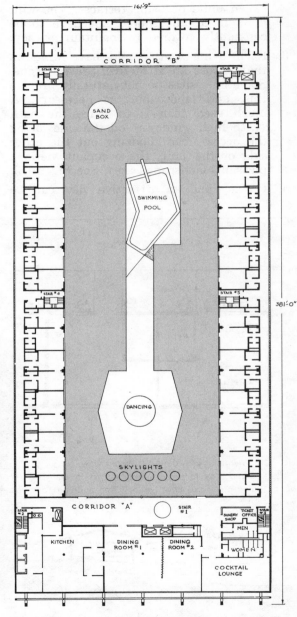

Fig. 1012. Exterior view and floor plan of Sahara Motor Hotel, Cleveland, Ohio. (Motel/Motor Inn Journal)
Note that all exterior walls are solid, and all units face on the garden park area. At upper right, adjacent to stairway No. 7, is a private elevator for guests in swimsuits.

Rooms facing corridor B are for conferences, private meetings and parties — all completely separated from guest rooms. Also, note arrangement of dining rooms with folding partition, permitting combining both dining areas into a large banquet room.

utilize hills and screens to reduce traffic sounds. Noise reduction is discussed in the residential portion of this book.

2. Privacy for each living unit is important. Frequently this is provided for by zig-zagging the units, using bushes or screens between entrances, placing carports between units or using terraces. The windows in a unit should not have to be constantly covered to maintain privacy.

3. Each living unit should have windows that expose an attractive, private scene. Sometimes sites do not naturally provide this, and landscaping is necessary. A much used plan is to place the bath (with high windows) on the side facing the access road. Looking out the other side of the unit, the occupant views a pleasant, landscaped area. See Fig. 1013.

4. Privacy and an attractive view can be provided, in some cases, by building on a sloping lot or by locating the living units on a second floor, above the ground-level parking area. This latter arrangement, however, does require the guest to carry luggage up and down a flight of stairs. See Fig. 1014.

5. A two-story building may have to be constructed on a small site, to provide the number of units needed. This reduces privacy and complicates parking and the moving of baggage, but it does provide an economical structure to build and operate.

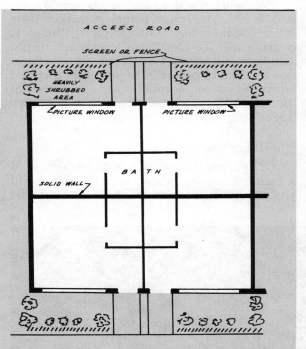

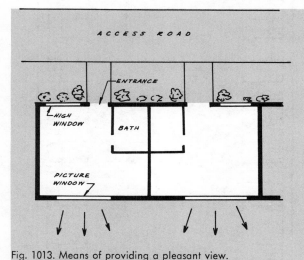

Fig. 1013. Means of providing a pleasant view.

Left. Good way to provide easy access to unit and yet offer a pleasant view. Effective only for buildings one-unit wide.

Right: Means for providing pleasant view for buildings two-units wide. Area between the unit and access road could be fenced and made into a private terrace. Parking area tends to be quite a distance from the unit.

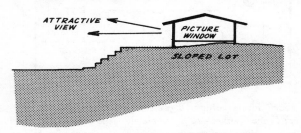

Fig. 1014. Utilizing a sloping lot.

Left. Elevated living units provide privacy from passers-by and a view high over access road and cars.

Right. Two-story structure built into the side of the hill.

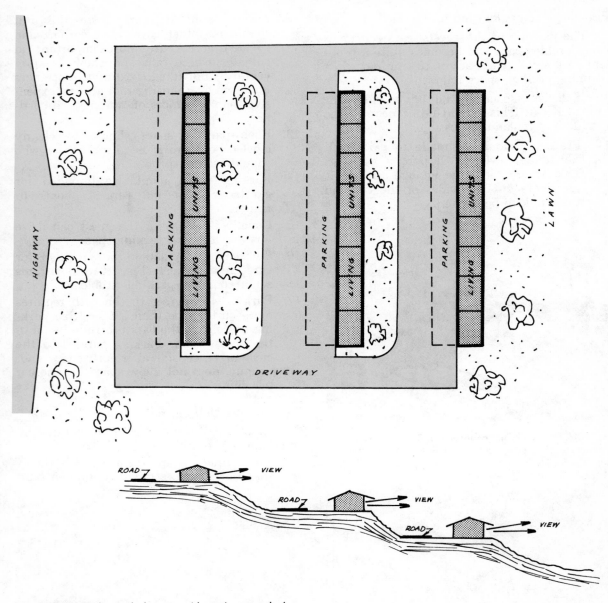

Fig. 1015. Properly used slope provides privacy and view.

6. Single units built on gently sloping ground can be terraced, to offer privacy and a view. See Fig. 1015.

7. The entire site should be utilized as a part of the overall planning procedure. This would include such features as a swimming pool, children's play area, restaurant facilities and a garden or park area.

8. The overall appearance should be one of unity and relaxation. It is necessary to put a pleasant "face" to the highway to encourage guests to stop for the night.

9. An attractive sign that invites the overnight guest is important. It should be located so it can be seen for some distance before the guest reaches the motel entrance. This location is a necessary part of site utilization. See Fig. 1016 on page 390.

Planning Factors Related to Parking

The parking of the guests' cars consumes considerable space and becomes quite a problem on a small site. Factors to consider when planning parking space follow.

10. Sufficient space should be provided for each car. This should be as near to the door of the unit as possible.

11. Provision should be made to park each car under cover. A carport is popular. This should be large enough to permit the doors on both sides of the car and the trunk to be opened.

Fig. 1016. A motor inn designed to fit the climate and atmosphere of its geographic location. Notice the attractive sign. This facility is located in San Diego, California. (Motel/Motor Inn Journal)

12. Access from the parking to the unit should be under cover. The carport and covered access are more important in climates where rain and snow are prevalant. Individual, exterior entrances under an overhanging roof are less expensive than entrances off an enclosed corridor.

13. Each parking space should be clearly labeled so there is no dispute over who should use the space.

14. Parking space should be provided for guests with second cars or boats or trailers.

15. Usually it is best if the guest can drive forward into the parking space.

16. Sufficient room should be provided for cars to maneuver. Fig. 1018 illustrates some common parking problems.

17. Parking 45 degrees to the curb requires more curb space than a 90-degree parking angle, but the cars protrude less into the access road. Parking parallel to the curb takes considerable curb space and, usually, does not allow space for one car per unit.

Planning the Unit Shape

The shape of a motel is often dictated by the shape of the site.

18. The simplest shape for a motel is the *I*-shape or a long, straight, unbroken unit.

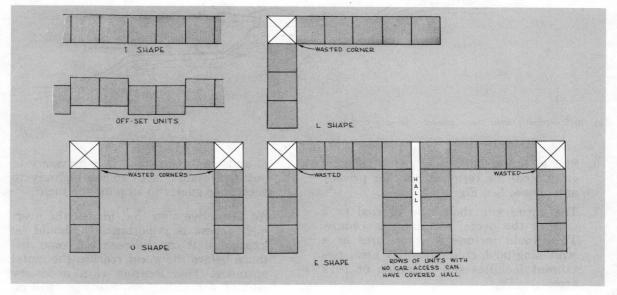

Fig. 1017. Typical motel building shapes.

This is economical to build, but is rather monotonous in appearance.

19. Frequently the building has offsets to break the monotony. This also helps to achieve some privacy.

20. The *U*-shape and the *L*-shape have corners that usually are waste space. These corners can be utilized for storage, furnaces and water heaters.

21. The *E*-shape has wasted corners and also

a wing that has no close auto access. Fig. 1017 illustrates various shapes. In large motels, the footage lost due to corners is not significant enough to bar their use.

22. Shape can influence the use of land. For example, if units are designed as shown in Fig. 1019, the use of carports between units increases the length of road and roof, but the unit can be built on a nar-

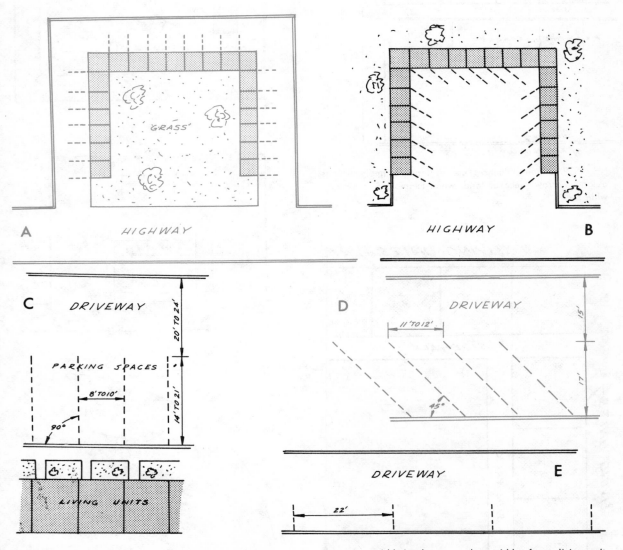

Fig. 1018. Parking plans and space requirements.

A. U-shape plan works best with parking around outside.

B. Inside the U, parking crowded and difficult. Also it is noisy and eliminates some privacy.

C. 90° parking allows space for one car per unit. Park-

ing space width is about equal to width of one living unit.

D. 45° parking requires more curb space, but less depth from curb to curb, than perpendicular parking.

E. Parallel parking space is about as long as two living units; therefore, it will not provide sufficient parking space.

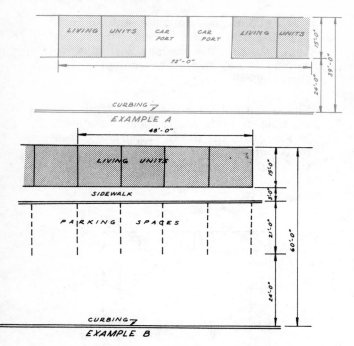

Fig. 1019. Shape influences use of land. Example A uses a long, narrow piece of land, while Example B is a short, wide site.

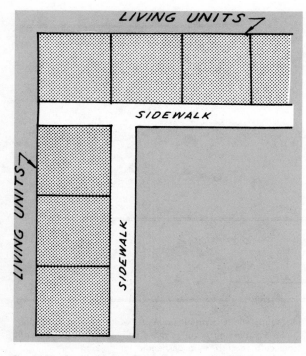

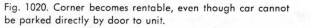

Fig. 1020. Corner becomes rentable, even though car cannot be parked directly by door to unit.

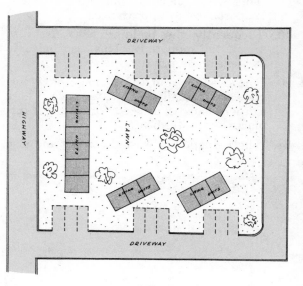

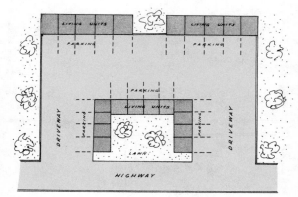

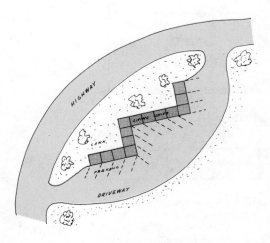

Fig. 1021. Ideas for motel planning.

rower strip of land than can one which has the parking in front.

23. The wasted corner in an *L*- or *U*-shaped building frequently is opened into a passageway, thus making all footage under roof rentable space. See Fig. 1020.

24. The alert planner utilizes those basic shapes that best fit the shape and contour of the building site. Some possible layouts are shown in Fig. 1021.

25. The combination of individual units into a large structure influences the shape of the overall building. The location of baths is the primary consideration. The more baths using a single plumbing stack, the less construction costs will be. Information pertaining to stack location and size can be found in Chapter 9.

26. As individual units are combined, privacy and a pleasant view always should be considered.

27. In general, the shapes requiring the least amount of exterior wall are the most economical to build.

Planning the Individual Unit

It is poor practice to design one good living unit and then repeat it until the required number of rental units are available. This may facilitate construction and maintenance, but it does not offer maximum occupancy potential. Motels should have a variety of rental units. These could vary from a small unit for one person to several units that could make a suite. The following factors should be considered when planning the individual units.

28. The unit should provide space for bathing, dressing, sitting, sleeping and some storage. The area allotted to each unit varies with the proposed functions for it. Cooking and dining facilities are provided in some units.

29. Some of the same area can be used for several activities. For example, a large portion of the sleeping area can be used as a part of the sitting area during the day. In some units, the beds make up into sofas and thus comprise the major portion of the sitting area.

30. Early in the planning, it is necessary to determine what furniture will be used in each unit. The area must be large enough to accommodate this furniture and still

permit unrestricted movement about the room.

31. Furnishings should be made from durable materials requiring little maintenance. Some furniture could be upholstered with plastic sheet, and floor coverings could be long-wearing carpet.

32. Two double beds could be used instead of twin beds. The additional cost for the beds and linens is nominal, and such an arrangement permits sleeping four persons. Since double beds occupy considerable floor space, twin beds plus a sofa bed could be used instead. This is saving on floor space, but increases furniture costs. The designer needs to consider all factors such as this in his attempt to provide the most rental return for the least investment. See Fig. 1022.

33. Furniture should be arranged so employees can easily clean the room and make the beds. Since this is a daily task, it becomes a significant operating expense.

34. Good reading lighting should be provided both in the sitting area and over the bed.

35. Unnecessary furniture should be eliminated. For units rented mainly to overnight guests, suitcase racks of chair height are more convenient and less expensive than dressers. Units to be occupied by guests staying several days would profit by having some drawer storage.

Fig. 1022. A spacious room designed to accommodate four persons. It is large enough for guests who wish to stay for extended periods of time. (Motel/Motor Inn Journal)

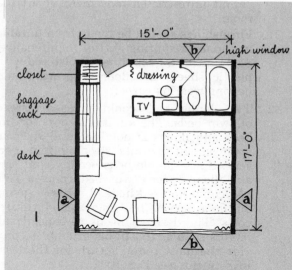

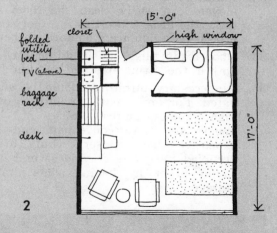

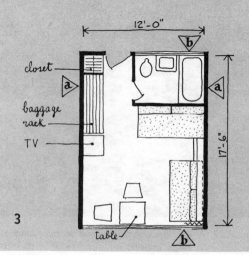

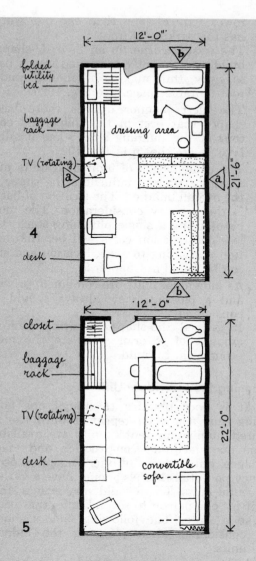

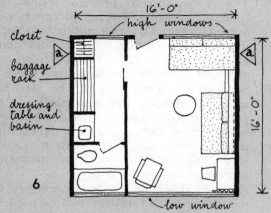

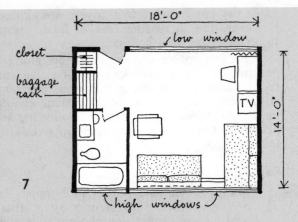

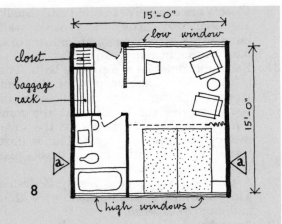

Fig. 1023. (opposite and above) Basic plans for various types of living units. (Reprinted from *Motels* by Baker and Funaro, Reinhold Publishing Co., by permission)

These almost-minimum room plans are arranged and furnished to fit the special requirements of one-night occupants (e.g. baggage racks instead of bureau drawers). Most of the rooms shown have entrance on one side and outlook on the other. Although seldom found in existing motels, this type of arrangement seems to be almost essential, unless site limitations prevent it. Windows are indicated diagrammatically; they do not have to run from wall to wall. No consideration is given to the possibility of overlapping and interlocking one unit with another. . . . Some features are shown in one plan, some in another; almost all are, of course, interchangeable. If two double beds are used, more space will be required.

1. Minimum depth *b* in this plan is made up of the pair of twin beds, with night table and clearances, plus the bathroom which cannot be fitted into less than 5 feet. Minimum width *a* is fixed by bed length plus space for sitting group. Hanging closet and baggage rack are close to both the entrance and the dressing-bath area. The TV here is built-in and the washbasin moved into the dressing alcove.

2. Some detail changes are shown here within a room of exactly the same size and shape as (1), above. The washbasin is still in a plastic-topped counter, but is in a conventional position in the bathroom. The closet space has been enlarged to allow for storage of a folding utility cot.

3. With sofa-beds set against the walls, the unit width can be reduced from 15 ft. to 12 ft. The controlling factor *a* is then a total of bathroom plus passageway plus closet and baggage rack depth. The slight increase in unit length *b* is accounted for by the bed and night table arrangement; the bathroom is identical with that in plan (2). The movable card table is suggested as an alternative to the conventional wall desk. There is ample space for a conventional TV cabinet.

4. By increasing the unit length *b* from 17'-6" to 21'-6", there is space for quite a large dressing room, fitted with a washbasin set into a make-up counter. There is space

in the closet for storing a folding utility cot. The dressing-bathroom area is self-contained. It does not extend into the sleeping-sitting area and might even have a different flooring, such as washable tile.

5. A double bed and convertible sofa show clearly the difficulties of placing furniture of such a size in a rental unit of minimum dimensions. The convertible is more expensive than a sofa bed, which in turn is far more expensive than a folding utility bed. Yet most visitors will still consider the convertible to be no better than extra, emergency sleeping accommodations. The bathroom shown is of conventional plan with a separate make-up table in the dressing area.

6. In plans (6), (7), and (8), the bathroom-dressing area is located along the side instead of across one end of the rental unit. This causes the unit to be less deep but wider, so it is more extravagant in frontage. On the other hand, it can offer two-way daylighting and cross ventilation.

The minimum width *a* is the result of bathroom plus entry plus bed length. The whole bathroom-dressing area can be closed off by a sliding door from the sitting area, an attractive feature for a resort motel. The entrance, on the other hand, opens directly into the main unit space, but it could be shielded with an exterior screen.

7. This rental unit type would be well suited to a site plan where entrance and view are on the same side. It presupposes, however, that a wide planting bed, or a difference in level, will protect the big outlook window from passersby. Furniture could be placed as in the plan above, but with the bed group reversed for a saving of 2 feet in width over the alternative arrangement drawn here.

8. Unit width *a* is reduced by using a pair of twin beds conventionally placed at right angles to the wall, but recessed in an alcove. The beds are hidden during the day by a curtain drawn across to close off this alcove. Yet at night, when this curtain is drawn back, the beds are in a spacious room with good through-ventilation. This plan, like (7), is well suited to a site plan where entrance and view are on the same side.

36. Closets are expensive to build and usually are used very little. Inexpensive, wall-hung racks with hangers are adequate in most overnight rental units.

37. Each unit must have a private bath. This is the most expensive part of the unit. However, proper design can allow several people to use the facilities at the same time. It is desirable to locate the toilet in a compartment by itself. This is illustrated by the baths in the basic plan types in Fig. 1023.

38. A tub with a shower is highly desirable. This provides a double facility, with a minimum of expense.

39. An exhaust fan in the bath helps expel odor and hot air to the outside. This reduces the load on the air conditioner and freshens the room.

40. Luggage racks should be near the entrance to the unit.

Basic Room Plans

Suggested room plans built around basic unit sizes are shown on pages 394 and 395.

Planning Utilities

41. Already discussed was the value of locating plumbing so a central stack could be used to accommodate the maximum number of baths.

42. Quick-acting heating and cooling units should be provided. When a guest wants additional heat or cooling, he wants it right away.

43. The heating or cooling for each unit should be controlled by the occupants of the unit. This calls for a very flexible system. Chapter 10 on heating, air conditioning and insulation discusses the various systems available.

44. The heating and cooling system should provide a supply of fresh air to the unit, to remove odors and stale air.

45. The heating and cooling system should be so installed that it is easily accessible for rapid maintenance and repair.

46. A plentiful supply of hot water is vital.

Parking Facility Design

A basic decision that must be made when planning a parking facility is whether it will be self-parking or attendant operated. Facilities utilizing attendant parking require less space per car because the drivers are skilled. However, the increasing cost of labor seems to be offsetting this savings.

The two major objectives in designing a parking facility are efficient use of space and rapid handling of incoming and outgoing automobiles. All design considerations should implement these two objectives. Following are principles to consider when planning a parking facility.

Ramp Parking Facilities

1. The size of the auto stall must be decided. Since auto sizes vary a great deal, a size must be chosen that will accommodate the majority of cars. A study of popular lengths and widths currently on the road is necessary. Some experts recommend a stall 19'-0" long by 9'-6" wide.

2. The length of the auto includes not only the wheel base, but also the body overhang.

3. The stall should be wide enough that auto doors can be opened with minimum of conflict with the next car and so that the average driver can park without difficulty.

4. The width of the aisles handling traffic flow on the parking deck varies with the width of the parking stall. The narrower the stall, the wider the aisle required. See Table 56.

5. Pedestrians usually can use the auto traffic aisles to get to and from their parked autos. Special sidewalks take considerable space from the parking area and reduce the number of parking stalls available.

6. A decision must be made concerning the angle of the parking stall. Usually a 60-degree or 90-degree stall angle is used. Convenience and speed of parking are

Table 56
Suggested Aisle Widths for Parking

STALL WIDTH	60° PARKING		90° PARKING
	Stall Length to Curb (19' Stall)	Aisle Width[1]	Aisle Width[2]
8'-6"	20.7	18'-6"	25'-0"
9'-0"	21.0	18'-0"	24'-0"
9'-6"	21.2	18'-0"	24'-0"

[1]Aisle accommodates one-way traffic and provides room to back out of stall.
[2]Aisle accommodates two-way traffic and provides room to back into or out of stall.
Reproduced with permission from George Baker and Bruno Funaro, Parking, Reinhold Publishing Company, New York.

the major considerations. Fig. 1024 illustrates a ramp system utilizing 90-degree parking.

7. The angle of the parking stall influences the distance required from the curb to the rear edge of the parking stall as well as the number of stalls that can be located along a wall. Design tables prepared by Baker and Funaro in their book *Parking* indicate that a 19'-0" stall on a 30-degree angle requires 16'-6" from curb to rear of stall, while a 90-degree stall requires 19'-0". However 20 stalls 9'-6" wide on a 60-degree angle require 382'-0" lineal wall length, while 90-degree parking accommodates the same number of stalls in 190'-0".

8. Consideration must be given to approaches from the street into the parking area and to fast and easy access to the street for cars leaving the facility.

9. Parking facilities on more than one level require ramps or elevators to transport autos to upper levels (or lower levels if it is an underground facility).

10. The minimum land requirement for a ramp-type facility is about 20,000 square feet.

11. The slope of the ramp is critical. If it is too steep, the front and rear of the auto will strike the pavement. A 7-degree slope is commonly accepted as maximum. The steeper the ramp, the less floor area consumed.

12. The floor-to-floor height of the multistory facility influences ramp length. The greater this height, the longer the ramp needed. A height of 8'-0" is common. Table 57 gives data for selected angles of ramps and floor-to-floor height.

13. The change of grade between the ramp and the floor must be gradual. Usually the slope at the beginning and end of the ramp is reduced. This reduced slope should cover a distance equal to the wheel base of the average auto (about 10'-0" to 12'-0"). See Fig. 1025.

14. Sufficient space is needed at the end of the ramp for the car to turn a corner. This is based upon the turning radius of the auto. A one-way aisle requires about 30'-0" to 32'-0", and a two-way aisle about 42'-0" to 45'-0".

Table 57
Ramp Length for Straight Ramps (In Feet)

ANGLE (Degrees)	Ramp Grade (Percent)	Floor-to-Floor Height		
		8'-0"	9'-0"	10'-0"
4	7	114	128	143
5	9	89	100	111
6	10	80	90	100
7	12	67	75	83
8	14	57	64	72

Reproduced with permission from George Baker and Bruno Funaro, Parking, Reinhold Publishing Company, New York.

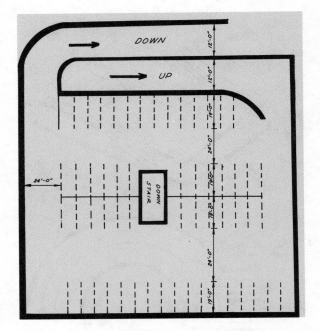

Fig. 1024. A suggested parking deck on top of a one-story building. Ramp length varies with the height of the building. The ramp system could be altered slightly to permit the addition of parking levels above this.

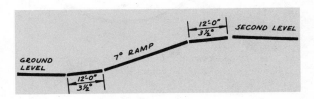

Fig. 1025. Ramps require a lesser slope at the beginning and end to prevent autos from bumping the floor. This slope should be half the ramp angle.

15. In most cases, a single system of ramps in a self-parking garage is adequate to handle all traffic. Only in an extremely large facility would more than one ramp system be needed. See Fig. 1026.

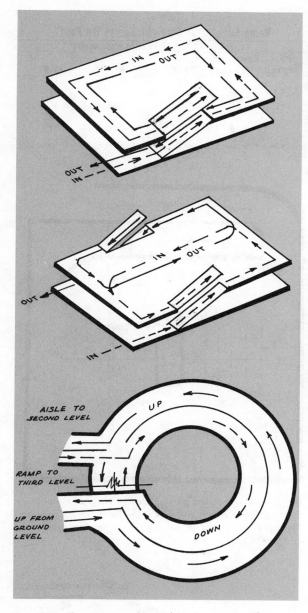

Fig. 1026. Three commonly used ramp systems. There are many other ways of locating ramps.

Fig. 1027. A parking garage using helical ramps. The ramps are protected from the weather by plastic panels. (Alsynite Division of Reichhold Chemicals, Inc.)

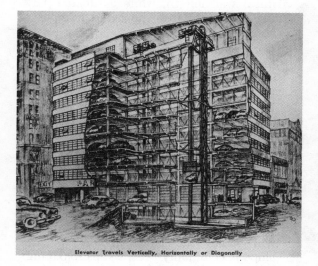

Elevator Travels Vertically, Horizontally or Diagonally

Fig. 1028. A multistory, elevator-equipped parking garage. Notice how the facility was adapted to a small, narrow site. (Montgomery Elevator Co.)

16. Helical ramps are used instead of straight ramps in some facilities. These can be one-way or two-way traffic aisles as shown in Fig. 1026.

17. The diameter of the helical ramp is controlled by the turning radius of the auto. A two-way helical ramp requires 42'-0" to 45'-0" *radius* to the outside edge of the outer lane. A one-way helical ramp could have a *diameter* of 30'-0" to 32'-0" to the outside edge of the lane. An exterior view of a helical ramp facility is shown in Fig. 1027.

18. Attendant-parking facilities with ramps require some means for allowing the employees to return rapidly to the entrance level. The autos are driven up the usual ramp system. Elevators or firepoles usually are used to return attendants.

19. Building columns in a multistory building should be located so a number of autos can be parked between them with no wasted space.

20. Provision for moving pedestrians from upper-level, self-service parking to the street is necessary. A two- or three-story

facility usually provides stairways. Larger facilities have elevators or escalators. Even with an elevator, a stairway should be included for emergency use. Stairs should be located so the customer does not have to walk a great distance from his car to reach them.

21. Since parking customers do not arrive at an even pace, provision should be made for accommodating a number of waiting autos to prevent them from blocking traffic in the street.

Elevator Parking

22. The elevator parking facility is especially effective when a site is too small or so shaped that it cannot use ramps. Several elevators are manufactured for this purpose. Fig. 1028 illustrates a multistory parking garage with elevator parking.

23. Elevators move horizontally and vertically at the same time. The attendant drives the auto on the elevator and operates the elevator from a control panel, while still in the driver's seat. Stalls

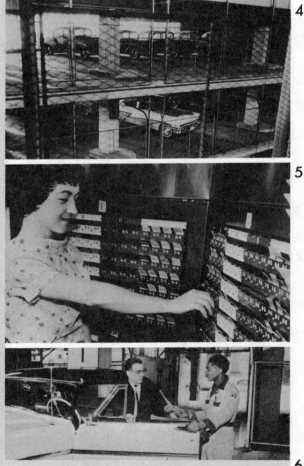

Fig. 1029. Operational cycle of elevator parking facility. (Courtesy, Montgomery Elevator Co.)

1. Customer arrives and receives parking stub from attendant.

2. Attendant drives car onto elevator and activates switch on elevator control panel. This automatically closes the safety gates and moves the elevator car to the assigned level and stall.

3. Safety gates closed, the elevator car starts to move.

4. Vehicles are stored in a minimum of space.

5. When customer claims his car, the cashier pulls the matching claim stub from the master control panel. This signals the attendant on the elevator who secures the vehicle.

6. Attendant drives auto off the elevator and delivers it to the waiting customer.

that are occupied are shown on a control panel in the checker's room. When a customer wants his car, the cashier removes the ticket from her panel, a number lights on a panel on the elevator and the elevator operator secures that vehicle. Frequently, an intercommunication system is used in addition. See Fig. 1029.

24. The major advantages of an elevator system as compared to a ramp system are: (1) minimum site requirements are less (5,000 square feet), (2) space required per stall is less, (3) the building construction cost is less, (4) total operating costs are less and (5) automobiles are moved less and, therefore, are less apt to be damaged.

25. Elevator parking facilities should be planned in multiples of 20'-0" lengthwise and 8'-0" sidewise. Fig. 1030 illustrates a typical plan.

26. A one-way traffic pattern must be created.

27. The entrance drive to the elevator should be straight, with any necessary turns located on the exit side. This is not mandatory, but is highly desirable.

28. For elevator garages, the receiving area should be allotted at least 6 percent of the garage capacity. The exit area should be planned so autos not removed immediately by the owner will not block the exit flow.

29. One elevator is needed for each 135 stalls. These should be divided into units of 45 stalls on each side of the hatchway, with one side two autos deep. If storage capacity exceeds 400 autos, the number of stalls per elevator should be reduced somewhat.

30. Elevator garages storing over 400 autos need more than one street entrance; a single entrance cannot handle the traffic.

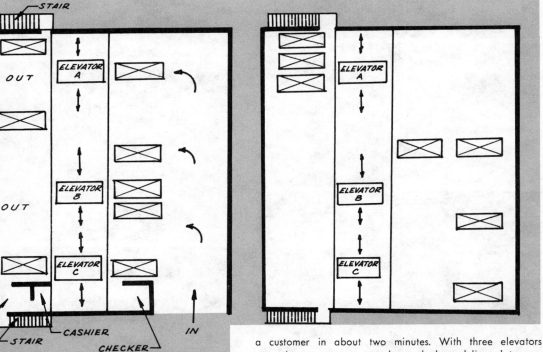

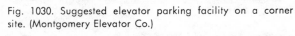

Fig. 1030. Suggested elevator parking facility on a corner site. (Montgomery Elevator Co.)

Vehicles enter on the right, where space is available to hold eleven autos waiting to be moved up and parked. Elevators move to right and left to pick up cars, and move vertically and horizontally to open storage areas where the cars are driven off. An auto can be stored or returned to a customer in about two minutes. With three elevators operating, many cars can be parked or delivered to customers in an hour. During peak periods, the entrance aisle is also used to store autos waiting to be parked.

The upper deck parking accommodates autos one deep on the left and two deep on the right. The right rear stalls of upper floors are usually reserved for long-term storage. The left section could be expanded to two deep if desired.

Notice that the column spacing accommodates three autos with no wasted space.

Class Activities

1. Visit a motel. Try to envision problems facing a customer as he checks in at the office, parks his car, carries his bags into the room and makes himself comfortable. List the good and poor planning features of the motel. Special consideration should be given to parking.

2. Visit a motel and determine its ability to withstand hard use. Prepare a report listing things that seem to have become unusually worn. Then explain what improvements you recommend, by revising the plan or substituting a different material. For example, a motel owner may try to reduce costs by using plastic tile in the bath. Due to heavy use, it may be loose or may present a poor appearance. What would you do to remedy this problem?

3. Working with other students, plan a motel and adjoining food service. The work could be divided according to interest. Both units must attract the passing customer and entice him to stop. Refer to the previous chapter for food service planning.

4. Visit with attendants at a parking facility. Be familiar with the principles of planning such a facility, so you can ask questions. Prepare a report listing the special problems they cite concerning the design and use of their installation.

5. Plan a two-story or higher parking facility to accommodate the automobiles driven daily to your school. This entails a careful count over a period of a week, plus selecting a suitable building site.

Additional Reading

Motels

Architectural Record (Editorial Staff), *Motels, Hotels, Restaurants and Bars*.

Baker, Geoffrey, and Funaro, Bruno, *Motels*.

Hattrell, W.S., *et. al., Hotels, Restaurants and Bars*.

Parking Facilities

Baker, Geoffrey, and Funaro, Bruno, *Parking*.

CHAPTER SEVENTEEN

PLANNING
SHOPPING CENTERS

Today's shopper tends to purchase needed items from stores in close proximity to one another. No longer is he content to drive from store to store to make his purchases. A popular plan to meet these demands is the grouping of a variety of stores, so the customer can easily walk from one to another. Store owners have found their combined drawing power enables them to increase business, because a larger number of potential customers pass their doors.

Recreational facilities have followed much the same development. The grouping of such activities has proven quite successful.

In this chapter, principles for planning shopping centers are presented, as well as one type of recreational grouping — the bowling center combined with other activities.

Shopping Centers

A shopping center is a carefully integrated area of merchandising facilities. The types of merchandise to be offered must be ascertained before any other planning starts. This information must be obtained from a study of the shopping needs of the geographic region to be served. Then, a plan can be developed to meet all these needs. In this sense, therefore, a row of small stores located along a busy thoroughfare is not a true shopping center. Some of the principles to consider when planning a shopping center follow.

Preliminary Planning

1. Before a center is built, much preliminary planning must be done. Of first importance is an analysis of the potential marketing area. Usually the center needs a well populated, residential area or a new, rapidly expanding area, for maximum economic success.

2. The selection of the site is another preliminary planning factor. A careful study must be made of such features as the shape of the plot, orientation, access roads to the site, availability of utilities (sewers, water, gas, electricity), slope of the land and drainage possibilities, and soil conditions influencing construction costs.

3. Sites of an unusual shape cause planning difficulties and should be avoided.

4. A popular trend is the utilization of sloping sites, thus enabling a center to be planned with entrances on two levels.

5. The site selected should be large enough to accommodate a center that will meet the needs of the marketing area. If the area is growing, room must be allowed on the site for future expansion of the sales area and parking.

6. A study of subsurface soil conditions is strongly advised before a site is purchased. Unsuitable conditions may require excessively expensive foundations. This may make the site development cost prohibitive.

7. The building site is best if it is in one tract of land. Some sites with a minor street cutting through them can be developed, but special consideration of auto and pedestrian traffic is necessary. The

street could be spanned by a pedestrian overpass. Sometimes stores are built on both sides of the street and are connected at several levels by passways built over the street. This enables customers to cross over the street, without leaving the sales building.

8. Utilities should be at the site or close enough for economical connections.

9. As is true with any construction, zoning regulations should be studied to see that the site can be used as intended.

10. The site should have suitable access roads to handle the heavy flow of traffic. Heavily traveled, major thoroughfares usually are not the best choice; the additional traffic from the shopping center can cause severe difficulties.

11. After the site location is decided, the architect can begin preliminary building design and site layout drawings. As this is done, many other decisions need to be made, such as the types of stores to be in the center, their location in relation to other stores, the architectural styles to be used, and the locations of parking areas and malls.

Access Roads and Parking

12. The site layout must provide roads connecting the passing thoroughfares.

13. For large centers, traffic patterns should separate truck traffic from customer traffic. Very large centers may have subsurface shipping and receiving tunnels leading to basement receiving, shipping and storage areas.

14. Large areas for customer parking are a must. Usually these areas surround the shopping complex on all sides, thus reducing the distance a customer must walk. A distance of 300 to 400 feet from the parking area to the store is considered maximum.

15. The amount of parking space needed varies with the size and type of center. The most common plan for neighborhood centers is to allow 2 square feet of parking area for each square foot of building area (including upper floors, basements and mezzanine areas); for larger centers, allow 3 square feet of parking for each square feet of building.

Each auto requires 300 square feet of area (including traffic aisles). If portions of the parking area are to be landscaped or if pedestrian walks are a part of the parking area, these need to be added to the allotment. Suggestions for arranging the parking area can be found in Chapter 16.

16. The parking area is best if it is all in one tract of land and is not cut by cross-traffic streets.

17. If land is expensive, a multideck parking building can be used. Some stores provide parking area on the roof. See Chapter 16.

18. Traffic congestion can be relieved by the use of drive-in windows for services such as cleaning, laundry and banking.

19. Raised pedestrian walks between the rows of parked autos generally are not used. Most people walk in the auto traffic aisles. The walks take considerable space, and the cost is prohibitive in areas where land is expensive.

20. Within the shopping center, pedestrian traffic is directed over walks, courts and malls. See Fig. 1050. These areas frequently have roofs for protection from sun and inclement weather.

21. The center should contain areas filled with plants, trees and sculpture to create

Fig. 1050. A shopping center with a mall. Notice the plastic covered canopies and attractive planting. Customers can move freely with no fear of automobile traffic. (Alsynite Division of Reichhold Chemicals, Inc.)

a pleasant atmosphere. Benches for rest and fountains for beauty are common.

Grouping the Stores

22. A basic principle in store grouping is that closely related stores, which can be of mutual benefit to one another, should be placed together. Success has been experienced by locating department stores and food stores next to each other, stores catering to women together, stores providing service and repairs together, and food stores and variety stores together. In general, doctors' offices are most satisfactorily located in a separate building. Second-floor locations seem to be inferior, except for businesses which have regular customers who park for short times, such as dance studios.

23. The center should be built around one or two large stores such as department stores. The addition of small shops adds to the completeness of the center and gives it a balance of services. The customer should find all services he needs in the one center. This frequently includes restaurants and banks.

24. Large stores attract great numbers of customers. For this reason, they should be located so that customers, to reach them, must pass the many small shops in the shopping center. Their "pulling power" is used to provide a flow of customers to the smaller stores.

25. A small neighborhood center usually uses a food store, a junior department store or a drugstore as a major customer attraction. Other stores, such as cleaners, jewelers and novelty shops, rely heavily upon the customers that the larger stores attract.

26. It is desirable to have more than one large store. These are placed in different sections of the center, so customers must pass the small stores.

27. If only one major store is planned, usually it is located in the middle of the shopping complex, and the smaller stores are grouped around it.

28. Store locations must be arranged to promote maximum customer traffic throughout the shopping center. This is best accomplished by assigning locations to each type.

29. It is desirable to have several stores of each kind in a center. This provides the opportunity for comparison shopping and keeps the store managers alert to competition.

30. Opinions vary on the best way to group stores. Some architects desire to group like stores together. For example, two food stores could be adjacent, with other food services such as bakeries nearby. This has worked in actual practice, but it does cause some difficulties such as parking congestion.

    Other designers prefer to separate the types of stores. Since most centers are a complex of buildings, these designers attempt to balance the types of stores in each building. For example, each building might include a jewelry store, clothing store, barber shop and a shoe store.

31. Stores handling mainly impulse items generally are located on the portions of the mall with heavy traffic or on the main court. Stores handling demand items, such as appliance stores, can be located on the outskirts or outside walks.

32. In a residential area, it may be necessary to provide a buffer zone of trees and shrubs around the shopping center, to soften the impact of the buildings and parking areas.

Exterior Design

33. The architecture of the entire center should be integrated. The center should present a uniform facade, yet each store should exhibit an individual character.

34. Store signs, while they can reflect individuality, should be controlled by an overall plan so as to preserve the unity of the center.

35. Materials, colors and other features should be used to individualize each store and to prevent it from being lost among the other stores.

36. Each store front should be designed to complement, rather than overshadow, its neighbor.

Illustrative Examples

The following four centers illustrate the application of some of the principles of planning a shopping center.

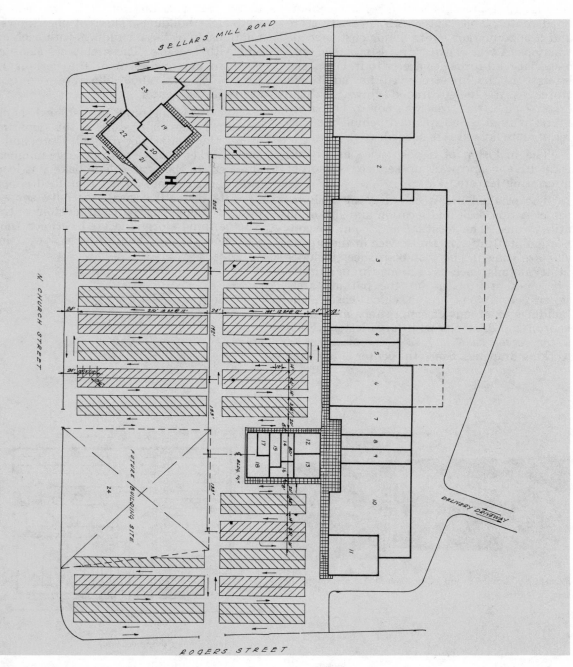

Fig. 1051. An abbreviated plan for a small shopping center. This is the Cum Park Plaza Shopping Center, Burlington, North Carolina. (Alley, Williams, Carmen and King, Inc., Engineers and Architects)

Key to Buildings:

1. Supermarket.
2. Hardware store.
3. Variety store.
4. Shoe store.
5. Ladies clothing.
6. Drugstore.
7. Clothing store.
8. Men's clothing.
9. Gift shop.
10. Dry goods.
11. Clothing store.
12. Dairy bar.
13. Family stamp store.
14. Barber shop.
15. Beauty shop.
16. Shoe store.
17. Bakery.
18. Specialty shop.
19. Post office.
20. Laundromat.
21. Dry cleaners.
22. Bank with drive-in window.
23. Post office truck maneuvering area.
24. Site for future building.

Fig. 1051 presents a plan for a neighborhood center. This center uses a variety store and a supermarket as its major customer attractions. A rear delivery area is provided, and a special road furnishes access to it. Of special interest is the area reserved for additional stores as the neighborhood grows. On the original plan, this area was not to be paved. Stores may also be expanded behind the center, if more floor area is needed.

The inclusion of a post office and bank, with drive-in and walk-up service, is another interesting feature.

The original architect's drawing includes the elevation data and location and size of all utility lines. The location and point of connection of utilities to the service in the streets also are shown. The plot plan sheet includes utility details, such as sections through drainage pipes and plates for the parking area, sewer connections and a catch basin. The buildings or groups of small shops are identified on the drawings with large letters. Each letter serves as a key to a complete set of working drawings. Since the center is too large

to be drawn as one set, it is drawn as if it were eight buildings. The plot plan shows the relationship of these buildings with each other and with the site. The architects also developed an enlarged plan of the parking area. Figs. 1052 and 1053 illustrate two of the stores in this center.

Fig. 1054 illustrates an *L*-shaped shopping center. Three main stores — the department store, the junior department store and the supermarket — serve to draw large numbers of shoppers to the center. The bakery is located near the supermarket, so that food shoppers pass its door. The small specialty shops are located along the path of customer traffic. The clothing store is located between the department stores. This insures a flow of inter-

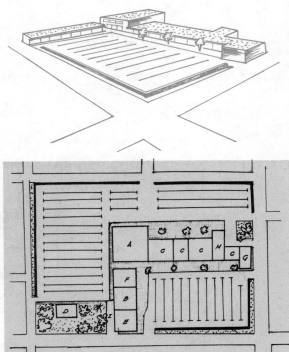

Fig. 1052. A women's shop in the Cum Park Plaza Shopping Center. (Natcor)

Fig. 1053. A drugstore in the Cum Park Plaza Shopping Center. (Natcor)

Fig. 1054. *L*-shaped shopping center.

Key to Buildings:
A. Major department store.
B. Junior department store.
C. Specialty shops (jewelry, shoes, etc.).
D. Bakery.
E. Supermarket.
F. Clothing store.
G. Drugstore.
H. Restaurant.
I. Truck zone.

ested customers and increases the competition between these stores, which is necessary to a successful shopping center.

All stores are easily reached from either parking area. One problem with a small center is the receiving and shipping of merchandise. This activity could become entangled with customer traffic, since no special provi-

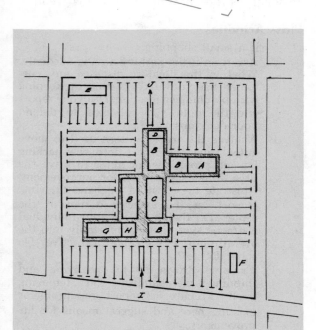

Fig. 1055. Center with parking on four sides.

Key to Buildings:

A. Supermarket.
B. Specialty shops (jewelry, shoes, etc.)
C. Department store.
D. Drugstore.
E. Medical building.
F. Service station.
G. Restaurant.
H. Hardware store.
I. Ramp to unloading area below.
J. Truck exit ramp.

sion is made for it, except for the area behind the supermarket.

Fig. 1055 illustrates a comprehensive shopping center, offering a medical center and a service station, in addition to the usual shopping facilities. A department store and supermarket serve as the major customer attractions. Considerable space is devoted to specialty shops in an attempt to provide all the services a shopper needs, such as shoe repair, jewelry, dry cleaning and barber and beauty shops. A center of this size could also include a branch office for a bank.

The buildings are arranged in an irregular pattern, giving all stores maximum exposure to the mall and parking areas.

Of special interest is the receiving and shipping area below the shopping center. Notice the ramps leading into and out of this basement area. The lower level can be used for storage, uncrating merchandise and wrapping items for delivery to customers.

The service station, of necessity, is located on a corner, so it is convenient for passing motorists. Since it is easily reached from the parking area, it can do a fine business in auto accessories, tires and batteries.

The medical complex is located on the outskirts of the center. Usually those desiring medical attention do not wish to be delayed by shopping traffic. Since the extreme corner of a parking area is the last to be used by shoppers, it serves this special purpose very well. The patients also have excellent parking facilities near the center. The drugstore is located in the shopping center, but on the end nearest the medical center. In this way, it can serve both areas.

Fig. 1056 illustrates a shopping center utilizing another plan for receiving and shipping merchandise. The department store has an area screened off from the view of the customer for this activity. The specialty shops have an area between them, while the supermarket and adjoining stores have a drive hidden by shrubbery.

Since a supermarket has a high concentration of parked autos, this plan provides a large parking area adjacent to the store. This area usually will not be used by customers shopping in other parts of the center.

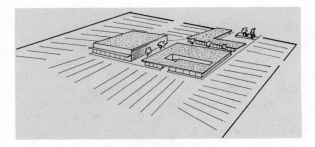

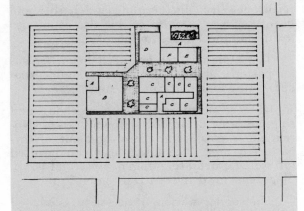

Fig. 1056. Shopping center with concealed loading areas.
Key to Buildings:
A. Shop service areas.
B. Department store.
C. Specialty shops.
D. Supermarket.
E. Drugstore.
F. Clothing store.

A Look to the Future

The typical retailer today operates a small store as a part of a neighborhood shopping center or a large regional center. His store is one of a cluster of small shops built side-by-side. In the future, this typical shopping center may give way to the *one-stop shopping center.* This single store will handle a comprehensive variety of goods. Everything from drugs to furniture and food will be available in one store, thus offering the customer great convenience in shopping. Obviously, such a plan will greatly change the type of store facility that must be built.

European stores are experimenting with one solution — the use of a shopping card system. All the items in the facility (except produce and meat) are for display only. The customer detaches a card from the rack containing the merchandise he desires and presents this card at the check-out counter.

When the shopper enters the store, he picks up a number card divided into four sections. One section is attached to produce he selects and another to the selected meat. These purchases are sent by a conveyor to the stock room. The third section is presented to the check-out clerk, along with the collected merchandise cards. These are sent via a pneumatic tube to a basement stock room. Here the purchases are assembled, together with the meat and produce sent down. The customer gets his auto, drives to a pick-up window and presents the fourth section of the card as a claim check for all the purchases.

Such a system eliminates all problems of maintaining stock on the sales floor and removes the need for push carts, thereby reducing congestion. Fig. 1057 illustrates how this concept might work. Large multimillion dollar, regional centers may not follow this trend.

Class Activities

1. Visit a small shopping center.
   A. Ascertain if the parking area is adequate. What is the greatest distance any customer has to walk? Is this in keeping with planning suggestions? In your report cite the data you collected to defend your decisions.
   B. Analyze the traffic pattern used to move autos from the street into the parking lot and provisions for autos to leave the area. Make suggestions for improvement. Illustrate these with a freehand drawing.
   C. Report on the exterior design of the center. Do the stores have an individual character, yet blend comfortably into the overall plan? Is the center attractive? Do signs detract?
   D. Examine provisions for receiving and shipping merchandise and removing trash. Prepare a report on problems existing here and suggest means for improvement.
   E. Analyze the types of stores in the center. Do they meet the suggested principles for the selection of occupants? Consider the relationship of a store to its neighbor. Is the choice of adjoining stores sound? What changes would you suggest?

2. A class could undertake to design a small shopping center. This is a large project and could involve every class member. A building site should be selected and the grade ascertained. Then decisions must be made concerning the types of stores to include. Stu-

dents could then begin to plan each store as subgroups. Space allocations and final decisions concerning the overall size and shape of the center will need to be made. The completed plan then could be constructed as a three-dimensional model.

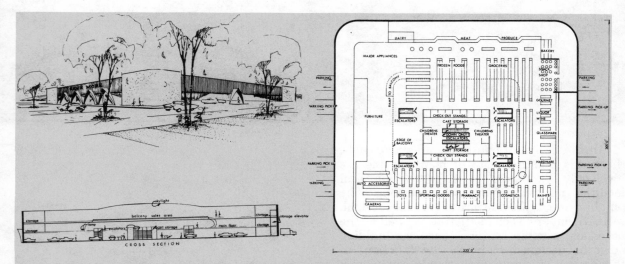

Fig. 1057. A comprehensive, one-stop shopping center. It appears that in the future this type of facility will replace the typical small shopping center. (Beverly Willis, Industrial Designer)

Possible shell for the 300' x 335' one-stop shopping center with sales area on the second level. The ground floor of the building is open on three sides. The arches are decorative and serve to break up the immense front span. The skylight is not visible on the exterior of the building.

Cross section of the one-stop shopping center shows the relationship of the ground floor, main shopping floor and balcony. There is sufficient space on the 80-foot-deep balcony for men's and women's wear, children's apparel, shoes, carpeting and drapery, TV-radio and hi-fi, optometrist, jewelry and bank.

This floor plan, an overall 100,500 square feet, provides 68,750 square feet of sales area and 31,750 square feet of storage on the main floor; 51,700 square feet for sales and 31,750 square feet for storage on the balcony; plus a total of 120,450 square feet for merchandise display and sales and a total of 63,500 square feet of storage. Parking is on the ground level, beneath the store. The market totals 22,800 square feet.

CHAPTER EIGHTEEN

PLANNING CHURCHES

In the design of churches and synagogues, the needs and interests of many people are involved. Differences exist in the physical facilities needed by different religions. The building must provide areas for educational, recreational and social activities, as well as the necessary worship centers. Since the building must be designed to house the functions of the church effectively, it should take on a form that is, in reality, a symbol to the world of the church and what it believes. This form must reflect the purpose of the church. Because the objectives vary from congregation to congregation within a denomination, they can be ascertained only by the minister and the congregation. These decisions should be revealed to the architect, as he tries to unite the needs and purposes of the church into a building that is functional and representative.

General Planning Considerations

1. When a church building is planned, the congregation must determine what activities are to take place and what type of facility is needed for them. Then the architect can design a building to house these activities.

2. The architect must know the theology and history of the church and the meaning of the liturgy. He must also be informed about the educational methods and procedures. While the theology and worship procedures are the work of the congregation, the structural design is the responsibility of the architect, as is the development of an interior and exterior

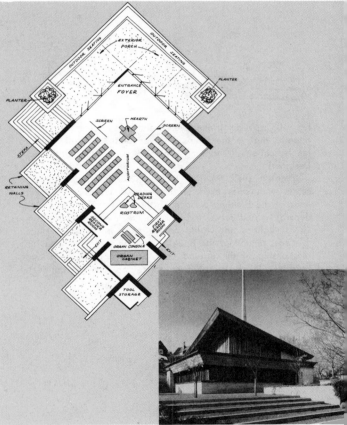

Fig. 1080. First Church of Christ, Scientist, Belvedere, California. (California Redwood Assoc., Charles Warren Callister, Designer) Notice the special requirements for this denomination and the terms used to identify the parts of the church. The narthex is a foyer, the nave an auditorium and the chancel a rostrum. Special provision must be made for the first and second readers.

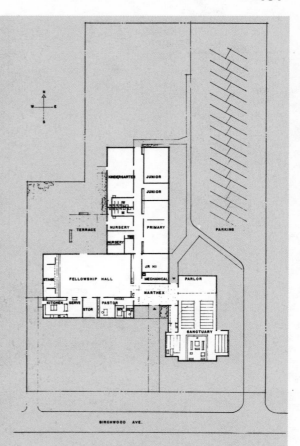

Fig. 1081. A small Presbyterian Church in Bellingham, Washington. (Durham, Anderson and Freed, Architects) The interior is lighted with cone-shaped spotlights and a skylight above the altar. The structural members are laminated wood arches and the exterior is a blending of native materials.

The church office is compact, but contains the desirable features of an outer secretary's office, enclosed workroom and a private office for the pastor. The kitchen and social hall are adjoining, and a storage room is readily available.

The narthex serves the fellowship hall and the sanctuary with equal effectiveness. The parlor serves to accommodate overflow congregations. The mechanical room is centrally located so as to serve all three wings of the building.

design that reflects the spirit of the church. Figs. 1080 through 1084 illustrate solutions for five denominations.

3. A careful study of the site must be made before the building design is started. It is best if the architect can be employed before the site is selected, so he can assist the congregation in their decision.

4. Adequate parking space should be located so the congregation can easily enter the church. It should not be so obvious as to ruin the exterior setting.

5. Exterior gardens and plantings should be in harmony with the building.

6. Churches and church school buildings should have year-round air conditioning.

7. Churches have a special heating problem. Some portions need to be kept at a comfortable temperature for daily activities, while other areas need not be fully heated, except for special times during the week. A zoned heating system is recommended.

8. Drinking fountains should be provided throughout the entire church building.

9. Janitors' closets need to be located in space of little value, yet be convenient to the areas to be maintained.

10. An exterior storage room is needed for items such as a lawn mower, hose, and snow removal equipment.

11. Ramps instead of steps are of value

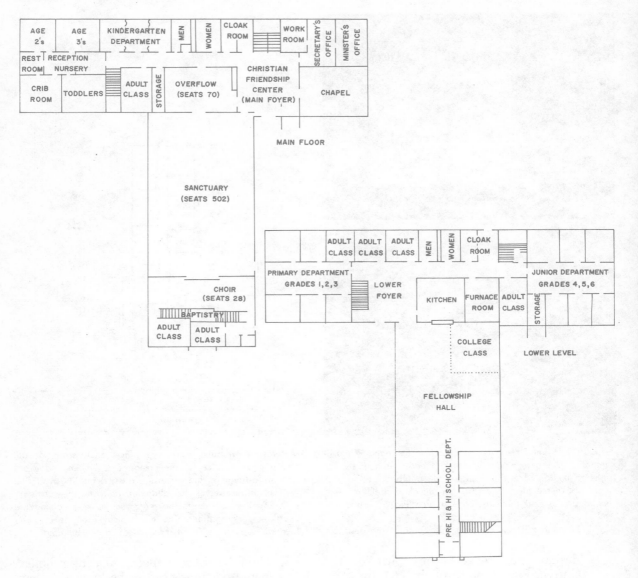

Fig. 1082. Eastview Christian Church, Bloomington, Illinois. (Goodman Church Builders)

The seating capacity of the sanctuary is extended by use of the overflow area at the rear of the auditorium. Exten- sive Bible school activity was planned in the building with 33 classrooms provided from a crib room in the nursery to seven adult study rooms. A chapel is provided for private or group meditation or for small weddings.

wherever they can be used. They reduce the possibility of accident and are especially helpful to the aged.

12. Occasionally a congregation feels a parlor is needed. This should be furnished in a manner similar to a typical living room. The furnishings should be in keeping with the architecture of the church.

Fig. 1082. (Cont.) Warm wood paneling and stone are used to create natural beauty for the platform area. The exterior is stone and uses a lighted aluminum cross rising from a lattice-work tower to denote the architectural purpose of the building.

Fig. 1083. A Catholic Church in Alhambra, California. (J. Earl Trudeau, AIA, Architect) This building is steel framed with a 2-inch, pneumatically applied, concrete roof surface over a plywood diaphragm. The windows are chipped glass set in concrete. Interior ceiling is sprayed acoustical plaster and the floors are terrazzo. The altar is of marble and the reredos is flagcrete.

13. Lack of funds to complete the entire church plant occasionally requires that some rooms be used for several purposes. The sanctuary frequently serves also as a social hall and sometimes houses church school classes. Such measures should be only temporary. Fig. 1083 illustrates an expandable plan.

14. Suitable flooring materials include oak and maple wood flooring, carpeting, asphalt, vinyl asbestos, vinyl and rubber tile, flagstone, terrazzo and marble. Carpeting in the sanctuary seems to be generally favored. Not only is it attractive, but it helps to deaden sounds, thus promoting a worshipful atmosphere.

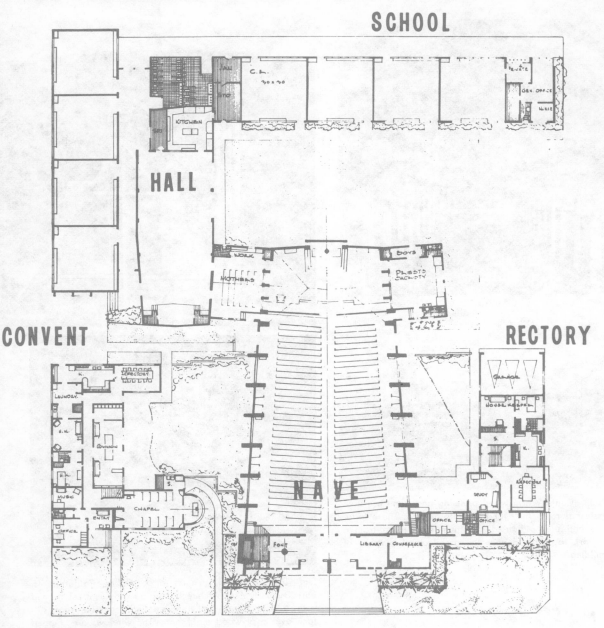

Fig. 1083. (Cont.)

15. Flooring materials should be carefully chosen so they are in harmony with the other building materials. Only the best quality materials should be used.

16. The church office is a busy place. If it is to function properly, the activities to be performed there must be decided. The principles of planning offices (Chapter 14) must be carefully observed. In many church offices, the Sunday bulletin and a church newspaper are printed, financial records are kept, mail is answered, appointments are made and church records of all kinds are filed and kept up-to-date. It is desirable to plan a work and storage room off the main office. This removes noise and clutter from the office.

17. The clergy should have private offices,

Main entrance to a large shopping center. (Western Wood Products Association)

The design of the exterior mall requires consideration of traffic flow, customer rest areas, and a pleasant atmosphere. (Cold Spring Granite Co.)

On the mall of an area shopping center. (Western Wood Products Association)

The lobby of a motel or motor inn must be attractive and comfortable. (Holiday Inns, Inc.)

A motel should have a large, attractive sign. An inn can be designed as a multistory structure. (Holiday Inns, Inc.)

Many motels and motor inns have extensive dining facilities with a warm, comfortable atmosphere. (Holiday Inns, Inc.)

A typical motel room. (Motel/Motor Inn Journal)

A second lavatory is often located outside the bath. (Motel/Motor Inn Journal)

An outdoor swimming pool is an important part of the planning of motels and motor inns. (Motel/Motor Inn Journal)

Large hotels and inns have special suites for important guests. (Holiday Inns, Inc.)

This church interior was designed for large audiences. (National Forest Products Association)

This exterior view reflects the architectural function of this building in its design. (National Forest Products Association)

The architectural design of this church compliments its setting. (National Forest Products Association)

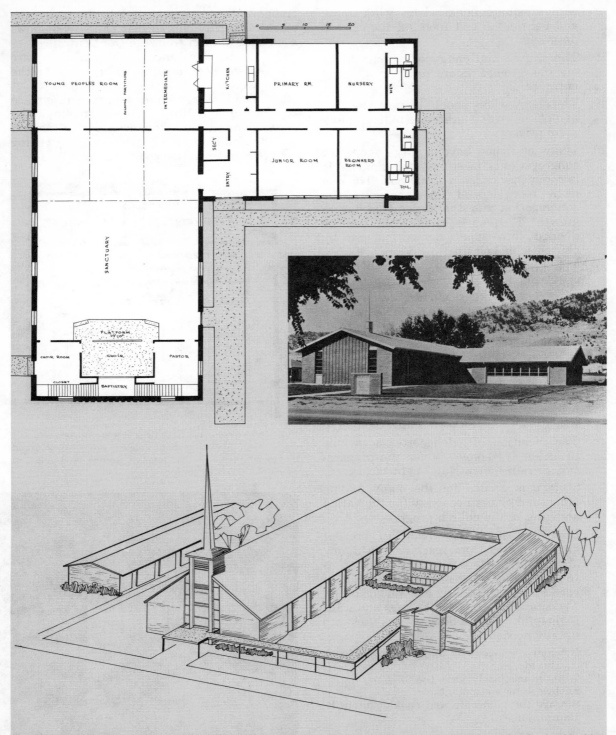

Fig. 1084.   Broadway Baptist Church, Boulder, Colorado. (Robert W. Ditzen, Architect) Photo shows the first unit of a church that is to be expanded into a campus-type facility. This unit will serve the congregation as a sanctuary and church school until a larger separate church school building and a large separate sanctuary can be built, when it becomes the fellowship hall. Perspective shows the eventual development planned.

with adequate bookshelves, work space and lighting. A rest room off the office is desirable.

18. The church and clergy offices should be on the ground floor, near an exterior entrance.

19. The clergy offices should be near the general offices, yet so located as to have maximum privacy.

20. Many churches have a large room for congregational meetings and dinners. It is commonly called a social hall. The size of the room depends upon the size of the congregation and the anticipated future growth. Frequently, this room can be divided into small rooms for use by church school classes.

21. The kitchen is next to the social hall, since the hall serves as a dining area. Most church kitchens are designed to prepare food and provide table service. Some provide cafeteria service instead. The choice of service, location, and selection of equipment requires a study of food preparation and serving techniques and equipment. The section in Chapter 15 pertaining to planning restaurants and cafeterias can prove helpful here. See Fig. 1085.

22. The inclusion of kitchenettes accessible to assembly rooms enables the preparation of refreshments and light meals.

23. Storage is needed for the many folding tables and chairs necessary for the varied activities of the church program.

24. Provision should be made to prevent kitchen noises from reaching the dining area. The most satisfactory solution is to place the kitchen on one side of a corridor and the dining area on the other. Acoustical treatment of ceilings and walls is helpful. The following facilities are usually needed:

Efficient arrangement to prepare and cook the food.
Units to efficiently serve the food.
Dishwashing equipment.
Storage for tableware and cooking utensils.
Refuse removal.

The Narthex

The narthex refers to the vestibule, foyer or entrance hall of a church. The main entrance to the church opens into this area. It is essential to any church plan. Fig. 1086 shows a narthex as seen from the front entrance.

1. The narthex should contain 2 square feet of floor area for every seat in the nave.

2. Since this area serves as a gathering place before and after services, it should be separated from the nave with a sound-deadening wall and should have ceiling treatment to reduce noise.

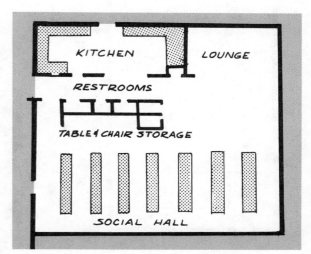

Fig. 1085. Means of separating kitchen noise from the dining area. Notice the relationship of the two areas and the sound barrier in the form of storage area and rest rooms plus a serving corridor.

Fig. 1086. A view from the narthex into the nave of the Hope Lutheran Church, Colma, California. (California Redwood Assoc., Mario Corbett, Architect)

3. The narthex should have special racks for coats. One foot of hanging space for every fifteen seats in the nave is recommended.

4. Rest rooms should be located conveniently off the narthex; however, their doors should not open directly off this area. The room size depends upon the number of people in the congregation.

5. A sufficient number of outside doors should open off the narthex to enable rapid exit.

6. To reduce chilling drafts, a double set of outside doors can be used. This is not necessary in warm climates.

7. The exterior church doors should attract attention and extend a welcome. They can be emphasized by use of color or contrasting materials, such as a stone frame around the door of a brick church.

8. The doors into the church and nave should be wide enough to allow passage of pallbearers carrying a casket. Minimum width is 5½ feet.

9. Provision should be made in the narthex for a guest register, literature racks and displays.

The Nave

The nave is that portion of the church used for seating the congregation during the worship service. It adjoins the narthex and is entered from it. Fig. 1087 illustrates a nave in a contemporary church.

1. An overall plan of traffic flow must be developed for the nave. A center aisle is almost universally used. It should be at least 5'-0" wide, since it is used for processionals and as a main exit upon conclusion of the service. Other aisles should be at least 4'-0" wide, to accommodate two persons side-by-side.

2. A major cross aisle should be located between the chancel and the front row of pews.

3. The use of secondary side aisles greatly facilitates traffic flow. Only very small churches should have just one center aisle for all traffic.

4. The most frequently used plan for a nave is based on a rectangle of a 2 : 1 or 1½ : 1 proportion. This is then split into two sections of pews, with a main center aisle.

5. The arrangement and spacing of the pews should be such that the maximum number of people can be comfortably seated and see and hear the service. This could involve working around columns. The size and design of the pews must be known before this planning can be done.

6. The Lutheran Church suggests planning nave seating capacity for 50 percent of membership, if this membership is over 400 persons. If under 400, but more than 175, seating capacity should be planned for 65 to 75 percent.

7. Building codes usually limit seating to fourteen persons per pew if both ends open onto aisles, or seven persons per pew if one end is against a wall and the other opens onto an aisle.

8. The average person occupies 20 inches of pew seat. If finances permit, 22 to 24 inches is a better allowance. Rows should

Fig. 1087. A view of the nave and chancel of the Methodist Church, Linwood Heights, Pennsylvania. (Pennsylvania Wire Glass Co., Carroll, Grisdale and Van Alen, Architects)

be spaced 36 inches apart, from the back of one pew to the back of that in the next row. See Fig. 1088 for suggested pew dimensions.

9. The selection of pews depends primarily upon the congregation and the interior styling of the nave. Some prefer uncushioned, hardwood pews, while others prefer cushioned or upholstered pews.

10. Some churches require movable kneelers.

11. Provision should be made for storage of hymnals in the pew.

12. Pews should be of such design and color that they are inconspicuous and, therefore, do not detract from the worship service or fight the architecture of the building. Any upholstery material should be durable and of a neutral color.

13. The location of exits, columns, heat sources and other obstructions must be considered when planning a seating layout.

14. The use of individual, upholstered, folding seats, as found in the theatres, is to be avoided. They detract from the religious atmosphere. Individual chairs of certain types, such as a straight-back, rush-bottomed chair, are attractive and suitable.

15. The nave should be designed so the minister can be clearly heard everywhere and instrumental and choral music do not reverberate. The job of designing the acoustics requires a trained engineering specialist.

16. The floor of the nave should be level. A sloping floor, such as in a theatre, increases the cost of construction and makes pew installation difficult.

17. The nave floor should be of a durable, easily cleaned material such as vinyl tile. The aisles should be carpeted.

18. It is desirable to design the structure so the nave is free of columns.

19. The nave should be shielded from all noises from other rooms or outside the building.

20. The communion rail, when used, is placed at the front of the nave and on the same floor level. The kneeling step in front is approximately 6 inches high, and the rail is about 24 inches high.

It should accommodate at least 10 percent of the seating capacity of the nave. The center section should be removable to provide access to the chancel during the worship service. A minimum opening of 4'-0" is needed.

21. The chancel rail separates the chancel from the nave. It is on the floor level of the chancel. The rail may be solid or pierced and is usually 36 inches high.

22. At least 3'-0" of open floor space should separate the communion rail and the chancel rail. Clergy must walk here during communion services.

23. The interior walls of a nave may be any suitable material such as wood, brick, stone, plaster, glass or marble. The natural beauty of the materials provides the needed decoration. Different wall materials frequently are used within a church. For example, the chancel may have walls of stone, while the nave might have painted, plastered walls.

24. While most churches in the Western World are rectangular in plan, some are beginning to follow an Eastern World plan of a round church with the altar in the center. This is commonly referred to as a church-in-the-round. The altar rail surrounds the altar on all sides. The cross is suspended from the ceiling above the altar. The pulpit is on one side, and the baptismal font is placed on the other. This in effect creates a religious amphitheater, with the congregation gathered around the altar.

With such a plan, the congregation tends to stare across the altar at each other, rather than concentrate on the liturgy. Acoustics become a problem, since the listeners are spread over a wide arc and some may even be behind the clergy. To enable everyone to see the

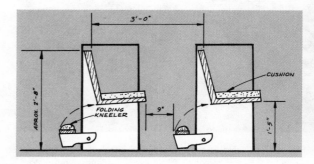

Fig. 1088. Suggested pew dimensions.

raised altar, the nave floor must be sloped or stepped in tiers. Fig. 1089 illustrates a church-in-the-round.

The Chancel

The chancel is reserved for the clergy to use to lead the worship service. See Figs. 1090 and 1091.

1. The floor of the chancel should be elevated above the floor of the nave. It should be high enough that all liturgical acts can be seen by the entire congregation.
2. The chancel should be designed to accommodate the ritual of the church. This varies with the denomination, and these requirements should be studied carefully.

3. There should be no physical separation between the chancel and nave. The chancel, which contains the altar, is the dominant feature of the church and the focal point of attention. As previously mentioned, some denominations place a low communion rail between the chancel and nave.
4. The chancel should be spacious enough to accommodate ceremonies such as confirmations, ordinations and weddings.
5. The choir and organ sometimes are placed in the chancel.
6. Also located in the chancel are: the pulpit, lecturn, altar, cross, baptismal font and other items used in the services.

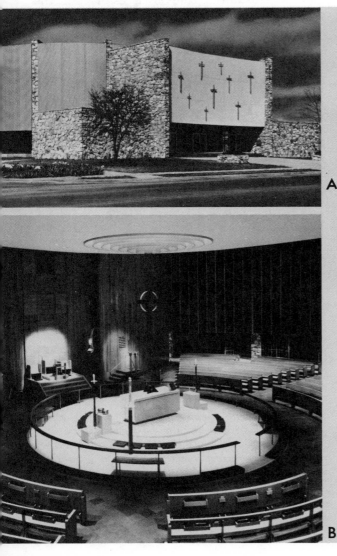

Fig. 1089. St. Luke's Episcopal Church, Dallas, Texas.

A. The mass and form of the structure plus the textures of the materials selected combine to form this striking church exterior. It was designed in a round shape to accommodate the interior seating and altar.

B. The altar and surrounding communion rail support the theology of the Lord's Supper that it is the Lord's people gathered around the Lord's Table. Notice the specially designed, circular pews and the accent lighting of the pulpit and lecturn. The cross is hung above the altar.

C. Of special interest is the pulpit shown on the left. Notice it is raised and of considerable prominence as compared to the lecturn. The choir, organ and organ pipes are strikingly accommodated on a balcony. Notice the ceiling and walls of the choir space are plaster so they will reflect the music. General illumination is by spotlights in the ceiling. High-intensity illumination over the altar focusses attention upon it, and the altar is raised so it is visible to the entire congregation.

7. The predella is a part of the chancel. It is a platform, usually one step above the chancel floor, on which the altar is placed.

8. The predella should be wide enough to permit the clergy to walk while administering holy rites. Usually 36 inches is necessary.

The Sacristy

Some denominations require two sacristies — a working sacristy and a clergy's sacristy. Nonliturgical churches usually do not have a clergy's sacristy. The working sacristy is a room used for the storage, preparation and care of vestments, sacred utensils, paraments and other items used in the chancel. The clergy's sacristy is a private room devoted to personal meditation. The clergy also don their robes and vestments here.

1. Storage cabinets and drawers are needed to store linens so they have a minimum of folds. They may be rolled on tubes, hung on rods or laid flat in drawers.

2. Special cabinets for storing communion trays, the chalice, missal stand, flower vases and candlesticks must be designed.

3. A sink and counter space are needed for the preparation of floral arrangements.

4. Direct access to the chancel is necessary.

5. Sometimes linens are washed and ironed in the working sacristy; therefore, a large sink and ironing facilities are needed. Communion vessels and glasses are also washed here.

6. A substantial safe is necessary for the storage of silver utensils.

7. The size of the sacristy varies with the

Fig. 1090. A chancel. Notice the chancel floor is raised two steps above the nave floor. The altar is on the predella which is three steps above the chancel floor, with an open altar rail of simple design. The predella allows ample room for the clergy to walk around the altar to perform the ritual. Behind the altar, rising to the ceiling, is a magnificent reredos.

Fig. 1091. Hendrix Avenue Baptist Church, Jacksonville, Florida. (Sunday School Board of the Southern Baptist Convention, Reynolds, Smith and Hills, Architects and Engineers)

In this contemporary Baptist church, the locations of the pulpit, altar table and choir are important. The organ is located to the right of the pulpit behind the planter. Flush spotlights in the ceiling furnish general illumination, and lights hidden in the planters provide interesting side lighting. The greatest concentration of light is on the pulpit, thus focusing attention there.

denomination, since some require more liturgical items.

8. The decoration should be simple and in keeping with the church proper. It should not appear to be a kitchen.

9. A water closet and lavatory are necessary, especially in the clergy's sacristy.

10. Storage closets are needed for vestments and robes.

11. The clergy's sacristy should connect with the minister's study.

12. Storage is needed for bibles, prayer books, hymnals and other books used by the clergy in the service.

The Chapel

Consideration should be given to the inclusion of a chapel. Large churches frequently have a small worship area for special services or private occasions such as weddings. Fig. 1092 illustrates a typical chapel included as a part of a larger church plant.

1. The planning of a chapel is similar to that of the sanctuary. A thorough study of the types of services that are to occur there must be made so they can be accommodated. For example, a baptismal

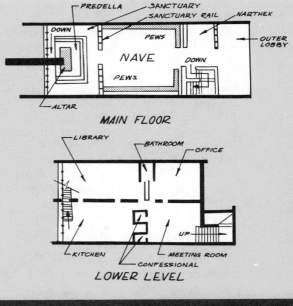

MAIN FLOOR

LOWER LEVEL

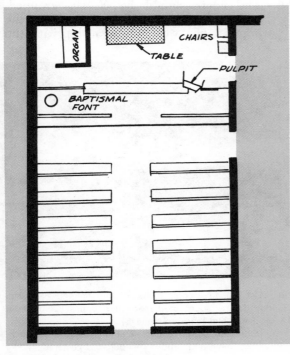

Fig. 1092. A typical small chapel plan.

Fig. 1093. Chapel of the Holy Cross, Sedona, Arizona. (Anshen and Allen, Architects) This Roman Catholic church is situated in a magnificent setting, and the structure is well suited to the site. Notice the use of the architectural principles of mass, scale, surface and texture of materials. The building shell is reinforced concrete, 12 inches thick, and forms the interior and exterior walls. Glare is reduced by using smoke-colored glass. The congregation is seated in pews along the side walls. Individual chairs are used to seat the remainder of the congregation.

font is needed if the chapel is to be used for baptisms.

2. The maximum seating capacity for a chapel is usually 75 to 100 persons. Most are smaller.

3. The chancel should have a side door for access to the area from outside the chapel.

4. The chapel should be located so it is as accessible as the main sanctuary for weddings, baptismals and other services. It should be near the main entrance so it is accessible to the public during the week for prayer and meditations.

5. Choir space usually is omitted.

6. A small electric organ is needed.

7. Provision should be made to seat at least two people in the chancel.

8. Fig. 1093 illustrates a chapel designed as an independent structure, rather than as a part of a large church.

Choir and Organ Placement

The church choir serves three basic functions: to lead congregational singing; to add to the inspiration of the worship service; and to provide appropriate responses and transitions in the service.

1. The placement of the choir is limited to the chancel, a rear balcony or an alcove off the side of the nave. The exact location depends upon the congregation. The primary consideration is to locate the choir so it can best serve its desired function. Each location has advantages and disadvantges; no one place is perfect in all respects. A decision has to be made concerning the importance of music and the recommendations of the denomination involved.

2. A chancel location is most frequently chosen. In one seating arrangement, the choir is placed across the chancel and facing the congregation. Usually this is not a good situation, because the choir and congregation stare at each other. It also places the choir behind the altar, which separates the choir members from the worship service. See Fig. 1094.

3. A much used chancel location places the choir on one side of the chancel, with the organ on the other. An alternate method divides the choir, so the members are opposite one another. This permits the

music to be coordinated and produces a satisfactory area for the blending of voices and organ. However, it does tend to remove the choir from participation in the service since they are behind the pulpit. In no case should the altar be blocked from view by the choir seats.

4. The rear-balcony location is ideal for the production and projection of music. The choir can be directed easily, and their actions do not detract from the service. However, the choir members tend to feel that they are not a part of the worship service. Also, processionals are eliminated. Some denominations use this location, because they want to concentrate attention on the altar and desire the choir out of sight. Coordination between the clergy and choir is more difficult.

5. The choir may be located in an alcove off to the side of the nave. Here it is on the same level as the congregation, and members feel a part of the worship service. On the other hand, this location could cause a structural imbalance of the nave. It also can cause acoustical problems, since the voices do not blend before reaching the congregation.

6. The choir should be closely grouped, and the organ should be located so the organist has a close relationship with the

Fig. 1094. Ruhama Baptist Church, Birmingham, Alabama. (Sunday School Board of the Southern Baptist Convention, Turner, Smith and Batson, Architects)

A traditional Baptist church interior — notice the location of the choir and organ. The pulpit is centered on the chancel.

choir. This helps coordinate their activities and blends the organ music and choir voices.

7. Usually it is best to elevate the choir above the nave floor.

8. A chancel location is most desirable for special choir programs.

9. The choir members should be able to see and hear the clergy and to participate in the service.

10. The choir area should be maintained at a comfortable temperature and should have adequate ventilation.

11. The choir needs a room (called a vestry) in which members can put on their robes, secure their music and rehearse. It should have facilities for the storage of robes and music and should be conveniently located for forming the procession to the nave. Sounds of the choir rehearsing before the worship service should be inaudible in the nave.

12. The size of the choir should be decided. Twenty members is a common minimum.

13. If a processional is desired, a traffic plan for moving the choir to the main aisle in the nave must be made. It is undesirable to block late-arriving worshipers from entering the nave.

14. An office for the minister of music is desirable. It need not be as readily accessible as the church office or the offices of the clergy, but it should be in or near the vestry.

15. The pipe organ should be in the main body of the church. It is poor practice to locate it in an alcove off to the side of the nave, since three sides of the instrument should be exposed. Sufficient space must be allowed for proper installation. Exact space requirements vary, depending upon the instrument selected.

16. It is proper to expose the organ pipes to the view of the congregation. However, they should be so placed that they do not compete with the altar for attention.

17. Some prefer to hide the organ pipes from view, by covering them with a metal or plastic grille. However, this reduces the effectiveness of the organ; exposed pipes produce the best sound.

18. Organ pipes can be placed at the sides of the chancel or the back of the nave.

19. The walls behind a pipe organ, and the ceiling above, should be of a hard material to give resonance to the music.

20. The electronic organ is replacing the pipe organ in some churches. Since no stacks of pipes are necessary, it is especially helpful for churches with limited floor space.

21. The speakers for electronic organs must be located as unobtrusively as possible, yet be able to function properly. They should be well above the heads of the congregation.

Furnishings

Any furnishings in the chancel that play no part in the practice or spirit of the liturgy should be discarded. Secular symbols should not be permitted to share honors with the symbols of God's presence in His church.

The final and lasting impression given by the interior of a church is mainly made by the furniture and accessories. The selection of pews, altar, pulpit, communion table, sculpture, special windows and other art pieces is greatly significant in the total picture. A structurally sound, church building with a fine floor plan is incomplete if the furniture and accessories are poorly selected.

1. The pulpit, lectern and other furnishings should be in harmony with the architecture of the building, not only in design but also in materials. In traditional churches, these were always wood. In contemporary churches, they are of wood, iron, stone, brick or any other suitable material.

2. In most churches, the pulpit is placed at one side of the chancel and the lectern at the other. Some churches place the pulpit in the center. The Christian Science church has two reading desks.

3. The design of the lectern and that of the pulpit should harmonize. The pulpit is of greater importance and should be larger and more impressive.

4. It is recommended that the architect design the altar, baptismal font and other needed items, rather than using items chosen from a catalog. Only in this way can they reflect the church plan and be in harmony with it.

5. The altar is always raised at least one step above the chancel floor. More common is a three-step rise. The exact plan

varies with the denomination. Refer to Fig. 1090, page 429.

6. A current trend in ecclesiastical architecture is to place the altar away from the wall, so the clergy can go behind it and face the congregation as he performs the rites of worship.

7. The altar or altar table (used in some churches) is the focal point of the entire building. It should be located so all can see it. Basically, the church is planned around the altar. It is of first importance.

8. The altar should be in proportion with the size of the chancel. In general practice, it is from 36 to 40 inches in height, 30 to 48 inches wide and 6 to 8 feet long. If designed for a small chapel, it should be scaled down. Each denomination has specific size recommendations.

9. A reredos is placed in back of the altar in many churches. This is a screen of wood or stone intended to enhance the impressive appearance of the altar. See Fig. 1090, page 429.

10. A dossal is a fabric hanging on the wall in back of the altar, to give prominence to the worship center. See Fig. 1091. A church usually has either a reredos or a dossal, but not both.

11. In many churches, the baptismal font is located within the chancel. It is placed inside the altar rail to the side, so it will not interfere with the altar. The font should occupy an important position. It is second only to the altar. Some churches place their baptismal font in a separate baptistry chapel, where baptismal services are held. Other denominations place it in the narthex near the main entrance. Still others practice immersion and need a baptismal pool under the chancel floor.

12. The typical baptismal font is 36 to 40 inches high and contains a removable, metal, noncorrosive bowl, 9 to 15 inches in diameter, with a removable lid. Usually provision is made to drain it to a dry well or the earth.

13. The needed liturgical fittings vary greatly between denominations. Their selection and design should be done by someone knowledgable of the church and its requirements. Items such as altar lamps, censers, crosses, chalices, tabernacles and candlesticks are included in this category.

Color

When lighting is planned, color must be considered at the same time. The colors chosen depend a great deal upon the character and intensity of the light. A wall color may look quite different under artificial lighting.

1. Color balance is necessary. This is done by painting portions of the church in contrasting colors. This pleases the eye and emphasizes areas of importance. For example, the color of the chancel might contrast with that of the nave.

2. Too much wood paneling of the same color reduces the importance of the pulpit and altar or communion table. Instead of blending in with wood wainscoting, these items should stand out against the walls and become the center of attention.

3. The communion table is emphasized in some churches by use of brilliant table coverings.

4. The dossal serves to draw attention to the communion table or altar. Its color should not match anything in the chancel or nave. Scarlet is a frequently used color.

5. A carpet runner extending down the central aisle to the altar can add color and focus attention on the altar. It should be a strong color, but should not match the dossal.

6. Usually the nave walls are a pastel shade, at the opposite side of the color spectrum from that used for the chancel.

7. Drapes in a nave could have strong colors, but should not match the dossal. They could be the same color as pew cushions and carpets.

8. Warm colors that give a friendly, welcome feeling should be chosen.

9. Exterior church doors should appear inviting. They should contrast with the exterior color. Such doors could be painted red, green or blue, if they are a part of a white church exterior. If the exterior of the church is dark, the doors should be very light.

10. Church school rooms, social halls, offices and other rooms should be cheerful and should receive thoughtful color planning.

11. Color selection for the exterior of the church is vital. White has been a most satisfactory color and remains so today.

The use of brick and stone is common. The natural color of the material dominates, and a pleasing color must be selected for the wood trim. Here again, white is good, but not the only suitable color.

Lighting

Church lighting should enhance the beauty of the architecture and preserve the spiritual values of the ecclesiastical atmosphere. The lighting plan should be developed as the building plans are made. Lighting can be used to create different moods and to focus attention on important features.

1. The nave needs well distributed, low-intensity, general illumination. This should be variable from darkness to reading level, by means of a dimmer system.

2. The chancel should receive 20 to 30 footcandles of light.

3. The altar or communion table and the pulpit should receive 50 footcandles of light.

4. Controls for the dimmer system should be in the narthex, since they are operated by someone specially assigned to this task. The clergy never should be expected to do this from the pulpit.

5. The effective use of dimmers is shown by the following example. The general illumination is at a low level during the organ prelude. When the choir processional enters, the illumination is increased to reading level (10 footcandles). It is kept at this level during the service, because the congregation must use their hymnals. As the sermon begins, the sanctuary and choir lights are dimmed, and the pulpit is spotlighted. After the sermon, the pulpit spotlight is diminished, and the choir lights in the nave are increased in intensity. At the conclusion of the service, all lights are increased to full illumination.

6. Light fixtures should be in harmony with the architectural styling of the church.

7. Floodlights and spotlights can be used to illuminate the church interior with indirect light. No fixtures even need to be visible. This directs attention to the surface upon which the light falls, rather than to the light source.

8. Two systems of indirect lighting are in common use. In the first, floodlights are concealed in coves along the upper part of the wall. The light is directed to the ceiling, where it is reflected to the floor. This requires powerful light sources, since much light is absorbed by the ceiling. In the second system, the light is aimed directly toward the surface it is to illuminate. This is done by putting the bulb inside a metal tube, which concentrates the light and sends it in one direction. As the light leaves the tube, it spreads in a cone shape. A number of these tubes directing light straight down into the nave provides adequate general illumination and utilizes more of the light from the bulb than does floodlighting. These tubes can be recessed into the ceiling or hung as conventional light fixtures.

9. Fluorescent lighting generally is unsatisfactory for sanctuary use. It does not accent architectural details, since it casts no shadows. Its cool light causes color distortion, and such lighting cannot be dimmed.

10. The lighting controls should be as simple as possible, since inexperienced persons most often operate them.

11. The lighting system should be easy to maintain. It should not be difficult to replace bulbs or to clean fixtures.

12. Colored light is used in church lighting. The changes should be subtle, rather than dramatic as in a theatre. A slight change in the color of the light in the chancel from that in the nave tends to focus attention upon the chancel. The congregation will be unaware of this difference. When planning, remember that color has psychological implications.

13. The altar, pulpit, lectern, choir, cross, and other specific areas need supplementary lighting. Generally this is used only for a short time, to call attention to the particular activity.

14. The pulpit and lectern should be lighted from two sources, in order to reduce shadows and reflections. Usually an overhead spotlight and a small reading light are adequate. Care must be taken to avoid reflection on the minister's face or glasses. Glare of any kind should be eliminated.

15. The lighting of the sanctuary and altar varies, depending upon the textures, colors and materials used. A smooth material, such as marble, requires a different lighting combination than wood or fabric. The shape and detail of the surface, such as an altar heavily carved, influence the type and location of lighting.

16. In the past, church windows were formally and evenly spaced. However, windows in a contemporary church are placed wherever they will contribute to the effect desired. They may be concentrated in one wall or a portion of a wall. For example, windows may be located only in the chancel, to provide a dramatic lighting effect on the altar.

17. Careful use of natural light by means of precisely placed windows and skylights is a fine source of dramatic illumination. A skylight could be so located as to light an altar. See Figs. 1087 and 1097.

18. A congregation should never be seated so they face windows directly. The eyestrain caused by looking into such a bright source of light is considerable. It also tends to distract attention from the altar. An alternate plan is to place windows at the side of the chancel, thus removing them from the direct view of the congregation.

19. The halls and stairs of the church building require adequate illumination for night use. Classrooms, offices and meeting rooms need a high-level general illumination.

20. The architect can deliberately use lighting to cast shadows, creating a dramatic scene. All other shadows should be eliminated.

21. Exterior lighting that points up architectural features is necessary. Floodlights usually are hidden from view by shrubbery. Time switches may be used on exterior lights. See Fig. 1095.

22. Exterior steps, sidewalks and parking areas should be fully illuminated, and the church name should be visible at night. The use of electric crosses and neon signs should be avoided.

Art in Church Buildings

The integration of art in religious buildings is of great importance, and it demands the services of experts. Generally, a portion of the overall budget should be designated for utilization of the visual arts. It is recommended that the architect be given overall

Fig. 1095. Dramatic night lighting enables St. Lukes Episcopal Church, Dallas, Texas, to communicate its character to passersby.

Fig. 1096. Sculpture design complements the exterior architecture of the Church of the Transfiguration, Collingswood, New Jersey. (Rambush Decorating Co.)

control of the arts (sculpture, painting, murals, stained-glass windows) and that he employ artists to help plan these. See Figs. 1096 and 1097. This should be done as the structure is designed. Each art medium should serve a specific, preplanned purpose and should directly contribute to the *total* architectural picture of the church building.

The art should meet the requirements of the modern congregation. Man no longer lives as he did in past centuries. The Gothic and Romanesque Periods are past. Art should reflect the new age and should interpret the spirit of the present. It should contribute to the atmosphere of worship.

The Church School

One of the most important parts of a church building is the educational facility. The exact requirements must be ascertained by the congregation, and some details vary from one denomination to another. Fig. 1081 illustrates a small church school plan.

Fig. 1097. Chapel of Manhattenville College, Purchase, New York. (Rambush Decorating Co.)

Stained-glass windows are designed to complement the interior and exterior architecture. Notice the altar lighted from the side by a window.

*Courtesy Division of National Missions of the Methodist Church.

Most denominations operate a church school on the holy day. This should accommodate classes from the nursery level through the adult level. Each church should ascertain its needs. The following planning principles pertain to a facility for the usual Sunday School or Church School and not for full-time day schools.

1. The division of classes is established by the denomination. Most follow the same age grouping as the public schools.

2. Two different plans for room arrangement are in use. In one plan, each level has a self-contained classroom; in the second, a large assembly room is planned, with many small classroom cubicles located off it. The decision here varies with the denomination and its procedures for Christian education. In any case, the second plan is not satisfactory for lower-age groups. Usually the self-contained classroom is used through the third grade.

3. Younger children require more space per child in the classroom.

    Following are the recommended number of square feet per person for church school classrooms.*

	Good	Fair	Poor
Crib, toddlers, 2, 3, 4 and 5 year olds	35	30	25
First grade through sixth grade	30	25	20
Seventh grade through twelfth grade & older youth	25	20	15
Adults	20	15	12

4. The younger the children, the smaller the number that can be assigned per room. The maximum number of pupils recommended per room is:*

Crib to two years	8 to 10
2 years old	10 to 15
3 years	12 to 18
4 and 5 years	20 to 25
6 to 8 years	25
9 to 12 years	25 to 30
13 to 21 years	35
Adults	Up to 50

5. In a large church, each grade is a separate class. For small churches, often two or three grades must meet in one classroom. Boys and girls are usually in the same class.

6. It is advisable to vary classroom sizes to accommodate different class sizes. This provides some flexibility in handling unusually large or small classes. A minimum size is about 300 square feet; a maximum size, about 750 square feet. Most rooms should be from 400 to 600 square feet.

7. Adequate storage cabinets and bookshelves are vital. These also make the room useful for several different activities. The activities that take place vary, but include such things as religious instruction on Sunday morning and recreational activities on Sunday and weekday evenings. Children, youths and adults have weekday activities that must be housed in the church school building.

8. The classrooms should be airy and well lighted. Chalkboards and bulletin boards should be provided. Provision for darkening the rooms for use of films and slides is necessary.

9. Classrooms should be rectangular — approximately a 3 : 4 proportion.

10. The lower grades and the nursery should be housed on the ground level.

11. A large social hall in which to hold meetings, dinners and youth programs is necessary. Church school offices and general storage rooms must be provided.

12. Usually a library is desired. It should be located so all have access to it without going through other rooms. Preferably, it should be accessible during the week; therefore, frequently it is located near the church office.

13. Halls and stairs should be wide enough to accommodate the expected traffic. Classroom doors should swing out into the hall; therefore, it is necessary to recess the doors to keep the hall clear.

14. Furniture and coatroom racks should be scaled to the size of those using the room. The nursery should have playpens and cribs.

15. All classrooms should be accessible from a corridor. Doors should be near a corner of the room and of sufficient thickness to block hall noises.

16. Doors should be placed so all classes can move into the hall at the same time without congestion. Several doors opening into the hall at the same location is poor planning.

17. All materials, especially floors and walls, should be durable and easily cleaned.

18. Some congregations desire a stage as part of the church school.

19. The classroom for very small children should have a lavatory with direct access from the room.

20. The church school can be housed in a building that is an integral part of the main church building, or it can be in a wing off this area. It can be one or more stories. Fig. 1098 illustrates a multistory youth building.

21. Classroom furniture should be strong and durable, yet lightweight and easily movable. Teachers often need to rearrange furniture to suit their planned activities.

22. A helpful guide for ascertaining anticipated percentages of total enrollment by grades follows:

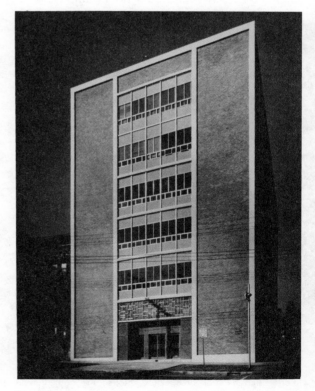

Fig. 1098. Youth Building, First Baptist Church, Columbia, South Carolina. (Sunday School Board of the Southern Baptist Convention, Lafaye, Fair, Lafaye and Associates, Architects)

Age Group*	Percentage
Nursery	7
Kindergarten	8
Grades 1, 2, 3	12
Grades 4, 5, 6	12
Junior high	11
Senior high	10
Older youth	5
Adult	35

23. Drinking fountains and rest rooms should be conveniently located off the corridor.

24. The church school should be properly heated and cooled and should have adequate ventilation.

25. Classrooms should have a 9'-0" ceiling.

26. Racks must be available for coats.

27. Acoustical treatment of the ceiling and walls is necessary in the classroom and corridors. Solid masonry walls between the classroom and corridor are most satisfactory.

28. Exterior windows are necessary in every classroom. Continuous windows placed about 2'-6" from the floor and extending near the ceiling are recommended.

29. If partitions between classrooms can be non-load-bearing, it is possible to enlarge or reduce the size of a room easily.

30. Stairways should be kept to a minimum. Short flights of one, two or three steps cause accidents, since usually they are not seen in time. If slight elevation changes are necessary, a ramp should be used, provided space permits. Handrails are necessary.

Designing the Exterior

The styling of a church exterior will and should vary considerably from one congregation to another. The most frequent problem faced by the congregation is whether to copy an established style of the past or to design a building that reflects the purpose of the church today. The congregation and the architect should establish the needs of the church and plan the use of space to serve these needs. Once this is resolved in an interior plan, then the exterior should be considered. The exterior grows out of the plan and shelters it. It should be in tune with the times. The designer works with form, proportion, balance,

*Courtesy Division of National Missions of the Methodist Church.

Fig. 1099. The Church of the Savior, Paramus, New Jersey. (California Redwood Assoc., Shreve, Lamb and Harmon, Associates, Architects)

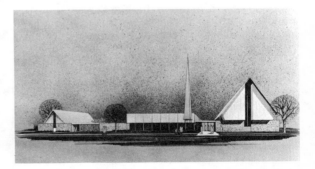

Fig. 1100. The First Baptist Church, Arabi, Louisiana. (Sunday School Board of the Southern Baptist Convention, Oubre and Wagner, Architects)

scale, texture, color, light and shade to achieve a structure that is an expression of the religious beliefs of the congregation. The building should have an effect upon the worshippers and passersby. It should stir the imagination and emotions and should reflect the purpose for which the structure was planned. See Fig. 1099.

A church should reflect strength and courage. It should present a welcome atmosphere, yet be sincere, simple and restrained. It should draw people inside by symbolizing harmony, peace and dignity. See Fig. 1100.

The interior and exterior should be unified. As a worshipper approaches the building, enters the narthex and is seated in the nave, he should feel the continuity of design. This is true not only of the architecture, but of the detail. A church building with a simple exterior should be just as simple inside. Excess decoration in the nave would be in disharmony with the exterior.

Consideration should be given to the prevailing style and available materials in the area in which the church is to be built. While the Georgian style church is widely accepted in New England, it would tend to be out of its environment on the West Coast. It is best to utilize materials readily available in the area. They fit the overall scene and are less expensive.

Climate also influences styling. Warmer climates can utilize a plaza or other open areas. Northern churches must withstand cold and heavy snows and must make provisions for a long heating season.

Build Your Vocabulary

Following are words that you should understand and use as a part of your working vocabulary. Write a brief explanation of each.

Liturgy
Nave
Chancel
Pulpit
Lectern
Reredos
Dossal
Vestry
Narthex
Sacristy

Class Activities

1. Visit the church of your choice and talk with the minister about the meaning of the liturgy. Report on the space and items needed in the various church ceremonies.

2. Plan a small church for a denomination with which you are most familiar. This project would be of value, if a congregation could be found which actually needed a new building. Ascertain the congregation size, and design the building to suit their needs and projected growth.

3. Plan a small chapel. Many institutions, such as large churches, colleges and hospitals, have a chapel available. If it is on a campus, usually it is a separate building. If it is a part of a large hospital, usually it is a room on the first floor. If possible, visit several to ascertain details.

4. Visit a church office. Record all the activities that must take place there. Then design a facility to handle these tasks. Consult Chapter 14 containing principles of office planning.

5. The design of church furniture is an art. Try designing a church pew, chancel rail, altar, pulpit and matching lectern.

6. Visit the ministers of several churches having their choirs located in different places. Ascertain from them the advantages and disadvantages of each location.

7. Examine the exterior of several churches. Select the one you believe has the most outstanding exterior styling. In a paper, report the reasons you selected this church.

8. Make a survey of art inside and outside of church buildings. Report the type of art work found, its location in the building or on the site and the subject matter represented.

9. Design a small church school building. If some in the class are designing churches, as suggested in Item 2, plan a church school to go with the church building.

Additional Reading

Anson, Peter, *Churches, Their Plan and Furnishing* (Catholic).

Atkinson, C. Harry, *Building and Equipping for Christian Education.*

Betts, Darby W. (ed.), *Architecture and the Church.*

Board of Church Extension, Presbyterian Church in the United States. Numerous booklets.

Board of Jewish Education of Chicago, "Jewish School Building Manual."

Commission on Church Architecture, Lutheran Church in America. Various booklets.

Division of National Missions of the Methodist Church, "Church School Planning." *Also:* "Sanctuary Planning."

Hammond, Peter, *Liturgy and Architecture.*

Horland, Richard, *Compilation: Planning Christian Education in the Local Church.*

Illuminating Engineering Society, "Church Lighting."

McCarty, Margie, *The Church Plans for Children.*

McClinton, Katherine (Morrison), *The Changing Church.*

Mills, Edward D., *The Modern Church.*

National Council of Churches of Christ in the U.S.A. Publishes a comprehensive list of inexpensive booklets on church planning.

Sherman, Jonathan G. (ed.), *Church Buildings and Furnishings*.

Southern Baptist Convention, "Planning Better Church Buildings."

Thery, Paul, Bennett, Richard M., and Kamphoefner, H. L., *Churches and Temples*.

Union of American Hebrew Congregations, "An American Synagogue for Today and Tomorrow."

Watkins, William W., *Planning and Building the Modern Church* (Protestant).

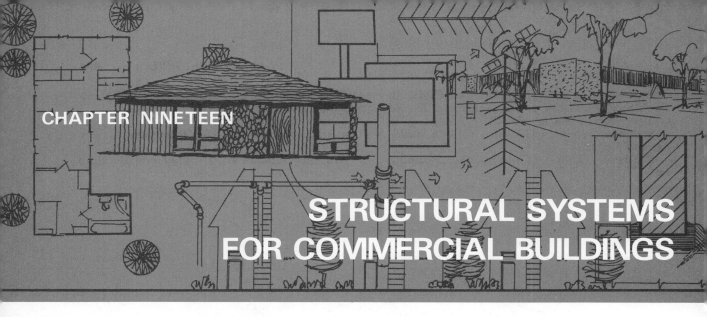

STRUCTURAL SYSTEMS FOR COMMERCIAL BUILDINGS

The structural systems discussed in this chapter are based upon the use of stock members. No attempt is made to discuss the designing of structural members. This is an engineering function and is beyond the scope of this text. Small commercial buildings can be designed and built satisfactorily with stock members. Multistory buildings present engineering problems that are not considered. All discussion pertains to one-story structures. However, some illustrations show multistory applications of structural members.

The systems presented in this chapter are for light construction. If heavy or concentrated loads are involved or if the building will be subject to heavy impact loads or vibration of machinery, special design considerations are necessary. All of the prefabricated systems presented should be designed and built under the supervision of a competent architect or design engineer.

They are presented here for student use to provide a means of designing a structural system to house small commercial establishments. The student should realize that each business and building presents special design problems that can be solved only by professional architects and engineers.

The method for ascertaining the load on a structural member is explained in Chapter 7. This process is not explained in this chapter.

Footings

The design of footings has been discussed in Chapter 6. These principles apply to small commercial construction.

Pile Foundations

When a soil investigation reveals that it would be unwise to pour a foundation upon the soil, the building should be supported upon a pile foundation. The type of piling, its depth, size and spacing vary with the building and soil characteristics. Pile types vary considerably, but fall generally into three groups — steel, concrete and timber or some combination of these. While the design of a pile foundation is beyond the scope of this text, the following comments are informative.

Soil Investigations

Careful study of the character and physical properties of the rock or soil upon which a building is to be built is of great importance, if the structure is to remain stable and structural damage be avoided. This is true for light buildings, such as a service station, as well as large multistory buildings. In a soil investigation, specialists bore into the soil in the area where a building is to be constructed. The soil samples brought up provide the engineer with the information necessary to design the foundations. A structure can be properly designed above the ground, but be damaged due to the yielding of the soil supporting the structure. Damage is especially great when soil conditions permit one portion of the structure to settle more than another.

Many companies conduct soil investigations before they purchase property upon which to erect a building. This data gives the engineer an idea of the foundation costs.

The most frequently used procedure of foundation test borings is the Gow method. In this method, a small-diameter borehole is sunk into the ground. At each change of soil formation, or at more frequent intervals when desired, a sample tube is retrieved; it is opened so that the soil can be examined, classified and sealed in a sample jar. Where hard strata or ledge rock must be penetrated, a rotary or diamond drill is used. See Fig. 1120.

Types of Piles

Step-taper piles consist of a hollow steel core that is in sections, each one inch larger in diameter than the next. The step-taper shells are helically corrugated to provide strength against ground pressure, and they are available in a variety of steel gauges and lengths. The joints between the sections are screw-connected. The pile is closed at the point by a steel plate, welded to the bottom, driving ring. Usually the pile is driven with a rigid steel core. After it is in place, it is inspected and filled with concrete. See Fig. 1121.

Fig. 1122 illustrates four types of steel pile. At the left is a uniform-taper pile driven with an expandable mandrel which, after driving, can be contracted to permit withdrawal without disturbing the driven shell. The pile is then filled with concrete. Second from the

Fig. 1120. Equipment for the Gow method of soil investigation. (Raymond Concrete Pile Co.)

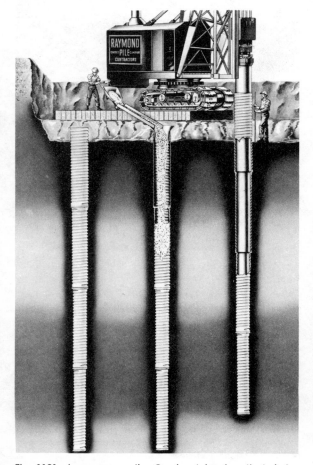

Fig. 1121. A step-taper pile. On the right, the pile is being driven with a steel core and in the center, it is being filled with concrete. At left is a finished pile. (Raymond Concrete Pile Co.)

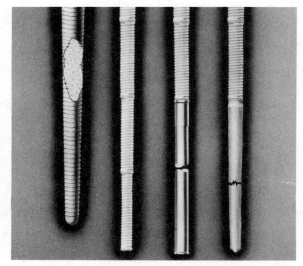

Fig. 1122. Variations of the steel-shell, concrete pile. From left to right: the uniform-taper pile; the step-taper pile; the pipe, step-taper pile; and the wood, step-taper pile. (Raymond Concrete Pile Co.)

left is the step-taper pile. Next is a step-taper pile, with a closed-end steel pipe as the lower section. This type is used where the required pile length is beyond the limits of available equipment to drive the all-steel shell or where the soil and driving conditions warrant. On the right is a step-taper pile, with a timber-pile, lower section. The timber section is untreated and is driven entirely below the permanent, ground water table. The permanent, concrete-filled, steel shell extends through the zone of fluctuating water level.

Also in use is a concrete pile, employing a concrete shell rather than one of steel. See Fig. 1123. The concrete shells are threaded on a steel mandrel. The bottom section is closed by a solid concrete shoe, and joints between the sections are sealed by recessed steel bands.

After being driven the required depth, the mandrel is withdrawn and the shell is filled with concrete. During the driving, the mandrel bears directly on the concrete closure shoe, and the driving head engages the upper end of the concrete shell.

Cast-in-place piles are used extensively also. In simple terms, a hole is drilled into the

soil, and this is filled with concrete. One variety of this procedure is to insert a pipe into the hole and pump concrete grout through it, thus filling the hole from the bottom. See Fig. 1124. This prevents dirt from falling into the hole, as frequently happens when con-

Fig. 1124. Cast-in-place pile. Hole is being filled with concrete grout from a pressure pumping station. Notice the auger used to bore the piling hole. (Intrusion Prepakt, Inc.)

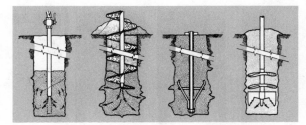

Fig. 1125. Types of concrete piles, left to right. (Intrusion Prepakt, Inc.)

I-P Cast-in-Place Pile: An advanced design of a basic pile for self-supporting soils. Augered hole is filled with intrusion mortar through inserted pipe. Depths and diameters as required.

I-P Pakt-in-Place® Pile: For stable or unstable soils. No casing required. Intrusion mortar, pressure injected into hole through auger shaft, is forced into fissures and compacts weak soil zones. Superior skin friction. Depth and diameters as required.

I-P Locked-in-Place®, Post-Tensioned Pile: For use where bending stress or uplift action may be present. Same placing procedure as Pakt-in-Place. Rod and sleeve assembly permits post-tensioning after setting.

I-P Mixed-in-Place® Pile: Intrusion mortar, pressure injected through auger shaft, combines with in-place soil to form pile. Excellent for cut-off walls in most soils. For moderate loading in sandy soils.

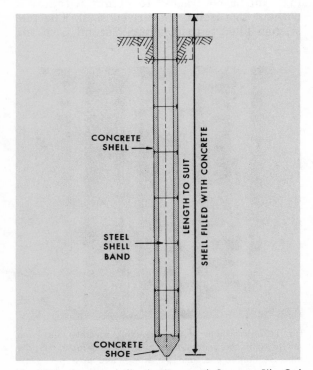

CONCRETE SHELL

STEEL SHELL BAND

LENGTH TO SUIT

SHELL FILLED WITH CONCRETE

CONCRETE SHOE

Fig. 1123. Concrete-shell pile. (Raymond Concrete Pile Co.)

crete is poured from the top. See Fig. 1125 for this and other procedures used for cast-in-place concrete piles. These piles can be accurately cast close together. See Fig. 1126.

Precast Concrete Structural Systems for Large Spans and Heavy Loads

Available from a number of companies are complete systems of precast concrete structural members. These are beams and girders, joists, roof and floor decking and bents. See Fig. 1127.

Concrete members usually are cast in a factory and transported to the building site where they are rapidly erected. They provide a fireproof system that requires little maintenance.

The designer should carefully observe the recommended spans and the maximum allowable loads permitted on the members of various sizes. The following systems illustrate those available from one company. Other systems with different capacities are available.

Precast Columns

Precast concrete columns are available in a wide variety of cross-sectional dimensions and lengths. They have a steel base plate welded to the main reinforcing members, which are cast integrally with the column. Holes are drilled in the base plate to receive anchor bolts that are cast into the foundation.

Construction crews erect these columns by raising them into position, lowering them to the foundation, placing the anchor bolts through the base plate holes and tightening

Fig. 1126. Cast-in-place concrete piles exposed by excavation for an addition. Notice the accurate placement. (Intrusion Prepakt, Inc.)

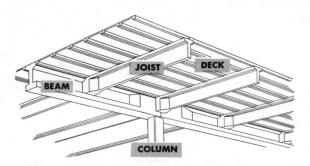

Fig. 1127. A structural detail showing a precast concrete column, beam, tee joists and channel-roof decking.

Fig. 1128. A precast concrete column being plumbed and bolted to the footing. (Flexicore Manufacturers Assoc.)

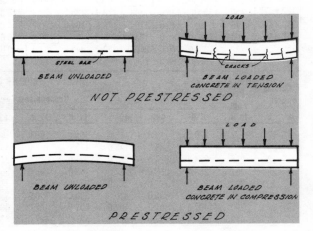

Fig. 1129. Visualization of load on plain and prestressed concrete beam.

the anchor-bolt nuts. See Fig. 1128. Below the base plate, 1¼ inches of nonshrinking grout is placed. Table 60 gives stock column data.

Precast Beams and Girders

Precast concrete beams and girders are available in unlimited lengths and sizes. They can be designed to accommodate all types of loadings. Usually they are cast in an *I* or rectangular shape. See Tables 61 and 62. A precast, prestressed beam requires a depth of

only one-half to two-thirds that of ordinary concrete construction, thus permitting extra headroom and the spanning of longer distances. In a prestressed beam, the steel reinforcing members inside the beam are drawn to a predetermined tension before the concrete unit is cast around them.

Fig. 1129 illustrates why prestressing increases the load-carrying capacity of a member. Any beam (when loaded) tends to sag in the center, thus stretching the material at

Table 60
Design Data for Pre-Cast Concrete Columns[1]
Loads below heavy line are short column loads.

Column Size	Weight Per Foot In #	ROUND COLUMNS Unsupported Column Height													Remarks
		8'-0	9'-0	10'-0	11'-0	12'-0	13'-0	14'-0	15'-0	16'-0	17'-0	18'-0	19'-0	20'-0	
6" ø	29	24.0	22.4	20.6											For One Story Structures
7" ø	40	32.9	31.0	29.6	27.0					Concrete f'c = 3000 psi Int. Grade Vert. Bars					
8" ø	52	47.0	44.5	42.5	40.0	38.0	35.4								
9" ø	66	63.5	61.0	58.5	56.7	53.0	50.5	48.0	45.5						
10" ø	82	82.6	80.5	77.5	74.0	71.5	68.5	65.0	62.5	59.5					
11" ø	99	92.0	92.0	89.0	86.5	83.0	80.0	77.2	74.5	71.5	68.0				
12" ø	118	107.0	107.0	107.0	104.0	100.0	97.5	94.0	91.0	88.0	84.5	81.0	78.0	75.0	For Multiple Story Structures
13" ø	138	132.0	132.0	132.0	132.0	128.0	124.0	120.0	116.0	113.0	109.0	105.0	102.0	99.0	
14" ø	160	145.0	145.0	145.0	145.0	143.0	141.0	137.0	133.0	129.0	125.0	122.0	117.5	113.0	
15" ø	184	177.0	177.0	177.0	177.0	177.0	175.0	170.0	166.0	163.0	158.0	155.0	151.0	145.0	
16" ø	209	210.0	210.0	210.0	210.0	210.0	210.0	206.0	202.0	198.0	194.0	189.0	185.0	179.0	

Column Size	Weight Per Foot In #	SQUARE COLUMNS Unsupported Column Height													Remarks
		8'-0	9'-0	10'-0	11'-0	12'-0	13'-0	14'-0	15'-0	16'-0	17'-0	18'-0	19'-0	20'-0	
6" x 6"	38	29.0	26.8	24.6											For One Story Structures
7" x 7"	51	43.5	41.0	39.2	35.8					Concrete f'c = 3000 psi Int. Grade Vert. Bars					
8" x 8"	67	63.0	60.0	57.0	53.5	51.0	47.5								
9" x 9"	84	83.0	79.0	76.0	73.0	69.0	66.0	62.5	59.0						
10" x 10"	104	105.0	103.0	99.0	94.0	90.0	87.0	83.0	80.0	76.0					
11" x 11"	126	116.5	116.5	112.0	109.0	104.0	101.0	98.0	94.0	91.0	86.0	81.0			
12" x 12"	150	134.0	134.0	134.0	130.0	125.0	122.0	118.0	114.0	111.0	106.0	102.0	98.0	94.0	For Multiple Story Structures
13" x 13"	176	170.0	170.0	170.0	170.0	164.0	160.0	154.0	150.0	146.0	141.0	136.0	131.0	128.0	
14" x 14"	204	186.0	186.0	186.0	186.0	184.0	180.0	175.0	171.0	166.0	160.0	156.0	151.0	146.0	
15" x 15"	238	240.0	240.0	240.0	240.0	240.0	237.0	230.0	226.0	221.0	214.0	209.0	204.0	197.0	
16" x 16"	267	268.0	268.0	268.0	268.0	268.0	268.0	262.0	256.0	251.0	246.0	241.0	235.0	227.0	

Column Size a b	Weight Per Foot In #	CORNER COLUMNS Unsupported Column Height												
		8'-0	9'-0	10'-0	11'-0	12'-0	13'-0	14'-0	15'-0	16'-0	17'-0	18'-0	19'-0	20'-0
8" 12"	133	120.5	118.0	113.0	108.0	105.0	100.0	95.0	92.0	87.0		Concrete f'c = 3000 psi Int. Grade Vert. Bars		
8" 15"	183	186.0	186.0	178.0	175.0	167.0	163.0	158.0	150.0	147.0	138.0			
8" 18"	233	224.0	224.0	224.0	224.0	217.0	210.0	204.0	197.0	192.0	186.0	179.0	172.0	168.0
8" 20"	267	268.0	268.0	268.0	268.0	265.0	260.0	252.0	246.0	238.0	230.0	225.0	217.0	209.0
8" 22"	300	277.0	277.0	277.0	277.0	277.0	274.0	266.0	260.0	255.0	246.0	241.0	235.0	227.0
8" 24"	333	330.0	330.0	330.0	330.0	330.0	330.0	323.0	317.0	310.0	304.0	297.0	290.0	280.0
12" 22"	399	407.0	407.0	407.0	407.0	407.0	407.0	407.0	407.0	394.0	386.0	378.0	370.0	362.0
12" 24"	449	427.0	427.0	427.0	427.0	427.0	427.0	427.0	427.0	427.0	417.0	410.0	401.0	389.0

[1]Safe axial load is in kips.
Data are for columns manufactured by Shlagro Steel Products Corp.

Table 61
Safe Superimposed Loads for Prestressed Beams
(Lbs. per Lineal Foot)

Beam No.	M In.K	\multicolumn{12}{c}{CLEAR SPAN IN FEET}											
		15	20	25	30	35	40	45	50	55	60	65	70
20-10	655	1940	1090	700									
20-15	982	2900	1630	1045	725								
20-20	1310	3870	2175	1395	965	710							
20-25	1640	4840	2720	1740	1205	890	680						
20-28	1830	5410	3040	1950	1350	995	760	600					
24-10	780		1300	835	575								
24-15	1170		1950	1250	870	640							
24-20	1560		2600	1665	1155	850	650						
24-25	1950		3250	2085	1445	1065	815	640					
24-30	2340		3900	2500	1735	1280	975	775	625				
24-36	2810		4680	3000	2080	1530	1170	925	750	620			
30-10	1012			1080	750								
30-15	1520			1620	1125	825	630						
30-20	2025			2160	1500	1100	845	665					
30-25	2535			2700	1875	1375	1055	835	675				
30-30	3040			3240	2250	1650	1265	1000	810	665			
30-35	3545			3780	2625	1930	1475	1165	945	780	655		
30-40	4050			4320	3000	2200	1690	1330	1080	890	750	640	
30-45	4560			4860	3375	2480	1900	1500	1215	1000	845	720	615

Beam Size 20" D. x 12" W. Wt. Approx. 145# per LF.

Beam Size 24" D. x 13" W. Wt. Approx. 190# per LF.

Beam Size 30" D. x 15" W. Wt. Approx. 235# per LF.

Data are for beams manufactured by Southern Cast Stone Co., Inc.

BEAM No. 20-10 = 20" DEEP WITH 10 WIRES
fc = .4 f'c, INITIAL fs = .7 f's, FINAL fs = .85 INITIAL fs, $M = \frac{WL^2}{8}$

Table 62
Safe Loads for Rectangular Concrete Beams
Safe load is in kips.
Beams are designed for simple support.
Top reinforcing used for possible moment developed by handling.

\multicolumn{10}{c}{PRE-CAST CONCRETE f'c = 3000 #/□"}									
Span	Width	Depth	Area	Weight Per Foot	Top Reinforcing	Bottom Reinforcing	\multicolumn{2}{c}{Stirrups}		Allowable Load Per Foot of Beam
Feet	Inches	Inches	Square Inches	Pounds	Size	Size	Size	Spacing	Kips
20	13	22½	292.5	320	#5	#8	#3	12"	1.71
	14	26	364.0	380	#5	#9	#3	12"	2.72
22	13	28	364.0	380	#5	#8	#3	12"	1.89
	17	28	476.0	496	#5	#9	#4	12"	3.11
25	17	28	476.0	496	#5	#9	#4	12"	1.76
	20	34	680.0	710	#5	#9	#4	12"	3.76

\multicolumn{7}{c}{PRESTRESSED CONCRETE f'c = 5000 #/□"}						
Span	Width	Depth	Area	Weight Per Foot	Size of Wires	Allowable Load Per Foot of Beam
Feet	Inches	Inches	Square Inches	Pounds	Inches Diameter	Kips
20	6	23	138	143	0.2	1.69
	8	26	208	216	0.2	2.57
22	7	24	168	175	0.2	1.73
	8	30	240	250	0.2	2.80
25	12	26	312	325	0.2	1.61
	12	32	384	400	0.2	3.45

Data are for beams manufactured by Shlagro Steel Products Corp.

Table 63
Safe Superimposed Loads for Precast Concrete Tee Joists
(Lbs. per Linear Foot)

12" HIGH UNITS																	
Purlin No.	Total M In-K	Clear Span in Feet															
		16	17	18	19	20	21	22	23	24	25	26	27	28	29	30	31
12T9	186	411	365	309	275	236	207										
12T10	237	543	471	413	363	320	283	252	225								
12T11	286	670	585	513	452	382★	327★	276★	233★								
12TC	292			530	469	415	370	330	297	265							
12TC8	444						605	545	493	445	405	369					
D = 12" W = 12" T = 3" B = 3½"																	

16" HIGH UNITS																	
		Clear Span in Feet															
		20	21	22	23	24	25	26	27	28	29	30	31	32	33	34	35	36
16T10	346	469	417	374	334	297	267	240									
16T11	408	589	574	471	424	380	344	311	283	256							
16T9/9	504	749	673	606	545	493	448	401★	351★	304★	263★						
16TC	565	849	760	699	622	560	511	464	426	389	354	327	299	276			
16TC/9	829								669	614	564	522	483	448	417	386	359	334
D = 16" W = 12" T = 3" B = 3½"																	

20" HIGH UNITS																	
		Clear Span in Feet															
		27	28	29	30	31	32	33	34	35	36	37	38	39	40	41	42	43
20T10	435	291	263	238													
20T11	529	377	343	311	284	259											
20T9/9	662	499	457	418	384	361	324	299	275	253	234						
20T9/10	745	575	526	483	445	408	388	350	312★	276★	247★						
20TC	799	624	573	526	485	347	413	383	353	328	303	282					
20TC/9	1,140			797	738	683	635	593	552	513	480	449	419	393	368	345		
20TC/10	1,230					753	702	653	609	568	532	498	466	436	409	383	362	342
D = 20" W = 12" T = 3" B = 3½"																	

Data are for joists manufactured by Southern Cast Stone Co., Inc.

fc = 6000 psi, $m = \dfrac{WL^2}{8}$

the bottom. This causes cracking and failure of the underside of the member. In a prestressed beam, the steel reinforcing is placed under tension as the concrete is poured. After the concrete sets, the tension is removed, thus compressing the concrete at the bottom of the beam. When a load is applied, the downward force tends to further compress the material. Since concrete resists compression, the beam can support the load without cracking.

The only way to overcome the tendency of an ordinary beam to crack is to increase its size. Therefore, a small prestressed beam can carry the same load as a large beam that is not prestressed.

Precast Tee Joists

The precast joist, usually *T*-shaped, is placed between beams to carry the roof decking. See Table 63.

This structural system is suitable for supporting concrete slab roof decks, steel decking, wood-fiber decking, gypsum decking and poured-in-place concrete and wood decking. Fig. 1130 illustrates a roof framed with these

Fig. 1130. A roof framed with precast tee joists and decked with wood fiber planks. (Tectum Corp.)

members and decked with wood-fiber planks. The planks form the finished ceiling, as well as the roof deck.

Precast Roof Decking Systems

Available are many concrete roof decking members, including channels, planks and double tees. Design data for some stock units manufactured by the Southern Cast Stone Co., Inc. are shown in Table 64 (channels), Table 65 (longspan channels) and Table 66 (double tees).

Precast Concrete Planks

Precast concrete tongue-and-groove planks are suitable for floors and for flat and sloped, roof decking. Since they are reinforced with galvanized mesh on both sides, they are reversible, allowing either side to face up. This type of plank can be nailed to the supporting members. The planks are available with dif-

ferent structural capabilities. See Table 67 for design data and construction details.

Light-Duty Precast-Concrete-Joist Floor System

The Portland Cement Association has developed a system of precast concrete joists suitable for small building construction. Seldom are these used for imposed loads over 100 pounds per square foot. In cross section, these are *I*-shaped, Fig. 1131. Placed in the top and bottom of the joist are steel bars with metal stirrups located at predetermined intervals. See Fig. 1132. The size of the bars varies with the load and span the member is designed to serve. The *stirrup* is a wire hanger placed around the reinforcing bars to hold them apart and to add reinforcement to the joist. It extends above the joist and is embedded in the concrete floor slab, thus tieing

Table 64
Safe Superimposed Loads for Six-Inch Concrete Roof Channels
(Lbs. per Square Foot)

Unit No.	M In. K	Clear Span in Feet								
		8	9	10	11	12	13	14	15	16
633	19.2	82	61	46	35					
644	34.5	162	124	97	77	62	50	40	33	27
655	53.2			159	128	105	87	73	60	51
666	75.4					155	129	108	92	79

$f'c = 4000$ psi, $fc = 1800$ psi, $fs = 20,000$ psi, $M = \dfrac{WL^2}{8}$

Data are for channels manufactured by Southern Cast Stone Co., Inc.

Table 65
Safe Superimposed Loads for Longspan Concrete Roof Channels
(Lbs. per Square Foot)

Unit No.	M In. K	Clear Span in Feet													
		10	11	12	13	14	15	16	17	18	19	20	21	22	23	24
9-88	220	704	575	480	404	344	295	256	224	196	173	153	136	121	109	97
9-77	171	540	441	366	308	261	224	190	167	146	127	112	99	88	78	69
9-66	124	384	312	257	215	180	154	131	113	97	84	73	64	56	49	42
9-55	88	268	217	178	147	122	103	87	73	62	53	45				
9-44	60	169	135	108	88	72	58	48								

$f'c = 4000$ psi, $fc = 1800$, $fs = 20,000$, $M = \dfrac{WL^2}{8}$

Data are for channels manufactured by Southern Cast Stone Co., Inc.

Table 66
Safe Superimposed Loads for Double Tee Concrete Roof Decking
(Lbs. per Square Foot)

Unit No.	M In. K	DL lbs./ft²	20	21	22	23	24	25	26	27	28	29	30	31	32	33	34	35	36	37	38	39	40
12" HIGH UNITS												Clear Span in Feet											
6T127	236	27	38	32	27																		
6T128	310	27	59	51	44	38	32	28															
6T129	392	27	82	72	63	55	49	42	37	33	29												
6T1210	470	28	103	91	80	71	63	56	49	44	39	34	30										
6T1211	571	28	133	115	107	92	82	73	66	59	51	47	42	38	33	30							
14" HIGH UNITS												Clear Span in Feet											
6T147	284	29	50	42	36	30																	
6T148	372	29	74	65	57	49	43	37	32	28													
6T149	471	29	102	90	79	70	62	55	48	43	38	33	29										
6T1410	585	30	133	117	105	93	82	74	66	59	53	47	42	38	33	30							
6T1411	690	30			128	115	102	93	83	75	68	61	55	49	45	40	36	32					
16" HIGH UNITS												Clear Span in Feet											
6T167	330	31	60	52	45	38	32	27															
6T168	432	31	88	76	67	59	51	44	39	34	29												
6T169	547	32	120	105	94	83	73	65	57	51	45	40	35	31	27								
6T1610	685	32		140	126	112	100	89	80	72	65	58	52	47	43	38	34	30					
6T1611	824	32			141	126	117	103	97	85	76	69	63	57	52	47	42	38	34				

$$f'c = 4000 \text{ psi}, \quad fc = 1800, \quad fs = 20{,}000, \quad M = \frac{WL^2}{8}$$

Data are for decking manufactured by Southern Cast Stone Co., Inc.

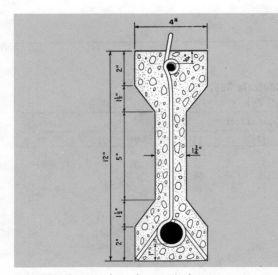

Fig. 1131. Section through a typical precast concrete joist. (Portland Cement Association)

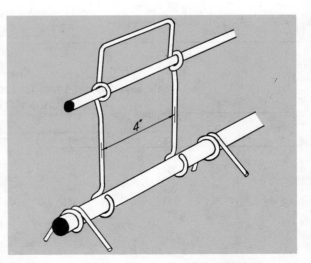

Fig. 1132. A stirrup used in precast concrete joists. Proper spacing distances of stirrups can be found in the design tables.

Table 67
Design Data and Construction Details for Precast Concrete Planks[1]
(Safe Loads in Lbs. per Square Foot)

Thick – Wgt.		2' 0"	3' 0"	4' 0"	5' 0"	6' 0"	7' 0"	8' 0"
2 "	14 lbs.	200	150	125	100	75		
2¾"	19 lbs.				150	105	75	60

[1]Planks are made to a maximum of 9' 0" in length with the allowable support spacing being 4'-0" or less.
Data are for planks manufactured by Southern Cast Stone Co., Inc.

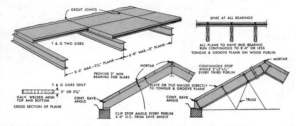

The following discussion illustrates two methods of using these members. One is with precast joists and a cast-in-place floor slab designed as *T*-beams, and the other is with precast joists designed as independent beams.

Selecting Precast Joists with Concrete Cast-In-Place Slab Designed as T-Beams

Assume that it is desired to design a precast joist system with a poured concrete floor for the building shown in Fig. 1133. The imposed floor loads must be computed, as explained in Chapter 6. For this example, assume that the total floor load is 100 pounds per square foot. The span of some of the joists is 13'-0", while that for others is 11'-0".

Since this is to be precast joists with a cast-in-place slab designed as *T*-beams, either Table 68 or 69 can be used. However, Table 69 is applicable only when the joists are shored up at their midpoints, prior to the floor slab being poured. For purposes of this illustration, assume that no shoring is used. Examine the columns in Table 68 entitled "Superimposed loads — psf" and "Clear span — ft." Since one

the joist and slab together. If a joist is to serve as an independent beam, the stirrup loop does not extend above the top. The stirrups are placed according to the data shown in the design tables. They are located, as shown, at each end of the joist, and are spaced 18" o.c. through the remainder of the member.

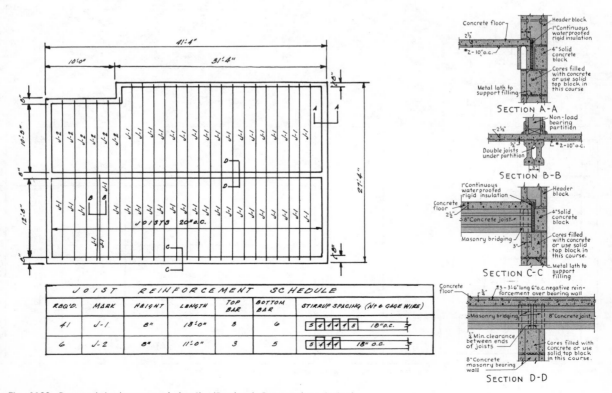

Fig. 1133. Precast joist layout and details. (Portland Cement Association)

Table 68
Design Data and Loads for Joists and Slab Designed as T-Beams
No shoring used during construction

One row of bridging should be used at mid-span in residential floor construction having spans over 20 ft. and in all other floor construction having spans over 16 ft. Bridging is not usually required for roof construction.

Stirrup spacings at each end of joist — in. Use additional stirrups 18 in. o.c. between end spacings shown below. Use No. 6 gage wire for stirrups	Joist size in.	Size of deformed reinforcing bars[1]		Weight of joist and slab psf	Slab thickness in.	Joist spacing c. to c. in.
		Top	Bot.			
`5 4 4 4`		#3	#5	34	2	20
				32	2	24
				32	2	27
				37	2½	30
				36	2½	33
`5 4 4 4 4 4`	8	#3	#6	34	2	20
				32	2	24
				32	2	27
				37	2½	30
				36	2½	33
`5 4 2 4 4 4 4 4 4 4`		#3	#7	34	2	20
				32	2	24
				32	2	27
				37	2½	30
				36	2½	33
`5 4 5 4 5 4`		#3	#6	37	2	20
				35	2	24
				34	2	27
				39	2½	30
				38	2½	33
`5 4 5 4 5 4 5 4`	10	#3	#7	37	2	20
				35	2	24
				34	2	27
				39	2½	30
				38	2½	33
`5 4 2 4 5 4 5 4 5 4`		#3	#8	37	2	20
				35	2	24
				34	2	27
				39	2½	30
				38	2½	33
`5 4 6 4`		#3	#6	44	2	20
				41	2	24
				39	2	27
				43	2½	30
				42	2½	33
`5 4 6 4 6 4`		#3	#7	44	2	20
				41	2	24
				39	2	27
				43	2½	30
				42	2½	33
`5 4 6 4 6 4 6 4`	12	#3	#8	44	2	20
				41	2	24
				39	2	27
				43	2½	30
				42	2½	33
`5 4 2 4 4 4 6 4 6 4 6 4`		#3	#9	44	2	20
				41	2	24
				39	2	27
				43	2½	30
				42	2½	33

[1]Bar sizes are given in numbers based on the number of eighths of an inch included in the nominal diameter of the bars as specified in ASTM A305.

Superimposed loads shown in table are the loads that the floor or roof is designed to support in addition to the weights shown for the precast joists and concrete slab.

Load values are limited by maximum allowable moment or shear and will produce deflections less than $1/360$th.

					Superimposed loads — psf									
					Clear span — ft.									
10	11	12	13	14	15	16	17	18	19	20	21	22	23	24
	113	88	69	53	40	30								
118	90	69	53	40	29									
101	76	57	42	31										
85	61	43	29											
74	52	36	23											
			113	91	73	59								
		113	90	72	57	45								
	122	96	75	59	46	36								
139	106	81	61	46	33	22								
123	93	70	53	38	26									
				137	113	94								
			134	110	90	74								
			115	93	76	61								
		125	99	78	61	48								
	128	111	87	68	53	40								
				124	103	85	70	57	47	38				
			122	99	81	66	53	43	34	27				
		131	105	85	69	55	44	35	27					
		113	89	70	54	41	31	22						
	128	100	78	60	46	34	25							
						129	109	92	78	66				
					124	103	87	72	61	50				
				129	107	89	74	61	51	42				
			137	111	90	73	59	47	37	28				
			121	98	79	63	50	39	30	22				
								134	115	99				
							125	107	91	78				
						127	108	92	78	66				
				138	125	110	91	76	63	52				
				122	111	97	80	66	54	44				
					126	104	86	71	59	48	39	31		
				123	100	83	68	55	44	35	27			
			131	106	87	70	57	46	36	28				
			113	90	72	57	44	33	24					
		126	99	79	62	48	36	27						
							135	115	97	83	70	59	50	42
						128	108	91	77	64	54	45	37	30
					133	111	93	78	65	54	45	37	30	23
					115	95	78	63	51	41	32	25		
				124	101	82	67	54	43	34	26			
										123	107	93	81	69
								133	114	98	85	73	62	53
							135	115	99	85	72	62	52	44
							117	98	83	69	58	48	39	32
						123	103	86	72	60	49	40	32	25
												131	115	102
										137	120	105	92	80
									137	119	103	90	78	68
								138	118	101	87	74	63	54
								122	104	89	75	64	54	45

Courtesy Portland Cement Association

Table 69
Design Data and Loads for Joists and Slab Designed as T-Beams
Shoring used at midspan during construction

One row of shoring at midspan must remain in place until the slab has attained the required strength.
One row of bridging should be used at midspan in residential floor construction having spans over 20 ft. and in all other floor construction having spans over 16 ft. Bridging is not usually required for roof construction.

Stirrup spacings at each end of joist — in. Use additional stirrups 18 in. o.c. between end spacings shown below. Use No. 6 gage wire for stirrups	Joist size in.	Size of deformed reinforcing bars[1] Top	Bot.	Weight of joist and slab psf	Slab thickness in.	Joist spacing c. to c. in.
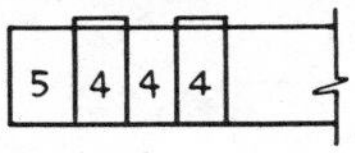 5 4 4		#3	#5	34	2	20
				32	2	24
				32	2	27
				37	2½	30
				36	2½	33
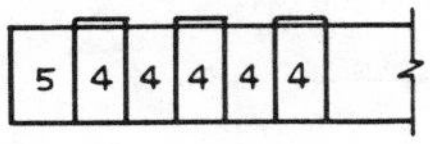 5 4 4 4 4	8	#3	#6	34	2	20
				32	2	24
				32	2	27
				37	2½	30
				36	2½	33
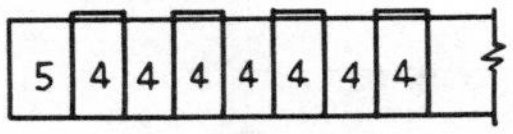 5 4 4 4 4 4 4		#3	#7	34	2	20
				32	2	24
				32	2	27
				37	2½	30
				36	2½	33
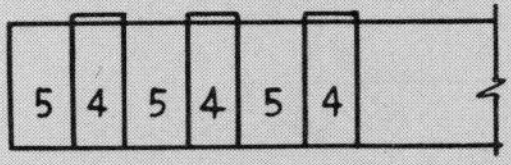 5 4 5 4 5 4		#3	#6	37	2	20
				35	2	24
				34	2	27
				39	2½	30
				38	2½	33
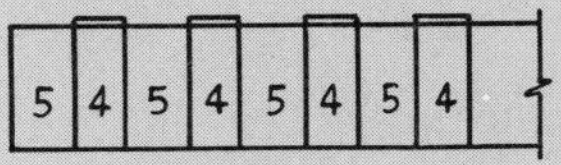 5 4 5 4 5 4 5 4	10	#3	#7	37	2	20
				35	2	24
				34	2	27
				39	2½	30
				38	2½	33
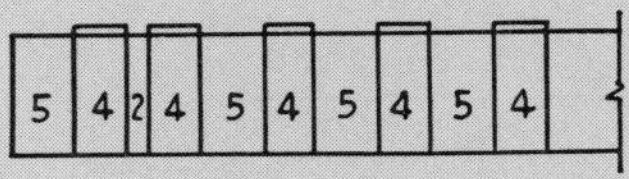 5 4 2 4 5 4 5 4 5 4		#3	#8	37	2	20
				35	2	24
				34	2	27
				39	2½	30
				38	2½	33
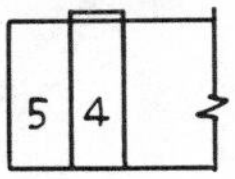 5 4		#3	#6	44	2	20
				41	2	24
				39	2	27
				43	2½	30
				42	2½	33
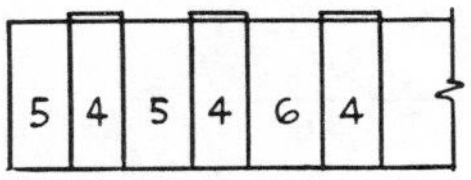 5 4 5 4 6 4	12	#3	#7	44	2	20
				41	2	24
				39	2	27
				43	2½	30
				42	2½	33
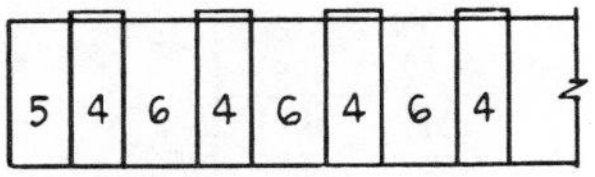 5 4 6 4 6 4 6 4		#3	#8	44	2	20
				41	2	24
				39	2	27
				43	2½	30
				42	2½	33
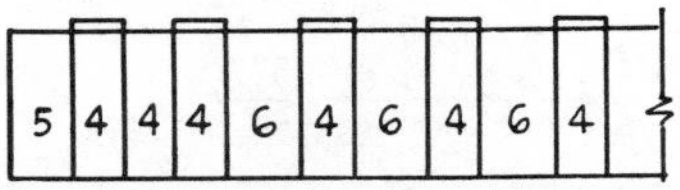 5 4 4 6 6 4 6 4 6 4		#3	#9	44	2	20
				41	2	24
				39	2	27
				43	2½	30
				42	2½	33

[1] Bar sizes are given in numbers based on the number of eighths of an inch included in the nominal diameter of the bars as specified in ASTM A305.

Superimposed loads shown in table are the loads that the floor or roof is designed to support in addition to the weights shown for the precast joints and concrete slab.

Load values are limited by maximum allowable moment or shear and will produce deflections less than $1/360$th.

						Superimposed loads — psf								
						Clear span — ft.								
10	11	12	13	14	15	16	17	18	19	20	21	22	23	24
	124	99	79	64	51	41								
128	100	80	63	50	39	30								
111	86	67	52	41	31									
100	76	58	44	33	24									
89	67	50	38	28										
			123	102	84	70								
		123	100	82	67	55								
	133	106	86	70	57	46								
	121	96	76	61	48	38								
138	108	85	67	53	42	32								
					124	105								
				120	101	85								
			126	104	87	72								
			115	94	77	63								
		126	102	83	68	55								
			133	112	94	79	66	55	46					
			130	108	89	75	62	51	42	35				
			113	93	77	63	52	43	35	28				
		125	101	82	66	53	43	34	26					
	112	90	72	58	46	37	29							
							118	101	87	75				
					132	112	95	81	69	59				
				137	115	97	82	69	59	50				
				123	102	85	71	59	49	40				
			134	110	91	75	62	52	42	35				
									124	109				
							133	115	100	87				
						136	116	100	86	75				
					137	122	104	88	75	64				
				134	123	109	92	78	66	56				
					134	112	95	80	67	56	47	39	32	26
				130	109	90	75	63	52	43	35	29		
				114	94	78	65	54	44	36	29			
			124	101	83	67	55	44	35	28				
		136	110	89	72	58	47	37	29					
								123	106	92	79	68	59	50
						136	116	99	84	72	62	53	45	38
						119	101	86	73	62	53	44	37	31
					126	105	89	75	63	52	43	35	29	
				135	112	93	78	65	54	44	36	29		
										133	116	102	90	79
									123	106	93	81	70	61
								123	106	92	80	69	61	52
							128	109	94	81	69	59	50	43
						134	114	97	83	71	60	51	43	36
													125	111
											128	113	100	88
										127	111	98	86	76
									129	113	98	85	75	65
								133	115	99	86	75	65	56

span of the building is 13'-0", look down the safe load figures under this heading, until a loading of 100 pounds per square foot or slightly larger is found. The first such reading is 113. Referring to the columns to the left, note that an 8-inch joist with a No. 3 top bar and a No. 6 bottom bar, spaced 20 inches on center, is the required member.

Repeat this process for the joists spanning 11'-0". Two choices are evident. An 8-inch joist with a No. 3 top bar and a No. 5 bottom bar, spaced 20 inches on center, will serve, as will an 8-inch joist with a No. 3 top bar and a No. 6 bottom bar, spaced 30 inches on center. If a 2½-inch concrete floor is desired, the latter is the best choice. The joists for the 13'-0" span are designed for a 2-inch slab, but can also be used for a 2½-inch slab, since the total additional weight is small.

The 2½-inch slab floor is used if plumbing and conduit are to be buried in the floor.

Selecting Precast Joists Designed
As Independent Beams

Follow the same procedure as that used for the precast joists with slab, designed as *T*-beams. Design data is found in Table 70.

Construction Details

While exact details for construction with precast concrete structural systems vary, the following discussion illustrates a typical example for a small building.

The footings are designed to support the calculated load, and then these are poured. The foundation wall is constructed. Usually this is poured concrete. Concrete blocks can be used, but the blocks upon which the joists will rest should be of solid masonry. This helps distribute the load over the wall.

The girder is set into place, and the floor joists are then placed according to the building plan. They are temporarily braced to hold them erect. The ends of the joists are permanently secured by filling between them with masonry bridging placed on top of the foundation. This could be brick, concrete block or precast masonry units. See Fig. 1134.

The forms for the cast-in-place floor slab are placed between the joists, and welded fabric wire is placed on top as reinforcement for the slab. See Fig. 1135. If electrical conduit and plumbing are to be cast in the floor, they are installed now. The concrete is poured and

finished. After it has attained sufficient strength, the forms are dropped and removed.

Where floor loads are expected to be heavier than the planned uniform load, the joists can be doubled. Double joists can be placed several inches apart, to permit space for plumbing and heating ducts.

A 2-inch floor slab is adequate to carry the 100 pounds per square foot imposed load used in this system. The tops of the precast joists should be embedded ½ inch into the slab.

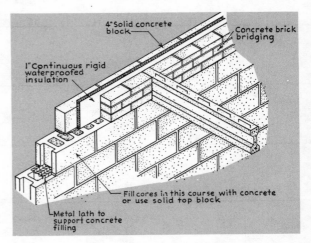

Fig. 1134. Precast concrete joist as designed by Portland Cement Association. Notice recommended construction details.

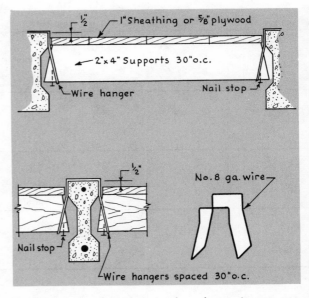

Fig. 1135. One method of placing forms for pouring concrete slab over precast concrete joists. (Portland Cement Association)

The interior lighting system of this corridor compliments the natural light from the windows. The lights are 2'-0" x 2'-0" recessed luminaries spaced on six-foot centers. (Columbia Lighting, Inc.)

This ceiling design creates a skylight effect with lights of gold and white baffles. Gold down light reflectors are used. (Columbia Lighting, Inc.)

Lighting design can create interesting ceilings. These luminaries are mounted in 5' x 5' vaulted ceiling sections. (Columbia Lighting, Inc.)

Precast concrete panels with exposed aggregate. (Mo-Sai Institute, Inc.)

These wall panels are precast concrete. They are secured to the structural frame with metal fasteners. (Mo-Sai Institute, Inc.)

The Los Angeles Music Center Memorial Pavillion. It has double-tapered and fluted precast concrete columns. (Mo-Sai Institute, Inc.)

This building uses white quartz window wall units. They were cast 34' high to cover both stories with a single unit. (Mo-Sai Institute, Inc.)

The granite exterior material enables this building to project a feeling of dignity and permanence. (Cold Springs Granite Co.)

These slender columns with a flared top give a graceful appearance. (Mo-Sai Institute, Inc.)

Precast concrete curtain walls are used on high-rise structures. (Mo-Sai Institute, Inc.)

Laminated wood arches. (National Forest Products Association)

A structure using precast concrete members. (Precast Concrete Institute)

The windows form the design element for this apartment building. (Andersen Corporation)

Precast Bents

A wide variety of precast concrete bents is available in stock sizes. Design data are shown in Fig. 1137. These bents are suited for channel slab decks, wood, steel or any other decking material. They are fireproof and maintenance free.

Precast concrete bents are spaced according to the load they must carry and the distance the proposed roof decking can span.

Details of construction and a layout for a small building are illustrated in Fig. 1136. The details concerning the joining of the bents at the ridge are shown in Section 3. The bent first is bolted to the grade beam, as shown in the details, and then grouting is placed between it and the grade beam to secure it in a level position. The finished floor is poured over the connection and tie rod. The tie rod extends under the floor to the mating bent at the opposite side of the building. This serves to contain the tension put upon the bent coupling at the grade beam. See the cross section through the building for details.

Section 1 illustrates how the 6-inch, precast concrete channels are secured to the

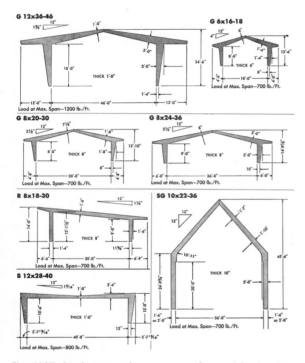

Fig. 1137. Stock precast bents as manufactured by Southern Cast Stone., Inc. Notice the allowable load at maximum span in pounds per foot.

Fig. 1139. Precast concrete bents for a church erected with a precast channel roof decking. (Southern Cast Stone Co., Inc.)

Fig. 1138. Precast, concrete bents being secured and leveled. (Southern Cast Stone Co., Inc.)

Fig. 1140. Interior of church with exposed precast bents and roof channels. (Southern Cast Stone Co., Inc.)

Table 70
Design Data and Loads for Joists Designed as Independent Beams
No shoring used during construction

One row of bridging should be used at midspan for all floor construction having spans over 16 ft. Bridging is usually not required for roof construction.

For the 8 in. joists the stirrups, which are made in pairs, have been lapped to provide 2-in. spacings as shown above.

Stirrup spacings at each end of joist in. Use additional stirrups 18 in. o.c. between end spacings shown below. Use No. 6 gage wire for stirrups	Joist size	Size of deformed reinforcing bars[1]		Weight of joist and slab	Joist spacing c. to c.	
	in.	Top	Bot.	psf	in.	
5 2 2 2 2 4		#3	#5	34 / 32 / 32	20 / 24 / 27	
5 2 2 2 2 2 2 2 2 2	8	#4	#6	34 / 32 / 32	20 / 24 / 27	
5 2 2 3 2 2 2 3 2 2 2 3 2 2 2		#6	#7	34 / 32 / 32	20 / 24 / 27	
5 4 4 4		#3	#6	37 / 35 / 34	20 / 24 / 27	
5 4 4 4 4 4 4 4	10	#5	#7	37 / 35 / 34	20 / 24 / 27	
5 4 4 4 4 4 4 4 4 4 4 4		#6	#8	37 / 35 / 34	20 / 24 / 27	
5 4 5 4		#3	#6	44 / 41 / 39 / 43 / 42	20 / 24 / 27 / 30 / 33	
5 4 5 4 5 4	12	#3	#7	44 / 41 / 39 / 43 / 42	20 / 24 / 27 / 30 / 33	
5 4 5 4 5 4 5 4		#4	#8	44 / 41 / 39 / 43 / 42	20 / 24 / 27 / 30 / 33	

[1]Bar sizes are given in numbers based on the number of eighths of an inch included in the nominal diameter of the bars as specified in ASTM A305.

Superimposed loads shown in table are the loads that the floor or roof is designed to support in addition to the weights shown for the precast joists and concrete slab.

Load values in *light-face* type are limited by deflection of $1/360$th.

Load values in **bold-face** type are limited only by maximum moment or shear and will produce deflections greater than $1/360$th.

	Superimposed loads — psf													
	Clear span — ft.													
10	11	12	13	14	15	16	17	18	19	20	21	22	23	24
112	86	67	52	40	31									
					21									
89	68	52	40	30	**22**									
76	57	43	32	23										
					49	23								
		106	85	69	**56**	**45**								
					30	8								
	107	85	67	54	**43**	**34**								
				42	16									
	92	72	56	**44**	35									
					69	39								
				103	**85**	**71**								
				79	46	21								
			100	**82**	**67**	**55**								
				60	30	8								
		106	86	**69**	**56**	**46**								
									26					
				100	82	68	56	46	**37**					
								29						
			98	79	64	52	42	**34**						
		104	84	68	54	44	35							
								70	43	21				
						104	88	**74**	**63**	**53**				
								46	23	5				
					99	82	69	**58**	**48**	**40**				
							57	32	12					
				102	85	70	**59**	**49**	**40**	**33**				
								85	56	32				
							89	**107**	**93**	**80**				
							100	**85**	**73**	**63**				
							70	43	22	4				
						102	**86**	**73**	**62**	**53**				
					105	87	72	60	49	40	32	26		
				102	83	68	56	45	36	29	23			
			109	88	72	58	47	38	30	23				
			90	71	57	45	35	26						
		100	79	62	49	38	29							
													39	19
							96	81	69	58	49		**41**	**34**
													20	
						106	89	75	63	53	44	37	**30**	
													28	10
						92	77	65	54	45	37	**30**		**24**
												21		
					91	75	61	50	40	32	**25**			
				98	80	65	53	43	34	26				
												75	50	28
										103	90	**78**	**67**	**58**
												50	28	10
									95	81	70	**60**	**52**	**44**
												37	18	2
								96	82	70	60	**51**	**44**	**37**
												30	9	
							93	78	66	55	**46**	**38**	31	
											41	19		
						97	82	68	57	**47**	**39**	32		

Courtesy Portland Cement Association

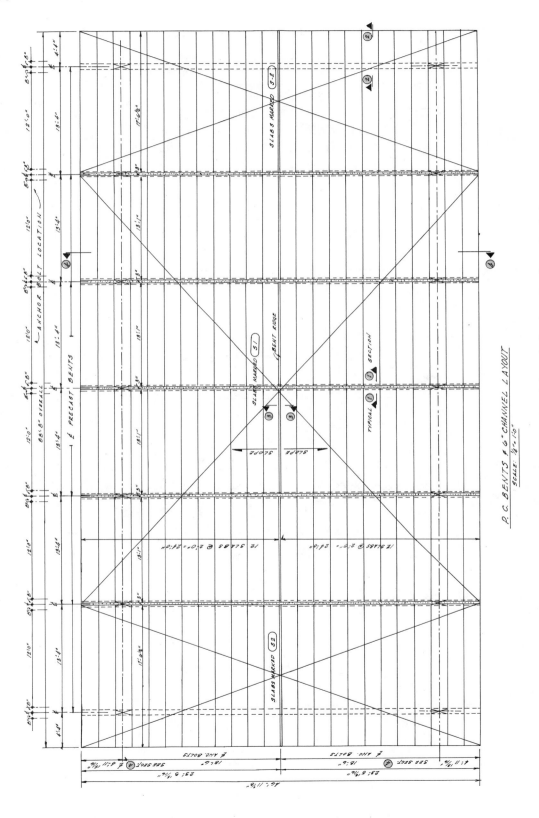

Fig. 1136. Details for a small commercial building using precast, concrete bents and roof channels. (Southern Cast Stone Co., Inc.)

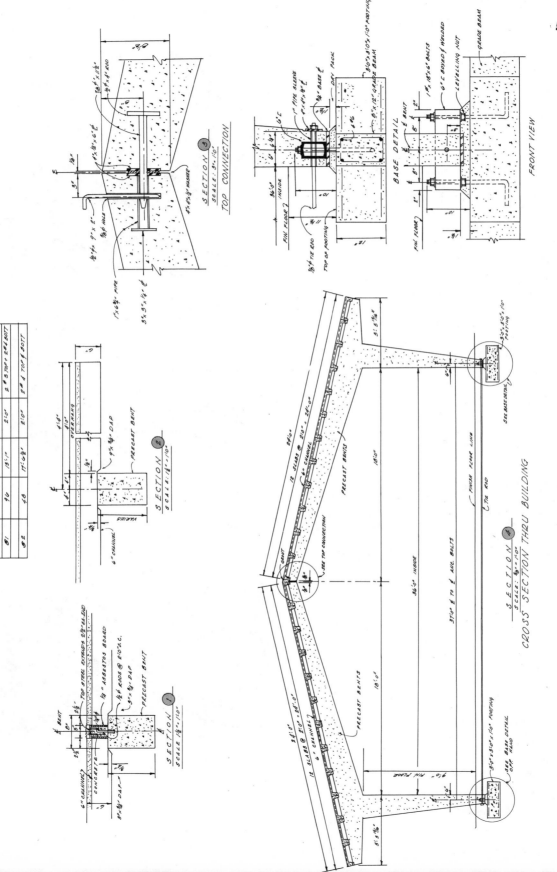

Fig. 1136. Continued.

bents. The space between the channel ends is filled with concrete.

Bents are rapidly erected. Usually a crane is used to raise each half section and to hold it in place as it is leveled and secured. See Figs. 1138 and 1139.

Fig. 1140 illustrates the interior of a church with exposed, precast concrete bents and precast roof channels. These can be decorated or colored in several ways, to contribute to the atmosphere of the building.

Monolithic Reinforced Concrete Construction

A monolithic reinforced concrete structure is one in which the concrete structural system is strengthened with steel reinforcing rods. Monolithic means that the concrete members are cast as a solid, continuous unit.

The concrete columns and beams are made by building forms on the job. The forms are in the places the columns and beams are wanted. Steel reinforcing rods are tied in place inside the forms. The concrete is poured into the forms to form the columns and beams into a single unit. See Fig. 1141A.

Fig. 1141A. This is a monolithic, cast-in-place reinforced concrete structure. As each floor is cast, the reinforcing steel and forms are moved up to form the next level. Notice the forms and shoring on the top level. The tower at the left is a lift for moving men and materials. (Martin K. Eby Construction Co., Inc.)

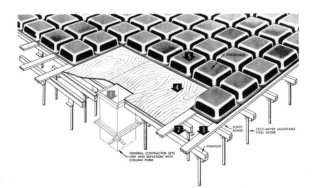

Fig. 1141. Erection procedure for monolithic, reinforced concrete construction. (Ceco Corp.)

1. Forms for columns, beams and column capitals below the joist level are put into place.

2. Wood stringers and metal shores are erected.

3. Soffit boards are placed on the stringers and spaced to support the steel forms.

4. Flat forms are placed for all solid areas.

5. Steel forms are placed and nailed to soffit boards.

6. Plumbing sleeves, electrical outlet boxes and reinforcing steel and mesh are placed.

7. Concrete is poured over and between domes.

Fig. 1142. A roof ready to be poured. Notice the steel domes, the reinforcing rod in the spaces forming the ribs and the wire mesh for the roof slab. In the center of the photo is an area without domes, which is to be a solid slab. (Ceco Corp.)

A much-used procedure is to pour monolithically the concrete joists and the floor or roof slab. The joists are generally arranged in one direction. They are formed by placing removable steel forms on top of wood stringers that are supported by shoring. See Fig. 1141 for erection procedures. Figure 1142 shows the forms with steel reinforcing rods in place. The job is ready for the concrete to be poured.

After the concrete has gained proper strength, the shoring, stringers, and soffit boards are removed. The steel domes are removed with compressed air, Fig. 1143. After

Fig. 1143. The steel domes are removed by air pressure without damaging the concrete. When the flanges of the steel domes are butted, a 6-inch rib is formed. If a wider rib is desired, a filler strip is placed between the flanges. This photo illustrates two wide ribs and several standard 6-inch ribs. (Ceco Corp.)

Fig. 1144. An exposed, concrete-joist ceiling sprayed with acoustical plaster and paint. Notice the suspended acoustical panels and spotlights. (Ceco Corp.)

they are cleaned and oiled they can be used again.

The interior ceiling can be painted or sprayed with acoustical asbestos to present a pleasing appearance. Figure 1144 illustrates one such ceiling. A suspended ceiling can also be installed.

Concrete is made from portland cement, water, sand, and gravel. The strength and appearance varies with the quantity and quality of these materials.

Concrete has good compressive strength. Compressive strength is the ability of a material to withstand forces tending to shorten it. See Fig. 1144A. The tensile strength of concrete is low. Tensile strength is the ability of a material to withstand forces tending to lengthen it. See Fig. 1144A. Steel has a high tensile strength. This is why steel reinforcing rods are added to structural concrete members. The concrete resists the compressive forces. The steel resists the tensile forces.

Reinforced Concrete Drawings

The design of reinforced concrete members is a difficult assignment. Those who make the drawings from the engineer's design data must be very knowledgeable. The American Concrete Institute has prepared a book, *A Manual of Standard Practice for Detailing Reinforced Concrete Structures*, that gives standard drafting practices.

Following are some terms used that the engineer and draftsman must know.

Bars are round steel reinforcing rods placed in a concrete member to strengthen it. Bars are specified by a number. The larger the number, the larger the bar diameter.

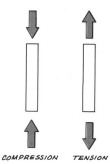

COMPRESSION   *TENSION*

Fig. 1144A. Compression forces tend to shorten a member. Tension forces tend to lengthen a member.

Dowels are round metal bars used to splice together two reinforcing bars in a column. They are usually the same diameter as the bars joined. They are welded in place. See Fig. 1144B.

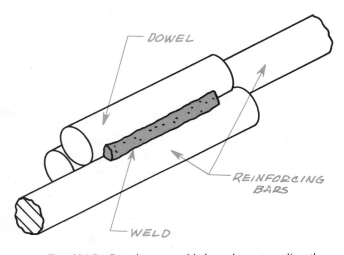

Fig. 1144B. Dowels are welded to bars to splice them together.

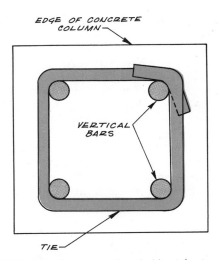

Fig. 1144D. Wire ties are used to hold reinforcing bars in place.

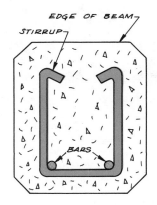

SECTION THRU RECTANGULAR CONCRETE BEAM

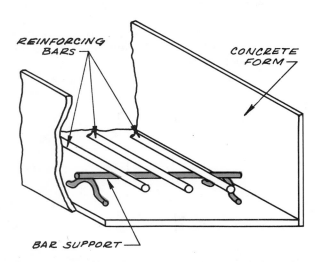

Fig. 1144C. Bar supports hold the reinforcing bars above the bottom of the form.

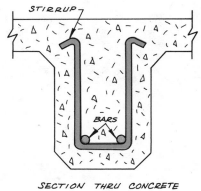

SECTION THRU CONCRETE T-BEAM

Fig. 1144E. Stirrups are used to locate and hold bars in place.

Bar supports are round metal bars used to hold the reinforcing bars the proper distance above the bottom of the form. They prevent the bars from moving when the concrete is poured. There are several standard types in use. See Fig. 1144C.

Ties are made from a small diameter metal wire. They are used to hold bars in place in columns. They prevent the bars from moving when the concrete is poured. See Fig. 1144D.

Stirrups are round metal bars usually bent in the shape of a U. They are used to hold bars in the proper position when the concrete is poured. See Fig. 1144E.

Mark is a term used for identifying the floor and type of member. See the following listing for mark abbreviations. A typical mark would be 2B3. This indicates the second floor, beam number 3.

Member	Mark
Beam	B
Column	C
Footing	F
Girder	G
Joist	J
Lintel	L
Slab	S
Wall	W

Marks used on structural drawings, American Concrete Institute

Beams are the main horizontal structural members. They run from column to column or column to foundation.

Joists are smaller horizontal structural members. They run between beams. They provide support for the floor or roof slab.

Bent refers to bending reinforcing bars. These strengthen the structural members. See Fig. 1144F.

There are two types of drawings used to show the concrete structure. These are engineering drawings and placing drawings.

Engineering Drawings

Engineering drawings are made by the engineer. They show the general arrangement of the structural members. They also show the size of the members and the required reinforcing. Notes are used to give complete information. An example is in Fig. 1144G.

Engineering drawings give all the design information through a drawing, note, or schedule. The engineer gives the draftsman the data he needs to draw the members and schedule the bending of the bars.

Engineering drawings include a typical concrete slab, joist, beam, and column detail.

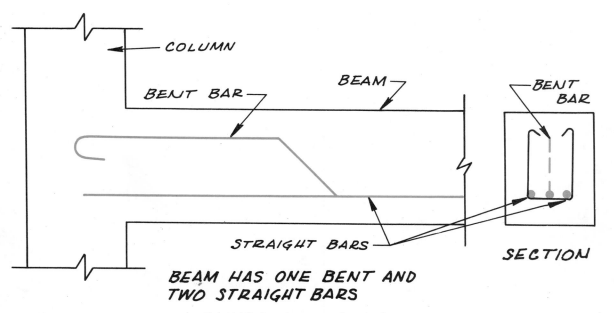

BEAM HAS ONE BENT AND TWO STRAIGHT BARS

Fig. 1144F. Bent bars strengthen the beam.

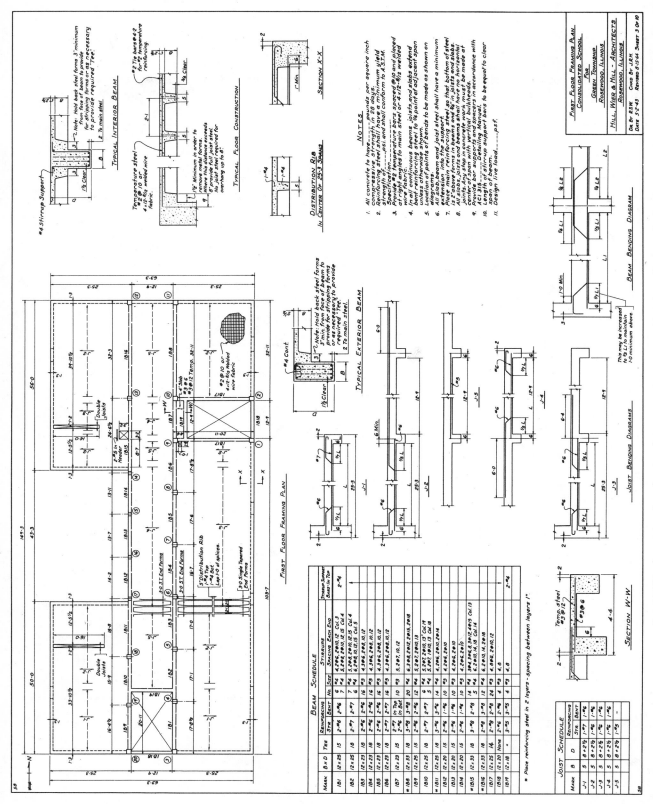

Fig. 1144G. An engineering drawing for a concrete structure. (American Concrete Institute)

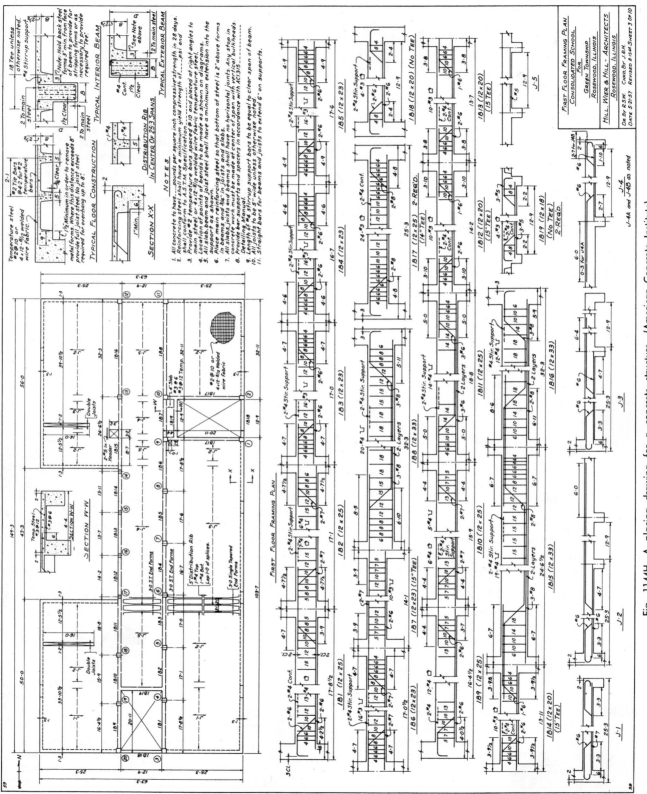

Fig. 1144H. A placing drawing for a concrete structure. (American Concrete Institute)

They show how the reinforcing bars are to be arranged.

The engineer shows where the bars are to be bent and to what points they should be extended. He does not work out all the dimensions. This is the work of the draftsman.

To be shown are the quality of the concerte and the type and grade of reinforcing bars. The engineer notes the live loads the structure will carry and other design data as the load bearing capabilities of the soil.

The engineering drawing in Fig. 1144G shows the plan for the first floor of a school. The dimensions of the building and column spacing are given. The direction of the joists is shown. Each joist is identified by a number.

The beam schedule gives the data needed by the draftsman to make the placing drawing. The following explanation will show how to read the beam schedule. Illustrated is beam 1B1. The *mark 1B1* means first floor, beam number 1. *B x D* gives the width and thickness of the beam. This beam is 12″ by 25″. The beam uses two no. 6 straight bars. It uses two no. 6 bars that are to be bent on the end. The beam contains six stirrups made from no. 4 bar. These six are for the end of the beam next to the number 3 column. The first stirrup is 4″ from the end of the beam. The next two are spaced 6″ apart. The next two are spaced 10″ apart. The last stirrup is 12″ from the last 10″ stirrup. From the end of the beam next to column 4 are seven stirrups made of number 4 bar. The first stirrup is 5″ from the end of the beam; the next two are spaced 8″ apart; the next two are spaced 10″ apart; the next one is spaced 12″; and the last is 15″. The last entry for beam 1B1 means that two no. 4 bars are used to support the stirrup. These directions are detailed on the placing drawing. See Fig. 1144H.

On the placing drawing in Fig. 1144H find the detail for beam 1B1. Notice that the stirrups are drawn in their exact location and are dimensioned.

The engineering drawing gives a typical section through a beam. It shows the two straight bars as round, black circles. The bent bars are shown as round, black circles with the bent portion shown by dashed lines.

The beam and joist bending diagrams show how the engineer wants the bars bent. The sections through the floor slab shows typical floor construction.

Study the notes in Fig. 1144G. What information do they give that cannot be shown with drawings?

Placing Drawings

A placing drawing is shown in Fig. 1144H. Placing drawings are detail drawings. They show the plan for placing the structural members. Also shown are the details for making each member. This includes the placing of reinforcing bars. The only dimensions needed are those showing the location of the bars. They show the size, shape and location of each bar.

The detailed design information on the engineering drawing is used by the draftsman to make the placing drawing. The beam design information is shown as a graphic detail on the placing drawing. Notice that the stirrup support bars are shown. Compare the detail of beam 1B1 with the data on the engineering drawing.

The concrete slab reinforcement is shown. The size of reinforcing bar is shown on the detail.

Column reinforcement is shown in a column schedule much like the beam and joist schedule. This has a section for showing ties and bent bars. It has diagrams showing the arrangement and bending of the ties. The ties are used to keep the bars from buckling. They hold them in place as the column is cast. See Fig. 1144D. Standards for spacing ties are given in the American Concrete Institute Standards manual.

Study the placing drawing in Fig. 1144H. Notice that each beam and joist is completely dimensioned. The draftsman gets these dimensions from the floor framing plan. He also dimensions the bent bars. The information for figuring these dimensions comes from the beam bending diagram on the engineering drawing.

Reinforced concrete drawings are made to scale. The most commonly used scale is ¼″ = 1′-0″. A larger scale is generally used for sections and detail drawings.

Dimensions are placed in feet and inches. The number of feet are given first, followed by a dash and the number of inches. Example: 149-3 means 149 feet and 3 inches; 56-0 means 56 feet even. The foot mark (′) and the inch

mark (″) are sometimes used. Study Fig. 1144G and 1144H to observe standard dimensioning practices.

A Precast Concrete Floor and Roof System

Another precast floor and roof system is manufactured by Flexicore Manufacturers Association. The two basic design considerations are span and load. Table 71 illustrates the safe loads for one of the stock sizes.

These units are set in place as shown in Fig. 1145, and a concrete grout is placed between them. Fig. 1146 shows a typical section through a slab, with the keyslot grouted between it and the next slab. The load tables are based upon superimposed load, which includes

Fig. 1145. Flexicore units being set into place to form a roof deck. Notice the hollow cores. (Flexicore Co., Inc.)

Table 71
Maximum Safe Superimposed[1]Working Loads for 6" x 16" Precast Concrete Decking
(Lbs. per Square Foot)

Safe superimposed $W = \dfrac{6M}{L^2} - 45.8$ lb. (W in lb. per sq. ft. of floor area.)

The maximum span without stirrups $= \dfrac{1926}{W_{D+L}}$. With stirrups used it is $\dfrac{5136}{W_{D+L}}$

The table is based upon dead load plus grout of 61 lb. plf. or 45.8 psf.
Stirrups are needed for all loadings indicated in light figures above the heavy stepped dashed line.
The safe loads shown in light figures in shaded area produce deflection in excess of $1/360$ of the span.
The above tabulated loads contemplate a depth, d, to the centroid of the steel of 4.875 in.
Minimum total wall thickness (b') = 2.59 in.
Load computations are in accordance with 1951 ACI 318 Code.

Standard Designation	Tensile Steel Area Sq. In.	8'-0"	9'-0"	10'-0"	11'-0"	12'-0"	13'-0"	14'-0"	15'-0"	16'-0"	17'-0"	18'-0"	19'-0"	20'-0"	21'-0"	22'-0"	23'-0"	24'-0"
									Simple Spans in Feet									
S 99	0.994				310	253	208	174	145	122	103	87	73	62	51	43	35	29
S 94	0.942			364	292	238	196	163	136	114	96	80	67	56	47	39	32	25
S 90	0.896			344	276	225	185	153	127	106	89	74	62	51	42	34	28	
S 89	0.890			342	274	224	184	152	126	105	88	74	61	51	42	34	27	
S 84	0.837		406	320	257	208	170	141	117	97	81	67	55	46	37	30		
S 79	0.785		378	298	238	192	157	129	107	88	73	60	49	40	32	25		
S 74••	0.739	460	354	278	222	179	146	119	98	81	66	54	44	35	27			
S 70	0.699	434	334	262	208	168	136	111	91	74	60	49	39	31				
S 69	0.693	430	330	259	206	166	134	109	89	73	59	48	38	30				
S 65	0.647	399	306	239	190	152	123	99	81	65	53	42	33	25				
S 61••	0.614	377	288	225	178	142	114	92	74	60	48	38	29					
S 60	0.601	367	280	218	172	138	110	89	71	57	46	36	27		For Roof Slabs Only			
S 56	0.561	340	260	202	158	126	100	80	64	51	40	30						
S 53	0.528	319	242	188	147	116	92	73	58	45	35	26						
S 52	0.522	315	239	185	145	114	91	72	57	44	34	25						
S 50••	0.497	300	227	176	137	108	85	67	53	40	31							
S 48	0.482	288	218	168	130	102	80	63	49	37	28							
S 44	0.442	263	198	152	117	91	71	55	42	31								
S 39••	0.393	228	171	130	99	76	58	44	32									
S 38	0.381	220	164	124	95	72	55	41	30									
S 32	0.319	178	131	97	72	54	38	27										
S 31••	0.307	170	124	92	68	50	36				Do Not							
S 30••	0.301	165	121	89	66	48	34				Extrapolate							
S 26	0.258	136	98	70	50	35					Values							
S 22••	0.221	111	78	55	37													
S 20	0.196	94	65	44	28													

[1]Includes the live load plus any dead load that is additional to the weight of the bare grouted slabs in place.
••Indicates slabs with 2 rods for tensile steel.
Data are for 6" x 16" Flexicore as manufactured by The Flexicore Co., Inc.

the live load plus any dead load over and above the weight of the bare, grouted slab. A floor fill of at least 1 inch of concrete is placed over the slabs. This is a part of any superimposed load.

The roof decking usually consists of the application of rigid insulation with a built-up roof covering. Fig. 1147 illustrates roof details at a parapet and fascia and when cantilevered.

Flexicore units are precast as a monolithic unit. The steel reinforcement is prestressed,

and the slabs are kiln-cured. Holes for pipes can be drilled with masonry drills or cut with a chisel. The slabs are adaptable to cantilevered construction, and overhangs up to 9 feet are practical.

These slabs can be used with masonry, reinforced concrete or steel framing systems. Fig. 1148 illustrates construction details. The

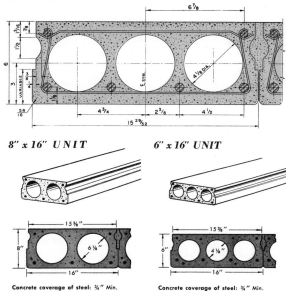

8" x 16" UNIT   *6" x 16" UNIT*

Concrete coverage of steel: ¾" Min.

Grouted weight psf: 55 lbs. (based on 150 pcf concrete)

Usual minimum bearing:
    On steel: 2"
    On concrete: 3"
    On masonry: 3"

Concrete coverage of steel: ¾" Min.

Grouted weight psf: 46 lbs. (based on 150 pcf concrete)

Usual minimum bearing:
    On steel: 2"
    On concrete: 3"
    On masonry: 3"

Fig. 1146. Details of Flexicore slab and installation. (Flexicore Co., Inc.)

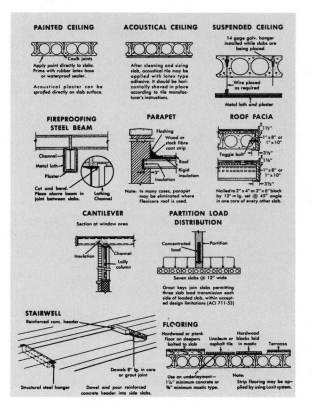

Fig. 1147. Construction details for Flexicore slabs. (Flexicore Co., Inc.)

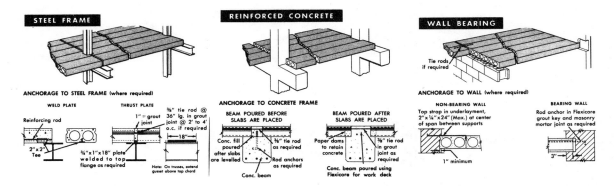

Fig. 1148. Details of framing for Flexicore slabs. (Flexicore Co., Inc.)

minimum bearing of the slab on framing systems is recommended as: on steel, 2 inches; concrete, 3 inches; and masonry, 3 inches. Other details are shown in Fig. 1147. A considerable saving in finishing costs can be achieved by painting the smooth interior surface of the slab. Fig. 1149 illustrates such an installation.

The hollow cores can be used for running electrical conduit. An underfloor electrical system of metal raceways is available. These raceways are placed on top of the precast slab, and 1½ inches of concrete is poured as a floor topping. This enables electrical outlets to be located anywhere needed along the system, at any time during or after construction. Fig. 1150 illustrates this system. By running wiring through the core, circuits are made available in one direction; other circuits are run at right angles to these through the metal header ducts.

Details for ceiling receptacles and surface-mounted conduit are shown in Fig. 1151.

Fig. 1152 presents one design for a small store with a basement. Notice that the load conditions limit the width and make beams or supporting walls necessary. The length of the building is not limited.

Fig. 1149. Flexicore slabs painted, and electrical receptacles surface-mounted. The wiring is run through the cores in the slabs. (Flexicore Co., Inc.)

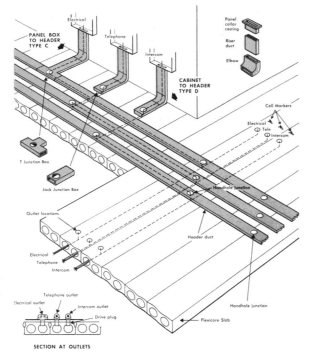

Fig. 1150. Electrical system used with precast, hollow-core, concrete decking. (Flexicore Co., Inc.)

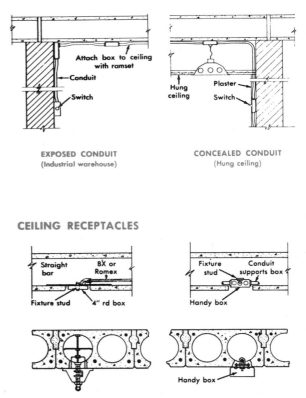

Fig. 1151. Typical electrical details. (Flexicore Co., Inc.)

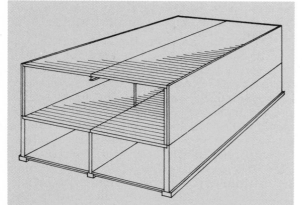

ONE STORY WITH BASEMENT (Multiple Bay)

Flexicore Roof and Floor

TYPICAL EXAMPLE

Width: 44' 0"
Length: As Required
Ceiling Height: First Story
  12' 0" Average.
  Basement 9' 0"
Storeroom Width: 42' 0"
Storerooms: One

Walls: First Story—Brick Exterior, Block Plastered Interior. Basement—Block or Concrete Exposed
Roof: 8" x 16" Flexicore
Floors: 8" x 16" Flexicore
Floor Load: 100 PSI

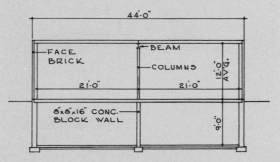

CROSS SECTION

LONGITUDINAL SECTION

Fig. 1152. Design data for small store with basement. (Flexi-core Co., Inc.)

Poured Gypsum Roof Systems

Gypsum roof decks are formed by pouring gypsum concrete over permanently installed formboards that are supported by structural steel framing. The poured gypsum concrete is reinforced with welded wire mesh and is covered with built-up roofing materials. See Figs. 1175 and 1176. The steel framing is usually formed in one of two ways — with subpurlins or without subpurlins.

With subpurlins (the most commonly used method), lightweight structural steel members are spaced and welded 32⅝ inches on center, running perpendicular to the main

Fig. 1175. Construction of poured gypsum roof. (Bestwall — Certain-Teed Sales Corp.)

A. After the structural steel is erected, the steel subpurlins are welded at right angles to the structural steel. The formboards are placed between the flanges of the subpurlins.

B. After the formboard is in place, welded wire mesh is placed on top.

C. Next the gypsum is poured in place. It usually sets up in 30 minutes.

structural steel members. Formboards are laid between the main steel members and are supported on the edges by the subpurlins. See Fig. 1177.

Without subpurlins, the formboards are laid directly on the roof joists. Usually bar joists are used, since the maximum, clear span between the joists should not exceed 36 inches.

See Fig. 1177. Tables 72 and 73 illustrate one type of subpurlin available.

Formboards are usually made of asbestos-cement, gypsum or insulation board. Data for these are given in Table 74.

The poured gypsum deck most frequently used is 2 inches thick. This material weighs 50 pounds per cubic foot. A 2-inch thick deck weighs 8.32 pounds per square foot. When the dead load of the roof is computed, the weight of the gypsum deck, formboard and purlins must be totaled. Tables 72 and 74 give weight data for formboard, purlins and built-up roof covering.

Table 72
Weights of Bulb Tees Per Foot
Bulb Tee type numbers refer to manufacturer's numbers (See Fig. 1175).

Bulb Tee Type	Wt./ft. (lbs.)
1120 (B)	1.40
158 (I)	1.50
1480 (B)	1.55
1680 (B)	2.00
168 (I)	2.00
168 (C)	2.00
1780 (B)	2.40
178 (I)	2.50
178 (C)	2.50
200 (C)	2.90
2025 (B)	3.00
218 (C)	3.00
200 (I)	3.00
218 (I)	3.00
2180 (B)	3.05
2140 (B)	3.65
228 (C)	3.65
2258 (B)	4.67
258 (C)	4.67

Courtesy National Gypsum Co.

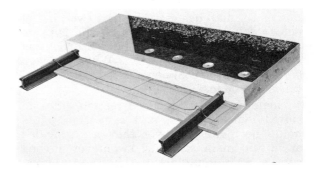

Fig. 1176. Section of a poured gypsum roof. (National Gypsum Co.)

The purlins are steel members. A formboard insert is placed between the purlins, and a wire mesh is set on top. The gypsum is poured over this. After it has set, two plies of roofing felt are nailed to the slab. The balance of the built-up roof is mopped over these sheets.

Table 73
Design Data and Safe Loads for Bulb Tee Sub-Purlins

Table is based on design stress of 27,000 psi, providing a 1.85 safety factor, based upon bulb tee manufacturers' yield point of 50,000 psi. For design stress of 20,000 psi, use 75% of tabulated load.

Sub-purlin spacing is 32⅝"; $M = \dfrac{WL}{10}$.

Minimum recommended design load, 35 psf, or as required by local code.

Table is based on steel stress only; if deflection is design criterion, check deflection. For deflections in semi-continuous spans, use formula $D = \dfrac{3WL^3}{384EI}$;

for 2 span continuous members, use formula $D = \dfrac{.005416WL^4}{EI}$ (Kidder Parker, 18th Ed., Chap. 18, Para. 10.)

Suppliers of sub-purlins whose data have been used in this table and whose literature provides further detail are: Buffalo Steel Corp., Inland Steel Co. and Connors Steel Div. II. K. Porter Co., Inc.

Maximum eave overhang should not exceed 44% of purlin span.

Bulb Tee Group	Manufacturer's Number			Section Modulus Range	Safe Total Uniform Loads — Pounds per Square Foot (Spans in Feet and Inches)																
	Buffalo	Connors	Inland		3-0	3-6	4-0	4-6	5-0	5-6	6-0	6-6	7-0	7-6	8-0	8-6	9-0	9-6	10-0	10-6	11-0	11-6	12-0
I	1120			.119	109	81	62	49	39	33													
II	1480		158	.172-.174	117	89	70	57	46	40	34	29											
III	1680	168	168	.240-.261	162	124	98	79	65	55	47	41	35										
IV	1780	178	178	.332-.367		172	137	110	91	76	65	56	49	43	38	34	31						
V	2025	200	200	.460-.474			188	152	125	105	91	78	67	60	53	47	42	38	35				
VI	2180	218	218	.520-.527				142	120	101	88	76	67	60	53	47	43	39	36	33			
VII	2140	228	228	.736-.745					169	145	124	108	95	84	75	68	61	55	51	46	43		
VIII	2258	258		1.05-1.06											108	97	87	78	72	66	61		

Courtesy National Gypsum Co.

After a roof slab has been poured, it usually sets to full-load capacity in 30 minutes. Workmen can move ahead rapidly on newly poured areas, and roof coverings can be be applied as successive areas are finished. The gypsum slabs dry from the bottom through the formboard. Adequate heat and ventilation below the slab are necessary to remove moisture.

A suspended ceiling, if used, should be hung from the structural steel — never from the gypsum slab. If suspended from the subpurlins, this extra weight must be considered when selecting the purlin, so that excessive deflection does not occur.

The roof covering should be installed as soon as the slab has set. The first two plies of roofer's felt should be nailed to the gypsum slab. The remainder of the built-up roof can be mopped on over the felt. While built-up roofing is most commonly used, other materials can be installed.

Some expansion and contraction occur in poured gypsum roofs, and expansion joints should be made wherever they are provided for in the main structure, wherever a wing joins a main building or wherever a long, narrow slab needs to be broken. The maximum recommended distance between expansion joints is 200 feet in the direction of the subpurlins or in the direction of the direct primary supports when subpurlins are not used. Expansion strips should be used at the junction between roof slabs and curbs, parapets and chimneys.

Buildings subject to excessive moisture or high temperature, such as a steam laundry, should not be constructed with a gypsum roof, since these conditions tend to damage the slab over a long period of time.

It is recommended that roofs to be made of poured gypsum not exceed a pitch of 9 inches in 12 inches.

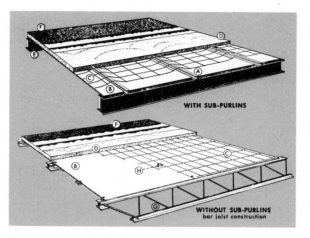

Fig. 1177. Details of built-up roof construction. (National Gypsum Co.)

With Subpurlins: End joints of formboard may fall between main purlins, if supported by joint tees or connector clips (recommended only where suspended ceilings are used).

Without Subpurlins (bar joist construction): End or edge joints occur over bar joists. Adjacent edge of formboard is supported with joint tees or connector clips as shown (recommended only where suspended ceilings are used). When clear span between bar joints exceeds 36", subpurlins must be used.

A. Subpurlins.
B. Formboards.
C. Wire, reinforcing mesh.
D. Gypsum concrete.
E. Main purlins.
F. Built-up roofing.
G. Bar joists.
H. Connector clips.

Table 74

Data on Component Parts of Typical Poured Gypsum Deck[2]

Characteristics	Gypsum Form-board	Insulation Formboard			Econacoustic Formboard			Acousti-fibre Form-board	Asbestos-Cement Formboard			Metro Mix		Typical 4-Ply Built Up Roof Covering	Inside Air Surface		Outside Air Surface (Wind 15 Mph)
															Heat Up	Flow Down	
Thickness	½"	¾"	1"	1½"	1"	1¼"	1½"	1"	¼"	⅜"	½"	2"	2¼"	⅜"			
Widths Available	32", 48"	32"	24" 32"	24" 32"	24" 32"	24" 32"	24" 32"	24"	24" 32"	24" 32"	24" 32"						
Lengths Available (Purlin Length)	to 12'0"	to 8'0"	to 12'0"	to 12'0"	to 12'0"	to 12'0"	to 12'0"	24"	4'	4'	4'						
Weight — P.S.F.	2.1	1.21	1.55	2.34	1.40	1.75	2.24	1.52	2.4	3.6	4.8	8.33	9.37	2.2			
Thermal Conductance (C Value [1,2])	2.25	.49	.38	.25	.38	.30	.25	.38	16.	10.6	8.	.83	.74	3.	1.63	1.08	6. [1]
Thermal Resistance (R Value [2,3])	.45	2.06	2.63	4.00	2.63	3.30	4.00	2.63	.06	.09	.12	1.20	1.35	.33	.61	.92	.17[1]
Noise Reduction Coefficient					.60	.60	.60	.65									
Light Reflectivity — Natural	.66	.10	.38	.38	.38	.38	.38	.49	.49	.49	.49						
Light Reflectivity — Factory Coated White			.78	.78	.72	.72	.72	.81									

[1]C Value is conductance of materials for specific thickness shown
[2]R Value is resistance — R=1/c U Value=1/Rt
[3]Reference = Heating, Ventilating, and Air Conditioning (A.S.H.R.A.E.) Guide — 1959 edition.
Courtesy National Gypsum Co.

Fig. 1178. A tilt-up panel being trowelled to final finish. Notice the bolts extending through the panel. These will be used to assist in the raising of the panel.

Fig. 1179. A tilt-up wall panel ready to be poured.

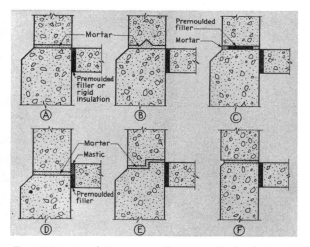

Fig. 1180. Foundation — wall joints. (Portland Cement Association)

These are typical joints subject to many variations. A and C are the simplest and most commonly used. The offset from the floor level in D and the offset in the foundation or lower wall is sloped or offset slightly as shown in these sketches so that there is no horizontal surface to catch the water, there is little possibility of leakage. Certainly there is no more possibility of leakage at this point than with any unit masonry wall.

Tilt-Up Concrete Construction

In tilt-up construction, reinforced concrete wall sections are cast in a horizontal position and then are lifted to a vertical position to form the walls of the building. The panels are framed with wooden forms, the reinforcement rods are tied into place and the concrete is poured. Electrical conduit may be cast in the panel. After the concrete is placed and screeded, it is permitted to stiffen. The forms are removed as soon as the concrete is firm enough to hold its shape, and the surface is trowelled and given its final finish. See Fig. 1178. When the panel has set long enough to achieve sufficient strength to be lifted, it is tilted into place and temporarily braced. While there are many ways of lifting, a crane is most frequently used.

The reinforcing rods are permitted to extend outside the concrete panel, and the panels are erected with a gap between them. Vertical columns are cast in place at each opening between the panels. The reinforcing rods are treated so they will not adhere to the column, thus allowing some movement at the joint.

Before the wall panel is cast, the concrete floor upon which it is cast must be treated to prevent adherence. This treatment is usually a liquid form treatment material or a form oil. Sheet materials such as paper, felt, plywood and canvas also are used. Any imperfection in this surface will show on the wall panel. Fig. 1179 shows a wall panel ready to be poured.

The panel reinforcement is the same as that used in cast-in-place walls. It could be bars or welded wire mesh. A quantity of small bars gives better crack control than the same weight of larger bars.

If openings are cast in the panel, extra reinforcement should be used on all sides of the opening.

Several types of joints are used between the panel and its supporting foundation. See Fig. 1180. The most common procedure is to spread a layer of portland cement mortar on the foundation and tilt the wall on top of it. Some use of a premolded joint filler has been made. This can be sealed with portland cement mortar. Wedges are sometimes placed on top of the foundation and the panel lowered on top of them. These permit the panel to be leveled easily, and then they can be re-

moved when the mortar in the joint sets. Fig. 1181 shows a panel being raised.

Columns can be cast first and the panels fitted to them, or the panels can be erected first and the columns cast between them. The latter is most generally used. See Fig. 1182. The column usually overlaps the panel. This hides any rough edges and makes variances in spacing unnoticed. It also hides differences in panel thickness. See Fig. 1183.

Since movement between the column and the panels is necessary to permit expansion and contraction, provision for preventing bonding between the column and the panel must be made. This may be paper, felt, premolded joint filler, cork gasket or some similar material. Even the reinforcing bars extending from the panels into the column must be coated to prevent bonding. An exception to this is in areas such as the West Coast, where earthquakes are likely to occur; the panels are joined together as firmly as possible.

The reinforcing bars usually extend from 2 to 6 inches from the panel into the column. They should extend into the column, just beyond the column reinforcement. See Fig. 1184.

Tilt-up construction is adaptable to a wide variety of one-story buildings and has been used on multistory structures. Construction time is short, since the time-consuming framing necessary for poured-in-place walls is greatly reduced. Also, tilt-up construction tends to be less expensive.

The wall panels must be designed to meet two conditions. First, the panel should serve as the wall of the building and support the load of the roof. The design for this condition is the same as for a conventionally-built reinforced concrete wall. Second, it must withstand the stresses placed upon it during the tilt-up operation.

Fig. 1182. A column joining two tilt-up panels formed and ready to pour.

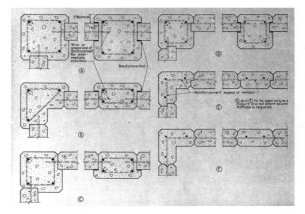

Fig. 1183. Column — wall joints. (Portland Cement Co.)

A to D are typical joints for use where movement at the joints is desired. They can also be used for rigid joints by lapping the reinforcement and omitting the bond-prevention material. Note that even where movement is desired at intermediate columns, the corner columns are bonded to the wall panels. V-joints should be used wherever the face of the wall is flush with the column.

Fig. 1181. A panel being raised into position on a continuous foundation.

Fig. 1184. Tilt-up panels in vertical position ready to have a column formed and poured. Notice the reinforcing rods extending from the panel into the column.

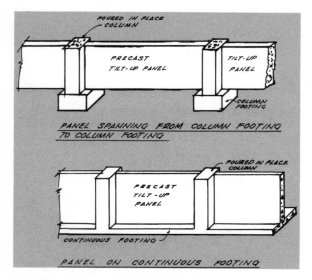

Fig. 1185. Column and continuous footings.

The method to be used for the lifting process must be known before the bending stresses can be ascertained. With some pickup systems, an analysis of stress becomes very involved. For small panels with a steel channel or angle bolted to the top edge of the panel, the panel should be designed as a simple slab that is supported on two ends. It is common practice to lift the panel by cables attached to the top edge. If the pick-up points are located one-quarter of the way down the panel from the top edge, the stresses are greatly reduced.

Special consideration must be given to panels whose length is greater than their height. They tend to develop stresses longitudinally as well as horizontally.

If openings are cast into a panel, it is necessary to consider the effect of these when designing the panel to accommodate lifting stresses.

The most commonly used wall thickness is 6 inches. Usually this meets structural requirements and is of sufficient strength that average-size panels can be lifted with minimum danger of cracking.

Panel design also is influenced by whether the walls are to be supported on a continuous footing or to be supported on the column footings only. If the panel extends from column footing to column footing, it serves as a deep beam, carrying its own weight plus the imposed weight from the roof. This also requires special consideration when designing the column footings, since they must carry considerably more load than with the continuous foundation. See Fig. 1185.

Another design consideration is whether the tilt-up wall is to be load bearing or non-load-bearing. If the roof is supported by the columns, walls can be of lighter construction.

Structural Steel Members

There is a wide variety of steel framing members available for small commercial building construction. Some design tables and procedures are presented in this chapter. Since structural members are subject to a number of stresses, these also are discussed, and their influence upon the design and selection of structural members is considered.

Solid-Web Joists

The solid-web joist provides greater beam strength than the open-web joist and, therefore, usually permits wider spacing. The smaller ones frequently are referred to as "junior" beams.

Concrete floors and roof are formed by placing standard plywood forms between the beams. These are held in place by metal clips located on top of the beams. Wire mesh is placed on top of the forms, and the concrete floors are poured. After the concrete has hardened, the clips are broken from below, and the plywood forms are removed. No special shoring or bracing is necessary.

Light Steel Beams

Another type of steel structural member is available in a series of beams slightly heavier and stronger than the solid-web joists. These provide even greater spans and wider spacing. The designer can select the steel members he wants from the vast array of stock structural members manufactured.

Open-Web Steel Joists

The open-web steel joists are placed close together, and they support a thin concrete floor slab. The usual slab thickness is 2½ inches. The joists are widely used on single-story buildings and increasingly are being used on multistory structures. This system is popular because it can be rapidly erected (in all kinds of weather) and is economical. As soon as the joists are in place and are decked, a working platform is available for immediate use. See Fig. 1186.

The joists are set in place, braced and welded. Metal lath, paper-backed wire mesh, or light corrugated-steel sheets form the decking upon which a concrete slab is poured. The slab must have wire mesh or reinforcing rods in it to add strength. Many other manufactured roof decking materials are used. These are explained in other portions of this chapter.

The ceiling below the open-web joists can be formed by fastening ribbed metal lath or gypsum lath to the bottom flange and plastering this. Any of the suspended-ceiling systems mentioned in this chapter also can be used. See Fig. 1187.

The open webs are used as runs for electrical conduit and plumbing. This is easily done and speeds construction.

The lightness of the open-web steel joist permits the use of light framing and footings.

Wide-Flange Beams

The main supporting structure of a steel-framed building is built of wide-flange beams.

The floor and roof decking are supported by open-web joists, solid-web joists or light steel beams that are supported by the structural-steel framing.

The design of the structural-steel framework is a complex engineering task and requires the services of a person licensed to do such work. Furthermore, a structural design must conform to the building codes in the locality where the structure is to be built.

These members are now made from a steel designated as A-36. All steel tables published before 1964 are for an A-7 steel; this generally has been replaced by the A-36 steel. The A-36 steel is an all-purpose steel of greater strength and improved weldability. The tables that follow and the discussion presented are for the A-36 steel, wide-flange members.

High-strength steels, such as A-242, A-440 and A-441, are not considered in this text.

A wide selection of steel shapes and structural properties is available from steel mills.

Fig. 1186. Open-web steel joists ready to receive the roof decking. (Builders Structural Steel Corp.)

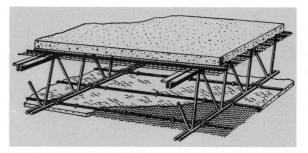

Fig. 1187. Open-web steel joists with metal lath decking and a concrete slab. Notice the ribbed, metal lath and plaster ceiling.

The Regular Series Shapes are most commonly used and are the only kind presented.

Simple Stresses in Structural Steel Members

Stress is internal resistance to external load or force. Structural members are subject to a number of stresses. Simple or direct stress (except for bending stress) can be expressed by the formula $f = \dfrac{P}{A}$. These terms refer to the following:

f_c — Compressive stress
f_t — Tensile stress (psi or ksi)
f_v — Shearing stress (psi or ksi)
f_b — Bending stress (psi or ksi)
P — Applied load (in kips)
A — Cross-sectional area of the member (in square inches). For vertical shear, A refers to the area of the web.

This formula, $f = \dfrac{P}{A}$, refers to direct stresses that are uniformly applied over the cross section of the member; bending stress is excluded because it is not uniform on the cross section.

When designing a steel framing system, the engineer must consider the kinds of stresses to which the individual members are subjected. Three different kinds of stresses are considered — tension, compression and shear. The allowable unit stresses for A-36 steel are shown in Table 75.

Tensile Stress

A member that is under *tensile stress* is under a force that tends to lengthen it. For example, if a steel rod with a cross-sectional area (A) of 2 square inches is hung from a beam and has a load of 15,000 pounds (P) hung from it, the computed tensile stress (f_t) would be 7,500 pounds per square inch of the rod cross section.

$$f_t = \frac{P}{A} = \frac{15,000}{2.0}$$
$f_t = 7,500 \text{ lb./in.}^2 \text{ or } 7.5 \text{ kips/in.}^2$

Compressive Stress

Compressive stress refers to forces acting upon a member, which tend to shorten it. If the steel rod in the previous illustration were under compression, the compressive stress would be 7,500 pounds per square inch of the rod cross section.

Table 75
Allowable Unit Stresses for Structural Steel with 36,000 psi Specified Yield Point (A-36 Steel)

Type of Stress	Description	Unit Stress (psi)
Tension	Tension on net section, except at pin holes. Tension on net section at pin holes.	$f_t = 22,000$ $f_t = 18,000$
Shear	Shear on gross section; allowable unit stress for girder webs are reduced somewhat. Consult tables in *Manual of Steel Construction.*	$f_v = 14,500$
Compression	Axial compressive strength permitted in absence of bending stress is given in tables in *Manual of Steel Construction.* These are given for main and secondary members with a $\dfrac{Kl}{r}$ not over 120, main members $\dfrac{Kl}{r}$ of 121 to 200 and secondary members $\dfrac{1}{r}$ of 121 to 200.	
Bending	Tension and compression for compact, adequately braced beams having an axis of symmetry in the plane of loading. (For other data, see *Manual of Steel Construction.*) Tension and compression on pins. Bearing on projected area of bolts and rivets.	$f_b = 24,000$ $f_b = 33,000$ $f_p = 48,500$

Shearing Stress

Vertical shear refers to forces which tend to cause a member to fail by a cutting action at each support. Fig. 1188 illustrates a member suspended between two supports. As a

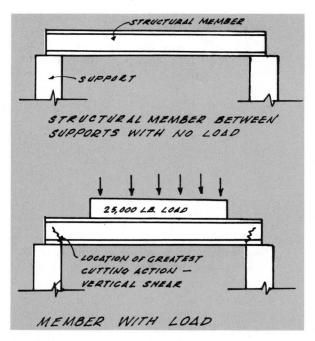

Fig. 1188. Forces on structural members.

load is applied, the member tends to drop down between the supports, but is restrained by the resistance of the material from which the beam is made. The end of the member tends to remain on the supports. If sufficient load is applied, the member may break near the supports. This type of stress is often critical in short beams carrying very heavy loads. In beams, the vertical and horizontal shearing stresses generally cause a 45-degree fracture upon failure.

When vertical shear is computed, it is customary to calculate the *area of the web only*, ignoring the area of the flanges. A large portion of the material in a steel beam is in the flanges. The maximum horizontal-shearing stresses occur at the neutral surface and are zero at the extreme fibers. Since this is true, the area of the web is used when computing vertical shear, rather than the area of the entire member (including the flanges).

The allowable vertical-shearing stresses for various structural items are usually specified in building codes. For steel beams, they are usually 12,000 to 13,000 pounds per square inch. Table 75 gives commonly accepted, allowable unit stresses.

The computation of the vertical shearing stress is illustrated in the following example. If a structural member is 10 x 8 WF 45 steel beam, with a load of 25,000 pounds distributed over its length, what is the vertical shear? The tables giving the shapes for designing indicate the web thickness is ⅜ inch and the depth of the beam is 10⅛ inches. The web area is, therefore, ⅜" x 10⅛" or 3.8 square inches. If the beam is supported at its ends, the load is divided equally between each support or 12,500 pounds on each end of the beam. These data are placed into the formula, and the shear stress is computed.

$$f_v = \frac{P}{A} = \frac{12,500}{3.8}$$

$f_v = 3,289.4$ pounds per square inch.

Again, it should be pointed out that the value is an average stress over the cross section. Technically, this value is not correct, but it is the way shearing stress is used in actual practice.

Horizontal shear is the tendency of the material in the structural member to slide horizontally. This can be best illustrated by stacking several boards between two supports.

When a load is applied, the boards bend and tend to slide horizontally, thus becoming uneven on the ends. This same horizontal force is present in any beam under load. See Fig. 1189.

The formula $f = \frac{P}{A}$ does not apply to horizontal shear. Its computation is not discussed in this text, but its presence should be noted. For rectangular cross sections, the formula $f = \frac{3V}{2bh}$ is used.

On short spans, allowable beam loads may be limited by the shearing strength of the web, instead of the maximum bending stress allowed in the member. The shear limit of the web is indicated in the allowable uniform load tables of the American Institute of Steel Construction (AISC) "Manual of Steel Construction." The loads in kips shown above the dark horizontal lines are the maximum allowable shear forces on the web.

Shear also occurs in fasteners such as rivets or bolts. The engineer must ascertain the shear strength of these connectors, so they will not fail under load. Fig. 1190 illustrates a rivet in shear. The formula $f = \frac{P}{A}$ can

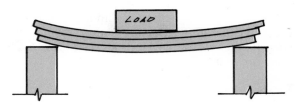

Fig. 1189. Horizontal forces exist in a structural member under load; these tend to cause material to slide horizontally.

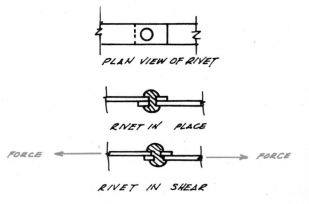

Fig. 1190. Shear force on rivet.

be used to ascertain the shear stress of a rivet. *P* is force applied and *A* is the cross-sectional area of the rivet body. If the rivet in Fig. 1190 has a cross-sectional area of .425 and is subject to an applied load of 6,000 pounds, the shear stress is 14,117 pounds per square inch of cross section of the rivet body.

Bending Stress

Stresses caused by *bending* are indirect stresses and, in this way, differ from tensile, compression and shear stresses. The formula f=$\frac{P}{A}$, therefore, does not apply.

When a beam is supported at its ends and is loaded from above, the top portion is under compression and the lower portion is under tension. See Fig. 1191. This occurrence also was illustrated in the discussion of prestressed concrete members.

A horizontal plane through the center of a beam subjected to bending stress is a neutral zone, with compression stresses occurring above it and tension stresses occurring below. These stresses are greatest at the exterior or extreme surfaces of the beam, and they decrease as the center or neutral zone is approached.

The important point to consider when working with bending stress is the extreme fiber stress. In A-36 steel beams, for example, the allowable stress is 24,000 psi, and the engineer must design a beam of sufficient cross section that the extreme fiber stress does not exceed this limit. If stock sizes are to be fastened together, such as in forming a spandrel beam, the same principle applies. A beam must be selected with sufficient cross section that the extreme fiber stress limit is not exceeded.

Elastic Limit, Yield Point, and Ultimate Strength

As a structural member is placed under a load, the member changes in length or shape. This change is referred to as *deformation*. If a

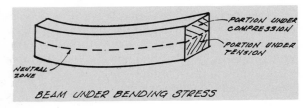

Fig. 1191. Beam under bending stress.

member is under tension, the deformation occurring is a lengthening of the member; while if it is under compression, the deformation is a shortening. (When a member is subjected to bending, the deformation is called *deflection*. This is discussed in detail in a later section of this chapter.)

Up to a point, when a member is subjected to a load, the deformation is proportional to the stress. In other words, increasing the load causes a uniform and proportional deformation. This proportion continues until the member reaches its *elastic limit*. This is the point at which increased stress or load causes deformation to occur at a faster rate than that at which the load is increased. If a member is loaded to its elastic limit and then the load is removed, the member will return to its original length. If the elastic limit is exceeded, the member will have an increased length, rather than returning to its original length. This increase in length is called *permanent set*.

If the elastic limit is exceeded slightly, a small amount of deformation occurs, even though the load is not increased. The point at which this occurs is called the *yield point*. For A-36 steel, the yield point is 36,000 psi. For all steels, the elastic limit and the yield point are close together.

As the load is increased beyond the elastic limit and the yield point, rapid deformation occurs. When the greatest stress is attained (just before beam failure), the *ultimate strength* of the member has been reached. Any stresses beyond the ultimate strength bring failure or rupture to the member. This is called the *breaking strength*.

Modulus of Elasticity

The *modulus of elasticity* of a material is its degree of stiffness. The greater the modulus of elasticity, the less deformation that occurs under load. The modulus of elasticity for various materials must be obtained from tables in architectural standards or manufacturers' publications. The modulus of elasticity for steel is 29,000,000 pounds per square inch.

The following formula is useful in ascertaining what the modulus of elasticity must be for a member subject to known stress and deformation. Any factors in the formula may be found if four of the five parts are known.

$$E = \frac{Pl}{Ae}$$

E = Modulus of elasticity in pounds per square inch.

P = Applied force in pounds.

l = Length of member in inches.

A = Cross-sectional area of member in square inches.

e = Total deformation of member in inches.

For example, if a steel member has a cross-sectional area (A) of 4.5 square inches, has a modulus of elasticity of 29,000,00 psi (E), is 120 inches long (l), and has an applied load of 10,000 pounds (P), the unknown deformation (e) can be computed by substituting into the formula:

$$29,000,000 = \frac{10,000 \times 120}{4.5 \times e}$$

By converting the formula to the unknown, we get the deformation:

$$e = \frac{Pl}{AE} = \frac{10,000 \times 120}{4.5 \times 29,000,000} = 0.009 \text{ inches}$$

The total deformation of the steel member with the above characteristics is 0.009 inches.

Deflection

As a downward load is placed on a joist or beam, the member is subject to bending stresses. The deformation associated with these stresses is called deflection. *Deflection* is the vertical distance a beam moves from a straight line. It is often so slight it is not visibly noticeable, but, it is always present in a member under load.

The engineer must ascertain the deflection in a beam under the design loads. While the beam may be strong enough to sustain the stresses of bending, the deflection may be great enough to cause cracking of the plaster ceiling or the floor surface. Deflection is usually limited by building codes to $\frac{1}{360}$ of the span of the member.

The longer the span, the more likely that excessive deflection will occur. The deflection of a beam varies directly with the fiber stress and inversely with the depth of the beam. When a beam is selected, therefore, it is best to select one having the greatest practical depth, since depth reduces deflection. If two beams of similar cross-sectional area and capacity are under consideration, such as one 10″ x 12″ and one 8″ x 14″, the 8″ x 14″ will have less deflection because of its greater depth. Of course, the deeper beam tends to reduce ceiling height.

In tables giving allowable uniform load in kips for beams laterally supported, the deflection for the various spans is given for beams supporting the full, tabulated, allowable loads. If it is necessary to compute maximum deflection of any symmetrical beam or girder, uniformly loaded, the following formula can be used:

$$\text{Deflection} = \frac{5Wl^3}{384 \, EI}$$

W = Total uniform load (including the weight of the beam) in pounds.

l = Span in inches.

E = Modulus of elasticity (29,000,000 pounds per square inch for steel).

I = Moment of inertia of the beam cross section in inches for X-X Axis (found in steel design tables).

For concentrated loads, other equations must be used.

After the actual deflection is found, it is necessary to compute the maximum allowable deflection in inches. This is normally 1/360 of the span. The following formula can be used:

$$\text{Max. allowable deflection} = \frac{\text{span in in.}}{360}$$

The actual deflection must be compared with the allowable deflection, to see if the actual deflection is greater than that permitted. If it is, another beam must be selected. Remember, the beam may be able to carry the imposed load safely, yet the deflection could be too great.

Using Safe Load Tables for Beams

The AISC "Manual of Steel Construction" gives design data for all common steel shapes, and many special designs. Included are tables giving allowable uniform loads, in kips, for beams laterally supported.

Using these tables, the designer can select the proper beam for a uniformly distributed load, without involved computation.

The tables in this chapter are for A-36 steel, having an extreme fiber stress of 24,000 lbs./in.[2]. The loads are assumed to be uniform and supported laterally. The safe load, in kips (1,000 pounds), includes the weight of the beam. The safe superimposed load is found by deducting the weight of the beam from the safe load.

2-37

A36 Steel F_y = 36 ksi

BEAMS
American Standard beams
Allowable uniform loads in kips for beams laterally supported

6-5-4-3

I

Nominal Depth & Width Weight per Foot	6 × 3⅜ 17.25	12.5	Deflection Inches	5 × 3 14.75	10.0	Deflection Inches	4 × 2⅝ 9.5	7.7	Deflection Inches	3 × 2⅜ 7.5	5.7	Deflection Inches
L_c	3.9	3.6		3.6	3.3		3.0	2.9		2.7	2.5	
L_u	9.7	9.1		9.7	8.9		9.3	8.9		9.9	9.2	
d/A_f	4.69	5.02		4.67	5.11		4.89	5.13		4.60	4.95	
Span in Feet												
2	69.6	40.0	.02	48.0	30.5	.02	26.4	22.0	.02	15.2	13.6	.03
3	46.4	38.9	.04	32.0	25.6	.04	17.6	16.0	.06	10.1	9.1	.07
4	34.8	29.2	.07	24.0	19.2	.08	13.2	12.0	.10	7.6	6.8	.13
5	27.8	23.4	.10	19.2	15.4	.12	10.6	9.6	.16	6.1	5.4	.21
6	23.2	19.5	.15	16.0	12.8	.18	8.8	8.0	.22	5.1	4.5	.30
7	19.9	16.7	.20	13.7	11.0	.24	7.5	6.9	.30	4.3	3.9	.41
8	17.4	14.6	.26	12.0	9.6	.32	6.6	6.0	.40			
9	15.5	13.0	.34	10.7	8.5	.40	5.9	5.3	.50			
10	13.9	11.7	.41	9.6	7.7	.50						
11	12.7	10.6	.50	8.7	7.0	.60						
12	11.6	9.7	.60			.70						
13	10.7	9.0	.70									

Properties and Reaction Values

	6 × 3⅜		5 × 3		4 × 2⅝		3 × 2⅜	
S in.³	8.7	7.3	6.0	4.8	3.3	3.0	1.9	1.7
V kips	40.5	20.0	35.8	15.2	18.9	11.0	15.2	7.4
R kips	**53.4**	**26.4**	**55.9**	**23.7**	**36.3**	**21.2**	**38.3**	**18.6**
R_1 kips	12.6	6.2	13.3	5.7	8.8	5.1	9.4	4.6
N_6 in.	2.5	2.5	2.0	2.0	1.5	1.5	1.0	1.0
A242 C.F.	1.38	1.38	1.38	1.38	1.38	1.38	1.38	1.38
A440 L_c	3.3	3.1	3.0	2.8	2.6	2.4	2.3	2.1
A441 L_u	7.2	6.7	6.1	6.5	6.8	6.5	7.2	6.7

See page 2-12 (deflection)

For explanation of deflection see page 2-12

Values of R in boldface exceed maximum web-shear V.
Load above heavy line is limited by maximum allowable shear.

AMERICAN INSTITUTE OF STEEL CONSTRUCTION

Table 76

2-36

A36 Steel F_y = 36 ksi

BEAMS
American Standard beams
Allowable uniform loads in kips for beams laterally supported

10-8-7

I

Nom. Depth and Width Wt. per Foot	10 × 4⅝ 35.0	25.4	Deflection Inches	8 × 4 23.0	18.4	Deflection Inches	7 × 3⅝ 20.0	15.3	Deflection Inches
L_c	5.4	5.0		4.5	4.3		4.2	4.0	
L_u	11.0	10.4		10.1	9.7		9.8	9.3	
d/A_f	4.12	4.37		4.51	4.71		4.62	4.88	
Span in Feet									
2	172.3		.01	102.3		.01	91.4		.01
3	155.7	89.9	.02	85.3	62.6	.03	64.0	50.8	.03
4	116.8	78.1	.04	64.0	56.8	.05	48.0	41.6	.06
5	93.4		.06	51.2	45.4	.08	38.4	33.3	.09
6	77.9	65.1	.09	42.7	37.9	.11	32.0	27.7	.13
7	66.7	55.8	.12	36.6	32.5	.15	27.4	23.8	.17
8	58.4	48.8	.16	32.0	28.4	.20	24.0	20.8	.23
9	51.9	43.4	.20	28.4	25.2	.25	21.3	18.5	.29
10	46.7	39.0	.25	25.6	22.7	.31	19.2	16.6	.35
11	42.5	35.5	.30	23.3	20.7	.38	17.5	15.1	.43
12	38.9	32.5	.36	21.3	18.9	.45	16.0	13.9	.51
13	35.9	30.0	.42	19.7	17.5	.52	14.8	12.8	.60
14	33.4	27.9	.49	18.3	16.2	.61	13.7	11.9	.70
15	31.1	26.0	.56	17.1	15.1	.70	12.8	11.1	.80
16	29.2	24.4	.64	16.0	14.2	.79			
17	27.5	23.0	.72	15.1	13.4	.90			
18	26.0	21.7	.80						
19	24.6	20.5	.90						
20	23.4	19.5	.99						
21	22.2	18.6	1.09						

Properties and Reaction Values

	10 × 4⅝		8 × 4		7 × 3⅝	
S in.³	29.2	25.4	16.0	14.2	12.0	10.4
V kips	86.	45.	51.	31.	46.	25.
R kips	**72.**	**38.**	**52.**	**32.**	**52.**	**29.**
R_1 kips	16.0	8.4	11.9	7.3	12.2	6.8
N_6 in.	4.4	4.4	3.4	3.4	2.9	2.9
A242 C.F.	1.38	1.38	1.38	1.38	1.38	1.38
A440 L_c	4.5	4.3	3.8	3.7	3.5	3.4
A441 L_u	8.1	7.6	7.4	7.1	7.2	6.8

See page 2-12 (deflection)

For explanation of deflection see page 2-12

Values of R in boldface exceed maximum web shear V.
Load above heavy line is limited by maximum allowable shear.

AMERICAN INSTITUTE OF STEEL CONSTRUCTION

Data for American Standard I-Beams, Wide-Flange Beams, Junior Beams, and Light Beams — Uniform Load in Kips — (Tables 76-79)

Information across the top of the table gives the depth and width of the beam and its weight per lineal foot. Beneath this are the following symbols:

L$_c$ — The maximum, unbraced length (in feet) of the compression flange, at which the allowable bending stress may be taken at 0.66 F$_y$ (feet).

L$_u$ — The same function as L$_c$, except the stress is 0.6 F$_y$ (feet).

d/A$_f$ — The depth of the beam or girder (in inches), divided by the area of the compression flange (in square inches).

The column at the extreme right gives the deflection that will occur if the indicated load is placed on the beam at the listed span, in feet.

The bottom of the table gives data on properties and reaction values.

S in.^{3} — The elastic section modulus, (in.^{3}).

V kips — Statical shear on the beam, in kips.

R kips — Reaction (or concentrated transverse load) applied to the beam or girder, in kips.

R$_i$ kips — Increase in reaction (R), in kips, for each additional inch of bearing.

N$_e$ in. — Length at end bearing to develop maximum web shear, in inches.

Below these are data for high-strength steels, which are not considered here.

Data for Wide-Flange Beams, Light Beams, and Junior Beams — Dimensions for Detailing — (Tables 80-82)

The column headings give data about the beam size, its weight, flange dimensions and web dimensions. These are followed by dimensions giving exact sizes for all parts of the beam. (The beam parts are indicated by symbols on a drawing of the beam.) The column headings indicate that some data is in pounds and other, in inches.

Data for Wide-Flange Beams, Light Beams, and Junior Beams — Properties for Designing — (Tables 80-82)

The column headings give data about the weight per lineal foot of the beam, the cross-sectional area of the entire beam (web plus flanges), the actual depth of the beam, flange dimensions and web thickness. These are fol-

lowed by the symbol d/A$_f$, in which d is the depth of the beam or girder (in inches) and A$_f$ is the area of the compression flange (in square inches).

The last six columns give design data for the beam in relation to the X-X axis and the Y-Y axis. The following data are given: I is the moment of inertia of the section (in.^{4}); S is the elastic section modulus (in.^{3}); r is the governing radius of gyration (inches). This latter factor is discussed in detail in a later section of this chapter.

Factor of Safety

Most building codes have some regulations pertaining to a *factor of safety*. This number can be calculated by dividing the ultimate strength or yield of a material by the allowable or actual stress. For example, if the ultimate strength of a material is 66,000 pounds per square inch and the actual stress is 16,000 pounds per square inch, the factor of safety is 4.1. The larger the factor of safety, the smaller the allowable stress. Some building codes specify the allowable stress, rather than a safety factor.

Steel Columns

A *column* is a structural member erected in a vertical position and subject to compression stresses parallel to its longitudinal axis. The most commonly used steel member is the wide-flange column. The standard *I*-beam is not as effective as a wide-flange column, because it has a small radius of gyration and, therefore, has a greater tendency to bend under load. Where fireproofing is not required, the most effective shape for columns is the hollow cylinder. That is why the Lally columns used in light construction are round and hollow in cross section.

Radius of Gyration

The *radius of gyration* of a cross section of a steel structural member is an index of the stiffness of the member when it is used as a column. The radii of gyration (r$_x$ and r$_y$) are listed in tables of properties of rolled steel sections. These are given for the two major axes, X-X and Y-Y. For use in column design, the least of the two radii (the Y-Y axis) should be used, because buckling is likely to occur in the path of least resistance.

It is important for the designer to know how much load a column can withstand be-

2 - 29

8 WF — BEAMS, WF shapes — **A36 Steel, $F_y = 36$ ksi**

Allowable uniform loads in kips for beams laterally supported
For beams laterally unsupported, see page 2‑46

Nominal Depth and Width	8 × 8		8 × 6½		8 × 5¼		
Weight per Foot	35	†31	28	24	20	17	Deflection Inches
L_c	8.7	—	7.1	7.0	5.7	5.7	
L_u	22.2	19.7	17.1	14.8	11.1	9.2	
d/A_f	2.05	2.31	2.66	3.07	4.08	4.95	

Span in Feet:

Span	35	†31	28	24	20	17	Deflection
4					58.5	53.4	.05
5			66.6	56.3	54.4	45.1	.08
6	74.2	66.8	64.8	55.5	45.3	37.6	.11
7	71.1	57.4	55.5	47.5	38.9	32.2	.15
8	62.2	50.2	48.6	41.6	34.0	28.2	.20
9	55.3	44.7	43.2	37.0	30.2	25.1	.25
10	49.8	40.2	38.9	33.3	27.2	22.6	.31
11	45.2	36.5	35.3	30.3	24.7	20.5	.38
12	41.5	33.5	32.4	27.7	22.7	18.8	.45
13	38.3	30.9	29.9	25.6	20.9	17.4	.52
14	35.5	28.7	27.8	23.8	19.4	16.1	.61
15	33.2	26.8	25.9	22.2	18.1	15.0	.70
16	31.1	25.1	24.3	20.8	17.0	14.1	.79
17	29.3	23.6	22.9	19.6	16.0	13.3	.90
18	27.6	22.3					
19	26.2	21.2					
20	24.9	20.1					
21	23.7						
22	22.6						

Properties and Reaction Values

	35	†31	28	24	20	17
S in.³	31.1	27.4	24.3	20.8	17.0	14.1
V kips	37.	33.	33.	28.	29.	27.
R kips	37.	34.	33.	29.	28.	26.
R_1 kips	8.5	7.8	7.7	6.6	6.7	6.2
N_e in.	3.5	3.5	3.5	3.4	3.7	3.7

		35	†31	28	24	20	17
A242	C.F.	1.25	†1.36	1.38	1.25	1.38	†1.25
A440	L_c	—	—	6.0	10.9	4.8	—
A441	L_u	16.3	14.4	12.5		8.2	6.7

Deflection Inches — For explanation of deflection see page 2‑12

Values of R in boldface exceed maximum allowable web shear V.
Load above heavy line is limited by maximum allowable web shear.
† Non-compact for A36, A242, A440 and A441 steels. See Quick Reference Notes on beams.
‡ Non-compact for A242, A440 and A441 Steels.

AMERICAN INSTITUTE OF STEEL CONSTRUCTION

Table 77

2 - 28

10 WF — BEAMS, WF shapes — **A36 Steel, $F_y = 36$ ksi**

Allowable uniform loads in kips for beams laterally supported
For beams laterally unsupported, see page 2‑46

Nominal Depth and Width	10 × 10				10 × 8			10 × 5¾		
Weight per Foot	66	60	54	†49	45	39	†33	29	25	21
L_c	11.0	10.9	10.9	—	8.7	8.7	—	6.3	6.2	6.2
L_u	33.2	30.5	27.9	25.4	22.3	19.3	16.1	12.9	11.1	9.0
d/A_f	1.37	1.49	1.63	1.79	2.04	2.36	2.83	3.52	4.08	5.07

Span in Feet:

Span	66	60	54	†49	45	39	†33	29	25	21	Deflection
5					103			82	74	69	.06
6					98	92	83	70	70	57	.09
7		123	108	99	87	84	73	62	60	49	.12
8	138	119	107	89	79	75	64	55	53	43	.16
9	131	107	97	80	71	68	57	49	47	38	.20
10	118	98	88	73	65	61	51	45	42	34	.25
11	107	89	81	67	60	56	47	41	38	31	.30
12	98	83	74	62	56	52	43	38	35	29	.36
13	91	77	69	57	52	48	39	35	32	26	.42
14	84	72	64	53	49	45	37	33	30	25	.49
15	79	67	60	50	46	42	34	31	28	23	.56
16	74	63	57	47	44	40	32	29	26	22	.64
17	69	60	54	44	41	38	30	28	25	20	.72
18	66	57	51	42	39	36	29	26	23	19	.80
19	62	54	48	40	37	34	27	25	21	18	.90
20	59	51	46	38	36	32	26	23	20	17	.99
21	56	49	44	36			24			16	1.09
22	54	47	42	35							
23	51	45	40	33							
24	49	43	39	32							
25	47	41	37								
26	45	40	36								
27	44	38	35								
28	43	37									
29	41	36									
30	39										

Properties and Reaction Values

	66	60	54	†49	45	39	†33	29	25	21
S in.³	73.7	67.1	60.4	54.6	49.1	42.2	35.0	30.8	26.4	21.5
V kips	69.	62.	54.	49.	51.	46.	41.	43.	37.	34.
R kips	59.	53.	46.	42.	44.	39.	35.	34.	29.	27.
R_1 kips	12.3	11.2	9.9	9.2	9.5	8.5	7.9	7.8	6.8	6.5
N_e in.	4.3	4.3	4.3	4.3	4.3	4.3	4.3	4.6	4.6	4.6

		66	60	54	†49	45	39	†33	29	25	21
A242	C.F.	1.38	1.25	1.25	†1.36	1.38	1.25	†1.36	1.38	1.38	†1.25
A440	L_c	9.3	—	—	—	7.4	—	—	5.3	5.3	—
A441	L_u	24.3	22.4	20.4	18.6	16.3	14.1	11.8	9.5	8.2	6.6

Deflection Inches — For explanation of deflection see page 2‑12

Load above heavy line is limited by maximum allowable web shear.
† Non-compact for A36, A242, A440 and A441 steels. See Quick Reference Notes on beams.
‡ Non-compact for A242, A440 and A441 steels.

AMERICAN INSTITUTE OF STEEL CONSTRUCTION

Table 78

2-33 — A36 Steel, $F_y = 36$ ksi — 10-8

BEAMS — Junior beams and Junior channels
Allowable uniform loads in kips for beams and channels laterally supported

Nominal Depth and Width	12 × 3	10 × 2¾	8 × 2¼	7 × 2⅛	6 × 1⅞	12 × 1½	10 × 1½	10 × 1⅝
			Beams				Channels	
Weight per Foot	11.8	9.0	6.5	5.5	4.4	10.6	8.4	6.5
L_c	—	—	—	—	—	—	—	—
L_u	2.6	2.5	2.4	2.3	2.0	1.8	1.9	1.0
d/A_f	17.4	18.1	18.6	18.7	19.0	25.9	23.8	44.2

Span per Foot

Span	12 × 3	10 × 2¾	8 × 2¼	7 × 2⅛	6 × 1⅞	12 × 1½	10 × 1½	10 × 1⅝
2		45.0	31.3	25.6	19.2	66.1	47.7	32.3
3	60.9	41.6	25.1	18.7	12.8	45.5	31.8	21.5
4	48.0	31.2	18.8	14.0	9.6	34.1	23.8	16.1
5	38.4	25.0	15.0	11.2	7.7	27.3	19.1	12.9
6	32.0	20.8	12.5	9.3	6.4	22.7	15.9	10.8
7	27.4	17.8	10.7	8.0	5.5	19.5	13.6	9.2
8	24.0	15.6	9.4	7.0	4.8	17.0	11.9	8.1
9	21.3	13.9	8.4	6.2	4.3	15.2	10.6	7.2
10	19.2	12.5	7.5	5.6	3.8	13.6	9.5	6.5
11	17.5	11.3	6.8	5.1	3.5	12.4	8.7	
12	16.0	10.4	6.3	4.7	3.2	11.4	7.9	
13	14.8	9.6	5.8	4.3	3.0	10.5	7.3	
14	13.7	8.9	5.4	4.0		9.7		
15	12.8	8.3	5.0	3.7		9.1		
16	12.0	7.8	4.7			8.5		
17	11.3	7.3	4.4			8.0		
18	10.7	6.9						
19	10.1	6.6						
20	9.6	6.2						
21	9.1	5.9						
22	8.7							
23	8.3							
24	8.0							
25	7.7							

Properties and Reaction Values

	12 × 3	10 × 2¾	8 × 2¼	7 × 2⅛	6 × 1⅞	12 × 1½	10 × 1½	10 × 1⅝
S in.³	12.0	7.8	4.7	3.5	2.4	9.3	6.5	4.4
V kips	30.5	22.5	15.7	12.8	9.9	33.1	24.7	21.8
R kips	4.8	16.5	14.1	13.2	**11.9**	21.2	18.4	15.7
R_1 kips	5.9	4.9	3.6	3.4	3.1	5.1	4.6	4.1
N_1 in.		4.9	3.9	3.4	2.8	5.8	4.9	5.0
A242 — C.F.	±1.25				1.38			1.38
A440 — L_c	1.9				1.7			1.7
A441 — L_u	1.8				1.8			1.8

Values of R in boldface exceed maximum web shear V.
Load above heavy line is limited by maximum allowable web shear.
‡ Non-compact for A242, A440 and A441 steels.

AMERICAN INSTITUTE OF STEEL CONSTRUCTION

2-32 — A36 Steel, $F_y = 36$ ksi — 8-6

BEAMS — Miscellaneous shapes (M) and Light beams (B)
Allowable uniform loads in kips for beams laterally supported
For beams laterally unsupported, see page 2-46

Nom. Depth and Width	8 × 5¼			8 × 4				6 × 4		
Wt. per Foot	22.5	20	18.5	17	15	13	†10	16	12	†8.5
L_c	5.8	5.8	5.7	5.7	5.8	5.8	4.6	4.4	4.3	4.3
L_u	10.8	9.3	10.5	9.1	7.1	5.8	4.6	11.8	8.4	6.0
d/A_f	4.21	4.89	4.33	5.00	6.44	7.87	9.83	3.84	5.38	7.63

Span in Feet

Span	22.5	20	18.5	17	15	13	†10	16	12	†8.5
3	87.0	81.1	74.7	55.7	57.7	52.7	38.9	47.1	38.6	28.7
4	68.4	60.8	56.0	44.8	47.2	39.5	31.2	40.4	29.0	24.8
5	54.7	48.6	44.8	37.8	37.8	31.6	24.9	32.3	23.2	18.6
6	45.6	40.5	37.3	31.5	31.5	26.3	20.8	26.9	19.3	14.9
7	39.1	34.7	32.0	27.0	27.0	22.6	17.8	23.1	16.5	12.4
8	34.2	30.4	28.0	23.6	23.6	19.8	15.6	20.2	14.5	10.6
9	30.4	27.0	24.9	21.0	21.0	17.6	13.9	18.0	12.9	9.3
10	27.4	24.3	22.4	18.9	18.9	15.8	12.5	16.2	11.6	8.3
11	24.9	22.1	20.4	17.2	17.2	14.4	11.3	14.7	10.5	7.4
12	22.8	20.3	18.7	15.7	15.7	13.2	10.4	13.5	9.7	
13	21.0	18.7	17.2	14.5	14.5	12.2	9.6	12.4	8.9	
14	19.5	17.4	16.0	13.5	13.5	11.3	8.9		8.3	
15	18.2	16.2	14.9	12.6	12.6	10.5	8.3		7.7	
16	17.1	15.2	14.0	11.8	11.8	9.9	7.8			
17	16.1	14.3	13.2	11.1	11.1	9.3	7.3			

Properties and Reaction Values

	22.5	20	18.5	17	15	13	†10	16	12	†8.5
S in.³	17.1	15.2	14.0	14.0	11.8	9.88	7.79	10.1	7.24	5.07
V kips	43.5	40.6	39.6	27.8	26.7	19.5	18.4	23.6	20.0	14.4
R kips	43.0	39.6	27.1	27.3	25.2	18.4	18.1	29.4	25.2	18.1
R_1 kips	10.1	6.2	6.5	6.6	6.2	4.6	3.7	7.0	6.2	4.6
N_1 in.	3.5	3.6	3.6	3.7	3.7	3.7	3.4	2.7	2.7	2.7
A242 — C.F.	±1.25	±1.25	±1.25	±1.25	±1.25	±1.36	±1.36	±1.38	±1.38	±1.36
A440 — L_c	7.9	7.7	7.7	6.7	5.2	3.7	3.4	8.7	6.2	4.4
A441 — L_u	16.1	14.3	16.2	13.2						

Values of R in boldface exceed maximum web shear V.
Load above heavy line is limited by maximum allowable web shear.
† Non-compact for A36, A242, A440 and A441 steels. See Quick Reference Notes on beam.
‡ Non-compact for A242, A440 and A441 steels.

AMERICAN INSTITUTE OF STEEL CONSTRUCTION

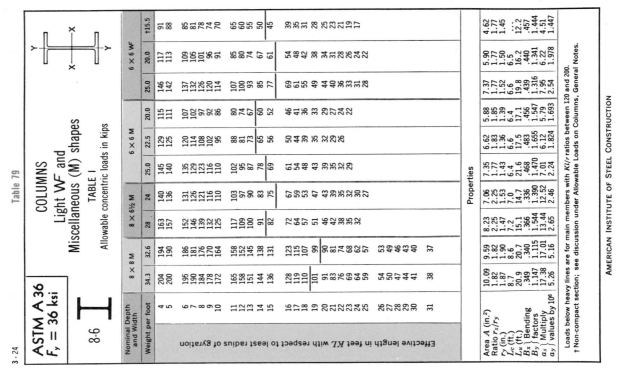

Table 79   3-24

ASTM A36 $F_y = 36$ ksi   8-6

COLUMNS
Light WF and Miscellaneous (M) shapes
TABLE I — Allowable concentric loads in kips

Effective length in feet *Kl* with respect to least radius of gyration

Nominal Depth and Width	8 × 8 M		8 × 6½ M		6 × 6 M			6 × 6 WF		
Weight per foot	34.3	32.6	28	24	25.0	22.5	20.0	25.0	20.0	†15.5
4	204	194	163	140	145	129	115	146	117	91
5	200	190	157	136	140	125	111	142	113	88
6	195	186	152	131	135	120	107	137	109	85
7	190	181	146	126	129	114	102	132	105	81
8	184	176	139	121	123	108	97	126	101	78
9	178	170	132	116	116	102	92	120	96	74
10	172	164	125	110	110	95	86	114	91	70
11	165	158	117	103	102	88	80	107	85	65
12	158	152	109	97	95	81	74	100	80	60
13	151	145	100	90	87	73	67	93	74	55
14	144	138	91	83	78	65	60	85	67	50
15	136	131	82	75	69	56	52	77	61	45
16	128	123	72	67	61	50	46	69	54	39
17	119	115	64	59	54	44	41	61	48	35
18	110	107	57	53	48	39	36	55	42	31
19	101	99	51	47	43	35	33	49	38	28
20	91	90	46	43	39	32	29	44	34	25
21	83	81	42	39	35	29	27	40	31	23
22	76	72	38	35	29	26	24	36	28	21
23	69	68	35	32			22	33	24	19
24	64	62	32	30				31	22	17
25	59	57		27				28		
26	54	53								
27	50	49								
28	47	46								
29	44	43								
30	41	40								
31	38	37								

Properties

	8 × 8 M 34.3	8 × 8 M 32.6	8 × 6½ M 28	8 × 6½ M 24	6 × 6 M 25.0	6 × 6 M 22.5	6 × 6 M 20.0	6 × 6 WF 25.0	6 × 6 WF 20.0	6 × 6 WF 15.5
Area A (in.²)	10.09	9.59	8.23	7.06	7.35	6.62	5.88	7.37	5.90	4.62
Ratio r_x/r_y	1.82	1.82	2.25	2.25	1.77	1.83	1.85	1.77	1.77	1.77
r_y (in.)	1.87	1.90	1.47	1.53	1.43	1.36	1.39	1.52	1.50	1.45
L_c (ft.)	8.7	8.6	7.2	7.0	6.4	6.6	6.4	6.6	6.5	...
L_u (ft.)	20.9	20.7	15.1	14.7	21.6	17.5	17.1	19.8	16.2	12.2
B_x } Bending	.349	.340	.366	.340	.468	.483	.456	.439	.440	.457
B_y } factors	1.147	1.115	1.544	1.390	1.470	1.655	1.547	1.316	1.341	1.444
a_x } Multiply	17.38	17.01	13.44	12.52	7.01	6.12	5.79	7.95	6.22	4.51
a_y } values by 10⁶	5.26	5.16	5.16	2.46	2.24	1.824	1.693	2.54	1.978	1.447

Loads below heavy lines are for main members with Kl/r ratios between 120 and 200.
† Non-compact section; see discussion under Allowable Loads on Columns, General Notes.

AMERICAN INSTITUTE OF STEEL CONSTRUCTION

---

fore it will bend. The longer the unsupported length of a column, the less weight it can withstand before bending. For example, place a one-inch stick between your finger and thumb; then apply pressure to it until it breaks. Repeat this, using a two- or three-inch stick of the same diameter. The longer the stick, the easier it is to break.

Slenderness Ratio

The tendency of a column to bend under load varies with the ratio of the unsupported length of the member to its least radius of gyration (r_y). This is illustrated by the formula $\dfrac{l}{r_y}$, where l is the unsupported length of the column in inches and r_y is the least radius of gyration in inches. This ratio is referred to as the *slenderness ratio*.

Building codes usually specify the maximum acceptable slenderness ratio. For main structural members, a maximum slenderness ratio of 120 is common, while 200 is frequently used for secondary members.

The computation of the slenderness ratio is illustrated by the following example. An 8″ x 8″ WF 35 member is to be used as a column, with an unsupported length of 15′-0″.

The slenderness ratio should be less than the maximum 120. What is the actual ratio?

The unsupported length is 15′-0″ or 180 inches. The radius of gyration for the weak or minor axis (Y-Y) is 2.03 (found in steel column tables).

$$\text{Slenderness ratio} = \frac{l}{r_y} = \frac{180}{2.03} = 88.6$$

This is less than the 120 maximum. Therefore, this column can be used as a main structural member.

What is the maximum permissible unsupported length of this column, without exceeding the maximum, permissible ratio of 120?

$$120 = \frac{l}{r_y}$$
$$120 = \frac{l}{2.03}$$
$$l = 2.03 \ (120)$$
$$l = 243.6 \text{ inches or } 20.3 \text{ feet.}$$

The *effective length* (Kl) of a column is the unbraced length (l in the slenderness ratio) multiplied by a factor referred to as K. K involves the restraint at the ends of the unbraced length and the resistance to lateral movements. It can be seen, therefore, that the means of restraint influences the effective

1-17

ROLLED STEEL SHAPES

WF SHAPES
Properties for designing

Weight per Foot Lb.	Area In.²	Depth In.	Flange Width In.	Flange Thickness In.	Web Thickness In.	$\dfrac{d}{A_f}$	AXIS X-X I In.⁴	S In.³	r In.	AXIS Y-Y I In.⁴	S In.³	r In.
112	32.92	11.38	10.415	1.248	.755	.876	718.7	126.3	4.67	235.4	45.2	2.67
100	29.43	11.12	10.345	1.118	.685	.961	625.0	112.4	4.61	206.6	39.9	2.65
89	26.19	10.88	10.275	.998	.615	1.06	542.4	99.7	4.55	180.6	35.2	2.63
77	22.67	10.62	10.195	.868	.535	1.20	457.2	86.1	4.49	153.4	30.1	2.60
72	21.18	10.50	10.170	.808	.510	1.28	420.7	80.1	4.46	141.8	27.9	2.59
66	19.41	10.38	10.117	.748	.457	1.37	382.5	73.7	4.44	129.2	25.5	2.58
‡60	17.66	10.25	10.075	.683	.415	1.49	343.7	67.1	4.41	116.5	23.1	2.57
‡54	15.88	10.12	10.028	.618	.368	1.63	305.7	60.4	4.39	103.9	20.7	2.56
†49	14.40	10.00	10.000	.558	.340	1.79	272.9	54.6	4.35	93.0	18.6	2.54
45	13.24	10.12	8.022	.618	.350	2.04	248.6	49.1	4.33	53.2	13.3	2.00
‡39	11.48	9.94	7.990	.528	.318	2.36	209.7	42.2	4.27	44.9	11.2	1.98
†33	9.71	9.75	7.964	.433	.292	2.83	170.9	35.0	4.20	36.5	9.2	1.94
29	8.53	10.22	5.799	.500	.289	3.52	157.3	30.8	4.29	15.2	5.2	1.34
25	7.35	10.08	5.762	.430	.252	4.08	133.2	26.4	4.26	12.7	4.4	1.31
‡21	6.19	9.90	5.750	.340	.240	5.07	106.3	21.5	4.14	9.70	3.4	1.25
67	19.70	9.00	8.287	.933	.575	1.16	271.8	60.4	3.71	88.6	21.4	2.12
58	17.06	8.75	8.222	.808	.510	1.32	227.3	52.0	3.65	74.9	18.2	2.10
48	14.11	8.50	8.117	.683	.405	1.53	183.7	43.2	3.61	60.9	15.0	2.08
40	11.76	8.25	8.077	.558	.365	1.83	146.3	35.5	3.53	49.0	12.1	2.04
‡35	10.30	8.12	8.027	.493	.315	2.05	126.5	31.1	3.50	42.5	10.6	2.03
†31	9.12	8.00	8.000	.433	.288	2.31	109.7	27.4	3.47	37.0	9.2	2.01
28	8.23	8.06	6.540	.463	.285	2.66	97.8	24.3	3.45	21.6	6.6	1.62
‡24	7.06	7.93	6.500	.398	.245	3.07	82.5	20.8	3.42	18.2	5.6	1.61
20	5.88	8.14	5.268	.378	.248	4.08	69.2	17.0	3.43	8.50	3.2	1.20
‡17	5.00	8.00	5.250	.308	.230	4.95	56.4	14.1	3.36	6.72	2.6	1.16

† Non-compact shape in A36, A242, A440 and A441.
‡ Non-compact shape in A242, A440 and A441.

AMERICAN INSTITUTE OF STEEL CONSTRUCTION

Table 80

1-16

REGULAR SERIES

WF SHAPES
Dimensions for detailing

$c = \frac{1}{2}\,web + \frac{1}{16}''$

Nominal Size In.	Weight per Foot Lb.	Depth In.	Flange Width In.	Flange Thickness In.	Web Thickness In.	Web Half-Thickness In.	Distance a In.	T In.	k In.	k₁ In.	g₁ In.	c In.	Usual Gage g In.
10×10	112	11⅜	10⅜	1¼	¾	⅜	4⅞	7⅞	1¾	⅞	3¼	7/16	5½
	100	11⅛	10⅜	1⅛	11/16	⅜	4⅞	7⅞	1⅝	⅞	3¼	7/16	5½
	89	10⅞	10¼	1	⅝	5/16	4⅞	7⅞	1½	13/16	3	⅜	5½
	77	10⅝	10¼	⅞	9/16	5/16	4⅞	7⅞	1⅜	13/16	3	5/16	5½
	72	10½	10⅛	13/16	½	¼	4⅞	7⅞	1⅜	¾	2¾	5/16	5½
	66	10⅜	10⅛	¾	7/16	¼	4⅞	7⅞	1¼	¾	2¾	5/16	5½
	‡60	10¼	10⅛	11/16	7/16	¼	4⅞	7⅞	1⅛	11/16	2½	¼	5½
	‡54	10⅛	10	⅝	⅜	3/16	4⅞	7⅞	1⅛	11/16	2½	¼	5½
	†49	10	10	9/16	⅜	3/16	4⅞	7⅞	1 1/16	11/16	2½	¼	5½
10×8	45	10⅛	8	⅝	⅜	3/16	3⅞	7⅞	1⅛	11/16	2½	¼	5½
	‡39	10	8	½	5/16	3/16	3⅞	7⅞	1 1/16	11/16	2½	3/16	5½
	†33	9¾	8	7/16	5/16	3/16	3⅞	7⅞	15/16	11/16	2½	3/16	5½
10×5¾	29	10¼	5¾	½	5/16	3/16	2¾	8½	⅞	½	2¼	¼	2¾
	25	10⅛	5¾	7/16	¼	⅛	2¾	8½	13/16	7/16	2¼	3/16	2¾
	‡21	9⅞	5¾	5/16	¼	⅛	2¾	8½	11/16	7/16	2¼	3/16	2¾
8×8	67	9	8¼	15/16	9/16	5/16	3⅞	6⅜	1 5/16	1	3	⅜	5½
	58	8¾	8¼	13/16	½	¼	3⅞	6⅜	1 3/16	15/16	2¾	5/16	5½
	48	8½	8⅛	11/16	7/16	3/16	3⅞	6⅜	1 1/16	⅞	2¾	¼	5½
	40	8¼	8⅛	9/16	⅜	3/16	3⅞	6⅜	15/16	⅞	2¾	¼	5½
	‡35	8⅛	8	½	5/16	3/16	3⅞	6⅜	⅞	13/16	2¾	¼	5½
	†31	8	8	7/16	5/16	3/16	3⅞	6⅜	13/16	13/16	2¾	¼	5½
8×6½	28	8	6½	7/16	5/16	⅛	3⅛	6⅜	13/16	½	2¼	3/16	3½
	‡24	7⅞	6½	⅜	¼	⅛	3⅛	6⅜	13/16	½	2¼	3/16	3½
8×5¼	20	8⅛	5¼	⅜	¼	⅛	2½	6¾	11/16	7/16	2	3/16	2¾
	‡17	8	5¼	5/16	¼	⅛	2½	6¾	11/16	7/16	2	3/16	2¾

AMERICAN INSTITUTE OF STEEL CONSTRUCTION

1-23

ROLLED STEEL SHAPES

MISCELLANEOUS SHAPES (M) and LIGHT BEAMS (B)
Properties for designing

Weight per Foot (Lb.)	Area (In.²)	Depth (In.)	Flange Width (In.)	Flange Average Thickness (In.)	Web Thickness (In.)	d/A_f	AXIS X-X: I (In.⁴)	S (In.³)	r (In.)	AXIS Y-Y: I (In.⁴)	S (In.³)	r (In.)
31	9.12	15.84	5.525	.442	.275	6.49	372.5	47.0	6.39	11.57	4.19	1.13
†26	7.65	15.65	5.500	.345	.250	8.25	298.1	38.1	6.24	8.71	3.17	1.07
26	7.65	13.89	5.025	.418	.255	6.61	242.6	34.9	5.63	8.26	3.29	1.04
†22	6.47	13.72	5.000	.335	.230	8.19	197.4	28.8	5.52	6.40	2.56	.99
17.2	5.05	14.00	4.000	.272	.210	12.9	147.3	21.0	5.40	2.65	1.32	.72
22	6.47	12.31	4.030	.424	.260	7.20	155.7	25.3	4.91	4.55	2.26	.84
19	5.62	12.16	4.010	.349	.240	8.69	130.1	21.4	4.81	3.67	1.83	.81
†16.5	4.86	12.00	4.000	.269	.230	11.2	105.3	17.5	4.65	2.79	1.39	.76
†14	4.14	11.91	3.970	.224	.200	13.4	88.2	14.8	4.61	2.25	1.13	.74
†29.1	8.55	9.88	5.935	.389	.425	4.28	131.5	26.6	3.92	11.2	3.7	1.14
†22.9	6.73	9.88	5.750	.389	.240	4.42	116.6	23.6	4.16	9.9	3.5	1.22
†21	6.10	9.90	5.750	.338	.240	5.09	104.4	21.1	4.14	9.2	3.2	1.22
19	5.61	10.25	4.020	.394	.250	6.47	96.2	18.8	4.14	4.19	2.08	.86
17	4.98	10.12	4.010	.329	.240	7.67	81.8	16.2	4.05	3.45	1.72	.83
15	4.40	10.00	4.000	.269	.230	9.29	68.8	13.8	3.95	2.79	1.39	.80
†11.5	3.39	9.87	3.950	.204	.180	12.3	51.9	10.5	3.92	2.01	1.02	.77
†28	8.23	8.00	6.650	.398	.390	3.02	90.1	22.5	3.31	17.73	5.33	1.47
†24	7.06	8.00	6.500	.398	.240	3.09	83.8	21.0	3.45	16.52	5.08	1.53
‡22.5	6.61	8.00	5.395	.352	.375	4.21	68.3	17.1	3.23	7.5	2.8	1.08
‡20	5.88	8.00	5.360	.305	.350	4.89	60.7	15.2	3.22	6.6	2.46	1.06
‡18.5	5.44	8.00	5.250	.352	.230	4.33	62.1	15.5	3.38	6.9	2.6	1.13
‡17	5.00	8.00	5.250	.305	.240	5.00	56.0	14.0	3.35	6.16	2.35	1.11
15	4.43	8.12	4.015	.314	.245	6.44	48.0	11.8	3.29	3.30	1.65	.86
†13	3.83	8.00	4.000	.254	.230	7.87	39.5	9.88	3.21	2.62	1.31	.83
†10	2.95	7.90	3.940	.204	.170	9.83	30.8	7.79	3.23	1.99	1.01	.82
16	4.72	6.25	4.030	.404	.260	3.84	31.7	10.1	2.59	4.32	2.14	.96
12	3.53	6.00	4.000	.279	.230	5.38	21.7	7.24	2.48	2.89	1.44	.90
†8.5	2.50	5.83	3.940	.194	.170	7.63	14.8	5.07	2.43	1.89	.96	.87

† Non-compact shape in A36, A242, A440 and A441.
‡ Non-compact shape in A242, A440 and A441.

AMERICAN INSTITUTE OF STEEL CONSTRUCTION

Table 81

1-22

REGULAR SERIES

MISCELLANEOUS SHAPES (M) and LIGHT BEAMS (B)
Dimensions for detailing

$c = \frac{1}{2}\,\text{web} + \frac{1}{16}''$

Nominal Size and Designation (In.)	Wt. per Foot (Lb.)	Depth (In.)	Flange Width (In.)	Flange Avg. Thickness (In.)	Web Thickness (In.)	Web Half Thickness (In.)	Distance a (In.)	T (In.)	k (In.)	k_1 (In.)	g_1 (In.)	c (In.)	Max. Flg. Rivet (In.)	Usual Gage g (In.)
16×5½ B	31	15⅞	5½	7/16	¼	⅛	2⅝	14	15/16	9/16	2½	3/16	⅞	2¾
	26	15⅝	5½	3/8	¼	⅛	2⅝	14	13/16	9/16	2½	3/16	⅞	2¾
14×5 B	26	13⅞	5	7/16	¼	⅛	2⅜	12⅛	⅞	9/16	2¼	3/16	⅞	2¾
	22	13¾	5	5/16	¼	⅛	2⅜	12⅛	13/16	9/16	2¼	3/16	⅞	2¾
14×4 B	17.2	14	4	¼	3/16	3/32	1⅞	12⅝	9/16	½	2	3/16	¾	2¼
12×4 B	22	12⅜	4	7/16	¼	⅛	1⅞	10¾	¾	7/16	2¼	3/16	¾	2¼
	19	12⅛	4	3/8	¼	⅛	1⅞	10¾	11/16	7/16	2¼	3/16	¾	2¼
	16.5	12	4	¼	¼	⅛	1⅞	10¾	⅝	7/16	2¼	3/16	¾	2¼
	14	11⅞	4	¼	3/16	⅛	1⅞	10¾	9/16	7/16	2	3/16	¾	2¼
10×5¾ M	29.1	9⅞	5 15/16	3/8	7/16	3/16	2¾	8¼	13/16	⅝	2¼	¼	⅞	2¾
	22.9	9⅞	5¾	3/8	¼	⅛	2¾	8¼	13/16	9/16	2¼	3/16	⅞	2¾
	21	9 9/16	5¾	3/8	¼	⅛	2¾	8⅜	¾	…	2¼	3/16	⅞	2¾
10×4 B	19	10¼	4	3/8	¼	⅛	1⅞	8⅞	11/16	7/16	2¼	3/16	¾	2¼
	17	10⅛	4	5/16	¼	⅛	1⅞	8⅞	⅝	7/16	2¼	3/16	¾	2¼
	15	10	4	¼	¼	⅛	1⅞	8⅞	9/16	7/16	2¼	3/16	¾	2¼
	11.5	9⅞	4	3/16	3/16	⅛	1⅞	8⅞	½	7/16	2	3/16	¾	2¼
8×6½ M	28	8	6⅝	3/8	3/8	3/16	3⅜	6¼	⅞	…	2¼	¼	⅞	3½
	24	8	6½	3/8	¼	⅛	3⅜	6¼	⅞	…	2¼	3/16	⅞	3½
8×5¼ M	22.5	8	5⅜	3/8	3/8	3/16	2½	6⅛	¾	9/16	2¼	¼	⅞	2¾
	20	8	5⅜	5/16	3/8	3/16	2½	6⅜	11/16	…	2¼	¼	⅞	2¾
	18.5	8	5¼	3/8	¼	⅛	2½	6⅜	11/16	½	2	3/16	⅞	2¾
	17	8	5¼	5/16	¼	⅛	2½	6⅜	11/16	…	2	3/16	⅞	2¾
8×4 B	15	8⅛	4	5/16	¼	⅛	1⅞	6⅞	⅝	7/16	2	3/16	¾	2¼
	13	8	4	¼	¼	⅛	1⅞	6⅞	9/16	7/16	2	3/16	¾	2¼
	10	7⅞	4	3/16	3/16	⅛	1⅞	6⅞	½	7/16	2	3/16	¾	2¼
6×4 B	16	6¼	4	3/8	¼	⅛	1⅞	4⅞	11/16	3/8	2¼	3/16	¾	2¼
	12	6	4	¼	¼	⅛	1⅞	4⅞	9/16	3/8	2	3/16	¾	2¼
	8.5	5⅞	4	3/16	3/16	⅛	1⅞	5	7/16	3/8	2	3/16	¾	2¼

Gage g permissible near beam ends; elsewhere Spec. may require reduction in fastener size.

AMERICAN INSTITUTE OF STEEL CONSTRUCTION

1-21

ROLLED STEEL SHAPES

LIGHT WF COLUMNS · MISCELLANEOUS COLUMNS (M) and JUNIOR BEAMS AND CHANNELS
Properties for designing

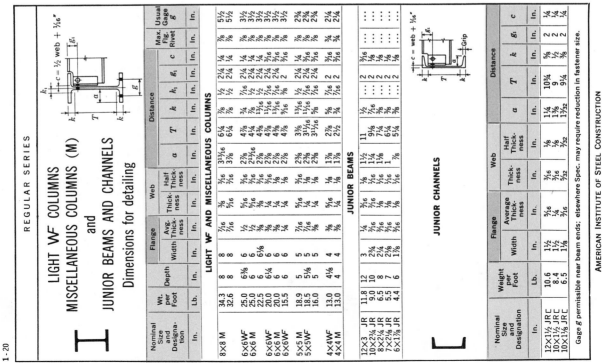

LIGHT WF AND MISCELLANEOUS COLUMNS

Weight per Foot (Lb.)	Area (In.²)	Depth (In.)	Flange Width (In.)	Flange Average Thickness (In.)	Web Thickness (In.)	d/A_f	Axis X-X I (In.⁴)	S (In.³)	r (In.)	Axis Y-Y I (In.⁴)	S (In.³)	r (In.)
‡34.3	10.09	8.00	8.000	.459	.375	2.18	115.5	28.9	3.40	35.1	8.8	1.87
‡32.6	9.59	8.00	7.938	.459	.313	2.20	112.8	28.2	3.45	34.2	8.6	1.90
25.0	7.37	6.37	6.080	.456	.320	2.30	53.5	16.8	2.69	17.1	5.6	1.52
25.0	7.35	6.00	5.938	.481	.313	2.10	47.0	15.7	2.53	14.9	5.0	1.43
‡22.5	6.62	6.00	6.063	.367	.375	2.60	41.0	13.7	2.49	12.2	4.2	1.50
‡20.0	5.90	6.20	6.018	.380	.258	2.81	41.7	13.4	2.66	13.3	4.4	1.36
20.0	5.88	6.00	5.938	.380	.250	2.66	38.8	12.9	2.57	11.4	3.8	1.39
‡15.5	4.62	6.00	6.000	.269	.240	3.72	30.3	10.1	2.56	9.69	3.2	1.45
18.9	5.56	5.00	5.000	.417	.313	2.40	23.8	9.5	2.08	7.85	3.1	1.20
18.5	5.45	5.12	5.025	.360	.265	2.43	25.4	9.94	2.16	8.89	3.5	1.28
16.0	4.70	5.00	5.000	.360	.240	2.78	21.3	8.53	2.13	7.51	3.0	1.26
13.0	3.82	4.16	4.060	.345	.280	2.97	11.3	5.45	1.72	3.76	1.9	.99
13.0	3.82	4.00	3.937	.372	.250	2.73	10.4	5.20	1.65	3.39	1.7	.94

JUNIOR BEAMS

Weight per Foot (Lb.)	Area (In.²)	Depth (In.)	Flange Width (In.)	Flange Average Thickness (In.)	Web Thickness (In.)	d/A_f	Axis X-X I (In.⁴)	S (In.³)	r (In.)	Axis Y-Y I (In.⁴)	S (In.³)	r (In.)
†11.8	3.45	12.00	3.063	.225	.175	17.4	72.2	12.0	4.57	.98	.64	.53
†9.0	2.64	10.00	2.688	.206	.155	18.1	39.0	7.8	3.85	.61	.45	.48
6.5	1.92	8.00	2.281	.189	.135	18.6	18.7	4.7	3.12	.34	.30	.42
5.5	1.61	7.00	2.078	.180	.126	18.7	12.1	3.5	2.74	.25	.24	.39
4.4	1.30	6.00	1.844	.171	.114	19.0	7.3	2.4	2.37	.17	.18	.36

JUNIOR CHANNELS

Weight per Foot (Lb.)	Area (In.²)	Depth (In.)	Flange Width (In.)	Flange Average Thickness (In.)	Web Thickness (In.)	d/A_f	Axis X-X I (In.⁴)	S (In.³)	r (In.)	Axis Y-Y I (In.⁴)	S (In.³)	r (In.)	x (In.)
10.6	3.12	12.00	1.500	.309	.190	25.9	55.8	9.3	4.23	.39	.32	.35	.27
8.4	2.47	10.00	1.500	.280	.170	23.8	32.3	6.5	3.61	.33	.28	.37	.29
6.5	1.91	10.00	1.125	.201	.150	44.2	22.1	4.4	3.47	.12	.13	.25	.19

† Non-compact shape in A36, A242, A440 and A441.
‡ Non-compact shape in A242, A440 and A441.

AMERICAN INSTITUTE OF STEEL CONSTRUCTION

1-20

REGULAR SERIES

LIGHT WF COLUMNS · MISCELLANEOUS COLUMNS (M) and JUNIOR BEAMS AND CHANNELS
Dimensions for detailing

c = ½ web + ¹/₁₆″

LIGHT WF AND MISCELLANEOUS COLUMNS

Nominal Size and Designation (In.)	Wt. per Foot (Lb.)	Depth (In.)	Flange Width (In.)	Flange Avg. Thickness (In.)	Web Thickness (In.)	Web Half Thickness (In.)	a (In.)	T (In.)	k (In.)	k₁ (In.)	g₁ (In.)	c (In.)	Max. Usual Flg. Rivet Gage g (In.)
8×8 M	34.3	8	8	7/16	3/8	3/16	3¹¹/₃₂	6¼	7/8	1/2	2¼	1/4	5½
8×8 M	32.6	8	8	7/16	5/16	3/16	3⅞	6¼	7/8	1/2	2¼	1/4	5½
6×6 WF	25.0	6⅜	6	1/2	5/16	3/16	2⅞	4¾	7/8	7/16	2¼	1/4	3½
6×6 M	25.0	6	6	1/2	5/16	3/16	2¹³/₁₆	4¼	7/8	1/2	2¼	1/4	3½
6×6 WF	22.5	6	6	3/8	3/8	3/16	2⅞	4¾	3/4	7/16	2¼	1/4	3½
6×6 M	20.0	6¼	6	3/8	1/4	1/8	2⅞	4⅝	13/16	7/16	2¼	3/16	3½
6×6 WF	20.0	6	6	3/8	1/4	1/8	2⅞	4¾	11/16	7/16	2¼	3/16	3½
6×6 M	15.5	6	6	1/4	1/4	1/8	2⅞	4⅞	9/16	7/16	2¼	3/16	3½
5×5 M	18.9	5	5	7/16	5/16	3/16	2⅜	3⅜	13/16	1/2	2¼	1/4	2¾
5×5 WF	18.5	5⅛	5	7/16	1/4	1/8	2⅜	3¹¹/₁₆	11/16	7/16	2¼	3/16	2¾
5×5 WF	16.0	5	5	3/8	1/4	1/8	2⅜	3¹¹/₁₆	11/16	7/16	2¼	3/16	2¾
4×4 WF	13.0	4⅛	4	3/8	5/16	3/16	1⅞	2⅞	5/8	7/16	2	3/16	2¼
4×4 M	13.0	4	4	3/8	1/4	1/8	1⅞	2½	3/4	7/16	2	3/16	2¼

JUNIOR BEAMS

Nominal Size and Designation (In.)	Wt. per Foot (Lb.)	Depth (In.)	Flange Width (In.)	Flange Avg. Thickness (In.)	Web Thickness (In.)	Web Half Thickness (In.)	a (In.)	T (In.)	k (In.)	k₁ (In.)	g₁ (In.)	c (In.)	g (In.)
12×3 JR	11.8	12	3	1/4	3/16	3/32	1½	11	1/2	…	2	3/16	…
10×2¾ JR	9.0	10	2¾	3/16	3/16	3/32	1¼	9⅝	7/16	…	2	1/8	…
8×2¼ JR	6.5	8	2¼	3/16	1/8	1/16	1⅛	7¼	3/8	…	2	1/8	…
7×2⅛ JR	5.5	7	2⅛	3/16	1/8	1/16	1	6¼	3/8	…	2	1/8	…
6×1⅞ JR	4.4	6	1⅞	3/16	1/8	1/16	7/8	5¼	3/8	…	2	1/8	…

JUNIOR CHANNELS

c = web + ¹/₁₆″

Nominal Size and Designation (In.)	Weight per Foot (Lb.)	Depth (In.)	Flange Width (In.)	Flange Avg. Thickness (In.)	Web Thickness (In.)	Web Half Thickness (In.)	a (In.)	T (In.)	k (In.)	g₁ (In.)	c (In.)
12×1½ JR ⊏	10.6	12	1½	5/16	3/16	3/32	1¼	10¾	5/8	2	1/4
10×1½ JR ⊏	8.4	10	1½	1/4	3/16	3/32	1⅜	9	1/2	2	1/4
10×1⅛ JR ⊏	6.5	10	1⅛	3/16	5/32	3/32	1³/₃₂	9¼	3/8	2	1/4

Gage *g* permissible near beam ends; elsewhere Spec. may require reduction in fastener size.

AMERICAN INSTITUTE OF STEEL CONSTRUCTION

length of a column. In the "Commentary on the AISC Specifications," a guide is given to the selection of K. It gives six idealized cases, a theoretical K for each and a recommended design value for use when ideal conditions are approximate.

A more precise and effective means of computing K is explained in the "Manual of Steel Construction."

In the tables giving allowable concentric loads on WF columns of A-36 steel, the safe loads above the heavy horizontal line are for columns for which Kl/r is equal to or less than 120. Loads where Kl/r is greater than 120 are given below the heavy horizontal line. The radius of gyration (r_y) is taken about the minor or Y-Y axis. This property is shown at the bottom of the steel column tables.

The following example illustrates the use of the table for steel columns with Kl/r less than 120 for the Y-Y axis. If the slenderness ratio is not known, it must be computed. Assume a column has an unbraced length of 10 feet and an axial load of 205 kips. If the base is pinned and the top fixed, with sway at the fixed end, the K factor is 2.0, Table 83. The approximate effective length is 2 x 10' or 20 feet. Examining steel column tables reveals that an 8 x 8 WF 67 column, with an effective unbraced length of 20 feet, can carry 221 kips. This is more than the required load; therefore, this column would prove satisfactory. The slenderness ratio is Kl/r_y or $2 \times \dfrac{120 \text{ inches}}{2.12}$ or 113.2, which is less than 120.

The tables are designed to give the safe load with respect to the minor axis of the section. Sometimes it is necessary to investigate the allowable load with respect to both axes — Y-Y and X-X. The bottom of the wide-flange column tables gives the ratio r_x/r_y. This is used to investigate the strength of the column with respect to the major (X-X) axis.

To obtain the allowable effective length with respect to the major axis (X-X), corresponding to the minor axis for which loads are tabulated, multiply the effective unbraced length (Kl) for the minor axis (Y-Y) by this ratio (r_x/r_y). If the product is greater than the actual effective length for the major axis (X-X), the column is satisfactory. If the product is less than the actual effective length relative to the major axis (X-X), the X-X axis is critical. In this case, enter the tables with an actual effective length with respect to the major axis (X-X) divided by r_x/r_y, and select a column to satisfy the calculated concentric load. A more detailed explanation can be found in the "Manual of Steel Construction."

It can be seen, therefore, that although one WF column may support the design load in respect to the Y-Y axis, a heavier column may be needed if the X-X axis is critical. Before deciding to use the heavier column, compute a more accurate and effective K. The K values in Table 83 are conservative, and a more accurate K may influence the computations enough that the lighter column will satisfy all load and radius of gyration requirements. A detailed explanation of a more effective K, along with the necessary tables, can be found in the AISC "Manual of Steel Construction."

Data for WF Shapes as Columns — Allowable Concentric Loads — (Table 84)

Data across the top of the table give the nominal depth and width of the member and its weight per lineal foot. The body of the table is the allowable concentric loads, in kips, for the various-sized members, at the effective length in feet (Kl), with respect to the least radius of gyration. The column of figures at the extreme left is the effective length of the column.

Various properties are given at the bottom of the table.

Area A (in.²) — Cross-sectional area of the column (in square inches).

Ratio r_x/r_y — Ratio of: radius of gyration with respect to the X-X axis (r_x), and radius of gyration with respect to the Y-Y axis (r_y).

L_c — Maximum, unbraced length (in feet) of the compression flange, at which the allowable bending stress may be taken at 0.66 F_y (feet).

L_u — Same function as L_c, except the stress is 0.6 F_y (feet).

Table 83
K Factors

	K	Approx. K
Both ends fixed	0.5	0.65
One end fixed, one pinned	0.7	0.80
Fixed ends with sidesway	1.0	1.2
Both ends pinned	1.0	1.0
Sidesway at a pinned end	2.0	2.1
Sway at fixed end, other end pinned	2.0	2.0

Table 84   3-23

COLUMNS — WF shapes
TABLE I
Allowable concentric loads in kips

ASTM A36 — $F_y = 36$ ksi

Nominal Depth and Width	8 × 5¼	8 × 5¼	8 × 6½	8 × 6½	8 × 8	8 × 8	8 × 8	8 × 8	8 × 8	8 × 8
Weight per foot	**17**	**20**	**24**	**28**	**†31**	**35**	**40**	**48**	**58**	**67**
Effective length in feet KL with respect to least radius of gyration										
6	86	102	133	155	178	201	230	277	335	387
7	81	97	128	150	174	197	225	270	327	379
8	75	90	123	144	169	191	219	264	319	370
9	69	84	118	138	164	186	213	257	311	360
10	63	76	113	132	159	180	206	249	302	350
11	56	69	107	125	154	174	200	241	293	339
12	48	60	101	118	148	168	193	233	283	328
13	41	52	94	111	142	162	185	224	273	316
14	36	45	88	103	136	155	177	215	262	304
15	31	39	81	95	130	148	170	206	251	292
16	27	34	73	86	123	141	161	197	239	279
17	24	30	66	78	117	133	153	187	228	265
18	22	27	59	69	110	125	144	176	215	251
19	19	24	53	62	102	117	134	165	202	236
20		22	47	56	95	109	125	154	189	221
21			43	51	87	100	115	143	175	206
22			39	46	79	91	105	131	161	190
23			36	42	72	83	96	120	147	174
24			30	39	66	76	88	110	135	159
25			28	36	61	70	81	101	125	147
26				33	57	65	75	94	115	136
27				31	52	60	70	87	107	126
28					49	56	65	81	100	117
29					45	52	60	75	93	109
30					42	49	56	70	87	102
31					40	46	53	66	81	96
32					37	43	50	62	76	90
33					35	40	47	58	72	84
34							44	55	67	79
35									64	75
Properties										
Area A (in.²)	5.00	5.88	7.05	8.23	9.12	10.30	11.76	14.11	17.06	19.70
Ratio r_x/r_y	2.90	2.86	2.12	2.13	1.73	1.72	1.73	1.74	1.74	1.75
r_y (in.)	1.16	1.20	1.61	1.62	2.01	2.03	2.04	2.08	2.10	2.12
L_c (ft.)	5.7	5.7	7.0	7.1	...	8.7	8.8	8.8	8.9	9.0
L_u (ft.)	9.2	11.1	14.8	17.1	19.7	22.2	24.8	29.7	34.4	39.2
B_x Bending factors	.355	.346	.339	.339	.333	.331	.331	.327	.328	.326
B_y Bending factors	1.923	1.838	1.261	1.247	.991	.972	.972	.941	.937	.921
a_x Multiply values by 10⁶	8.41	10.31	12.30	14.60	16.36	18.80	21.8	27.4	33.9	40.4
a_y values by 10^6	1.003	1.262	2.73	3.22	5.49	6.32	7.29	9.10	11.21	13.19

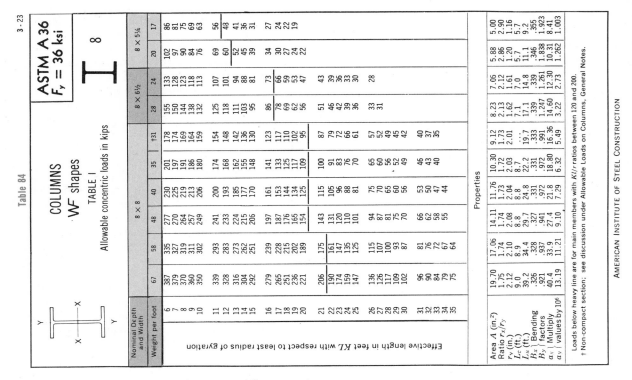

Loads below heavy line are for main members with Kl/r ratios between 120 and 200.
† Non-compact section; see discussion under Allowable Loads on Columns, General Notes.

AMERICAN INSTITUTE OF STEEL CONSTRUCTION

B_x and B_y — Bending factors, with respect to the X-X axis and Y-Y axis, for determining the equivalent axial load in columns subjected to combined loading conditions.

A_x and A_y are components of amplification factor for solving Equation (7a — see "Manual for Steel Construction"), when bending is about the X-X axis and Y-Y axis respectively.

Information pertaining to properties for designing with light, wide-flange columns is found in Table 82.

Round and Square Columns

Many other types of columns are available. Most frequently found are round and square types. Table 85 gives design data for selected areas and lengths.

Fireproofing

One disadvantage of steel framing is that it loses its strength when subjected to heat. To overcome this, in buildings where fireproofing is required, steel columns are encased in a fireproof material such as metal lath covered with vermiculite plaster, or they have a concrete shell cast around them. See Fig. 1192.

Steel beams are commonly fireproofed by installing concrete floors above and fireproof

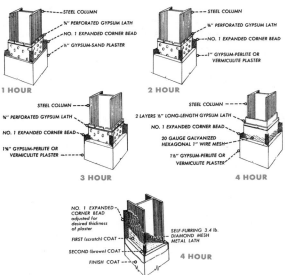

Fig. 1192. Typical ways of fireproofing a steel column. (National Gypsum Co.)

ceilings below. Such a ceiling usually is metal lath covered with one-inch, vermiculite plaster.

Consult an architectural standards book for other ways of fireproofing and the rating of the various methods. The common rating

Table 85
Allowable Loads for Concrete-Filled Steel Columns
Safe load is in kips (thousands of pounds).
Data apply to concentric loads. If eccentric loading is to occur, special tables must be consulted.

ROUND, EXTRA HEAVY COLUMNS

Diam. of Column Inches	Weight Per Foot Lbs.	Area of Steel Sq. In.	Area of Concrete Sq. In.	6	7	8	9	10	11	12	13	14	15	16	17	18	19	20	24	28	32	36	40
											Unbraced Length of Column — In Feet												
4	21	3.68	8.89	63	59	55	51	47	43	39	35												
4½	27	4.41	11.50	78	74	70	66	62	57	52	47	43	39										
5½	39	6.11	18.19	117	113	108	104	99	94	89	84	79	74	70	65	60	55	51					
6⅝	56	8.41	26.07	169	164	159	153	148	143	137	132	126	121	115	110	104	99	93					
8⅝	91	12.76	45.66	279	272	265	258	250	244	239	232	225	219	212	206	199	192	185	157	125			
10¾	133	16.10	74.66	385	378	370	364	356	349	342	335	328	321	314	306	298	292	285	255	225	197	169	
12¾	178	19.24	108.44	495	490	484	476	468	460	452	444	436	428	420	412	405	397	389	360	328	296	264	232

SQUARE COLUMNS

Exterior Dimensions Inches	Weight Per Foot Lbs.	Area of Steel Sq. In.	Area of Concrete Sq. In.	6	7	8	9	10	11	12	13	14	15	16	17	18	19	20	21	22	23	24
											Unbraced Length of Column — In Feet											
3 x3 x³/₁₆	14	2.11	6.89	37	34	31	28	25	23	20												
3 x3 x¼	16	2.75	6.25	43	40	37	33	30	27	24												
3½x3½x³/₁₆	18	2.49	9.76	47	45	43	40	37	34	31	28	26										
3½x3½x¼	20	3.25	9.00	56	53	50	47	43	40	37	33	30										
4 x4 x³/₁₆	23	2.87	13.13	59	56	53	51	48	45	42	39	37	34	31	28							
4 x4 x¼	26	3.75	12.25	71	67	64	60	57	53	50	46	43	40	36	33							
4 x6 x¼	36	4.75	19.25	94	90	85	80	76	71	66	62	57	53	48	44	39	34	30				
4 x8 x¼	46	5.75	26.25	118	112	106	100	94	88	83	77	71	65	60	54	46	43	37				
5 x5 x¼	37	4.75	20.25	102	98	94	90	86	83	80	76	72	68	64	61	57	53	50	46	42		
6 x6 x¼	50	5.75	30.25	135	131	127	123	119	115	111	107	103	100	96	92	88	84	80	76	72	68	64

Data are for columns manufactured by the Lally Column Company.

Table 86
Design Data for Corrugated Panels
Maximum span-siding and panels — 20 lbs./sq. ft. total load; roofing — 40 lbs./sq. ft. total load.
Weights based on gross squares for roofing and siding and net squares for panels.

TYPE OF SECTION	U.S.S. Gauge	Steelbestos			Galvanized			B. & S. Gauge	Aluminum		
		Wt./Sq.	Roofing	Siding	Wt./Sq.	Roofing	Siding		Wt./Sq.	Roofing	Siding
2½" Corrugated Roofing & Siding (Maximum length 25'-0")	18	267	7-6	8-0	235	7-6	8-0	18	62	5-2	7-3
	20	213	6-6	7-0	181	6-6	7-0	20	50	4-7	6-6
	22	185	5-9	6-0	153	5-9	6-0	22	39	4-0	5-7
	24	158	5-0	5-3	126	5-0	5-3				
	26	131	4-3	4-6	99	4-3	4-6				
Ribbed Roofing & Siding (Maximum length 25'-0")	18	276	9-4	11-9	243	9-4	11-9				
	20	219	7-10	10-5	186	7-10	10-5	16	82	8-7	12-0
	22	191	6-11	9-0	158	6-11	9-0	18	64	7-7	10-3
	24	163	6-0	7-7	130	6-0	7-7	20	51	6-7	8-9
	26	135	5-0	6-3	102	5-0	6-3				
Long Span Roofing & Siding (Maximum length 12'-2")	18	289	9-4	11-10	255	9-4	11-10	16	86	8-10	11-10
	20	230	8-1	11-6	196	8-1	11-6	18	67	8-0	11-4
	22	200	7-5	10-6	166	7-5	10-6	20	54	7-2	10-1
	24	171	6-7	9-3	137	6-7	9-3				

C—2½" CORR. ROOFING & SIDING Maximum length 25'-0"
33" 29¾" TO WEATHER

B—RIBBED ROOFING & SIDING Maximum length 25'-0"
30" TO WEATHER 32⅝" 1"

L—LONG SPAN ROOFING & SIDING Maximum length 12'-2"
30½" 26¾" TO WEATHER 1¾"

Courtesy Bowman Steel Company

method is to report how many hours of fire-proofing will protect the beam at both the indicated temperature and the type and thickness of the fireproofing.

Structural Steel Drawings

A structural steel framed building is shown in Fig. 1192A. The location, size, and type of each steel member is planned by an engineer.

Fig. 1192A. A structural steel framed building. (Martin K. Eby Construction Co., Inc.)

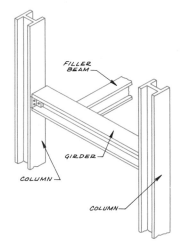

Fig. 1192B. Typical structural members.

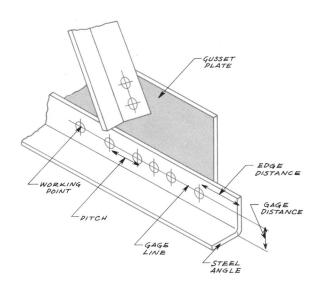

Fig. 1192C. Terms used in structural drafting.

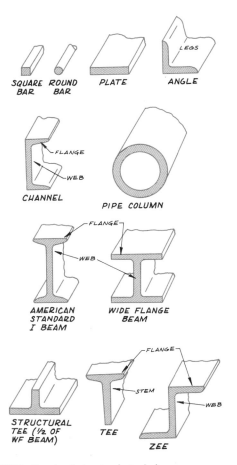

Fig. 1192D. Standard structural steel shapes.

A draftsman must understand the terms used before he can effectively make structural drawings. Some of the common terms follow:

Columns are vertical steel members used to support the roof and floor. See Fig. 1192B.

Girders are structural members running horizontally between columns. See Fig. 1192B.

Filler beams are structural members running horizontally between girders. See Fig. 1192B.

Pitch is the distance between the center lines of fasteners or holes. See Fig. 1192C.

Gage line is a continuous center line passing through holes or fasteners. See Fig. 1192C.

Gage distance is the distance the gage line is from the back of the structural member. See Fig. 1192C.

Edge distance is the distance the first hole or fastener is from the end of the member. See Fig. 1192C.

Slope is an indication of the angle a member makes with the horizontal.

Gusset plates are used on trusses to join the structural members. See Fig. 1192C.

Structural Steel Shapes

The most commonly used structural steel shapes are shown in Fig. 1192D. These members are made in a wide variety of sizes. Tables give the maximum load each can carry.

Abbreviations and Symbols

A standard system of recording data in the form of notes on drawings is used. It was developed by the American Institute of Steel Construction. The system does not use inch or pound marks. They are understood as the symbol is read. Some of the most frequently used abbreviations are in Fig. 1192E.

Joining Steel Members

Structural steel members are joined by riveting, bolting, or welding. Rivets are installed by heating them to a cherry red color. They are inserted in the hole and a head is formed on the straight end. See Fig. 1192F. The rivet is held in the hole with a dolly. It is a tool that fits over the head. While one worker holds the dolly another forms the other head with a rivet gun.

When members are riveted together in a structural steel shop they are called *shop rivets*. When rivets are installed on the building site they are called *field rivets*. Shop rivets are shown on drawings as open circles. Field

Fig. 1192E. Symbols and abbreviations for structural steel members.

STRUCTURAL SHAPE	SYMBOL	ORDER OF PRESENTING DATA	SAMPLE OF ABBREVIATED NOTE
Square Bar	□	Size, Symbol, Length	½ □ 5'-3
Round Bar	○	Size, Symbol, Length	⅝ ○ 7'-5
Plate	PL	Symbol, Width, Thickness, Length	PL 4 x ¼ x 11
Angle, Equal Legs	∟	Symbol, Leg, Leg, Thickness, Length	∟ 2 x 2 x ¼ x 9'-4
Angle, Unequal Legs	∟	Symbol, Long Leg, Short Leg, Thickness, Length	∟ 4 x 3 x ¼ x 6'-6
Channel	⊏	Depth, Symbol, Weight, Length	6 ⊏ 10.5 x 12'-2
American Standard Beam	I	Depth, Symbol, Weight, Length	10 I 35.0 x 13'-4
Wide Flange Beam	WF	Depth, Symbol, Weight, Length	16 WF 64 x 20'-7
Structural Tee	ST	Symbol, Depth, Weight, Length	ST 12 60 18'-6
Tee	T	Symbol, Flange, Stem, Weight, Length	T 4 x 4½ x 11.2 x 10'-4
Zee	Z	Symbol, Web, Flange, Weight, Length	Z 4 x 3 x 12.5 x 7'-9
Pipe	○	Nominal Diameter, Name	3½" extra strong pipe

rivets are drawn as a solid black circle. See Fig. 1192G.

The holes to receive rivets are made about $\frac{1}{16}''$ larger than the rivet diameter.

Structural bolts are widely used to erect steel structures. Special high tensile steel bolts are used. The selection of the proper size bolt is critical to structural soundness. Each bolt must be tightened to the proper tension. These data are given in the publication "Structural Joints Using ASTM A325 Bolts," published by the American Institute of Steel Construction. Symbols for drawing bolts are in Fig. 1192G.

Welding is another way of joining steel members. The fillet weld is most commonly used. Specifications for welding are in the "Manual of Steel Construction" published by the American Institute of Steel Construction. Some welding details are in Fig. 1192Z.

Spacing Bolts and Rivets

The gage line locates the center line of the fastener that is parallel with the length of the structural member. The pitch is the distance between the actual centers of each fastener. See Fig. 1192C.

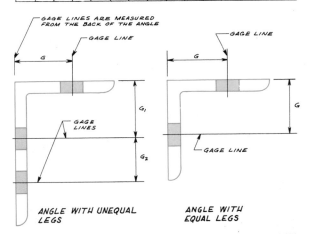

LEG	8	7	6	5	4	3½	3	2½	2	1¾	1½	1⅜	1¼	1
G	4½	4	3½	3	2½	2	1¾	1⅜	1⅛	1	⅞	⅞	¾	⅝
G 1	3	2½	2¼	2										
G 2	3	3	2½	1¾										

Fig. 1192H. Hole gages for angles in inches. (American Institute of Steel Construction)

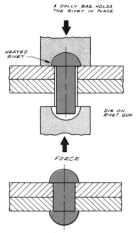

Fig. 1192F. Rivets are installed by heating the rivet, putting it in place, and forming a second head with a die on a rivet gun.

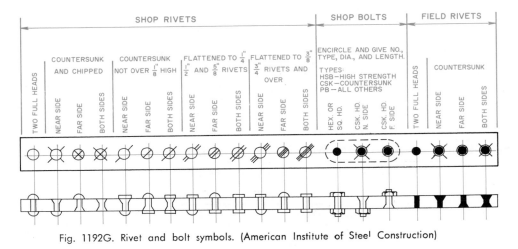

Fig. 1192G. Rivet and bolt symbols. (American Institute of Steel Construction)

The location of gage lines has been standardized for various connections. They vary with the length of the leg. In Fig. 1192H are gage line distances for angle connections. The gage line is located by measuring from the back of the angle.

The pitch between holes of angle connectors is usually in 3″ units. See Fig. 1192I. The angle connection is used to fasten a girder to a column.

The spacing of gage lines in I beams is shown in Fig. 1192J. The gage lines are measured from the center of the flanges. See Fig. 1192K. Spacing is usually 3″, 3½″, and 5½″. These holes are spaced along gage lines in 3″ units.

For structural strength, holes must be kept specified distances from the edge of a member. The minimum distances are in Fig. 1192L. Notice they vary with the diameter of the rivet.

Standard Connections

Connections are used to fasten beams to other structural members. They are standard-

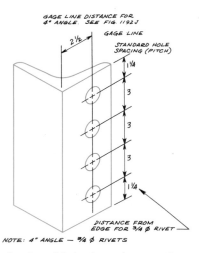

Fig. 1192I. Spacing of holes in angle connections.

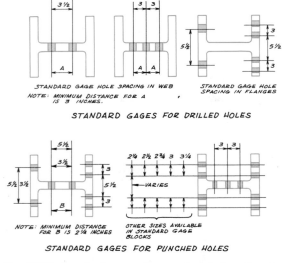

Fig. 1192J. Standard gages for punched holes. (American Institute of Steel Construction)

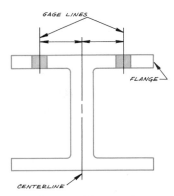

Fig. 1192K. Gage lines are located from the center of I beam flanges.

Fig. 1192L. Minimum edge distance in inches for punched holes. (American Institute of Steel Construction)

Minimum Edge Distance (Inches) for Punched Holes			
Rivet Diameter (inches)	In Sheared Edges	In Rolled Edge of Plate	In Rolled Edge of Structural Shapes*
½	1	⅞	¾
⅝	1⅛	1	⅞
¾	1¼	1⅛	1
⅞	1½	1¼	1⅛
1	1¾	1½	1¼
1⅛	2	1¾	1½
1¼	2¼	2	1¾

*May be decreased ⅛ inch when holes are near end of beam.

ized by the American Institute of Steel Construction. The two types used are framed and seated. See Fig. 1192M. The framed connections are fastened to the side of the beam. The seated connections are fastened to the column and the beam rests on them.

Other types of connections are plates, Tee and double-angle hangers, and bracket plates. See Fig. 1192N. Column connections are in Fig. 1192O.

Structural Steel Drawings

Three types of drawings are commonly used. These are a steel framing drawing, an erection drawing, and shop drawings. The

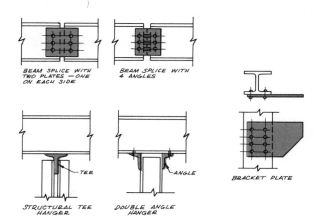
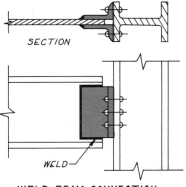
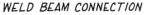

Fig. 1192N. Other types of standard connections.

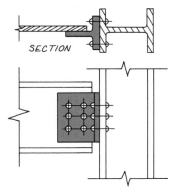

TEE BEAM FRAMING

WELD BEAM CONNECTION

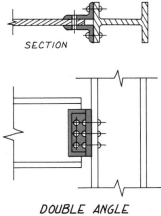

DOUBLE ANGLE
FRAMED CONNECTION

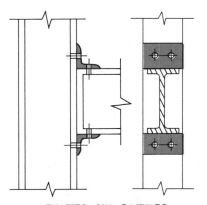

BOLTED AND RIVETED
SEATED BEAM CONNECTIONS

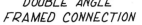

Fig. 1192M. Beam connections.

sample drawings that follow are for the small building shown in Fig. 1192P.

Framing and erection drawings are usually made to the scale of $\frac{1}{4}'' = 1'\text{-}0''$. They can be made to a larger scale if desired. See Fig. 1192Q and 1192R. Shop drawings are usually drawn $\frac{3}{4}'' = 1'0''$ to $1'' = 1'\text{-}0''$. See Fig. 1192T.

Steel Framing Drawings

The steel framing drawing shows the location of beams, columns, and other steel members. See Fig. 1192Q. This is the roof of a one story building. It shows the size and location of each. This drawing is made by the engineer. It is the result of his calculations and decisions concerning the design of each structural member.

Notice that each structural member is shown by a solid line. The main beams are wide flange. These carry the roof load to the column. Filler beams made from channel and angle members are used to support the roof decking.

The size of each member is shown on the member. The actual length of each member is not shown. This is figured and shown on the shop drawings.

The framing drawing dimensions the location of each member to the center line of the member. The columns are also located.

Buildings several stories high have a separate framing plan for each floor plus one for the roof.

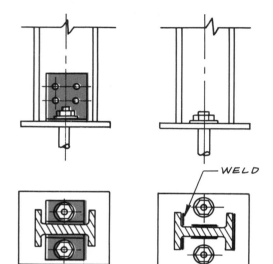

BOLTED COLUMN BASE CONNECTION   WELDED COLUMN BASE CONNECTION

Fig. 1192O. Column connections.

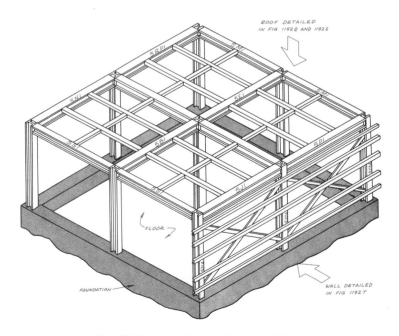

Fig. 1192P. A small steel framed building.

Erection Plans

The erection plan for the roof in Fig. 1192Q is shown in Fig. 1192R. Erection plans are really a type of assembly drawing. They show how the various members are put together.

Erection plans show those putting the framework together where each member belongs. Each member is made to the correct length in the structural shop. They are numbered. These numbers are shown on the erection plan. The construction crew finds a member with the number as shown on the plan and puts it in the place shown. They do not need to know the size data since they are only assembling the members.

The erection plan only has the dimensions locating the columns. Since each member is marked and all holes for assembly drilled, no measuring is necessary. Many of the connections are shop-assembled.

Sometimes the framing plan and erection plan data are placed on one drawing. This can be done if the structure is not too complex. See Fig. 1192S.

If the building is several stories, an erection plan is made for each floor and the roof.

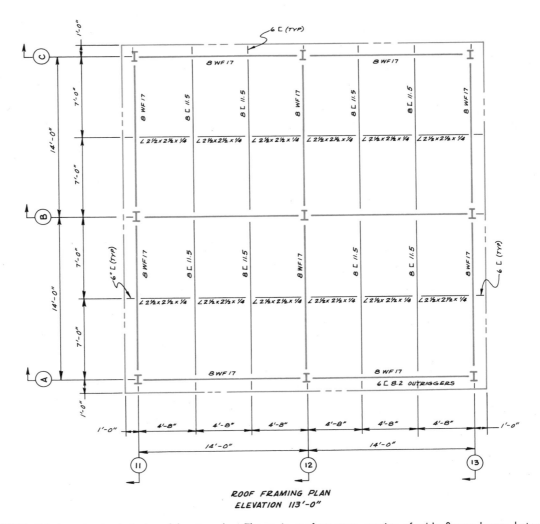

ROOF FRAMING PLAN
ELEVATION 113'-0"

Fig. 1192Q. This is a structural steel roof framing plan. The main roof structure consists of wide flange beams between the columns. Roof decking is supported by filler beams made from steel channel and angle members.

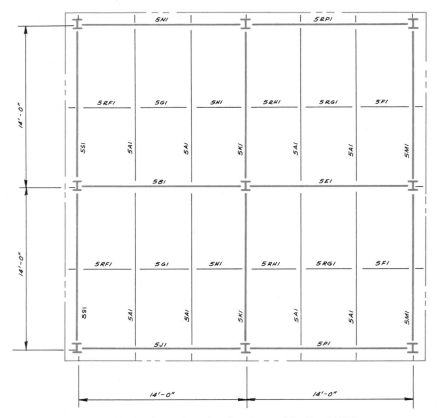

Fig. 1192R. Steel erection plan for the roof in Fig. 1192Q.

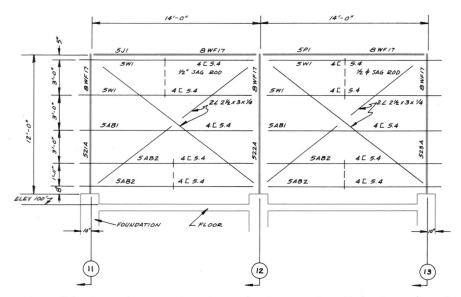

Fig. 1192S. An exterior wall framing and erection plan. This is a combination plan with framing and erection data. Can you find this wall on the roof framing and erection plans in Figs. 1192Q and 1192R?

Wall Plans

If exterior walls are composed of structural steel members, framing and erection plans are made for each wall. The same principles apply here as just discussed for the roof plan. A combined framing and erection plan for one wall of the building in Fig. 1192P is in Fig. 1192S.

Notice that the identification numbers for the columns appear on the wall plan. This does not appear on the floor or roof plan because they are not a part of that section of the structure.

Any structural member that appears in several drawings uses the same identification number on all drawings. In Fig. 1192S beams 5J1 and 5P1 appear at the roof line. Find these on the erection drawing in Fig. 1192R.

This wall is to be covered with metal siding in large sheets. To support this steel, channel and angle members are used between the columns.

Shop Drawings

Shop drawings are detail drawings of each structural member. The draftsman secures the needed information from the framing plan. He must know how structural members are joined and the design of connections.

Shop drawings show the size and length of the member. They detail the connections used. All hole locations are given. Dimensions must be complete because the member is made in the shop from this drawing. It must be able to be connected to the adjoining members in the field or shop with no addi-

tional machine work. Shop drawings include notes giving special instructions.

The scale used should produce a drawing large enough to be clear. A common scale is $\frac{3}{4}'' = 1'\text{-}0''$. Very long members do not have the length to scale. Break lines are not used. The member is simply drawn shorter but dimensioned true size. The height and width are always drawn to scale.

Each part of a structural system is given a number. This must appear on the shop drawing and erection drawing. It is used whenever the piece appears on a drawing. The number is painted on each member after it is made. If several members are identical they are given the same number.

In Fig. 1192T is a shop drawing of a beam. It is Beam 5J1 as shown in Figs. 1192P, 1192R, and 1192S. This beam has welded connections. The detail of 1192T shows how welded and bolted connections would be detailed.

Notice the shop and field rivet symbols. Whenever possible the structure is designed so holes line up on a common gage line. Each connection requires the location of gage lines, edge distance and pitch.

Connections usually extend beyond the end of the beam. This set back distance is the difference between the overall length of the assembled member and the length of the beam alone with the connections. In Fig. 1192T the beam alone is $13'\text{-}9\frac{5}{8}''$ long. With the connections it measures $13'\text{-}10\frac{5}{8}''$. This is the actual distance between the columns to which it is to be attached.

The left end view shows the angle connection holes and their dimensions. When the right end connections are the same they need not be drawn. The beam is not shown in the end view.

A shop drawing of a riveted steel column is in Fig. 1192U. Usually it can be described with a view of two faces. The section view is actually a view from the top of the column.

The angle connections on this column are shop riveted to the column and plate. Notice that the top connections extend $\frac{1}{2}''$ beyond the end of the beam forming the column. The faces of columns are marked with a letter. The surface facing north is marked. This helps in the erection of the building. When two faces are the same only one need be drawn. The

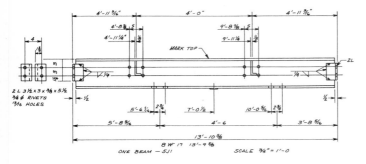

Fig. 1192T. A typical welded steel beam shop drawing. All parts of this type of drawing are to scale except the length of the beam. This is a beam from the building in Fig. 1192P.

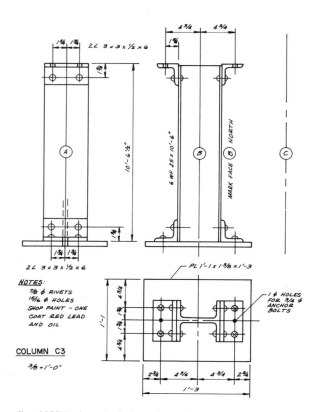

2 L 3 x 3 x ½ x 6

COLUMN C3

NOTES:
⅞ ∅ RIVETS
¹³⁄₁₆ ∅ HOLES
SHOP PAINT - ONE
COAT RED LEAD
AND OIL

Fig. 1192U. A typical riveted steel column shop drawing.

other can be indicated with a center line and an identifying letter.

A welded steel column is in Fig. 1192V. All shop assembly was welded. The parts to be field-assembled have holes drilled for rivets or bolts. This column is the one in the center of the building in Figs. 1192P, 1192Q, and 1192R.

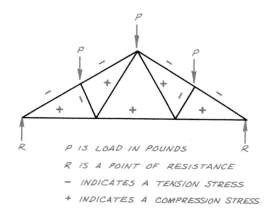

P IS LOAD IN POUNDS
R IS A POINT OF RESISTANCE
− INDICATES A TENSION STRESS
+ INDICATES A COMPRESSION STRESS

Fig. 1192W. Roof load places members of a truss under tension and compression stresses.

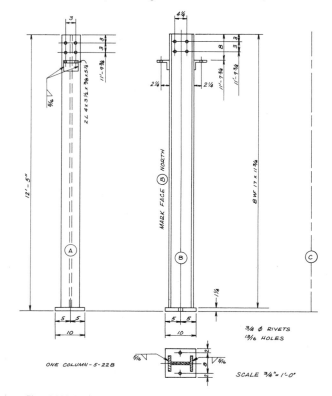

ONE COLUMN - 5-22B

¾ ∅ RIVETS
¹³⁄₁₆ HOLES

SCALE ¾" = 1'-0"

Fig. 1192V. A typical welded steel column shop drawing.

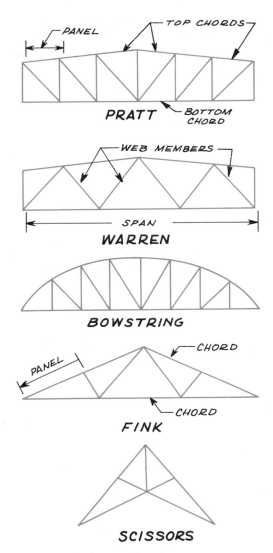

Fig. 1192X. Typical types of steel trusses.

Drawing Steel Trusses

Trusses are used to span distances too great for girders. Steel trusses are made from tees, wide flange beams, or angles.

Trusses must be carefully designed. The engineer must design them to withstand tension and compression stresses. The truss in Fig. 1192W shows these stresses in a fink truss. The common types of steel trusses are the Warren, Pratt, Fink, scissors, and bowstring. See Fig. 1192X.

The Warren and Pratt trusses are used to carry floor and roof loads. They are also good to use if the roof has to carry an extra load, as an overhead crane.

The Fink truss is used for roofs where a steep slope is desired. It usually carries only the roof load.

The bowstring truss can span long distances. It gives the roof good slope.

The scissors truss is used for high pitched roofs.

Draftsmen must know the terms used in truss design. These are chord, web member, panel, and span. See Fig. 1192X.

A *chord* is one of the principle structural members that is braced by web members.

Web members are internal braces running between the chords.

Panels are the distances between two web members measured along a chord.

Span is the horizontal distance covered by the trusses with no support from columns or walls.

The engineer decides which type of truss will do the job best. The engineer then computes the stresses on each member. Next he makes a simple design drawing. See Fig. 1192Y. It shows tension and compression in

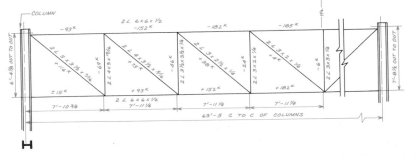

Fig. 1192Y. A design drawing for a truss is prepared by the engineer. The shop drawing for this truss is in Fig. 1192AA. The term "out to out" on the height dimensions refers to the outside surface ot the top and bottom members. (American Institute of Steel Construction)

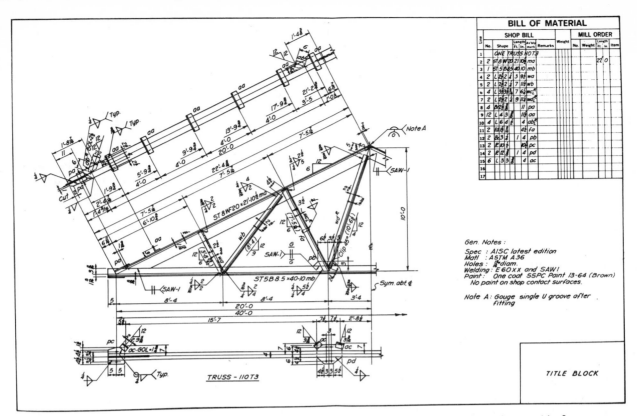

Fig. 1192Z. A simple welded Fink truss. The web members are made of steel angles. The top chord is a wide flange T-beam. The bottom chord is a T-beam. (American Institute of Steel Construction)

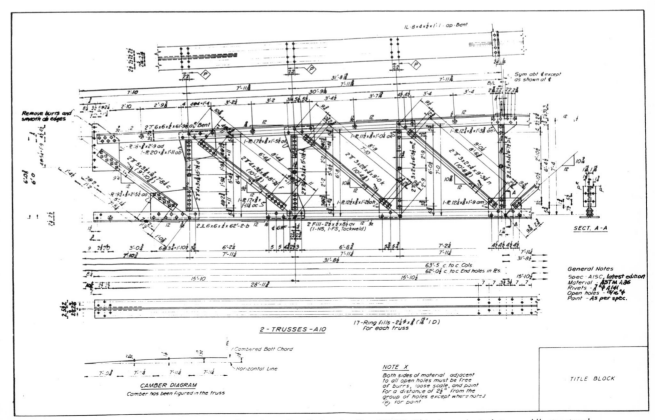

Fig. 1192AA. A Pratt truss shop drawing. It is based on the design in Fig. 1192Y. This is a riveted truss. All structural members are angles. Notice the great dimensioning detail required. (American Institute of Steel Construction)

pounds. Tension is shown by a minus (−) and compression by a plus (+). The engineer then selects structural members for each part of the truss. These are recorded on the design drawing. The shop drawing is made from the data on this design drawing.

The *shop drawing* shows all information needed to make the truss. Uusually the truss is drawn in the assembled position. Individual pieces are not usually detailed separately since they are usually few in number and simple in design. An example is in Fig. 1192Z. This is a welded Fink truss. Notice the use of welding symbols. Usually only half a truss is drawn since the other half is identical. Study carefully the data in the bill of material.

In Fig. 1192AA is the shop drawing for the truss design in Fig. 1192Y. Notice that the size of each piece is recorded. The gusset plates are fully dimensioned. Hole locations are indicated according to standard design practices. Some drawings can become very crowded. Fig. 1192AA is such a drawing. The placement of dimensions must be very carefully planned. Such a drawing is very difficult to check, therefore the draftsman must work very carefully. If there are details that can be clarified with a section they are drawn.

Generally each piece of a truss is not identified with a number. The entire assembled truss is numbered. It apears on an erection drawing as a single member. Therefore, it only needs a single identifying number. They are usually shop-assembled. Extremely large trusses might be shipped to the site in two pieces. These are field-joined.

Trusses are drawn to scale. All parts of the truss use the same scale. Details may be drawn larger.

Rigid Frame Drawing

The members of rigid frames are steel, girder-like members. They are assembled by welding, riveting, or bolting. They form the column and roof structure.

A drawing of a low rigid frame is in Fig. 1192BB. It is drawn assembled. Notice the use of large scale detail drawings to clarify assembly information.

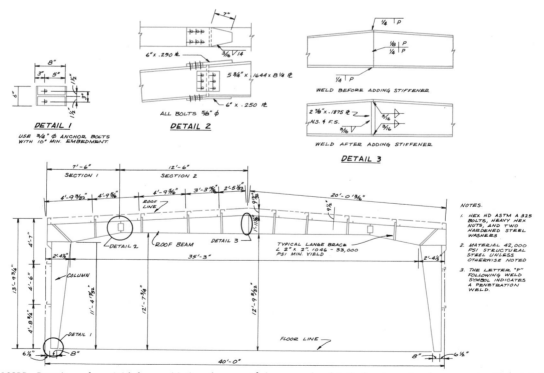

Fig. 1192BB. Drawing of a rigid frame. Notice the use of large scale detail drawings to show construction details. (Butler Manutacturing Co.)

Steel Roof Decking and Wall Panels

Numerous steel decking systems are manufactured. Some decking types are exposed to the weather, while others are used as forms for supporting a poured concrete roof or floor. Still others provide electrical and heating systems to be built into the floor. Selected examples of these are illustrated in the following paragraphs.

Corrugated Panels

Table 86 gives design data for three types of corrugated roof and wall panels. Steelbestos is a trade name for a steel sheet to which is applied an adhesive, a layer of asphalt-impregnated asbestos felt and a plastic outer coating. The plastic coating is available in a variety of colors. The power plant in Fig. 1193 has corrugated, roof and wall panels.

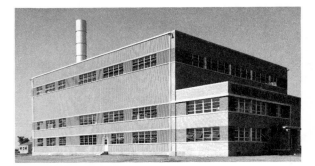

Fig. 1193. Steel panels were used for roof decking and wall panels in this building. (Bowman Steel Corp.)

Table 87
Allowable Loads for Steel Roof Decking

LONG SPAN

Type Span			5-75-18 A	5-75-18 B	5-75-16 A	5-75-16 B	5-75-14 A	5-75-14 B	5-75-12 A	5-75-12 B
16'-0"			84*		144		183		261	
17'-0"			79*		128		162		231	
18'-0"			74*		114		145		206	
19'-0"			71*		102		130		185	
20'-0"			67*		92		117		166	
21'-0"			64*		84		106		151	
22'-0"			60		76		97		138	
23'-0"			55		70		89		126	
24'-0"			50	50	64		81		116	
25'-0"					59	58	75	74	107	106
26'-0"					55	51	69	65	99	94
27'-0"					51	46	64	59	92	84
28'-0"					47	41	60	52	85	75
29'-0"					44	37	56	47	79	68
30'-0"					41	33	52	43	74	61
31'-0"					38	30	49	39	69	55
32'-0"					36	27	46	35	65	51

Type Span	5-45-18 A	5-45-18 B	5-45-16 A	5-45-16 B	Type Span	5-30-18 A	5-30-18 B	5-30-16 A	5-30-16 B
10'-0"	141				10'-0"	81		102	
11'-0"	116				11'-0"	67	64	85	85
12'-0"	98		124		12'-0"	56	49	71	65
13'-0"	83		106		13'-0"	47	39	61	51
14'-0"	72		92		14'-0"	41	31	52	41
15'-0"	62		80		15'-0"	36	25	45	34
16'-0"	55	53	70	70	16'-0"	31	21	40	28
17'-0"	49	44	62	58	17'-0"	28	18	35	23
18'-0"	43	37	55	49	18'-0"			32	20
19'-0"	39	32	50	42	19'-0"			28	16
20'-0"	35	27	45	36					
21'-0"	32	23	40	31					
22'-0"	29	20	37	27					
23'-0"			34	24					
24'-0"			31	21					
25'-0"			29	18					

SHORT SPAN

Type Span	3-20 A	3-20 B	3-18 A	3-18 B	3-16 A	3-16 B	3-14 A	3-14 B	3-12 A	3-12 B
5'-0"	139	121	182	168	231	215	288	278	403	398
5'-6"	115	91	150	126	190	161	238	208	334	300
6'-0"	99	70	127	97	160	124	200	161	280	230
6'-6"	82	55	108	76	136	98	170	126	239	182
7'-0"	71	44	93	61	118	78	147	101	206	145
7'-6"	62	36	81	50	102	64	128	82	179	118
8'-0"	54	30	71	41	90	52	112	68	157	97
8'-6"	48	25	63	34	80	44	100	56	140	81
9'-0"	43	21	56	29	71	37	89	48	125	68
9'-6"			50	24	64	31	80	40	112	58
10'-0"			45	21	57	27	72	34	101	50
10'-6"					52	29	65	30	91	43
11'-0"					47	20	59	26	83	37
11'-6"							54	23	76	33
12'-0"							50	20	70	29
12'-6"									64	25

Column A gives total, uniformly distributed loads (in lbs./sq. ft.) which unit will carry at a stress not to exceed 18,000 psi, premised on simple span ($\frac{1}{8}$ WL).

Column B gives uniformly distributed loads per square foot on a simple span which will cause unit to deflect not more than 1/240th of span.

Q-3 sheets are available in metallic coated steel up to 31'-0"; Q-5-45 and Q-5-30 sheets in 25'-0" lengths; and Q-5-75 in 40'-0" lengths.

Numbers at the top of each column, as 3-20, mean No. 3 Q-deck of 20-gauge steel.

Data are for Q deck No. 3 as manufactured by H. H. Robertson Co.

Steel Roof Deck

Many types of steel roof decking are available. Two of these are presented. Manufacturers' catalogs should be consulted for other types.

One type designed for short spans is illustrated in Fig. 1194. This spans up to 12'-6", carrying a normal roof load. The units have interlocking side joints. They are fastened to

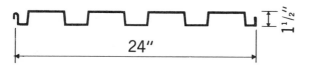

Fig. 1194. Section through short-span, steel roof decking (Q-deck, No. 3). (H. H. Robertson Co.)

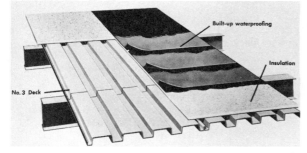

Fig. 1195. Steel roof decking (Q-deck, No. 3) with built-up roof. (H. H. Robertson Co.)

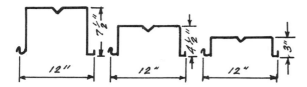

Fig. 1196. Section through long-span, steel roof decking, (Q-deck, No. 5). (H. H. Robertson Co.)

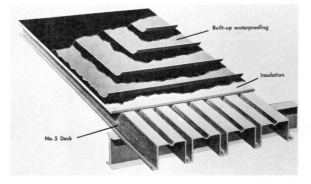

Fig. 1197. Steel roof decking (Q-deck, No. 5) with built-up roof. (H. H. Robertson Co.)

the supporting roof structure by arc welding. The safe loads for various spans and gauges of steel are given in Table 87.

After the steel is welded in place, it is covered with insulation board and a built-up roofing. See Fig. 1195.

A decking designed for long, unsupported spans of roof is shown in Fig. 1196. The safe load varies with the depth of the decking and the gauge of the steel. See Table 87. When this decking rests on masonry walls or steel beams, the hollow space between the webs should be closed with a pressed metal filler that is welded in place. The decking sheets are welded to the structural-steel frame. A built-up roof is applied over the decking, as shown in Fig. 1197.

Fig. 1198. Exposed steel decking forms ceiling. (H. H. Robertson Co.)

Fig. 1199. Steel decking placed over structural-steel frame and welded in place. The welded deck provides a working surface for other trades. (Granco Steel Products Co.)

Steel roof decking can be rapidly erected in any weather. The corrugated undersurface provides an attractive ceiling; however, suspended ceilings can be used. See Fig. 1198.

Another type of steel floor and roof panel is designed to serve as a form for poured concrete roof or floor decks. It is zinc-coated to insure permanence. The zinc coating also unites with the cement in the concrete, thus forming a strong bond.

The steel sheets are welded to the structural-steel frame. A special washer is placed on the sheet; the welder strikes an arc in the washer hole and burns through the sheet. This builds a plug weld from the structural steel member up into the washer, thus greatly strengthening the weld. See Fig. 1199.

The steel sheets then are covered with an insulating concrete, Fig. 1200. This serves as thermal insulation and as an effective vapor barrier, preventing moisture from penetrating the roof.

Special vent clips are attached at the side laps of the sheet, to provide an opening for venting cast-in-place, insulating concrete roof fills. See Fig. 1201. This type of roof construction is lightweight. A built-up roof is applied over the insulating concrete. See Fig. 1202.

The floor slab is structural concrete with a reinforcing mesh, Fig. 1203. The steel sheets may be used over precast concrete joists, to serve as a permanent deck for a cast-in-place concrete floor.

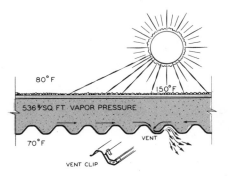

Fig. 1201. A section through a roof with steel decking, insulating concrete layer and a built-up roof. Notice the vent clip detail and how it permits venting moisture from the concrete. (Granco Steel Products Co.)

Fig. 1202. After the concrete slab has hardened, a built-up roof is laid. This is composed of layers of building felt and tar. (Granco Steel Products Co.)

Fig. 1200. Insulating concrete being poured and screeded over steel decking. This type of roof is rapidly erected. (Granco Steel Products Co.)

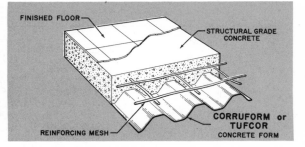

Fig. 1203. A section through a floor with steel decking, reinforced concrete slab and a finished floor. (Granco Steel Products Co.)

Table 88
Design Data for Steel Roof Decking and Insulating Concrete Slab

First consider the structural steel framing for the most economical purlin spacing; then select the type of decking; and finally choose the thickness of insulating concrete fill for desired "U" factor.

"S" signifies Standard Corruform and "T" Tufcor. Gauge of Tufcor is indicated by number preceding "T"

Product gauge and pattern recommended are based on actual laboratory and field experience. Recommendations limit stress under total dead and live load to less than 30,000 psi, for two or more spans. Dead load of 13 psf is composed of 1½psf for Tufcor, 6 psf for insulating concrete and 5½ psf for built-up roof.

"U" factors were derived using average thickness of insulating concrete (d), and using "K" value of 0.70 for 25 pcf density concrete.

Refer to insulating concrete aggregate manufacturers' literature for specific data on insulating properties of their material.

"U" factors have been calculated for winter condition.

Uniform Design Live Load (lbs./sq. ft.)	DECK SELECTION															
	Purlin Spacing (Center to Center)															
	3'-0"	3'-6"	4'-0"	4'-6"	5'-0"	5'-6"	6'-0"	6'-6"	7'-0"	7'-6"	8'-0"	8'-6"	9'-0"	9'-6"	10'-0"	10'-6"
20	S	S	S	S	26T	26T	26T	26T	24T	24T	24T	24T	22T	22T	20T	20T
30	S	S	S	26T	26T	26T	26T	24T	24T	24T	24T	22T	22T	20T	20T	20T
40	S	S	S	26T	26T	26T	26T	24T	24T	22T	22T	20T	20T	20T	——	

INSULATING CONCRETE SELECTION						
	Type of Roof System	Total Thickness "D"	"U" Factor for 25 pcf Density Concrete			
			Tufcor		Corruform	
			1⁵⁄₁₆" Corrg. Depth	⅞" Corrg. Depth	⁹⁄₁₆" Corrg. Depth	
Exposed Underside	Tufcor/Corruform with low density concrete such as Perlite, Vermiculite or cellular types.	2½"		.24	.23	
		3 "	.22	.21	.20	
		3½"	.19	.18	.18	
		4 "	.17	.16	.16	
Metal Lath and Plaster Ceiling	Roof system as listed above with the addition of a suspended ceiling of metal lath and ¾" of lightweight aggregate plaster.	2½"		.19	.18	
		3 "	.17	.16	.16	
		3½"	.15	.15	.14	
		4 "	.14	.13	.13	

Data are for decking manufactured by Granco Steel Products Co.

Table 89
Design Data for Floor Construction with Steel Decking and Concrete Slab

Slab capacity is the safe superimposed load which slab will carry when reinforced as shown. When galvanized material is used, add slab weight to values shown above to determine safe superimposed load.

Form material symbols: S - Standard Corruform; HD - Heavy Duty Corruform; T - Tufcor; numeral preceding T indicates gauge.

Total slab weight and construction load equals 50 psf minimum, or greater.

Deflection under concrete load equals ¹⁄₂₄₀ or less.

Recommendations based on actual construction and laboratory experience. Care should always be exercised to prevent concentrated loads and excessive buggy use over unprotected form materials.

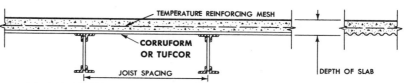

For 2½" and 3" slabs. (For 3½" deep slab or over, see "long span construction" detail)

TEMPERATURE REINFORCING MESH
CORRUFORM OR TUFCOR
JOIST SPACING
DEPTH OF SLAB

Depth of Slab	Slab Weight	Minimum Reinforcement Recommended		Span (Center to Center)													
				1'-6"	2'-0"	2'-6"	3'-0"	3'-6"	4'-0"	4'-6"	5'-0"	5'-6"	6'-0"	6'-6"	7'-0"	7'-6"	8'-0"
2½"	28	6 x 6 — 10/10	Form Material	S	S	S	S	S									
		As = .029	Slab Capacity	365	193	113	70	44									
3 "	35	6 x 6 — 10/10	Form Material	S	S	S	S	S	HD								
		As = .029	Slab Capacity	519	277	164	103	66	35								
3½"	41	6 x 6 — 4/4	Form Material			S	HD	HD	HD	HD	24T	24T	24T	24T			
		As = .080	Slab Capacity			459	294	215	161	124	81	61	46	34			
4 "	47	6 x 6 — 4/4	Form Material			S	HD	HD	HD	24T	24T	24T	22T	22T	22T	20T	
		As = .080	Slab Capacity			556	370	272	205	140	108	83	64	49	36	26	
4½"	53	4 x 4 — 6/6	Form Material			S	HD	HD	HD	24T	24T	24T	22T	22T	20T	20T	
		As = .087	Slab Capacity			725	489	362	274	194	151	119	93	73	56	43	
5 "	60	4 x 4 — 4/4	Form Material			S	HD	HD	24T	24T	24T	24T	22T	20T	20T	20T	
		As = .120	Slab Capacity			1178	810	605	434	340	271	218	177	143	117	114	

Data are for decking manufactured by Granco Steel Products Co.

While construction details vary, Figs. 1204 and 1205 illustrate commonly used design details.

Design data for roof construction are presented in Tables 88 and 89.

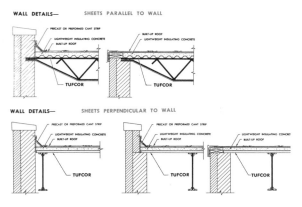

Fig. 1204. Typical design details for Tufcor® steel decking in roof construction. (Granco Steel Products Co.)

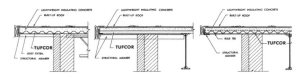

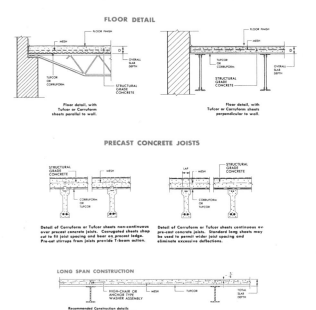

Fig. 1205. Typical design for steel decking in floor construction. (Granco Steel Products Co.)

Cellular-Steel Floor Systems

A number of floor systems are manufactured using load-bearing cellular-steel units for electrical distribution and heat and cooling distribution. Fig. 1230 illustrates one such system, in which the cellular-steel units serve for load bearing and electrical distribution. The cellular-steel decking is placed upon the structural members of the building. On top of this, placed at right angles, is a crossover header. This carries wiring across the decking and permits it to extend into the cellular units, thus allowing electrical outlets and telephones to be located wherever needed. These outlets can be easily moved at any time.

A variation of this system is shown in Fig. 1231. In this system, certain cells in the floor are considerably wider than others. They carry hot and cold air and can have an outlet set into them wherever needed. These ducts must be insulated.

The trade name for this system is Q-Floor, and it is manufactured by the H. H. Robertson Company. It is used on large multistory buildings. See Fig. 1232.

A similar floor system manufactured by the R. C. Mahan Company is illustrated in Fig. 1233. The steel floor decking serves as a load-carrying base, upon which electrical headers and a concrete floor are laid. Details are shown in Figs. 1234 through 1236.

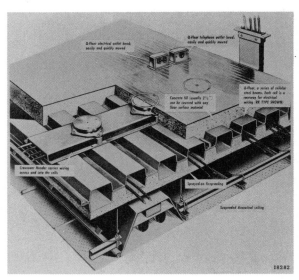

Fig. 1230. A cellular-steel floor used to carry a load and serve as electrical raceway. Notice the sprayed-on fireproofing layer on the bottom of the steel. (H. H. Robertson Co.)

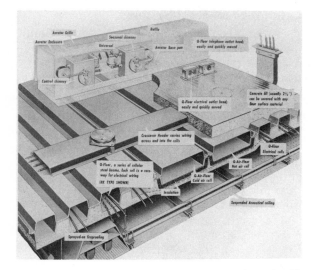

Fig. 1231. A section through a cellular-steel floor. (H. H. Robertson Co.)

Notice the cells used for electrical raceways and heat and cooling distribution. The crossover headers carry wiring across the floor into the cells where needed. A 2½-inch concrete floor is poured on top of the steel. In this installation, a suspended acoustical ceiling is used with lights set flush with the ceiling.

Fig. 1232. Cellular-steel, load-bearing units as they are installed in a multistory building. This illustration shows both electrical-wiring cells and heat and cooling cells. A concrete floor is poured over the steel deck. (H. H. Robertson Co.)

Glued, Laminated Wood Structural Members

Data concerning butterfly, peaked, peaked and cambered, tapered and simple straight beams are given in Chapter 7. In this chapter,

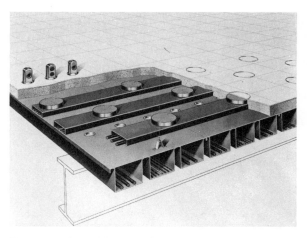

Fig. 1233. A cellular-steel floor system permitting rapid erection in any weather. The units are welded to the structural frame. (R. C. Mahon Co.)

Fig. 1234. Floor extension panels positioned to be welded in place. They are designed to provide openings for perimeter heating and cooling equipment. (R. C. Mahon Co.)

structural members designed for use in larger buildings are discussed. The types presented include rigid frames; two-hinged or barrel arches; three-hinged arches; bowstring trusses; glued, laminated domes, and laminated wood post and beam construction.

Rigid Frames

The rigid-frame unit provides an economical method of achieving low-pitched roofs, while maintaining desired clearances. It accomplishes the same thing as the three-hinged arch, without the radius at the haunch. Each half bent is composed of separate leg and arm members, precision fabricated and joined by a patented haunch connection that maintains the correct roof slope under design loads.

Table 90
Design Data for Laminated Structural Members - Rigid Frame Units

SPAN	ROOF SLOPE 3:12					ROOF SLOPE 6:12				
	Loading Per Lineal Foot	Leg Height	Dimension			Loading Per Lineal Foot	Leg Height	Dimension		
			A	B	C			A	B	C
40'	600 lbs.	12'	7" x 19½"	10"	10"	600 lbs.	12'	5¼" x 19½"	8"	10"
		16'	7" x 21⅛"	10"	11"		16'	5¼" x 21⅛"	8"	10"
		20'	7" x 21⅛"	10"	11"		20'	7" x 19½"	10"	10"
	800 lbs.	12'	7" x 22¾"	10"	11"	800 lbs.	12'	7" x 19½"	10"	10"
		16'	7" x 24⅜"	10"	12"		16'	7" x 21⅛"	10"	11"
		20'	7" x 24⅜"	10"	12"		20'	7" x 22¾"	10"	11"
	1,000 lbs.	12'	7" x 26"	10"	14"	1,000 lbs.	12'	7" x 21⅛"	10"	11"
		16'	7" x 27⅝"	10"	14"		16'	7" x 24⅜"	10"	12"
		20'	7" x 27⅝"	10"	14"		20'	7" x 26"	10"	13"
50'	600 lbs.	12'	7" x 24⅜"	10"	12"	600 lbs.	12'	7" x 21⅛"	10"	11"
		16'	7" x 26"	10"	13"		16'	7" x 22¾"	10"	11"
		20'	7" x 26"	10"	13"		20'	7" x 22¾"	10"	11"
	800 lbs.	12'	7" x 27⅝"	10"	16"	800 lbs.	12'	7" x 22¾"	10"	12"
		16'	7" x 29¼"	10"	15"		16'	7" x 26"	10"	13"
		20'	9" x 26"	12"	13"		20'	7" x 26"	10"	13"
	1,000 lbs.	12'	9" x 27⅝"	12"	16"	1,000 lbs.	12'	7" x 26"	10"	15"
		16'	9" x 29¼"	12"	15"		16'	7" x 29¼"	10"	15"
		20'	9" x 29¼"	12"	15"		20'	7" x 29¼"	10"	15"
60'	600 lbs.	12'	7" x 27⅝"	10"	16"	600 lbs.	12'	7" x 22¾"	10"	12"
		16'	7" x 29¼"	10"	15"		16'	7" x 24⅜"	10"	12"
		20'	9" x 26"	12"	13"		20'	7" x 27⅝"	10"	14"
	800 lbs.	12'	9" x 27⅝"	12"	16"	800 lbs.	12'	7" x 27⅝"	10"	16"
		16'	9" x 29¼"	12"	15"		16'	7" x 29¼"	10"	15"
		20'	9" x 30⅞"	12"	15"		20'	9" x 27⅝"	12"	14"
	1,000 lbs.	12'	9" x 30⅞"	12"	20"	1,000 lbs.	12'	9" x 29¼"	10"	19"
		16'	9" x 34⅛"	12"	17"		16'	9" x 27⅝"	12"	14"
		20'	9" x 34⅛"	12"	17"		20'	9" x 30⅞"	12"	15"
70'	600 lbs.	12'	9" x 27⅝"	12"	16"	600 lbs.	12'	7" x 26"	10"	14"
		16'	9" x 30⅞"	12"	15"		16'	7" x 27⅝"	10"	14"
		20'	9" x 30⅞"	12"	15"		20'	9" x 26"	12"	13"
	800 lbs.	12'	9" x 32½"	12"	21"	800 lbs.	12'	7" x 29¼"	10"	19"
		16'	9" x 34⅛"	12"	18"		16'	9" x 27⅝"	12"	14"
		20'	9" x 35¾"	12"	18"		20'	9" x 30⅞"	12"	15"
	1,000 lbs.	12'	9" x 35¾"	12"	26"	1,000 lbs.	12'	9" x 29¼"	12"	19"
		16'	9" x 39"	12"	22"		16'	9" x 32½"	12"	16"
		20'	11" x 35¾"	14"	18"		20'	9" x 34⅛"	12"	17"
80'	600 lbs.	12'	9" x 30⅞"	12"	20"	600 lbs.	12'	7" x 29¼"	10"	17"
		16'	9" x 32½"	12"	17"		16'	9" x 27⅝"	12"	14"
		20'	9" x 34⅛"	12"	17"		20'	9" x 29¼"	12"	15"
	800 lbs.	12'	9" x 35¾"	12"	25"	800 lbs.	12'	9" x 29¼"	12"	18"
		16'	11" x 34⅛"	14"	18"		16'	9" x 32½"	12"	16"
		20'	11" x 35¾"	14"	18"		20'	9" x 34⅛"	12"	17"
	1,000 lbs.	12'	11" x 35¾"	14"	26"	1,000 lbs.	12'	9" x 32½"	12"	22"
		16'	11" x 39"	14"	23"		16'	9" x 35¾"	12"	20"
		20'	11" x 40⅝"	14"	20"		20'	11" x 34⅛"	14"	17"

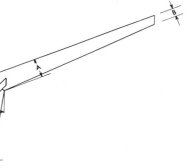

Courtesy Timber Structures, Inc.

Fig. 1235. Floor panels being positioned prior to welding. Notice the steel roof decking overhead. (R. C. Mahon Co.)

Fig. 1236. A building with steel decking in place, electrical headers located and reinforcing wire mesh being positioned, prior to pouring of the concrete deck. The steel decking provides a working platform for all trades, even before the concrete deck is poured. (R. C. Mahon Co.)

Fig. 1237. A rigid frame with a slight concave curve to the roof arm, giving a graceful sloping roof. (Timber Structures, Inc.)

Table 90 illustrates a rigid frame and gives design data for selected spans and roof slope. Fig. 1237 illustrates one of these units.

Two-Hinged Barrel Arches

The two-hinged arch, sometimes called the barrel arch, is adaptable for wide spans. It has been used for spans of 250 feet and can be designed for even wider spaces. There are three basic types — the foundation arch, the tied arch and the buttressed arch. See Fig. 1238. With *foundation arches*, the horizontal thrust is contained by foundation piers, with or without tie rods below the floor. *Tied arches* are supported by columns or bearing walls, with tie rods placed at the top of the column or wall. The use of tie rods is an important means of containing horizontal thrust. The horizontal thrust of *buttressed arches* is contained by concrete buttresses. Soil conditions and height of buttresses are determining factors as to fitness and cost.

Of course, special consideration must be given to the design of foundations, bearing walls or buttresses, to contain the horizontal thrust; however, this is not considered in this

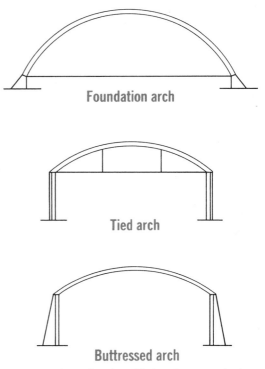

Fig. 1238. Two-hinged arches. (Timber Structures, Inc.)

text. Table 91 gives the spans, rise and radius for selected arches; it also gives data concerning horizontal thrust.

The arches are connected with purlins which support the roof decking. Since the loading on the purlins is considerably less than that on the arches, they are much smaller in cross section. Glued, laminated beams serve as purlins. Design data for safe loads are found in Chapter 7. Fig. 1239 gives design details for this construction. Fig. 1240 illustrates one of these units.

Three-Hinged Arches

Three-hinged arches add greatly to the interior beauty of a structure, and they are

Table 91
Design Data for Two-Hinged Arches

The spacing of the arches depends upon imposed load. The load data given are per lineal foot of span.

Data are provided for horizontal thrust. This must be contained by the foundation buttresses or tie rods.

Data are based on conservative design criteria, for construction with suitable structural grade combinations, but are subject to local considerations and specific job requirements. Normal lateral support is assumed.

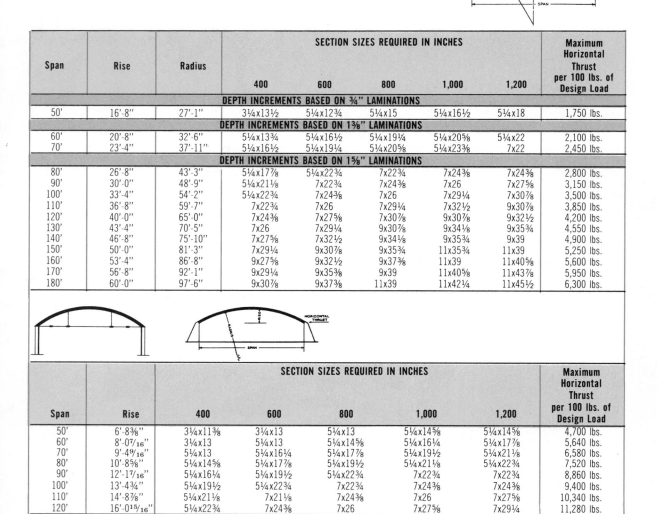

Span	Rise	Radius	SECTION SIZES REQUIRED IN INCHES					Maximum Horizontal Thrust per 100 lbs. of Design Load
			400	600	800	1,000	1,200	
DEPTH INCREMENTS BASED ON ¾" LAMINATIONS								
50'	16'-8"	27'-1"	3¼x13½	5¼x12¾	5¼x15	5¼x16½	5¼x18	1,750 lbs.
DEPTH INCREMENTS BASED ON 1⅜" LAMINATIONS								
60'	20'-8"	32'-6"	5¼x13¾	5¼x16½	5¼x19¼	5¼x20⅝	5¼x22	2,100 lbs.
70'	23'-4"	37'-11"	5¼x16½	5¼x19¼	5¼x20⅝	5¼x23⅜	7x22	2,450 lbs.
DEPTH INCREMENTS BASED ON 1⅝" LAMINATIONS								
80'	26'-8"	43'-3"	5¼x17⅞	5¼x22¾	7x22¾	7x24⅜	7x24⅜	2,800 lbs.
90'	30'-0"	48'-9"	5¼x21⅛	7x22¾	7x24⅜	7x26	7x27⅝	3,150 lbs.
100'	33'-4"	54'-2"	5¼x22¾	7x24⅜	7x26	7x29¼	7x30⅞	3,500 lbs.
110'	36'-8"	59'-7"	7x22¾	7x26	7x29¼	7x32½	9x30⅞	3,850 lbs.
120'	40'-0"	65'-0"	7x24⅜	7x27⅝	7x30⅞	9x30⅞	9x32½	4,200 lbs.
130'	43'-4"	70'-5"	7x26	7x29¼	9x30⅞	9x34⅛	9x35¾	4,550 lbs.
140'	46'-8"	75'-10"	7x27⅝	7x32½	9x34⅛	9x35¾	9x39	4,900 lbs.
150'	50'-0"	81'-3"	7x29¼	9x30⅞	9x35¾	11x35¾	11x39	5,250 lbs.
160'	53'-4"	86'-8"	9x27⅝	9x32½	9x37⅜	11x39	11x40⅝	5,600 lbs.
170'	56'-8"	92'-1"	9x29¼	9x35⅜	9x39	11x40⅝	11x43⅞	5,950 lbs.
180'	60'-0"	97'-6"	9x30⅞	9x37⅜	11x39	11x42¼	11x45½	6,300 lbs.

Span	Rise	SECTION SIZES REQUIRED IN INCHES					Maximum Horizontal Thrust per 100 lbs. of Design Load
		400	600	800	1,000	1,200	
50'	6'-8⅜"	3¼x11⅜	3¼x13	5¼x13	5¼x14⅝	5¼x14⅝	4,700 lbs.
60'	8'-0⁷/₁₆"	3¼x13	5¼x13	5¼x14⅝	5¼x16¼	5¼x17⅞	5,640 lbs.
70'	9'-4⁹/₁₆"	5¼x13	5¼x16¼	5¼x17½	5¼x19½	5¼x21⅛	6,580 lbs.
80'	10'-8⅝"	5¼x14⅝	5¼x17⅞	5¼x19½	5¼x21⅛	5¼x22¾	7,520 lbs.
90'	12'-1⁷/₁₆"	5¼x16¼	5¼x19½	5¼x22¾	7x22¾	7x22¾	8,860 lbs.
100'	13'-4¾"	5¼x19½	5¼x22¾	7x22¾	7x24⅜	7x24⅜	9,400 lbs.
110'	14'-8⅞"	5¼x21⅛	7x21⅛	7x24⅜	7x26	7x27⅝	10,340 lbs.
120'	16'-0¹⁵/₁₆"	5¼x22¾	7x24⅜	7x26	7x27⅝	7x29¼	11,280 lbs.

Courtesy Timber Structures, Inc.

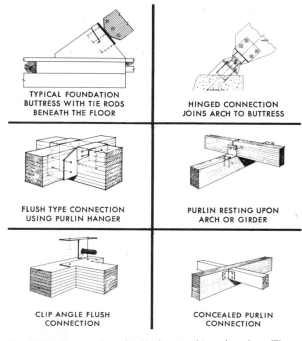

TYPICAL FOUNDATION BUTTRESS WITH TIE RODS BENEATH THE FLOOR

HINGED CONNECTION JOINS ARCH TO BUTTRESS

FLUSH TYPE CONNECTION USING PURLIN HANGER

PURLIN RESTING UPON ARCH OR GIRDER

CLIP ANGLE FLUSH CONNECTION

CONCEALED PURLIN CONNECTION

Fig. 1239. Construction details for two-hinged arches. (Timber Structures, Inc.)

used where appearance requirements are most rigid, such as in churches and auditoriums. See Fig. 1241 for one application of these units. There are three principal types — Tudor, Gothic and continuous. Standard spans are from 30 feet to 100 feet, though wider spans can be designed. Fig. 1242 illustrates these types and gives details of construction. Construction is much the same as for the two-hinged arch, and purlins are used between the

Fig. 1240. A two-hinged barrel arch spanning 200 feet to form a fieldhouse. (Timber Structures, Inc.)

Table 92
Design Data for Selected Three-Hinged Arches
Depth increments based on ¾" laminations.
All sections shown are dictated by vertical loading. On slopes steeper than 10:12, wind load may govern.

SPAN 40 FEET — Vertical Loadings—Pounds per Lineal Foot of Span

Roof Slope	Wall Ht. (Ft.)	400	600	800	1,000	1,200
3/12	10	5¼x9¾	5¼x13½	5¼x16½	5¼x20¼	7x17¼
	12	5¼x12	5¼x14¼	5¼x16½	5¼x20¼	7x18
	14	5¼x13½	5¼x16½	5¼x18¾	5¼x21	7x20¼
	16	5¼x14¼	5¼x17¼	5¼x20¼	7x18¾	7x21¾
	18	5¼x15	5¼x18¾	7x18	7x21	7x22½
4/12	10	5¼x9¾	5¼x12	5¼x16½	5¼x20¼	7x17¼
	12	5¼x12	5¼x15	5¼x16½	5¼x19½	7x17¼
	14	5¼x13½	5¼x16½	5¼x18¾	5¼x21	7x20¼
	16	5¼x14¼	5¼x17¼	5¼x20¼	7x19½	7x21¾
	18	5¼x15	5¼x18¾	7x18	7x21	7x22½
6/12	10	5¼x10½	5¼x13½	5¼x15	5¼x16½	5¼x18
	12	5¼x12	5¼x15	5¼x17¼	5¼x18¾	5¼x20¼
	14	5¼x13½	5¼x16½	5¼x18¾	5¼x21	7x19½
	16	5¼x14¼	5¼x17¼	5¼x20¼	7x19½	7x21
	18	5¼x15	5¼x18¾	5¼x21	7x21	7x21¾
8/12	10	5¼x11¼	5¼x14¼	5¼x16½	5¼x18	5¼x19½
	12	5¼x12	5¼x15¾	5¼x16½	5¼x20¼	7x18
	14	5¼x13½	5¼x16½	5¼x18¾	5¼x21	7x20¼
	16	5¼x15	5¼x18	5¼x20¼	7x19½	7x21¾
	18	5¼x15	5¼x18¾	5¼x21	7x21	7x22½
10/12	10	5¼x11¼	5¼x13½	5¼x15	5¼x17¼	5¼x18¾
	12	5¼x12	5¼x15	5¼x17¼	5¼x18¾	5¼x21
	14	5¼x13½	5¼x15¾	5¼x18	5¼x20¼	7x19½
	16	5¼x13½	5¼x16½	5¼x19½	7x18¾	7x20¼
	18	5¼x14¼	5¼x17¼	5¼x20¼	7x19½	7x21¾
12/12	10	5¼x11¼	5¼x14¼	5¼x15¾	5¼x18	5¼x19½
	12	5¼x12	5¼x15	5¼x17¼	5¼x19½	5¼x21
	14	5¼x13½	5¼x16½	5¼x18¾	5¼x21	7x20¼
	16	5¼x14¼	5¼x17¼	5¼x20¼	7x19½	7x21
	18	5¼x15	5¼x18	7x18	7x20¼	
16/12	10	3¼x12¾	5¼x12¾	5¼x14¼	5¼x16½	5¼x18
	12	5¼x11¼	5¼x13½	5¼x15¾	5¼x18	5¼x19½
	14	5¼x12	5¼x14¼	5¼x17¼	5¼x18¾	5¼x21
	16	5¼x12¾	5¼x15¾	5¼x18	5¼x20¼	7x18¾
	18	5¼x13½	5¼x16½	5¼x18¾	5¼x21	7x19½

SPAN 60 FEET — Vertical Loadings—Pounds per Lineal Foot of Span

Roof Slope	Wall Ht. (Ft.)	400	600	800	1,000	1,200
3/12	12	5¼x16½	7x17¼	7x21	7x24¾	9x24
	14	5¼x18¾	7x19½	7x21¾	7x26¼	9x24¾
	16	5¼x20¼	7x21	7x24	7x27	9x26¼
	18	7x18¾	7x22½	7x25½	9x25½	9x27¾
	20	7x20¼	7x24	7x27¾	9x27¾	9x30
4/12	12	5¼x16½	5¼x20¼	7x19½	7x24	9x23¾
	14	5¼x18¾	7x19½	7x21¾	7x24¾	9x24
	16	5¼x20¼	7x21	7x24	7x26¼	9x25½
	18	5¼x21	7x21¾	7x25½	9x24¾	9x27¾
	20	5¼x21¾	7x22½	7x27¾	9x27	9x29¼
6/12	12	5¼x16½	5¼x20¼	7x19½	7x21¾	7x24
	14	5¼x18	7x18¾	7x21	7x24	7x26¼
	16	5¼x19½	7x20¼	7x23¼	7x26¼	9x24¾
	18	5¼x21	7x21¾	7x24¾	7x27¾	9x26¼
	20	5¼x21¾	7x22½	7x26¼	7x29¼	9x27¾
8/12	12	5¼x17¼	5¼x20¼	7x20¼	7x21¾	7x24
	14	5¼x18¾	7x19½	7x21¾	7x24¾	7x27
	16	5¼x19½	7x20¼	7x23¼	7x26¼	9x25½
	18	5¼x20¼	7x21¾	7x24¾	7x27¾	9x27
	20	5¼x21	7x22½	7x26¼	7x29¼	9x28½
10/12	12	5¼x15¾	5¼x19½	7x19½	7x21¾	7x23¾
	14	5¼x17¼	5¼x21	7x21	7x23¾	7x25½
	16	5¼x18	7x19½	7x22½	7x24¾	7x27
	18	5¼x19½	7x20¼	7x23¾	7x26¼	9x25½
	20	5¼x20¼	7x21	7x24¾	7x27¾	9x26¼

tudor arches — 3-hinged depth increments based on ¾" laminations

SPAN 80 FEET — Vertical Loadings—Pounds per Lineal Foot of Span

Roof Slope	Wall Ht. (Ft.)	400	600	800	1,000	1,200
3/12	14	7x20¼	7x24	9x25½	9x30	9x34½
	16	7x22½	7x27	9x27¾	9x30¾	9x35¼
	18	7x24	9x25½	9x29¼	9x32¼	9x36
	20	7x24¾	9x26¼	9x30¾	9x33¾	11x33¾
	22	7x25½	9x27	9x31½	9x35¼	11x35¼
4/12	14	7x19½	7x24¾	7x27¾	9x27¾	9x32¼
	16	7x21¾	7x27	9x27	9x29¼	9x33
	18	7x23¼	9x24¾	9x28½	9x31½	9x34½
	20	7x24¾	9x26¼	9x30	9x33¾	9x36
	22	7x26¼	9x27	9x30¾	9x35¼	11x33¾
6/12	14	7x18¾	7x23¼	7x27	9x27¾	9x28½
	16	7x20¼	7x24¾	7x25½	9x28½	9x30¾
	18	7x21¾	7x26¼	9x27	9x30	9x32¼
	20	7x23¼	9x24¾	9x27¾	9x31½	9x34½
	22	7x24¾	9x25½	9x29¼	9x33	9x36
8/12	14	7x19½	7x23¼	7x27	9x26¼	9x28½
	16	7x20¼	7x24¾	7x25½	9x28½	9x30¾
	18	7x21¾	7x26¼	9x27	9x30	9x32¼
	20	7x22½	7x27¾	9x28½	9x31½	9x33¾
	22	7x23¼	9x25½	9x29¼	9x32¼	9x35¼
10/12	14	5¼x21	7x22½	7x26¼	9x25½	9x27¾
	16	7x20¼	7x24	7x27¾	9x27	9x30
	18	7x21	7x25½	9x25½	9x29¼	9x31½
	20	7x21¾	7x27	9x27	9x30	9x33
	22	7x23¼	9x24¾	9x27¾	9x31½	9x34½

(diagram: ROOF SLOPE, 0.5 × HAUNCH DEPTH, HAUNCH DEPTH, WALL HEIGHT, SPAN, 0.75 × HAUNCH DEPTH)

Courtesy Timber Structures, Inc.

arches, to carry the roof decking. Design data vary with the roof slope. Table 92 gives design data for selected slopes and spans. Many other sizes are available, and manufacturers' catalogs should be consulted for a complete listing.

Bowstring Trusses

The bowstring truss is one of the most practical and most used of all truss types. It is designed to provide a high degree of fire safety and freedom from dimensional changes. While the design data in Table 93 includes spans up to 150 feet, units as wide as 250 feet are in use. When provided for in the design, these trusses can support an overhead monorail or other unusual loading. Another type of truss is illustrated in Fig. 1243.

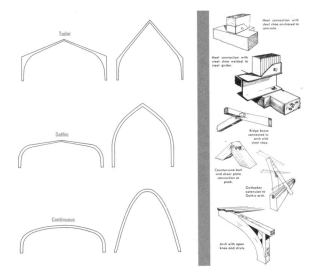

Fig. 1242. Three-hinged arches and typical construction details. (Timber Structures, Inc.)

Fig. 1241. A church using three-hinged, Tudor arches. Notice the purlins running perpendicular to the arches. The roof decking is a wood fiber product. (California Redwood Assoc.)

Fig. 1243. A lenticular type truss over a supermarket. It spans 124 feet with chords extending 13'-6" beyond the sidewalls to provide overhangs. (Timber Structures, Inc.)

Table 93
Design Data for Typical Bowstring Trusses with Dimensions of Bearings[1]

Span	No. of Panels	Truss Height[2]	Roof Height	Arc Length[1]	Camber	Heel Width[3]	Length of Bearings[3]	Truss Weight	
40'	6	5' 9"	6' 9½"	41' 10¹¹/₁₆"	1½"	6"	5"	950 Lbs.	Heel connection uses heavy steel U-Strap and shear plates.
50'	6	7' 2⅛"	8' 2⅝"	52' 4⁵/₁₆"	2"	6"	6½"	1,120 Lbs.	
60'	6	8' 7¾"	9' 8¼"	62' 10"	2½"	6"	8"	1,530 Lbs.	
70'	6	10' 0¾"	11' 1¼"	73' 3¹¹/₁₆"	2¾"	6"	9"	2,180 Lbs.	Web members are connected to chords with bolts and heavy steel straps. Shear plates are added when the stress requires.
80'	8	11' 6⅜"	12' 6⅞"	83' 9⁵/₁₆"	3"	6"	10"	2,700 Lbs.	
90'	8	12' 11½"	14' 0"	94' 3"	3½"	6"	11½"	3,330 Lbs.	
100'	8	14' 4½"	15' 5"	104' 8¹¹/₁₆"	4"	6"	12½"	3,710 Lbs.	
110'	10	15' 6⅛"	16' 7¼"	115' 2⅜"	4½"	7¾"	11½"	5,100 Lbs.	
120'	10	16' 11¾"	18' 0¼"	125' 8"	4¾"	7¾"	11½"	6,230 Lbs.	Tim-Truss with heel connected to steel I-beam column.
130'	10	18' 4¾"	19' 5¼"	136' 1¹¹/₁₆"	5"	7¾"	12½"	7,050 Lbs.	
140'	12	19' 9⅞"	20' 10¼"	146' 7⅜"	5½"	7¾"	13½"	8,170 Lbs.	
150'	12	21' 3"	22' 3½"	157' 1"	5¾"	7¾"	14"	9,460 Lbs.	

[1]Tabular values are for average conditions. Individual designs may vary.
[2]Truss height is the vertical distance from bearing line to top of truss at mid-span. Roof height, as shown, is truss height plus depth of typical roof joists and thickness of 1" nominal sheathing.
[3]Dimensions as determined for typical case of 40 lbs./sq. ft. total loading and 20 foot spacing, i.e., 800 pounds per linear foot of truss span. Heel width is also minimum pilaster width.
Courtesy Timber Structures, Inc.

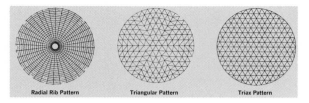

Fig. 1244. Typical structural patterns for glued, laminated wood domes. (Timber Structures, Inc.)

Fig. 1245. A glued, laminated, structural dome over a gymnasium spanning 132'-6". (Timber Structures, Inc.)

Domes

Glued, laminated, structural domes have been built with clear spans up to 300 feet, and they are practical for even greater spans. With a tension ring to resist horizontal thrust, side walls need not be buttressed, and no tying members are needed. The ratio of rise to span is low. Since the members are in compression and need not be designed to resist bending, section sizes are relatively small. Before the domes are raised into position, they usually are assembled in sections. Some typical construction patterns are shown in Fig. 1244, and one application is shown in Fig. 1245.

Drawing Laminated Wood Structural Systems

After the engineer produces the preliminary design of the structure, the draftsman makes carefully dimensioned drawings. In Fig. 1245A is a pictorial of parts of a wood structural system. Notice that the long spans are made with large beams. Shorter spans are made with smaller beams and girders. The areas between these have purlins to help sup-

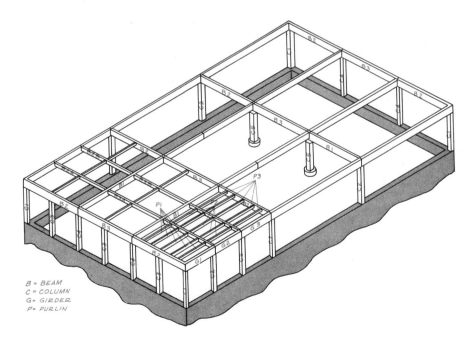

B = BEAM
C = COLUMN
G = GIRDER
P = PURLIN

Fig. 1245A. Partially completed view of frame of a laminated wood structure. Compare identified members with Figs. 1245B and 1245E.

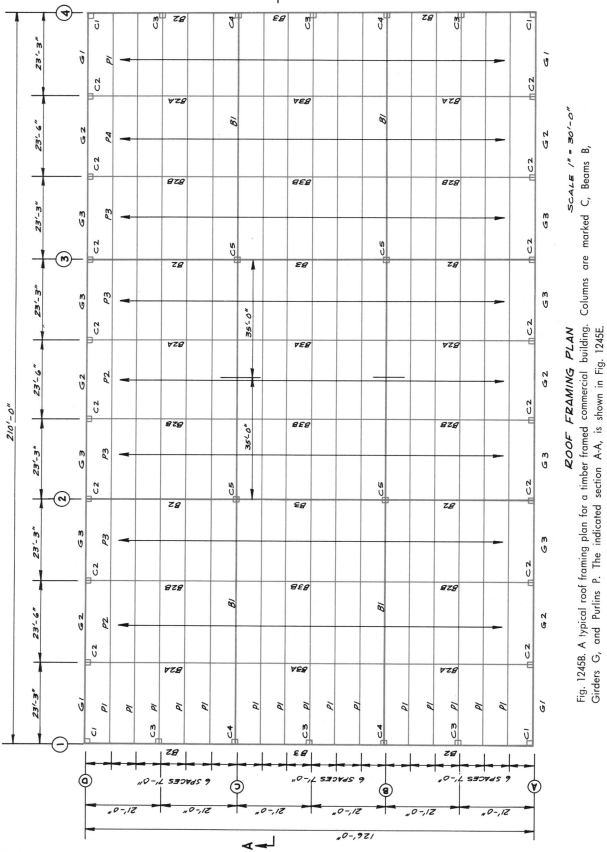

ROOF FRAMING PLAN

SCALE 1" = 30'-0"

Fig. 1245B. A typical roof framing plan for a timber framed commercial building. Columns are marked C, Beams B, Girders G, and Purlins P. The indicated section A-A, is shown in Fig. 1245E.

COLUMN SCHEDULE

COLUMN	SIZE	LENGTH	NO. REQUIRED	TOP FAB	BOTTOM FAB
C1	9 x 9 3/4	25'-10 1/8	4	DET. T	CORNER DET.
C2	9 x 16 1/4	25'-10 1/8	16	DETAIL OF C2	TYP C1
C3	9 x 17 7/8	25'-10 1/8	6	DETAIL OF C1	TYP C1
C4	12 1/2 x 14 5/8	25'-10 1/8	4	DETAIL OF C1	TYP C1
C5	12 1/2 x 16 1/4	24'-6 1/8	4	TYP INTERIOR	COP AND ANCHOR

Fig. 1245D. Typical column schedule.

BEAM SCHEDULE

BEAM NO.	SIZE	LENGTH	NO. REQUIRED
B1	9 x 48 3/4	105'-0"	4

Fig. 1245C. Typical beam schedule.

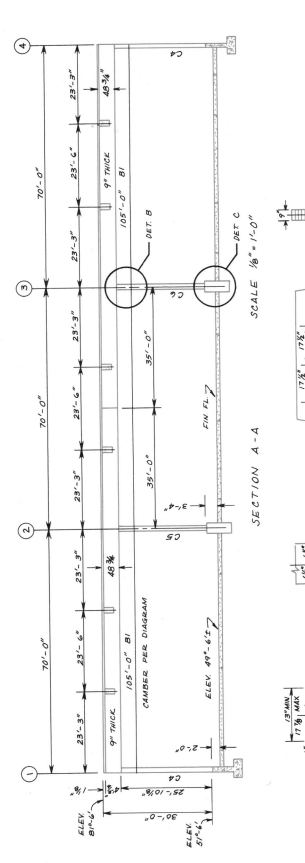

SECTION A-A   SCALE 1/8" = 1'-0"

DETAIL B   SCALE 1 1/2" = 1'-0"

DETAIL C   SCALE 1 1/2" = 1'-0"

Fig. 1245E. This is the section through the timber framed commercial building in Fig. 1245B. Typical large-scale construction details are shown.

port the roof deck. A complete roof framing plan for this structure is in Fig. 1245B. It shows the columns, beams, girders, and purlins. Each of these is identified by a letter and a number. The exact size is given in schedules which are a part of the drawing. Examples are in Fig. 1245C and 1245D. Notice that each member is dimensioned to its center line. The beams and girders are drawn much thicker than the purlins.

It is usually necessary to draw some sections to help clarify construction details. A typical example is in Fig. 1245E. It locates the structural members shown. The elevation of the foundation, roof, and finished floor are given.

The roof beams are designed with camber. This is a slightly convex (curved) condition. Engineers record the design data for the camber on the drawing.

Various special construction details are necessary. In Fig. 1245E are some details showing how the columns are anchored to the foundation. Another shows how the beams are joined to the column.

Wood-Fiber Roof Planks

Numerous types of wood-fiber roof planks are available. In Chapter 7, design data are given for one such product in 1½-, 2-, and 3-inch thicknesses. Other thicknesses are available, and data should be obtained from manufacturers' catalogs.

Fig. 1246. Wood fiber decking applied to open-web steel joists. (Tectum Corp.)

In commercial construction, this type of decking is used with steel, wood and concrete structural systems. Fig. 1246 shows decking

Fig. 1247. Wood fiber decking applied to box-section subpurlins. (Tectum Corp.)

Table 94
Design Data for Box Section Subpurlins

Loads given are for three span conditions. For one and two span conditions, multiply these by .9.

Loads are based upon tests conducted by Pittsburgh Testing Laboratories and Ohio State Engineering Experimental Station.

Deflections of spans in bold face type exceed $\frac{1}{240}$ of span, but are less than $\frac{1}{180}$ of span.

Total Loads P.S.F.	Spacing O.C.	Spans 16 Ga.	18 Ga.	20 Ga.
30	32"	9'-9	8'-7	7'-1
	36"	9'-2	8'-2	6'-8
	42"	8'-6	7'-7	6'-2
	48"	7'-11	7'-0	5'-9
35	32"	9'-0	8'-0	6'-6
	36"	8'-6	7'-7	6'-2
	42"	7'-10	6'-11	5'-8
	48"	7'-4	6'-6	5'-4
40	32"	8'-5	7'-6	6'-1
	36"	7'-8	6'-10	5'-7
	42"	7'-4	6'-6	5'-4
	48"	6'-10	6'-1	4'-11
45	32"	7'-11	7'-0	5'-9
	36"	7'-6	6'-8	5'-5
	42"	6'-11	6'-2	5'-0
	48"	6'-6	5'-9	4'-8
50	32"	7'-7	6'-8	5'-6
	36"	7'-1	6'-4	5'-1
	42"	6'-7	5'-10	4'-10
	48"	6'-2	5'-6	4'-6
55	32"	7'-2	6'-4	5'-2
	36"	6'-9	6'-0	4'-11
	42"	6'-3	5'-7	4'-6
	48"	5'-10	5'-2	4'-2

being applied to open-web steel joists, and Fig. 1247 shows it over a metal, box-section subpurlin. It is nailed to the steel joists in a nailing groove provided in the top member. Steel clips are used to secure it to box-section subpurlins. Design data for box-section subpurlins are shown in Table 94. Another method of framing a roof is to use bulb-tees. Design data for these are given in Table 95. The space between the bulb-tee and the fiber deck is filled with a lightweight concrete grout, as shown in Fig. 1248. See Fig. 1249 for other methods used to secure wood-fiber roof decking to structural members.

This decking can be left exposed on the interior of a building, thus forming a finished ceiling as well as the roof decking and insulation. See Fig. 1250.

Table 95
Maximum Spans for Three Span Bulb Tees

All deflections should be checked, if limiting deflection is critical.
Tabulated spans below are calculated on the basis of $Fs = 20,000$ psi.
For high strength steels ($Fs = 27,000$ psi), multiply span below by 1.16.
For one and two span conditions, multiply below spans by 0.9.

Type of Bulb Tee	Spacing CC	Loading in psf						
		25	30	35	40	45	50	55
I 158	23¾	7-7	6-11	6-5	6-0	5-8	5-4	5-1
	31¾	6-7	6-0	5-7	5-2	4-11	4-8	4-5
I 168	23⅞	8-11	8-2	7-7	7-1	6-8	6-4	6-0
	31¾	7-9	7-1	6-6	6-1	5-9	5-6	5-3
I 178	24	10-8	9-9	9-0	8-5	7-11	7-6	7-2
	31⅞	9-3	8-5	7-10	7-3	6-11	6-6	6-3
I 200	24⅛	12-5	11-4	10-6	9-9	9-3	8-9	8-4
	32	10-9	9-9	9-1	8-6	8-0	7-7	7-3
I 218	24⅛	13-2	12-0	11-2	10-5	9-10	9-4	8-10
	32	11-5	10-5	9-8	9-0	8-6	8-1	7-8
I 228	24¼	15-8	14-3	13-3	12-3	11-8	11-1	10-7
	32⅛	13-7	12-5	11-5	10-9	10-1	9-7	9-2

Data are for bulb tees manufactured by Inland Steel Co.

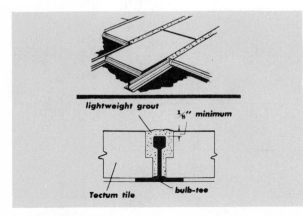

Fig. 1248. Wood-fiber roof planks installed with metal bulb-tees. Notice the grout placed between the planks and around the bulb-tee.

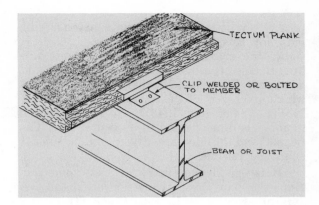

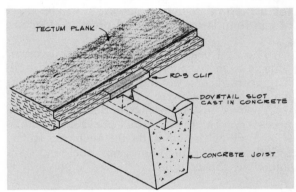

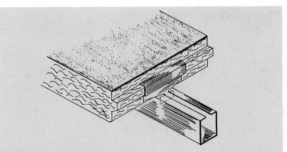

Fig. 1249. Various types of metal clips are used to secure wood fiber roof decking structural members. (National Gypsum Co.)

Fig. 1250. Wood-fiber roof decking used as exposed ceiling, roof decking and roof insulation. (Tectum Corp.)

Fig. 1251. The factory-manufactured steel framework is rapidly assembled on the site. (Butler Manufacturing Co.)

Factory-Manufactured Commercial Buildings

Available from a number of manufacturers are small commercial buildings built of standard, preengineered components which are manufactured on a production basis. Some assembly is done in the factory. The components are fitted together on the job. See Fig. 1251.

Such a structure can be rapidly erected with some saving in cost, since much on-the-site labor is eliminated due to factory cut and fitted components. These buildings can be easily expanded by adding on another unit; the components removed to attach the addition are utilized in the new structure. No demolition is necessary. See Fig. 1252.

Large, column-free, interior areas can be enclosed. See Fig. 1253. The area is free of obstructions from wall to wall and from floor to roof peak.

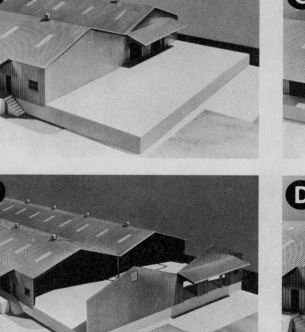

Fig. 1252. Building an addition to a factory-manufactured building. (Butler Manufacturing Co.)

A. Foundation and floor of addition poured.

B. Ends of units removed and placed in position for reuse on new addition.

C. Steel frame and purlins frame the new addition.

D. Metal roof and siding secured to frame; building ready to be occupied.

Basically, the design procedure is simple. The footings and foundation are designed to support the necessary load. Since the steel frame carries the total load of the roof, heavy concrete footings are needed only at the uniformly spaced piers, not around the entire building. Factory-fabricated wall panels are designed to hang on the steel frame. If these are replaced with a conventional masonry wall, the footings for the wall need to support its own weight.

Each company has a variety of standard framing systems available. See Fig. 1254. Since some are better suited to certain types of buildings than others, a decision must be made concerning the system to be used. Design data for one system is given in Table 96. The needed span and roof pitch are two primary considerations.

Another decision is the selection of exterior siding. Two metal types are available.

One is a metal panel rolled in some form of ribbed or corrugated pattern. Generally, these panels are used on buildings which do not require insulation; however, they may be insulated after erection, if desired. A second type

Fig. 1253. Interior of a warehouse built with low rigid frames and stamped metal roof and walls. Notice the wide, column-free, floor area. (Butler Manufacturing Co.)

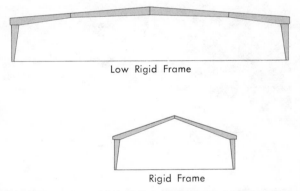

Fig. 1254. Two rigid-frame designs. The low rigid frame has a roof pitch of 1 in 12, and the other rigid frame has a pitch of 1 in 4. (Butler Manufacturing Co.)

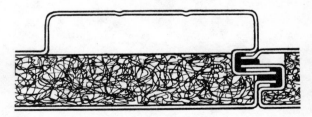

Fig. 1255. Section through an insulated wall panel. (Butler Manufacturing Co.)

This is a hollow metal panel completely insulated. The double tongue-and-groove design creates a strong panel-to-panel joint. Double vinyl gaskets seal out moisture and wind.

Table 96
Data for Stock, Rigid Frame Steel Buildings

	LOW RIGID FRAME (LRF)									
	Clear Span Standard Widths									
	24	32	36	40	50	60	70	80	100	120
Eave Heights	10	10	10							
	12	12	12	12	12	12	12			
				16	16	16	16	16	16	16
				20	20	20	20	20	20	20
				24	24	24	24	24	24	24

	Building		**Canopy**		**Width Extension**		
Bay lengths	18',20',21',24'		18',20',21',24'		18',20',21',24'		
Total length	Unlimited		Unlimited		Unlimited		
Roof slope	1 in 12		1 in 12		1 in 12		
Design loadings[1]	2, 4, 6, 8		2, 4, 6, 8		2, 4, 6, 8		
Widths			6', 10'		24', 48'		

	RIGID FRAME (RF)									
	Clear Span Standard Widths									
	20	24	28	32	36	40	50	60	70	80
Eave Heights	10	10	10	10	10	10	10			
	12	12	12	12	12	12	12	12		
	14	14	14	14	14	14	14	14	14	
						16	16	16	16	16
						20	20	20	20	20
						24	24	24	24	24

	Building		**Canopy**		**Width Extension**		
Bay lengths	18',20',21',24'		18',20',21',24'		18',20',21',24'		
Total length	Unlimited		Unlimited		Unlimited		
Roof slope	4 in 12		1 in 12		1 in 12		
Design loadings[1]	1, 2, 4, 6		2, 4, 6		2, 4, 6		
Widths			6', 10'		24', 48'		

[1]Key to design loadings:
 1 - Roof live load 10 psf or wind load 15 psf
 2 - Uniform Building Code
 4 - Southern Standard Building Code, Inland and Coastal
 6 - Roof live load 30 psf and wind load 20 psf
 8 - Roof live load 40 psf and wind load 20 psf
 Data are for buildings as manufactured by Butler Manufacturing Co.

is a hollow metal panel, completely insulated when manufactured. The type illustrated in Fig. 1255 is available in a variety of colors. The edge joint between the panels is a double tongue-and-groove with vinyl gaskets.

After the steel structure is erected, brick, stone or other conventional materials can be used for the exterior wall. See Fig. 1256. Since the total load of the structure is on the steel frame, the wall need only be self-supporting.

Build Your Vocabulary

Following are words that you should understand and use as a part of your working vocabulary. Write a brief explanation of what each means.

Compressive stress
Tensile stress
Shear stress
Bending stress
Kips
Vertical shear
Elastic limit
Yield point
Ultimate strength
Deformation
Deflection 522
Permanent set
Breaking point
Modulus of elasticity
Radius of gyration 524
Slenderness ratio

Problems for Study

1. A one-story structure is to have precast concrete columns having an unsupported length of 14'-0". The load on each column was computed to be 64 kips. What size round column

Fig. 1256. A small manufacturing building assembled from stock low-rigid frames, with stone and metal panels as exterior siding. (Butler Manufacturing Co.)

should be used? What is the weight per foot of this column? What size square, precast column should be used? What is the weight per foot of this column? Which column would seem to be the more economical? Explain.

2. A building requires a prestressed concrete *I*-beam to span 40'-0" in the clear. It must carry a superimposed load of 800 pounds per lineal foot. What beam should be used? What should be the depth and width of the beam? How many prestressed wires must be cast in the beam?

3. A rectangular, precast concrete beam is required to span 20 feet and carry a load of 1600 pounds per foot of beam. What beam would carry this load? What is the width and depth of this beam? What size reinforcing bars must be used?

4. Precast concrete *T*-joists are to be used to form the roof structure. They must span 24'-0" in the clear. The superimposed roof load is 285 pounds per lineal foot. What size joist must be used?

5. A roof is to be built of double-tee, precast roof decking. It must span 30'-0" in the clear. If the computed roof load is 40 pounds per lineal foot, what size decking unit should be used? What should be the width of the unit?

6. A roof is to be decked with precast concrete planks. The planks are to span 6'-0". The roof load is 70 pounds per square foot. What thickness plank must be used?

7. A building is to use a light-duty, precast concrete joist system. The floor is to be cast in place. Shoring at midspan is to be used during construction. The joist must span 16'-0" in the clear. The superimposed floor load is 110 pounds per square foot. What joist should be used? What size reinforcing bars should be used? How many stirrups are required, and what is the spacing between them? How far apart should the joists be spaced? How thick should the concrete floor slab be for this system?

If no shoring is used during construction, what size joist must be used?

8. A building is to use precast concrete Flexi-core units for floor and ceiling. The floor units span 12'-0" and the roof units, 22'-0". The floor loading is 150 pounds per square foot and the roof, 30 pounds per square foot. A 6" x 16" section is to be used. What are the stock units that should be used for each?

9. A round, extra-heavy steel column has an unbraced length of 12'-0". It must support a load of 85,000 pounds. What diameter

column must be used? What is the area of steel and concrete in the column?

10. A steel rod, 1½" in diameter, supports a tensile load of 20,000 pounds. Compute the tensile unit stress.

11. If the allowable tensile unit stress on a rod is 18,000 pounds per square inch and if the rod supports a load of 80,000 pounds, what must be its cross-sectional area? If the rod is rectangular with a thickness of ½ inch, what would be its width? If the rod is round, what diameter would be required?

12. If an 8 x 8 WF 35 beam has a load of 74,000 pounds imposed upon it, what is the vertical shear stress? Assume the load is uniformly placed and the beam is supported at each end.

   If the beam spans 12'-0", what is the allowable shear limit of the web? (Read from tables.) Is the shear stress greater than the shear limit of the web?

13. A ½-inch-diameter rivet resists a shearing stress of 5,000 pounds. Compute the shearing unit stress.

14. A 2-inch-diameter steel member (modulus of elasticity 29,000,000 pounds per square inch), 8 feet long, has an applied tensile load of 8,000 pounds. Compute the total deformation (elongation) in inches.

15. If an 8 x 8 WF 35 beam spans 15'-0" with a uniform load of 30,000 pounds, what is the actual deflection?

   What is the maximum permissible deflection in inches? Will this beam carry the assigned load without excess deflection?

16. A WF column must support a load of 200 kips. The unsupported length is 15'-0". Assume K to be 1.0. Select the appropriate column. Check the Y-Y axis.

17. A concrete roof slab, 3½ inches thick, is to be poured over a corrugated steel decking. The decking spans 5'-0" between joists. What form material should be used? If the steel decking has a 1 5/16-inch corrugation depth and the underside is exposed, what is the U factor (insulation factor) of the slab if it is of low-density concrete?

18. Long-span, steel roof decking (as manufactured by H. H. Robertson Co.) is used with a built-up roof covering. It spans 30'-0" in the clear with a stress not to exceed 8,000 psi. If it carries a load of 40 pounds per square foot, what stock decking should be used?

19. A building is to use corrugated, galvanized-steel panels for exterior siding. If the panels are to be 8'-0" high, what gauge steel is necessary? What is the maximum span for steel panels of this gauge if used for roof decking?

20. A roof is to be framed of wood bowstring trusses that must span 100'-0". What are the height and weight of the truss?

21. A church is to be built using three-hinged wood arches. They must span 60 feet, with a roof slope of 8 to 12. The wall height is 14'-0", and the vertical loading is 800 pounds per lineal foot of span. What is the depth increment of the arch frame?

22. A two-hinged wood arch must span 90'-0" and carry a load of 400 pounds per lineal foot of span. What are the rise and radius of the arch? What thickness of lamination is used in constructing this arch? What is the total horizontal thrust activated by this member?

23. A roof is to be framed with steel box-section subpurlins and wood-fiber roof decking. If the roof load is 40 pounds per square foot and if the spacing is 32 inches on center, what is the maximum span for these subpurlins?

   If the same roof is to be framed with three-span, steel bulb-tees, what is the maximum span allowed for the bulb-tee members?

Additional Reading

American Institute of Steel Construction, "Commentary on the AISC Specification." *Also:* "Manual of Steel Construction."

American Iron and Steel Institute, "Light Gage Cold-Formed Steel Design Manual."

Bethlehem Steel Company, "Structural Steel Shapes."

Gaylord, Edwin H., and Gaylord, C. N., *Design of Steel Structures.*

Kaylor, Harry, *Prestressed Concrete Simply Explained.*

"Manual of Standard Practice for Detailing Reinforced Concrete Structures", American Concrete Institute, Box 4754, Redford Station, Detroit, Michigan.

Orchard, Dennis E., *Concrete Technology* (2 vols.).

Parker, Harry, *Simplified Design of Structural Steel.*

———, *Simplified Engineering for Architects and Builders.*

Portland Cement Association, "Continuity in Concrete Building Frames;" "Handbook of Frame Constants;" "Precast Concrete Joists;" and "Tilt-Up Construction."

"Structural Joints Using ASTM A325 Bolts", American Institute of Steel Construction, 101 Park Avenue, New York, New York.

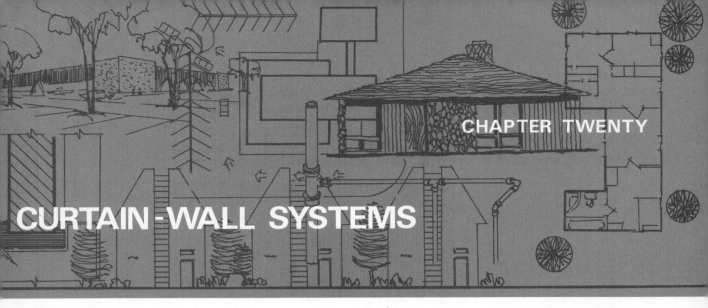

CURTAIN-WALL SYSTEMS

A curtain wall is a non-load-bearing wall erected on the exterior of a building to provide a barrier between the outer elements and the interior. More specifically, it is an entire enclosure element, which is complete with exterior finish, interior finish, insulation, structural independence and a means of attachment to a building. It is an engineered series of units designed for specified wind loads, structural requirements, insulating factors and expansion and contraction, together with weathertightness. A curtain wall provides all the advantages of a masonry wall, plus the advantages of speedier erection, lighter weight and better insulation. It has a long, maintenance-free life.

Curtain walls can be made of many materials. Combinations of extruded sections and insulation, patterned sheets, rigidized sheets, honeycombed panels, porcelain on aluminum or steel, or aluminum anodized sheets are used. The basic materials of aluminum, steel, stainless steel, bronze, cement-asbestos panels, plate glass and plastic panels are used. Other systems use precast concrete, glass blocks, and ceramic-tile panels.

Windows are a prime component of these walls and must be engineered as a part of the entire unit. Generally, it is recommended that the designer use the window units suggested by the manufacturer of the curtain-wall system to be used.

Porcelain-Enamel Curtain-Wall Systems

Porcelain enamel is a hard, durable, glass-like coating applied to a metal base and produced by fusing to the base a carefully compounded mixture of mineral substances such as cryolite, feldspar, quartz, borax, silica, tin and zirconium oxides and clays.

The panels are available in a wide array of permanent colors and are resistant to acid and severe abrasive action. They can be cleaned by a simple washing. They are so durable they can withstand severe atmospheric and climatic conditions. Another feature is their fireproof quality.

The porcelain-enamel, curtain wall is lightweight, thin, extremely weatherproof, and is easily framed. It is available in large sections, thus reducing the number of joints, and it is economical. These walls save an average of 6 inches in thickness at each wall. In a large building, this adds thousands of square feet of usable floor space. Since the wall is light in weight, the foundation and steel framing can be reduced. If the Empire State Building had been constructed with curtain walls, it could have been 13 stories higher with no weight increase.

The two types of metal panels used in porcelain-enamel, curtain-wall systems are steel and aluminum. Design details vary, depending upon the manufacturer; it is best to consult the catalogs of each supplier.

There are three types of porcelain-enamel panels in general use — the single-sheet panel, the laminated panel, and the mechanically assembled panel. See Fig. 1285.

Porcelain-enamel, curtain walls are classified into four types depending upon their appearance. These types are (1) *sheath*, in

567

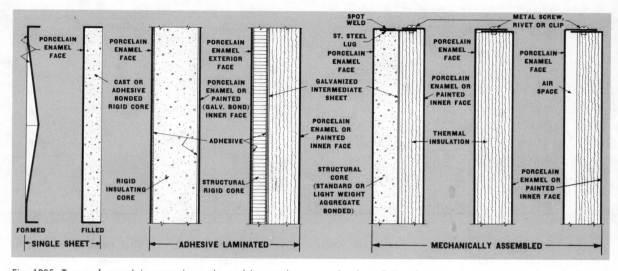

Fig. 1285. Types of porcelain-enamel panels used in curtain-wall construction.

Single-Sheet Panels: These are metal units which form the exterior face and provide the required weather barrier. A back-up material is used to supply thermal insulation and fire resistance or to meet code requirements. The panel and the back-up material together comprise the composite type of curtain-wall construction.

Laminated Panels: In a laminated panel, assembly of the components is accomplished by use of adhesives. Either flat or formed metal sheets or pans may be used.

Mechanically Assembled Panels: Exterior and interior components are fastened together by mechanical means. When the flanged pans are used back-to-back, they form a "box-type" panel with an interior space in which a variety of insulating materials may be held.

which no structural elements are indicated; (2) *grid,* in which an equal emphasis and expression of horizontal and vertical, structural elements is given; (3) *mullion,* in which vertical structural elements are emphasized; (4) *spandrel,* in which horizontal structural elements are emphasized.

Moisture within a panel system might adversely affect the insulating material or damage the framing or panel. It is necessary to control moisture that may enter the wall from either penetration or condensation. Several methods are used to permit this moisture to escape. One system provides vent holes at the bottom of the panel to allow for drainage. Another system provides a vented air space between the porcelain-enameled face and the insulation, thus venting the interior of the panel. This produces a chimney effect, and air movement allows the panel to breathe. See Fig. 1286.

Vapor barriers are necessary to prevent infiltration of moisture into the panel through the joints. These may be metal foil, paint or a plastic film placed on the warm side of the panel.

A Porcelain-Enamel-on-Aluminum Curtain-Wall System

Porcelain enamel over aluminum has been thoroughly tested in actual use for many years and has proven very satisfactory. While uncoated aluminum sheets are excellent for exterior use, the glass coating increases their resistance to abrasion and corrosion and lends rigidity and flexure resistance. In effect, the coated panel is stronger. With the use of vitreous coatings, a wide variety of colors and surface texture is obtainable.

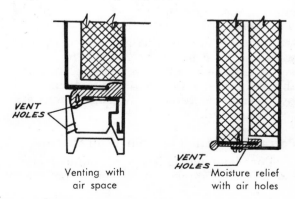

Venting with air space

Moisture relief with air holes

Fig. 1286. Methods of venting panels.

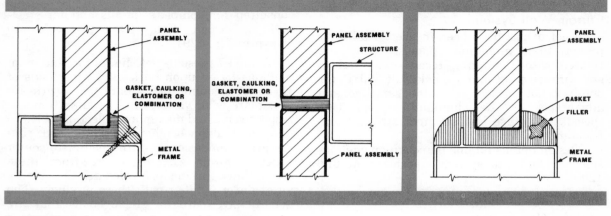

Fig. 1287. Typical ways of sealing porcelain-enamel panels.

After being coated, the panels can be sawed or drilled, with no spalling from the cut edge and with very little corrosion of the exposed metal. This allows on-the-job cutting when panels are fitted in difficult places.

The panels may be sealed with extruded, neoprene rubber or polyvinyl-chloride weatherproofing gaskets. These seals have a longer life than caulking and can be installed faster. Caulking and elastomer compositions are also extensively used. The latter type develops a strong adhesive bond to the porcelain-enamel surface and has great flexibility and elasticity. It also has a longer life than usual caulking compounds. See Fig. 1287.

Design Data

The following information pertains to an aluminum curtain-wall system as manufactured by Ceco Steel Products Corporation. Data are presented for single-story buildings only; manufacturer's catalogs should be consulted for complete details. Other companies manufacture competitive systems.

The installation details are typical of panel arrangements, ventilating areas, and fixed windows. These systems are based upon the stock aluminum windows manufactured by Ceco Steel Products Corporation. They have a wide variety of aluminum extrusions used as mullions and spandrels. Design data are given in this chapter. These, in combination with stock windows and porcelain-enamel panels, are fabricated into curtain-wall sections to suit the desire of the architect. Stock window sizes should be obtained from manufacturers' catalogs.

Details for projected windows and double-hung windows, as used in single-story buildings, are illustrated in Figs. 1288 and 1289.

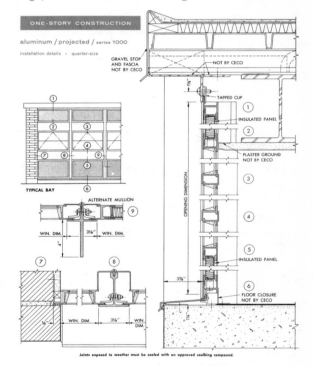

Fig. 1288. Detail of projected window installation. (Ceco Corp.)

In this single-story application, the curtain wall is anchored at head and sill. There is a drop ceiling, with an insulated panel covering structural members. This is standard window construction. Note the strong, simple mullion and cover (detail 8) and the alternate mullion (detail 9). Subsills may be simply applied to suit various masonry conditions. An insulated panel from floor to sill level conceals convectors, pipes, etc. from outside view.

A Porcelain-Enamel-on-Steel Curtain-Wall System

Steel panels have been in use for a longer period than aluminum panels. They are treated with Bonderite, receive one coat of gray primer paint and are baked at 300°F. for one-half hour. They have the same general advantages as the aluminum panels. One special advantage is their great strength and resistance to denting.

Design details for one porcelain-enamel-on-steel, curtain-wall system are shown in Fig. 1290.

Mullion Design Data for Porcelain-Enamel Curtain-Wall Systems

The data that follow are for mullions to be used in the design of aluminum curtain walls that are manufactured by the Ceco Cor-

poration. Manufacturer's catalogs should be consulted for complete details and for steel-mullion, design data. Typical details are shown in Fig. 1291.

Table 97 presents safe limits for aluminum mullions based upon horizontal wind loads of 15 and 20 pounds per square foot (with approximate wind velocities of 60 and 70 m.p.h. respectively) and maximum deflection of 1/175 of span. Mullion heights are established, conservative dimensions for the center-to-center widths shown. Any departure from these should have specific load calculations made by an engineer familiar with these products. The heights given are for single spans that are unsupported between anchorages. An increase in the limit of length can be made when full tubular mullions are continuous and anchored over two spans in the curtain wall.

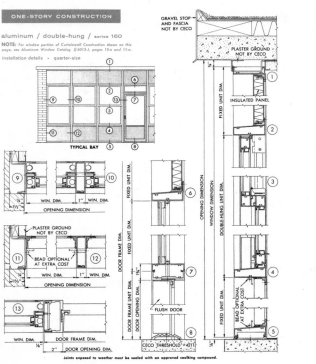

Fig. 1289. Detail of double-hung window installation. (Ceco Corp.)

Details of double-hung, intermediate-weight, aluminum windows are shown for typical curtain-wall construction for one-story and multistory buildings. Combinations of a double-hung and fixed windows may be used in almost any arrangement. Sleeving mullions are an integral part of each window; thus adjacent units are bolted together for fast, easy and low-cost installation.

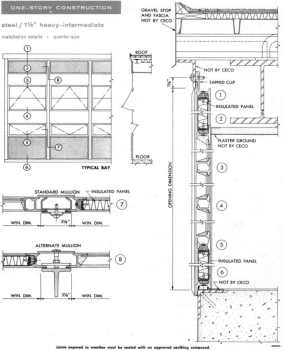

Fig. 1290. Design details of a porcelain-enamel-on-steel, curtain-wall system. (Ceco Corp.)

This is a single-story detail with 1½″, heavy-intermediate, steel sections featuring simple window construction and anchored head and sill. It is arranged to receive the insulated panel at the head and to conceal the structural steel. A drop ceiling returns to the window. The insulated panel at the sill conceals convectors, pipes, etc. from outside view.

Stainless-Steel Curtain Walls

Stainless-steel, curtain-wall panels are in use on all types of buildings from single-story structures to skyscrapers. See Fig. 1292. While single-thickness sheets of stainless steel have been applied as an outer covering on buildings, the most successful applications have occurred when laminated panels have been used. Several types are in use. These have a core made from mineral, vegetable, inorganic or plastic materials. The core is then faced on both sides with cement-asbestos panels, and a veneer of stainless steel is bonded to them. These panels are usually custom-fabricated and may vary in thickness from 11/16″ to 3″, depending upon the design requirements.

Another type of veneer panel consists of a stainless-steel veneer laminated to a cement-asbestos or hardboard veneer. A variation of this is a panel with a rubber-impregnated,

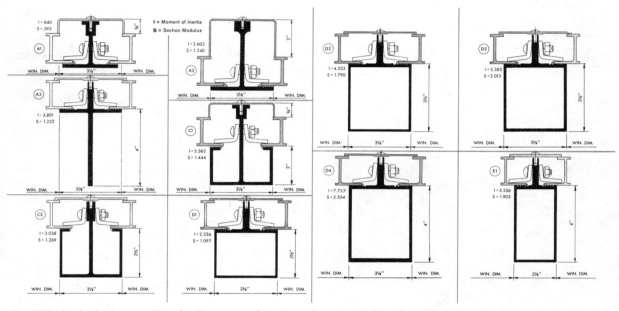

Fig. 1291. Stock aluminum mullion detail, moment of inertia and section modulus data. (Ceco Corp.)

Table 97
Safe Limits for Aluminum Mullions - Rectangular Loading

I = Moment of inertia.

S = Section modulus.

To select the mullion, ascertain the width and height of the curtain wall section being designed. From the table, determine the moment of inertia (I) and the section modulus (S) required. From the mullion detail (Fig. 1291), select the size with I and S factors of equal or greater capacity.

For example, a wall section 4'-0" wide and 10'-0" high, with a 15 psf wind load, has an I value of 1.912 and an S value of .844. An examination of Fig. 1291 reveals that mullion A2 would be satisfactory because the I factor of 2.602 and S factor of 1.240 are greater than those required. Mullion A1 has factors less than those indicated and is therefore not usable.

	Ht.	15 P.S.F. WIND LOAD									20 P.S.F. WIND LOAD														
W.		8'-0"	8'-6"	9'-0"	9'-6"	10'-0"	10'-6"	11'-0"	11'-6"	12'-0"	8'-0"	8'-6"	9'-0"	9'-6"	10'-0"	10'-6"	11'-0"	11'-6"	12'-0"	12'-6"	13'-0"	13'-6"	14'-0"	14'-6"	15'-0"
3'-6" I		.856	1.027	1.220	1.434	1.674	1.937	2.227	2.544	2.891	1.141	1.369	1.625	1.911	2.229	2.580	2.967	3.390	3.852	4.353	4.897	5.484	6.116	6.795	7.523
S		.473	.533	.598	.666	.738	.814	.893	.977	1.063	.631	.713	.799	.891	.987	1.087	1.194	1.304	1.422	1.542	1.667	1.798	1.934	2.074	2.220
3'-9" I		.916	1.099	1.304	1.534	1.790	2.072	2.382	2.722	3.093	1.218	1.461	1.735	2.040	2.380	2.755	3.167	3.619	4.112	4.648	5.228	5.855	6.530	7.255	8.032
S		.506	.571	.640	.713	.791	.872	.957	1.046	1.139	.676	.763	.856	.953	1.057	1.165	1.278	1.397	1.522	1.651	1.786	1.926	2.071	2.222	2.378
4'-0" I		.979	1.174	1.394	1.639	1.912	2.213	2.545	2.908	3.304	1.304	1.565	1.857	2.184	2.548	2.950	3.391	3.875	4.403	4.976	5.598	6.269	6.992	7.768	8.599
S		.540	.610	.684	.762	.844	.930	1.021	1.116	1.215	.722	.815	.913	1.018	1.127	1.243	1.365	1.491	1.624	1.762	1.906	2.055	2.210	2.371	2.537
4'-6" I		1.101	1.321	1.568	1.844	2.151	2.490	2.863	3.271	3.717	1.467	1.760	2.089	2.457	2.866	3.318	3.815	4.359	4.952	5.598	6.297	7.051	7.864	8.737	9.673
S		.608	.686	.769	.857	.949	1.047	1.149	1.256	1.367	.812	.916	1.027	1.145	1.269	1.398	1.535	1.678	1.827	1.982	2.144	2.312	2.487	2.667	2.854
5'-0" I		1.224	1.468	1.742	2.049	2.390	2.767	3.181	3.635	4.130	1.631	1.956	2.322	2.731	3.185	3.687	4.239	4.844	5.504	6.221	6.997	7.836	8.740	9.709	10.749
S		.675	.762	.854	.952	1.055	1.163	1.276	1.395	1.519	.902	1.018	1.142	1.272	1.410	1.553	1.706	1.864	2.030	2.203	2.382	2.569	2.767	2.963	3.172

Courtesy Ceco Corp.

cork-fiber core. This permits the panel to be bent around columns where a radius is needed. This radius can be as small as 6 inches. See Fig. 1293.

The stainless steel most commonly used in curtain-wall construction is of the austenitic type. It is nonmagnetic and has chromium (approximately 17 to 19 percent) and nickel (approximately 8 to 10 percent) as the major alloying elements. This type of stainless steel is not heat-treated and hardens with age.

Surface finishes range from a coarse mill to a highly polished surface. The most popular finish is a dull, satin surface.

The following designations are used to indicate surface finish:

No. 2D — Dull cold rolled, full finished. Gives a nonreflective effect.

No. 2B — Bright cold rolled, full finished. Brighter than 2D, but does not have the high luster of a polished finish.

No. 4 — Polished. Bright finish with good luster.

No. 2D — Architectural. Dull cold rolled as 2D, but is finish rolled through special rolls to produce a matt finish.

No. 6 — Polished and tampico brushed. Is a fine, soft finish with low reflectivity.

Some types of stainless-steel panels can be field cut with a special power saw. Others require expensive cutting operations or must be returned to the factory to be cut.

Stainless steel requires no surface treatment, since it resists corrosion. It can be used in direct contact with brick, stone, or ceramics, since it is not affected by the alkalies and caustics in lime and mortar. Because it has a high tensile strength, it can be used in thinner gauges than other metals. Due to its mechanical properties, it can be stamped, deep-drawn, press-braked or roll-formed into almost any design desired, thus allowing the architect great freedom of expression.

Mullions of stainless steel have the same long-wearing, lightweight qualities as the panels. They are frequently used with such panel types as porcelain enamel, as well as with stainless steel.

Copper and Copper-Alloy Curtain-Wall System

Copper and bronze curtain-wall panels, available in a variety of forms and shapes, exhibit all the desirable characteristics of other metal curtain-wall systems. They vary in color from bright red and yellow through dark brown and ebony. There are five archi-

Fig. 1292. Four Gateway Center, a building using stainless-steel panels and mullions. (Crucible Steel Company of America)

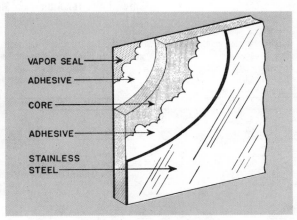

Fig. 1293. A laminated, stainless-steel, curtain-wall panel. (Mirawal Division, Birdsboro Corp.)

tectural metals of this type in use — Copper, Red Brass, Architectural Bronze, Yellow Brass and Nickel Silver.

They are available in the grid-type system, as discussed for the other metal panels. The mullions are extruded of the copper or copper alloy to be used. Exact design details vary from the other systems, and manufacturers' catalogs should be consulted.

Steel Wall Panels

Data concerning steel wall panels are presented in Chapter 19, along with steel roof-decking systems.

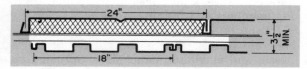

Fig. 1294. A typical aluminum curtain-wall panel.

Fig. 1295. A building utilizing translucent plastic curtain walls. These walls admit a diffused, natural light. (Panel Structures, Inc.)

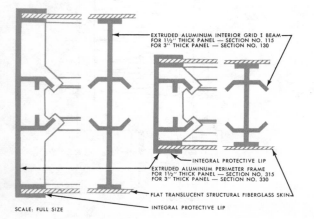

Fig. 1296. A section through translucent fiber glass, plastic-skin curtain-wall panel bonded to an extruded aluminum frame and gridwork. (Panel Structures, Inc.)

Aluminum Wall Panels

Aluminum wall panels are available in a wide variety of stamped designs. They are backed, as are steel panels, with an insulation material such as fiber glass. One such panel is illustrated in Fig. 1294. They have excellent insulation qualities, and the aluminum face requires no painting, thus eliminating maintenance costs.

The stock lengths vary, depending upon the type of panel, but range up to 30'-0".

Translucent Plastic Curtain-Wall Panels

The translucent plastic, curtain-wall panel is a structural sandwich fabricated of two skins of glass fiber-reinforced, polyester plastic, laminated to an extruded aluminum grid-work core. Permanent lamination is accomplished by means of a rubber-based adhesive, which is activated by heat and pressure.

These panels offer full translucency with a wide range of color skins and color inserts. They admit an evenly diffused, natural light. See Fig. 1295.

They are available in several types; manufacturers' catalogs should be consulted for specific details. They also are available in 48-inch widths and in lengths of 8, 10, 12 and 20 feet. The standard thicknesses of the panels are 1½ and 3 inches. The standard skin is 2-ounce, glass fiber-reinforced, polyester plastic; however, heavier skins are available.

Fig. 1296 illustrates a section through a typical panel.

Cement-Asbestos Curtain-Wall Panels

Cement-asbestos, curtain-wall panels are manufactured with a stable, unicellular, plastic insulation core. The cement-asbestos skins are adhered with epoxy resin to this core. See Fig. 1297. While the thickness of panels varies, Table 98 illustrates data for the panel most commonly used for exterior, curtain-wall construction. This panel is faced with a .018-inch, polyester, glass fiber cloth face over the

Table 98
Design Data for Cement-Asbestos Curtain-Wall Panels

Thickness (inches)	"U" Factor	Weight (lbs./sq. ft.)	Maximum Bending Moment (inch pounds)
1¼	.24	2.9	723
2¼	.12	3.07	1410

Table 99
Design Data for Ceramic-Tiled Curtain-Wall Panels Over Insulated Concrete Units

Panel Thickness	COMPONENT THICKNESSES				Wgt. p.s.f.	U Value	Maximum Area Sq. Ft.	Maximum Length Lin. Ft.
	Insulation	Concrete		Tile				
		Inner	Outer					
1¾"	1"	¼"	¼"	¼"	9.0	.28	12	4
2"	1¼"	¼"	¼"	¼"	9.5	.25	15	5
2¼"	1½"	¼"	¼"	¼"	10.0	.20	20	5
2"	1"	⅜"	⅜"	¼"	14.0	.27	32	8
2½"	1½"	⅜"	⅜"	¼"	16.0	.18	40	8
3"	2"	⅜"	⅜"	¼"	18.0	.16	50	10
3¼"	1"	1"	1"	¼"	25.0	.25	72	12

Courtesy Ceramic Tile Panels, Inc.

cement-asbestos board. These panels are available in a wide range of colors and in sizes up to 4'-0" by 12'-0".

Ceramic-Tile-Faced Curtain-Wall Panels

Curtain-wall panels faced with ceramic tile are available in two types — tile over a cast concrete panel and tile over a metal sandwich core.

The ceramic-tile facing is grouted with a specially formulated, weatherproof, flexible latex grout. The tile is self-cleaning, requires no maintenance and has a low-reflective surface.

Fig. 1298 illustrates a section through a tile-on-concrete panel. The panel has a rigid-insulation core. A ⅛-inch clearance should be allowed between all edges of the panel, framing members and framing stops.

Table 99 gives design data for the tile-over-concrete panels. Notice the variety of thicknesses and maximum panel sizes. Special sizes and shapes can be manufactured to suit the designs of the architect.

Tile-faced, curtain-wall panels over a metal skin are available in a wide range of sizes and thicknesses. Design data are presented in Table 100.

The metal skins are either aluminum or galvanized steel, bonded to a rigid insulation

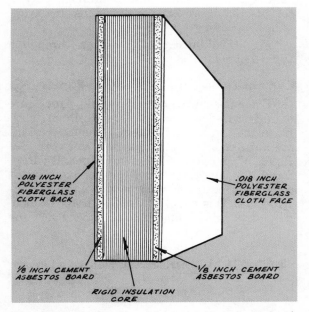

.018 INCH POLYESTER FIBERGLASS CLOTH BACK

.018 INCH POLYESTER FIBERGLASS CLOTH FACE

⅛ INCH CEMENT ASBESTOS BOARD

⅛ INCH CEMENT ASBESTOS BOARD

RIGID INSULATION CORE

Fig. 1297. A typical cement-asbestos curtain-wall panel with polyester fiber glass cloth face.

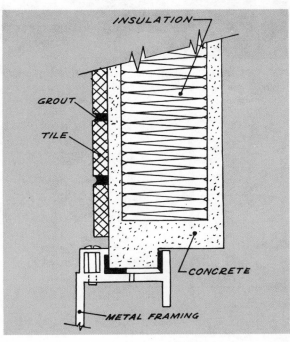

INSULATION

GROUT

TILE

CONCRETE

METAL FRAMING

Fig. 1298. A section through a reinforced concrete panel with a ceramic-tile facing. The interior of the panel is filled with a rigid insulation. (Ceramic Tile Panels, Inc.)

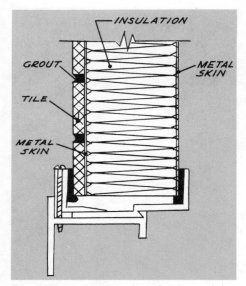

Fig. 1299. A section through a metal-skin panel with ceramic-tile facing. (Ceramic Tile Panels, Inc.)

Fig. 1300. A two-story building with glass curtain walls. The horizontal and vertical framing members are extruded aluminum with clear glass window panels and heat-strengthened, colored glass spandrels. (Libbey-Owens-Ford Glass Co.)

core. The tile is bonded to the metal skin. To prevent delamination of the panels due to humidity, temperature variation, aging or chemical attack, a resilient, moisture-resistant adhesive is used to adhere the skin to the core. Moisture penetration will not affect the insulation, because the rigid insulation will not absorb it. Flexible, weatherproof grout is used between the exterior tiles. Fig. 1299 illustrates a typical section through this type of panel. The tile may be adhered to one or both sides, thus providing an attractive, tiled, interior surface as well as a tiled exterior surface. Manufacturers' catalogs should be consulted for complete design details.

Table 100
Design Data for Ceramic-Tiled Curtain-Wall Panels Over Insulated Metal Panels

Panel Thickness	Insulation Thickness	Tile Thickness	WT psf	"U" Value		Max. Size
				Styrofoam	Paper Honeycomb	
1⅜"	1"	¼"	6.6	.20	.27	4' x 8'
1⅞"	1½"	¼"	6.6	.15	.22	4' x 12'
2⅜"	2"	¼"	6.7	.11	.19	4' x 12'
2⅞"	2½"	¼"	6.7	.09	.17	4' x 12'
3⅜"	3"	¼"	6.8	.08	.16	4' x 12'

Courtesy Ceramic Tile Panels, Inc.

Glass Curtain-Wall Panels

Glass curtain walls are made in many ways. One frequently used system uses ¼-inch clear plate glass panels for wall areas where it is desired to see outside the building and makes the opaque spandrels from ¼-inch heat-strengthened, polished plate glass with ceramic color fire-fused on the back surface of the glass. This becomes an integral part of the glass panel. The color is sun-fast, and the panel resists weathering, crazing and checking, exactly the same as clear, plate glass does.

Glass curtain walls have the same advantages as mentioned for porcelain-enamel and stainless-steel curtain-wall systems.

The opaque, glass panels are available in a wide variety of colors, permitting considerable variety of architectural expression. They are nonporous and nonabsorbent and resist most atmospheric acids and temperature changes.

The heat-strengthened panels are twice as strong and three times as resistant to thermal shock as ordinary plate glass.

The standard maximum size for these panels is 48 inches by 84 inches. On special order, they can be as large as 60 inches by 84 inches.

The panels are usually set in metal mullions and sealed with caulking or neoprene gaskets. The glass panel should have a ¼-inch clearance on all edges from the mullion to provide space for expansion.

It is necessary to provide a system of ventilation in the space between the back of the glass panel and insulating material. Usually, perforations are made in the horizontal members of the curtain-wall framing, to provide for drainage and ventilation in the spandrel area. Fig. 1300 illustrates a building with glass curtain walls.

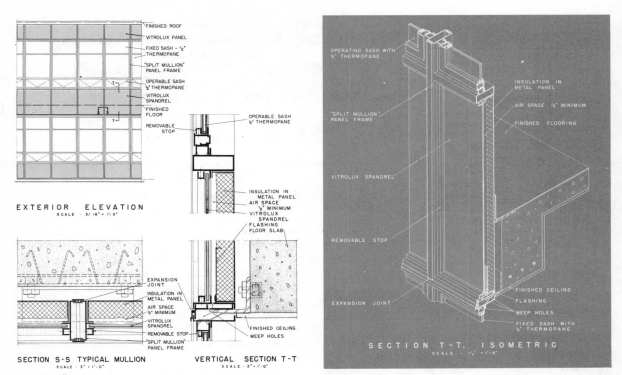

Fig. 1301. Details of one glass curtain-wall installation. (Libbey-Owens-Ford Glass Co.)

Fig. 1301 illustrates a typical detail of a glass curtain-wall installation. Numerous methods of construction are in use, and manufacturers' catalogs should be consulted for full details.

In Fig. 1301, notice the use of metal panel frames and how the glass spandrels and clear glass windows are set into this frame. Also notice that a ½-inch air space is maintained between the glass panels and the insulation. "Weep holes" are provided in the frame to drain condensation.

Glass-Block Curtain Walls

A wide selection of glass-block units for use in curtain-wall construction is available. These units are supplied in many sculptured and intaglio forms and in a variety of colors. They provide a wall that is low in maintenance cost, low in surface condensation, and high in insulation values. They can admit sunlight while excluding hot rays.

Since a wide array of shapes, colors and sculptured surfaces is available, design opportunities are great.

Standard glass blocks are available in a number of stock sizes. These are commonly

Table 101
Heat Transmission "U" Values of Glass Blocks

Glass Block Size and Type	"U" (Btu./hr./sq.ft./°F.)
6" square — single cavity	0.60
8" square — single cavity	0.56
8" square — double cavity	0.48
12" square — single cavity	0.52
12" square — double cavity	0.44
4" x 12" — single cavity	0.60
4" x 12" — double cavity	0.52

Courtesy Pittsburgh Corning Corporation

6, 8 and 12 inches square and a 4 x 12 inch unit. Some are available with one dead air space inside, while others have two such spaces. The blocks are formed by fusing two sections of pressed glass together at elevated temperatures. The colored blocks have a fired-on, ceramic enamel coating on one face.

The thermal insulation values of these blocks are shown in Table 101. Their average sound reduction is 38.0 decibels.

The compressive strength of glass blocks, when uniformly loaded, is 400 to 600 pounds per square inch. While this is higher than many masonry constructions, these blocks are not used for load-bearing walls.

Fig. 1302. Curtain walls formed from 4″ x 8″ oval and 8″ x 8″ hourglass intaglio glass blocks. This building is a library. (Pittsburgh Corning Corp.)

Fig. 1304. Interior view of glass-block curtain wall illustrated in Fig. 1305. (Pittsburgh Corning Corp.)

Fig. 1303. A curtain wall built of sculptured glass blocks. These units are hollow and have the design on both faces. While the blocks are colored, they remain translucent. (Pittsburgh Corning Corp.)

Fig. 1305. Exterior view of curtain wall made from clear glass blocks, set in terra cotta framing to light the public foyer of a county courthouse. The glass blocks have fire-polished faces to allow vision through them. They are 4 inches thick, with a hollow interior being at a partial vacuum. They have an insulating value equivalent to an 8-inch mansonry wall. (Pittsburgh Corning Corp.)

Intaglio glass blocks are pressed, all-glass units in which the outer surfaces of each unit provide molded, translucent patterns, masked in a ceramic frit. They are available in 4″ x 8″ and 8″ x 8″ units.

These units provide the same advantages as the regular glass blocks and are installed in the same manner.

Two of the stock units are shown in Fig. 1302. The curtain walls are a combination of oval and hourglass units.

Also available are sculptured glass blocks. These are used, as are other glass blocks, for interior and exterior walls. They offer light transmission and insulation values.

The patterns in these units are pressed about 1½ inches into the surface on both sides. They are available in a variety of colors. The color is weather-resistant and withstands scratches and abrasives almost as well as the basic glass to which it is fused.

Fig. 1303 illustrates a curtain wall built of sculptured glass blocks.

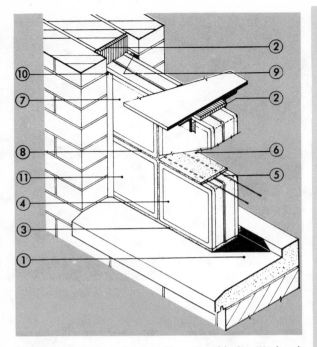

Fig. 1306. Procedure for installing glass blocks. (Pittsburgh Corning Corp.)

1. Check that sill area to be covered by mortar has a heavy coat of asphalt emulsion.

2. Adhere expansion strips to jambs and head with asphalt emulsion. Make sure expansion strip extends to sill.

3. When emulsion on sill is dry, place full mortar bed joint — do not furrow.

4. Set lower course of block. All mortar joints must be full and not furrowed. Steel tools must not be used to tap blocks into position.

5. Install panel reinforcements in horizontal joints where joints were required as follows:
   a. Place lower half of mortar bed joint. Do not furrow.
   b. Press panel reinforcement into place.
   c. Cover panel reinforcement with upper half of mortar bed and trowel smooth. Do not furrow.
   d. Panel reinforcement must run from end to end of panels and, where used continuously, must lap 6 inches. Reinforcement must not bridge expansion joints.

6. Place full mortar bed for joints not requiring panel reinforcement. Do not furrow.

7. Follow above instructions for getting succeeding courses of blocks.

8. Strike joints smoothly while mortar is still plastic and before final set. At this time, rake out all spaces requiring caulking to a depth equal to the width of the space. Remove surplus mortar from faces of glass blocks and wipe dry. Before mortar takes final set, tool joints smooth and concave.

9. After mortar sets, pack oakum tightly between glass-block panel and jamb and head construction. Leave space for caulking.

10. Caulk panels as indicated on details.

11. Final cleaning of glass-block faces should not be done until after final mortar set.

Glass blocks can be cast in frames made from other materials. Figs. 1304 and 1305 illustrate blocks cast in a terra cotta frame.

When large wall sections are to be built of glass blocks, expansion strips are necessary. Manufacturer's recommendations should be followed.

The glass-block panels require a reinforcement of galvanized-steel, double-wire mesh. This reinforcement should be embedded in the horizontal mortar joints on approximately 24-inch centers and in joints above and below all openings within the panel. The reinforcement should run continuously from end to end of the panels and should be lapped at least 6 inches when it is necessary to use more than one length in a joint. Expansion joints should not be bridged with reinforcement.

The panels are anchored to the walls or masonry columns with perforated, steel-panel anchor strips, 24 inches long and 1¾ inches wide. They should be crimped with expansion joints, so movement is possible. Usually, the panel anchors are placed 24 inches apart and in the same mortar joint as the wire-mesh, panel reinforcement.

The glass blocks are set in portland cement that has a waterproof ingredient added.

The blocks are cushioned at jambs, heads and intermediate supports with oakum. Caulking should be a waterproof mastic. Installation details are shown in Fig. 1306.

Details concerning installation vary from manufacturer to manufacturer and depend upon the type of building structure. Fig. 1307 illustrates some common construction details. Manufacturers' catalogs should be consulted for complete construction information.

Precast Concrete Facing and Curtain-Wall Panels

Precast panels are available in a wide variety of sizes and surfaces. Manufacturers' catalogs should be consulted for information on these many kinds.

Precast facing units are most economically cast in sizes from 20 to 60 square feet and in

2-inch thicknesses. Larger units can be cast, if the thickness is increased according to steel-reinforcement requirements. While the weight varies according to the type of panel, 25 pounds per square foot is a common design weight for 2-inch thick panels. Exact weights must be ascertained from manufacturers' catalogs.

These panels are cast in mold boxes and are reinforced with welded, galvanized, wire mesh. The crushed aggregate, cement and reinforcing mesh are compacted in the mold box with high-frequency vibrations to assure good bond and maximum strength and density.

The panels are designed for placement in a vertical position and must be stored, transported and handled in this position. Fig. 1308 illustrates ways of handling these panels for low structures.

The panels can be mechanically fastened to a steel or wood frame or to a masonry wall. They may also be used as forms against which

a masonry wall can be cast. Special fastening devices are manufactured to provide this connection. See Fig. 1309.

Precast curtain-wall units are available with built-in insulation. Lightweight insulation concrete can be cast as a core of the unit, or various types of rigid insulation can be cast in the slab. See Fig. 1310.

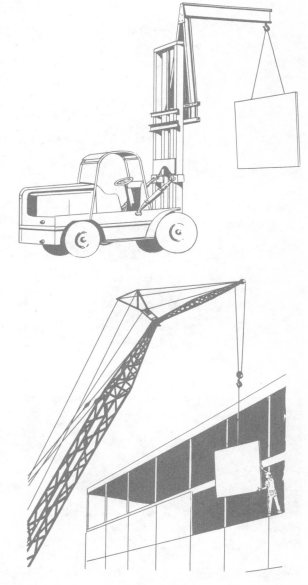

Fig. 1308. Methods of handling precast concrete facing and curtain-wall panels. (The George Rockle and Sons Co.)

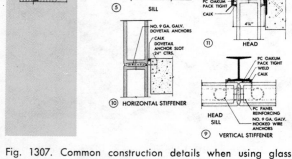

Fig. 1307. Common construction details when using glass block. (Pittsburgh Corning Corp.)

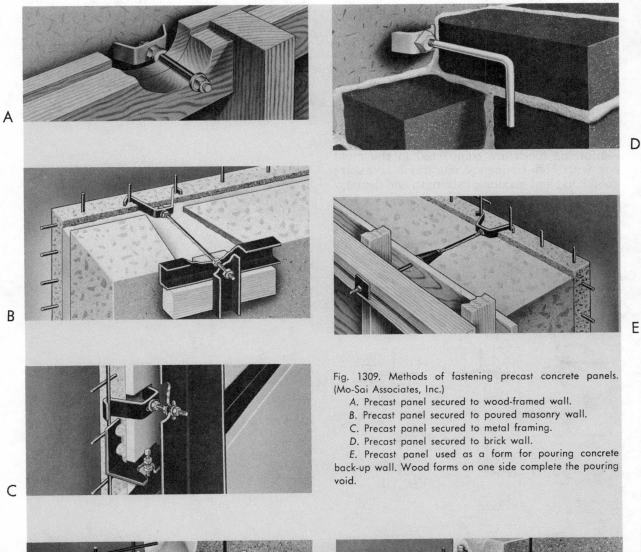

Fig. 1309. Methods of fastening precast concrete panels. (Mo-Sai Associates, Inc.)

    A. Precast panel secured to wood-framed wall.

    B. Precast panel secured to poured masonry wall.

    C. Precast panel secured to metal framing.

    D. Precast panel secured to brick wall.

    E. Precast panel used as a form for pouring concrete back-up wall. Wood forms on one side complete the pouring void.

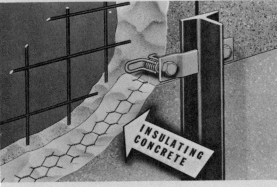

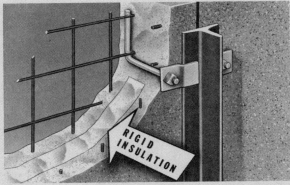

Fig. 1310. Insulating precast concrete curtain walls. (Mo-Sai Associates, Inc.)

    A. Precast panel with insulating concrete back-up and metal back strip.

    B. Precast panel with sandwich-style, rigid insulation and metal back strip.

Build Your Vocabulary

Following are words that you should understand and use as a part of your working vocabulary. Write out a brief explanation of what each means.

Curtain wall
Expansion joints
Caulking
Unicellular plastic core
Anodizing
Grid system
Glass fiber panels
Mullion
Grout

Class Activities

1. Explore your community and find commercial buildings using curtain-wall construction. Prepare a report giving the street address and name of the company occupying the building and identify the type of curtain-wall system used. Find as many different kinds as possible.

2. Examine manufacturers' catalogs and compile a list of companies manufacturing the various curtain-wall systems.

WORKING DRAWINGS FOR SMALL COMMERCIAL BUILDINGS

The complete set of drawings for a small commercial building represents the work of a team of specialists. The original planning and design are done by an architect who spends considerable time in conferences with his clients. The architect must first ascertain exactly what functions are to be performed in the building; then he must plan the interior arrangement and finally design a shell to enclose the required activities. For small structures, he may do the structural, mechanical, and electrical design. For larger buildings, he often relies upon engineers to design these systems. These tasks usually are assigned to a firm of consulting engineers.

A detailed set of specifications is written to accompany the information given on the working drawings. Usually this is written by specialists in this field. For small buildings, the architect may use a standard specification form and supplement it with specifics for the building under consideration.

Since the working drawings usually involve a large number of sheets and many type-written pages of specifications, it is not possible to present a complete set in this text. Complete sets of plans and specifications, for classroom use, frequently can be obtained from architectural firms. Careful examination of these will reveal the many necessary layouts and details.

Placement of Drawings on the Sheets

While the placement of the various drawings and details on sheets varies, an attempt should be made to keep related parts together.

The following is only a suggested plan to illustrate this point.

Sheet 1 — plot plan; roof plan; list of abbreviations; section symbols; material indications; index of drawings; and sections and details of miscellaneous items such as stairs, curbing, and parking area drains.

Sheet 2 — Basement plan; floor plans; door and window schedule; room finish schedule; details of door and window framing, such as mullions and jambs; door and window elevations; cabinets; elevations; sections; and details.

Sheet 3 — Exterior elevations; sections through the building; construction details such as cornice sections and structural framing details.

Sheet 4 — Construction details such as: wall sections; sections through the entire

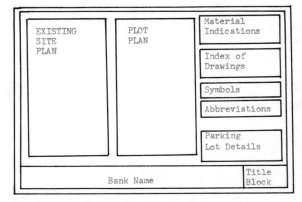

Fig. 1318. Layout of Sheet 1 of bank plans.

building; roof sections; window sections; cornice details; structural details such as steel framing, concrete columns and beams, and wood structural members; foundation plan.

Sheet 5 — Roof framing plan; floor framing plan; other construction details needed; beam schedule; column schedule.

Sheets 6 and 7 — Heating, air-conditioning, and plumbing layout; details of heating

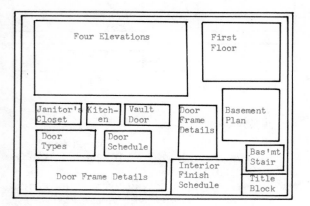

Fig. 1319. Layout of Sheet 2 of bank plans.

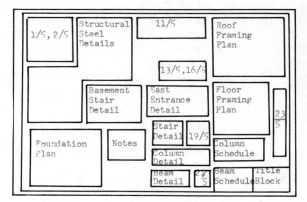

Fig. 1322. Layout of Sheet 5 of bank plans.

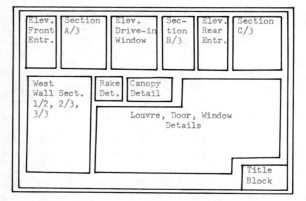

Fig. 1320. Layout of Sheet 3 of bank plans.

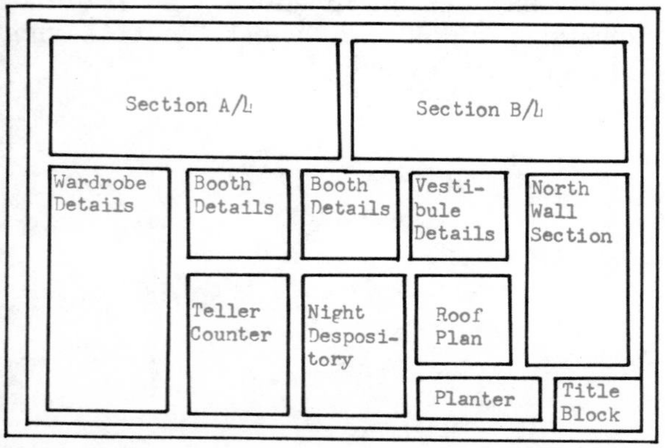

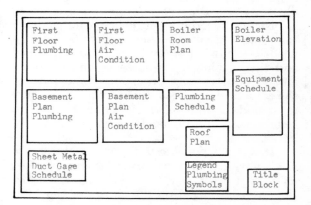

Fig. 1323. Layout of Sheet M-1 of bank plans.

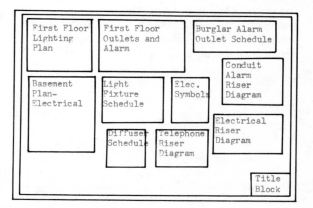

Fig. 1321. Layout of Sheet 4 of bank plans.

Fig. 1324. Layout of Sheet E-1 of bank plans.

and plumbing connections, duct connections, water heater connection, furnace elevations, and furnace room layout. (Also referred to as M-1, M-2, etc.)

Sheet 8 — Electrical plan, light fixture schedule, and electrical symbols. (Also referred to as E-1.)

The title block is placed in the lower right corner of each sheet. While the exact layout will vary, a typical example is shown in Fig. 1325.

The most frequently used sheet size is 24 inches by 36 inches. A ½-inch border is common.

A Set of Working Drawings

The drawings that follow were selected from a set of drawings for a building to house a branch of a large bank. The design was done by architects and engineers of Louis C. Kingscott and Associates, Kalamazoo, Michigan. Since the quantity of details is numerous, it is not possible to show them all. Those shown illustrate the type of information presented. Decisions concerning details must be made as the building is designed. Details usually needed are window and door heads, jambs and sills, cabinets, stairs, eaves and cornices, and structural connections. If some part of the structure can be clarified by a detail, then it should be drawn. Everything about the structure should be set forth in an elevation, detail, or note.

It was not possible to reproduce the sheets as they were drawn, because of their size. Figs. 1318-1324 show the manner in which the drawings were arranged on the sheets of the total set of plans.

Note the coding: Detail 12/5 is Detail Number 12 found on Sheet 5. Since the scale for each detail may vary, the actual scale must be shown by each drawing. (The drawings presented are reduced for use in this text, so the indicated scale is for illustrative purposes only.)

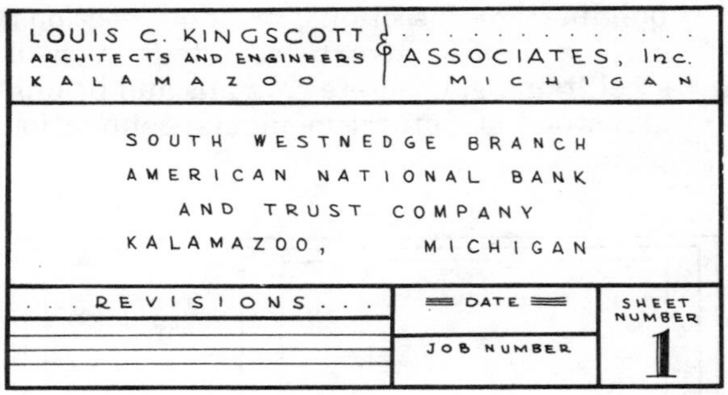

Fig. 1325. Title block.

Details of Sheet 1

The plot plan (Fig. 1326) gives the location of the building, drive and parking areas, sidewalks, curbs, sewers, gas, water and electrical lines, parking layout, grade lines, and lawns. It also indicates who is responsible for providing the various services. Notice that the power company is to furnish service to a pole east of the building and that the electrical contractor is to provide underground electrical and telephone conduit to the building. Also shown are existing utilities, such as the 8-inch gas main in the street at the front of the building.

The grades shown on the parking area indicate it slopes toward the building and is below the lawn area surrounding it.

Details concerning curbing, catch basins, and storm sewers for removing water from the parking area are included on the original drawings. A detail illustrating the construction of the curbs and retaining walls is shown in Fig. 1327. See section 1/1 indication on the plot plan.

Also included on Sheet 1 are the material indications, index of drawings, symbols, and a list of abbreviations.

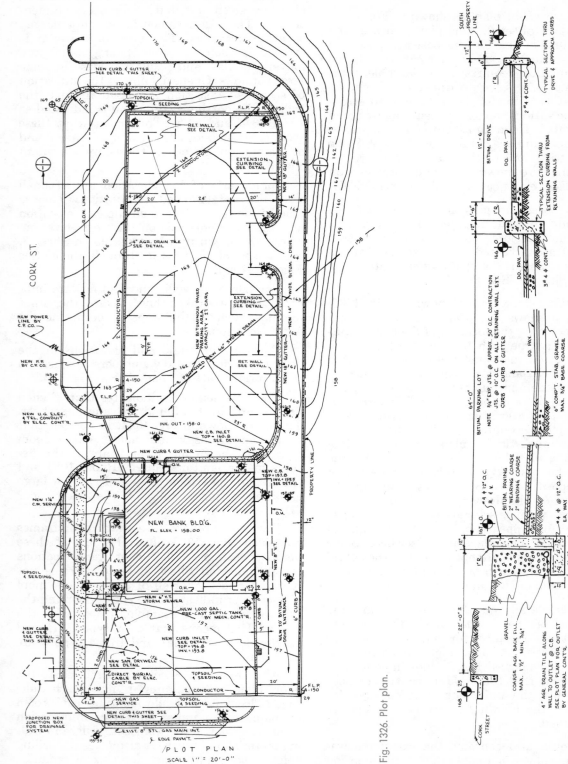

Fig. 1326. Plot plan.

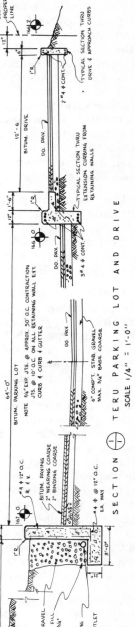

Fig. 1327. Section through parking lot and drive.

Details of Sheet 2

The basement plan, as shown in Fig. 1329, was part of Sheet 2. This plan indicates the overall dimensions for the basement, as well as the location for the interior partition. Since the foundation requires a considerable number of notes, a separate drawing is included on Sheet 5, with details pertaining to structure. The various rooms are identified by name and number. Doors are identified by a standard symbol and are detailed on Sheet 2. Since the electrical and mechanical systems are detailed, they are shown as separate drawings on Sheets E-1 (electrical) and M-1 (mechanical).

The basement plan includes dimensions pertaining to wall thickness and room size. The various fixtures (in this case, rest room fixtures) are indicated. The cafeteria contains a kitchen. This is detailed as a separate drawing on Sheet 2. See Fig. 1334.

The first-floor plan is shown in Fig. 1330. This plan shows the overall exterior dimensions, including the location of doors and windows. As is true with the basement plan, the electrical and mechanical systems are shown on Sheets E-1 and M-1. The rooms are identified by name and number, and their sizes are given. Of special importance to this particular building is the location of the fixtures, such as the tellers' counters, work counters, counter in the vestibule, planter boxes, railing separating the bank offices' area, and the private booths for individual examination of safe deposit boxes. Since these can only be indicated on the drawing, elevations and sections are shown as separate details on Sheet 4. These could appear on Sheet 2, but lack of space forced their placement elsewhere. Since the fixture details are not related to the actual room sizes, they can be placed on later sheets with no lack of continuity.

Other details on the floor plan are the elevation of the finished floor, the recessed areas at the entrances for mats, and the type of finished floor. The night depository is located and marked N.I.C. (not in contract). This means that the building contractor does not supply the unit, but is responsible for preparing the building to receive the unit to be installed.

Sheet 2 also contains the exterior elevations, as shown in Fig. 1331. An examination of these reveals that major overall dimensions are given, but that no details are dimensioned. These are dimensioned on enlarged separate drawings. The type of material is indicated, such as stone facing, aluminum louvers, fascias, and insulating glass in some large windows. Of special note is the indication of sections. A section is passed through the wall on the north elevation and is indicated as 22/4, 23/4 and 24/4. This means that these sections (numbers 22, 23, and 24) are found as details on Sheet 4. These are shown in Fig. 1332.

Some parts of the elevation are so small that the details need elaboration. This is true of the rear entrance on the east elevation and the front entrance on the west elevation. These are drawn to a larger scale on Sheet 3, and a section is passed through them. See Figs. 1337 and 1339.

The basement walls and footings are indicated with a broken line, as are the other footings, such as the stepped footing on the north elevation.

The door schedule and elevations of the door types and the key numbers assigned to them form a part of Sheet 2. See Fig. 1335.

The basement plan indicates that kitchen details are to be found on another sheet. These are shown in Fig. 1334. It was felt that simple elevations would suffice. Other room elevations shown on Sheet 2 are of the fixtures in the janitor's closet (Room 108) and the rest rooms (Rooms B-4 and B-5). A large elevation giving details of the vault door (D/6) also is included.

Sections through the various door frames are given. Fig. 1333 illustrates one of these detailed sections. Other door frame sections are included on Sheet 3, since there is not room on Sheet 2 for all of these. The symbol at each door indicates the type of door and the type of frame. For example, a door with the symbol H/3 means that door type H (found on the door schedule) and frame type 3 are used here.

Also shown on Sheet 2 and related to the floor plan is the interior finish schedule, Fig. 1336. This schedule identifies each room by name and number and gives information about the floor, base, wainscot, wall, and ceiling material and finish. It also gives the ceiling height and allows space for special remarks.

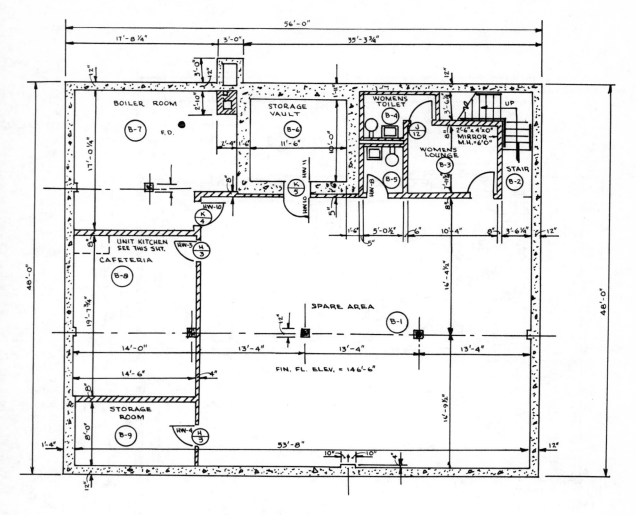

BASEMENT PLAN
SCALE 1/8'' = 1'-0''

Fig. 1329. Basement plan.

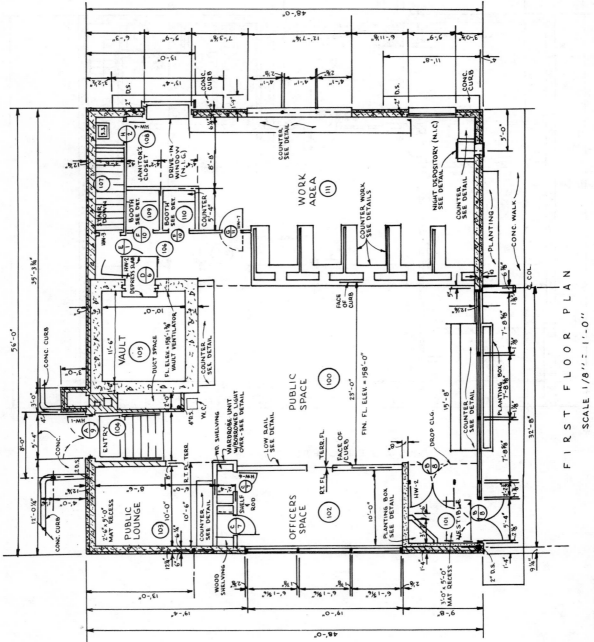

FIRST FLOOR PLAN

SCALE 1/8'' = 1'-0''

Fig. 1330. First-floor plan.

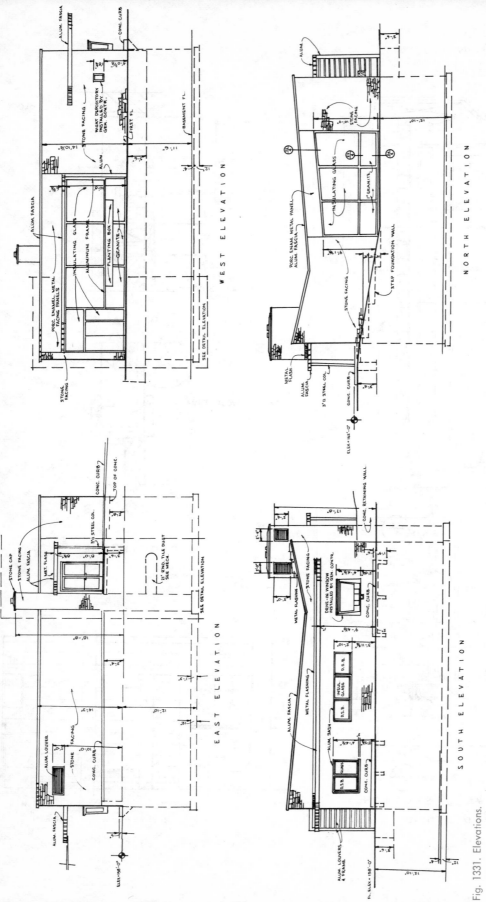

Fig. 1331. Elevations.

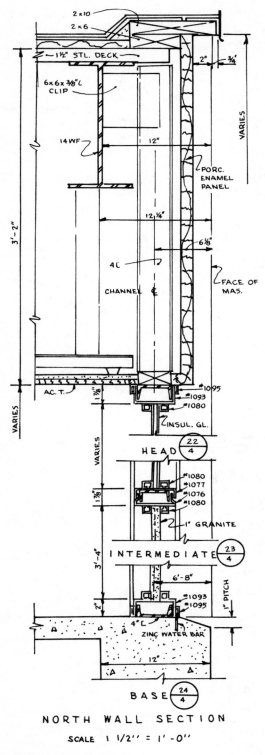

NORTH WALL SECTION

SCALE 1 1/2'' = 1'-0''

Fig. 1332. North wall section.

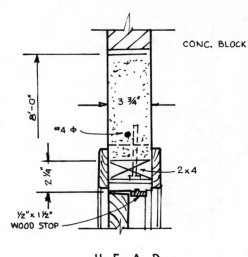

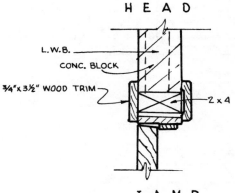

HEAD

JAMB

DOOR FRAME #3

Fig. 1333. Door frame detail.

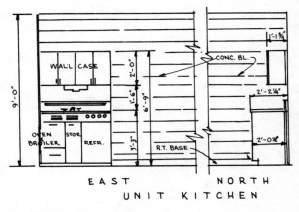

EAST **NORTH**

UNIT KITCHEN

Fig. 1334. Kitchen unit.

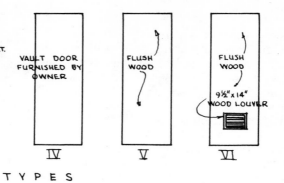

I	II	III	IV	V	VI	VII
GLASS	GLASS	½" SQUARE EDGE PANELING SEE. DET.	VAULT DOOR FURNISHED BY OWNER	FLUSH WOOD	FLUSH WOOD — 9½" x 14" WOOD LOUVER	FLUSH METAL "B" LABEL

DOOR TYPES

DOOR SCHEDULE

MARK	TYPE	SIZE	MAT'L.	REMARKS
A	I	1 PR. - 2'-6" x 7'-0" x 1¾"	ALUM.	EXT. DOOR – MET. THRESHOLD
B	II	1 PR. - 2'-8" x 7'-0" x ¾"	GLASS	EXT. DOOR (1) MET. THRESHOLD
C	III	2'-6" x 6'-8" x 1⅜"	WOOD	PANEL FACING: SEE D.F. #7
D	IV	3½' VAULT DOOR	METAL	FURNISHED BY OWNER INSTALLED BY GEN. CONTR.
E	V	2'-8" x 7'-0" x 1¾"	WOOD	
F	V	2'-6" x 5'-8" x 1¾"	WOOD	
G	V	2'-6" x 2'-7⅜" x 1¾"	WOOD	
H	VI	2'-8" x 7'-0" x 1¾"	WOOD	
J	VI	2'-6" x 7'-0" x 1¾"	WOOD	
K	VII	3'-0" x 7'-0" x 1¾"	METAL	"B" LABEL FIRE DOOR

Fig. 1335. Door types and door schedule.

INTERIOR FINISH SCHEDULE

ROOM NAME	ROOM NO.	FLOOR MAT.	FLOOR FIN.	BASE MAT.	BASE FIN.	WAINSCOT MAT.	WAINSCOT HT.	WAINSCOT FIN.	WALL MAT.	WALL FIN.	CEILING MAT.	CEILING FIN.	CLG. HT.	REMARKS
PUBLIC SPACE	100	TERR.	—	TERR.	—	—	—	—	SEE REMARKS		A.C.T.	—	VARIES	PL. EAST WALL & PAINT SEE DETAILS.
VESTIBULE	101	TERR.	—	TERR.	—	—	—	—	STONE	—	CEM.PL.	P.	10'-8⅛"	
OFFICERS SPACE	102	R.T.	—	R.T.	—	—	—	—	SEE REMARKS		—	—	VARIES	E. WALL WOOD W. WALL GLASS SEE DETS.
PUBLIC LOUNGE	103	R.T.	—	R.T. STONE	—	—	—	—	G. PL. STONE	P.	A.C.T.	—	VARIES	E. & S. WALLS PL. N. WALL STONE W. WALL WD.
ENTRY	104	TERR.	—	TERR.	—	—	—	—	G.PL.	P.	A.C.T.	—	VARIES	
VAULT	105	R.T.	—	R.T.	—	—	—	—	CONC.	P.	CONC.	P.	9'-10⅝"	
CORRIDOR	106	R.T.	—	R.T.	—	—	—	—	G.PL. WD.	P.	AG.PL.	P.	8'-4"	
STAIR	107	CONC.	BRM.	—	—	—	—	—	G. PL.	P.	G. PL.	P.	SEE. DET.	
JANITORS CLOS.	108	C.T.	—	C.T.	—	—	—	—	L.W.B.	P.	CEM.PL.	P.	8'-0"	
BOOTH	109	R.T.	—	R.T.	—	—	—	—	W.D.	SEE SPECS.	—	—	—	WD. PART'NS PARTIAL HT.
BOOTH	110	R.T.	—	R.T.	—	—	—	—	W.D.	SEE SPECS.	—	—	—	WD. PART'NS PARTIAL HT.
WORK AREA	111	R.T.	—	R.T.	—	—	—	—	G. PL.	P.	A.C.T.	—	8'-8"	AG.PL. CLG. OVER TELLERS CAGES - SEE DET.
SPARE AREA	B-1	A.T.	—	R.T.	—	—	—	—	CONC. CO.B	P.	EX.P.	P.	SEE DETAIL	
STAIR	B-2	CONC.	BRM.	—	—	—	—	—	G.PL.	P.	G.PL.	P.	SEE DETAIL	
WOMENS' LOUNGE	B-3	A.T.	—	R.T.	—	—	—	—	CO.B.	P.	A.C.T.	—	8'-0"	
WOMENS' TOILET	B-4	C.T.	—	G.S.U.	—	G.S.U.	5'-4"	—	CO.B.	P.	CEM.PL.	P.	8'-0"	
MENS' TOILET	B-5	C.T.	—	G.S.U.	—	G.S.U.	5'-4"	—	CO.B.	P.	CEM.PL.	P.	8'-0"	
STORAGE VAULT	B-6	A.T.	—	—	—	—	—	—	CONC	P.	CONC.	P.	10'-1⅜	
BOILER ROOM	B-7	CONC.	—	—	—	—	—	—	CONC. CO.B	—	EX.P.	—	SEE DETAIL	
CAFETERIA	B-8	A.T.	—	R.T.	—	—	—	—	CONC. CO.B	P.	A.C.T.	—	9'-0"	
STORAGE ROOM	B-9	CONC.	—	—	—	—	—	—	CONC. CO. B	P.	EX.P.	—	—	

Fig. 1336. Interior finish schedule.

Details of Sheet 3

This sheet is devoted entirely to exterior details. The enlarged elevation and section of the front entrance referred to on the building elevations on Sheet 2 are shown here and are detailed in Fig. 1337. An examination of this drawing shows the value of enlarged details. It reveals many things about the structure that are not clearly shown on Sheets 1 and 2. Critical dimensions are given, materials are identified and sections are indicated. Note that related details are drawn together, so that the complete relationship is shown. Sections 1/3, 2/3 and 3/3 illustrate how individual details can be shown, while still retaining the relationship of these sections. Fig. 1338 presents these details. Note that every part involved in the section is shown and that the various items are identified. For example, these details indicate a 32-ounce copper lining, the steel angles in the planter, and the sizes of each wood member. Nothing can be left out of these enlarged details.

An enlarged detail elevation and section of the rear entrance are shown in Fig. 1339. Notice how these clarify the change in levels from the parking lot to the bank lobby. While this is referred to on the floor plan, the exact change is not clear until this detail is examined. Here again, various sections are indicated. Sections 36/3, 38/3 and 39/3 are drawn so their relationships are established, Fig. 1340. This also establishes the details for one of the many door frames in the building, as well as showing other construction information.

Any unique features of a building must be carefully detailed. The drive-in window indicated on the floor plan is one such example. Fig. 1341 illustrates how this is done. Many enlarged details are necessary, as indicated in this figure. Space does not permit the reproduction of these details, but they all become part of the many special details that must be drawn complete.

In addition to the door frame sections, the various types of windows must be completely detailed. One window shown on the elevation in Fig. 1341 indicates sections 22/3, 23/3 and 25/3 are drawn on Sheet 3. These are illustrated in Fig. 1342. This is only one example of a number of different window details that are necessary. Whenever a window is framed differently, a new number can be used to refer to the common section. Assistance in designing these and other sections, such as door frames, can be obtained from the catalogs of manufacturers of the doors and windows. They publish details illustrating the most satisfactory methods for this construction.

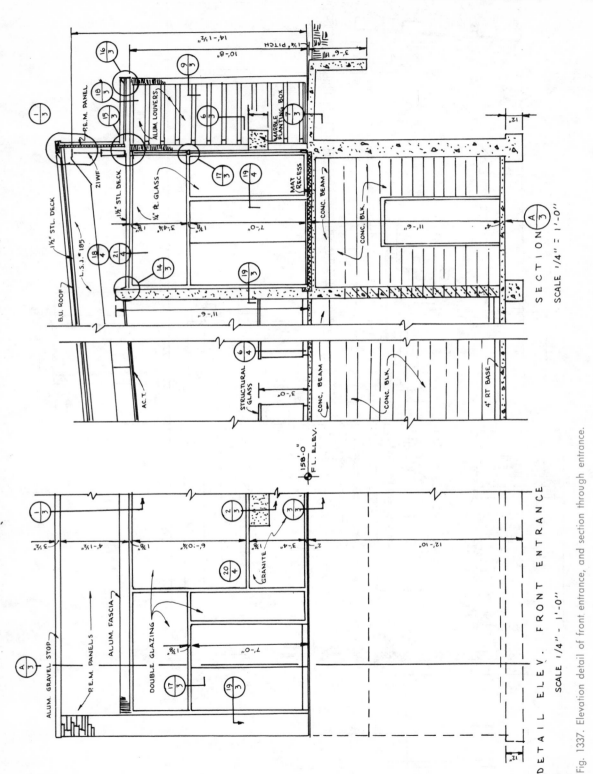

Fig. 1337. Elevation detail of front entrance, and section through entrance.

594

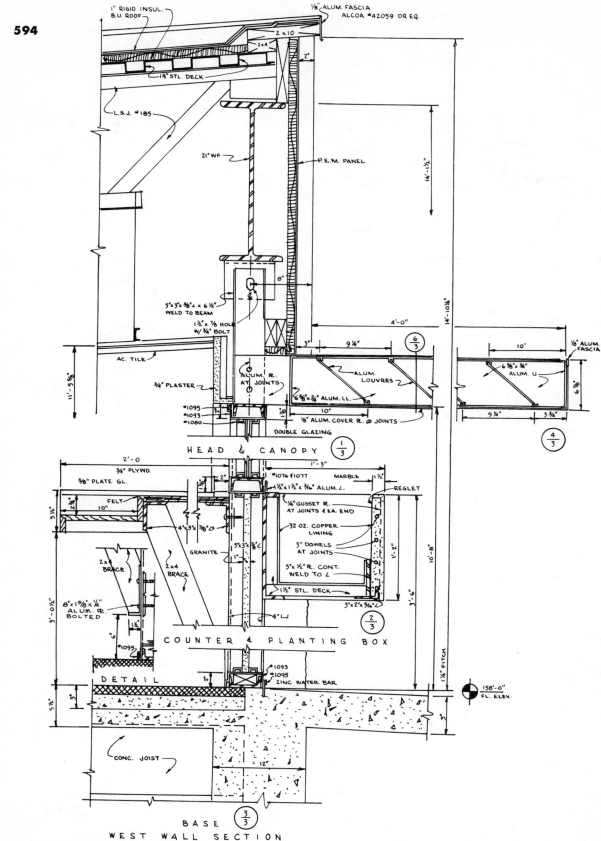

WEST WALL SECTION

Fig. 1338. West wall section.

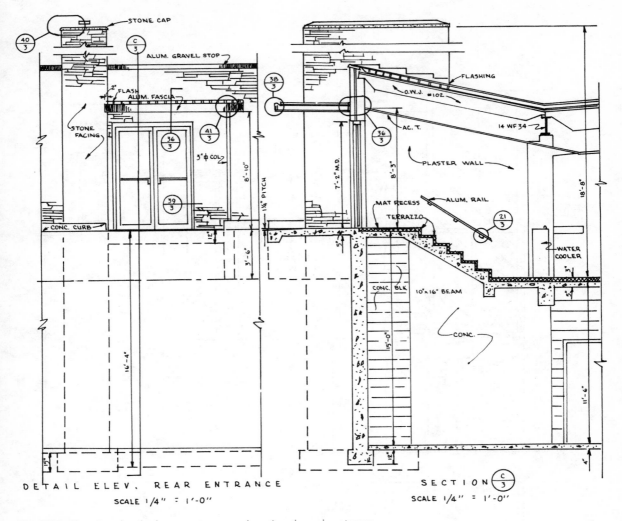

DETAIL ELEV. REAR ENTRANCE
SCALE 1/4" = 1'-0"

SECTION $\frac{C}{3}$
SCALE 1/4" = 1'-0"

Fig. 1339. Elevation detail of rear entrance and section through entrance.

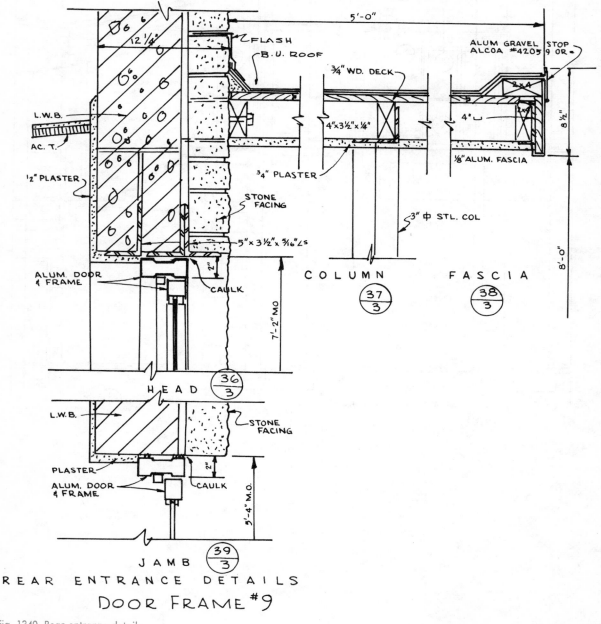

Fig. 1340. Rear entrance details.

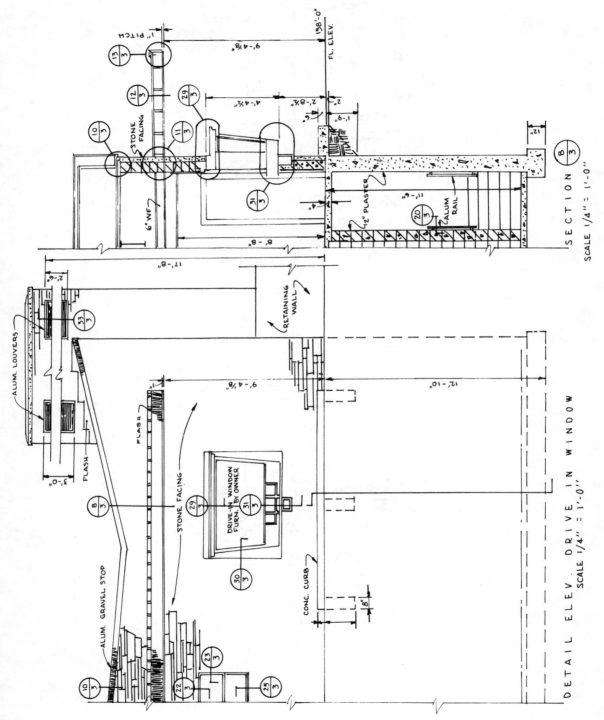

Fig. 1341. Drive-in window — elevation and section.

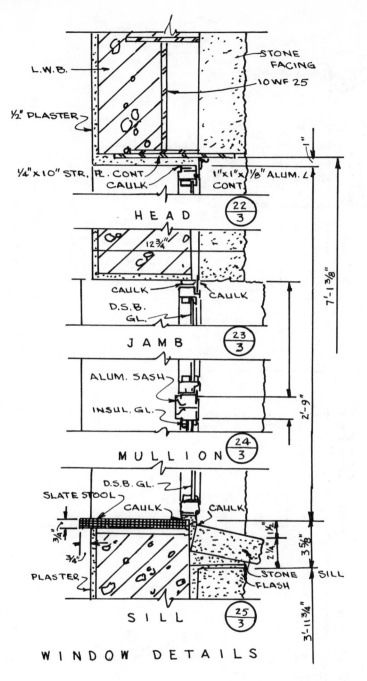

Fig. 1342. Window details.

Details of Sheet 4

Sheet 4 is devoted to interior details. Usually it is helpful to reveal interior details and indicate necessary sections through cabinets, counters and other fixtures by passing appropriate sections through the entire building. Two such sections are used in detailing this bank building. Sections are made through the vault and public space in an east-west direction and through the officers' space and public space in a north-south direction. This reveals most of the counters and other fixtures. Fig. 1345 illustrates the east-west section and Fig. 1344, the north-south section.

In Fig. 1345, the elevation of the public counter is shown as it appears to the customer. A section (10/4) is passed through the counter to illustrate construction details. This is shown in Fig. 1343. Details of the vault construction are also shown, as is the plan for placing the long-span steel joists and for hanging the acoustical-tile ceiling. In addition, the roof pitch and information about roof construction are given.

Many other cabinet details are given on Sheet 4. These include details of the wardrobe partition rail, counter divider, safe deposit booths, teller's work counter, planter box, and public counter. Since the night depository is an unusual item, it also requires a detail, as shown in Fig. 1346.

Sheet 4 also contains a simple roof plan, Fig. 1347. This locates the canopies, chimneys, and exhaust vents and indicates the direction of slope. A roof framing plan is shown on Sheet 5.

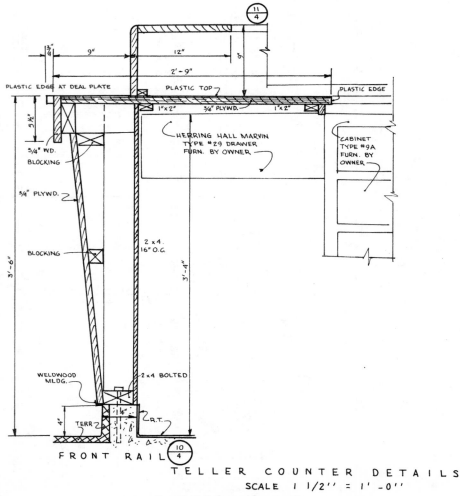

Fig. 1343. Teller counter details.

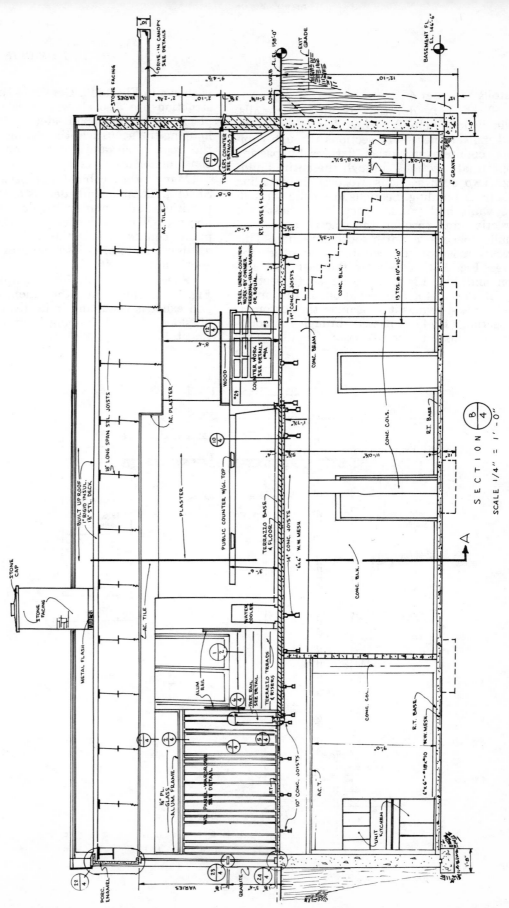

Fig. 1344. Section B-4 — through officers' space and public space, north to south.

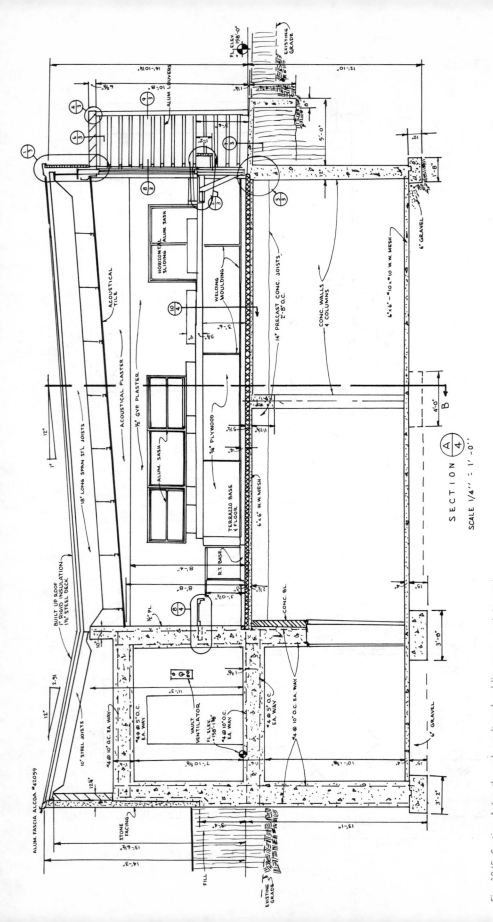

Fig. 1345. Section A-4 — through vault and public space, east to west.

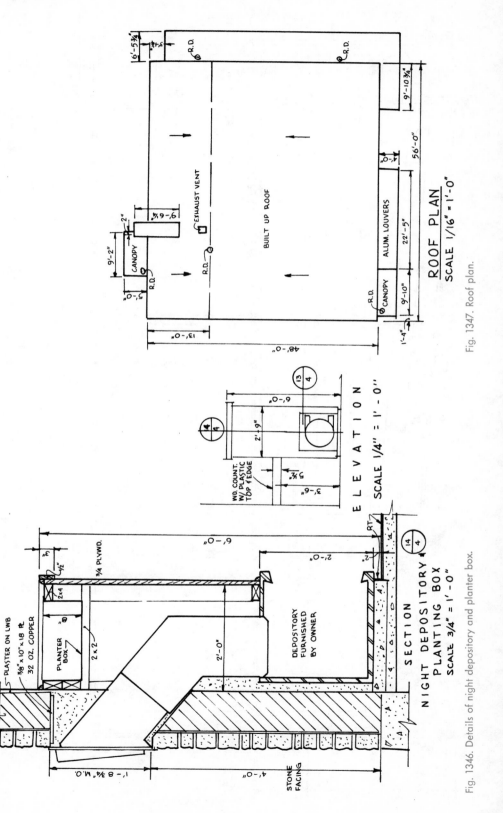

ROOF PLAN
SCALE 1/16" = 1'-0"

Fig. 1347. Roof plan.

ELEVATION
SCALE 1/4" = 1'-0"

NIGHT DEPOSITORY
PLANTING BOX
SCALE 3/4" = 1'-0"

SECTION

Fig. 1346. Details of night depository and planter box.

Details of Sheet 5

Sheet 5 is devoted to structural details. This involves, first of all, a detailed drawing giving full information concerning the foundation. The foundation plan is shown in Fig. 1350. This includes dimensions locating the various foundation walls and pilasters and indicating their thickness. Also included are data pertaining to the steel reinforcement required. Footings are located and sizes are recorded. Some items, such as the chimney footing, require enlarged details that are placed on Sheet 5. Notice that the vault requires foundation walls running to grade. This space in the basement enclosed by these walls is used as a fireproof storage vault, thus taking advantage of this needed extra foundation. The partitions in the basement are concrete block and require a padding-type footing. The design of this footing is detailed, as shown in Fig. 1348.

The floor-framing plan (Fig. 1351) is a part of Sheet 5. It is closely related to the foundation plan. The columns are located on the foundation plan, but are identified by number on the floor-framing plan. Details concerning size, reinforcement, and ties for columns are shown in a table, as found in Fig. 1349. Details concerning column bases are necessary. The base required for the steel columns is shown in Fig. 1352. The size of these columns is shown on the roof-framing plan, since they support the roof.

The floor-framing plan also locates the beams and identifies them by number. The design data are shown in a beam schedule, which gives beam size, reinforcing bars needed and stirrup locations, Fig. 1353.

The placement of the precast concrete joists is indicated. Sections through the joists and at other places needing clarification are identified. These details are drawn to a larger scale and form a part of Sheet 5. Examples of these are Section 23/5 (Fig. 1354) through the precast concrete joists; Section 21/5 (Fig. 1355) through joists where floor level changes; Section 17/5 (Fig. 1356) through the east entrance stair detail; and Section 19/5 (Fig. 1357) showing the typical joist detail at a bearing wall. Other sections are given, but are too numerous to present here. Notice that complete information is given on each detail.

The roof-framing plan (Fig. 1359) and the many details necessary to the roof structure are a part of Sheet 5. The placement of the open-web, long-span, steel joists is shown, and the joists are identified by the standard system of joist-size specification. For example, the long-span joists are designated as L.S.J. 185, and the joists over the short section of roof are S.J. (steel joists) 102.

The joists meet and are supported by a 16 WF 36 (wide flange) steel beam. Other steel beams are used and identified. Section 16/5 (Fig. 1358) gives the details for this connection, and Section 13/5 shows the connection between the open-web, steel joists and the exterior wall.

A number of other sections are needed. Some of these are shown here to illustrate typical needed details. Sections 1/5 and 2/5 (Fig. 1360) detail the requirements for placing the wide-flange steel beams to support the open-web, steel roof joists. Section 11/5 (Fig. 1361) gives details on the canopy over the drive-in side of the bank and shows the bracing used between the roof joists. Notice that other details are indicated on this detail. Details 10/5, 12/5 and 15/5 (not shown in text) are drawn to a larger scale to clarify these portions of the structure.

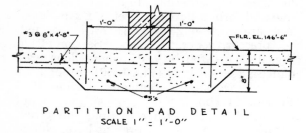

PARTITION PAD DETAIL
SCALE 1" = 1'-0"

Fig. 1348. Partition pad detail.

COLUMN SCHEDULE			
NO.	SIZE	VERT. BARS	TIES
1	12 x 12	4 - #6	#3 @ 12" O.C.
2	12 x 12	4 - #6	#3 @ 12" O.C.

Fig. 1349. Column schedule.

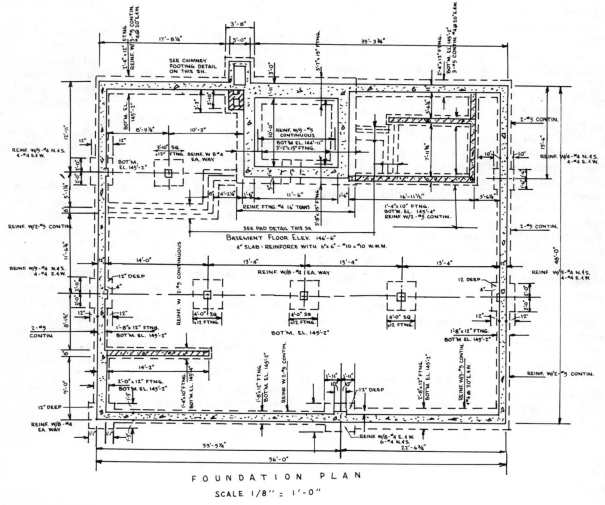

FOUNDATION PLAN
SCALE 1/8" = 1'-0"

Fig. 1350. Foundation plan.

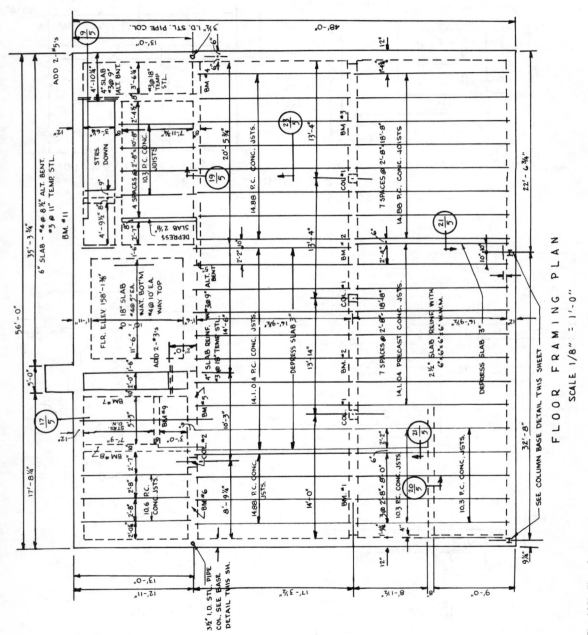

Fig. 1351. Floor-framing plan.

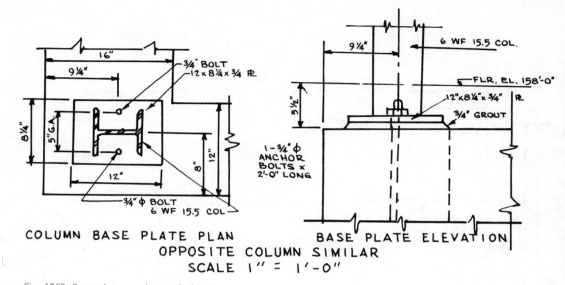

COLUMN BASE PLATE PLAN
OPPOSITE COLUMN SIMILAR
SCALE 1″ = 1′-0″

Fig. 1352. Base plate — plan and elevation.

BEAM SCHEDULE				
NO.	SIZE	STRAIGHT BARS	BENT BARS	NO. 3 STIRRUPS - TOP BARS
1	12×22″×25″	2 - #7	2 - #8	1 @ 2″ COL. FACE, 1 @ 5½″, 1 @ 7½″ O.C. EA. END
2	12×22″×25″	2 - #8	2 - #8	1 @ 2½″- COL. FACE, 1 @ 5½″, 1 @ 8″ O.C. EA. END
3	12×22″×25″	2 - #7	2 - #8	1 @ 2½″- COL. FACE, 1 @ 6″, 1 @ 8½″ O.C. EA. END
4	8 × 22	2 - #4		ADD 2 - #4 ≤ TOP 4′-6″ LONG
5	12×22 ¹25	2 - #7	2 - #7	1@ 2½″ COL. FACE, 3 @ 5½″, 1@ 8½″, 1@ 12″ NORTH END 2@ 2″, 1@ 4″ SOUTH END
6	12 × 25	2 - #6	2 - #6	2 @ 3″, 1@ 4″ EA. END
7	10 × 16	2 - #6	1 - #6	
8	10 × 16	2 - #7	1 - #7	
9	8 × 12	2 - #6	1 - #6	
10	8 × 22	2 - #4		ADD 2 - #4 TOP, 6′-6″
11	8 × 20	2 - #4		

Fig. 1353. Beam schedule.

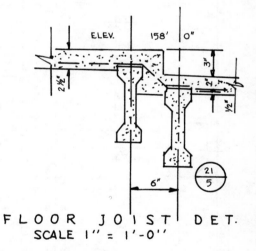

FLOOR JOIST DET.
SCALE 1″ = 1′-0″

Fig. 1355. Floor joist detail.

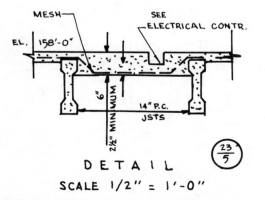

DETAIL
SCALE 1/2″ = 1′-0″

Fig. 1354. Detail 23-5 — section through precast concrete joists.

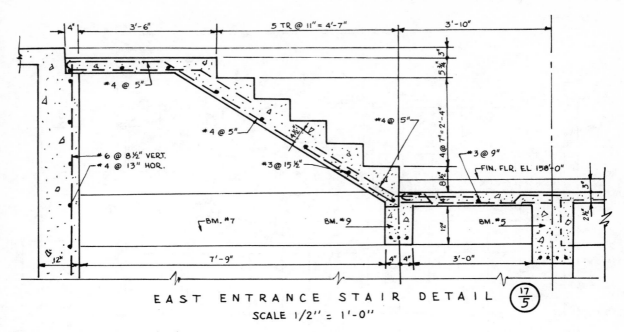

EAST ENTRANCE STAIR DETAIL 17/5
SCALE 1/2'' = 1'-0''

Fig. 1356. East entrance stair, detail.

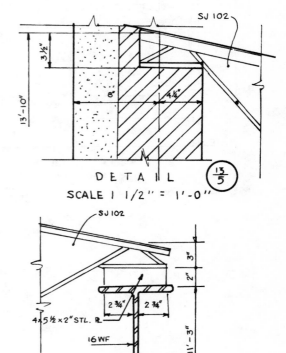

DETAIL 13/5
SCALE 1 1/2'' = 1'-0''

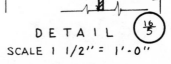

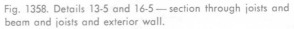

DETAIL 16/5
SCALE 1 1/2'' = 1'-0''

Fig. 1358. Details 13-5 and 16-5 — section through joists and beam and joists and exterior wall.

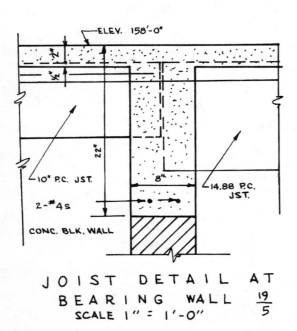

JOIST DETAIL AT
BEARING WALL 19/5
SCALE 1'' = 1'-0''

Fig. 1357. Joist detail at bearing wall.

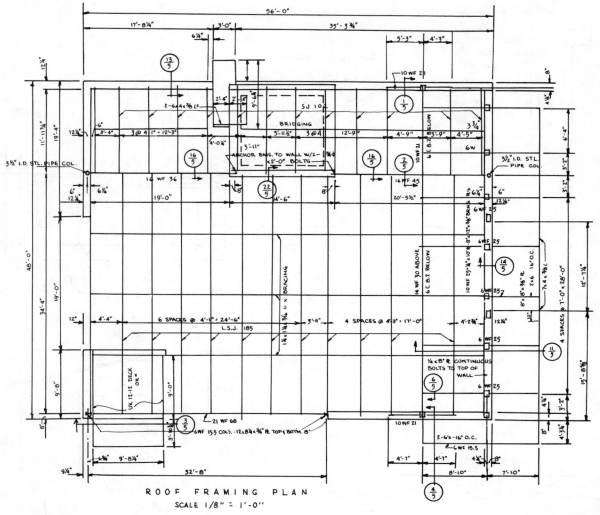

R O O F   F R A M I N G   P L A N
SCALE 1/8" = 1'-0"

Fig. 1359. Roof-framing plan.

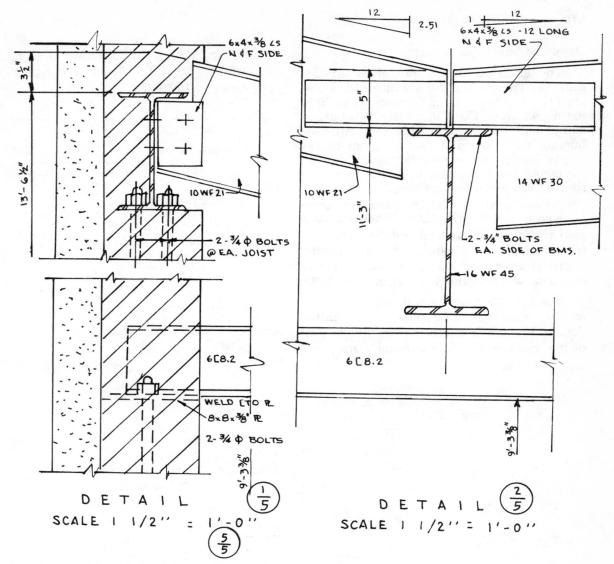

$3\frac{1}{2}''$

$13' - 6\frac{1}{2}''$

6x4x⅜ LS
N & F SIDE

10 WF 21

2 - ¾ φ BOLTS
@ EA. JOIST

12   2.51   1   12
                         6x4x⅜ LS -12 LONG
                              N & F SIDE

5"

1'-3"

10 WF 21

14 WF 30

2 - ¾" BOLTS
EA. SIDE OF BMS.

16 WF 45

6 ⸢8.2

6 ⸢8.2

WELD ⸢ TO R
8x8x⅜" R
2 - ¾ φ BOLTS

$9' - 3\frac{3}{8}''$

$9' - 3\frac{3}{8}''$

D E T A I L $\frac{1}{5}$
SCALE 1 1/2'' = 1'-0''

$\frac{5}{5}$

D E T A I L $\frac{2}{5}$
SCALE 1 1/2'' = 1'-0''

Fig. 1360. Details 1-5 and 2-5 — placement of beams to support roof joists.

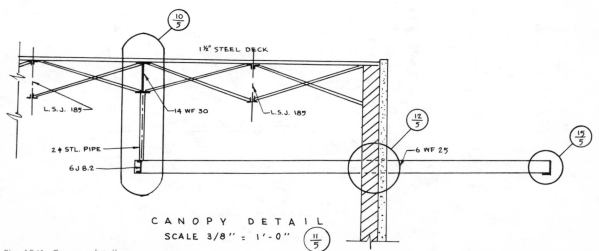

$\frac{10}{5}$

1½" STEEL DECK

L.S.J. 185

14 WF 30

L.S.J. 185

2 φ STL. PIPE

6 J 8.2

$\frac{12}{5}$

6 WF 25

$\frac{15}{5}$

C A N O P Y   D E T A I L
SCALE 3/8'' = 1'-0'' $\frac{11}{5}$

Fig. 1361. Canopy detail.

Details of Sheet E-1

The electrical details are given on this drawing. Three schedules are included. These are (1) a key to electrical symbols; (2) a light fixture schedule, Fig. 1363; and (3) a burglar alarm outlet schedule. Included with the burglar alarm schedule is a diagram of the empty conduit for the burglar alarm system. An empty conduit diagram for the telephone riser is also given on this sheet.

An electrical plan for the basement rooms is given in detail (Fig. 1364). Shown on this plan are lights, outlets, and switches. The electrical panels are located, and a separate, electrical riser diagram is necessary to give complete details of the panel wiring, Fig. 1365.

The first-floor electrical details are shown on two drawings. One plan gives lighting details, Fig. 1366; another gives outlet, telephone, clock, ventilating fan and alarm loca-tions, Fig. 1367. This separate drawing is necessary because the detail is too great to place on one drawing.

TYPE NO	WATTS	LIGHT FIXTURE SCHEDULE
		DESCRIPTION
A	300	SILVRAY "SKYLIKE," NO. RA 50F/300 - SILVER BOWL LAMP
B	2-40	MODERN TROFFER NO. 12240-RAPID START-LOUVERED
C	3-40	MODERN TROFFER NO. 12340-RAPID START-LOUVERED
D	150	KIRLIN NO. 1211 RECESSED - LOUVERED
E	75	ART METAL NO. 3305 RECESSED R-30 LAMP
F	150	KIRLIN NO. 1208 RECESSED
G	100	ART METAL NO. 3364 RECESSED SILVER BOWL LAMP
H	100	ART METAL NO. 1738 DRUM TYPE
I	–	NOT USED
J	2-75	ART METAL NO. 3361
K	75	ART METAL NO. 3395 BRACKET LIGHT
L	2-100	ART METAL NO. 3362
M	150	BENJAMIN NO. 7642 RLM PENDANT- M.H. 8'-0"
N	150	KIRLIN NO. 1511 RECESSED
O	–	NOT USED
P	150	KIRLIN NO. 1208 SUR. SURFACE MOUNTED
Q	1 LIGHT	HUBBELL NO. 40462 PORCELAIN SOCKET- PULL CHAIN
R	4-150	REVERE NO. 199-620 POLE, 4 LIGHT ASSEMBLY w/#3281 FLOODS

Fig. 1363. Light fixture schedule.

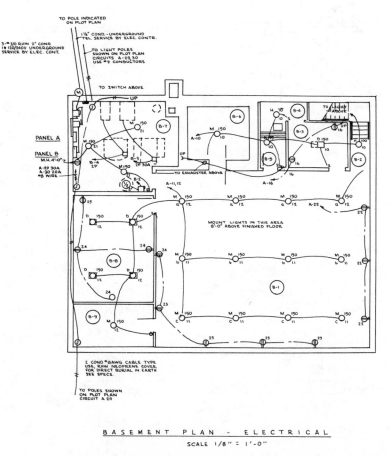

BASEMENT PLAN - ELECTRICAL

SCALE 1/8" = 1'-0"

Fig. 1364. Basement plan — electrical.

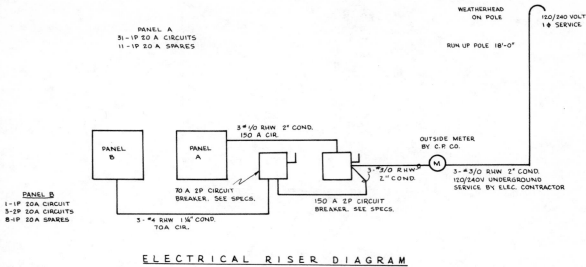

ELECTRICAL RISER DIAGRAM

NO SCALE

Fig. 1365. Electrical riser diagram.

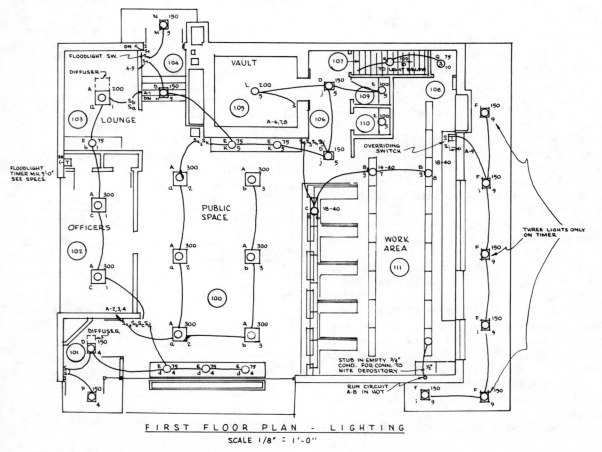

FIRST FLOOR PLAN - LIGHTING

SCALE 1/8" = 1'-0"

Fig. 1366. First-floor plan — lighting.

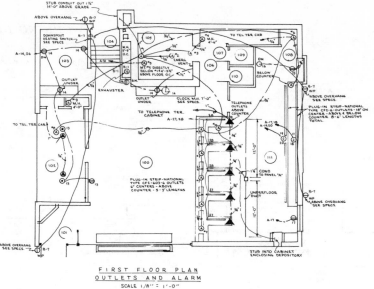

FIRST FLOOR PLAN
OUTLETS AND ALARM
SCALE 1/8" = 1'-0"

Fig. 1367. First-floor plan — outlets and alarm.

Details of Sheet M-1

This sheet is devoted to details of plumbing, air conditioning, and boiler room layout. The schedules given are: (1) a legend of symbols; (2) a diffuser schedule, Fig. 1369; (3) a plumbing schedule, Fig. 1370; and (4) an equipment schedule, Fig. 1373.

A simple roof plan is given to show the location of plumbing vents, exhaust outlets, roof drains and downspouts. See Fig. 1374.

Separate plans showing the plumbing layout are given for the basement and the first floor. See Figs. 1371 and 1372.

On the basement plumbing plan, notice the use of a common plumbing wall between the rest rooms. The boiler room and unit kitchen are also located on the front of the building, so that all plumbing is confined to one section of the building.

Since the piping in the boiler room is complex, an enlarged drawing of this area is made (Fig. 1377). This plan shows the location of the incinerator, evaporator water cooler, heating and cooling air-conditioning unit, exhaust ducts, hot water heater, gas and water meters, gas lines, hot and cold water lines, and sewer lines. The major pieces of equipment are numbered. These refer to the numbers on the equipment schedule, where detailed information about each item is recorded.

The first floor plumbing plan indicates the location of the service sink in the janitors' closet, the water cooler, a sill cock, the required water and sewer lines, and the vent pipes.

Separate plans are made for each floor level to locate air-conditioning ducts. These are shown in Figs. 1375 and 1376. Since the enlarged detail of the boiler room gives details concerning this part of the air-conditioning system, this is not repeated on the duct layout. Notice that the ducts are reduced in size as they approach the end of a run. Especially note how the duct sizes and the required cubic feet per minute flow are indicated. The fresh-air intake is located and is run to a wall cavity that also serves as the space for the conditioned air flow to the rooms to be heated and cooled. Notice the direction of flow on the fresh-air intake, the ducts to the rooms, and the air return from the public space to the boiler room.

DIFFUSER	SCHEDULE		
ROOM NO.	QTY.	DIFF. SIZE	C.F.M. (COOL.)
100	2	24 × 24	450
101	1	12 × 12	130
102	1	24 × 24	650
103	1	24 × 24	330
104	1	12 × 12	185
111	1	24 × 24	600
	2	24 × 24	300
B-1	2	16 × 5 (WALL REG)	210
B-3	1	12 × 12	150
B-8	1	24 × 24	200

ABOVE DIFFUSERS BASED ON "ANEMOSTAT" TYPE E.

Fig. 1369. Diffuser schedule.

PLUMBING SCHEDULE						
FIXTURE	QTY.	C. W.	H. W.	WASTE	VENT	TRAP
WATER CLOSETS F.M. – F.V.	2	1"		4"	4"	INT.
LAVATORIES	2	½"	½"	1-¼"	1-¼"	1-¼"
SERVICE SINK	1	¾"	¾"	3"	3"	INT.
FLOOR DRAIN	1			3"	3"	3"
ROOF DRAIN (AS SHOWN)	3					

NOTE: CONNECTIONS TO EQUIPMENT SHALL CONFORM TO MANUFACTURERS SPECIFICATION. SCHEDULE GIVEN AS A GUIDE TO FIGURING AND SHALL NOT BE CONSIDERED AS ABSOLUTE OR BINDING. ANY MODIFICATIONS NECESSARY TO THE COMPLETE AND SATISFACTORY CONNECTING UP OF FIXTURES SHALL BE MADE FOR A COMPLETE INSTALLATION.

Fig. 1370. Plumbing schedule.

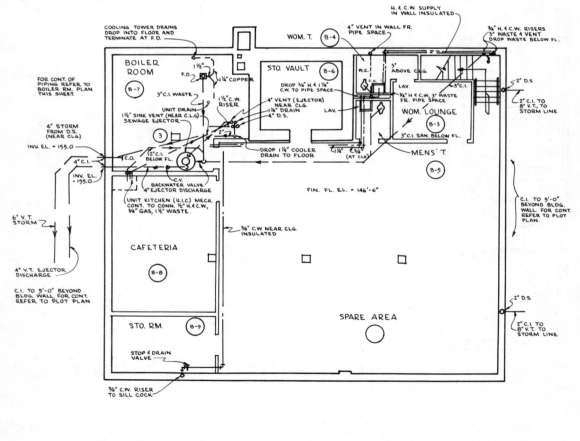

BASEMENT FLOOR PLAN - PLUMBING

SCALE 1/8'' = 1'-0''

Fig. 1371. Basement floor plan — plumbing.

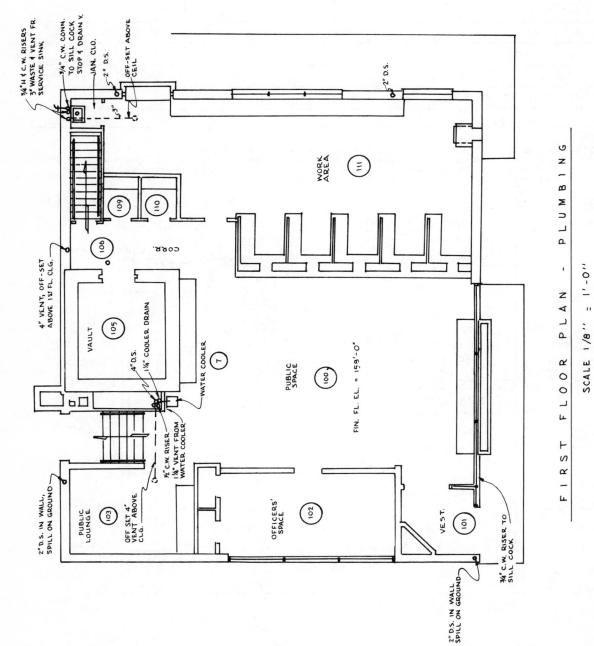

FIRST FLOOR PLAN - PLUMBING

SCALE 1/8" = 1'-0"

Fig. 1372. First-floor plan — plumbing.

EQUIPMENT SCHEDULE

(1) <u>AIR CONDITIONING UNIT :</u>

GAS OPERATED, HEATING CAPACITY 144,000 B.T.U.H. COOLING CAPACITY 65,000 B.T.U.H. (5.4 TONS), INLET WATER TEMP. 75°F., INLET AIR TEMP. 80°F. D.B. & 67°F. W.B. RATED AIR CAPACITY 2,000 C.F.M. @ 38 S.P., 1 H.P. 240 VOLT, 60 CYCLE, 1 PHASE MOTOR. SIMILIAR AND EQUAL TO "SERVEL" DE-144-G UNIT.

(2) <u>AIR CONDITIONING UNIT :</u>

GAS OPERATED, HEATING CAPACITY 96,000 B.T.U.H. COOLING CAPACITY 40,000 B.T.U.H. (3.3 TONS), INLET WATER TEMP. 75°F., INLET AIR TEMP. 80°F., D.B. & 67°F. W.B. RATED AIR CAPACITY 1200 C.F.M. @ .38 S.P., 1/2 H.P. 240 VOLT, 60 CYCLE, 1 PHASE MOTOR. SIMILIAR AND EQUAL TO "SERVEL" DC-96 G UNIT.

(3) <u>SEWAGE EJECTOR :</u>

SINGLE, SCREENLESS, CAPACITY 50 G.P.M. AGAINST 22 FT. HEAD. 3/4 H.P., 1 PHASE, 60 CYCLE, 240 VOLT, 1140 R.P.M. MOTOR. SIMILIAR AND EQUAL TO "WEIL"

(4) <u>HOT WATER HEATER :</u>

GAS FIRED, 30 GAL. STORAGE WITH 30 GAL/HR RECOVERY @ 100°F TEMP. RISE. SIMILIAR AND EQUAL "RUUD" 30-30 HI-SPEED.

(5) <u>INCINERATOR :</u>

PORTABLE TYPE, 4 BU. CAPACITY, SIMILIAR AND EQUAL TO "GODAR".

(6) <u>EXHAUSTER :</u>

ROOF TYPE, CAPACITY 500 C.F.M. @ 1/4" S.P., FAN TIP SPEED 4080 F.P.M., 1/3 H.P., 1 PHASE 60 CYCLE, 120 VOLT, 1725 R.P.M. MOTOR. SIMILIAR AND EQUAL TO "SWARTWOUT" AIRLIFT JUNIOR.

(7) <u>WATER COOLER :</u>

REFER TO SPECIFICATIONS.

(8) <u>EVAPORATIVE WATER COOLER :</u>

SELF-CONTAINED UNIT TO SUPPLY 15 G.P.M. OF 74° WATER @ 67°F W.B. AIR. FAN TO HANDLE 2200 C.F.M. AIR @ .10" W.G. FAN & PUMP MOTORS 1/2 H.P., 60 CYCLE, 1 PHASE, 120 VOLT. SIMILIAR & EQUAL TO "SERVEL" TE-15.

(9) <u>EVAPORATIVE WATER COOLER :</u>

SELF-CONTAINED UNIT TO SUPPLY 10 G.P.M. OF 74° WATER @ 67°F W.B. AIR. FAN TO HANDLE 1500 C.F.M. AIR @ .10 W.G. FAN & PUMP MOTORS 1/3 H.P., 60 CYCLE, 1 PHASE 120 VOLT. SIMILIAR & EQUAL TO "SERVEL" TE-10.

Fig. 1373. Equipment schedule.

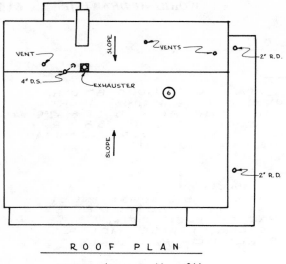

ROOF PLAN

SCALE 1/16" = 1' - 0"

Fig. 1374. Roof plan.

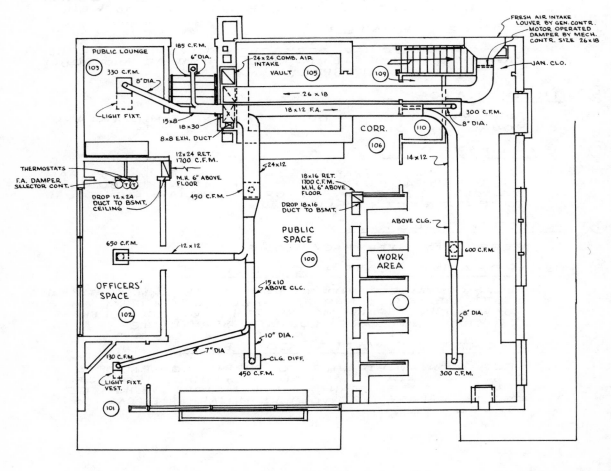

FIRST FLOOR PLAN - AIR CONDITIONING

SCALE 1/8" = 1'-0"

Fig. 1375. First-floor plan — air conditioning.

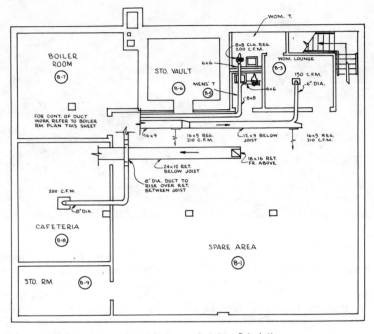

BASEMENT FLOOR PLAN

AIR CONDITIONING

SCALE 1/8" = 1'-0"

Fig. 1376. Basement floor plan — air conditioning.

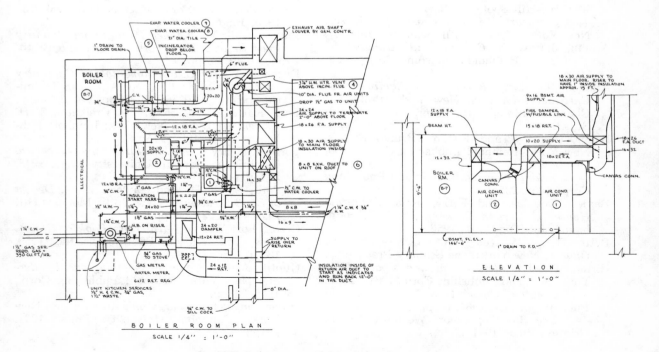

BOILER ROOM PLAN

SCALE 1/4" = 1'-0"

ELEVATION

SCALE 1/4" = 1'-0"

Fig. 1377. Boiler room — plan and elevation.

REFERENCE LIST

Books

Anson, Peter. *Churches, Their Plan and Furnishing* (Catholic). Milwaukee: Bruce Publishing Co., 1948, 242pp.

Architectural Record (Editorial Staff). *Motels, Hotels, Restaurants and Bars* (2nd. ed.). New York: McGraw-Hill Book Co., 1960.

————. *Record Houses.* (An Annual Series). New York: McGraw-Hill Book Co. Yearly.

————. *The Second Treasury of Contemporary Houses.* New York: McGraw-Hill Book Co., 1959.

————. *Time Saver Standards.* New York: McGraw-Hill Book Co., 1954.

————. *Treasury of Contemporary Houses.* New York: McGraw-Hill Book Co., 1954.

Aronin, Jeffrey E. *Climate and Architecture.* New York: Reinhold Publishing Corp., 1953, 304pp.

Atkinson, C. Harry. *Building and Equipping for Christian Education.* New York: Protestant Church Buildings, Publisher, 27 East 39th Street.

Baker, Geoffrey, and Funaro, Bruno. *Motels.* New York: Reinhold Publishing Corp., 1955, 264pp.

————. *Parking.* New York: Reinhold Publishing Corp., 1958, 202pp.

Bayles, Douglas, and Perry, Joan. *California Houses of Gordon Drake.* New York: Reinhold Publishing Corp., 1956.

Betts, Darby W. (ed.). *Architecture and the Church.* New York: The Seabury Press, 1960.

Birren, Faber. *Color, Form, and Space.* New York: Reinhold Publishing Corp., 1961, 128pp.

————. *Creative Color.* New York: Reinhold Publishing Corp., 1961, 128pp.

————. *The Story of Color.* Westport, Conn.: Crimson Press, 1941, 336pp.

Buss, Truman C., Jr. *Simplified Architectural Drawing.* Chicago: American Technical Society, 1946, 258pp.

Choate, Chris. *Architectural Presentation in Opaque Watercolor.* New York: Reinhold Publishing Corp., 1961, 158pp.

Close, Paul D. *Building Insulation* (4th ed.). Chicago: American Technical Society, 1951, 402pp.

Commery, Eugene W., and Stephenson, C. E. *How to Decorate and Light Your Home.* New York: Coward-McCann, Inc., 1955, 256pp.

Dalzell, James R. *Blueprint Reading for Home Builders.* New York: McGraw-Hill Book Co., 1955, 138pp.

Dana, Arthur W. *Kitchen Planning for Quantity Food Service.* New York: Harper and Brothers, 1949, 229pp.

Durbahn, Walter E. *Fundamentals of Carpentry* (3rd. ed.). 2 vols. Chicago: American Technical Society, 1950. Vol. 1, 383pp; Vol. 2, 544pp.

Ford, Katherine (Morrow), and Creighton, T. H. *Designs for Living.* New York: Reinhold Publishing Corp., 1955, 215pp.

Forman, Henry C. *Architecture of the Old South.* Cambridge: Harvard University Press, 1948, 203pp.

Gaylord, Edwin H., and Gaylord, C. N. *Design of Steel Structures.* New York: McGraw-Hill Book Co., 1957, 540pp.

Green, Lois W. (ed.). *Interiors Book of Offices.* New York: Whitney Publications, Inc., 1959, 163pp.

Guptill, Arthur. *Color in Sketching and Rendering.* New York: Reinhold Publishing Corp., 1945, 348pp.

Hammond, Peter. *Liturgy and Architecture.* New York: Columbia University Press, 1961, 191pp.

Harada, Jiro. *The Lesson of Japanese Architecture.* London, England: The Studio Limited, 1954, 192pp.

Harling, Robert (ed.), *et. al. House and Garden Small Homes.* Greenwich, Conn.: Conde Nast Publications, LTD., 1961, 208pp.

Hattrell, W. S., *et. al. Hotels, Restaurants, and Bars.* New York: Reinhold Publishing Corp., 1962, 146pp.

Hollis, Harold F. *Teach Yourself Perspective Drawing.* New York: Roy Publishers, 1956, 198pp.

Horland, Richard. *Compilation: Planning Christian Education in the Local Church.* Valley Forge, Pa.: Judson Press, 1962.

Kautzky, Theodore. *Pencil Broadsides.* New York: Reinhold Publishing Corp., 1960, 64pp.

Kaylor, Harry. *Prestressed Concrete Simply Explained.* New York: John Wiley and Sons, 1961, 158pp.

Kenney, Joseph E. *Blueprint Reading for the Building Trades* (2nd. ed.). New York: McGraw-Hill Book Co., 1955, 120pp.

Ketchum, Morris. *Shops and Stores.* New York: Reinhold Publishing Corp., 1957, 264pp.

Kirk, Paul H., and Sternberg, E.D. *Doctors' Offices and Clinics.* New York: Reinhold Publishing Corp., 1955, 224pp.

Klaber, Eugene H. *Housing Design.* New York: Reinhold Publishing Corp., 1954, 247pp.

Koeppe, Clarence E., and DeLong, G. C. *Weather and Climate.* New York: McGraw-Hill Book Co., 1958, 341pp.

Kotschevar, Lendal H., and Terrell, M. E. *Food Service Planning: Layout and Equipment.* New York: John Wiley and Sons, Inc., 1961, 449pp.

Limbach, Russell T. *American Trees.* New York: Random House, 1942, 34pp.

Little, R. Keith. *Kitchen Layout Logic.* New York: Ahrens Publishing Co., 1959, 92pp.

Manasseh, Leonard, and Cunliffe, Roger. *Office Buildings.* New York: Reinhold Publishing Corp., 1962, 216pp.

Matthias, Arthur J., and Smith, E. *How to Design and Install Plumbing.* Chicago: American Technical Society, 1960, 446pp.

May, Cliff. *Sunset. Western Ranch Houses.* Menlo Park, California: Lane Publishing Co., 1958.

McCarty, Margie. *The Church Plans for Children.* Kansas City, Missouri: The Methodist Publishing House, 1953.

McClinton, Katherine (Morrison). *The Changing Church.* New York: Morehouse-Gorham Co., 1957, 144pp.

Means, Robert S. (ed.). *Building Construction Cost Data.* 2 vols. (V.19-20). Duxbury, Mass.: Robert Snow Means Co., 1961-62.

Mills, Edward D. *The Modern Church.* New York: Frederick A. Praeger, 1956, 188pp.

Newcomb, Rexford. *The Old Mission Churches and Historic Houses of California.* Philadelphia: J. P. Lippincott Co., 1925, 379pp.

Norling, Ernest. *Perspective Made Easy.* New York: The Macmillan Co., 1939, 203pp.

Norton, Dora M. *Freehand Perspective.* New York: Sterling Publishing Co., 1957, 92pp.

Orchard, Dennis F. *Concrete Technology.* 2 vols. New York: John Wiley and Sons, 1962. Vol. 1, 358pp; Vol. 2, 241pp.

Pagani, Carlo. *Italy's Architecture Today.* Milan, Italy: Copyright by Ulrico Hoepli, 1955, 293pp. Parallel text in English and Italian.

Parker, Harry. *Simplified Design of Stuctural Steel* (2nd. ed.). New York: John Wiley and Sons, 1955, 244pp.

———. *Simplified Engineering for Architects and Builders* (3rd. ed.). New York: John Wiley and Sons, 1961, 325pp.

Parnes, Louis. *Planning Stores That Pay.* New York: McGraw-Hill Book Co., 1948, 313pp.

Pilcher, Donald E. *The Regency Style, 1800-1830.* New York: B. T. Batsford, LTD., 1948, 120pp.

Pollman, R. B. *123 Unicom Modular Component Designs.* Detroit: Home Planners, Inc., 16310 Grand River Road

Ramsey, Charles G., and Sleeper, H. R. *Architectural Graphic Standards* (6th ed.), New York: John Wiley and Sons, Inc., 1970, 695pp.

Ray, J. Edgar. *Graphic Architectural Drafting.* Bloomington, Ill.: McKnight and McKnight Publishing Co., 1960, 256pp.

Richardson, Albert E. *Georgian Architecture.* New York: Pellegrini and Cudahy, 1950, 256pp.

Salwey, Jasper. *Sketching in Lead-Pencil; for Architects and Others.* New York: Charles Scribner's Sons, 1926, 174pp.

Sherman, Jonathan G. (ed.). *Church Buildings and Furnishings.* New York: The Seabury Press, 1958, 130pp. (Sponsored by Joint Commission on Architecture and the Allied Arts of the Protestant Episcopal Church in the U.S.A.)

Simon, Maron J. (ed.), and Libbey-Owens-Ford Glass Co. *Your Solar House.* New York: Simon and Schuster, 1947, 125pp.

Stewart, Ford. *Protestant Church Buildings and Equipment.* New York: Ford, Stewart, Publisher, 27 East 39th Street.

Stokes, John W. *Food Service in Industry and Institutions.* Dubuque, Iowa: William C. Brown, Co., 1960, 261pp.

Summerson, Sir John N. *Architecture in Britain, 1530 to 1830.* Baltimore: Penguin Books, 1954, 372pp.

Thery, Paul, Bennett, R. M., and Kamphoefner, H. L. *Churches and Temples.* New York: Reinhold Publishing Corp., 1953.

Townsend, Gilbert, and Dalzell, J. R. *How to Plan a House* (3rd. ed.). Chicago: American Technical Society, 1958, 591pp.

Turner, William W. *Shades and Shadows: Their Use in Architectural Rendering.* New York: The Ronald Press Co., 1952, 115pp.

Visher, Stephen S. *Climatic Atlas of the United States.* Cambridge: Harvard University Press, 1954, 403pp.

Waterman, Thomas T. *The Dwelling of Colonial America.* Chapel Hill: The University of North Carolina Press, 1950, 312pp.

Watkin, William W. *Planning and Building the Modern Church* (Protestant). New York: F. W. Dodge Corp., 1951, 163pp.

Watson, Ernest W. *How to Use Creative Perspective.* New York: Reinhold Publishing Corp., 1955, 160pp.

Wright, Frank L. *The Natural House.* New York: Horizon Press, 1954, 223pp.

Yorke, Francis R. *The Modern House* (5th ed.). London, England: The Architectural Press, 1946, 221pp.

Yoshida, Tetsuro. *The Japanese House and Garden.* New York: Frederick A. Praeger, 1955, 204pp.

Government Publications [1]

"Capacities of Stacks in Sanitary Drainage Systems for Buildings," U.S. Federal Housing Administration, 1961, 52pp. Catalog No. C 13.44:31.

"Condensation Control in Dwelling Construction," U.S. Housing and Home Finance Agency, 1950, 73pp. Catalog No. HH 1.2: C 75/2d print.

"Crawl Spaces," U.S. Housing and Home Finance Agency, 1950, 16pp. Catalog No. HH 1.9/a:1.

"Design for Livability," U.S. Housing and Home Finance Agency, 1951, 10pp. Catalog No. HH 1.9/a:12.

"Fireplaces and Chimneys," U.S. Department of Agriculture, 1963 (rev.), 23pp. Catalog No. A 1.9:1889/2.

"Heat Loss Calculations," U.S. Federal Housing Administration, 1959 (rev.), 54pp. Catalog No. HH 2.12:7/2.

"Insulation, Where and How Much," U.S. Housing and Home Finance Agency, 1950, 9pp. Catalog No. HH 1.9/a:4.

[1] Government publications may be obtained from the Superintendent of Documents, Washington, D.C. 20402. They request that all orders specify title, agency, and catalog number.

"Manual of Individual Water Supply Systems," U.S. Federal Housing Administration, 1962 (rev.), 121pp. Catalog No. FS 2.6/2: W 29/2.

"Minimum Property Standards for One and Two Living Units," U.S. Federal Housing Administration, May 1963 (*being revised*), 22pp. Catalog No. HH 2.17/4:963.

"Plumbing Fixture Arrangement," U.S. Housing and Home Finance Agency, 1952, 18pp. Catalog No. HH 1.18:1.

"Plumbing Manual," National Bureau of Standards, U.S. Department of Commerce, 1962 (rev.), 70pp. Catalog No. C 13.29:66.

"Septic Tanks, Their Use in Sewage Disposal," U.S. Housing and Home Finance Agency, 1951, 16pp. Catalog No. HH 1.8:18.

"Wood-Frame House Construction," U.S. Department of Health, Education and Welfare, 1955, 235pp. Catalog No. A 1.76:73.

"Wood Roof Trusses for Small Buildings," U.S. Housing and Home Finance Agency, 1950, 4pp. Catalog No. HH 1.9/a:2.

Other government sources include:

National Bureau of Standards, Building Technology Division (Numerous publications).

U.S. Department of Agriculture, Agricultural Marketing Service, Marketing Research Division (Bulletins concerning marketing).

U.S. Forest Products Laboratory, U.S. Department of Agriculture, Madison, Wisconsin (Numerous bulletins and design reports).

Magazines

American Builder. (Catalog Directory). Monthly. Simmons-Boardman Publishing Corporation, 30 Church Street, New York, New York 10007.

Architectural Forum. Monthly (10 nos. per year). American Planning and Civic Association, 111 W. 57th Street, New York, New York.

Architectural Record. Monthly. McGraw-Hill, Inc., 330 W. 42nd. Street, New York, New York 10036.

Engineering News-Record. Weekly. McGraw-Hill, Inc., 330 West 42nd. Street, New York, New York 10036.

House and Home. Monthly. McGraw-Hill, Inc., 330 W. 42nd. Street, New York, New York 10036.

Practical Builder. Monthly. Industrial Publications, Inc. (Subsidiary of Cahners Publishing Co., Inc.), 5 South Wabash Avenue, Chicago 3, Illinois.

Association and Industrial Publications

Air Conditioning and Refrigeration Institute, 1815 North Fort Meyer Drive, Arlington, Virginia.

"Air Conditioning and Refrigeration Institute Standards."

American Institute of Steel Construction (AISC), 101 Park Avenue, New York 17, New York. Numerous booklets.

"AISC Specification for the Design, Fabrication, and Erection of Steel for Buildings."
"Manual of Steel Construction."
"Commentary on the AISC Specification."

American Institute of Timber Construction (AITC), 1757 K Street, N.W., Washington 6, D.C. Numerous bulletins and design reports.

American Iron and Steel Institute (AISI), 150 East 42nd Street, New York 17, New York.

"Light Gage Cold Formed Steel Design Manual."

American Machine and Foundry Company, Bowling Equipment Division, 6500 N. Lincoln Avenue, Chicago, Illinois.

"Bowling Lane Architectural Design Data."

American Society of Civil Engineers (ASCE), 345 East 47th Street, New York 17, New York.

"Light Wood Trusses," by R. F. Luxford, Paper 1838, 1958.

American Society of Heating, Refrigerating and Air-Conditioning Engineers (ASHRAE), 345 East 47th Street, New York 17, New York.

"Heating, Ventilating and Air Conditioning Guide."

American Society of Mechanical Engineers (ASME), 345 East 47th Street, New York 17, New York.

"National Plumbing Code."

Bastian-Blessing Company, 4201 W. Peterson Avenue, Chicago 46, Illinois.

"Cafeteria Planning."

Bell and Gossett Company, Morton Grove, Illinois.

"Engineering Manual."

Bethlehem Steel Company, Bethlehem, Pennsylvania.

"Structural Steel Shapes."

Better Kitchens Institute, 1120 Chester Avenue, Cleveland 14, Ohio.

"Kitchen Planning Book."

Board of Church Extension, Presbyterian Church in the United States, 241B Ponce De Leon Avenue, N.E., Atlanta, Georgia. Many booklets.

Board of Jewish Education, Chicago, Illinois.
"Jewish School Building Manual," 1954.

Brunswick Corporation, Bowling Division, 623 S. Wabash Avenue, Chicago, Illinois.

"Planning Brunswick Bowling Centers."

Canadian Wood Development Council, Ottawa 2, Ontario, Canada.

"Post and Beam Construction for Residential Buildings," Wood Data Manual No. 2.

Champion Dish Washing Machine Company, Box 8927, Winston-Salem, North Carolina.

"Dish Pantry Layouts."

Commission on Church Architecture, Lutheran Church in America, 231 Madison Avenue, New York, New York. Many booklets.

Concrete Reinforcing Steel Institute (CRSI), 38 South Dearborn Street, Chicago 3, Illinois.

"Concrete Reinforcing Steel Institute Handbook."

Division of National Missions of the Methodist Church, 1701 Arch Street, Philadelphia, Pennsylvania. Many booklets.

"Sanctuary Planning" and "Church School Planning," by Norman Byar.

American Plywood Association, 1119 A Street, Tacoma 2, Washington. Numerous bulletins.

"Fir Plywood Technical Data Handbook."

Edison Electric Institute, Commercial Department, 750 Third Avenue, New York 17, New York.

"Handbook of Residential Wiring Design."

Electrical Information Publications, Inc., Madison, Wisconsin.

"Fact Book, Electric Heating and Cooling."

General Electric Company, Plant Layout and Materials Handling Service Section, Schenectady, New York.

"An Approach to Office Building."

General Electric Company, Wiring Department, Providence, Rhode Island.

"Remote Control Wiring."

General Electric Company, Construction Materials Division, Bridgeport, Connecticut.

"Wiring for Residential Outdoor Lighting."

Gerber Plumbing Fixtures Corporation, 232 North Clark Street, Chicago.

"Tips from Your Plumber."

Illuminating Engineering Society (IES), 345 East 47th Street, New York 17, New York.

"Lighting Keyed to Today's Homes."
"IES Lighting Handbook."
"Church Lighting."

Industry Committee on Interior Wiring Design, 420 Lexington Avenue, New York, New York.

"Residential Wiring Handbook."

Institute of Boiler and Radiator Manufacturers (IBR), 608 Fifth Avenue, Suite 408, New York 20, New York. Numerous bulletins.

Insulation Board Institute (IBI), 111 West Washington Street, Chicago 2, Illinois.

"Fundamentals of Building Insulation."

International Business Machines Corporation, 112 East Post Road, White Plains, New York.

"Planning for an IBM Data Processing System."

International Conference of Building Officials (ICBO), 50 South Los Robles, Pasadena, California.

"Uniform Building Codes."
"National Electrical Code."
National Association of Retail Grocers of the U.S., 360 North Michigan Avenue, Chicago 1, Illinois.

"Super Markets and Shopping Centers."
"Exterior Designs and Interior Arrangements for 17 Food Stores."
"Modern Food Stores."
"Self-Service Meats."
National Board of Fire Underwriters, 85 John Street, New York 38, New York.

"The National Building Code."
National Council of Churches of Christ in the U.S.A. (NCC), 475 Riverside Drive, New York 27, New York. Many inexpensive booklets.

National Electrical Manufacturers Association (NEMA), 155 East 44th Street, New York 17, New York.

"Manual for Electric House Heating," Pub. No. HE-1-1957; AIA File No. 30-C-44.
National Lumber Manufacturers Association (NLMA), 1619 Massachusetts Avenue, N.W., Washington 6, D.C.

"Maximum Spans for Joists and Rafters in Residential Construction."
"Manual for House Framing."
"Plank and Beam Finishing for Residential Buildings."
"The Unicom Method of House Construction." Manual No. 1.
"Fabrication of Components," Manual No. 2, 1962.
National Warm Air Heating and Air Conditioning Association, 640 Engineers Building, Cleveland 14, Ohio.

"Warm Air Heating and Air Conditioning Library."
Plywood Fabricator Service, Inc., Box 7, Riverdale Station, Chicago, Illinois.

"Stressed Skin Panels."
Portland Cement Association, 33 West Grand Avenue, Chicago 10, Illinois.

"Tilt-Up Construction."
"Handbook of Frame Constants."

"Continuity in Concrete Building Frames."
"Precast Concrete Joists."
Sears, Roebuck and Company, Chicago, Illinois.

"Simplified Electric Wiring Handbook."
Small Homes Council, University of Illinois, Urbana.

"Financing the House."
"Business Dealings with Architect and Contractor."
"Land Design."
"Household Storage Units."
"Kitchen Planning Standards."
"Separate Ovens."
"Laundry Areas."
"Garages and Carports."
"Basements."
"Wood Framing."
"Crawl-Space Houses."
"Flooring Materials."
"Insulation."
"Moisture Condensation."
"Chimneys and Fireplaces."
"Window Selection Principles."
"Heating the Home."
"Plumbing."
"Septic Tank Systems."
"Summer Comfort."
"Interior Design."
"Handbook of Kitchen Design."
Southern Baptist Convention, Department of Church Architecture, 127 Ninth Avenue, Nashville 3, Tennessee.

"Planning Better Church Buildings," by W. A. Harrell (1962).
Sweets' Catalog Service, F. W. Dodge Corporation, New York.

"Sweets' Architectural Catalog File."
Timber Engineering Company, 1619 Massachusetts Avenue, N.W., Washington 6, D.C. Numerous bulletins and design reports.

Union of American Hebrew Congregations, 838 Fifth Avenue, New York 21, New York.

"An American Synagogue for Today and Tomorrow," edited by Peter Blake.
West Coast Lumbermen's Association, 1410 S.W. Morrison Street, Portland 5, Oregon. Numerous bulletins and design reports.

INDEX

A

Abbreviations, of steel members, 535
Access roads, to shopping centers, 453
Acoustical engineer, 318
Acoustical material, 315, 316
  factors in selection of, 318
Acoustics, 315-318
  in banks, 401
  in churches, 466, 468, 479
  in data processing centers, 396
  in food stores, 414
Air —
  flow of heated, 269
  used in heat pump, 282
Air-conditioning —
  benefits of yearly, 269
  of clinics, 407
  gas, 282, 285-286
  installing room, 277, 278
  in modular system, 161, 166
  see also Cooling
Air-cooled systems, 273, 274
Aisles —
  in churches, 467
  data processing office, 396
  in food stores, 419
  in offices, 390
  parking in shopping centers, 453
  planning shopping, 352, 353
  in planning displays, 354
  width for parking, (table) 446
Alarm system, planning in banks, 399
Altar, 469, 473, 474
Altitude, and building a home, 19, 20
Aluminum, curtain-wall panels, 567-570, 573

Aluminum sandwich panels, 183
American Institute of Architects, 117
American National Standards Institute, 175
Amortization, rate of, 325, 326
Ampere, defined, 236
Analogous colors, in renderings, 346
Angle beams, loads for, (table) 233
Annunciators, electrical system needed for, 250
Apartments, modular system for, 166-174
Appliances —
  circuits for, 237, 238, 240
  and kitchen planning, 35
Appliance stores, planning, 368-370
Arches, 554, (table) 555, 556
Architect —
  and church planning, 460
  common duties of, 321, 322
  communicates through renderings, 338-347
  landscape, 16, 17
  relationship with owner, 321-322
  renderings and models by, 328
  selecting an, 320
  studies objectives of food store, 412
Architect's scales, reading, 103
Architectural Graphic Standards, 115
Architectural renderings, and model construction, 328-348
Architecture —
  American since 1900, 81-100
  Dutch Colonial, 74-75
  early American residential, 69-81
  French Colonial, 75-76
  integrating shopping center, 454
  Japanese influence on American, 83-86

  Old World residential, 64-69
  Southern colonial, 70-71
  Spanish, 76-79
  in transition, 97-100
Art, in churches, 476
Artist, draws renderings, 338-347
Assembly line, modular, 164, 166
Asymmetry, of building design, 60
Atmosphere, planning consideration of merchandising facilities, 353
Attic —
  insulating, 312
  storage and joist selection, (table) 208
  temperature and, 296
  ventilation of, 315
Automatic grace period, in home payment plan, 326
Automobile, parking facilities for, 446-450
Azimuth, and building site, 20

B

Bakery, 414, 415, 420, 454
Balance, in exterior design, 60
Balustrade, in Federal house style, 79
Banks, planning, 397-403, 454, 457
Baptismal font, 469, 471, 473, 474
Barber shops, planning, 378-379, 454
Bars, for reinforcing concrete, 503
Bar supports, reinforced concrete, 504, 505
Baseboard heaters, 270, 278, 288
Basement plan, drawing, 113
Basements —
  and condensation, 314
  dimensioning on working drawings, 110

Basements (*continued*)
  excavating, 131
  footings and foundation
    construction, 187-206
  as garage space, 49
  and heat loss, 297
  in house design, 11-12, 63
  lighting and electric service in,
    246-247
  planning, 49-52
  planning homes without, 49
  uses for, 50
Bathrooms —
  basement, 51
  lighting and electric service in,
    244, 245
  in mobile homes, 176, 177
  planning, 41-44
  planning motel, 446
Batter boards, 131
Batt insulation, 310
Beams, 146-148
  and columns, in monolithic
    concrete construction, 502-509
  dimensioning, 110
  glued laminated and purlin sizes,
    (tables) 225, 226
  light steel, 518
  precast concrete, 486-488
  using safe load tables for, 522-532
  wide-flange steel, 518
Beam schedule, in engineering
    drawings, 508
Bedrooms —
  lighting and electric service in,
    244
    planning, 38-39
  planning windows in, 53
Bending stress, 521
Bents, precast concrete, 499-502,
    505
Bevel siding, 135, 136
Bids —
  obtaining house, 321
  specifications and, 117
Blanket insulations, 310
Block system, in merchandising
    facility, 352
Boilers, in heating systems,
    286-292, 294
Bolting, steel member, 535
Bolts, structural steel, 536
Bonding, of contractor, 324
Booths, in restaurants, 425
Bowstring trusses, 544, 557
Box beams, 181-182, 222-225
Breaking strength, and stress, 521
Breezeway, garage to house, 48
Brick —
  construction with, 140-141
  patterns of, 140
  used in curtain wall, 200
  used for fireplaces, 298, 301, 304
Bridging, 137, 138
British Thermal Units (BTU), 295
Bronze curtain-wall panels, 572, 573

Budget, building house within, 323
Builders, house plan source, 321
Builder's felt, to waterproof
    foundation, 197
Building codes, 13-15
  influence home styling, 63
  protect homeowner, 14
Building site —
  and codes, 14, 15
  factors in choice of, 14-18
  planning, 14-15
  purchasing, 15
Building supply dealers, source of
    house plans, 320
Building supply stores, planning,
    373-375
Built-up cased beams, 146-148
Bulb tees —
  spans for, (table) 562
  table of weights, 513
Bungalow house style, 81
Butterfly roof, 64
Buttressed arches, 554

——— C ———

Cabinets —
  dimensioning, 111
  drawing details of, 115-116
  kitchen, 37-38
  scale of details, 103
Cables, electric heating, 278-279
Cafeteria, sample plan for, 432
California house style, 91-92
California Spanish mission, 77, 78
Canopies —
  in drive-in restaurant planning,
    434
  service station, 382, 383
Cantilevers, with steel framing, 149
Cape Cod house style, 11, 75
Carpentry, in specifications, 119
Carpeting, as acoustical material
    318
Carports —
  in motel planning, 440
  planning garages and, 47-49
Cases, display for merchandise, 354
Cast-in-place piles, 484
Ceiling purlins, in modular system,
    166
Ceiling line, in dimensioning, 110
Ceilings —
  insulating, 310, 311, 312
  in modular system, 166
  in monolithic concrete
    construction, 503
  and noise control, 317
  service station, 382
Cellular glass slabs, as
    insulations, 311
Cellular-steel floor systems, 551-552

Cement-asbestos panels, in curtain-
    wall system, 571, 572, 573
Cement-asbestos shingles, 135, 136
Center line, in spacing bolting, 536
Ceramic tile, curtain-wall panels,
    574
Chancel —
  location of choir and organ, 472
  planning church, 469-470
Chapel, planning church, 471-472
Characteristics, identifying
    exterior design, 62
Charts, perspective, 334
Check-out stations, in food stores,
    417, 418
Chemical, to prevent termites,
    197, 198
Chimes, electrical system for, 249
Chimney footings, 193
Chimneys, fireplace, 306-308
China, architectural influence on
    Japan, 83
Choir, planning church area for,
    472-473
Chord, member of truss, 544
Churches —
  arches in, 554-557
  exterior design, 479-480
  harmonizing furnishings in,
    473-474
  planning, 460-481
  use precast vents, 499
Chute, laundry, 46
Circuits —
  number needed in home, 238
  types of electrical, 237
  typical low-voltage, 251
Circulation, of heated air, 269, 270
Classrooms, church school, 477-479
Cleaning shops, planning, 376-377
Climate —
  affects garage planning, 47
  influences home styling, 63
Clinics, planning, 404-410
Closets —
  in halls, 7
  lighting, 246
  motel room, 446
  planning, 39-40
Closing costs, of loan, 326
Clothing stores —
  planning men's and women's,
    370-372
  in shopping centers, 454, 456
Coal, in steam heating system,
    293, 294
Codes —
  building service station, 381
  electrical, 236
  zoning and building in planning
    banks, 402
Coefficient of heat transmission,
    295, (table) 299, 300
Coefficient of noise reduction, 315
Coils, heating, 291, 292
Cold water system, 265-266

Collar beams, 211
Colonial house styles, 70-81
Color —
  in architectural renderings, 342
  in building design, 62
  in church planning, 474
  for food store planning, 414
  hue and intensity in renderings, 346, 347
  media in renderings, 345
  in office planning, 394
  in planning merchandising facilities, 358
  in shopping center design, 454
  used for contrast, 61
Columns —
  and beams in monolithic concrete construction, 502-509
  loads on structural, (tables) 216
  piers and curtain walls, 198-200
  and pier footings, 192-193
  precast concrete, 485, (table) 486
  steel, 524, 527, 530, 531-533
  in tilt-up concrete construction, 516
Commercial buildings —
  factory-manufactured, 563-565
  overview of planning, 349-350
  structural systems used in constructing, 482-566
  working drawings for small, 582-617
Common rafters, 143
Communication systems, 249-250
Communion rail or table, 468, 469, 474
Community center, building in mobile home parks, 179-180
Complementary colors, 346, 347
Composition, principle of, 60
Compressive stress, 519
Concrete —
  in basement foundations, 195
  in curtain-wall panels, 574
  engineering drawings for construction, 505-508
  insulating, 311
  insulating steel roof decking, 549
  in modular system, 173, 174
  monolithic reinforced construction, 502-509
  and noise control, 316
  in pile foundations, 483, 484
  pilings, 201
  pouring footing, 187, 188
  precast curtain-wall panels, 578-580
  precast panels, 183, 184
  precast reinforced lintels, (tables) 231, 232
  reinforced drawings, 503, 505
  in slab foundations, 202-205
  in specifications, 118, 119
  strengths of, 503
  tilt-up construction, 515-517

used for piers, 198, (table) 199, 200
  used in pilasters, 200
Concrete blocks, in solid masonry construction, 141, 142
Condensation, controlling, 313-315
Condensers, in cooling system, 273, 275
Conductors, current carrying capacity of copper, (table) 240
Connections, standard steel, 537-539
Construction —
  methods of house, 131-186
  of modular apartments, 167-174
  new developments in house, 180-184
  with precast joists, 498
  scale of details, 103
  standards for mobile homes, 175-176
  structural members commonly used in, 207-235
  tilt-up concrete, 515-517
Consultation rooms, in medical clinics, 405
Contemporary house style, 86, 87-89
Contour lines, of building site, 16
Contract —
  binds owner and contractor, 117, 321
  general conditions of, 117, 118
  land to finance house, 325
Contractor —
  bonding of, 324
  estimates cost of house, 322-323
  relationship with owner, 117, 322
  responsibilities defined in specifications, 116
  selecting a, 321
Contrast, in exterior designing, 61-62
Convectors, heating devices, 279, 288, 289
Convenience merchandise, planning areas for, 351, 352
Conveyors, food handling, 420, 429, 431
Cooling —
  cold water systems, 292-293
  cycle of gas-fired air conditioner, 285, 286
  electric units for, 273-278
  forced-air, 273
  heating and insulating, 269-319
  motel room, 446
  with pump, 281
Copper curtain-wall system, 572-573
Core, planning rooms as, 47
Corners, framing, 134
Corrugated panels, steel, 547
Costs —
  closing on loan, 326
  estimating house, 322-323

and house shapes, 13
  of plans and specifications, 320, 321
  trade-in purchasing, 327
Cotswold, English house, 65, 66
Cottage, Cape Cod, 75
Counters —
  for displaying merchandise, 354-355
  in food service, 431
  for laundry, 45, 46
Crane, in module lifting, 161, 164, 167, 169
Crawl spaces —
  and condensation, 314
  foundations for, 195-196
  insulating, 312
Cul-de-sac lots, in mobile home parks, 179
Curtains, as acoustical material, 318
Curtain walls, 198-200, 567-581

——— D ———

Darkroom, for X-rays in clinics, 407, 408
Data, recorded on plot plan, 116
Data processing centers, planning, 396-397
Datum level, in plot plan, 15
Dead load, and footings, 189-193
Decible, measure of noise, 315
Decking —
  heavy roof, 213-215
  poured gypsum roof, 512-514
Decks, parking, 446
Deed, to land, 14
Deflection —
  of steel members, 522
  of structural members, 222
Deformation, in structural steel members, 521
Demand Merchandise, planning areas for, 351, 352
Dental offices, planning, 404-410
Department stores, in shopping centers, 454, 456, 457
Design —
  contrast in exterior, 61
  evaluating exterior home, 59-60
  exterior of merchandising facilities, 358-361
  of fireplaces, 298, 300-306
  of home exteriors, 59-101
  of individual rooms, 25-58
  mixing of exterior house, 59, 60
  principles of building, 59, 60-62
  rhythm in exterior, 61, 62
  standards for mobile homes, 174-176
  symmetrical and asymmetrical, 60
  unity in, 62

Design data —
for bow string trusses, 557
for box section subpurlins,
table) 561
for cement-asbestos curtain-wall
panels, (table) 573
for ceramic tiled curtain-wall
panels, (tables), 574, 575
for corrugated panels, (table)
533
for joists as independent beams,
(table) 496-497
loads for joists and slab
T-Beams, (tables) 492-495
on poured gypsum deck, (table),
514

Design data (*continued*)
for precast concrete columns,
(table) 486
for precast concrete planks, 491
for rigid frame units, (table) 553
safe loads for steel beams,
(tables), 525-530
for safe loads on subpurlins, 513
for steel columns, (tables)
527-533
for stud roof decking and slab,
(tables) 550
for stock rigid frame steel
buildings, (table) 564
for structural slab on ground,
203
for three-hinged arches, 556
for two-hinged arches, (table)
555

Designer, considerations of
commercial buildings, 349-350
Desks, office arrangements,
389, 390

Details —
dimensioning, 111
drawing, 114-116
of working drawings, 582-617

Dimensioning —
of details, 111
fireplaces, (tables) 301, 302,
303, 304
on place drawings, 508
of shop drawings, 542-543
steel framing drawings, 539
of truss drawings, 546
of working drawings, 103,
110-111

Dining areas —
planning in kitchens, 33-38
restaurants, 425

Dining rooms —
lighting and electric service in,
243
planning, 33-34
Dishwashing, area in restaurants,
428-429, 435

Display —
equipment for merchandise,
354-355
of food merchandise, 417-423
show windows for merchandise,
358-361
Dock, planning merchandising
facility, 357

Doctors' Parks, 408-410
Dolly, joining steel members, 535
Domes, 503, 558
Dormers, in house design, 11-12
Doorbells, systems for, 249

Doors —
in architectural renderings, 338,
340
classroom, 478
dimensioning, 110
double for church entrances, 467
exterior bank, 400
garage, 48, 49
and heat loss, 297
interior in modular system, 166
in modular system, 152
planning restaurant kitchen, 427
in room planning, 25, 32
sliding, 54, 56
store front, 361
storm, 312
and wall section symbols, 108

Dossal, 474
Dowels, for reinforcing concrete,
504
Downflow furnace, 271
Downpayment, for house, 325
Draftsman —
architectural, 320, 321
and lettering, 111, 112
and structural steel drawings,
535

Drainage, and building site, 15, 16
Drains —
house or building, 255
house in waste disposal system,
257-258
in restaurant kitchens, 427
sizing building, (table) 260, 261
sizing house, 259-260
Drain tile, and foundations, 196
Drawing boards, perspective, 334,
335

Drawings —
architectural presentation,
334-335
concrete placing, 508
engineering, 505-508
laminated wood structural
system, 558-561
making working, 102-130
pictorial, 328-335
reinforced concrete members,
503-505

rendering architectural, 338-347
steel framing, 539
steel truss, 544-546
structural steel, 534-546
structural steel shop, 542-543
working for commercial
buildings, 582-617
Dressing rooms, in medical clinics,
407
Drive-in, planning bank service,
397, 400, 401
Drugstores, planning, 383-386,
454, 455
Dry cleaning shops, planning,
376-377, 454
Dryer, planning space for, 45-47
Ducts, cooling and heating, 270,
271, 275
Dutch Colonial house style, 74-75

——— **E** ———

Easements, examining deeds for,
14
Eaves, framing, 138
Effective length, of steel columns,
527
Elasticity, modulus of, 521-522
Elastic limit, structural steel
members, 521
Electrical symbols, 104

Electrical systems —
low-voltage, remote-control,
251-253
planning, 241-249
for signaling and communication,
249-250

Electricity, 236-254
calculating entrance load,
240-241
in cellular-steel floor systems,
551-552
for data processing centers, 397
for display fixtures, 354, 356
food store needs, 419, 421
in forced-air heating systems,
270-272
heating with, 278-281
for hot water system, 266, 267
insulation when heating by, 312
for kitchens, 237, 238, 240
power centers for, 239-240
in precast concrete slabs, 511
see also Wiring
for service entrances, 238-239
for service stations, 383
in specifications, 121
system in mobile home
standards, 176
in tilt-up concrete construction,
515

Elevations —
drawing, 113-114
and fireplaces, 298
of house, 3, 4
influence home styling, 63
placement of drawings in
working drawing set, 582-584
in plot plan, 15
scale on drawings, 103
of shoe stores, 363, 364
Elevators —
freight in stores, 358
to move food trays, 429
parking, 449-450
planning in merchandising
facilities, 353
Elizabethan house, 66, 67
Ells —
dimensioning, 110
in house shape, 12, 13
in modular design, 162
Engineer —
acoustical, 318
computes stresses on
members, 544-545
responsible for structural
drawings, 505-508
Entrances —
planning traffic pattern, 5
to restaurants, 424
store, 360, 361
Equipment —
list of restaurant kitchen, 427
planning for in clinics, 405, 408
planning for in food stores, 414
planning space in banks, 400, 401
for service station, 383
Equity, in house, 323, 326
Erection plans, 540-541
Escalators, planning in
merchandising facilities, 353
Europe, architectural styles of, 64
Evaluation, of exterior home
designs, 59-60
Examining rooms, in medical
clinics, 405
Excavating, in specifications, 118
Experimental Housing Program,
Federal Housing
Administration's, 166
Exposure, of sidings, 135, 136
Exteriors —
design of church, 479-480
designing home, 59-101
and floor plans, 2
mixing designs of house, 59, 60

——— F ———

Factory-manufactured commercial
buildings, 563-566
Factory-manufactured house, 150
Fahrenheit, 295

Family, meeting home needs
of, 1-6
Fans, exhaust to prevent
condensation, 314
Federal house style, 79
Federal Housing Administration —
and building codes, 13-15
and window requirements, 53
using in financing home, 325
Fiberboard, for sheathing walls,
134, 135
Files, locating in offices, 393
Fill, and slab foundations, 205
Filling, in specifications, 118
Financing, methods of house,
324-327
Finishing, of modular units on the
site, 161-162
Fink truss, 544-545
Fire, home insured against, 324
Fire alarms, electrical system
needed for, 250
Fireplaces, 298-309
and chimneys, 306-307
in design proportion, 61
dimensioning, 110, 111
drawing details of, 114
placement of, 51, 306
in room designing, 32
Fireproofing, of steel framing, 532
Fixtures —
in clothing stores, 370, 371
display in jewelry stores, 365
display in shoe stores, 362, 363
for florist shop, 377
in food store planning, 414-419
in hardware store, 374
merchandise display, 354-355
placement in bath, 43
symbols, 105
Fixture unit values, for measuring
waste flow, 260
Flat roof, 64
Flemish Colonial house style, 74, 75
Floor decking, 144, 145, 146
Floor line, in dimensioning, 110
Floor plans —
affected by exterior design, 2
checking usability, 2
developing, 1-6
dimensioning on working
drawings, 110
drawing, 112-113
and economical lumber usage, 2-3
finalizing, 4
and lot, 2
of mobile homes, 175, 176
for modular apartments, 171, 172
of modular townhouse, 170
and roof framing, 4
revising to meet family needs, 1-6
scale on drawings, 103
sketching, 2
summary of steps for, 4
Floor purlins, in modular
system, 166

Floors —
cellular-steel system, 551-552
insulating, 311, 312, 313
materials for church, 463, 464
in modular system, 158, 159, 166
plank, 146
precast concrete, 509, 512
slab, 202-205
slab with steel roof decking,
549, 551
Florida, Spanish influence on
architecture of, 76-77
Florida house style, 89-91
Florist and nursery shops,
planning, 377-378
Flues, 306, 307, 308
Flying gable, roof design, 64
Food stores —
placement of departments in,
419-423
planning, 412-423
planning cleaning ease, 414
in shopping centers, 454, 456, 457
Footings, 131, 132, 187-206
chimney, 193
and construction material
weights, (table) 190
depth of, 193-194
design problems of, 190-192
determining size, 188-194
example of load calculation of
pier, (table) 193
factors in constructing
rectangular, 187
and fireplaces, 302
flared, 187
pier and column, 188, 192-193
porch and stair, 193
standard size residential,
(table) 189
stepped, 188
Forced circulation, in heating
system, 287
Formboards, 513
insulation, 310
Foundation arches, 554
Foundation plan —
dimensioning of working
drawings, 110
drawing, 113
scale on drawings, 103
Foundations, 187-206
for crawl spaces, 195-196
and fireplaces, 302
layout and digging of, 131, 132
in modular systems, 153, 154,
158, 169
pier and curtain wall, 198-200
and pilisters, 200
piling, 201, 482-485
protecting from termites, 197-198
slab, 202-205
standard thicknesses for
residential walls, (table), 195
waterproofing, 196
Foyers, planning church, 466-467

Framing —
  of house, 132-134
  of joists, 135, 137
  in modular system, 153, 159,
    160, 166
  roof, 143
  of steel houses, 148-149
  steel on modular units, 162, 163
  systems of, 144, 145
  systems for factory-manufactured
    buildings, 564
  of walls in house, 133-134
Free-flow system, in merchandising
  facility, 352, 353
Freestanding fixture, to display
  merchandise, 354
French Colonial house style, 75-76
Freon, in cooling units, 273
Frost line —
  and footings, 193, 194
  and foundations, 195, 201
Furnaces —
  contain cooling unit, 275
  electric, 280
  horizontal forced-air, 271
  placement in basement, 51
  upflow and downflow, 271
Furnishings, harmonizing church,
  473-474
Furniture —
  in motel planning, 443-445
  in offices, 390
  in perspective drawings, 332, 333
  in planning rooms, 25-33
  and stairs, 8
  typical sizes of, 25-33
  and window placement, 53
Furniture stores, planning, 366-368
Furring strip, in solid masonry
  construction, 140, 141

——— G ———

Gables —
  in modular component assembly,
    154, 156
  roof design, 63, 64
Gage line, in bolting steel, 536, 537
Gambrel, roof design, 64
Garages —
  fireproofing, 49
  and heat loss, 297
  lighting and electric service
    for, 247
  planning carports and, 47-49
  see also Parking facilities
Gas —
  for air conditioning, 282, 285-286
  in cooling units, 273
  in forced-air heating, 270-272
  for heating, 286
  to operate water heater, 266, 267
  service to appliance stores, 369
  in steam heating system, 293, 294

Gases, in waste disposal system,
  262, 263
Georgian Colonial house style,
  71-74
Georgian house style, 67
Gingerbread, Victorial house
  style, 80
Girders —
  computing load area of, 218-220
  and joist framing, 135, 137
  precast concrete, 486-488
  spans of solid wood, (tables)
    220, 221, 222, 223
  steel, 227-228
  wood, 216, 218-227
Glass —
  cellular slabs to insulate, 311
  curtain-wall panels, 575
Glass blocks, as curtain walls,
  576-578
Glued laminated wood structural
  members, 552-561
Gondolas, display of foods, 417, 420
GOW method, of soil
  investigation, 483
Grade beam, 201
Grading, of building site, 15, 118
Greek Revival house style, 79-80
Grid, curtain-wall panels, 568, 573
Groceries, displaying in food
  stores, 420
Gropius, 81
Gypsum, poured roof system,
  512-514
Gyration, radius of steel
  columns, 524, 527

——— H ———

Half-timbered house, 66, 67
Halls —
  lighting and electric service in,
    246
  planning, 7
Handrail, for stairs, 8
Hardboard siding, 135, 136
Hardware, in specifications, 120
Hardware stores, planning, 373-375
Hawaiian house style, 85, 86
Hearth, *see* Fireplaces
Heaters —
  electric, 278-281
  hot water, 266-267, 287, 288-292
Heating —
  ASHRAE guide for, 296
  calculating adequacy of
    systems, 295-298
  of churches, 461
  and condensation control,
    313-315
  cooling, and insulating, 269-319
  and cooling unit placement,
    269-270

cycle of gas-fired air conditioner,
  286
electric, 240, 278-281
electric and insulation for, 312
fireplaces and, 298-309
food store needs of, 419, 421
forced-air system, 270-272
with heat pump, 281-284
hot water system, 286-292
and insulation, 309-313
in modular systems, 161, 166, 167
motel room, 446
new electrical developments, 281
planning room for in
  merchandising facilities, 358
service station, 383
in specifications, 120
by steam, 293-294
system in mobile home
  standards, 176
Heat loss —
  calculations of, 295-298
  and insulation, 312
Hip rafters, 143
Hip roof, 63, 64
Hoffman, 81
Holes, minimum edge distance for
  punched, (table) 537
Horizon, in perspective drawings,
  329
Horizontal fixture branch,
  computing size of, 261
Horizontal wood siding, 135, 136
Hot water, in specifications, 120
Hot water system, 266-267
Houses —
  around the world (pictorial),
    93-97
  assembling with modular
    components, 153-156
  basic types of, 11-12
  business factors in building,
    320-327
  common shapes of, 12-13
  designs of, 59-101
  estimating cost of, 322-323
  factors in choosing building
    sites, 13-23
  factory-manufactured, 150
  financing, 324-326
  fitting costs into family budget,
    323
  methods of constructing, 131-186
  from modular units, 157-162
  new construction developments,
    180-184
  panelized metal, 183
  planning new, 1-24
  positioning correctly, 21-23
  steel framed, 148-149
  styles of, 64-101
  styles in U.S. since 1900, 81-100
  values of in choosing site, 14, 15
  wiring for electricity, 236-254
  wiring for prefabricated, 250, 251
  zoning, 6-7

Hue, and intensity in renderings, 346, 347
Humidity —
  and condensation, 134, 313
  control in data processing centers, 397
  in florist shop, 378
  controlling, 269

——— I ———

I beams, 227
  joist framed into, 137
Illustrations, black and white, 343, 344
Impulse merchandise, planning areas for, 351, 352
Infiltration heat loss, 295, 297
Inks, colored for renderings, 345
Inspectors, and building codes, 13-15
Insulation, 269-319
  in curtain-wall panels, 567-580
  design data on slab heating requirements, (table) 204
  of electrically- and non-electrically-heated living units, 312
  and electric heat, 278
  and heat loss, 312
  in modular system, 156, 166
  and noise control, 316
  in roof decking, 145
  and steel roof decking, 549
  types of, 309-312
Insurance, cost in house payment, 323, 324
Interest, on home loan, 323, 325
Interest rates, limited by government, 325
Interiors, perspective drawings of, 332-334
Interpolation, process of, 22, 23
Intrusion mortar, in pile foundations, 484
Island fixture, to display merchandise, 354
Islands, service station, 381
Italian house styles, 68

——— J ———

Jacobean house, 67
Japanese Modern house style, 83-86
Jewelry stores, planning, 365-366, 454
Joining, of structural steel members, 535

Joists —
  dimensioning, 110
  framing, 135, 137
  loads for independent beam, (table) 496-497
  in modular component system, 152
  in monolithic reinforced concrete construction, 503
  open-web steel, 228, (table) 229, 230, 518
  precast concrete flooring, 489
  precast concrete tie, (table) 488
  selecting, 207-209
  solid-web steel, 517
  spacing standards for plywood sheathing, (table) 211
  spans for floor and ceiling, (table) 208

——— K ———

K factor, 295
  in steel column tables, 531
Kips, 228, 524
Kitchens —
  accessible from garages, 47
  areas in restaurants, 425-428
  in cafeteria, 431
  in churches, 466
  indrive-in restaurants, 434
  electrical circuits for, 237, 238, 240
  lighting and electric service in, 245, 246
  in mobile homes, 176, 177
  planning, 34-38
K values, 215

——— L ———

Laboratory, in medical clinics, 406
Laminated wood structural systems, 552-561
  drawing, 558-561
Lamps, types of, 247-249
Land, advantages of sloping, 15
Land contract, financing house purchase, 325
Landings, for stairs, 8
Landscaping —
  of motels, 438
  plan for, 16-17
  and privacy, 18
  for privacy in mobile home parks, 178
Latitude, and house location, 20-23
Laundry —
  basement area for, 51
  facilities in garage, 47, 49
  facilities in kitchen, 38
  lighting and electric service in, 246
  planning facilities for, 45-46

Lavatories, in master bedroom, 42
Laws —
  control module transportation, 157, 158, 176
  limits mortgages, 324
Layout —
  of architectural renderings, 342
  of food stores, 415, 416, 420, 421, 422
  of foundation of house, 131
  making office, 388-395
  steps of perspective drawing, 329-332
  of views and plans in working drawings, 582-584
Lean-to-house style, 70
Le Corbusier, 81
Lecturn, 469, 473
Lettering, of drawings, 111-112, 335
Liability, insurance for, 324
Library, church school, 478
Light —
  in drawing renderings, 344
  windows give natural, 53

Lighting —
  in basements, 246, 247
  for bathrooms, 244
  for bedrooms, 244
  cafeteria, 429
  of churches, 474-475
  in closets, 246
  in clothing stores, 370, 372
  in data processing centers, 396
  in drugstores, 386
  electrical needs for, 240
  in florist shop, 377, 378
  in food stores, 414
  for furniture stores, 368
  for garages and carports, 247
  in hardware stores, 375
  halls and stairs, 246
  in jewelry stores, 365, 366
  for kitchens, 245
  in laundry and utility areas, 246
  motel room, 443
  in offices, 390, 393, 394
  planning requirements for home, 241-242
  for porches, 247
  restaurants, 424
  for sales areas of merchandising facilities, 356
  service station, 381
  in shoe stores, 364
  of show windows, 360
  types of fixtures, 247-249
Lime, in stucco, 139
Lineal feet, in house shapes, 12
Lintels, 228, 231-234
Lithium bromide, 285, 286, 292
Live loads —
  common design loads for, (table) 189
  and footings, 189-193

Living areas, motel, 443-446
Living rooms —
  lighting and electric service in, 242, 243
  in mobile homes, 176, 177
  planning factors, 31-33
Loads —
  allowable for steel roof decking, (table) 547, 548
  allowed for concrete-filled steel columns, (table) 533
  dead and live, 189-193
  dead and live on joists, 207, (table) 208
  dead and live on rafters, 209, (table), 210
  example of residential calculation of, (table) 191
  for joists and slab T-Beams, (tables) 492-495
  on precast concrete beams, (tables) 487
  safe concrete roof channels, (tables) 489, 490
  safe limits for aluminum mullions, (table) 571
  safe for open-web steel joists, (table) 229, 230
  safe on precast concrete decking, (table) 509
Loan, figuring interest on, 325
Loan agency —
  approves plans and specifications, 321
  governmental, 325
Lobby, restaurant, 424
Loggia, in Italian house style, 68
Loop perimeter heating, 273
Loose-fill insulations, 310, 311
Lot —
  building codes, 14
  determining needed size, 14
  and floor plan, 2
  types of for mobile home park, 178-179
Lounge, in medical clinics, 405
Lumber —
  allowable unit stresses for structural, (table) 224
  economical use of, 2-3
Lumber (*continued*)
  for sheathing walls, 134, 135
  species for girders, 221-223
Luminaries, 248
Luncheonettes, planning, 431-433

Magazines, source of house plans, 320
Malls, shopping center arrangements, 453

Mandrel, in pile foundation forming, 484
Mansard, roof design, 64
Mantels, 307, 309
Manufacturers, source of house plans, 321
Mark, identification of floors and members, 505
Masonry —
  chimneys of, 306-308
  and noise control, 317
  solid construction, 140-142
  pilasters, 200
  in specifications, 119
  used for piers, 198, (table) 199, 200
Masonry veneer, over frame construction, 142-143
Mass, in building design, 62, 338
Materials —
  average weights of construction, (table) 190
  considering for merchandising facilities, 358
  for exterior design contrasts, 61
  influence home styling, 63
  listed in specifications, 116-121
  in shopping center design, 454
Matting, of architectural renderings, 343
Meat departments, in food store 419-423
Medical offices —
  planning, 404-410
  in shopping centers, 457
  space requirements, (table) 407
Mediterranean house styles, 68
Merchandise —
  display equipment for, 354-355
  placement in stores, *see* Type of store
Merchandising facilities —
  coordination of products in, 353
  exterior design of, 358-361
  planning, 351-387
  planning sales area of, 351-356
  planning shopping centers, 452-459
Midwest Ranch house style, 82, 83
Millwork —
  fireplace mantels, 307, 309
  in specifications, 119
Mineral wool, as insulation, 310
Mirrors, in store planning, 364, 366, 372, 379
Missions, Spanish architectural influence of, 77-79
Mobile Home Manufacturers Association, 174
Mobile homes, 174-180
  expandable, 176
  parks for, 177-180
Models, architectural renderings and construction of, 328-348
Modern style house, 81-82

Modular components —
  application of, 153
  assembling house with, 153-156
  to construct buildings, 150-156
Modular system, construction and design specifications, 165, 166
Modular units —
  for apartment construction, 166-174
  building with, 157-174
  for commercial buildings, 162-166
  laws governing transporting, 157, 158
  lifting, 161
  in residential design, 157-162
  typical sizes, 157, 158
Module —
  sizes, 150
  using principle of in room planning, 2, 3
Modulus of elasticity, in steel members, 521
Moisture, controlling, 313-315, 568
Molding, used with stucco, 139
Money —
  influences home styling, 63
  sources of for building house, 325
Monitor, roof design, 64
Monolithic reinforced concrete construction, 502-509
Monterey style house, 78, 79
Mortgage, house, 323, 324
Motels, planning, 436-446
Motor hotels, planning, 436-446
Mount Vernon, style of, 72, 73
Mullions, curtain-wall panel, 568, 570, 571, 572
Multistory building, heating, 292
Multistory parking facilities, 446-450
Muntins, block window view, 52

Nails —
  in applying stucco, 138
  power staples replace, 184
Narthex, church foyers, 466-467
National Fire Protection Association, 175
National Housing Act, 325
National Lumber Manufacturers Association, 150
Nave, planning church, 467-469
Neighborhood, influences home styling, 63
Neutra, 81
New England houses, early 17th century, 69, 70
New Orleans, French influence on architecture in, 75-76

Noise —
    airborne, 315, 316
    control of, 315-318
    direct, 315
    in food stores, 414
    human reaction to, 315
    and motel planning, 437
    transmission of, 316
    and zoning, 6
Norman house style, 65, 66
Nosings, of stairs, 9
Notes, on working drawings, 110
Nurseries —
    church, 477, 478
    and landscape plans, 16, 17
    planning, 377-378
Nurse's station, in medical
    clinics, 406

O

Offices —
    analyzing employee needs, 388
    planning, 388-411
    planning in bank, 399, 400
    planning church, 464, 466
    planning principles, 388-395
Oil, in heating systems, 270,
    293, 294
Old English house, 65, 66
One-story house, drawing floor
    plan of, 113
Open plan, in modern house, 81
Operatories, in dental clinics, 408
Organ, planning placement in
    churches, 472-473
Orientation, of house, 18-23
Outlets —
    for appliance stores, 368
    in barber shops, 378
    in basements, 246, 247
    in bathrooms, 244
    in bedrooms, 244
    convenience, 241, 242
    for dining areas, 243
    in furniture stores, 368
    for garages and carports, 247
    graphical electrical symbols
        for, 242
    in halls, 246
    in kitchen, 245, 246
    in laundry and utility areas, 246
    for living rooms, 242, 243
    for merchandise displaying, 354
    for porches, 247
    split-wired, 242
    television, 250
Overhang, dimensioning, 111

Owner —
    relationship with architect,
        321-322
    relationship with contractor,
        117, 322
    responsibilities defined in
        specifications, 116

P

Pacific house style, 86, 87
Painting, in specifications, 120
Paints —
    peeling due to condensation, 314
    water-soluble for renderings, 345
Panelized metal houses, 183
Panels —
    acoustical, 317
    aluminum sandwich, 183
    corrugated steel, 547
    hot water heating, 289, 290
    members of trusses, 544
    precast concrete, 183, 184
    stressed-skin, 216, 217
    tilt-up concrete, 515-517
Paper —
    drawing for architectural
        renderings, 329, 345
    and insulation, 310, 311
    for presentation drawings, 335
    sizes for working drawings, 102
Parking —
    advantages of elevator, 450
    area for guest, 48
    church, 461
    for doctors' parks, 408, 410
    drive-in restaurant, 434
    facilities in mobile home parks,
        178, 179
    motel and motor inn, 440
    for multi-story motor hotels, 436
    planning bank, 397
    planning for clinics, 407, 408
    planning facilities for, 446-450
    planning food store, 413, 414
    planning service station, 381
    shopping center, 453
Parks —
    doctor's, 408-410
    for mobile homes, 177-180
Parlor, church, 462
Partitions —
    dimensioning, 110
    and framing joists, 137
    solid laminated, 180-181
Pastel sticks, for renderings, 345
Patterns, pronounced and
    secondary, 61, 62
Payments, plans for house,
    323, 325, 326
Perimeter heating, 270
Perlite, insulating material, 311

Permanent set, of steel members,
    521
Perspective, architectural, 328-335
Perspective drawings, preliminary
    rendering step, 342
Pews, arrangement in churches,
    467-468
Picture plane, in perspective
    drawing, 329, 330, 331
Piers, 198, 200
    and column footings, 192-193
    dimensioning, 110
Pilasters, 200
Pile foundations, 482-485
Pilings, foundation, 201
Pine —
    columns, 216
    for girders, 222
    joists and rafters, (tables)
        208, 210
Pipes —
    soil and waste, 255
    system in hot water heating, 287
    water supply, (table) 265
Piping symbols, 104-105
Pitch —
    in bolting, 536, 537
    calculating roof, 209
    of stairs, 9
Placing drawings, in concrete
    construction, 508-509
Planks —
    precast concrete, 489, (table) 491
    wood-fiber roof, 561-562
Plans —
    contour, 16
    developing exterior, 60
    developing floor, 1-6
    drawing erection, 540
    foundation, 3
    for food store layouts, 415, 416,
        420, 421, 422
    landscape, 16-17
    for new home, 1-24
    placement in working drawings,
        582-584
    plot, 15, 16
    sample shopping centers, 455-459
    sources of, 320, 321
    and specifications in estimating
        costs, 322, 323
    for stairs and halls, 7-11
    for stores, *see* Type of store
    structural steel wall, 542
    wall, 542
Plaster, applying in modular
    system, 168
Plastic —
    curtain-wall panels, 573
    polystyrene slabs to insulate,
        311, 312
Plate, and double plate in
    framing, 134
Platforms, for displaying
    merchandise, 354-355

Plenum, in furnaces, 271
Plot plan —
    drawing roof and, 116
    scale on drawings, 103
    surveyor makes, 15
Plumbing, 255-268
    in bathroom planning, 42
    and beam construction, 146
    for clinics, 407
    controlling noise of, 317
    factory-installed modular, 167
    food store needs of, 419
    in modular component
        assembly, 156
    in modular units, 161
    motel, 443, 446
    plastic, 184
    for room core units, 47
    in specifications, 120, 121
    system in mobile home
        standards, 176
    unit values of fixtures, 260
Plywood —
    sheathing standards for roofing,
        (table) 211
    for sheathing walls, 134, 135
    siding, 135, 136
    standards for subflooring,
        (table), 213
Polyethylene film, to waterproof
    foundation, 197
Polystyrene plastic slabs,
    insulations, 311, 312
Porcelain-enamel, curtain-wall
    system, 567-570
Porches, lighting and electric
    service for, 247
Portico, in Colonial Georgian
    house style, 71-74
Portland cement —
    in concrete, 503
    in installing glass blocks, 578
    stucco base, 138, 139
Positioning, of house, 21-23
Post office, feature in shopping
    center, 456
Post, plank and beam construction,
    143-148
Pratt truss, 544, 545
Precast concrete —
    facing and curtain-wall panels,
        578-580
    in structural systems, 485-502
Precast concrete lintels, 231-232
Precast concrete panels, 183, 184
Predella, 470
Presentation drawings,
    architectural, 334-336
Privacy —
    and building site, 17-18
    of clergy offices, 465, 466
    factor in office planning, 391
    in mobile home parks, 178
    motel units, 438, 439, 441
    and traffic patterns, 4, 5
    and use of windows, 53

Produce, displaying and
    processing, 417, 421
Projections, in perspective
    drawing, 329, 330
Proportion, as design element,
    60, 61
Pulpit, 469, 473
Pump, heat, 281-284
Purlins, and laminated beam sizes,
    (tables) 225, 226
Pylons, in storefront design,
    412, 413

——— Q ———

Quality, specifications list
    material, 116-121

——— R ———

Racks, for displaying merchandise,
    354-355, 417
Radial lots, in mobile home
    park, 179
Radial perimeter heating, 273
Radiators, heat emitters, 288, 289
Radius of gyration, 524, 527
Rafters —
    and roof trusses, 211, 212
    selecting, 209-211
    spans for joists and, (table), 210
    types of roof, 143
Ramps —
    in churches, 461
    lengths for, (table) 447
    parking facility, 446-449
Ranch house style, 82, 83
Receiving area, planning in
    merchandising facility, 357, 358
Recreation, room for in
    basements, 51
Redwood, for girders, 222
Reflective insulations, 311
Regency house style, 67, 68
Registers, placement of heat,
    269, 270
Reinforcement bars, in tilt-up
    concrete, 515
Reinforcing rods, steel, 502-509
Renderings —
    drawing architectural, 338-347
    preliminary black and white,
        343, 344
Renaissance, and house styles,
    66, 67
Repair, areas in stores, 365, 369
Reredos, 474
Residences, *see* Houses

Restaurants —
    planning, 423-429
    planning drive-in, 433-435
    planning short-order, 431-433
    in shopping centers, 454
Rest rooms —
    in banks, 400
    in churches, 467, 479
    in clinics, 405, 406, 408
    office, 392, 394
    in restaurants, 424
    service station, 382, 383
Reverberation, characteristics and
    time, 315
Rhythm, of design, 61, 62
Ridgepole, in roof framing, 143
Rigid frames, 552, (table) 553
Risers, of stairs, 8, (table) 9, 10
Rivets, joining steel members with,
    535-537
Roads, access to shopping
    centers, 453
Roof —
    calculating pitch and slope, 209
    collar beams, 211
    drawing in perspective
        drawings, 332
    drawing the plan, 116
    and floor plan, 4
    framing the, 143
    influences home styling, 62
    and live loads, 189
    in modular unit construction, 160
    poured gypsum system of,
        512-514
    precast concrete system, 509-512
    and rigid frames, 552
    types, 63-64
Roof decking, 144, 145, 213-215
    insulated, 309
    precast concrete systems, 489,
        (table) 490
    steel, 547-551
Roofing —
    in modular system, 166
    and sheet metal in specifications,
        119, 120
Roof planks, wood-fiber, 561-562
Roof trusses, 211, 212
    in modular system, 152, 155, 156
Rooms —
    designing factor, 25-33
    identifying when dimensioning,
        110
    planning in basement, 49-52
    planning as core units, 47
    planning dining, 33-34
    planning kitchen, 34-38
    planning living, 31
    planning utility, 46-47
Row houses, colonial, 73

—— S ——

Sacristy, planning church, 470-471
Safety —
  and allowable stress on steel
    members, 524
  and mobile home standards,
    175-176
  in wiring system, 237
Sales area, planning efficient and
    attractive, 351-356

Saltbox house style, 70
Sanctuary, *see* Nave
Sand, in stucco, 139
Sash, window, 53, 54, 57
Scale —
  drawing to, 102-103
  drawing trusses to, 546
  of drawings vary in set, 584
  models made to, 336-337
  in proportioning design, 61
  of structural steel drawings, 539
Scales, architect's, 102, 103
Schools —
  and choosing building site, 14
  planning church, 461, 477-479
Scissors truss, 544
Sealer, installing strip, 133
Sections —
  beam in engineering drawings,
    508
  drawing wall, 114
Septic tanks —
  located on plot plan, 116
  in waste disposal system, 264-265
Service areas, planning in
    merchandising facilities,
    356-358
Service stations —
  planning, 379-383
  in shopping centers, 457
Sewer —
  house or building, 255
  house in waste disposal system,
    258
  lines located on plot plan, 116
  sizing building, (table) 260, 261
Shadows —
  in architectural renderings,
    342, 344
  determining cast of, 21-23
Shape, motel units, 440-443
Shearing stress, 519, 520
Sheath, curtain-wall panels, 567
Sheathing, 211-213
  insulation board, 310
  of walls, 134-135
Shed roof, 64
Sheet metal, and roofing in
    specifications, 119, 120
Shingles, as siding, 135, 136
Shiplap siding, 135, 136

Shoe stores —
  planning, 362-364
  in shopping centers, 454
Shop drawings, structural steel,
    542-543
Shopping centers —
  future developments, 458
  planning, 452-459
Shoring, 503
Show windows, in merchandising
    facilities, 358-361
Shrubs, and trees in architectural
    renderings, 341, 342
Siding, 135, 136
  in modular system, 168, 169
Signaling systems, 249-250
Signs —
  coordinating stores in shopping
    centers, 454
  for dry cleaning shops, 376
  to identify store, 361
  planning motel, 439
  service station, 381
Sills, in house construction, 133
Simplicity, in modern house, 81, 82
Site —
  and building codes, 14, 15
  influences home styling, 63
  planning bank, 397
  planning motel, 437-439
  planning service station, 380-381
  selecting church, 461
  selection of shopping center,
    452, 453
Skylights —
  in church design, 476
  and halls, 7
Slabs —
  concrete and condensation, 314
  concrete and steel roof decking,
    549
  foundation and floor, 202-205
  glass and plastic to insulate,
    311, 312
  installation of heating system
    in, 271, (pictorial) 272
  insulating houses built on,
    311, 312
  precast concrete floor and roof,
    509-512
  precast concrete with joists,
    491-495
Slenderness ratio, of steel columns,
    527
Slope, calculating roof, 209
Social halls, in churches, 466
Soffit boards, 503
Soil —
  average safe loads of, (table) 191
  examining before building, 14
  and footings, 187, 188
  investigating for slab
    foundations, 205-206
  investigation for pile
    foundations, 482-483

and septic tank usage, 264
  testing shopping center
    site's, 452
Soil pipes, in waste disposal
    system, 255-264
Solid beams, 146-148
Sound, control of, 315-318
Southern Colonial houses, 70-71
Southwest, Spanish architecture
    in, 77-79
Southwestern Ranch house
    style, 82
Spaced beams, 146-148
Spacings, *see* Spans
Spandrel, curtain-wall panel, 568
Spanish house styles, 68, 69, 76-79
Spans —
  of glued laminated wood beams,
    (tables), 225, 226
  maximum for bulb tees,
    (table) 562
  maximum for roof decking, 214
  permissable in joists, (table) 208
  permissable in roof joists and
    rafters, (table) 210
  permissable in solid wood
    girders, (tables) 220, 221,
    222, 223
  sheathing, 211, 213
  of trusses, 544
Specifications, 102-130
  and owner-contractor
    relationship, 116
  for modular system, 166
  and plans in estimating
    costs, 323
  precedence over working
    drawings, 117
  purpose of, 116
  sample set of, 118-121
  sources of, 320, 321
  writing, 117
Split level house, 12
Split-level house, drawing floor
    plan of, 113
Split ring, in truss construction,
    211, 213
Stainless-steel curtain walls,
    571-572
Stairs —
  in church schools, 478, 479
  dimensioning, 111
  drawing details of, 115
  figuring sizes, 8, (table) 9, 10, 11
  interior to basement, 50
  lighting, 246
  planning in homes, 7-11
  planning in merchandising
    facilities, 353
  and moving furniture, 8
  and *Time Saver Standards,* 11
  types of, 9-10
Stalls, angles of parking, 446-447

Standardization, of modular
components, 150-153
Standards, design for mobile
homes, 174-176
Staplers, power, 184
Station point, in perspective
drawing, 329
Steam heat, 293-294
Steel —
connections for members, 537-539
to frame modular units, 162, 163
lintels, 232-234
loads on columns, 215,
(table), 216
in modular system, 173, 174
porcelain-enamel on panels, 570
prefabricated fireplaces, 304-306
reinforcing rods for concrete
construction, 502-509
stainless curtain-wall panels,
571-572, 573
stresses on members, 519-521
structural members, 517-534
used in pile foundations, 483, 484
Steel columns, 524, 527, 530,
531-533
Steel-framed houses, 148-149
Steel roof decking, 547-551
Step-taper piles, 483
Stirrups —
and joists, 137
for reinforcing concrete, 504, 505
Storage —
in banks, 399, 400
in halls, 7
in merchandising facilities,
356-358
in mobile homes, 175, 176
planning for, 39-40
planning motel room, 443-446
in stores, *see* Type of store
Stores —
grouping in shopping
centers, 454
planning food, 412-423
planning various, 362-387
see also Merchandising facilities
in house designs, 11-12
Storm doors, and insulation, 312
Storm sash, and insulation, 312
Stressed-skin panels, 182-183,
216-217
Stresses, on structural steel
members, 519-521
Structural insulation board, 309
Structural members —
glued laminated wood, 552-561
typical terms, 535
Structural steel drawings, 534-546
Structural steel members, 517-534
Structural systems —
precast concrete members in,
485-502
used in commercial construction,
482-566

Stucco, applying exterior, 138-139
Studs —
in framing walls, 133-134
partition in modular system, 166
utilizing in modular plans, 2
Styling, factors influencing home,
2, 62-63
Subcontractor, 322
Subfloor —
and bridging, 138
in modular system, 154, 155, 166
and noise control, 316
standards for plywood,
(table) 213
Subpurlins —
design data for, (table), 561
in gypsum roof system, 512,
(table) 513
Sun, in planning house location,
18-23
Supermarkets, *see* Food stores
Swimming pool, in motel
planning, 439
Switches —
for electric circuits, 242
in low-voltage remote-control
system, 252
Symbols —
architectural, 103-108
plumbing, 258
structural steel members, 535
wiring, 253
Symmetry of building design, 60

——— T ———

Tables, in restaurants, 425
Taking off, method of estimating
cost, 323
Taxes —
in choosing building site, 14
on home, 323
T-beams, precast concrete, 491-495
Tee joists, 488
Telephones, electrical system for,
249, 250
Television, electrical system
needed for, 250
Temperature —
attic space design, 296, 297
and crawl spaces, 297
in data processing rooms, 397
garage and basements, 297
outside and inside design, 296
Templates —
for architectural drafting, 103
using furniture in room
designing, 25
Tensile stress, 519

Termites —
protecting sills from, 133
subterranean and
nonsubterranean, 197
Termite shield, installing in
foundations, 197-198
Texture —
in building design, 62
methods of showing in
renderings, 338, 339
Thermal insulation, 309
Thermostats, 295
Tied arches, 554
Tile, terra cotta in solid masonry
construction, 141, 142
Tilt-up concrete, 515-517
Time Saver Standards, 115
to figure stairs, 11
Timber, allowable unit stresses for
structural, (table) 224
Title blocks, of working
drawings, 111
Tongue-and-groove construction,
154, 155
Topography, and building
house, 15-17
Townhouse, modular, 170
Trade-in, purchasing house by,
326-327
Traditionalists, in house design, 59
Traffic —
customer and employee, 357
flow in churches, 467, 478
flow of parking facilities, 446-450
in merchandising facilities,
352, 353
in office areas, 390
patterns in cafeterias, 430, 431
in food store planning, 412,
413, 414
patterns of home, 2, 4-6
patterns in kitchens, 37
patterns in restaurants, 425
patterns in room planning, 32, 33
plan for church choir, 473
planning stair and hall, 7-11
problem to solve, 6
and service station location,
380, 381
and shopping centers, 453
and store design, 361
Trailer Coach Association, 175
Trailers —
to move modular units, 168, 169
see also Mobile homes
Traps, in waste disposal system,
262
Treads, of stairs, 8, (table) 9, 10
Trees, and shrubs in architectural
renderings, 341, 342
Trenches, in constructing footings,
187
Trim, exterior in modular system,
166

True-length line, in perspective drawing, 332
Trusses —
bowstring, (table) 557
drawing steel, 544-546
roof, 211, 212
in roof framing, 143
typical steel, 544
Tudor house, 66
Two-point perspective, architectural drawings, 328-334
Two-story house, drawing floor plan of, 113

——— U ———

U factor, 295, 298
Ultimate strength, stress and, 521
Unit heaters, 288, 289
Units, planning motel, 440-446
Unity, of design, 62
Upflow furnace, 271
Utilities —
and choosing building site, 14
cost in house payment, 323
for display of merchandise, 354
for drugstores, 385
in mobile home parks, 178, 179
planning motel, 446
on site of shopping centers, 453, 456
Utility rooms, planning, 46-47
U values, 215, 312

——— V ———

Valley rafters, 143
Values —
house and building site, 14, 15
use of in renderings, 345-346
Valves, in water system, 265, 266
Vanishing points, in perspective drawings, 329, 332
Vapor barrier, 314
in curtain-wall panels, 568
in foundation, 196
and slab foundation, 205
Vault, planning in bank, 397, 398
Vegetable fibers, insulating, 310
Veneer —
brick over concrete or tile, 141-142
masonry, 142-143
Ventilation —
and attic, 296
in bathrooms, 42
in bedrooms, 39
to control condensation, 314, 315
in crawl space, 297

of curtain-wall panels, 568
in kitchen, 36
of restaurant kitchens, 427
in utility rooms, 46
and window designs, 52-55
Vents —
descriptions of waste disposal system, 255-256
usual residential disposal system sizes, (table) 264
in waste disposal system, 262-264
Vermiculite, insulating material, 311
Vestibules, planning church, 466-467
Veteran's Administration G. I. Loans, 325
Vibration, controlling noise of, 315, 317
Victorian house style, 80
View —
and building site, 17-18
from motel units, 438, 439
of store in planning merchandising facilities, 353
Views —
placement of on working drawings, 582-584
in shop drawings, 542-543
three-dimensional rendering, 338
in two-point perspective drawings, 329-332
in working drawings, 112-117
Vitrified-clay pipe, in waste disposal system, 258
Volt, defined, 236

——— W ———

Waiting rooms, in clinics, 404, 408
Wall fixture to display merchandise, 354
Wall plans, of structural steel drawings, 542
Walls —
brick or stone, 140-141
checking squareness of, 134
condensation in, 313
curtain systems, 567-581
directional of home and sun, 18-19
exterior in modular system, 166
framing house, 133-134
insulating, 310, 312
interior in modular system, 166
interior in specifications, 119
in modular system, 152, 154, 158-159, 168
sheathing, 134-135
washable restaurant kitchens, 428

Wall sections —
dimensioning, 111
drawing, 114
scale on drawings, 103
symbols for, 106-108
Warranty deed, 15
Warren steel truss, 544
Washer, planning space for, 45-47
Waste, of lumber by poor planning, 3
Waste disposal system, 255-264
Waste pipes, in waste disposal system, 255-260, 263, 264
Water —
air cooling with cold, 292-293
in cooling systems, 273, 275
in gas-fired air conditioner, 285, 286
heating with hot, 286-292
surface and slab foundations, 205, 206
used in heat pump, 281, 282
Watercolors, for renderings, 345
Water pipe, 267
Waterproofing —
of foundations, 196
insulation, 310
Water system, 265-267
Watt, defined, 236
Weather stripping, and insulation, 312
Web members, of trusses, 544
Weight, *see* Dead or Live loads
Welding —
steel members, 535
of steel modular units, 174
steel roof decking, 549
Wells, located on plot plan, 116
Wide-flange beams, 227
Wind —
and piers, 198, 199
prevailing and building site, 17
protecting customer from, 360
Winders, corner stairs, 9, 10
Windows —
in architectural renderings, 338, 340
in basements, 51
in bathroom, 42
in bedroom planning, 39, 40
in church design, 476
curtain-wall, 567, 569, 570
drive-in bank, 400, 401, 403
dimensioning, 110
garage, 49
and heat loss, 297
in modular system, 152, 153, 166, 168
in motel planning, 438
in room planning, 25, 32
planning home, 52-58
show, 358-361
types of, 53-58
walk-up bank, 403
and wall section symbols, 106-107

Wire lath, in applying stucco, 138
Wire ties, for reinforcing concrete,
   504, 505
Wiring —
   accessibility of, 236
   capacity of system, 236
   characteristics and service
      requirements, 236-241
   control in operating system, 237
   electrical and beam construction,
      146
   house, 236-254
   isolation in system, 237
   for kitchens, 237, 238, 240
   low-voltage, remote-control,
      251-253
   of modular units, 161
   new developments in, 184
   power centers, 239-240
   prefabricated, 184
   safety in, 237
   see also Electricity
   for service entrances, 238, 239
   surface-mounted, 250
   symbols for low-voltage, 253
Wood —
   allowable unit stresses for
      structural, (table) 224

compressive strength of columns,
   (table) 218
glued laminated structural
   members, 552-561
loads on columns, (table) 216
span of girders, (tables) 220,
   221, 222, 223
used in roof decking, (table)
   214, 215
Wood lintels, 234
Wood shingles, as siding, 135, 136
Work —
   grouping office areas of, 389
   planning areas for banks, 397
   scope of in specifications, 118
Working drawings, 102-130
   dimensioning, 103, 110-111
   lettering, 111-112
   reading, 121-130
   sample set for bank, 584-617
   specifications take precedence
      over, 117
Workmanship, written in
   specifications, 116-121
Workrooms, planning in
   merchandising facilities,
   358, 370, 372
Wright, Frank Lloyd, 59

X-rays, planning for in clinics,
   407, 408

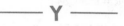

Yield point, of steel members, 521

—— Z ——

Zones —
   cooling, 293
   heating, 290
Zoning —
   house, 6-7
   regulations of building site,
      14, 15
   regulations for shopping centers,
      453

A contemporary residence using flush tongue and groove siding. (Western Wood Products Association)

The main entry creates the first impression of the home. (Western Wood Products Association)

Wood paneling can be used on the exterior to carry out the continuity of design. (Western Wood Products Association)

Dramatic lighting and warm wood interiors create an inviting atmosphere. (Western Wood Products Association)

A wide cantilever gives this house a soaring appearance. (Western Wood Products Association)

Outdoor rooms can be formed from fenced-in gardens. (Western Wood Products Association)

A wood deck can be used to tie the outside to the interior of the home. (Western Wood Products Association)

112C

The character of a house is strongly influenced by architectural detailing and window selection. (Andersen Corporation)

Modified ranch design. (The Garlinghouse Co., Inc.)

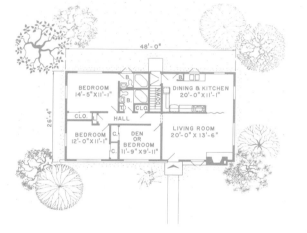

Contemporary two-story residence. (The Garlinghouse Co., Inc.)